Guide to the Pianist's Repertoire
Supplement

MAURICE HINSON

GUIDE TO THE PIANIST'S REPERTOIRE

SUPPLEMENT

INDIANA UNIVERSITY PRESS

Bloomington / London

TO THE MEMORY OF MY TEACHERS
Joseph Brinkman
(1901–1960)
AND
Olga Samaroff-Stokowski
(1882–1948)
WHOSE INTEGRITY AND DEVOTION TO
THE ART OF MUSIC WERE INSPIRING
MODELS FOR COUNTLESS ASPIRING PIANISTS

Manufactured in the United States of America

Library of Congress Cataloging in Publication Data
Hinson, Maurice.
   Guide to the pianist's repertoire—Supplement.
   Bibliography: p.
   Includes indexes.
   1. Piano music—Bibliography.   2.   Piano music—Bib-
liography—Graded lists.   I.   Title.
ML128.P3H5 Suppl.   016.7864′05   78-20430
ISBN 0-253-32701-6   1 2 3 4 5 83 82 81 80 79

Contents

Preface

Guide to the Pianist's Repertoire was published in 1973 (Bloomington: Indiana University Press), and this *Supplement* is intended to bring that volume up to date. The purpose of both the *Guide* and the *Supplement* is to make available in one practical listing the important solo piano literature. They are designed as basic textbooks for college piano literature courses and as special reference books for performers, teachers, librarians, music dealers, and all those interested in this rich and enormous repertoire.

A great quantity of solo piano music has appeared since 1973, and a book such as the *Guide* must be kept up to date if it is to provide the greatest assistance to the profession. The *Supplement* includes many new works published since 1973 as well as earlier compositions that were not included in the *Guide* either because of my oversight or simply because I was not familiar with them. Many unpublished pieces are now listed and described, as many composers have answered my request for scores and have generously supplied me with manuscripts.

This *Supplement,* like the *Guide* and *The Piano in Chamber Ensemble* (Bloomington: Indiana University Press, 1978) answers the questions: What is there? What is it like? Where can I get it?

Selection. In selecting works for this listing I have tried to cover all standard composers thoroughly and to introduce contemporary composers of merit, especially those of the United States (over 300 in this *Supplement*). Other criteria include: (1) No work is listed in the *Supplement* that was listed in the *Guide* unless the publisher has changed, or another publisher has added the work to his catalogue, or I have been able to analyze a work that was only listed by composer and title in the *Guide,* or I have improved or clarified a description that appeared in the *Guide.* (2) The time span covered is mainly from 1700 to the present, but a few works dating from before 1700 are included because of their special musical interest. The listing contains some music composed before the invention of the piano, but most of this literature is effective when performed on the piano. (3) Transcriptions of music originally written for other instruments, as a rule, are excluded, unless the arrangement was made by the composer, or, in my opinion, is highly effective. (4) Certain outstanding ragtime works are included as this type of music is a unique American contribution to piano repertoire. (5) Information on works listed but not described comes from publishers' catalogues. (6) New editions of standard works are added.

A certain amount of subjectivity is unavoidable in a book of this nature, but I have attempted to be as fair, objective, and clear as possible in my descriptions of the pieces. I am reminded of Elliott Carter's view on the limitation of words in describing music: "What impresses a composer about any attempt to verbalize about musical composition is the inadequacy of words to grasp something which is far more real to him in many important respects than words can be."[1] At one point after a detailed technical discussion of his own work he declares: "Perhaps the only consolation is that any such descriptive discussion as this has really consistently, although not intentionally, evaded the issues and visions most important and significant during the act of composing. . . . The reason for writing it . . . cannot be put into words."[2]

Even if Carter feels they are powerless to clarify the compositional process, however, "flawed words" are still useful. "It is entirely possible that many developments in the arts would never have taken place if there had not been critics to explain to listeners what they were hearing and to develop their judgment by drawing attention to qualities, subtleties—and faults."[3] Despite these verbal limitations I have tried to describe objectively the scores that were examined.

Composers who wish to submit compositions for possible inclusion in future editions are still encouraged to do so. Special effort has been made to examine as many contemporary works as possible, both published and unpublished. Recent avant-garde pieces are difficult to judge since most of them have not met the test of time, although many avant-garde techniques of the 1950s and 60s are becoming more refined and accepted into the compositional style of the 1970s. A number of contemporary composers use the piano strictly as a sonorous sound source, rather than identify the instrument with its past history. In any event, the piano still inspires almost all of our prominent and many of our less well known composers to write for it.

Because of constant change in the publishing world it is impossible to list only music currently in print. Some works known to be out of print were listed because of their merit, and many of them can be located at secondhand music stores, in the larger university or municipal libraries, or, more especially, in the Library of Congress.

Acknowledgments. Many people in many places have generously given me their help. I gratefully acknowledge the assistance of Martha Powell, Music Librarian of the Southern Baptist Theological Seminary; Rodney Mill of the Library of Congress; David Fenske, Librarian of the Indiana University School of Music; Marion Korda, Music Librarian of the University of Louisville; Fernando Laires of the piano faculty of Peabody Conservatory of Music; David Appleby, Professor of Music at Eastern Illinois University; my graduate assistant Wesley Roberts and the Southern Baptist Theological Seminary for making possible the typing of the manuscript and the aid of graduate assistants through the years. The American Composers Alliance Library and the Canadian Music Centre have been most helpful.

Without the generous assistance of numerous publishers this volume would not be possible. Special appreciation goes to Helen Deschler of Boosey and Hawkes, Inc.; Norman Auerbach of Theodore Presser Co.; Don Malin of Edward B. Marks Corp. and Belwin-Mills Publishing Corp.; Gertrud Mathys of C. F. Peters Corp.; Susan Brailove of Oxford University Press; Ronald Freed of European American Music Corp.; Ernst Herttrich of G. Henle Verlag; Barry O'Neal of G. Schirmer, Inc.; John Wiser of Joseph Boonin, Inc.; Robert Mabley of Galaxy Music Corp.; W. Ray Stephens of Frederick Harris Music Co., Ltd.; Mike Warren of Alphonse Leduc; Almarie Dieckow of Magnamusic-Baton, Inc.; Angelina Marx of McGinnis & Marx; Franz König of Tonos Verlag; B. J. Harrod of Alexander Broude, Inc.; Henri Elkan; and Frank L. Moore of Novello & Co., Ltd.

I also wish to express appreciation to my daughters, Jane and Susan, and to my wife, Peggy, for living with the inconvenience necessarily caused by the preparation of this book.

The death of Irwin Freundlich, my distinguished editor of *Guide to the Pianist's Repertoire,* has left a huge void, not only with me but with all who knew him. We remember his wisdom, encouragement, expertise, and goodness. I have missed his kind guiding hand and spirit throughout the compilation of this *Supplement.* Irwin Freundlich was a gentle man and a dear friend.

1. *The Writings of Elliott Carter: An American Composer looks at Modern Music,* compiled, edited, and annotated by Else Stone and Kurt Stone (Bloomington: Indiana University Press, 1977), p. 310.

2. Ibid., p. 364.

3. Ibid., p. 312.

Louisville, Kentucky   Maurice Hinson
September 1978

Using the Supplement

Arrangement of entries. In the "Individual Composers" section, all composers are listed alphabetically. Sometimes biographies and/or stylistic comments follow the composer's name and dates of birth and death. Under each composer's name, individual compositions are listed, by opus number, or by title, or by musical form, or by a combination of the three. The entries in the "Anthologies and Collections" section include the editor or compiler, the publisher, the composers, and sometimes the titles represented in the collection. (See p.xiv for further explanation of entries.)

Descriptions have been limited to general style characteristics, form, particular and unusual qualities, interpretative suggestions, and pianistic problems inherent in the music. Editorial procedures found in a particular edition are mentioned. The term "large span" is used when a span larger than an octave is required in a piece, and that occurs in many contemporary works. "Octotonic" refers to lines moving in the same direction one or more octaves apart. "Shifting meters" indicates that varied time signatures are used within the space mentioned (a few bars, a movement, the entire work). "Proportional rhythmic relationships," e.g., ⌐ ¯ ¯ ¯ 5"4 ¯ ¯ ¯ ¬, indicates 5 notes are to be played in the time space for 4. "3 with 2" means 3 notes in one voice are played with (against) 2 notes in another voice. "Chance music" (aleatory, aleatoric) is described or mentioned, not analyzed, since it has no definitely ordered sequence of events. "Synthetic scale(s)" are made up by the composer whose work is being discussed; the range may be less than one octave. "Stochastic techniques" refers to "a probabilistic compositional method, introduced by Iannis Xenakis, in which the overall contours of sound are specified but the inner details are left to random or chance selection" (DCM, p.708).

Grading. An effort has been made to grade representative works of each composer. Four broad categories of grading are used: Easy, Intermediate (Int.), Moderately Difficult (M-D), and Difficult (D). To provide a more thorough understanding of this grading, the following standard works will serve as guide:

Easy: Bach, dance movements from the *Anna Magdalena Notebook*
Leopold Mozart, *Notebook for Wolfgang*
Schumann, easier pieces from *Album for the Young*
Bartók, *Mikrokosmos,* Vols. I–II

Int. Bach, *Twelve Little Preludes and Fugues*
Beethoven, *Ecossaises*

Mendelssohn, *Children's Pieces* Op.72
Bartók, *Rumanian Folk Dances* 1–5
M-D: Bach, *French Suites, English Suites*
Mozart, *Sonatas*
Brahms, *Rhapsody* Op.79/2
Debussy, *La Soirée dans Granade*
D: Bach, *Partitas*
Beethoven, *Sonata* Op.57
Chopin, *Etudes*
Barber, *Sonata*

These categories must not be taken too strictly but are only listed for general indications of technical and interpretative difficulties.

Details of entries. When known, the date of composition is given after the title of the work. Then, in parentheses, are as many of the following as apply to the particular work: the editor, the publisher, the publisher's edition number, and the copyright date. When more than one edition is available, the editions are listed in order of preference, the most desirable first. The number of pages and the performance time are frequently listed. The spelling of the composers' names and of the titles of the compositions appear as they do on the music being described. Specifically related books, dissertations or theses, and periodical articles are listed following individual compositions or at the conclusion of the discussion of a composer's works (a more extended bibliography appears at the end of the book).

Sample Entries and Explanations

C. P. E. BACH
Six Sonatas 1761 W.51 (Juanelva Rose—TP 1973).

1761 is the year of composition; W.51 stands for Wotquenne (the cataloguer of C. P. E. Bach's music) and the number he assigned the pieces. Juanelva Rose is the editor, Theodore Presser is the publisher, and 1973 is the publication date.

FRANZ SCHUBERT
Four Impromptus Op.90 D.899 (Badura-Skoda—VU 50001). M-D.

Op.90 is the opus number; D.899 stands for Deutsch (the cataloguer of Schubert's music) and the number he has assigned the pieces. Badura-Skoda is the editor, Vienna Urtext is the publisher, and 50001 is their edition number. M-D means Moderately Difficult.

MILTON BABBITT
Playing for Time 1977 (Hinshaw) in collection *Twelve by Eleven* 12pp. M-D.

This work was composed in 1977, the publisher is Hinshaw, it is contained in the collection *Twelve by Eleven,* and it is 12 pages in length.

The work is classified as Moderately Difficult. Other pieces in the collection can be checked by looking in the "Anthologies and Collections" section under the title *Twelve by Eleven*.

Other assistance. See "Abbreviations" (pp.xvii) for terms, publishers, books, and periodicals referred to in the text; and the directories, "American Agent or Parent Companies of Music Publishers" (pp.xxi) and "Addresses of Music Publishers" (pp.xxiii), to locate publishers. Five special indexes—"Alphabetical List of Composers under Nationality Designations," "Black Composers," "Women Composers," "Compositions for Piano and Tape," and "Compositions for Prepared Piano"—direct the user to entries in the text for music in these categories. "New Dates" lists death dates of composers who have recently died as well as birth and death dates not available for the first printing of *Guide to the Pianist's Repertoire*.

Abbreviations

A	Allemande	ca.	circa
AA	Authors Agency of the Polish Music Publishers	CeBeDeM	CeBeDeM Foundation
		CF	Carl Fischer
		CFE	Composers Facsimile Edition
ABRSM	Associated Board of the Royal Schools of Music	CFP	C. F. Peters
		CK	*Contemporary Keyboard*
ACA	American Composers Alliance	CMC	Canadian Music Centre
AM	*Acta Musicologia*		
AME	American Music Editions	CMP	Consolidated Music Publishing
AMP	Associated Music Publishers	CPE	Composer/Performer Edition
AMS	American Musicological Society	D	Difficult
		DCM	*Dictionary of Contemporary Music,* ed. John Vinton (New York: E. P. Dutton, 1974).
AMT	*American Music Teacher*		
APS	Art Publication Society		
ASUC	American Society of University Composers	Dob	Doblinger
		DSS	Drustva Slovenskih Skladateljev
B	Bourrée		
B&VP	Broekmans & Van Poppel	DVFM	Deutscher Verlag für Musik
BB	Broude Brothers	EBM	Edward B. Marks
BI	(Brown Index) *Chopin: An Index of His Works in Chronological Order,* by Maurice J. Brown, 2d ed. (New York: Da Capo Press, 1972).	EC	Edizioni Curci
		ECS	E. C. Schirmer
		EFM	Editions Françaises de Musique/Technisonor
		EMB	Editio Musica Budapest
		EMH	Editions Musikk-Huset
BMC	Boston Music Co.	EMM	Ediciones Mexicanas de Música
Bo&Bo	Bote & Bock		
Bo&H	Boosey & Hawkes	EMT	Editions Musicales Transatlantiques
Br	Bärenreiter		
Br&H	Breitkopf & Härtel	ESC	Max Eschig
C	Courante	EV	Elkan-Vogel

FSV	Feedback Studio Verlag	K	Kalmus
G	Gigue	L	Longo, Alessandro
GD	*Grove's Dictionary of Music and Musicians,* 5th ed. (New York: St. Martin's Press, 1955).	LAMC	Latin American Music Center Indiana University
		LC	Library of Congress
		LG	Lawson-Gould
		L'OL	L'Oiseau-Lyre
Gen	General Music Publishing Co.	M	Minuet
		M&M	*Music and Musicians*
GM	Gehrmans Musikförlag	MAB	Musica Antiqua Bohemica (Artia)
GS	G. Schirmer		
GWM	General Words and Music Co.	MC	Mildly contemporary
		MCA	M.C.A. Music (Music Corporation of America)
Hin	Hinrichsen		
HV	Heinrichshofens Verlag	M-D	Moderately Difficult
IEM	Instituto de Extension Musicale Calle Compañia Universidad de Chile Compañia 1264 Santiago, Chile	Mer	Mercury Music Corp.
		MJ	*Music Journal*
		MJQ	MJQ Music
		ML	*Music and Letters*
		MM	*Modern Music*
		MMR	*Monthly Musical Record*
IMC	International Music Co.	MO	*Musical Opinion*
IMI	Israel Music Institute	MQ	*Musical Quarterly*
Int.	Intermediate difficulty	MR	*Music Review*
ITO	*In Theory Only* Journal of the Michigan Music Theory Society School of Music University of Michigan Ann Arbor, MI 48109	M-S	*Music-Survey*
		MS, MSS	manuscript(s)
		MT	*Musical Times*
		Nag	Nagel's Musik-Archive
		NME	New Music Edition
		NMO	Norsk Musikförlag
		NMS	Nordiska Musikförlaget
IU	Indiana University School of Music Library	Nov	Novello
		OBV	Oesterreichischer Bundesverlag
JALS	*Journal of The American Liszt Society*	OD	Oliver Ditson
JAMS	*Journal of the American Musicological Society*	OUP	Oxford University Press
		PAU	Pan American Union
JF	J. Fischer	PIC	Peer International Corporation
JWC	J. W. Chester		

PMP	Polish Music Publications	SHV	Státní hudbení vydavatelství
PNM	*Perspectives of New Music*	SP	Shawnee Press
		SSB	*Sonata Since Beethoven,* by W. S.
PQ	*Piano Quarterly*		Newman (Chapel Hill:
PWM	Polskie Wydawnictwo Muzyczne		University of North
R&E	Ries & Erler		Carolina Press, 1969;
Ric	Ricordi		2d ed., New York:
Ric Amer	Ricordi Americana S.A.		W. W. Norton, 1972).
		S&B	Stainer & Bell
Ric BR	Ricordi Brazil	SZ	Suvini Zerboni
S	Sarabande	TM	*Tonal Music,* by
SA	Sonata-Allegro		Jeffrey Kresky
Sal	Salabert		(Bloomington:
SB	Summy-Birchard		Indiana University
SBE	*Sonata in the Baroque Era,* by W. S. Newman		Press, 1977).
		TP	Theodore Presser Co.
	(Chapel Hill: University of North Carolina	UE	Universal Edition
		UFBA	Universidade Federal
	Press, 1959; rev. ed.		da Bahia
	1966; 3d ed., New	UME	Unión Musical
	York: W. W. Norton,		Española
	1972).	UMKR	Unbekannte Meister
	Sonata in the Classic		der Klassik und
SCE	*Era,* by W. S. Newman		Romantik (Boonin)
	(Chapel Hill: University of North Carolina	UMP	United Music Publishers
	Press, 1963; 2d ed.,	USSR	Mezhdunarodnaya
	New York: W. W.		Kniga (Music Publishers of the USSR)
	Norton, 1972).		
SDM	Servico de Documentacão Musical da	VU	Vienna Urtext Edition (UE)
	Ordem dos Músicos do	WH	Wilhelm Hansen
	Brazil Av, Almte.	WIM	Western International
	Barroso, 72–7° Andar		Music
	Rio de Janeiro, Brazil	YMP	Yorktown Music Press

American Agents or
Parent Companies of Music Publishers

1. Associated Music Publishers, Inc., 866 Third Avenue, New York, NY 10022.
2. Belwin-Mills Publishing Corp., 25 Deshon Drive, Melville, NY 11746.
3. Big 3 Music Corp., 729 Seventh Avenue, New York, NY 10019.
4. Boosey & Hawkes, Inc., P. O. Box 130, Oceanside, NY 11572.
5. Brodt Music Co., P. O. Box 1207, Charlotte, NC 28231.
6. Alexander Broude, Inc., 225 West 57th Street, New York, NY 10019.
7. Broude Bros., Ltd., 56 West 45th Street, New York, NY 10036.
8. Concordia Publishing House, 3558 South Jefferson Avenue, St. Louis, MO 63118.
9. Henri Elkan Music Publisher, 1316 Walnut Street, Philadelphia, PA 19107.
10. Elkan-Vogel Inc. (see Theodore Presser), Presser Place, Bryn Mawr, PA 19010.
11. European American Music Corp., 195 Allwood Road, Clifton, NJ 07012.
12. Carl Fischer, Inc., 56-62 Cooper Square, New York, NY 10003.
13. Mark Foster Music Co., P. O. Box 4012, Champaign, IL 61820.
14. Sam Fox Publishing Co., P. O. Box 850, Valley Forge, PA 19482.
15. Frank Music Corp., 119 West 57th Street, New York, NY 10019.
16. Galaxy Music Corp., 2121 Broadway, New York, NY 10023.
17. Hansen Publications, Inc., 1842 West Avenue, Miami Beach, FL 33139.
18. M C A Music, 25 Deshon Drive, Melville, NY 11746.
19. Magnamusic-Baton, 10370 Page Industrial Boulevard, St. Louis, MO 63132.
20. Edward B. Marks Music Corp., 1790 Broadway, New York, NY 10019.
21. Music Sales Corp., 33 W. 60th Street, New York, NY 10023.
22. Oxford University Press, Inc., 200 Madison Avenue, New York, NY 10016.
23. C. F. Peters Corp., 373 Park Avenue South, New York, NY 10016.
24. Theodore Presser Co., Presser Place, Bryn Mawr, PA 19010.
25. E. C. Schirmer Music Co., 600 Washington Street, Boston, MA 02100.
26. G. Schirmer, Inc., 866 Third Avenue, New York, NY 10022.

27. Shawnee Press, Inc., Delaware Water Gap, PA 18327.
28. Southern Music Publishing Co., 1740 Broadway, New York, NY 10019.
29. Summy-Birchard Co., 1834 Ridge Avenue, Evanston, IL 60204.
30. Warner Bros., Seven Arts Music, 75 Rockefeller Plaza, New York, NY 10019.
31. Location or American agent unverified.

Addresses of Music Publishers

A number following the name of a publisher corresponds to that of its American agent or parent company (see previous directory).

Ahn & Simrock
  Meinekestrasse 10
  1 Berlin 15, West Germany
J. Albert
  139 King Street
  Sydney, Australia
Alfred Publishing Co.
  15335 Morrison Street
  Sherman Oaks, CA 91403
Alier, Ildefonso
  Plaza Isabel II
  5 Barcelona, Spain
Allans
  Australia
Alsbach   23
  Amsterdam, Netherlands
Amadeus-Päuler   23
  Adliswil, Germany
American Composers Alliance—
  Composers Facsimile
  Edition
  170 W. 74th Street
  New York, NY 10023
American Music Editions   12
  263 E. 7th Street
  New York, NY 10009
American Society of
  University Composers   11
Amphion Editions Musicales
  (see E. C. Kerby, Ltd.)
AMS Press
  56 E. 13th Street
  New York, NY 10003

Amsco Music Publishing Co.   21
Edições Anacrusa
  San Eugenio 1053
  Lima, Peru
Andre   31
Antico Edition
  North Harton, Lustleigh,
    Newton Abbot
  Devon TQ 139SG, England
Antonio Inglesias—La Coruña   31
A-R Editions
  315 W. Gorham Street
  Madison, WI 53703
Collecion Arion   28
Arno Volk Verlag   18
  Cologne, Germany
Arrow Press   4
Ars Viva Verlag   2, 11
  Mainz, Germany
Artia   4
  Smečkách 30
  Prague I, Czechoslovakia
Ascherberg, Hopwood & Crew,
  Ltd. (England)   5, 14
Edwin Ashdown, Ltd.   4, 5
Ashley Dealers Service
  263 Veterans Boulevard
  Carlstadt, NJ 07072
Associated Board of the
  Royal School of Music
  (England)   2
Augener
  c/o Galliard
  Great Yarmouth, England

Authors Agency of the
  Polish Music Publishers
  ul. Hipoteczna 2, 00-950
  Warsaw, Poland
Bärenreiter Verlag   11, 19
  Heinrich Schütz Allee 35
  35, Kassel-Wilhelmshöhe,
  Germany
Barry & Cia. (Argentina)   4
Basil Ramsey   7
M. P. Belaieff   23
Belmont Music Publishers
  P. O. Box 49961
  Los Angeles, CA 90049
Bender, C. C.
  Amsterdam, Netherlands
Berandol Music Ltd. (Canada)   1
Bèrben   24
Biedermann   31
Gérald Billaudot, Editeur   24
  14, rue de l'Echiquier
  Paris 10, France
Blackwell's Music Shop
  38 Holywell Street
  Oxford, England OX1 4EY
Boelke-Bomart Music
  Publications   1
  Hillsdale, NY 12529
Bomart (see Boelke-Bomart)
F. Bongiovanni   2
  Bologna, Italy
Joseph Boonin (see Jerona
  Music Corp.)
Bosse Edition
  Postfach 417
  84 Regensburg 2, Germany
Boston Music Co.   15
  116 Boylston Street
  Boston, MA 02116
Bosworth & Co., Ltd.   2
Bote & Bock   1
  Hardenbergstrasse 9a
  1 Berlin 12, West Germany

Bowdoin College Music Press
  Department of Music
  Bowdoin College
  Brunswick, ME 04011
Branden Press, Inc.
  221 Columbus Avenue
  Boston, MA 02116
Braun (see Billaudot)
Breitkopf & Härtel   1
  Postschliessfach 74
  Walkmühlstrasse 52
  6200 Wiesbaden 1,
    West Germany
Breitkopf & Härtel   6
  Postschliessfach 107
  Karlstrasse 10
  701 Leipzig C1,
    East Germany
British and Continental
  Music Agencies Ltd.   18
  64 Dean Street
  London W1V 6AU,
    England
Broekmans & Van Poppel   23
  Amsterdam, Netherlands
Aldo Bruzzichelli,
  Editore (Italy)   1
Hans Busch Musikförlag
  Stubbstigen 3
  S-18146 Lidingo, Sweden
Editions J. Buyst
  76, avenue du Midi
  Brussels, Belgium
Canyon Press, Inc.
  Box 1235
  Cincinnati, OH 45201
Carisch, S. P. A.   4
  Via General Fara, 39
  20124 Milan, Italy
Valentim de Carvalho
  R. Nova do Almada 97
  Lisbon, Portugal

Editură Muzicala a Uniunii
Compozitorilor din
R. P. R.
Bucharest, Rumania

Edizioni Curci   3
4 Galleria del Corso
Milan, Italy

Edizioni De Santis
Via Cassia, 13
00191 Rome, Italy

Edizioni Suvini Zerboni   4
Via Quintiliano, 40
20138 Milan, Italy

Elkin & Co., Ltd.   16

Engström & Södring
(Denmark)   23

Enoch & Cie.   1, 5, 28
27, boulevard des Italiens
Paris 11, France

Max Eschig   1
48, rue de Rome
Paris 8, France

Eulenburg Pocket Scores   23

Faber Music   26

Fairfield, Ltd. (see Novello)

Edition Fazer
Postbox 260
SF-00101 Helsinki 10,
Finland

Feedback Studio Verlag
23 Genterstrasse
5 Cologne, Germany

Fermata do Brasil S.A.
Avenida Ipiranga, 1123
01039 São Paulo (SP),
Brazil

Finnish Information Centre
Runeberginkatu 15 A
SF-00100 Helsinki 10,
Finland

J. Fischer & Bro.   2
Harristown Road
Glen Rock, NJ 07452

Foetisch Frères, S.A.
(Switzerland)

Dan Fog Musikförlag
Graabrødretorv 1
DK 1154 Copenhagen K,
Denmark

Fondazione Carminignani
Rossini
Pesaro, Italy

Forberg   23

A. Forlivesi & Co.
Via Roma, 4
Florence, Italy

Arnaldo Forni, Editore
Via Triumvirato, 7
40132 Bologna, Italy

Forsyth Brothers, Ltd.   2
190 Grays Inn Road
London WC1X 8EW,
England

H. Freeman & Co.
64 Dean Street
London W1V 6AU,
England

Theodore Front
155 N. San Vicente
Boulevard
Beverly Hills, CA 90211

Galliard, Ltd. (England)   17

Carl Gehrmans Musikförlag   31
Post Box 505
S-101 26 Stockholm,
Sweden

General Music Publishing
Co., Inc.   28
P. O. Box 267
Hastings-on-Hudson,
NY 10706

General Words and Music Co.
525 Busse Highway
Park Ridge, IL 60068

Musikverlag Hans Gerig   3, 19
Cologne, Germany

Japan Federation of
  Composers
  c/o Ohminato Building
  14 Suga-cho Shinjuku-ku
  Tokyo, Japan
Japanese Society of Rights of
  Authors and Composers
  Tameike Meisan Building
  30 Akasaka Tameikecho,
  Minato-Ku
  Tokyo, Japan
Jaymar Music Ltd.   22
  P. O. Box 3083
  London 12, Ontario,
  Canada
Jerona Music Corp.
  14 Porter Street
  Hackensack, NJ 07601
Jean Jobert   10
  Paris, France
Johnson Reprint Corp.
  111 Fifth Avenue
  New York, NY 10003
Joshua Corp.
  (see General Music
  Publishers)
Jost & Sander
  Leipzig, East Germany
O. Junne
  Munich, Germany
P. Jürgenson
  Moscow 200, USSR
Alfred A. Kalmus, Ltd.
  2/3 Fareham Street
  London W1, England
Edwin F. Kalmus   2
A. Kalnajs
  719 W. Willow Street
  Chicago, IL 60614
Kenyon Publications
  17 W. 60th Street
  New York, NY 10023

E. C. Kerby Ltd.   11
  198 Davenport Road
  Toronto, Canada MR5 1J2
King's Crown   16
Kistner & Siegel   8
  P. O. Box 180201
  Gereonshof 38
  5 Cologne 1, Germany
L. Krenn
  Vienna, Austria
Kronos Press
  25 Ansdell Street
  London W8 5BN, England
Kultura   4
  P. O. Box 149
  Budapest 62, Hungary
Lawson-Gould Music
  Publishers, Inc.   2
Alphonse Leduc   5, 10
  175, rue Saint Honoré
  Paris 1, France
Leeds Music Corp.
  (see MCA Music)   18
Leeds Music Ltd. (Canada)   18
  2450 Victoria Park Avenue
  Willowdale, Ontario
  M2J 4A2, Canada
Henry Lemoine & Cie.   10
  17, rue Pigalle
  75 Paris 9, France
Alfred Lengnick & Co., Ltd.
  (see Frederick Harris
  Music Co.)
  421a Brighton Road
  South Croydon, Surrey,
  England
Lerolle
  Paris, France
Les Editions Ouvrières   16
F. E. C. Leuckart   1
  Nibelungenstrasse 48
  Munich 19, Germany

Rongwen Music, Inc.   7
Fondazione Carminignani
   Rossini
   Pesaro, Italy
E. Rouart, Lerolle & Co.
   (see Salabert)
   Paris, France
Rózsavölgyi
   P.O. Box 149
   Budapest, Hungary
Russian State Publishers   26
Editions Salabert
   575 Madison Avenue
   New York, NY 10022
   22, rue Chauchat
   Paris 9, France
San Andreas Press
   3732 Laguna Avenue
   Palo Alto, CA 94306
Sassetti & Cia.
   R. Nova do Almada, 60
   Lisbon 2, Portugal
Schaum Publications, Inc.
   2018 E. North Avenue
   Milwaukee, WI 53202
Wilhelm Schenk
   Munster, Germany
Arthur P. Schmidt Co.   29
Schmitt Co.
   110 N. Fifth Street
   Minneapolis, MN 55403
Schola Cantorum   9
Schott   11
   Schott and Co., Ltd.
   48 Great Marlborough
     Street
   London W2V 2BN, England
   B. Schott's Söhne
   Weihergarten 5
   6500 Mainz, Germany
Schott Frères   23
   Brussels, Belgium
Schroeder & Gunther   1
Musikverlag Schwann

Charlottenstrasse 80-86
   Düsseldorf, Germany
Charles Scribner's Sons
   597 Fifth Avenue
   New York, NY 10017
Seesaw Music Corp.
   1966 Broadway
   New York, NY 10023
Maurice Senart (see Salabert)
Serviço de Documentação
   Musical da Ordem dos
   Músicos do Brasil
   Av. Almte. Barroso,
   72-7° Andar
   Rio de Janeiro (RJ), Brazil
Hans Sikorski   2
   Johnsallee 23
   2 Hamburg 13, Germany
N. Simrock   1
   Hamburg, Germany
Slovenska Akademija
   Ljubljana, Yugoslavia
Smith Publications
   1014 Wilmington Avenue
   Baltimore, MD 21223
Ediciones Sonido 13
   Mexico City, Mexico
Sonos Music Resources
   1800 S. State Street
   Orem, UT 84057
Soviet Composer
   (Sovetskii Kompozitor)
   (see Otto Harrassowitz)
Stainer & Bell   16
Státní hudbení vydavatelskí   4
   (State Music Publishers—
   now Supraphon)
   Prague, Czechoslovakia
Státní Nakladtelstvi Krasne
   Literatury
   Hudby Umeni
   Prague, Czechoslovakia
Steingräber Verlag
   Auf der Reiswiese 9

Part I

Individual Composers,
Their Solo Piano Works
in Various Editions

and Facsimile Reproductions

A

HELGE AAFLÖY (1936–   ) Norway
Tre Bagateller (NMO   1968) 5pp. Allegro: 7/4, freely tonal, large span
 required. Allegretto e scherzando: 4/4, chromatic inner voice figuration. Allegro non troppo: 5/8, 6/8, 3/8, dancelike, strong rhythms,
 trio, attractive. M-D.

GAMAL ABDEL-RAHIM (–   ) Egypt
Variations on an Egyptian Folksong (Dob). Six variations, MC, plaintive
 folksong, large span required. M-D.

KOMEI ABE (1911–   ) Japan
3 Sonatinas for Children (Zen-On 330, 331, 332) published separately.
 I: F, three movements. II: G, three movements. III: c, three movements. MC with slight oriental flavor. Int.

EDOWARD ABRAHAMYAN (1923–   ) USSR
Preludes for Piano (USSR   1972) 139pp. Tetradi I–V.

JEAN ABSIL (1893–1974) Belgium
Passacaille Op.101 1959 (CeBeDeM) 10pp. In memoriam Alban Berg.
 Required piece for the 1960 Queen Elisabeth Competition. Chromatic theme and 20 variations treated in various ways. A few variations are relieved by short episodes. A calm and expressive mood is
 characteristic of the four middle variations while a brilliant coda
 concludes the work. D.
Alternances Op.140 (CeBeDeM   1971) 16pp. 14 min.
Sonatine Op.125   1966 (Metropolis) 7pp. Allegro moderato: fresh harmonies, clever rhythms. Pavane: imitative with mildly dissonant
 chords. Tarentelle: 6/8, dancelike, fleeting, attractive. Int.
Féeries Op.153 (CeBeDeM   1971) 22pp. 17 min. Lutins; Elfes; Korri-
 gans; Néréides; Choephores; Farfadets.

DIETER ACKER (1940–   ) Germany
Schichten I–IV (Gerig   1969) 11pp. Strato I–IV. Notes in English and
 German.

MARCIAL DEL ADALID (1826–1881) Chile
Vals brillante, Improvisación, Elegía, Andantino con variaciones (An-
 tonio Iglesias—La Coruña, Real Academia Gallega   1965) 72pp.
 Includes analysis and biographical commentary.

3

SAMUEL ADLER (1928–   ) USA
Adler teaches at the Eastman School of Music.
Canto VIII 1973 (CF) 5 min. String effects inside piano, harmonics.
   Quiet introduction is exploded by torrents of octaves, clusters,
   stopped notes—all make this a fun avant-garde concert etude. D.
   See: David Burge, "Five New Pieces," CK, 3 (December 1977):66.
Capriccio 1954 in collection *New Music for the Piano* (LG). Flexible
   meters and tonal centers, cross-relations, polymodality. Makes a fine
   one-minute encore. Int. to M-D.
Gradus: Forty Studies 1971 (OUP). Books I and II. Twenty studies in
   each volume that explore contemporary techniques. Volume II is
   more difficult than I. Notes explain each study. Int. to M-D.
See: Bradford Gowen, "Samuel Adler's Piano Music," AMT, 25 (January 1976):6–8.

ARKADII ARTEM'EVICH AGABABOV (1940–   ) USSR
Dvenadtsat' preliudii (Piano Preludes) (Sovetskii Kompozitor MK276-
   00367 1976) 46pp.

DENES AGAY (1911–   ) USA, born Hungary
Concertino Barocco (GS 1975) 15pp. Based on themes of Handel.
   Three contrasting movements, delightful. Int.
15 Little Pieces on Five-Note Patterns (BMC 1973). Great variety of
   five-finger positions. Easy to Int.
Four Dance Impressions (TP 1977). Night Music; Vibrations; Ballad
   without Words; Hommage à Joplin. Chromatic, strong rhythms, MC,
   sophisticated. Int. to M-D.
Petit Trianon Suite (GS). Ten tuneful short pieces in classic dance forms.
   M, S, Contredanse, Musette, etc. Easy.
Two Improvisations on Hungarian Folk Songs (TP 1973) 7pp. The
   Peacock. Gipsy Tune: modal, more fetching of the two, attractive.
   Int.

EMIL G. AHNELL (1925–   ) USA
Sonatine (MS available from composer: c/o Music Department, Kentucky
   Wesleyan College, Owensboro, KY 42301) 11pp. Allegro moderato;
   Adagio, ma non troppo; Allegro. Freely tonal, shifting meters, glis-
   sandi, neoclassic, exciting closing. M-D.

KARL AHRENDT (1904–   ) USA
Ahrendt was trained at the Cincinnati Conservatory and the Eastman
School of Music. For a number of years he was Director of the School of
Music at Ohio University. He resides at 5 Old Peach Ridge Road, Athens,
OH 45701.
Epigrams (MS available from the composer) 4 min. Eclogue; Let Down;
   Build Up; Five-Four; Valse; Sine nomine; Mirror; Accents. Short,

MC, titles dictate techniques used. Useful as a group or all pieces together. Interpretative problems are greater than technical. M-D.

Integrations (MS available from composer 1973) 10 min. Free fantasia form; varied techniques used including tone row, polychords, aleatoric contours, hence the title. B-A-C-H motive appears as a coordinating factor in a number of variations with melodic, harmonic, and tone-cluster treatment. Mature pianism required. D.

HUGH AITKEN (1924–   ) USA
Seven Bagatelles 1957 (MS available from composer: c/o Music Department, William Patterson College, Wayne, NJ 07470). Short, contrasting, mildly dissonant, subtle pedal effects. M-D.

YASUSHI AKUTAGAWA (1925–   ) Japan
La Danse—Suite pour Piano (Ongaku No-Tomo 1948) 14pp. 8 min. Two dance pieces with a presto intermezzo between them. Strong rhythms, freely chromatic, clusterlike sonorities. An attractive group. M-D.

ISAAC ALBÉNIZ (1860–1909) Spain
Azulejos (UME). 1. Prelude: this work was finished by Granados. M-D.
España Op.165 (Schott).
Fiesta de Aldea Op. posth. (UME 1973) 18pp. Apparently the first part of an unfinished composition intended for orchestra.
Rumores de la Caleta (Malaguena) (BMC; IMC) from *Recuerdos de Viaje.*
Songs of Spain Op.232 (IMC; GS) No.4 Cordova: Spanish dance rhythms, colorful imagination. M-D.
Suite Espagñole. (L. Lechner—Schott 5068; IMC).
My First Albeniz (Piero Rattalino—Ric). Six easy pieces. Easy to Int.
Iberia (IMC) in four vols.
Navarra (IMC).
A Book of Waltzes (K).
Collected Piano Works (K) 2 vols.
The Alhambra (Suite for piano) (La Vega) (K9477).
Deseo Op.40 Estudio de concert (K9480).

MATEO ALBÉNIZ (1760?–1831) Spain
Sonata D (Editorial Musica Moderna) 3pp. Presto, attractive, suggestion of Zapateado dance, fanfare effects. Fine program opener. Int.

EUGEN D'ALBERT (1864–1932) Germany, born Scotland
Blues see collection *Composer-Pianists* (Schaum Publications).

DOMENICO ALBERTI (ca. 1710–ca. 1740) Italy
Sonata B♭ (Zecchi, Fazzari—Carisch 1971) 10pp. Preface in Italian.

PER HJORT ALBERTSEN (1919–   ) Norway
Albertsen was educated as an architect before beginning his musical stud-

ies. He is an organist, choral conductor, and music teacher in Trondheim, Norway.

Sonata Op.4   1946 (Lyche) 12 min. Slättensonaten. Allegro—Gangar and Call; Andantino semplice—The Bridal March of the Miller's Boy; Allegro fuoco—Lofthusen.

Pastoral from "Little Suite" Op.14 (Lyche).

Hommage à J. S. Bach   1957 (Lyche). Published in volume III of *Pro Piano*. A three-voice fugue.

JOHANN GEORG ALBRECHTSBERGER (1736–1809) Germany

Six Fugues, Op.7 (Imre Sulyok—EMB & Litolff   1974) 32pp. For keyboard instrument. Informative preface in English and German deals with sources and editorial procedure. These pieces are good examples of contrapuntal skill using attractive subjects. Contains a few printed musical errors. M-D.

WILLIAM ALBRIGHT (1944–   ) USA

The Dream Rags   1970 (MS available from composer: c/o School of Music, University of Michigan, Ann Arbor, MI 48105) 25pp. 1. Sleepwalker's Shuffle: lazy, full chords, large span required; trio leads to a "Chicken Scratch" Harlem style. 2. The Nightmare Fantasy Rag—A Night on Rag Mountain: a kind of Lisztian "Mephisto Waltz rag"; wild, fantastic, involved, cadenza, coda (cruel rock tempo), a rag to end all rags! 3. Morning Reveries—a Slow Drag: highly chromatic. All three riotous rags are extremely effective. D.

Grand Sonata in Rag (Jobert   1974) 21pp. Three sweeping movements in ragtime. 1. Scott Joplin's Victory; 2. Ragtime Turtledove; 3. Behemoth Two-Step. Technically and musically demanding (especially the second movement). Any movement would also work well by itself. A blend of sonata form with rag characteristics. D.

Three Novelty Rags   1973 (Jobert) 17pp. Written with William Bolcom. Sleight of Hand, or Legerdemain Rag; Burnt Fingers; Brass Knuckles. Attractive, clever, tricky, delightful fun for performer and audience. M-D.

Sweet Sixteenths (EBM   1977) in collection *Ragtime Current*. Interesting irregular left-hand part. M-D.

See: David Burge, "William Albright," CK, 3 (March 1977):52. A discussion of Albright's newest work for piano, *Five Chromatic Dances,* and an interview.

RAFFAELE D'ALESSANDRO (1911–1959) Switzerland

4 Visions Op.49 (Gerig   1973) 8pp. Four short contrasting pieces. No. 3. "Somnambulique" has wide chord spacing. Large span required. M-D.

HAIM ALEXANDER (1915–   ) Israel

Patterns (IMI 325) 11pp. 6 min. Required piece for the first Arthur

Rubinstein International Piano Competition held in Israel in 1974. Strong rhythmic figurations throughout; wide span required. M-D.

JOSEF ALEXANDER (1910–) USA
Incantation in collection *New Music for the Piano* (LG).
Playthings (Gen).

ANATOLY ALEXANDROW (1888–) USSR
Three Pieces (GS 111). Prelude Op.10/3. Idyll Op.21/2. Melody Op.33/3.
Sonata No.4 Op.19 (GS 116).
Suite-Fantasy on motifs from the Opera "Bela" Op.51 (GS 123).
Echoes of the Theater Op.60 (GS 107). A suite.
Sonata No.10 Op.72 (GS 120).
12 Bashkir Melodies Op.73 (GS 105).
5 Pieces Op.75 (GS 112).
10 Russian Folk Melodies Op.76 Book 2 (GS 114).
Petite Suite Op.79 (GS 108).
Sonata-Fairy Tale (Sonata No.13) Op.90 (GS 121).
Sonata No.14 Op.97 (Soviet Composer 1971) 31pp.
6 Easy Pieces (GS 106).
Piano Works Vol. 2 (GS 4164).
Album of Pieces Book 2 (GS 4356).

HUGO ALFVEN (1872–1960) Sweden
See: Jan Olof Ruden, *Hugo Alfvens kompositioner* (Stockholm: NMS, 1972), 323pp. This thematic index contains a preface, introduction, and table of contents in English and Swedish.

ALEXANDER A. ALIABEV (1787–1851) Russia
Selections from His Piano Works (USSR). Consists mainly of short pieces in a post-Mozart style with some indebtedness to John Field. Int. to M-D.

HEITOR ALIMONDA (1922–) Brazil
O Estudo do Piano (Ric Brazil 1967) 10 vols. A piano course covering the main ingredients for developing a solid pianistic background. Easy to M-D.
Movimento Perpétuo (Ric Brazil 1966) 2pp. Ostinato treatment recalls Ibert's *The Little White Donkey*. M-D.
Estudo No.I (Ric Brazil 1956) 3pp. Romantic, tuneful. Int.
Estudo No.II (Wehrs 1958) 1 min.
Estudo No.III (Gerig 1957) 3pp. Moving thirds in right hand, then left hand; melody in opposite hand; contrary motion thirds in next to last bar. M-D.
Sonatina II (SDM 1960–1) 11pp. 8 min. Three movements. M-D.
Desafio (Wehrs 1956) 2 min.

Festa (Wehrs   1956) 1 min.
Modinha (Wehrs   1956) 2 min.

CHARLES HENRI VALENTIN ALKAN (1813–1888) France
The Alkan "boom" continues, and many of his works justify being rescued from oblivion.

Concerto da Camera I Op.10/1 a (Musica Obscura). Adagio is available separately from same publisher.

Concerto da Camera II Op.10/2 c♯ (Musica Obscura).

3 Etudes de bravoure (Improvisations) Op.12 (Billaudot).

3 Andantes Romantiques Op.13 (Billaudot).

3 Morceaux dans le genre pathétique Op.15 (Billaudot) 53pp. Aime-moi; Le vent; Morte.

3 Etudes de bravoure (Scherzi) Op.16 (Billaudot).

3 Nocturnes (Billaudot) No.1, Op.22; No.2, Op.57/1; No.3, Op.57/2.

Gigue et air de ballet dans le style ancien Op.24 (Billaudot).

Alleluia Op.25 (Billaudot; Musica Obscura) 5pp.

Le Chemin de fer Op.27 (Billaudot) etude.

25 Preludes Op.31 (Billaudot) for piano or organ, 62pp.

Sonata Op.33 "Les Quatre Ages" (Billaudot).

12 Etudes in Major Keys Op.35 (Joubert) 32 min. Some of Alkan's finest works.

3 Marches Op.37 (Billaudot) Quasi da Cavalleria.

12 Chants (Billaudot) 1st and 2nd suites, Op.38; 3rd Suite, Op.65; 4th Suite, Op.67; 5th Suite, Op.70. Six chants in each suite of Opp.65, 67, and 70. Op.38/9 Chant de Guerre (Musica Obscura).

5 Barcarolles (Billaudot) published separately. No.1 Op.38; No.2 Op.38; No.3 Op.65; No.4 Op.67; No.5 Op.70.

Etude de Concert Op.38/1 (Billaudot). Alkan gave the same opus numbers to different compositions; he also republished some works under different opus numbers. Therefore it is impossible for this list to be complete or completely accurate.

12 Etudes in Minor Keys Op.39 (Billaudot) in two suites, six pieces in each. 1. Comme le vent: 27 min. 2. Rhythme molossique. 3. Scherzo diabolico. 4. Allegro moderato. 5 Marche funèbre. 6. Menuet. 7. Finale. 8. Concerto: Allegro assai. 9. Concerto: Adagio. 10. Allegro alla Barbaresca. 11. Ouverture. 12. Le festin d'Esope. The Finale is somewhat like a cross between a bolero and a polonaise, an eclectic sprawling piece full of imagination, skill, craft, and virtuosity. Nos. 4–7 make up the *Symphony for Piano Solo*. This set contains some of Alkan's most interesting compositions. No. 12 is one of his finest achievements and shows Alkan at the height of his powers.

3 Petites fantaisies Op.41 (Billaudot) 35pp.

Réconciliation, petite caprice en forme de Zorcico Op.42 (Billaudot) 10pp. Contains some sonorous effects. M-D.

Salut cendre du pauvre Op.45 (Billaudot).

Capriccio alla solidatesca Op.50/1 (Billaudot). Left-hand clusters, fantastic writing.

Le Tambour bat aux champs Op.50/2 (Billaudot).

3 Minuets Op.51 (Billaudot).

Super flumina Babylonis, paraphrase Op.52 (Billaudot).

Quasi-caccia, caprice Op.53 (Billaudot).

Une Fusée Op.55 (Billaudot). Introduction and Impromptu.

Ma Chère Liberté Op.60/1 (Billaudot).

Ma Chère Servitude Op.60/2 (Billaudot).

Sonatine a Op.61 (Billaudot).

48 Esquisses Op.63 (Billaudot). Four suites, twelve pieces in each. Some are published separately by Billaudot. Nos.42 and 48 (Musica Obscura).

Laus Deo Op.63/49 (Billaudot; Musica Obscura).

Les Mois Op.74 (Billaudot). Twelve pieces in four suites published in four books. Six republished Op.8. No.7, Nue nuit d'été (Musica Obscura); No.12, l'Opera (Musica Obscura).

Toccatina Op.75 (Billaudot; Musica Obscura).

3 Grandes Etudes Op.76 (Billaudot). 1. Fantaisic A♭: left hand only. 2. Introduction, Variation, Finale: right hand only. 3. Mouvement semblable et perpetuel: for both hands. Published separately. D.

Perpetuum Mobile (Billaudot). Preparatory to Op.76.

Deux Fugues (Musica Obscura). Jean qui pleure. Jean qui rit.

Oeuvres choises (F. M. Delaborde, I. Philipp—Billaudot 1970). Super flumina Babylonis, Op.52; Paraphrase du psaume 137, Op.52.

See: Bryce Morrison, "Alkan the Mysterious," M&M, 22 (June 1974): 30–32. Mainly discusses *Sonata* Op.33.

DOUGLASS ALLANBROOK (1921–   ) USA

12 Preludes for all seasons 1974 (Bo&H) 25pp. One short prelude for each month of the year. Advanced compositional and pianistic techniques are used. Linear writing interspersed with vertical sonorities. For the artist student. D.

CARLOS VIANNA DE ALMEIDA (1906–   ) Brazil

Serenata à brasileira 1932 (Mangione 1941) 3 min.

Ritmos Cariocas 1st series 1937 (Napoleão 1964) 10 min.

Ritmos Cariocas 2nd series 1940 (Napoleão 1964) 10 min.

Seresta I 1943 (Fermata 1964) 5 min.

Divertimento 1962 (Fermata) 5 min.

Seresta IV 1966 (Napoleão 1970) 5 min.

CARLO ROQUÉ ALSINA (1941–   ) Argentina

Estudio II Op.6 1960 (SZ 1974) 15pp. Explanations in Italian and Spanish.

Klavierstück III Op.8 1962–65 (SZ 1974) 13pp.

4 Klavierstücke Op.23 (SZ   1969) One loose leaf. Explanations in Italian and German. Beria influence present. Avant-garde.

DELAMAR ALVARENGA (1952–   ) Brazil
Since 1962 Alvarenga has lived in São Paulo and has studied with Oliver Toni.
Ah Vous Dirai-Je Maman   1970 (Universidade de São Paulo   1972, Escola de Communicacões e Artes, São Paulo, Brazil) 7pp. Aleatoric, improvisational, new notation. Directions are given for three different realizations. Avant-garde.
Estudo a duas vozes   1969 (Ric) 2pp. This work attempts to integrate daily sounds into the context of a musical structure in two voices. Improvisational, graphic notation. On the 30th repetition the pianist must decide how to bring about the climax by using anything except the glissando. Avant-garde.

WILLIAM ALWYN (1905–   ) Great Britain
Alwyn teaches composition at the Royal Academy of Music in London. He is best known as a writer of music for over fifty films. He composes in an unashamed Romantic style that is full of instrumental color.
Sonata alla Toccata (Lengnick   1951) 21pp. Maestoso: C, basically diatonic, much rhythmic drive. Andante con moto e semplice: F, much use of thirds in melody and accompaniment. Molto vivace: F—f; triplet figuration prominent; requires good octave technique; concludes with an effective Presto furioso. M-D.
Fantasy-Waltzes (Lengnick   1956) 48pp. Eleven pieces inspired by Schubert and Ravel, cast in a MC harmonic idiom. Some charming, delectable writing, always grateful for pianist and audience. M-D.
Twelve Preludes (Lengnick   1959) 33pp. Each is written in a specific key, i.e., No.I in E♭, No.II in A, No.6 in G and F♯, etc., but with no key signature. Each piece is a complete entity and "fits the hand" beautifully. An impressive set that shows there is still plenty to be said in the key of C. M-D.

ANDRÉ AMELLER (1912–   ) France
Montreal (Leduc   1973) 3pp. 3 min. Short prelude that opens with an expressive recitative, octotonic writing interspersed with MC chords, modal. Impressionistic portrayal of Montreal, bell sonorities. M-D.

JUAN AMENÁBAR (1922–   ) Chile
Suite (IEM   1952) 13 min.

EMANUEL AMIRAN-POUGATCHOV (1909–   ) Poland
Lahat (Ecstasy) (IMI   1974) 20pp. A toccata for the adventurous pianist. M-D.

PIERRE ANCELIN (1934–   ) France
Prelude (Choudens   1965) 7pp.

THOMAS JEFFERSON ANDERSON (1928–   ) USA
Watermelon   1971 (IU M25.A552 W2; CFE) 11pp. 6 min.

VOLKMAR ANDREAE (1879–1962) Switzerland
Sechs Klavierstücke Op.20 (Hug   1911). Praeludium; Bacchantischer
    Tanz; Frage; Catalonisches Ständchen; Adagio; Unruhige Nacht.
    Post-Brahms writing, well-conceived pianistic sonorities. Available
    separately. M-D.

JURRIAAN ANDRIESSEN (1925–   ) The Netherlands
Roger's Sonatine (B&VP 1237). Outside movements are lively while the
    middle one is a sensitive sarabande. Refreshing. Contains no stretch
    larger than a seventh. Int.

JEAN-HENRI D'ANGLEBERT (1635–1691) France
Pièces de Clavecin (Kenneth Gilbert—Heugel   1975). This easy-to-read
    edition offers all of the 1689 collection plus 35 more pieces, 13 of
    which were previously unpublished. M-D.

ISTVAN ANHALT (1919–   ) Canada, born Hungary
Fantasia for piano (Berandol).

ANONYMOUS
A Scotish Gigg (Marie Zorn—A. Broude   1977). Recently discovered in
    the MS collection of the New York Public Library, this infectious
    sixteenth- or early seventeenth-century jig is of doubtful parentage,
    but keyboard players will be happy to "adopt" it. Int. to M-D.

ANONYMOUS
Presto d'incerto autore (D. Bishop, M. Hinson—Hinshaw   1977) 8pp. A
    delightful gigue-like piece in two-voice imitative style located in
    Muzio Clementi's *Introduction to the Art of Playing on the Piano
    Forte*, second part (1821). It is probably by an Italian composer of
    the second half of the eighteenth century. Preface includes discussion
    of style and interpretation, dynamics, ornaments, fingering. A perfect
    preparation piece for the J. S. Bach *Two-Part Inventions*. Int.

GEORGE ANTHEIL (1900–1959) USA
Sonata II "The Airplane" (NME   1931). Tricky rhythms; first move-
    ment has a funny twelve-bar repetitive sequence. D.

THEODORE ANTONIOU (1935–   ) Greece
Antoniou teaches at the Philadelphia Music Academy, 313 South St.,
    Philadelphia, PA 19107.
Sonata Op.7   1959 (MS available from composer) 15pp. Allegro mo-
    derato; Scherzino; Adagio; Presto. Freely tonal and chromatic; sec-
    onds, fourths, and sevenths are prevalent; vigorous rhythms. Osti-
    nato-like in Adagio, with secco left-hand octaves. Octotonic and
    shifting meters in finale. Greek flavor, interesting and effective. M-D.

Sil-ben (Syllables) (Gerig 1965) 4pp. in collection *Contemporary Greek Piano Music*. Six short pieces, each based on certain properties of letters or syllables in speech. Constructed on a twelve-tone row that also uses parameters of serial organization. 1. Parachesis: a sound group recurs frequently, like the recurring syllable creating this rhetoric figure in speech; dynamic extremes; hands crossed. 2. Anagram: the position of notes is interchanged in quick passages with different quantities that always end on a stressed note; short groups of fast chromatic notes stop on a long melody note. 3. Derivatives: a sound group or note induces others to sound as in language; addition of prefixes or suffixes leads to new words; pointillistic. 4. Epenthesis: middle register is altered in timbre by placing a book on the strings, giving a harpsichord-like sound; a motive has been transposed, therefore, and varied. Aphairesis: the Greek word means both subtraction and abstraction; glissando on string; plucked strings. Conclusion: a theme in a different style appears amid motives from the preceding movement; finally it is assimilated. Experimental. D.

Acquarelle (Edition Modern 1967) 14pp. in a package. 15 min. Ten separate pieces. Adagio espressivo; Vivo e secco; Largo mysterioso; Allegro ritmico; Andante espressivo; Allegro brioso; Andantino calmo; Presto scherzino; Largo amoroso; Allegro barbaro. Colorful and appealing pieces written in a freely tonal idiom with use of some serial technique. MC sonorities. Entire suite or a selection of the pieces would add strong interest to any program. One suggested grouping consists of Nos.2, 3, 8, 10. Requires above-average pianistic ability. M-D.

DAVIDE ANZAGHI (1936–   ) Italy
Segni (SZ 1971). Palinsesto I. Twenty-one loose leaves in cover.
Ritografia (SZ 1972) 19 loose leaves in cover. Reproduction of composer's MS. 10 min. Avant-garde.

GEORGES APERGHIS (1945–   ) France, born Greece
Simata (Amphion 1970) 14pp. for prepared piano or harpsichord.

RAFAEL APONTE-LEDÉE (1938–   ) Puerto Rico
Aponte-Ledée teaches composition in the Department of Music of the University of Puerto Rico.
Tema y seis diferencias (PIC 1963) 6pp. 3 min. Serial, six short contrasting and effective variations, frequent meter changes, contemporary treatment. M-D.

EDWARD APPLEBAUM (1938–   ) USA
Applebaum teaches at the University of California, Santa Barbara.
Sonata (WH 1965) 16pp. 12 min. Reproduction of the MS is not very legible, and there are a number of errors in the score. Serial, con-

temporary idioms. Mirrors: a mixture of contrasting sounds, i.e., dissonant chords, fast passagework, moderate tempo. Gestures: pedal effects, more colorful sonorities including a tremolo passage to be played "à la Errol Garner." D.

STAN APPLEBAUM (1929–   ) USA
Sound World (Schroeder & Gunther   1974) 23pp. A collection of new keyboard experiences. 31 short pieces that will open new worlds of sonorities for the intermediate pianist. Each new technique explained in detail. May be played separately or grouped in sets to form a miniature suite. Ideas developed include: major seconds, bitonality, perfect fourths contrasted with augmented fourths, clusters, twelve-tone piece. Int.
Frenzy-Toccata (Broude   1977) 4pp. In 6/8 with frequent hand alternations, bitonal, chromatic, thin textures, Vivace agilimente directions. M-D.
Bach Music—Simple Style (Schroeder & Gunther).

TITO APREA (1904–   ) Italy
15 Dances for Piano (Ric   1973) 39pp. Colorful illustrations. Range from folk to circus dances. Imaginative and some original writing. Pastorale Dance; Rustic Dance; Dance of the Ant; Dance of the Elephant; Dance of the Flea; Dance of the Chicks; Pierrot's Dance; Ponchinello's Dance; etc. Int.

BORIS ALEKSANDROVICH ARAPOV (1905–   ) USSR
Sonata (Sovetskii Kompozitor   1973) 39pp.

VIOLET ARCHER (1913–   ) Canada
4 Little Studies   1964 (Waterloo) 2pp. Each piece concentrates on one contemporary technique. Int.
3 Miniatures (Waterloo   1965) 4pp. Dreaming; Dark Mood; Determination. MC. Int.
Habitant Sketches (TP). Three scenes: Jig; Church Scene; Christmas in Quebec. Int.
Theme and Variations   1964 (Waterloo) 5pp. Flowing theme, six contrasting short variations. Int.
Four Bagatelles   1977 (CMC).

ANTON ARENSKY (1861–1906) Russia
12 Etudes Op.74 (C. Sorel—EBM). Excellent preface. Each piece is in a different key. Varied styles; fine recital material; excellent for developing flexible wrist motion, nimble fingers, and tonal control. Carefully edited with commentary. M-D.
Piano Selections (L. Prosypalova—USSR   1976) 61pp. Contains studies and other piano pieces. M-D.
Two Pieces (GS 139). In the Field, Op.36. No.24 Prelude in d, Op.63/10.

12 Selected Pieces (GS 4228).
Selected Piano Pieces (GS 8016).

ISABEL ARETZ (1913–   ) Venezuela, born Argentina
Since 1952 Dr. Aretz has been the director of the Inter-American Institute of Ethnomusicology and Folklore of the National Institute of Culture and Fine Arts in Venezuela.
Sonata (PAU   1965) 27pp. Moderato agitato: textures are thin and widely spread. Andante—Ostinato—Scherzando: mid-section scherzando breaks monotony of Andante—Ostinato. Toccata—Allegro: major seventh exploited in propulsive movement. M-D.

PAUL ARMA (1905–   ) France, born Hungary
Trois Epitaphes (EMT   1945) 9pp. 15 min. I. Pour Romain Roland: improvisatory, quietly moving harmonic sevenths with a chordal accompaniment, unbarred. II. Pour ceux qui ne sont jamais revenus: mes amis torturés, massacrés: written on four and five staffs; octotonic; chordal punctuation; builds to large climax, then subsides; *ppp* closing. III. Pour Béla Bartók, qui fut mon maître et mon ami: slow-moving chords, long-held sonorities; requires large span. Individual style. M-D.
Cinq Esquisses (EMT   1969) 4pp. 7 min. Parlando; Rubato; Con allegrezza; Lento rubato, con dolore; Con fretta. Contrasting, colorful, based on popular Hungarian melodies. Makes a fine set performed together. Int. to M-D.
A la decouverte du passé (Lemoine   1947) Fourteen easy pieces.
31 Instantanés   1949 (MS available from composer: 132 Ave. de Clamart, Issy (Seine), France) 10pp. 31 short pieces (some are less than two lines long) that capture fleeting ideas, moods, reactions. Prologue; à 4 Voix; Assurance; Esquisse; Humour; Courbes; Persistance; Laconisme; Tourbillon; Chant; Oppositions; Dans le rhythme "Akshak"; etc. Int. to M-D.

THOMAS ARNE (1710–1778) Great Britain
A Keyboard Allegro (C. Hogwood—OUP   1974). A graceful and melodically deft alternative for a Bach *Two-Part Invention*. Was originally the third movement of *Concerto* in C. Editor adds an improvised cadenza on the diminished seventh just before the close. A good student could and should expand this. Int.
See: Arthur Steiger, "Thomas Arne and His Keyboard Sonatas," *Clavier* 16 (May 1977). Brief remarks on the eight sonatas by Arne.

MALCOLM ARNOLD (1921–   ) Great Britain
Arnold is one of the most distinctive voices in English music.
Buccaneer (Lengnick). Healthy rhythmic drive. Int.
Variations on a Ukrainian Folk-Song (Lengnick   1944). Diatonic idiom.

Expressive theme harmonized in a mildly dissonant style. Ten variations cover the gamut of contrast; Var. 10 serves as a coda to the complete work. Has much audience appeal and could add excitement to a program. M-D.

Children's Suite—Six Little Studies Op.16 (Lengnick 1948). Prelude: study in fourths and fifths. Carol: study in legato thirds for left hand. Shepherd's Lament: study in triplets and accidentals. Trumpet Tune: study in trills and rhythmic playing. Blue tune: study in rhythms and color. Folk-Song: study in touch and phrasing. Short, attractive, clever. Int.

JUAN CRISOSTOMO ARRIAGA (1806–1826) Spain

Tres Estudios de Caracter (Dotesio). Allegro; Moderato; Risoluto. Classic style infused with some chromatic usage. Int. to M-D.

CLAUDE ARRIEU (1903–   ) France

Arrieu studied piano with Marguerite Long and composition with Jean Roger-Ducasse and Noël Gallon.

Marche, Etude, Choral (Heugel 1929).

La boite à malice (Lemoine 1931). Eight pieces.

Musique pour piano (Sal 1939).

Prélude, Forlane et Gigue (Enoch 1940).

Quatre pièces (Choudens 1946).

Sarabande (Chant du Monde 1946).

Trois improvisations (Amphion 1948).

Mouvement perpétuel (Amphion 1948).

Valse (Billaudot 1948).

Quatre Etudes-caprices (Ric 1954).

Toccata pour Clavecin (ou Piano) (Leduc 1963) 7 min. Registration leads to Allegro. A mid-section Commenciando Lento (quasi Cadenza) provides contrast before a return to faster tempi. Allegro sections have numerous ritards. M-D.

Les Petites Filles Modèles (Amphion 1975) 7pp.

Petit Récit. La Poupée Cassée (Billaudot 1976) 2pp.

Escapade et Cerf-Volant (Billaudot 1976) 4pp.

Promenade Melancolique et Questionnaire (Billaudot 1976) 4pp.

Prélude Pastoral. L'Enfant Sage (Billaudot 1976) 2pp.

All of these recent Billaudot publications are easy teaching pieces written in a traditional style.

JOHN H. ASHTON (1938–   ) USA

Ashton is a graduate of Carnegie-Mellon University and studied composition with Nikolai Lopatnikoff. He teaches at Fairmont State College in Fairmont, West Virginia.

Theme and Five Variations (Seesaw) 19pp. Var.I: March, *pp* and stac-

cato. Var.II: Andante, freely. Var.III: Very fast. Var.IV: Chorale
Prelude. Var.V: Finale, brightly. Solid neoclassical writing. M-D.

JAN ASTRIAB (1937–   ) Poland
Four Pieces (AA   1971) 8 min.
Sonores (AA   1972) 10 min.

GEORGES AURIC (1899–   ) France
Gaspard et Zoé (WH 3131).
Imaginées V   1976 (Sal) 7pp.
La Seine, au Matin (Sal   1975) Available separately. Light and spirited
mood. All French words are translated into English. M-D.

LARRY AUSTIN (1930–   ) USA
Austin teaches at the University of South Florida in Tampa. Some of his
recent works include theatrical, multimedia, and live electronic techniques.
Piano Set in Open Style (CPE   1964). Directions discuss space-time,
i.e., durations of single notes and/or groups of notes are determined
by the visual space between. Blank spaces are silent. Durational
gradations are obtained by use of the tie. Pointillistic, expressionistic.
Avant-garde. D.
Piano Variations (MJQ).

MENAHEM AVIDOM (1908–   ) Israel, born Poland
Hommage à Schoenberg   1974 (IMI 307) 6pp. 4½ min. Serial; based
on a hexachord derived from Schoenberg's name; displays strong
musical integrity. M-D.
Erste Stücke für Miriam (IMI 128).
Kleines Ballett für Daniela (IMI 129a).

JORGE GONZALEZ AVILA (1925–   ) Mexico
24 Invenciones (EMM   1964) 15pp. 2 vols. I: 1–9; II: 10–24. Atonal;
individual ideas for each invention are well developed. Displays a
fine craft. M-D.

THOMAS AVINGER (1929–   ) USA
Avinger lives in Houston, Texas. He received his Master's degree in com-
position from Baylor University.
Sonata   1968 (MS available from composer: 7622 Grape St., Houston,
TX 77036). Allegro ma non troppo; Lento e grazioso; Misterioso—
Presto ed agitato, sempre molto marcato. Effective rhythmic and
melodic writing throughout, some counterpoint and thick textures,
thoroughly contemporary. M-D.

JACOB AVSHALOMOV (1919–   ) USA, born China
Slow Dance (TP).

B

MILTON BABBITT (1916–) USA

3 Compositions for Piano (Bomart 1947).
> See: H. Wiley Hitchcock, *Music in the United States* (New York: Prentice-Hall, 1969), pp.232–35 for an analysis of this set.

Post Partitions (CFP 1973) 4 min. To be performed immediately after *Partitions* or independently. Atonal, pitch, rhythm, dynamics are all serial, complex. D.

Reflections (CFP) for piano and tape. 9½ min. Based on a scale of twelve dynamic values ranging from *ppppp* to *fffff* plus *mf* and *mp*. Three separate sections; in the first two the piano and tape exchange places while in the third the basic musical and sonorous materials are superimposed on each other. The title refers to the structure and content of the work, which is composed of reflections and interchanges between the piano and the loudspeakers, as well as to the organization of twelve-tone material. D.
> See: *Contemporary Music Newsletter,* May–June 1975, for a thorough analysis of this complex and highly sensitive piece.

Semi-Simple Variations (TP 1956).
> See: Christopher Wintle, "Milton Babbitt's Semi-Simple Variations," PNM, 14–15 (1976):111–54.

Tableaux (CFP 1973) 30pp. 9½ min. Pointillistic, complex rhythms, constant dynamic changes, proportional rhythmic notation. Virtuoso technique required. D.

Playing for Time 1977 (Hinshaw) in collection *Twelve by Eleven.* 12pp. Employs characteristically unfamiliar rhythmic notation in a simple context (3/4 meter). The underlying "set" finally evolves and appears explicitly in (and among other places) the final four measures. Highly organized musical syntax, pointillistic. Falls into place remarkably fast when read through even a few times. Contains some unique pianistic sonorities. M-D.

GRAZYNA BACEWICZ (1913–1969) Poland

Ten Studies (PWM 1958) 42pp. Covers pianistic problems such as leaps, extreme keyboard range, legato sixths, polyrhythms. Powerful writing. D.

Petit Triptyque (PWM 1966) 7pp. Three short complementary pieces using strong contemporary compositional techniques. M-D.

CARL PHILIPP EMANUEL BACH (1714–1788) Germany

Leichte Spielstücke (Hug 1971) 12pp. Menuett D; Allegretto C; Aria B♭; Rondo b; Arioso con Variazioni A; Polonaise a. Int.

4 Fantasias (Gát—EMB) No.18 Thesaurus Musicus.

Seven Pieces (E. Caland, F. P. Goebels—Heinrichshofen 1975) 48pp. Contains pieces from various collections: Sonatas W.51/4, 5; Rondos W.53/3, W.58/1, 3; and two short pieces, *La Stahl* and *Les languers tendres,* W.117/24. Editorial notes in German; editorial additions are confusing. A few interpretations of certain ornaments are questionable. M-D.

Sechs Sonaten mit veränderten Reprisen W.50 (Etienne Darbellay—Amadeus 1760, 1976) 72pp. Preface and critical report in German and English. Six sonatas with varied reprises. An exemplary edition including comprehensive critical material. "Play from the soul, not like a trained bird." This aphorism sums up the whole aesthetic approach of C. P. E. Bach, an approach that defines the style known as *Empfindsamkeit.* M-D.

Sonatas, Fantasias and Rondos (K 890). M-D.

Piano Works (Herrmann—CFP 4188). Sonatas and Pieces: W.50/5; 51/3; 52/3; 61/1; 65/48; 116/16, 17, 21. M-D.

Six Sonatas 1761 W.51 (Juanelva Rose—TP 1973). No.8 in Series of Early Music, University of California, Santa Barbara. These works appear here for the first time in a modern edition. They generally reflect the more conservative harmonic language favored by King Frederick. Table of ornaments and editorial notes are included. Interesting examples of works written between the Baroque and Classic periods. See especially No.6, g. M-D.

Kurze und leichte Clavierstücke (O. Jonas—UE). The word "easy" (*leichte*) is used rather loosely! Int.

18 Probestücke W.63 (L. Hoffmann-Erbrecht—Br&H 1957).

Fantasia C (J. Friskin—JF 8831). Sectional; exhibits a humorous liveliness; anticipates boisterous pranks of Haydn and Beethoven. Int.

Sonata G (Zingel—Br&H).

6 Sonatas (Hoffmann-Erbrecht—Br&H; Doflein—Schott 2 vols. 2353/4) written to go with *The Essay on the True Art of Playing the Keyboard.*

La Xenophone & La Sybille (Nemeth-Fiedler—OBV).

Keyboard Pieces with Varied Reprises (O. Jonas—UE 13311). These are C. P. E. Bach's "Inventions." Int.

14 leichte Klavierstücke (V. Luithlen, H. Kraus—UE 11015).

6 Sonatas (P. Friedheim—State University of N.Y., through Galaxy). W.65/9, 16, 23; 62/19; 52/2; 53/4. M-D.

3 Leichte Klaviersonaten (Zürcher—Schott 4707).

See: Eugene Helm, *A Thematic Catalog of the Works of Carl Philipp Emanuel Bach* (New Haven: Yale University Press, 1979).

Walter Schenkman, "Three Collections of Keyboard Works by C. P. E. Bach," Part I, *Bach,* 8 (October 1977):23–33; Part II, *Bach,* 9 (January 1978):2–14. Deals with three representative collections of keyboard works: the *Prussian* and *Wüttemberg Sonatas* and the *Sechs Sammlungen für Kenner und Liebhaber.*

JOHANN CHRISTIAN BACH (1735–1782) Germany

12 Keyboard Sonatas (Christopher Hogwood—OUP). A facsimile of the original eighteenth-century editions with an excellent introduction by the editor. Set I Op.5 (1768): 6 sonatas. Set II Op.17 (1779): 6 sonatas. All twelve show the *stile gallant* at its best. Both sets sound fine on the piano or harpsichord but even better on the fortepiano. Excellent preparation for Mozart sonatas. Int. to M-D.

Sonata A (Nag).

Sonata A Op.18/5 (Nag 115).

Leichte Spielstücke für Klavier (Hug 1971). Menuett F; Andantino F; Marsch C; Allegretto a; Menuett and Trio D; Theme and Variations G. Easy to Int.

JOHANN CHRISTOPH BACH (1642–1703) Germany

This Bach was a cousin of Johann Sebastian's father.

Aria a with 15 Variations (G. Birkner—Amadeus 1973) 12pp. Charming. Int. to M-D.

Sarabande mit 12 Variationen (H. Riemann—Steingräber).

Prelude and Fugue E♭ (Steingräber). Bischoff formerly attributed this work to J. S. Bach (S.Anh.177). Effective. M-D.

JOHANN CHRISTOPH FRIEDRICH BACH (1732–1795) Germany

Variations on "Ah, vous dirai-je Maman" (Barbé—Hug 1966). Theme and fourteen short, delightful variations. Int. to M-D.

Leichte Spielstücke für Klavier (Hug 1971). Arioso F; Menuett and Trio D; Andantino G; Allegretto c; Polonaise D; Andante F. Easy to Int.

JOHANN SEBASTIAN BACH (1685–1750) Germany

(K) has the keyboard works edited by Bischoff in miniature scores.

Two-Part Inventions (G. Anson—Willis) with performance suggestions and ornamentation. (Banowetz—GWM 1974) contains an extensive discussion of ornamentation, fingering, rhythmic conventions, tempi. Editorial suggestions in red print, excellent preface, helpful performance suggestions. (Landshoff—CFP; Pestalozza—Ric 1973; Solymos—EMB 1972).

See: TM, Analysis of Invention in d, pp.56–67.

Two- and Three-Part Inventions (Georg von Dadelsen—Br 1972). From Volume V/3 of the New Bach Edition. The appendix includes six of the sinfonias in the ornamented form in which they survive in two MSS belonging to Bach's pupils. (Ratz, Füssl, Jonas—VU 50042). Edited and annotated from autographs and MS copies. Contains a charming rhythmic variant of Invention I. Extensive critical notes and preface. (Lajos Hernardi—EMB; Alexander, Lofthouse—ABRSM).

See: Karl Heinz Füssl, "Bach's Secret Composition Course," PQ, 93 (Spring 1976):18–19. A discussion of the Inventions and Sinfonias as Bach's only manual on composition.

Six French Suites (Robert Kail—Ashley; T. Zaszkaliczky—EMB 1975, Epilogue in Hungarian, German, and English).

Six English Suites (A. Kreutz—CFP 4580A/B; Tamás—EMB 1977; Robert Kail—Ashley).

Six Partitas (Richard Douglas Jones—Br, part of the New Bach Edition; R. D. Jones—DVFM). Available separately: No.I B♭ (W. Palmer—Alfred).

See: Charles Joseph, "Performing Bach on the Piano," *Clavier,* 14 (November 1975):20, 36–39. Discusses Partita III a (S.827) and compares the tempi in three editions and in three different recordings.

French Overture S.831 (W. Emery—Br 5161 with the *Italian Concerto*) with early version of S.831a.

See: Frederick Neumann, "The Question of Rhythm in the Two Versions of Bach's French Overture S.831," in *Studies in Renaissance and Baroque Music in Honor of Arthur Mendel* (Kassel: Bärenreiter, 1974), pp.183–94.

Concerto in the Italian Manner S.971 (Klaus Engler—VU 1977) 19pp., facsimile. Fingering by Max Martin Stein, edited from first editions and MS copies. Preface and critical note in German and English. (W. Palmer, Linder—Alfred). With *French Overture* (Br 5161).

See: Wha Kyung Choi, "The Italian Concerto of J. S. Bach and Its Interpretation," Master's thesis, Southern Illinois University, 1965.

Four Duets S.802–805 (M. Tessmer—Br).

The Goldberg Variations S.988 (C. Wolff—Br 5162).

See: Wadham Sutton, "J. S. Bach: The Goldberg Variations," *Music Teacher,* 54 (August 1975):11.

14 Canons S.1087 (C. Wolff—Br 5153). From Vol.V/2 of the New Bach Edition. Recently discovered work that is based on the main subject of the *Goldberg Variations*. Published for the first time. Contains a facsimile of the original MS and reproduces the canons in their original notation; also offers suggestions by the editor for their solution and performance. (Sal 1976) with realizations by Olivier Alain.

The Well-Tempered Clavier I S.846–69 (Walther Dehnhard—VU 1977) 121pp. Contains two facsimiles. Score edited from the autograph and MS copies. Preface and critical note in German and English. Fingering by Detlef Kraus. (Amsco) 2 vols. Eight-page introduction and fingering by Glenn Gould, who presents a viable argument for performing both volumes on the piano. The text is the one edited by Franz Kroll and published by CFP over a hundred years ago. (Br&H) facsimile of Vol.I. (O. Morgan—Ashdown) 2 vols.
Available separately: Preludes and Fugues S.850, 851, 861, 871 (Schott).
Scc: Joseph Matthews, "Busoni's Contribution to Piano Pedagogy," DM diss., Indiana University, 1977, 120pp. See especially the chapter on Busoni's edition of Bach's *The Well-Tempered Clavier*.
Carl Schacter, "Bach's Fugue in B♭ Major, Well-Tempered Clavier, Book I, No.XXI," in *The Music Forum*, 3 (1973):239–67. A thorough analysis oriented toward a Schenkerian approach. Konrad Wolff, "Fugue Subjects without Leading Tone in the WTC," PQ, 100 (Winter 1977–78):11–12, 14. Paul Pisk, "A New Look at the 'Great 48,' " *Bach*, 8 (April 1977):23–25.

The Little Notebook for Anna Magdalena Bach. Bach himself started this collection with the two large partitas (Partita a S.827, Partita e, S.830) as a form of dedication. The *Klavierbüchlein*, with its patchwork of grave and gay, spontaneity and profound art, opens a door for us to the Bachs' daily life.

SEPARATE PIECES:

Chromatic Fantasia and Fugue d S.903 (Schenker, rev. Jonas—UE).
Capriccio, On the Departure of a Beloved Brother S.992 (Kreutz—Schott; Goldberger—GS), with added fingering and pedal, only as a legato aid.
Sonata C S.966 (K) in Various Works, Volume I: Praludium; Fuga; Adagio–Presto; Allemande; Courante; Sarabande; Gigue. Bach's transcription of a quartet by J. A. Reinken.
Sonata C S.966 (K) in Various Works, Volume I: Präludium; Fuga; Adagio; Allemande.
Aria with Variations in the Italian Manner S.989 (Amadeus/Paüler).
Fantasia c S.906 (Br 1976) facsimile edition with an introduction by R. L. Marshall. Preface in English and German, New Bach Edition.

COLLECTIONS for the Early Grades of Piano Study:

Kleine Präludien und Fughetten (Denhard—VU 1973). S.895, 899, 900, 902, 924–28, 930, 933–43, 952, 953, 961, 999. Edited from autograph and MS copies. Fingering added. Preface and critical notes in German and English.

20 Easy Pieces from Anna Magdalena Bach's Notebook (E. Sauer—CFP 3829).

The Young Bach (E. H. Davies—OUP).

Leichte Klavierstücke (H.-J. Schulze—CFP 9412 1974) 59pp. Preface and critical notes in German and English. Forty-five pieces compiled from various keyboard works. Int. to M-D.

Young Pianist's Guide to J. S. Bach (Y. Novik—Studio PR 1976) 24pp. with recording. Eleven pieces, mostly from the *Anna Magdalena Bach Notebook*. Well edited. Easy to Int.

The Young Pianist's Bach (H. Davies—OUP). Formerly titled "The Children's Bach."

Il Mio Primo Bach (E. Pozzoli—Ric E. R. 1951) 13pp. Vol.I: Minuets G, g, c, d, G, a; Musette G (from the Gavotte, English Suite g); Musette D; Polonaise g; Marches D, G; Prelude g. Easy to Int. Vol. II (Riboli—Ric 1973). Contains eight of the eighteen Short Preludes, three of the Two-Part Inventions. Fingering provided is used to indicate phrasing, mainly by thumb repetition. A few suggestions are given in footnotes but no dynamics or phrasing are indicated. Int.

Notenbuch der Anna Magdalena Bach (1725) (Sulyok Imre—EMB 1976) 27pp. Selections. Foreword in Hungarian, English, and German. Urtext edition.

Introduction to the Study of Bach (Mirovitch—GS 1955) 35pp. Contains a foreword, notes on interpretation, a Bach course of study (discussion of dance forms, the prelude, compositions in polyphonic form, the fugue, three-part inventions, English Suites and Partitas, Toccatas, *Well-Tempered Clavier*). Preparatory pieces by Hook, Zipoli, Chilcot, Kirnberger. Bach pieces include four Preludes and four movements from the French Suites. Int. to M-D.

Bach Easy Piano (Alfred). Seventeen easier selections of Bach's most familiar music from the suites and the *Anna Magdalena Bach Notebook*. Brief biography; notes concerning the style or origin of each piece; ornaments realized. Easy to Int.

Bach—Favorite Pieces (Alfred). Twenty-eight pieces with a few duplicates from the *Bach Easy Pieces* collection. Also includes more difficult works, such as 3 pieces from the *Wilhelm Friedemann Bach Notebook,* 4 Two-Part Inventions, 2 Preludes and Fugues from WTC I, dances from the suites, and transcriptions. A short biography and notes about each piece add interest. Int. to M-D.

J. S. Bach—An Introduction to His Keyboard Music (W. Palmer—Alfred). A varied selection of works with the usual fine introductory material providing a good understanding of the composer and his music. Int.

Easier Piano Pieces (H. J. Schulze—CFP 9412). A selection of 45 easy to M-D pieces and movements, either original or transcribed by Bach. With details of sources and comments by the editor in English and German.

Das Bach—Klavierbuch (Wiehmayer—Heinrichshofen 20). Fifty easy pieces.
J. S. Bach (Henry Duke—Freeman). In Keyboard Master Series. Prelude c (from *12 Short Preludes*); Courante G; Two-Part Inventions F, a, d; Three-Part Invention E; G from Partita I; Air on the G String; Prelude C from WTC I. Fingering, pedaling, and phrasing are added. Int. to M-D.

MORE DIFFICULT COLLECTIONS:

Sonatas and Partitas (PWM).
Keyboard Music (Dover) 312pp. A reprint of the Bach Gesellschaft edition, 1853 and 1863: 6 English Suites; 6 French Suites; 6 Partitas; Goldberg Variations; 15 Two-Part Inventions; 15 Three-Part Sinfonias. Clean edition. Int. to D.
14 Chorale Preludes (Zorn—Concordia). From the chorale preludes Bach wrote for the manuals alone.
Klavier und Lautenwerke (H. Eichberg, T. Kohlhase—Br 5044GA). Series V Vol.10 of the Neue Ausgabe Sämtlicher Werke. Contains following keyboard works: Ouverture F (Suite) S.820; Suite g, S.822; Suite f, S.823; Partie A, S.832; Praeludium e Partita del Tuono Terzo F, S.833; Sonata D, S.963; Aria Variata alla maniera Italiana a, S.989; Capriccio B♭ on the Departure of His Beloved Brother, S.992; Capriccio E In Honorem Joh. Christoph. Bachii, S.992. M-D.
Bach Album für Klavier (Istvan Mariassy—EMB 1973, 1974) 2 vols. Vol.I (58pp): Aria variata, S.989; Capriccio B♭, S.992; Duetto a, S.805; Fuga a, S.958; Gigue f, S.845; Menuet I G, S.841; Menuet II g, S.842; Menuett III G, S.843; Praeludium D, S.925; Praeludium F, S.928; Praeludium und Fuga A, S.896; Praeludium und Fughetta e, S.900; Praeludium und Fughetta F, S.901; Scherzo d, S.844; French Suite VI E, S.817. Clean edition. Vol.II: Duetto F, S.803; 2 Fughettas, S.679, 681; Partita a, S.827; Preambulum d, S.875a; Sonata D, S.963; Suites a, E♭, S.818, 819; Toccata e, S.914. M-D.
Bach, Keyboard Masterpieces (M. Gresh—GS 1976). 2 vols. Vol.I: English and French Suites; Vol.II: Partitas and Toccatas.
Bach: The Fugue (Charles Rosen—OUP). In Oxford Keyboard Classics series. Prelude and Fugue E, S.878; Prelude and Fugue F♯, S.858; Contrapunctus 1, 3, 9, 10, from *The Art of Fugue,* S.1080; Fantasie and Fugue a, S.904; Ricercars a³ and a⁶, S.1079. M-D to D.
Suiten, Sonaten, Capriccios, Variationen (Georg von Dadelsen—Henle 262). Fingering added by Hans-Martin Theopold. Preface in English, French, and German; critical notes and commentary in German. Urtext edition. Suite a, S.818a: Prelude, A, C, S, M, G. Suite a, S.818: A, C, S simple and S double, G. These two suites are similar in many ways. Suite E♭, S.819: A (another version of this A, S.819a), C, S, B, M I & II. Ouverture F, S.820: Entrée, M, B, G. Suite f,

S.823: Prélude, S en Rondeau, G. Suite A, S.832: A, Air pour les Trompettes, S, B, G. Präludium et Partita del Tuono Terzo, S.833: Präludium, A, C, S and Double, Air. 2 Menuettes from French Suites c, S.813a; E♭, S.815a. 3 Menuettes from the Notebook for Wilhelm Friedemann Bach: I G, S.841; II g, S.842; III G, S.843. Sonata D, S.963. Sonata a, S.967. Sonata after Reinken a, S.965. Sonata after Reinken C, S.966. Sonata d, S.964 (transcribed from a violin sonata). Adagio G, S.968 (transcribed from a violin sonata C). Capriccio on the Departure of His Beloved Brother, S.992. Capriccio E in Honor of Johann Christoph Bachii Ohrdruf, S.993. Aria Variata a, S.989. Int. to M-D.

TRANSCRIPTIONS:

The following arrangements, or "free paraphrases," by Wilhelm Kempff are similar to and compare well with those made by Ferruccio Busoni. Kempff makes clear distinctions between the various parts and carefully marks the score for beautiful legato (without relying totally on the pedal) by his use of ingenious fingering. He also seems to enjoy the interplay of tone colors, finding the right register, and establishing the particular timbre of each part in polyphonic writing. All the transcriptions listed are available separately (Bo&Bo). M-D.

Chorale, "Jesu, Joy of Man's Desiring," from Cantata No.147.

Chorale Preludes for Organ. "Befiehl du deine Wege," S.727; "Es ist gewisslich an der Zeit," S.734; "Ich ruf' zu Dir, Herr Jesu Christ," S.639; "In dulci jubilo," S.751; "Nun komm' der Heiden Heiland," S.659; "Wachet auf! ruft uns die Stimme," S.645; "Wir danken dir, Gott, wir danken dir," S.29.

Largo, from Keyboard Concerto in f, S.1056.

Siciliano, from Sonata II for Flute, S.1031b.

See: Putnam Aldridge, "Bach's Technique of Transposition and Improvised Ornamentation," MQ, 35 (January 1949):26–35. You may not agree with all of Aldridge's findings but his scholarship is beyond question.

Wallace Berry, "J. S. Bach's Fugue in D♯ Minor (WTC I #8): A Naive Approach to Linear Analysis," ITO, 2/10 (1977):4–7.

Beth Greenberg, "Bach's C Major Fugue (WTC I): A Subjective View," ITO, 2/3–4 (1976):13–17.

Charles M. Joseph, "Some Revisional Aspects of Bach's Keyboard Partitas, BWV 827 and 830," *Bach,* 9 (April 1978):2–16.

Edna Kilgore, "Time Signatures of the Well-Tempered Clavier: Their Place in Notational History," *Bach,* 4 (April 1973):3–16.

George Kochevitsky, "Performing Bach's Keyboard Music." Serialized in *Bach:* "The Choice of an Instrument," 3 (April 1972); "Phrasing," 3 (October 1972); "Articulation," 4 (January 1973); "Tempo," 4

(April 1973); "Notes Inégales—A Brief History and Summary," 4
(October 1973); "Embellishments," part I, 5 (July 1974), part II,
5 (October 1974).

Russell E. Lanning, *Bach Ornamentation* (Ann Arbor: J. W. Edwards,
1952), 61pp.

Walter Schenkman, "The Establishment of Tempo in Bach's *Goldberg
Variations*," Bach, 6 (July 1975):3–10.

Roy Travis, "J. S. Bach, Invention No.1 in C major: Reduction and
Graph," ITO, 2/7 (1976):3–7.

——. "J. S. Bach, Invention No.13 in A minor: Reduction and Graph,"
ITO 2/8 (1976):29–33.

Rosalyn Tureck, "Bach: Piano, Harpsichord or Clavichord," AMT, 11
(January–February 1962):8–9, 30.

Charles W. Wilkinson, *How to Play Bach's 48 Preludes and Fugues*
(London: Reeves, 1939).

WILHELM FRIEDEMANN BACH (1710–1784) Germany
Nine Sonatas (K).
Twelve Polonaises (PWM).
Klavierfantasien (Schott 6122   1972). Edited with preface in French,
German, and English; playing instructions and critical notes (only
in German) by Peter Schleuning. Nine fantasias that require much
finger dexterity. M-D.
Leichte Spielstücke für Klavier (Hug   1971). Menuetto and Trio a;
Allegretto B♭; Bourrée b; Menuetto and Trio d; Larghetto F; Largo
d; Polonaise d. Easy to Int.

FRIDTJOF BACKER-GRONDAHL (1885–1959) Norway
Kjaerlighetshymne Op.19 (NMO   1944).
Tre Klaverstykker Op.20 (NMO   1943) 10pp. Fragrance; Petite Chanson
Hereuse; Laengsel. M-D.
Dreaming Op.21 (NMO   1945). Thick harmonies, fast harmonic rhythm.
M-D.
Scherzo Op.22 (NMO   1944) 11pp. "Printer's Error." M-D.
All these pieces are written in a style similar to Grieg's.

CONRAD BADEN (1908–   ) Norway
Little Suite   1947 (Lyche).
Ten Small Pieces (NMO   1968) 8pp. Contrasting, MC. Int.
Ten Bagatelles (NMO   1972) 12pp. Off to School; Snooty; The Foun-
tain; Bruin the Bear; Piano Lesson; In the Evening; In the Chicken
Run; Big Secret; Dark Forest; Dance. Int.

HENK BADINGS (1907–   ) The Netherlands
Quaderni sonori   1976 (Donemus) 17pp. Photostat of MS.
Sonata VI   1947 (Donemus   1977) 36pp. Photostat of MS.

KJELL BAEKKLUND (1930–   ) Norway
Ostinato Ritmico (NMO   1975) 3pp.

RAYMOND BAERVOETS (1930–   ) Belgium
Hommage á Serge Prokofieff 1958 (Metropolis) 7pp. Secco style, strongly rhythmic, "tongue-in-cheek" melodic treatment, mildly dissonant. M-D.
Sonatine 1958 (Metropolis) 6pp. 5 min. Three movements with the finale, a toccata, the most successful. Int. to M-D.

CARLOS BAGUER (1768–1808) Spain
Siete Sonatas (UME   1976) 51pp. Transcription and introduction by María A. Ester Sala. Edited from MSS in the Biblioteca del Orfeó, the Biblioteca Universitaria, and the Biblioteca de Cataluña, in Barcelona.

JUNSANG BAHK (1938–   ) Korea
Mark (Litolff   1971) 10pp. Extensive explanation. Palm and forearm glissandi, clusters, trills, rolled chords, Stockhausen-inspired, rhythmically dull. Avant-garde. D.

WILLIAM BAINES (1899–1922) Great Britain
In his short life, this little-known Yorkshire composer composed some unusual and evocative music, skillfully written for the piano.
Coloured Leaves (Augener). Prelude; Valse; Still Days; Purple Heights.
Concert Study II: The Naiad (Elkin).
Four Poems (Augener). Poem-fragment; Elves; Poem-nocturne; Appassionata.
Pictures of Light (Elkin). Drift-Light: right hand ostinato, moving tune in left hand. Bursting Flames: octaves moving over keyboard. Pool-Lights: chromatic. M-D.
Seven Preludes (Elkin).
Silverpoints (Elkin). Labyrinth: right hand has accompaniment against sweeping left hand figuration. Water Pearles. The Burning Joss Stick. Floralia. M-D.
Tides: No. 2 Goodnight to Flamboro (Elkin).
Twilight Pieces (Elkin). Twilight Woods; Quietude; A Pause for Thought.
See: Peter J. Pirie, "William Baines," M&M, 21 (November 1972):36–40.

TADEUSZ BAIRD (1928–   ) Poland
Baird is professor of composition at the Warsaw Conservatory.
Little Suite for Children (PWM   1952) 8pp. 5½ min. Four short MC movements. Int.
Sonatina II (PWM   1952) 18pp. 12 min. Vivo e giocoso: changing tempi and mood, restless, moves into an improvisatory andante. Andante molto e calmato: peaceful, tranquil, overtones used. Finale: full of drive, vitality, final chords played with massive force. Strong folksong influences. Style is reminiscent of early Lutoslawski. M-D.

See: Alistair Wightman, "Tadeusz Baird at 50," MT, 1627 (October 1978):847–50.

DAVID A. BAKER (1949–   ) USA
Baker has degrees from the University of Kentucky and Florida State University. He studied composition with Carlisle Floyd and John Boda.
Five Pieces for Piano (CAP 1972) 15pp. Igor Stravinsky—in memoriam. No titles, only tempo indications. Neoclassic style, each piece has well-developed ideas. Closest in style to Stravinsky *Sonata*. No. 4 is followed by "attacca." M-D.

MICHAEL BAKER (–   ) Canada
Sonata Op.31 (Harris 1977) 20pp. 15 min. In one movement. Vigorous cadenza opening (returns later), freely tonal figuration, clusterlike sonorities, Larghetto choralelike section, enormous coda. Thoroughly contemporary. Requires dexterous fingers. D.

MILI BALAKIREV (1837–1910) Russia
Islamey (Christof Rüger—CFP).
Ausgewählte Klavierstücke (Christof Rüger—CFP P 9576a 1977) Vol. I, 97pp. Selected piano works including: Polka; Nocturne II; Mazurkas 1–3; Waltzes 4, 6; Scherzo II; Lullaby; Toccata. Epilogue in German and English. M-D. Vol.II (CFP P 9576b).
Cradle Song (GS 157).
Selected Piano Works (Roshchinoi—GS 8064).
Two Pieces (GS 158). Nocturne. Polka.

CLAUDE BALBASTRE (1729–1799) France
Pièces de clavecin, d'orgue et de fortepiano (Alan Curtis—Heugel) 93pp. Eighteen pieces including sonatas, sonatinas, overtures, and studies. Demonstrates a vigorous and brilliant style; Italian influence noted. Transition from harpsichord to pianoforte composition observed. The "Marche des Marseillois et l'air Ça ira" is an exciting battle piece. Excellent descriptive notes. Questionable editorial policy. M-D.
Livre de noëls (Schola Cantorum et Procure Generale) restitution J. Bonfils. 3 vols. Preface in French, 2 facsimiles.

LOUIS W. BALLARD (1931–   ) USA
Ballard, who is of Cherokee and Quapaw extraction, has used Indian folk music and traditions for inspiration in a number of his compositions. He is chairman of the music department at the Institute of American Indian Arts in Santa Fe, NM.
American Indian Piano Preludes (The New Southwest Music Publications, Box 4552, Santa Fe, NM 87502) 6 pieces. Well written. Indian influence gently permeates each piece but is not obvious. M-D.

CLAUDE BALLIF (1924–   ) France
Airs Comprimes Op.5 (EMT 1973) 17pp.
Erste Sonate Op.18 (Bo&Bo).

Cinquieme Sonate Op.32 (Choudens 1975) 32pp. One extended dramatic movement in contrasting sections. Serial, linear, arpeggi figuration, dynamic extremes, pointillistic, harmonics, proportional rhythmic relationships, low register *ppp* tremolo, varied tempi and moods, many ritards, expressionistic and intense. The color, character, and structure of this work are apparent. Contains characteristics similar to those of the Boulez sonatas. Requires mature pianism and large span. D.

Bloc-notes Op.37 (Bo&Bo).

ERNÖ BALOGH (1897–   ) Hungary
Conversation (Bo&H 1966) 2pp. In treble clef only, imitation. Easy.
Debate (Bo&H 1968) 3pp. Right hand on black keys, left hand mainly on white keys. Thin textures. Int.
Reel (Bo&H 1966) 2pp. All in treble clef, clever rhythmic combinations of 6/8 meter. Easy.

JACQUES BANK (1943–   ) The Netherlands
Blue Monk (Donemus 1974) 13pp. Photostat. For clavichord. Explanations in English.
Hitch (Donemus 1975) 11pp. Photostat. Notes in English.

OYO BANKOLE (1935–   ) Nigeria
Bankole had his early musical training in Lagos, followed by study in London and at UCLA.
Nigerian Suite (Chappell 1961) 11pp. 1. Forest Rains. 2. Ó Yá K'á Konga! 3. Orin Fún Òsùmàrè (Music for the Rainbow). 4. October Winds. 5. Warriors March. Contrasting, colorful, appealing. Unusual sonorities. Int.

GENNADII IVANOVICH BANSHCHIKOV (1943–   ) USSR
Piano Sonata No. 2 1973 (Sovetskii Kompozitor 1976) 32pp.

SAMUEL BARBER (1910–   ) USA
Ballade Op.46 (GS 1977) 6pp. Large ABA design, rich chordal sonorities, cadenza-like passages. Builds to enormous climax with octaves in alternating hands; colorful and effective; *pp* closing. M-D.

GIUSEPPE BARBERA (1911–   ) Italy
Toccata (EC 1972) 10pp.

RAMON BARCE (1928–   ) Spain
Estudio de Densidades (Editorial de Musica Española Contemporanea 1974) 10pp. A study in densities, of great difficulty.

ZBIGNIEW BARGIELSKI (1937–   ) Poland
7 Studiow na fortepian (AA 1957) 12pp.

ELAINE BARKIN (1932–   ) USA
Six Piano Pieces (ACA 1969) 11pp. Short, flexible meters, pointillistic,

extreme ranges exploited, expressionistic, rhythmic proportional relationships, percussive treatment, atonal, serial. M-D.

JEAN BARRAQUÉ (1928–1973) France
Sonate pour Piano (Margun 1978). D.

HENRI BARRAUD (1900–) France
Deux Préludes 1933 (Editions Françaises de Musique/Technisonor 1974) 9pp.

BÉLA BARTÓK (1881–1945) Hungary
4 Pieces 1905 (EMB).
Rumanian Dances Op.8a (EMB 1974) 38pp. Two Rumanian Dances, reprint of the original MS (Bartók Archives, with commentary by Laszlo Somfai). Commentary in Hungarian and English.
Marche funèbre from the symphonic poem *Kossuth* (EMB 1976) 4pp. Arranged by Bartók for piano, composed in 1903.
For Children (Banowetz—GWM) Authoritative edition; contains 42 pieces, or Vol.I only. Cassette available.
15 Hungarian Peasant Songs and Dances. See: Robert Dumm, "A Bartók Ballad," *Clavier*, 15 (March 1976):33–37. Discusses "Ballad" from this set.
Sonatine (Goldberger—GS) Based on original 1915 publication. Preface by editor. See: Guy Wuellner, "Béla Bartók's Sonatine: A Survey of Editions and Transcriptions," AMT, 25 (April–May 1976):28–31.
Rumanian Folk Dances 1915 (EMB) has a facsimile of two of these dances.
Mikrokosmos. None of these pieces are atonal, bitonal, or polytonal. Instead, each one, no matter how chromatically colored, is rooted in one key center.
See: Adele Franklin, "Bartók: Mikrokosmos, Book II," *Music Teacher*, 55 (November 1976):7–8; "Bartók: Mikrokosmos, Book III," *Music Teacher*, 55 (December 1976):12–13; "Bartók: Mikrokosmos, Book IV," *Music Teacher*, 56 (January 1977):17–18, and 56 (February 1977):15–16. Benjamin Suchoff, "Bartók's Musical Microcosm," *Clavier*, 16 (May–June 1977):18–20 (pp. 22–25 contain Nos.57 [Accente] and 140 [Free Variation] from the *Mikrokosmos*). Margit Varro, "Bartók's Mikrokosmos in Retrospect," in *Selections from the Piano Teacher 1958–1963* (Evanston: Summy-Birchard, 1964).
Tempo di Ciaccona and Fuga (György Sándor—Bo&H 1977) 17pp. 12½ min. From the *Sonata for Solo Violin,* adopted by Sándor along lines similar to those of Bartók's own piano adaptation of some of his *44 Violin Duets.* The full piano sonority works well in the monumental scope of the *Tempo di Ciaccona and Fuga.* D.
Bartók Easy Piano (Alfred). Twenty-four pieces selected from various

15 (December 1976):14–17. Includes "Out of the Depths" Op.130 for piano, pp.21–23; and "Twilight" Op.47/3 for piano duet, pp.24–25.

Burnet C. Tuthill, "Mrs. H. H. A. Beach," MQ, 26 (1941):197–310.

JOCHEN BECK (1941–   ) Germany
Klaviermusik II (Möseler 1972) 14pp.

JOHN BECKWITH (1927–   ) Canada
New Mobiles (Waterloo 1973) 6pp. Wind-harp: hands play independently and freely. Machine: perpetual motion. Tough Beans Charlie: repeated chords, skips, arpeggi. Int.
White Black (Waterloo 1973). One hand plays white keys while the other plays black keys. Glissandi. Int.

DAVID BEDFORD (1937–   ) Great Britain
Piano Piece II 1968 (UE) 6pp. Six notes must be prepared with rubber wedges; four milk bottles are to be placed on strings; etc. Avantgarde. M-D.

ANTONÍN BEDNÁR (1896–   ) Czechoslovakia
Sonatina (Urbánek 1922) 19pp. Moderato: G, cheerful ideas, chromatic. Andante: E, expressive, lyric, many triplets, unusual key relationships. Scherzo—Allegramente: C, Czechish dance, "splashing" figuration, octave chords, brilliant coda. Allegro ma non troppo: G, Slavic-sounding opening, contains techniques from other movements, fiery conclusion. Nationalistic style, à la Grieg, but Czech. M-D.

JACK BEESON (1921–   ) USA
Beeson is a graduate of the Eastman School of Music and Columbia University. He is presently in the Music Department, Columbia University, New York, NY 10027.
Fourth Sonata 1945, rev. 1951 (MS available from composer). 17pp. Slowly with freedom: motivic development, works to involved climax, complex figures, quiet ending. Squarely: thin legato textures thicken, flexible meters, brilliant conclusion. Flowing fluid figures throughout, freely dissonant lines. M-D to D.
Sketches in Black and White 1958 (MS available from composer) 17pp. Landscape: vagrant, rubato, flowing two-note motif. Portrait of a Slow Waltz: middle voice(s) important, freely tonal. Abstraction: fast and hard driving rhythms, motoric, mostly two-voiced. Still Life: an impressionistic tone poem, calm, subtle. Seascape: à la Chopin (Prelude G), constant sixteenth notes in both hands, alla cadenza. MC, colorful. M-D.
Fifth Piano Sonata 1946, rev. 1951 (TP 1973) 11pp., facsimile edition. Edited by John Kirkpatrick. Short, tightly knit, three-movement

work. Allegro moderato: shifting meters and emotions, restless, unstable tonality. Adagio: free, ornate, irregular rhythmic flow. Marziale: audacious, daring, strong rhythmic drive, dissonant percussive harmonies. D.

LUDWIG VAN BEETHOVEN (1770–1827) Germany

COMPLETE EDITIONS OF THE SONATAS:

(K) Miniature scores.

(Heinrich Schenker—Dover). This reprint is excellent but has a few minor flaws.

(Hans Schmidt—Henle). Part of the Neue Ausgabe sämtlicher Werke. Vol.I: Opp.2–26. Vol.II: Opp.27–57. Vol.III: Opp.79–111. Critical commentary volume forthcoming.

(Claudio Arrau, L. Hoffmann-Erbrecht—CFP). Combines research, based on authentic sources of revision, with the experience of international concert practice and established academic principles. Fingering and metronome marks are given (also Czerny's); measures are numbered. The fingering is unusually interesting.

(Germer—Litolff).

FACSIMILES AVAILABLE:

Op.27/2 (H. Schenker—UE).
Op.57 (CFP; Kesei Sakka—Ongaku No Tomo Sha   1972).

SEPARATE SONATAS AVAILABLE:

Op.2/1 (S. Scionti—Ric).
Op.2/3 (Schnabel—EC).
Op.7 (Schnabel—EC).
Op.10/1 (Schnabel—EC).
Op.10/2 (Schnabel—EC).
Op.10/3 (Schnabel—EC).
Op.13 (Banowetz—GWM with a cassette; Schnabel—EC; Podolsky—Volkwein).
    See: TM, Analysis of Op.13, 2nd movement, pp.92–107.
Op.26 (Schnabel—EC).
Op.27/2 (Schnabel—EC).
Op.28 (Schnabel—EC).
Op.31/1 (Schnabel—EC).
Op.31/2 (Schnabel—EC; Leo Weiner—EMB).
Op.31/3 (Schnabel—EC; Heugel).
Op.53 (Schnabel—EC; Leo Weiner—EMB).
Op.57 (Schnabel—EC; J. Fischer—CFP). Fischer edition contains epilogue in German and English, critical notes in German, and bars 340–66 of the first version of the last movement.

Op.78 (Schnabel—EC; Höpfel—Schott). Höpfel edition contains preface and critical notes in German and English.

Op.81a (Schnabel—EC).

Op.90 (Schnabel—EC).

Op.101 (Schnabel—EC).

Op.106 (Schnabel—EC; J. Fischer—CFP). Fischer edition contains epilogue in German and English, critical notes in German; fingered.

Op.109 (Schnabel—EC; Schenker—UE).

Op.110 (Schnabel—EC).

Op.111 (Schnabel—EC; Schenker—UE).

The Titled Sonatas (I. Kolodin—GS). Includes eight dramatic and programmatic sonatas: Pathétique, Moonlight, Pastorale, Tempest, Waldstein, Appassionata, Les Adieux, Hammerklavier. A most interesting and illuminating preface by Kolodin defends the use of these names. Urtext edition (the old Br&H) reprinted.

See: Roger Kamien, "Chromatic Details in Beethoven's Piano Sonata in E-flat major, Op.7," MR, 35 (August 1974):149–56.

William S. Newman, "K.457 and Op.13—Two Related Masterpieces in C Minor," PQ, 57 (Fall 1966):11–15; revised and enlarged version, MR, 28 (1967):38–44.

James Callahan, "Arrau vs. Schnabel in Beethoven's Op.28," PQ, 93 (Spring 1976):46–52.

Barry Cooper, "The Evolution of the First Movement of Beethoven's 'Waldstein' Sonata," M&L, 58 (April 1977):170–91.

James C. Kidd, "Wit and Humor in Tonal Syntax," *Current Musicology,* 21(1976):70–82. Discusses the first movement of Op.54 from the viewpoint of a subtle and comprehensive use of wit and humor by Beethoven.

Russell Bliss, "Late Beethoven—Playing Piano Sonata Op.109," *Clavier,* 15 (January 1976):19–22.

William Drabkin, "Some Relationships between the Autographs of Beethoven's Sonata in C minor, Op.111," *Current Musicology,* 13 (1972):38–47.

Kay Dreyfus, "Beethoven's Last Five Piano Sonatas. A Study in Analytical Method," PhD. diss., University of Melbourne, 1972, 385pp.

Willis H. Hackman, "Rhythmic Analysis as a Clue to Articulation in the Arietta of Beethoven's Op.111," PQ, 93 (Spring 1976):26–37.

H. A. Harding, *Analysis of Form as Displayed in Beethoven's 32 Pianoforte Sonatas* (London: Novello, 1890), 67pp.

Charles Timbrell, "Notes on the Sources of Beethoven's Op.111," M&L, 58 (April 1977):204–15.

EDITIONS OF THE VARIATIONS:

(Monike Holl, Bruno Seidlhofer—VU 1973). Vol.I: WoO 64, 65, 70, 71, 77, 80, Op.34, 35, 76, 120. Vol.II: WoO 63, 66, 68, 69, 72, 73,

75, 76, 78, 79. Urtext, performing format edition, fingered.
(Peter Hauschild—CFP 1970). Vol.I: Opp.34, 35, 76, 120; WoO 65, 80.
Vol.II: remaining variations. Urtext, preface in German and English,
fingered by Gerhard Erber.

Variationen über Volkweisen (Gerschon Jarecki—VU) Opp.105, 107.
Although an *ad libitum* flute part is included, these are mainly piano
variations making less than usual demands on the pianist. There are
numerous unexplained articulation and dynamic marks in this edition.

See: George A. Kochevitsky, "Beethoven's Variations in C Minor,"
Clavier (September 1967).

PIANO PIECES:

Fantasie für Klavier (Adolf Fecker—Möseler 1973) 48pp. Transcribed
from the "Kafka Note Book" (London, British Museum, Add. MS
#29,801) with missing portions completed by the editor. Epilogue
in German. M-D.

7 Bagatelles Op.33 (Henle 20).

Bagatelles Opp.33, 119, 126 (Brendel—VU 1973). Preface and critical notes in English and German.

Bagatelles Op.119 (Palmer—Alfred; Keller—CFP). Fingered.

Rondo alla ingharese ("The Rage Over the Lost Penny") Op.129 (Brendel
—VU).

EASIER COLLECTIONS AND PIECES:

Für Elise WoO 59 (Brendel—VU).

Two Easy Sonatas Op.49/1,2 (Henle 56).

Music for a Knightly Ballet (Hess—Br&H). Eight short pieces by Count
Ferdinand of Walstein but put together by Beethoven. The German
Song is repeated after each number like a refrain. Contains: Marsch;
Deutscher Gesang; Jagalied; Minnelied; Kriegslied; Trinklied; Tanz-
lied and Coda. A charming set that provides good sight-reading
material with some historical interest. Int.

DANCE COLLECTIONS:

Deutsche Tanze (Heinz Walter—Br&H).

12 German Dances (H. Kreutzer—Brodt 1968) 15pp.

COLLECTIONS:

Beethoven Album (EMB) Vol.I: 7 Bagatelles Op.33; Rondo Op.51/1;
Für Elise; Six Easy Variations on a Swiss Song; Seven Variations on
"Nel cor più non me sento"; 6 Ecossaises; 2 Minuets; 3 Contradances.
Vol.II: Rondo Op.51/2; 11 Bagatelles Op.119; 6 Bagatelles Op.126;
Rondo a Capriccio Op.129; Andante Favori. Int. to M-D.

Beethoven—An Introduction to His Piano Works (W. Palmer—Alfred
1970) 64pp. Contains: 3 Bagatelles; 3 Country Dances; 2 Ecossaises;

Für Elise; Lustig, Traurig; 3 Menuets; Theme from Rondo a Capriccio, Op.129; Sonata G Op.49/2; Sonatina G, Variations on a Swiss Song. Excellent introductory materials. Int.

Il Mio Primo Beethoven (Pozzoli—Ric E. R. 1952) 18pp. Three Country Dances D; Moderato semplice from Sonatina G; Scottish Tune; Romance from Sonatina G; Minuets C, G; Waltz D; Allegro from Sonatina F; Allemanda A; Rondo from Sonatina F. Int.

Sonatinen und Leichte Sonaten (Peter Hauschild—CFP 1973) 87pp. Fingering by Gerhard Erber. Contains Op.49; Op.79; WoO 47, 50–55; Kinsky Anhang 5. Preface in German and English, critical note in German.

A First Beethoven Book (K 3204) 16pp. German Dances F, D; Ecossaise E♭; Allemanda A; 3 Ländler D; Sonatina G: Moderato semplice; Rondo from Sonatina F; Six Easy Variations on a Swiss Air. Int.

Little Known Piano Pieces (P. Zeitlin, D. Goldberger—BMC 1972). Rondo (1783); Easy Sonata C; Two Bagatelles (1797, 1804); Two Piano Pieces (1821, 1818) are the most interesting. Int.

Beethoven Easy Piano (Alfred). Sixteen pieces that include the two possibly spurious Sonatinas, dance forms, and other familiar works. A short biography and notes on each piece are included. Easy to Int.

Beethoven—Favorite Piano (Alfred).

Beethoven—The First Book for Young Pianists (Palmer—Alfred) 24pp. The easiest pieces, Country Dances, Menuets, sonatina movements.

The Beethoven Sketch Books (Jack Werner—Chappell) 6 vols. Edited and arranged from the original MSS in a manner closely allied to Beethoven's own settings and style. 55 pieces in 6 volumes arranged progressively in order of difficulty. Helpful notes from the editor appear throughout. Easy to Int.

Young Pianist's Guide to Beethoven (Y. Novik—Studio P/R). Int.

See: Robert K. Formsma, "The Use of Pedal in Beethoven's Sonatas," PQ, 93 (Spring 1976):38–45.

William S. Newman, "Performance Practices in Beethoven's Time—A Selected Bibliographic Survey," PQ, 93 (Spring 1976):53–57. Compiled by a Seminar under the direction of W. S. Newman, held at the University of North Carolina during the summer of 1975. This is the single largest bibliography of sources on Beethoven performance practices that has yet been published.

——. "The Performance of Beethoven's Trills," JAMS, 29 (Fall 1976): 439–62.

Konrad Wolff, "Asides on Beethoven's Trills," PQ, 98 (Summer 1977): 37–39.

PAUL BEN-HAIM (1897–   ) Israel
Klaviermusik 1967 (IMI 650).
Melody and Variations (IMI 121).

ASHER BEN-YOHANAN (1929–   ) Israel
Prelude and Toccata (IMI   1969) 14pp. 6½ min.

GEORGE BENDA (1722–1795) Bohemia (Czechoslovakia)
Seven Sonatinas (H. B. Kreutzer—Brodt   1976) 16pp. Sonatinas a; F;
   C (Theme and Variations); D; G; G; g. Delightful and well written.
   Int.

RICHARD RODNEY BENNETT (1936–   ) Great Britain
Scena I   1975 (Nov) 14pp. 7½ min. A short, three-movement sonata in
   all but name. Clear, concise, with plenty of contrast, harmonics,
   fragmented style, unusual sonorities, half-pedal effects, musically
   vigorous. D.

WILLIAM STERNDALE BENNETT (1816–1875) Great Britain
Piano and Chamber Music (Geoffrey Bush—S&B   1972) 165pp. Edited
   from original English editions, the composer's MSS., and the German
   editions. Contains: Sonata I, Op.13; Suite de Pieces, Op.24 (available separately); Chamber Trio for violin, cello, piano, Op.26;
   Sonata—Duo for piano and cello, Op.32. Sonata Op.13 is a four-
   movement work in f with the two middle movements entitled
   Scherzo and Serenata. Dramatic and lyric contrasts are evident in
   each movement. Suite Op.24 (also available separately—S&B) contains six movements, each of which displays some aspect of piano
   technique. The final movement, Lento—Bravura is sonatalike and
   the most expansive. M-D.
3 Impromptus Op.12 (Ashdown).
3 Romances Op.14 (McFarren—Ashdown). Shows Bennett's lyrical invention at its best. M-D.
Fantasia A Op.16 (McFarren—Ashdown). In all but name a second
   sonata, with four continuous movements. D.
Sonata II A♭ ("The Maid of Orleans") (Cramer).
See: Geoffrey Bush, "William Sterndale Bennett (1816–75)," M&M, 23
   (February 1975):32–34.

NIELS VIGGO BENTZON (1919–   ) Denmark
Bentzon's sonatas probably represent the finest piano works to come out
of Scandinavia since Nielsen.
Sonata No.3 Op.44 (WH). Requires tremendous concentration and displays strong intellectual vitality. D.
Sonata No.5 Op.77 (WH). Compact, full of controlled vitality, impressive. D.
Sonata No.6 Op.90 (WH   1971) 56pp. 18 min. Includes some powerful
   and muscular fugal writing. Traces of serial procedure, à la Prokofiev with Lisztian pianism. D.
Sonata No.7 Op.121   1959 (WH) 40pp. 15 min. Three movements in
   the style of Nielsen's progressive tonality. Movements begin in one
   key, progress and end in another key. D.

Woodcuts Op.65 1951 (WH) Eleven pieces of varying difficulty. The art form of the title is reflected in the simple but well-defined motives, developed with much economy.

Paganini Variations "In Memoriam." Op.241 1968 (WH) 16pp. Dramatic, powerful. M-D to D.

Hydraulic Structures (WH). Commissioned by Carlisle (England) Festival, 1973. For prepared piano. Title alludes to the up-and-down movement of its patterns; improvisatory. M-D to D.

Klavermosaik 1970 (WH) Book 2: Scales. 10pp.

ARRIGO BENVENUTI (1925–   ) Italy
Cinque Invenzioni (Bruzzichelli 1958). New Notation. Avant-garde.

CATHY BERBERIAN (1925–   ) USA
Morsicat(h)y (UE 1969) 11pp. For piano or harpsichord. "A musical action (Morse code) based on my interest in onomatopoeia" (from the score). Includes detailed instructions for performer, a drawing, and two cards requesting receipt of performance code from the composer in a back cover pocket. The right hand simulates the sound of a mosquito while the left hand attempts to swat it with clusters. Aleatoric. A joke; could be very funny and fascinating, given the proper performance. Avant-garde. M-D.

GUNNAR BERG (1909–   ) Denmark, born France
Gaffky's Assortiment 2 (Dan Fog 1971) 10pp.

ARTHUR BERGER (1912–   ) USA
Two Episodes 1933 (LG) in collection *New Music for the Piano*.

Five Pieces 1969 (CFP 1975) 30pp. 13 min. Extensive preface, pointillistic, complicated skips, finger-picking effects, harmonics, special pedal effects. A few notes are prepared for the first two pieces. Avant-garde. D.

SVERRE BERGH (1915–   ) Norway
Bergh is conductor at "Den Nationale Scene" in Bergen.

To Norske Danser (NMO 1944) 7pp. Bjönnes'n: contrasting sections, lively. Gamel-Holin: subtle, flowing triplets, *ppp* ending. In style of Grieg. Int.

Gubben Noah (NMO 1946) 11pp. Theme and ten contrasting variations. Clever, delightful, attractive set based on story of Noah's Ark. Int. to M-D.

ERIK BERGMAN (1911–   ) Finland
Intervalles Op.34 1964 (Fazer) 24pp.

Aspekte 1968–9 (NMO) 15pp. Spektrum; Meditation; Metamorfos. Annotations in Norwegian, English, and German. Harmonics, aleatoric, pointillistic. D.

GÜNTER BERGMANN (–   ) Germany
Stationen: Musik für Klavier (Münster/Westf., Wilhelm Schenk 1972–
3). 7 vols. Vol:I: 1. Introduktion; 2. Brahms zum Gedenken. Vol.II:
3. Scherzo. Vol.III: 4. Ballade. Vol.IV: 5. Alster. Vol.V: 6. Intermezzo. Vol.VI: 7. September 1938. Vol.VII: August 1939 (Trauer-
marsch).

VITTORIO BERGONZINI (–   ) Italy
Scherzo II (EC   1970) 7pp.
Novelletta I (EC   1971) 11pp.
Inno al Trionfo (EC   1972) 6pp. Symphonic march.

LUCIANO BERIO (1925–   ) Italy
Berio studied with Giorgio Ghedini and Luigi Dallapiccola. He helped
establish the Studio di Fonologia di Musicale of the Italian Radiotelevision
in Milan and became its director. His interest in electronic music has
broadened tremendously in the last few years, and he has incorporated
serial principles in composing electronic music. He is one of Italy's leading
composers.
Cinque variazioni per Pianoforte (SZ   1953). Berio's excellent serial
craft shows through in all these variations. Nos.3 and 5 have codas;
No.3 also has a cadenza. An exciting vitality is evidenced in this
work. It is full of interesting sonorities and written in a style that
shows some influence of Stravinsky. Dynamic range: *ppppp* to *fff*.
M-D.
Sequenza IV (UE   1967) 7pp. Lyric, colorful, and grateful to performer.
This work is a series of constantly changing chords (continual vari-
ation). Much use is made of the sustaining pedal. The score is a
reproduction of the MS but it is fairly easy to read. M-D.
See: David Burge, "Luciano Berio's Sequenza IV," CK, 2 (September–October 1976):42. A fine discussion of this composition,
surely one of the original piano works of the last decade.
Erdenklavier (UE   1969) 2pp. "Pastorale." Performance directions.
Dynamics appear to be serialized. Unharmonized melody. Avant-
garde. M-D.
Wasserklavier (UE   1965) 2pp. Tonal, key signature, arpeggi. Entire
piece is *ppp*. Large span required. M-D.
Family Album (UE 15950   1975) 30pp. A collection of works by Berio's
father, Ernesto (a song); his grandfather, Adolfo (Maria Isabella—
a waltz for piano duet); and Berio's own *Petite Suite* for solo piano,
written in 1947. This neoclassical suite is the finest work in the collection but it demonstrates little or nothing of Berio's present style. M-D.

LENNOX BERKELEY (1903–   ) Great Britain
3 Piano Pieces (Galliard   1973). M-D.
Sonata A Op.20, 2d ed. 1974 (JWC).

3 Impromptus Op.7   1937 (W. Rogers).
6 Preludes Op.23   1948 (JWC).
　　See: Dennis Todd, "Berkeley: Six Preludes," *Music Teacher,* 57
　　(April 1978):14–15. A discussion and analysis of these pieces.
4 Concert Studies 1940 (Schott). Op.48 E♭; Op.14/2 e; Op.14/3 c;
　　Op.14/4 F.
4 Piano Studies 1972 (JWC 55076   1976) 15pp. Varied technical pur-
　　poses for each study; musical. M-D.

ISSAAK JAKOWLEWITSCH BERKOWITSCH (1902–   ) USSR
Selected Works for Piano (Musitschna Ukraina   1972) 71pp.

SOL BERKOWITZ (1922–   ) USA
Berkowitz studied composition with Karol Rathaus and Otto Luening
and piano with Abby Whitesides. Since 1960 he has written mainly for
theater and television.
Syncopations (LG   1958) in collection *New Music for the Piano.* Jazz
　　influence, chromatic. M-D.
Twelve Easy Blues (BMC). Varied blues style; good for developing
　　rhythmic flexibility. Int.
Four Blues for Lefty (TP   1976) 7pp. One-Sided Conversation; The
　　Tired Bugler; A Quiet Song; Movin' Along. Intriguing descriptive
　　pieces featuring left-hand melodies. Freely chromatic. Int. to M-D.
Nine Folk Song Preludes (Frank Music   1972) 21pp. Tunes are treated
　　to MC and modal harmonies; some are clever. Int.

JOHANN DANIEL BERLIN (1714–1787) Norway
Sonatina d (Lyche   1953) 9pp. Capricetto; Arietta; Gavotta; Menuet;
　　Giga. Eighteenth-century style, attractive. Int.

PETER BERNARY (1931–   ) Germany
Sonata (Möseler   1972) 15pp.

LORD GERALD TYRWHITT BERNERS (1883–1950)
　　Great Britain
The Triumph of Neptune   1926 (JWC   1975) 12pp. Edition for piano.
　　Three pieces that were originally part of a ballet. Witty, humorous,
　　MC. Harlinquinade; Intermezzo; Hornpipe. M-D.

SEYMOUR BERNSTEIN (1927–   ) USA
Birds (Schroeder & Gunther   1972). A suite of eight impressionistic
　　studies, each named after a feathered friend: Purple Finch; Humming-
　　bird; Woodpecker; Sea Gull; Chickadee; Vulture; Penguin; Eagle.
　　Complicated notation. M-D.
Birds II (Schroeder & Gunther). Nine descriptive pieces of birds: Myna
　　Bird; Swan; Robin; Owl; Roadrunner; Condor; Nightingale; Guinea
　　Hen; Phoenix. Helpful foreword and notes on performance. With

added narration, this would make a diverting collection for a student recital. M-D.

Insects (A. Broude). Eight characteristic studies. Witty, atonal, imaginative. Performing directions included. Hilarious introduction that relates the insects' origins. Carpenter Ant; Cockroach; Mosquito; Dying Moth; Humbug; Praying Mantis; Centipede; Black Fly. Player must clap hands, slap legs, etc. Int. to M-D.

Lullaby for Carrieann (A. Broude) 5pp. A reverie. Freely changing tonalities, meters, and tempi; restless at spots; contemporary sonorities. M-D.

Warblers and Flutters (A. Broude 1977). Book I of The Earth Music Series, an introduction to the trill. Nine short pieces that teach the student how to play this ornament. Presented in order of difficulty. Excellent performance commentary. "What better way to learn the trill than to think of birds whose trills are the envy of all instrumentalists!" (from the preface). Easy to Int.

Raccoons (A. Broude 1977) Book I. A musical adventure with nine descriptive pieces. Also includes a story and unusual photographs taken by Bernstein. M-D.

Out of the Nest (A. Broude 1977). Book II of The Earth Music Series. An introduction to the mordent. Eight short pieces with same approach as Book I in this series. Clever and effective. Easy to Int.

New Pictures at an Exhibition (A. Broude 1977) 40pp. Combining masterpieces of art, poetry by Owen Lewis, and music, this elegant book stimulates aural and visual senses. Nine pieces to be played as a suite although a few (Chagall, especially) can be extracted and performed separately. M-D.

WALLACE BERRY (1928–   ) USA
Eight Twentieth-Century Miniatures (CF   1967).

PAUL BERTHOLD (1948–   ) Germany
Klavierstück 68 (Sikorski). New notation. Avant-garde. D.

GÉRARD BERTOUILLE (1898–   ) Belgium
Bertouille studied composition with Jean Absil and André Souris. His music is basically tonal and expressed in classical form with great emphasis placed on melodic clarity.

Six Preludes and Fugues (CeBeDeM   1940–42) 2 vols. Imitation extensively employed. Varied moods, effective. All require solid pianistic equipment. M-D.

Sonata (Schott Frères   1945) 13pp. 12 min. Allegro; Nocturne; Final. Tonal, neoclassic; Nocturne is the most effective. M-D.

Introduction et Final (CeBeDeM   1970) 11pp. 8 min. Quiet opening, chromatic. Moves to contrapuntal development, dramatic conclusion. In Franck tradition. M-D.

Pour le Pianiste (CeBeDeM   1976) 12pp. 7 min.

FRANZ BERWALD (1796–1868) Sweden
Keyboard Music (Bengt Edlund—Br) 201pp. Complete works, XV. Includes: Three Fantasias, 1816–7, written for the melodicon, a Danish invention whose tone somewhat resembled that of the glass harmonica. These pieces contain variations on themes from *Don Giovanni* and *Die Zauberflöte*. Sixteen of the remaining pieces come from the *Musical Journals* that Berwald published in 1818–20. Most of these are salon pieces, many of them anonymous. Fantasia c on two Swedish Folk Melodies is one of the better Berwald works. The later pieces display a genuine individuality. Beautifully produced volume. Int. to M-D.

CHARLES BESTOR (1924–   ) USA
Sonata (Gen).

BRIAN BEVELANDER (1942–   ) USA
Sonata Op.2 (Branden Press   1966) 14pp. First movement: agitated, numerous meter changes, based on motivic development, rhapsodic pianistic style. Second movement: rondo, wide skips in left hand; returns to the opening section are treated in variation, scherzo style. No key signature but tonal. M-D.
Scherzo (Branden Press) 11pp. Flexible tempi, light and playful, slower expressive mid-section, sprightly ending. Requires fast shifts of hand position; large chords throughout. M-D.

FRANK MICHAEL BEYER (1928–   ) Germany
Variations (Heinrichshofen   1975) 32pp.

ANTONIO BIBALO (1922–   ) Born Trieste; in Norway since 1957 Bibalo has never made style the principal factor in his works, but in all of them one recognizes his personality immediately.
Four Balkan Dances (JWC   1956) 7½ min. Bartók influence noted. I. Allegro deciso e ben ritmato: left hand chordal octaves open and close the piece; 3+3+2 rhythms; toccata-like figurations alternate between hands. II. Andantino semplice: 5/4 meter, chromatic melodic line over chordal (second and seventh) accompaniment; lines sometimes three or four octaves apart; quasi echo effects. III. Adagio: a spun-out murmuring effect in upper register provides accompaniment; chordal punctuation in left hand adds rhythmic interest. IV. Presto: Sciolto e brillante in an ABABA design; tarantella-like rhythm with embedded melodic line worked into fabric; B sections rely on chromatic triplet for coloration; driving modal descending scales in right hand provide dramatic conclusion. M-D.
Fire Miniaturer (WH   1966). Four miniatures with folk-song and dance influence. Written in honor of Bartók. Reverie: vacillates between

tonic major and minor third. Allegretto con spirito: a fine left hand study in perpetual motion. Lonesome Doll. Little Finale. Int. to M-D.
Three Hommages (to Falla, Schönberg, Bartók) (WH).
Toccata (WH).
Sonata (WH 1974) 23pp.
Sonata II "La notte" (WH 1976) 11pp. 16 min.
Piano 'Solo' in the Evening (WH 1977).

MICHAEL VON BIEL (1937–) Germany
Für Klavier 1964–5. 12pp. *Etüden und Gesangsthemen* 1968. 5pp. (Feedback Studio 1971). Explanations in German only.

JOHN BIGGS (1932–) USA
Biggs has trained at the University of California, Los Angeles, and has studied composition with Leonard Stein, John Vincent, Lukas Foss, Roy Harris, Flor Peeters, and Halsey Stevens.
Theme and Variations (Consort 1959) 10pp. 8 min. A nine-bar theme and six variations with final variation serving as an exciting coda, neoclassic style. Highly pianistic, variations well contrasted. Good octave technique necessary for Var. 4. The composer's penchant for linear and unencumbered writing is obvious. M-D.
Invention for Piano and Tape (Consort 1970) 7½ min. Tape available from publisher. Tape cues notated on staff above piano staff. Changing meters, imitative, chromatic. Up to bar 112, tape sounds are made entirely with a piano with strings and hammers prepared in different ways. Following this is a live recording of a Kansas thunderstorm, with a train whistle faintly heard in the background. Explanation of closing section is included. M-D.
Sonatina "Clementiana" (Consort 1974) 8pp. 5½ min.
Sonatina II (Consort 1975) 11pp. 8½ min.
Both sonatinas are in three short movements, with much imitation. Tonal and freely chromatic. Well-turned and attractive writing. Int.

GORDON BINKERD (1916–) USA
Essays 1976 (Bo&H) 32pp. Intermezzo: parodies Brahms's Op.118/1, a kind of recasting of the whole piece. Adagietto. Allegresse. Lightly Like Music Running. She, to Him. Shut Out that Moon. These pieces are Binkerd's Lisztian transformations of some of his own songs— somewhat in the manner of Liszt's *Années de Pèlerinage*, Book II. Fanciful and imaginative writing. D.
See: David Burge, "New Pieces, Part II," CK, 4 (January 1978):50.
Five Pieces 1973 (Bo&H). Preambulum; Fugue à la Gigue; Zarabanda; Toccata; Fantasia. Highly contemporary writing. Demands pianistic expertise in all pieces. D.
Suite for Piano (Bo&H 1978) 33pp. Five Fantasies: Capriccio; Intermezzo on *Meine Lieder* (Brahms Op.106/4); Intermezzo on *Wenn*

du nur zuweilen lächelst (Brahms Op.57/2); Intermezzo on *Jung-fraülein, soll ich mit euch gehn* (Brahms *49 Deutsche Volkslieder,* Bk.II/11); Rhapsody. Style and approach similar to that of *Essays,* discussed above. The outer movements are especially concentrated. M-D to D.

JUAN CARLOS BIONDO (–   ) Brazil
Sonata I (Providence   1971) 16pp. Short, one movement. Contrasting sections; recurring Presto unifies work; cadenza-like sections; freely tonal. M-D.
Preludio Op.20/1 (Providence   1966) 2pp. Vision Fugaz. Fleeting, chromatic. Large span required. M-D.

KEITH BISSELL (1912–   ) Canada
Variations on a Folk Song (Waterloo   1970) 8pp. Asymmetrical theme, six variations plus coda. MC with a few rhythmic problems. Int.
Three Preludes (Harris   1973) 7pp. MC. Int.

BORIS LEONIDOVICH BITOV (1904–   ) USSR
Sonata III Op.44   1964 (Sovetskii Kompozitor   1975) 34pp.

MARCEL BITSCH (1921–   ) France
Le Livre de Noémie ("For Naomi") (Leduc   1949). Ten studies: Duet; The Little Railroad; When There Were Coaches; On the Water; Invention; In the Meadow; Lullaby; Chase; Fanfare; Ring for Matins. Each piece is devoted to some technical problem. Int.

JEAN BIZET (1924–   ) France
Sonata Op.12 (Technisonor   1969) 42pp.

ARNI BJÖRNSSON (1905–   ) Iceland
Björnsson studied at the Reykjavik School of Music. He was first flutist in the Icelandic Symphonic Orchestra and a teacher at the Reykjavik School of Music until 1952, when he suffered serious brain injuries, which put an end to his career.
Sonata Op.3 (Musica Islandica   1963) 17pp. Allegro con fuoco: SA, dramatic, much two with three. Andante cantabile: chordal, melodic; careful legato required. Rondo—Allegro ma non troppo: dancelike, contrasting sections and keys. M-D.

RICHARD BLACKFORD (1954–   ) Great Britain
Blackford was an honor graduate of the Royal College of Music, where he studied with John Lambert. He also worked privately with Elisabeth Lutyens and Hans Werner Henze.
Sonata   1975 (GS   1977) 22pp. 11 min. Molto vivace; Andante. The second movement has numerous contrasting sections. Pointillistic, expressionistic, many repeated notes, serial influence noted. Large span required. D.

DAVID BLAKE (1936–) Great Britain
Variations for Piano Op.1 (OUP 1964) 8pp. Linear theme, eight contrasting variations and a finale in four sections. Freely tonal; large span required. M-D.

EUBIE BLAKE (1884–) USA
Sincerely, Eubie Blake (Belwin-Mills 1975) 72pp. Transcribed by Terry Waldo. Nine original rags covering Blake's entire career. More sophisticated and difficult than the Joplin rags. Interesting foreword includes a discussion of the pieces and a biography of Blake. Includes: The Charleston Rag; Eubie's Classical Rag; Rhapsody in Ragtime; Eubie Dubie; Brittwood Rag; Kitchen Tom; Poor Katie Redd; The Baltimore Todolo; Poor Jimmy Green. M-D.

PAVEL BLATNY (1931–) Czechoslovakia
Meditace 1965 (Panton 1971) 8pp.

BRENNO BLAUTH (1931–) Brazil
Duas Peças Breves (Ric Brazil 1969) 4pp. Atonal, monothematic. Various timbres explored on the instrument. Second piece is aleatoric. Must be played as a group. M-D.
Sonata 1961 (MS available from composer: Rua Álvaro Neto 182-04-112, São Paulo, SP Brazil) 29pp. 16 min. Allegro deciso; Lento; Molto animato. Cheerful and rhythmic writing in outer movements. Dramatic qualities in Lento. M-D.
Suite Paulistinha (Ric Brazil 1968) 12pp. 12 min. 1. Tarde de Garôa. 2. A Capelinha de Juquitiba. 3. Nisseizinha. 4. A Valsa do Brotinho. Int.
Suite Parnanguara 1965 (Vitale) 15 min.
3 Dança Charrua (Vitale 1969) 5 min. each. Published separately.

HERBERT BLENDINGER (1936–) Germany
Three Preludes (Orlando 1974) 8pp. Photostat.

BLIND TOM (1849–1908) (Thomas Greene Bethune) USA
The Battle of Manassas (Musica Obscura) in collection *Piano Music in Nineteenth Century America,* Vol.I. A musical description of this famous battle. Variable keys, meters, and tempi. Uses patriotic tunes of the period, including "The Girl I Left Behind Me," "Dixie," "Yankee Doodle," "The Marseillaise." Clusters are used to simulate cannon fire; pianist must whistle and make locomotive noises. A fun piece from beginning to end. M-D.
See: Geneva H. Southall, "Blind Tom: A Misrepresented and Neglected Composer-Pianist," *The Black Perspective in Music,* 3 (May 1975): 141–59.

ARTHUR BLISS (1891–1975) Great Britain
Intermezzo (S&B 1912).

Triptych   1970 (Nov) 20pp. 14 min. Meditation; Dramatic Recitative; Capriccio. Excellent craft, pianistic. Second movement has the most interest. M-D.

WALDEMAR BLOCH (1906–   ) Austria
Bloch lives in Graz, Austria, and teaches composition there. He is also the author of an authoritative textbook on music theory.
Sonata E (Dob   1970) 19pp. Traditional forms SA and Rondo are used to give direction to the work. Strong tonal passages are interspersed with more MC lines. M-D.

JOHN BLOW (1648–1708) Great Britain
Compositions (K).
Ground in e (T. Dart—S&B) in collection *John Blow's Anthology*.

CHRISTOPHER BOCHMANN (1950–   ) Great Britain
Bochmann holds two degrees from Oxford University. He has studied composition with David Lumsden, Kenneth Leighton, Robert Sherlaw Johnson, and Richard Rodney Bennett.
Sonata (OUP   1974) 17pp. 15 min. In two parts: Preludio and Variazioni (written on 4 staves), then an Aria followed by a Postludio, to be played without a break between movements. Clusters, sharp dissonances, enormous skips, and wide dynamic range. Thematic material evolves from a five-note pattern. Skillful pedalling is essential. This is Bochmann's first published composition. D.

KONRAD BOEHMER (1941–   ) Germany
Potential (Tonos   1961) 29pp. 10½ min. Instructions in German. Versions I, II, III. Pointillistic, highly organized, proportional rhythmic relationships, many dynamic indications, clusters, unmeasured tempo at places, extreme ranges exploited, avant garde. Virtuoso technique required. D.

ALEXANDRE PIERRE FRANÇOIS BOËLY (1785–1858) France
Anthologie de Pièces pour Piano (Choudens). Contains some interesting, original, and even startling material. Individual Romantic writing. An unimpressive Capriccio opens the collection; the 16 other short pieces that follow are all somewhat better than the opening work. A contrapuntal flavor appears in most of the pieces, and they resemble J. B. Cramer's studies in this respect. Int. to M-D.

COR BOER (1933–   ) The Netherlands
Cantos in Modis Diversis (B&VP   1971) 9pp.

EDWARD BOGUSLAWSKI (1940–   ) Poland
Per Pianoforte (Ars Viva   1971) 5pp.

ROD DU BOIS (1934–   ) The Netherlands
As a composer du Bois was self-taught. Since 1959 he has been a member

of the group of composers associated with Gaudeamus, a Dutch society dedicated to performing new works. His works contain avant-garde characteristics.

Three Studies (Donemus 1966–7).

Just Like a Little Sonata (Donemus 1964) 7pp. Facsimile of composer's MS.

New Pieces—for Piano (Donemus 1972) 6pp. Reproduction of composer's MS.

Cadences (Donemus 1975) 7 min.

Mercy for John Vincent Moon (Donemus 1976) 6pp. Photostat of MS.

WILLIAM BOLCOM (1938–) USA

Bolcom studied composition with John Vincent, George McKay, and Darius Milhaud, and holds a DMA in composition from Stanford University. He presently teaches composition at the University of Michigan.

Twelve Etudes (Merion 1964). This set of pieces "while dealing with almost all aspects of piano technique, concentrates on control of textures, dynamics, pedals and the use of the strings of the piano" (from the preface). Each etude is devoted to one specific problem. No.1 concentrates on touch and dynamics; over- and under-hand technique in a small area. No.2 promotes smoothness and evenness of passage-work in both hands. Notation is proportional. Avant-garde. Performance directions provided. D.

Seabiscuits Rag (EBM 1974) 7pp. Cakewalk tempo, syncopation, swing. M-D.

Graceful Ghost Rag (EBM 1971) 4pp. Moderate rag-tempo, full chords, chromatic. Large span required. M-D to D.

The Garden of Eden (EBM 1974) 20pp. Four rags based on Genesis. A blend of rag characteristics with fine contemporary compositional techniques. Includes comments on the style of rag performance. Old Adam: a vigorous two-step in bouncy dotted rhythms. The Eternal Feminine: slow, languorous, elegantly shaped. The Serpent's Kiss: changing tempi and mood; slap the piano, stop time, click the tongue; two fingers tap dance; a virtuoso "Rag Fantasy." Through Eden's Gates: a casual cakewalk. M-D to D.

Raggin' Rudi (EBM 1974) 3pp. Clever. Large span required. M-D.

JOÃO DOMINGOS BOMTEMPO (1775–1842) Portugal

Sonate F (H. Costa 1972) 24pp. Copies available from Helena Costa, Largo Paz 53, Porto, Portugal. Allegro moderato: expressive melodies, quick arpeggi, broken octaves, extensive use of Alberti bass, development section in E, cadenza passages. Prestissimo assai: fast octaves, evolving figures, development section in D♭, melodic line woven into triplet usage, well crafted. M-D.

MARGARET ALLISON BONDS (1913–1972) USA
Troubled Water   1967 (Fox; IU) 7pp.

BENJAMIN BORETZ (1934–   ) USA
(*". . . my chart shines high where the blue milks upset. . ."*) (PNM, 14–15 [1976]:337–423). 87pp. 19 min. Highly organized, complex. Requires more musicianship than technique. M-D.

ELLIOT BORISHANSKY (1930–   ) USA
Borishansky holds degrees in composition from Queens College, Columbia University, and the University of Michigan. He is presently a member of the music faculty at Denison University, Granville, Ohio.
Three Pieces   1967 (MS available from composer) 10pp. Continuum; Trial Run; The Machine. *"Three Pieces* was my first theater piece. Theater pieces are concert pieces which have a visual as well as aural aspect. The two are inseparable, and one is an extension of the other. In Continuum I am trying to show that motion is a continuation of sound which contains motion and that all arts contain motion as a common denominator. I am also making the audience work in this piece, not that it should not always be working. In Trial Run the child is supposed to give up when he plays the glissando at the end" (from a letter to the author). The Machine has extensive directions. These are three of the funniest pieces ever conceived for the piano. Avant-garde. M-D.
Constellations   1972 (MS available from composer) 9pp. 5 min. Beautiful MS. Flexible meters, MC. Lyric lines contrast with punctuated rhythms; legato touch necessary, subtle and lovely sonorities. Large span required. M-D.

ALEXANDER BORODIN (1833–1887) Russia
Nocturne (Anson—Willis) from *Petite Suite*. Int.
Little Suite (Luise Vosgerchian—GS 195) 28pp.

SIEGFRIED BORRIS (1906–   ) Germany
Bagatelles Op.83 (Heinrichshofen   1973) 8pp.

JOHN BORSTLAP (1950–   ) The Netherlands
Sonata   1975 (Donemus   1976) 11pp. Photostat of MS. Explanations in Italian.
Trois préludes   1969 (Donemus   1977) 11pp. Photostat of MS.

SERGEY EDUARDOVICH BORTIKIEVICH (1877–1952) USSR
Bortikievich studied with van Ark and Liadov in St. Petersburg and then went to Germany, where he continued his musical training. He also lived in Constantinople for many years. "His compositions (for the greater part pianoforte works) are partly Russian, partly Oriental, with a slight inclination towards the new German style, recalling on occasions, especially in his preludes, the craftsmanship of Liszt and the expression of Chopin.

His music is based on sound principles and shows melodic invention, sincere feeling and romantic poetry" (GD, I, p.827). Many of his smaller works are excellent and are approximately late-intermediate level.

Seven Impressions Op.4 (Rahter 1907). Old Picture; Bird's Study; Storm; After the Rain; Shepherds and Shepherdesses; By Moonlight; Fancy-Dress Ball. Requires a certain amount of maturity for proper interpretation. Int. to M-D.

Deux Morceaux Op.7 (R&E 1976) Vol.I: 9pp; Vol.II: 11pp.

Sonata B Op.9 (Rahter 1909) 31pp. Allegro ma non troppo; Andante mesto e molto espressivo; Presto. A large work, well constructed. Late nineteenth-century idiom, highly pianistic; beautiful melodic writing infuses entire work. Does not sound too dated. D.

Six Pensées Lyriques Op.11 (Rahter 1909). Colorful short character pieces with Russian overtones. Int. to M-D.

From My Childhood Op.14 (Rahter 1911) 27pp. What the Nurse Sang; The Dark Room; The Dancing Lesson; First Love; First Sorrow; When I Am a Man. Int.

Ten Etudes Op.15 (Rahter 1911) 45pp. In Chopin tradition. All "sound" and are effective. M-D.

The Little Wanderer Op.21 (Rahter 1922). Eighteen pieces that take the little wanderer to many lands. The characteristics of each country are incorporated in the piece. Would make an attractive group project. Int.

Three Waltzes Op.27 (Rahter Elite Ed.108). La Gracieuse; La Mélancolique; La Viennoise. Delightful, attractive; titles indicate character and style. M-D.

From Andersen's Fairy Tales Op.30 (Rahter). Twelve musical pictures. Some impressionistic devices used. Unusually attractive collection that could be performed as a whole, integrating some of the prose from Hans Christian Andersen. Int.

Ten Preludes Op.33 (Rahter).

Ballade Op.42 (Litolff).

Marionettes Op.54 (Simrock 1938) 15pp. Nine short pieces. Int.

Lyrica Nova Op.59 (UE 1941). 10 min. Four character pieces. Con moto affettuoso; Andantino; Andantino; Con slancio. All are written in either five or six sharps. Mainly Romantic style with some Impressionistic influence. M-D.

Four Pieces Op.65 (Dob).

DMITRII STEPANOVICH BORTNIANSKII (1751–1825) Russia

Dvi Sonaty (Muzychna Ukrainia 1972) 27pp. Fingering by V. Klin. Two sonatas for piano C, F.

MAURO BORTOLOTTI (1926–   ) Italy

Cadenza per Transparencias (SZ 1968). One folded leaf.

Pour le Piano (SZ 1969) 14pp.

PIETER JOSEPH VAN DEN BOSCH (1736–1803) The Netherlands
Sonatine G (Metropolis E.M. 4720). Similar in style and length to the
    Kuhlau Sonatinas Op.55. Published with Three Sonatinas by F. Staes.
    Int.

ARTURO BOSMANS (1908–   ) Brazil, born Belgium
Clavinecdotes 1955 (Metropolis) 15pp. Five anecdotas for piano. Short,
    clever, colorful, freely tonal, MC. M-D.

KURT BOSSLER (1911–   ) Germany
So bauen wir ein Zwölftonhaus (Impero 1974) 9pp.

ANDRÉ BOUCOURECHLIEV (1925–   ) France, born Bulgaria
Boucourechliev completed his studies at the École Normale de Musique
in Paris. He worked at the Studio for Electronic Music of the Italian
Broadcasting in Milan and at the Research Center of the French Broadcasting in Paris. He has also written works in the field of esthetics and
criticism.
Archipel 4 (Leduc 1970). "Archipelago" is a mobile work, i.e., chang-
    ing in shape, character, articulation, and duration at each perfor-
    mance. In four sections, aleatoric; shown to best advantage in a con-
    cert performance in two different versions. Great piles of tone
    alternate with ringing sonorities; improvisation is as important as the
    written notes; hangs together remarkably well. Notation is almost
    unbelievable! Wildest sounds imaginable; extensive directions for
    performer; performer must literally chart his own course in this work.
    Avant-garde. D.
Six études d'après Piranese (Sal 1975) 7 leaves, photostat. Explanations
    in French.

PIERRE BOULEZ (1925–   ) France
No matter how variable and complex the organization of his music may
be, Boulez sticks tenaciously to the basic elements that have always characterized his art. One work grows out of another in his creativity, and so
too does Boulez stand before us today as a protagonist of a rightly com-
prehended link between tradition and progress.
Première Sonate (Amphion 1946). See: David Burge, "Untying Rhythmic
    Knots," CK, 3 (September 1977):52, which deals with the problem
    of meterless music using this work for the main discussion; and
    Burge, "Renotation," CK, 3 (October 1977):58, on the more com-
    plex passages from the same sonata.
Deuxième Sonate (Heugel 1948).
    See: David Burge, "Renotation revisited," CK 4 (March 1978):66.
    William Heiles, "The Second Piano Sonata of Pierre Boulez," AMT,
    22 (January 1973):34–37.
Troisième Sonate (UE 1961). Begun in 1957 and still not complete.

Only two of the proposed five movements have been published: Trope: Texte–Parenthese–Commentaire–Glose–Commentaire; Constellation–Miroir. One of the greatest pianistic creations of this century. D.

See: Anne Trenkamp, "The Concept of 'Alea' in Boulez's Constellation-Miroir," M&L, 57 (January 1976):1–10.

Mark Wait, "Aspects of Literary and Musical Structure as Reflected by the Third Piano Sonata of Pierre Boulez," unpub. diss., Peabody Conservatory, 1976, 81pp. Contains a very enlightening analysis.

ROGER BOUTRY (1932–   ) France

Boutry studied composition with Tony Aubin and won the Prix de Rome in 1954. He is professor of harmony at the Conservatoire de Paris.

Sonate—Scherzo (Leduc   1962) 16pp. 7½ min. Allegro con fuoco: driving rhythms (2/2 + 3/8); leads to more lyric section involving wide sweeps across the keyboard; opening section returns. Andante: sostenuto (quasi recitativo) leads to big climax, subsides, then leads through an octave stringendo to Allegro vivace: toccata-like, concludes vivacissimo. Effective virtuoso contemporary writing. D.

Scherzo Fantaisie (Leduc).

Toccata (Musique Contemporaine/Salabert   1970) 13pp.

Les danses extravagantes du gnome Farceur (ESC).

Le Voleur d'etincelles (Sal).

ANNE BOYD (1946–   ) Australia

Angklung (Faber   1974) 6pp. Reproduced from holograph. To be played as slowly as possible. No bar lines; only dynamic direction is "sempre *p* poss." Static harmonies built around E and b. M-D.

ATTILA BOZAY (1939–   ) Hungary

Intervalli Op.15   1969 (EMB) 15pp. Impressionistic, reminiscent of "Night Music" from Bartók's *Out of Doors* suite. M-D.

Postlude Op.19a   1970 (EMB) 5 leaves.

EUGÈNE BOZZA (1905–   ) France

Allegro de Concert (Leduc   1974) 10pp. 7 min. A big concert etude with full chromatic chords, fast octaves, alternation of hands, flexible meters, glissando at conclusion. Sounds more difficult than it actually is. M-D.

JOHANNES BRAHMS (1833–1897) Germany

Klavierwerke (Carl Seeman, Kurt Stephenson—CFP   1974) Vol.I: Sonatas Opp.1, 2, 5. Vol.II: Variations Opp.9, 21, 24, 35. Vol.III: Piano Pieces Opp.4, 10, 39, 76. Vol.IV: Piano Pieces Opp.79, 116, 117, 118, 119. Vol.V: Variations, Piano Pieces, Studies: Variations in d from Op.18; Sarabandes and Gigues; Waltzes, Op.39 (easy version); Hungarian Dances, Nos.1–10; Gavotte after Gluck; 5 Studies after Chopin, Weber, and J. S. Bach; 51 Exercises. This urtext edition is based on the Mandyczewski edition of the *Complete Works*. Contains interesting suggestions for distributing the material between the hands (Op.10/3) as well as for positioning the hands wherever they interlock. Editorial suggestions are indicated by use of brackets and dotted slurs. Brahms's original fingering appears in italics. Preface in German, English, and French.

> See: TM, Analysis Of Intermezzo Op.76/7, pp.120–34.

16 Waltzes Op.39 (Hans Höpfel—VU 1975; Seeman—CFP 3666a; Alfred). The Alfred edition contains both solo and simplified versions.

> See: Henry Levine, "Brahms Simplifies Brahms," *Clavier,* 13 (February 1974).

Variations and Fugue on a Theme by Händel Op.24 (S. Gerlach, H.-M. Theopold—Henle 272). Practical urtext edition. D.

Variations in d on a theme from String Quartet Op.18 (Seeman—CFP).

2 Rhapsodies Op.79 (Steegman—Henle; Stockman—VU).

> See: Edwin Smith, "Brahms: Two Rhapsodies for Piano Op.79," *Music Teacher,* 55 (May 1976):13–14, for analysis and discussion of these works.

3 Intermezzi Op.117 (Müller—VU).

> See: Harold Zabrack, "Projecting Emotion," *Clavier,* 16 (September 1975):27–34, for a lesson on Op.117/2.

5 Studies (Mayer-Mahr—Simrock). Setting of No.5, Chaconne after J. S. Bach for left hand, 1879, is closer to the original and more valid musically than Busoni's setting. M-D.

Klavierstücke Op.118 (Imogen Fellinger—VU 1974). Edited from the autographs and the original edition. Fingering added by Detlef Kraus. Preface and critical notes in German and English. M-D.

Klavierstücke, Op.119 (I. Fellinger—VU 1974). M-D.

> See: Brian Newbould, "A New Analysis of Brahms's Intermezzo in B minor, Op.119 No.1," MR, 38 (February 1977):33–43; and Robert Dumm, *Clavier* 13 (February 1974):24–32, for a performer's analysis of Op.119/2.

Klavierstücke (Monica Steegmann—Henle 36 1976) 120pp. Contains Opp.76, 79, 116, 117, 118, 119. Based on autographs and first editions. Fingering added by Walter Georgii. M-D.

See: Jane A. Bernstein, "An Autograph of the Brahms–Handel Variations," MR, 34 (August–November 1974):272–81.

Beth Greenberg, "Brahms Rhapsody in G Minor, Op.79/2: A Study of Analyses by Schenker, Schoenberg, and Jonas," ITO, 1/9–10 (1975–76):21–29.

Albion Gruber, "Understanding Rhythm in the [Brahms] Piano Music," *Clavier,* 13 (February 1974):9–13.

Denis Matthews, *Brahms Piano Music* (Seattle: University of Washington Press, 1978), 76pp. BBC Music Guides series.

THEO BRANDMÜLLER (1948–   ) Germany
5 Details (Bo&Bo   1975) 8pp. 8 min. Dramatic and violent tonal contrasts. D.

WIM BRANDSE (1933–   ) The Netherlands
Descriptions (Schmitt). Six pieces in varied tonal color and stylistic touches. Int.
Postcards from Holland (GS). A picturesque group of scenes including: An Old Abbey, Fields of Tulips, Windmills, Sailing on a Lake, An Old Church, Market Day. Mixture of Romantic and MC sonorities. Int.

PETER MICHAEL BRAUN (1936–   ) Germany
Reprise (Gerig   1959–74) 9pp. Explanations in German and English.

MICHAEL BRAUNFELS (1917–   ) Germany
Physiognomien (Nymphenburg   1970) 18pp. 7 character pieces.
Ritornell und Nocturno Op.8 (Nymphenburg   1971) 22pp.

ROBERT BREMNER (–1789) USA, born Great Britain
The Harpsichord or Spinnet Miscellany (J. S. Darling—University Press of Virginia) 32pp. Facsimile of original 1765 edition. The title page of this collection of popular eighteenth-century keyboard music describes it as "Being a Graduation of *Proper* Lessons from the Beginner to the tollerable Performer / Chiefly intended to save Masters the trouble of writing for their pupils. / To which are prefixed some Rules for Time." Includes dances, folksongs, grounds, and compositions by contemporary composers, Corelli among them, and "God Save the King." Contains music "that Jefferson and Washington enjoyed at Monticello and Mount Vernon" (from the preface). Also includes an informative preface by the editor. Int. to M-D.

CESAR BRESGEN (1913–   ) Germany
Impressionen (Gerig   1928–30/73) 2 vols.
Studies I (Dob) Kinderleichte Stücke.
Klavierstücke im Rumänische Stil (Dob).
Studies VII Romanesca (Dob   1971) 15pp. Seven varied pieces, neoclassic orientation. Int.

FRANK BRIDGE (1879–1941) Great Britain
Gargoyle (Thames   1977). An original, whimsical, and impressive scherzo. M-D.
See: Peter J. Pirie, "Frank Bridge's Piano Sonata," M&M, 24 (January 1976):28–30, 32.

ALLEN BRINGS (1934–   ) USA
Sonatine 1972 (MS available from composer: 199 Mountain Road, Wilton, CT 06897) 12pp. Poco allegro; Molto adagio ed espressivo; Allegro moderato. Freely tonal, excellent development of ideas, well conceived for the instrument. M-D.

CAREL BRONS (1931–   ) The Netherlands
Imaginations III (Donemus 1974) 10pp. Photostat of ms.

LÉO BROUWER (1939–   ) Germany
Sonata "pian e forte" (Ars Viva 1970). One folded loose leaf. About 10 min. Explanations in English, German, and Spanish. In addition to playing the piano, the performer is asked to play in and around the instrument. Calls for taped segments of the Gabrieli original and some improvisation by the performer. Aleatoric, avant-garde. D.

EARLE BROWN (1926–   ) USA
Twentyfive Pages for 1 to 25 pianos (UE 15587). Explanations in German and English, 1–25 leaves. "The *Twentyfive Pages* may be played in any sequence; each page may be performed either side up; events within each two-line system may be read as either treble or bass clef; the total time duration of the piece is between eight minutes and 25 minutes, based on 5 seconds and 15 seconds per two-line system as probable but not compulsory time extremities. After the 'Folio' experiments of 1952–3, this is the first extended work using what I call 'time notation' (durations extended in space relative to time, rather than expressed in metric symbols as in traditional notation) and which has since been called proportional notation" (from the score). Aleatoric, clusters, dynamic extremes, ten different attacks, performance directions, avant-garde. D.
See: David Burge, "Two Indeterminate Pieces," CK, 3 (January 1977):46, a discussion of Brown's "Twentyfive Pages" and John Cage's "Etudes Australes."

MERTON BROWN (1913–   ) USA
Brown studied composition with Wallingford Riegger and Carl Ruggles.
Arioso (NME 1949) 7pp. Chromatic, flexible meters, constant moving figuration, expressionistic. Second half to be played "sans nuance." M-D.

RAYNOR BROWN (1912–   ) USA
Sonata Breve (WIM 1974) 10pp.

ROSEMARY BROWN (–   ) Great Britain
The Rosemary Brown Piano Album (Nov 1973). Seven pieces inspired by Beethoven, Brahms, Chopin, Liszt, Schubert, and Schumann, claims Miss Brown. Opinion is still divided about her claim to have taken down pieces by the composers listed. The compositions look

and sound like good imitations of their respective styles but they have yet to be fully explained. An unusual collection. Int. to M-D.

Music from Beyond (Basil Ramsey   1977). Seven more pieces said to be inspired by J. S. Bach (Prelude), Beethoven (Scherzo), Brahms (Intermezzo), Chopin (Prelude), Liszt (Sonata movement), Rachmaninoff (Prelude), Schubert (Moment Musical). Miss Brown is still being "visited" by a host of music's immortals, who, she says, have dictated these pieces to her. Try them and judge for yourself. Int. to M-D.

Le Paon (B. Ramsey   1978) 2pp. The Peacock. Inspired by Debussy 15 Oct. 1967. Int.

See: Ian Parrott, *The Music of Rosemary Brown.* London: Regency Press, 1978.

MARK BRUNSWICK (1902–1971) USA
Brunswick studied composition with Rubin Goldmark and Ernest Bloch as well as with Nadia Boulanger.

Six Bagatelles (LG   1958) in collection *New Music for the Piano.* Brief, attractive, astringent contemporary style. M-D.

JOANNA BRUZDOWICZ (ca.1932–   ) Poland
Erotiques (Sal   1966) 8pp. 7½ min. Five short colorful sketches. Clusters are used in the second piece. M-D.

JOHN CALLIS BRYDSON (1900–   ) Great Britain
Fantasy (Freeman   1973) 12pp. Suite of five pieces: Frolic; Fairy Bells; Revelry; Will of the Wisp; Elfin Horns. Int.

ALBERTUS BRYNE (ca.1621–ca.1670) Great Britain
Musicks Handmaide (T. Dart—S&B   1969). Contains Bryne's only published keyboard music, five short pieces (in 1678 edition): Ayre, Corante, Sarabande, Ayre, Allemande, all in a. He did write several unpublished suites that have been overlooked until now. Three four-movement suites (almand, corant, sarabande, and "Jigg Allmaine") in Bodleian MS Mus. Sch. d.219 are among the finest English examples of their time. Of Bryne's English contemporaries only Matthew Locke has more surviving keyboard pieces. Bryne influenced many younger composers, particularly John Blow, and a suite ascribed to Blow in Brit. Mus. Add.31465, ff.36v–39, was actually written by Byrne.

See: Barry Cooper, "Albertus Bryne's Keyboard Music," MT, 113, No. 1548 (February 1972):142–43.

VALENTINO BUCCHI (1916–   ) Italy
Le Petit Prince (Ric   1971) 13pp. Five contemporary pieces.

WALTER BUCZYNSKI (1933–   ) Canada
Buczynski has studied composition with Earle Moss, Godfrey Ridout,

and Darius Milhaud and piano with Rosina Lhevinne. He has an extensive career as a concert pianist yet still manages to teach a large number of students.

Eight Epigrams for Young Pianists (Bo&H 1969) 10pp. Cheerful and forward-looking studies to help develop cantabile playing. MC harmony and compositional techniques. Analytical and performance directions. Int.

CAROLYN BULL (–   ) USA

Music for Haiku (CF 1971) 16pp. Inspired by Japanese poetry and music. Six musical postcards with a poem based on the Japanese verse form of *haiku*. Modal, MC. Int.

From Here to There (CF 1972) 23pp. Ten pieces, each stressing a specific interval. Clever, attractive. Int.

JOHN BULL (1562–1628) Great Britain

Twelve Pieces (T. Dart—S&B 1977) selected by John Steele from Volume XIX of *Musica Britannica*. A fine choice of works including: Chromatic Pavan; Prince's Galliard; Revenant; My Jewell; Bull's Goodnight. M-D.

ALAN BULLARD (1947–   ) Great Britain

Air and Gigue (OUP 1974) 6pp. 3½ min. For clavichord or piano. Air: melodic, cantabile, freely tonal around G. Gigue: driving rhythms, broken seventh chords. Int.

SAS BUNGE (1924–   ) The Netherlands

Etude I 1973 (Donemus 1977) 7pp.

Etude II 1973 (Donemus 1977) 10pp.

RICHARD BUNGER (1942–   ) USA

Two Pieces for Prepared Piano (Highgate 1977) 2pp. Preparations for both pieces include: plastic credit card, felt strip, clothespin wedges, screws, rubber erasers, dimes, bamboo wedge, vinyl tubing. I. Aria, 2½ min.: cantando; motivic figures sound over more sustained sonorities in left hand; long pedals; subtle; sensitive. II. Rondo for CK, 4 min. (published in *Contemporary Keyboard,* August 1977): ritmico; short, two–three-bar ideas frequently repeated; repeat to sign; flexible meters; thin textures; piece gradually fades away while repeating final three bars seven or more times. M-D.

Three Bolts Out of the Blue (Highgate 1977) 4pp. For prepared piano. Preparations are the same as listed above for *Two Pieces*. I. Eleven Bolt Bebop, 1 min.: syncopated, legato left-hand chords. II. One Bolt Blues, 2 min.: long pedals, quick chromatic arpeggi figures, slow closing. III. Stovebolt Boogie, 1½ min.: perpetual-motion boogie figures with each measure repeated the number of times indicated, tremolo closing in upper range of keyboard. M-D.

Money Music (Music of Change) 1978 (MS available from composer: c/o Music Department, California State College, Dominguez Hills, CA 02350) 12pp. For prepared piano. Uses coins as well as paper money woven onto and into the strings. Oligopoly: mechanically, like clockwork. Uncommon Cents. Small Changes. Clever. M-D.

Pianography (Fantasy on a theme by Fibonacci) (A. Broude).

See: Richard Bunger, "Prepared Piano—Its History, Development, and Practice," Part I, CK 3 (July 1977):26–28. Part II is found in CK, 3 (August 1977):14–16.

DAVID BURGE (1928–) USA

Eclipse II (Composer/Performer Edition 1967). New notation, pointillistic, dynamic extremes exploited, expressionistic, avant-garde. D.

JOHANN F. BURGMÜLLER (1806–1874) Germany

Burgmüller wrote mainly light salon music, but some of his studies, especially Opp.100 and 105, are useful.

25 Progressive Pieces (Alfred). Int.

25 Easy and Progressive Studies Op.100 (GS).

12 Brilliant and Melodious Studies Op.105 (GS).

12 Characteristic Studies Op.109 (GS).

Rondo alla Turca Op.68/3 (GS).

Bolero Op.76/2 (GS).

The Swallow (Harris).

NORBERT BURGMÜLLER (1810–1836) Germany

Younger brother of Johann F. Burgmüller. Robert Schumann valued Norbert greatly; he begins a memorial notice of him by saying that Burgmüller's death was the most deplorable that had happened since Schubert's early death (*Gesammelte Schriften*, Vol.III, p.145).

Rhapsodie b (UMKR No.26 1975) 7pp. An agitato section marked by an accented melody in the inner voices is contrasted with a Poco adagio, flowing, arpeggiated B section. Strong Romantic writing, colorful atmospheric closing. Would make a fine substitute for the Brahms *Rhapsodie* in g, Op.79/2. M-D.

WILLI BURKHARD (1900–1955) Switzerland

These three works are Reger- and Hindemith-oriented, tonally dissonant, and display a mastery of traditional techniques.

Variationen über ein Volkslied Op.8 (Br 1971) 12pp. Ten variations follow a simple theme. M-D.

Drei Präludien und Fugen Op.16 (Br 1971) 24pp.

Variationen über ein Menuett von Joseph Haydn Op.29 1930 (Br 1971) 12pp.

ALAN BUSH (1900–) Great Britain

Bush teaches composition at the Royal Academy of Music in London.

Suite Op.54 (CFP) for harpsichord or piano.

Variations, Nocturne, and Finale Op.60 (Nov). Diatonic, fine rhythmic vocabulary. Ornate decoration permeates all movements. Theme of all three movements is "Blow, ye winds." M-D.

GEOFFREY BUSH (1920–   ) Great Britain

Sonatina I (Nov) 8 min.

Sonatina II 1969 (Elkin 1974) 15pp. 7½ min. Reproduction of composer's MS; no fingering or pedalling indicated. Designed as an introduction to contemporary techniques. Neoclassical, contrapuntal. The three movements are based on a nine-note series. D.

FERRUCCIO BUSONI (1866–1924) Germany, born Italy

Piano Works (USSR 1969) 112pp. Contains Six Etudes Op.16; Op.33b (four pieces); All' Italia (in modo napoletano); Turandots Frauengemach (Intermezzo); Giga, Bolero and Variation (study after Mozart); Paganiniana. D.

Fantasia nach J. S. Bach alla Memoria di mio Padre Ferdinando Busoni (Br&H 1909) 15pp. Written in honor of Busoni's father, who died in 1909. Tranquil, serious opening leads to sonorous chordal section based on a Bach chorale. Figurative treatment of single voice chorale follows and leads to section based on "In Dulci Jubilo," Mancando conclusion. Holds together well in spite of sectionalization. M-D.

Variations on the Chopin Prelude c (Op.28/20) Op.22 (Br&H) 8½ min. One of Busoni's most ingenious works. Opens with the Prelude as Chopin wrote it, but from then on we have a catalogue of Busonian pianistic and contrapuntal complexities. D.

Sech kurze Stücke zur Pflege des polyphonen Spiels (Br&H 1922). These six short pieces for the development of polyphonic playing are based on nineteenth-century virtuoso concepts. D.

Die Nächtlichen (MS reproduced in Brazilian periodical *Musica Viva,* April 1936) 6pp. A chromatic, melodic, character piece. M-D.

Toccata: Preludio, Fantasia, Ciacona (Br&H 1921).

Trois Morceaux (Dob). Scherzo Op.4: lively, compound quadruple time. Prelude and Fugue Op.5: easy Prelude C, more difficult Fugue. Scène de Ballet Op.6: needs strong left-hand octaves; full chords in right hand. Polished writing. M-D.

Fantasia and Fugue on "Ad nos ad salutarem undam" 1897 (Br&H). This transcription of Liszt's arrangement for two players on the organ or pedal-piano is an awe-inspiring example of the Romantic imagination in full flower. Eminently pianistic. D.

SYLVANO BUSSOTTI (1931–   ) Italy

Musica per amici 1957, revised 1971 (Ric). Highly fragmented bits and pieces, variable meters, dynamic extremes, fists used on keys, avant-garde. D.

Foglio d'album 1970 (Ric). One folded loose leaf.

Novelleta 1973 (Ric). Pianist plays up and down the keyboard, on the cover of the keyboard, on his leg, on his arm, etc. All the clichés of contemporary piano writing, entertaining. M-D.

NIGEL BUTTERLEY (1935–   ) Australia

Letter from Hardy's Bay (J. Albert 224   1970) 8pp. 11½ min. Strings of four notes are to be prepared with eight metal bolts. Preparation directions included. Stemless notes indicate irregular rhythms. Clusters; harmonics; pointillistic; recurring gong-like chord halts the flow of the piece every time it appears; player stands to finish piece. Avant-garde. D.

Arioso (J. Albert   1960) 2pp. Freely dissonant moving lines. Int.

MAX BUTTING (1888–1976) Germany

Kinderspiel II (Neue Musik   1973) 11pp. Tänzchen I–IV Op.122b; Fürs Wunderkind Op.122c.

WILLIAM BYRD (1543–1623) Great Britain

9 Pieces from "My Ladye Nevells Booke" (A. Brown—S&B). Suggested directions. Int. to M-D.

6 Sets of Variations (A. Brown—S&B) from vols. 27 and 28 of *Musica Britannica*. Contains notes on history and performance. M-D.

3 Anonymous Keyboard Pieces attributed to William Byrd (O. Neighbour —Nov 1973). Prelude G: from Will Forster's Virginal Book. Prelude F. Alman C: especially attractive. Int.

The Carman's Whistle. Callino Casturame. Victoria (Farrenc—Leduc) Published together. M-D.

Compositions (K 3282).

THOMAS BYSTRÖM (1772–1839) Sweden

Polanaise C (Fazer 1973) 7pp., 2 facsimiles. From the collection Musikaliskt tidsfordrif 1805. Revised by Pentti Koskimes. Preface in English, Finnish, and Swedish by Einari Marvia. No.XIII of Documenta musicae fennicae.

Air Russe Variée (Fazer 1972) 11pp. No.XII of Documenta musicae fennicae.

C

JUAN CABANILLES (1644–1712) Portugal
See: Murray C. Bradshaw, "Juan Cabanilles: The Toccatas and Tientos,"
MQ, 59 (April 1973):285–301.

PETER CABUS (1923–   ) Belgium
Deux Danses (Metropolis   1965) 8pp. Introduction: Lento, rather leisurely, chromatic. Danse: alternating hands, *pp* opening, full chords,
strong rhythmic drive. M-D.

JOHN CAGE (1912–   ) USA
TV Köln (CFP   1960) 32 seconds. An early example of graphic music
notation, and thus subject to varying realizations by different performers. Its name comes from the television station in Cologne, Germany, which commissioned the work. Leaves the listener with the
wispiest of sensory impressions. Suggest it be played twice. Once
one learns to read the notation, the piece is about M-D.
The Perilous Night (CFP   1943–4) suite for prepared piano, six movements. Preparation requires weather stripping, flat pieces of bamboo,
and an assortment of nuts, bolts, and washers between the strings.
The effects are reminiscent of the Balinese gamelan. M-D.
Two Pieces for Piano   1946 (Henmar   1970) 8pp.
Two Pieces for Piano   1935 (Henmar   rev. 1974). Slowly; Quiet, Fast.
Two Pastorales (CFP   1960). Both involve chance operations derived
from the *I Ching* (Chinese Book of Changes).
Roots of an Unfocus   1944 (Henmar   1960) 3pp. For prepared piano.
Totem Ancestor   1943 (Henmar   1960) 5pp. For prepared piano.
And the Earth Shall Bear Again   1942 (Henmar   1960) 6pp. For pre-
pared piano.
Tossed As It Is Untroubled   1943 (Henmar   1960) 3pp. For prepared
piano.
Etudes Australes (CFP   1975) Four books of 32 etudes published in
two volumes. Fascinating format involving eight systems notated on
two pages, with each system having four staves. Extensive directions,
MS reproduction. Title comes from *Atlas Australis,* a book of star
maps used when writing these pieces. Terribly involved at places;
pointillistic, expansive range; tremendous leaps; both hands required
to play all over the keyboard at the same time. Avant-garde. D.

Water Music (CFP 6770   1960) 10 leaves. Chance composition, for a
pianist also using radio, whistles, water containers, deck of cards;
score to be mounted as a large poster.

Sonatas and Interludes (Henmar). For prepared piano. The sonatas attempt to express the permanent emotions of the Indian tradition.
The prepared piano produces some interesting Far Eastern sonorities.
Gentle percussive patterns. This set of pieces is Cage's "Well Tam-
pered Piano." M-D.

Cheap Imitation (CFP). 16 photocopied sides in a cover. 20 min. Three
movements. Melody from Erik Satie's *Socrate* is used with the *I Ching*
determinator. Some melodic doubling, sustaining pedal little used,
effective. Avant-garde. M-D.

31'57.9864" (CFP 6780   1960) 23pp. Chance composition, for prepared piano. Instructions (one leaf) inserted.

See: Doris M. Hering, "John Cage and the 'Prepared Piano,'" *Dance
Magazine,* 20, March 1946.

David Burge, "Two Indeterminate Pieces," CK, 3 (January 1977):46. A
discussion of Cage's "Etudes Australes" and Earle Brown's "Twentyfive Pages."

LOUIS CALABRO (1926–   ) USA

Calabro did graduate study at the Juilliard School and studied composition with Persichetti. Since 1955 he has taught composition at Benning-
ton College.

Young People's Sonatine (EV   1957) 7pp. Allegretto grazioso: mildly
dissonant lines. Lento assai: chordal, syncopated. Allegro: changing
meters, strong accents. Int.

Sonatina (EV   1959) 10pp. Allegro: freely tonal around B♭, expressive
lines, subito gestures, thin textures. Adagio: dissonant counterpoint
between hands. Allegro molto: driving rhythms in outer sections,
calm melodic mid-section. M-D.

Five for a Nickel Pie (EV   1975) 8pp. Fresh, original pieces using contemporary and modal harmonies. Int.

CHARLES CAMILLERI (1931–   ) Great Britain, born Malta

Camilleri writes in a style that is essentially new but at the same time very
old. He expresses himself in a contemporary approach based on well-tried
musical formulas used for centuries. His works for piano are prolific.

African Dreams (Roberton   1965). Six colorful pieces, explanations in
English. Hymn to Morning; Rain Forest Fantasy; Experience of Con-
flict; Festival Drumming; Children's Lagoon; A Dance—Ritual Celebration. M-D.

Three African Sketches (Roberton) 7½ min. Invocation and Dance.
Ulumbundu. Lament for an African Drummer. Pentatonic, thin textures, ostinati, contemporary Alberti bass treatment. Based on orig-

inal material, not African melodies. A folklike melody is introduced near the end of the third movement. Monotony sets in before piece concludes. Int. to M-D.

Due Canti (Roberton). Arabesque: decorated melodic line, modal harmonies. Cantilena: less-decorated melody, good for small hands. Int.

Etudes (Roberton). Book I: In Folk Song Style; Contrasts; Fantasy Waltz. Chords and broken chords; atonal; requires strong rhythmic control. Book II: Repliement; A Tranquil Song; Réjouissance; Chorale Prelude; Rondo. Technical problems explored are octaves, complex rhythms and chords, broken chords especially. Book III: "The Picasso Set." Composed as a response to an exhibition of Picasso's paintings. For Camilleri, Picasso represents in his art the dilemma facing all twentieth-century artists: the pull between representative and abstract art. Each piece in this book has a distinct flavor. Blues: the Blue period; Foxtrot; Gavotte; Mural; Primitif: very dissonant, with African rhythms; Circus Waltz: slightly chromatic. All are short and nondevelopmental. Int. to M-D.

Four Ragamats 1967–70 (Roberton) 26 min. The title is a combination of two musical forms: the Indian Raga and the oriental Maqamat. However the *Ragamats* do not try to emulate non-Western music. On the contrary, they try to fuse within themselves the philosophy of various different cultures. They use a technique that is concerned with widening the scope of rhythm, melody, and harmony. In this technique the beat is "atomized" into self-contained units that in themselves form part of the overall rhythmic and melodic form of the work involved. Small, innumerable, different, quick and slow melodic figures, each with a life of its own, may flow in a free, improvisatory manner while the metric beat remains steady—thus shifting the accents beyond the confines of any imaginary bar line. In their texture, fragments of ancient and modern scales, fragments of folk music, and other sources common to the music of the Mediterranean are to be found. But influences covering the music of Africa, the Orient, and the Americas are not uncommon. The pieces are freely tonal and may be played separately or together. No.1 centers around d, No.2 around F, No.3 B♭, No.4 around E♭. They may also be related to special times of day—morning, noon, evening, night. Highly chromatic; pointillistic in a few places.

Pieces for Anya (Roberton 1975). Morning Playtime (Hopscotch): delightful, staccato and legato. A Tender Melody. A Carol of Charms: all in treble clef. A Sad Folk Song: expressive. Little Caprice: rhythms make it the most difficult of the set. Int. to M-D.

Five Children's Dances Op.9 (Fairfield 1969) 12pp. For piano, voice and piano, or voices alone—with English and Maltese words. Boy's Football; One Two Three; Merry-go-round; The Children's Band; In Hyde Park. Int.

Petite Suite for Young Pianists (Roberton).

Sonatina Classica (Roberton   1974). Dedicated to the memory of the
Maltese composer Niccolo Isouard (1775–1818). Three movements
written in a style to suggest the period; an eighteenth-century pastiche. Int.

Sonatina semplice (Roberton).

Times of Day—Five Southern Impressions (Roberton   1958). These
five short pieces crystallize the mood of "A village island, primitive,
earthy and timeless," of the Maltese poet Dun Karn. Aubade: warm
melismatic chords in left hand and a shimmering right hand, which
possibly suggest a warm Mediterranean dawn with sunlight sparkling
on the water. Interlude I: short, octaves with disjointed rhythms,
improvisatory. Silent Noon: opens with a tolling bell; heavy chords
bring siesta as the A tonic chord is repeated fifteen times. Interlude
II: a lively presto with the right hand doing most of the work. Evening
Meditation: opening "Aubade" warm chords return; calm and le-
thargic mood. The pieces are fitted together in an arch form. The
entire work has a meditative and ritual effect. Notes in the preface
describe sources used for the pieces. M-D.

Sonatina I (Roberton   1960). The subtle first movement is developed
from the first Interlude in the *Times of Day* suite. The second and
third movements are more linearly conceived. Folklike melody is
introduced near the end of the third movement, which is a set of
variations. M-D.

Hemda (Nov   1962) 6 min. A quiet miniature aimed at capturing a
sense of magical stillness and tranquility evocative of sunrise on the
island of Malta. The middle section is a cantilena-type melody over
a guitar-like accompaniment. M-D.

Mantra (Nov   1969) 12 min. Camilleri tries to evoke the ethos and
spiritual state that is suggested by the oriental element "Mantra"—
the study and manipulation of sounds according to various planes of
consciousness. The beat remains steady while constantly fluctuating
patterns of melodic and rhythmic particles undergo a form of continual variation. D.

Noospheres   1978 (CMC).

Sonatina II (Roberton   1978).

See: Ates Orga, "Camilleri Premiere," M&M, 25 (November 1975):22,
24, 26, for a discussion of many of the piano works.

Christopher Palmer, *Introduction to the Music of Charles Camilleri* (London: Roberton Publications, 1974), 80pp. Illustrates Camilleri's
technique of composition.

LINA PIRES DE CAMPOS (1918–   ) Brazil

De Campos was assistant to Magdalena Tagliaferro for a number of
years. She founded her own music school in 1964 and turned to composition

after studying with Camargo Guarnieri. She has served as a member of the jury for several national piano competitions.

Acalanto   1959 (Vitale   1967) 4 min.

Ponteio 1   1959 (Ric BR   1970) 3 min.

Valsa 1   1960 (Ric BR   1970) 3½ min.

Circlo da boneca   1961 (Ric BR) 5 easy pieces. 4½ min.

7 Variações sobre o tema "Mucama bonita"   1962 (Ric BR) 5 min.

5 Peças infantis   1962 (Vitale   1967) 5 min.

Variações sobre tema brasileiro   1975 (Vitale   1977) 6 min.

3 Estorietas   1975 (Musicalia) 3 min.

Valsa 2   1975 (Musicalia) 4½ min.

Ponteio 2 (Homenagem a Guarnieri)   1976 (Vitale) 3 min.

HECTOR CAMPOS-PARSI (1922–   ) Puerto Rico

Tres Fantasies (Institute of Puerto Rican Culture, P.O. Box 4184, San Juan, Puerto Rico).

BRUNO CANINO (1935–   ) Italy

9 Esercizi per la Nuova Musica (Ric 1970–1) 16pp. Includes performance instructions in English, German, and Italian. 1. The Same Sound. 2. Play with the Stop Watch. 3. Play the Tempo, Well Counting the Eighth Notes. 4. Accelerando, Ritardando. 5. Quintuplets: requires two or three players. 6. As Fast As Possible. 7. The Three Pedals. 8. Secco, Morbido; PP, FF. 9. Little Maze. All pieces are designed to acquaint the pianist with avant-garde techniques on the piano. D.

Impromptu II (SZ   1973) 3pp. Note in Italian.

PHILIP CANNON (1929–   ) Great Britain

L'Enfant s'amuse Op.6 (Kronos) 21pp. L'Aube; Pas Seul; Pique-Nique des Marionettes; Berceuse pour une Souris; À Tricyclette. Attractive, MC, with a flair for interesting effects. M-D.

Sonatine Champêtre Op.17 (Galliard   1960). 19pp. 12 min. Three sparkling movements: Musette; Le Lac Gris; Colombine et Arlequin.

PHILIPPE CAPDENAT (1934–   ) France

Batteries (Amphion   1967) 15pp. For prepared piano.

MATILDE CAPUIS (1913–   ) Italy

Sei Preludi (EC   1972) 16pp.

Schizzi (EC   1976) 21pp.

CORNELIUS CARDEW (1936–   ) Great Britain

Cardew has been concerned mainly with graphic and experimental notation and with indeterminate or partly determined composition.

Volo Solo   1965 (CFP 7129A) for piano or prepared piano. For a virtuoso performer on any instrument! Instructions in English. 16 pages in a ring-bound plastic folder. Avant-garde.

Memories of You (UE 15447   1967). Avant-garde notation. Sounds
are "relative" to a grand piano. Durations and dynamics are free.
Any three objects may be used to create sounds (matchbox, comb,
hand, etc.). M-D.

LINDEMBERGUE CARDOSO (1939–   ) Brazil
Cardoso is professor of composition, folklore, and perception in the
School of Music and Scenic Arts of the Federal University of Bahia.
Toccata   1972 (Vitale) 13 min.

BENJAMIN CARR (1768–1831) USA, born Great Britain
*The Maid of Lodi. Four Pieces from 'Melange': Moderate; Waltz; Horn-
   pipe; Gavotte* (McClenny, Hinson—Belwin-Mills) in collection
   Early American Music. Also includes biographical material. Int.
Musical Journal (Scholarly Resources, Inc., 1508 Pennsylvania Ave.,
   Wilmington, Delaware 19806). 2 vols. This valuable collection of
   pieces (piano, voice, chamber music, etc.) provides a close look at
   the literature performed and heard during the last part of the eighteenth century and early part of the nineteenth century in America.
   It was the *Etude* of its day. Int. to M-D.
Musical Miscellany 1815–25 (Da Capo   1979) 300pp. This collection, issued in occasional numbers over a ten-year period, contained
   a large variety of musical types, reflecting the vogues and interests
   of the time: works by English composers and those popular in
   England—such as Hook, Haydn, Pleyel, Bishop, and Kelly; French
   and Italian songs; Scottish ballads and folklore. The series was almost evenly divided between vocal and instrumental music—the
   piano at this time was gaining popularity—and also contained a
   significant amount of sacred music by Carr as well as other composers, including Handel. The Da Capo reissue includes a new introduction by Eve Meyer that places both the *Miscellany* and Carr's
   career in historical perspective. This series is valuable not only for
   the picture it provides of American musical taste of the period but
   also as a collection whose artistic quality and range make it as useful
   for performance today as when the series first appeared. Int. to M-D.
   See: Eve R. Meyer, "Benjamin Carr's Musical Miscellany," *Notes*,
   33 (December 1976):253–65.

EDWIN CARR (1926–   ) Great Britain, born New Zealand
Carr studied at Auckland and Otago universities and the Guildhall School
of Music in London.
Five Pieces for Piano (Ric   1966). 11 min. Toccata; Aria 1; Sonata;
   Aria 2; Finale. Built on a twelve-note series. Large, solid hands
   needed. M-D.
Sonata (Ric   1955).

JULIAN CARRILLO (1875–1965) Mexico

Between 1885 and 1890 "Carrillo coined the term *sonido 13* (13th sound), referring to a specific microtonal pitch, the first two-octave harmonic on the fourth string of the violin. To Carrillo this was the first pitch to lie outside the traditional tuning system of 12 semitones to the octave; he later applied the term to his entire microtonal system, which he codified during the late teens and early 20s" (DCM, 126).

Preludio 29 de Septiembre (Sonido 13)   1949. For piano in 30ths.

Balbuceos (Sonido 13)   1959. For piano in 16ths.

ELLIOTT CARTER (1908–   ) USA

Carter is recognized as a composer of penetrating insight and provocative technique.

See: Robert Below, "Elliott Carter's Piano Sonata," MR, 34 (August–November 1974):282–93.

The Writings of Elliott Carter, compiled, edited, and annotated by Else Stone and Kurt Stone (Bloomington: Indiana University Press, 1977), 390pp.

DINORÁ DE CARVALHO (1905–   ) Brazil

De Carvalho, one of the foremost composers of Brazil, lives in São Paulo. Her early works were influenced by the "national school" of Mario Andrade. From 1967 on her compositions explore new combinations of timbre and harmony.

Lá vai a barquinha carregada de . . .   1939 (Ric BR   1941) 1 min.

O burrinho teimoso   1939 (Ric BR) 1 min.

Alegria dos pássaros   1940 (Vitale) 1 min.

Jogos no parque D. Pedro II   1940 (Vitale) 11 min.

Valsa I   1944 (Mangione   1948) 1½ min.

Cantilena   1945 (Ric BR   1961) 1½ min.

Festa do Santo Rei   1949 (Vitale   1955) 2 min.

Mural de pássaros ("Triste")   1960 (Vitale   1973) 2½ min.

Cavalinho de piche ("The Little Tar Horse")   1955 (Ric BR   1963) 2pp. Trotting 6/8 rhythm, melody shifts to left hand, picturesque. Int.

Contemplação   1963 (Gerig) 3½ min.

Suite   1968 (Ric BR) 8 min. Marcha; Angústia; Solidão; Polka; Allegro brilhante.

ROBERT CASADESUS (1899–1972) France

24 Préludes Op.5 (ESC   1924). 4 vols. In all the keys. M-D.

Trois Berceuses Op.8 (Sal) 8pp. Piquant, bluesy, quiet but contrasted, colorful, Romantic harmonies, nice. M-D.

8 Etudes Op.28   1941 (GS; Durand). 17 min.

Toccata Op.40 (Durand   1950).

See: Robert J. Silverman, "A Short Talk with Gaby Casadesus," PQ, 80 (Winter 1972–3):4–5. Includes a list of Casadesus's compositions.

Sacha Stookes, *The Art of Robert Casadesus* (London: The Fortune Press, 1960). Includes a biography and an analysis of his works.

ANDRÉ CASANOVA (1920–   ) France
Quatre Intermezzi Op.28 (Billaudot   1970) 15pp. 9½ min. Fantasque; Sarcastique; Douloureux; Flamboyant.

ALFREDO CASELLA (1883–1947) Italy
6 Studies Op.70   1944 (EC). Contains a piece based on thirds, on fourths, and another on major and minor sevenths; a Toccata; an Hommage to Chopin; and a fast repeated-note study. D.

PAOLO CASTALDI (1930–   ) Italy
Moll (UE   1970). One loose leaf in a roll. Avant-garde.
Definizione di 'grid' (Ric   1969). One folded loose leaf. Includes portions of Chopin's Etude Op.10/3 and Liszt's *Liebestraüme* No.III.
Left (SZ   1971) 14pp. 11 min.
Elisu (SZ   1964–67) 10pp.
Grid (SZ   1969) 3pp.
Scale (SZ   1971) 11pp.
Finale (Ric   1971–73) 84pp. 40 min.
Notturno (Ric   1971) 22 leaves. 20 min. Reproduced from holograph.
Study (Ric).
Studio   1971 (Ric) 9pp. 11 min.
Moderato   1975 (Ric   1977) 11pp. 9 min.

JOSEPH F. CASTALDO (1927–   ) USA
Moments (GS   1973) 5pp. Avant-garde writing that exploits the piano by damping strings and using a rubber mallet, fingernail glissandi, forearm clusters, etc. Wide dynamic range, exact pedal directions, economy of material. D.
Sonata (PIC   1961) 20pp.

MARIO CASTELNUOVO-TEDESCO (1895–1968) Italy
Melody is the essence of Castelnuovo-Tedesco's style.
Alghe   1919 (Forlivesi). The title refers to seaweeds that retain the perfume of the Italian seashores. M-D.
Questo fu il carro della Morte ("The House of Death") Op.2   1913 (Forlivesi). A descriptive work with a long quotation from Giorgio Vasari's "Vita di Pier di Cosimo" on the title page.
La Sirenetta e il pesce turchino ("The Little Mermaid and Dark Blue Fish")   1920 (Forlivesi). A fable of the sea.
Vitalba e Biancospino ("Clematis and Hawthorn")   1921 (Forlivesi). A sylvan fable.
La Danza del Re David (Forlivesi). Rhapsody on Jewish traditional themes. Strongly Impressionistic. M-D.
Epigrafe (Forlivesi). A gentle work. M-D.

Greeting Cards Op.170   1954 (Gen) Based on motives from the names of friends and colleagues. 1. Andre Previn: Tempo da Tango. 4. Walter Gieseking: Mirages, quiet and dreamy. 9. Amparo Iturbi: Tempo di Fandango. Op.170/2 (c.1975) is slow, with variations, on the name of Nicolas Slonimsky. M-D.

See: Nick Rossi, "Mario Castelnuovo-Tedesco: Modern Master of Melody," AMT, 25 (February–March 1976):13–14, 16.

——, ed. *Catalogue of Works by Mario Castelnuovo-Tedesco* (International Castelnuovo-Tedesco Society, 55 W. 73 St., New York, NY 10023   1977).

JACQUES CASTÉRÈDE (1926–   ) France
Capriccio (Sal).
Variations   1959 (Sal). Required piece of the Paris Conservatory, 1959. D.

MARISA CATALANOTTO (–   ) Italy
In Modo Burlesco (EC   1974) 4pp.
Piccola Toccata (EC   1974) 5pp.

NORMAN CAZDEN (1914–   ) USA
All MS copies are available from the composer, c/o Music Department, University of Maine, Orono, ME 04473.

Sonata Op.12 (MS   1941) 27pp. Allegro impetuoso: thematic contrast, multiple implied tonalities. Andante maestoso: dramatic gestures, scherzando section is giguelike. Allegro vivace: perpetual motion opening, slower mid-section, return to perpetual motion idea. M-D.

Three Modern Dances Op.42 (MS   1945) 11pp. Dance in Blue: slowly and intensely. Dance in Red: aggressively, varying tempi, slower and whitely, rolling on, full throttle (some of the directions). Polonaise: square set tempo, many skips for left hand. This set is representative of the numerous works Cazden has written for modern (stage) dance. Int to M-D.

Sonata Op.53/1 (MS 1958) 5pp. Freely chromatic. M-D.

Sonata Op.53/2 (LG 1958) In collection *New Music for the Piano*. More involved than Op.53/1, varied textures, bi-tonal. M-D to D.

Clefs, Crabs and Mirrors: A Group of Easy-to-Play Puzzles Op.79 (MS 1962) 7pp. Includes much practice in transposition. Easy.

A First Diatonic Reader Op.72 (MS   1962) 11pp. Pedagogic material.

First Steps Op.80 (MS   1964) 11pp. Pedagogic material.

New Pieces Op.95 (MS   1966) 44 short pieces.

The sets of pieces in Opp.72, 80, and 95 are indicative of the music Cazden has written for piano study on an elementary level.

The Sunshine Sonata Op.101 (MS   1971) 15pp. Sonata quasi una Fantasia. Linear, some broad gestures. Requires large span. M-D.

Six Preludes and Fugues Op.106 (MS   1974) 31pp. Each Prelude has a different subtitle: Promenade; Ceremonial Dance; Solfeggietto; "The Juggler"; Toccata; Ballad. Contrasting, freely tonal, intense, very difficult, abstract.

IGNACIO CERVANTES (1847–1905) Cuba

Cervantes studied piano with Louis M. Gottschalk and also attended the Paris Conservatoire. He wrote numerous drawing-room pieces in a popular French style. His piano suite *Danzas Cubanas* was the first work by a Cuban composer to incorporate native rhythms in a concert form.

Six Cuban Dances (GS).

Two Cuban Dances (JWC   1900). Gran Señora; Porque, Eh? 2pp. each. Appealing, with characteristic Cuban rhythms and folklike melodies. M-D.

Three Dances (JWC   1898). La Celosa; El Veloria; La Carcajada. 2pp. each. Latin-American rhythms. El Veloria is subtitled "Veillée funèbre," while the third dance is a brilliant "L'éclat de rire" with a quickly diminishing piano closing. M-D.

Ignacio Cervantes, a highlight collection of his best-loved original works (C. Hansen   1976) 48pp. Includes detachable portrait of the composer.

EMMANUEL CHABRIER (1841–1894) France

Pièces pittoresques   1880 (E. Klemm—CFP). Preface and critical notes in French, German, and English. These are musical pictures of nature and French and Spanish landscapes. Lithe rhythms and irregular phrases add much interest. M-D.

JOEL CHADABE (1938–   ) USA

Chadabe teaches at the State University of New York at Albany.

Three Ways of Looking at a Square (CPE   1967). New notation, avantgarde. Numbers with fermatas refer to seconds of silence. Numbers with dashes refer to seconds of holding sounds with the pedal. In either case they may be read freely, according to the piano, acoustics, etc. Pointillistic. D.

JACQUES CHAILLEY (1910–   ) France

Sketchbook (Martin Canin—Sal   1972) 20 easy pieces. Careful writing and titles, e.g., Lament of the Three Little Children, The Brooding Bagpipe, Prelude to the Evening of a Nymph, Three Hens Headed for the Fields. First ten pieces are based on French folk songs; second ten are original. Easy to Int.

LUCIANO CHAILLY (1920–   ) Italy

Variazioni nel sogno (Ric   1971) 14pp. 9 min. Theme, 12 variations, and coda. Complex and thorny avant-garde sonorities utilizing most of the keyboard. Traditional notation. D.

JULIUS CHAJES (1910–   ) USA, born Poland
Air Varié (Transcontinental). Theme, 4 variations, and coda. Int.

CÉCILE CHAMINADE (1857–1944) France
La Lisonjira ("The Flatterer") (Century). Delicate and imaginative with
    some unexpected happenings. Int. to M-D.
Piano Sonata c (Da Capo). Bound together with *Six Concert Etudes*.

PHILIPPE CHAMOUARD (1952–   ) France
Evocation (Choudens   1974) 7pp.

CLAUDE CHAMPAGNE (1891–1965) Canada
See: Anne Walsh, "The Life and Works of Claude Adonai Champagne,"
    diss., Catholic University, 1973, 183pp.

BRIAN CHAPPLE (1945–   ) Great Britain
Trees Revisited (JWC   1970) 16pp. 5½ min. Inspired by Oscar Ras-
    bach's *Trees*. Introductory bravura passage over long pedal note
    conceals original melody. Widely spaced chords, some dissonant and
    rich sonorities. M-D.

AARON CHARLOFF (1941–   ) Israel, born Canada
Etude for piano solo (IMI 270).

JACQUES CHARPENTIER (1933–   ) France
72 Etudes Karnatiques (Leduc   1960). Each study uses one of 72 Kar-
    natic modes of 7 notes each, which are listed in the Indian musical
    system known as the Karnatic. In this system the octave comprises
    7 main notes as well as 12 "regions" within which each note may
    move. Compared to dodecaphonic or tonal writing, the style of
    these Studies is extremely free. In 12 cycles, 6 pieces per volume.
    M-D to D.
Toccata (Leduc   1961) 1100. Varied groupings of 16th notes; alternating
    hands; widely spaced sonorities. D.
Allegro de Concert (Leduc   1965) 9pp. 6½ min. No meter or key sig-
    natures. A broad introduction (Vif) leads to a dolce *pp* section;
    increased intensity leads to section of trills in upper register, Dolce,
    pp; material from introduction rounds off the work. D.

ABRAM CHASINS (1903–   ) USA
Three Chinese Pieces (JF   1926) reissued 1974, slightly revised. 16pp.
    A Shanghai Tragedy: opens quietly, builds to climax, subsides. Flir-
    tation in a Chinese Garden: on white keys only, graceful, quiet. Rush
    Hour in Hong Kong: depicts a busy traffic scene, much activity. MC,
    interlaced with semi-oriental flavor (quartal and quintal harmonies),
    attractive. M-D.

ERNEST CHAUSSON (1855–1899) France
Piano Music (Herbert Haufrecht—Sal   1978) 26pp. Contains: Paysage,

Op.38; Interlude from *Poem de l'amour et de la mer;* Quelques
Danses: 1. Dedicace; 2. Sarabande; 3. Pavane; 4. Forlane. Well
edited, careful fingering. Int. to M-D.

CARLOS CHÁVEZ (1899–1978) Mexico
Sonata No.3 (EMM 1972) 20pp.
Estudio a Rubinstein (GS) 10pp. Brilliant, based on leaping conjunct
seconds. D.

CHEN SU-TI (1912–   ) China
Taiwan Sketches (available from composer: Tamsui, Taiwan) 21pp. Ten
descriptive, short, character pieces with colorful titles, e.g., Breezes
through the Banana Leaves; Black-bird on the Buffalo's Back; For-
mosan High-lander's Dance; Three Little Ducklings and a Toad. A
slight oriental flavor permeates some of the pieces. Int.
Etude Db (Divertimento). *Dragon Dance. Fantasie-Tamsui* (available
from the composer) 32pp. Bound in one volume. Nineteenth-century
gestures splash over the keyboard. M-D to D.

BRIAN CHERNEY (1953–   ) Canada
Cherney is a lecturer in theory and composition at the University of
Victoria. He is a graduate of the University of Toronto and has studied
composition with Samuel Dolin and John Weinzweig.
Intervals, Patterns, Shapes (Waterloo). Varied contemporary sonorities.
Int.
Jest (Jaymar) 3pp. A clever scherzo. M-D.
Pieces for Young Pianists (Jaymar) 3 books. Book II: four pieces, mu-
sically demanding; Int. Book III: three contrasting pieces, only the
last of which is titled—Dance for a Light Hearted Elephant; M-D.
Six Miniatures (Jaymar). Untitled, clever, MC. Int.

THOMAS CHILCOT (–   ) Great Britain
See: Gwilym Beechey, "Thomas Chilcot and His Music," M&L, 54 (April
1973):179–96, for a discussion of Chilcot's suites and concerti.

BARNEY CHILDS (1926–   ) USA
Childs teaches at the University of Redlands, Redlands, CA.
37 Songs (ACA 1971). A juxtaposition of short, simple ideas like
leitmotivs. Piano is prepared with a rubber eraser, a dime, and a
blackboard eraser. Specific instructions, e.g., "tap with knuckles on
keyboard cover behind keys"; "with left hand reach inside and push
eraser firmly against strings." Performer reads a given text to audience at conclusion of piece. Sensitive musicianship more important
than pianistic equipment. Will not work on a Baldwin grand because
the construction of the frame is such that one of the preparations
cannot be accomplished. Flexible meters, wide dynamic range, effective use of pedals. Mystifying and enchanting. Int. to M-D.

J.D. (ACA) for piano and tape. The tape consists of random extracts from John Dowland's lute song "I Saw My Lady Weep," sung a capella.

GABRIEL CHMURA (1946–   ) Israel, born Poland
Piece for Piano (IMI 182   1963) 10pp. 6 min. Avant-garde notation, clusters, improvisational, free rhythms, atmospheric. Large span required. M-D.

FRÉDÉRIC CHOPIN (1810–1849) Poland
Henle Verlag has continued to add to its projected complete edition of Chopin, an edition that cannot be recommended too highly. The Vienna Urtext Editions is also continuing to expand its Chopin catalogue, and both of these scholarly and urtext editions are gradually supplanting the older editions that have been available for many years. PWM has announced a new National Edition from Poland to supersede the Paderewski edition. This writer has seen only the Ballades.
"BI" (Brown Index) refers to Maurice J. E. Brown, *Chopin: An Index of His Works in Chronological Order,* 2d ed. (New York: Da Capo Press, 1972).
Henle now has available the Ballades, Etudes, Impromptus, Mazurkas, Nocturnes, Polonaises, Preludes, Scherzi, Sonatas (Opp.35 and 58), and Waltzes.
Some Chopin Institute volumes are now available in study scores: Vol. V: Scherzi; Vol.VIII: Polonaises; Vol.IX: Waltzes; Vol.XI: Mazurkas.
4 Ballades (E. Zimmermann—Henle; Jan Ekier—PWM, National Edition; Cortot—Sal with English text; Casella—EC with Fantasia Op.49; Agosti—EC). No.1. Op.23; No.2. Op.38; No.3. Op.47; No.4. Op.52. The Henle edition contains Chopin's fingering in italics as well as fingering added by Hans-Martin Theopold. Preface in French, German, and English. A highly commendable urtext edition.
See: Mark DeVoto, "Chopin, Ballade A♭, Op.47," ITO, 1/5 (1975): 31 (bars 140–43).
12 Etudes Op.10 (Badura-Skoda—VU; Esteban—Alfred), Op.25 (Badura-Skoda—VU; Cortot—Sal with English text; Friedheim—GS; Casella—EC), Opp.10 and 25 (Oborin, Milstein—USSR). VU edition contains fingerings and editorial additions in brackets; Friedheim—GS contains interesting fingering; Zimmermann—Henle is based on autographs, first, and early editions.
See: Edward Rothchild, "Slenczynska: On Playing the Chopin Etudes," *Clavier,* 15 (February 1976):14–21; Felix Salzer, "Chopin's Etude in F Major, Op.25, No.3. The Scope of Tonality," *Music Forum,* 3 (1973):281–90, which is mainly devoted to explaining the B major mid-section of this piece.

Impromptus (E. Zimmermann—Henle; Cortot—Sal; Jan Eiker—VU; Casella—EC). Henle edition contains Impromptus Op.29 A♭, Op.36 f♯, Op.51 G♭, and the Fantaisie-Impromptu Op.66 c♯ in both the Chopin and Fontana versions. These two versions show that we have been playing a great deal of Fontana for many years. VU edition has a preface and critical notes in French, English, and German, and added fingering.

Mazurkas (Zimmermann—Henle; Cortot—Sal in 3 vols.; Agosti—EC; EMB). Henle edition contains 57 mazurkas: Nos.1–49 were given opus numbers by Chopin; Nos.50–53 were published without opus numbers during Chopin's lifetime; and Nos.54–57 were published after his death. Fingering has been added by Hans-Martin Theopold. Early versions of some of the mazurkas that were later revised are given in the Supplement. Critical notes in German. This outstanding practical urtext edition is the most complete collection of mazurkas available.

See: TM, Analysis of Mazurka, Op.68/3, pp.80–91.

17 Selected Chopin Mazurkas (H. Levine—BMC). Highly edited.

Mazurka Op.68/4 f (Ronald Smith—Hansen House). A completely new realization of Chopin's final composition. M-D.

Nocturnes (Zimmermann—Henle) 21 nocturnes including two versions of Nocturne c♯ BI 49 (posth.). (Cortot—Sal) 2 vols. English text. Available separately: Nocturne c Posthumous (S. Askenase—Heuwekemeijer); Op.55/1 f (Anson—Willis).

3 Nocturnes (Cortot—Sal). Nocturnes c♯ BI 49 (posth.), Op.9/2 E, Op.55/1 f. English translation by Jerome Lowenthal.

See: Daniel Ericourt with the collaboration of Robert Erickson, "Melodic Elements in the Chopin Nocturnes," *Clavier*, 16 (September 1977): 35–39.

Polonaises (Zimmermann—Henle; Cortot—Sal; Agosti—EC). Henle edition contains Polonaises Op.26/1 c♯, 2 e♭; Op.40/1 A ("Militaire"), 2 c; Op.44 f♯; Op.53 A♭; Op.61 A♭ (Polonaise-Fantaisie); Op.71/1 (posth.) d, 2 B♭, 3 f (2 versions); g BI 1; B♭ BI 3; A♭ BI 5; g♯ BI 6; b♭ BI 13; G♭ BI 36. Based on autographs and first and early editions. Critical note in German.

Préludes (Zimmermann—Henle) Includes Op.28/1–24; Op.45; and BI 86 (Prélude A♭). (Thomas Higgins—Norton Critical Scores 1974). Contains Henle text without Op.45 and BI 86 plus analytical essays and historical background, which is supplemented by contemporary assessment by many of Chopin's champions and critics. The following do not contain Op.45 and BI 86: (Cortot—Sal with English text; Casella—EC; G. E. Moroni—Carisch). (Hansen, Demus—VU) alterations not always noted in musical text; critical notes must be read very closely to see where variations occur.

See: Maurice J. E. Brown, "The Chronology of the Chopin Preludes,"
MT, 98 (August 1957):423–44. Richmond Browne, "Chopin Preludes Forum: Back to Chopin," ITO, 1/4: 3–4. Ronald Cole, "Analysis of the Chopin Preludes, Op.28," Master's Thesis, Florida State
University, 1967. TM, Analysis of Op.28/4, pp.41–55.

Scherzi (E. Zimmermann—Henle; Cortot—Sal; Agosti—EC). No.1 Op.
20 b; No.2. Op.31 b♭; No.3. Op.39 c♯; No.4. Op.54 E. Henle
edition has a critical note in German.

Waltzes (E. Zimmermann—Henle) contains 18 waltzes with 2 versions
each of Op.69/2, Op.70/1, 2. Also contains in appendix Waltzes E♭
BI 133 and E♭ BI 46, which are of questionable authenticity. (Cortot
—Sal, with English translation by John Schneider; Casella—EC).

3 Valses Op.64, Op.69/1, 2. (Cortot—Sal). With English translation.

Valse f♯ (M. Dumesnil—Schroeder & Gunther). Not found in any collection.

Sonatas Op.35 b♭; Op.58 b. Published separately. (Zimmermann—Henle;
Cortot—Sal). Henle edition has preface and critical notes in French,
German, and English; based on the original German edition.

SEPARATE PIECES:

Berceuse D♭ Op.57 (Henle 320). Probably the most beautiful of all
Berceuses. M-D.

Fantaisie f Op.49 (Henle 321). One of Chopin's greatest works. D.

3 Ecossaises 1826 Op.72 (APS). These early works show a Schubert
influence. Int.

Marche Funèbre c, Op. Posth (CFP D-2796; Heuwekemeijer). This work
with dotted rhythms is similar to the slow movement of Sonata Op.35
B♭. Trio section is in major key. Octaves and large chords. M-D.

Waltz Op.70/1 G♭ and *Grand Valse Brillante* Op.18 E♭ (Byron Janis—
Edutainment, through GS). Contains two separate versions and
facsimile of these pieces. A few differences exist between these versions and other printed editions.

COLLECTIONS:

Album Chopina—L'Album de Chopin 1828–1831 (Jerzy Maria Smoter—
PWM   1975) 61pp. Polish and French. Bibliography, pp.61–62.

Chopin Album I (PWM). 5 preludes from Op.28; 7 mazurkas; 3 polonaises (g, c♯, A♭); 5 valses; 4 nocturnes; Revolutionary Etude. Fingering and pedal added.

Chopin—An Introduction to His Piano Works (W. Palmer—Alfred).
The 13-page introduction treats Chopin's style and rubato, but concentrates on a thorough explanation of Chopin's use of ornaments,
with many musical examples. Urtext edition with editorial additions
in gray print.

Chopin—Easy Piano (Alfred). 14 pieces including 6 mazurkas, 3 preludes, 3 waltzes, 2 unfamiliar posthumous works, plus a biography and notes about each piece. Int. to M-D.

Chopin—Favorite Piano (Alfred). 19 pieces including 4 mazurkas, 4 waltzes, Etude Op.10/5 E, Nocturne Op.9/2 E♭, Fantaisie-Impromptu. Biography and notes about each piece. Int. to M-D.

Il mio primo Chopin (Pozzoli—Ric ER2446) 14pp. Preludes Op.28/4 e, 6 b, 7 A; Mazurkas Op.7/5 C, part of Op.7/2 a, Op.67/2 B♭; Walzes Op.69/1 A♭, Op.69/2 b. Int.

Diverse Pieces (Cortot—Sal) Vol.I: Fantaisie; Barcarolle; Berceuse; Tarentelle. Vol.II: Allegro de Concert; Bolero; 3 Nouvelles Etudes; Prelude c; Variations Brillantes.

Introduction to the Cortot Editions of Chopin (Sal) 64pp. A sampler in English of Cortot's annotated editions. 4 preludes, 3 mazurkas, 3 nocturnes, 3 waltzes, ecossaises, Polonaise A.

Posthumous Works (Cortot—Sal). Sonata Op.4; Variations; 3 polonaises; 2 nocturnes; Marche Funèbre; 3 ecossaises; Polonaise g♯.

Klavierstücke (E. Herttrich, H.-M. Theopold—Henle 318). Includes Variations Op.12 B♭; Bolero Op.19; Tarantella Op.43; Allegro de Concert Op.46; Fantaisie Op.49; Berceuse Op.57; Barcarolle Op.60; Variations on a German National Air (Der Schweizerbub) BI 14; 3 Ecossaises Op.72. Based on autographs and first and early editions.

Young Pianist's Guide to Chopin (Y. Novik—Studio P/R). Includes record of the contents. Int.

See: Thomas Higgins, "Tempo and character in Chopin," MQ, 59 (January 1973), 106–20.

SHU-SAN CHOW (　　–　　) China
Chinese Short Pieces for Piano (Paterson　1973) 16pp.

DOMENICO CIMAROSA (1749–1801) Italy
Cimarosa's sonatas provide excellent alternatives to some of the overworked Clementi and Kuhlau sonatinas.

Sonatas (Arturo Sacchetti—Bèrben　1974) 19pp. Preface and performance notes in English. No.1 G is in the PWM collection listed below; Sonatas in F, F, C, B♭, and A published here for the first time. These are not the finest works by Cimarosa. All use much Alberti bass. Int.

32 Sonatas (Boghen—ESC　1925–26) 3 vols.

24 Sonatas (Ligteliyn, Ruperink—B&VP) 3 vols. Contains 24 of the sonatas from the Boghen collection.

Selected Harpsichord Sonatas (Z. Sliwinski—PWM　1971) 63pp. Preface in Polish only. Contains 20 sonatas, two of which are not in the Boghen collection. Well fingered; ornamentation written out.

31 Sonatas (V. Vitale, C. Brunno—Carisch) 2 vols. An edited "instructive" edition that duplicates only one sonata (No.27) in the Boghen edition. Uses MS numbers.

2 *Sonatas* (Lubomudrova—GS 211).

Comparison of Sonatas
in the ESC, B&VP, and PWM Editions
(Courtesy Rita Fucez)

	Eschig	Broekmans & Van Poppel	Polskie Wydawnictwo Muzyczne
Vols.I & II:	1	21	–
	2	17	5
	3	2	–
	4	22	1
	5	3	10
	6	20	3
	7	7	–
	8	19	–
	9	1	–
	10	23	–
	11	10	9
	12	18	–
	13	5	8
	14	4	7
	15	12	–
	16	8	16
	17	16	–
	18	14	–
	19	11	–
	20	24	18
Vol.III:	1 (21)	–	19
	2 (22)	–	4
	3 (23)	13	13
	4 (24)	–	15
	5 (25)	–	6
	6 (26)	–	2
	7 = MS 27	9	11
	8 (28)	–	–
	9 (29)	15	–
	10 (30)	–	20
	11 (31)	6	–
	12 (32)	–	14
	–	–	12
	–	–	17
Total: 32		Total: 24	Total: 20

EUGENE CINES (–   ) USA

Abbreviations (Bo&H 1974) 7pp. Three short works in contemporary idiom. Flexible meters, expressionistic. Requires large span. M-D.

OSCAR DE LA CINNA (–   ) Spain
3 Serenatas Vascas Op.113/1 (UME 6656) 9pp. Sérénade Basque I
(Pensée poétique) : syncopated outside sections with a cantabile waltzlike mid-section. II: energetic octaves, flowing melodies. III: 3/8
opening and closing sections, 6/8 mid-section with more florid
melismas. Int.

JEREMIAH CLARKE (ca.1673–1707) Great Britain
Selected Works for Keyboard (Eve Marsham—OUP 1975) 21pp. Preface and sources in English. Contains 27 short pieces. See especially
the expressive "Farewell," with its unusual dissonance. Int.

KENNY CLAYTON (1920–   ) Great Britain
The Secret Garden (UMP 1975) 20pp. An album of 8 pieces for young
pianists based on music for the recording of Frances Hodgson Bur-
nett's novel. Mistress Mary, Quite Contrary; Martha; The Robin;
The Secret Garden; Dickon; Colin, a Sick Boy—Colin, Well Again;
Ben Weatherstaff; Mother's Song (a duet for teacher and pupil).
Attractive MC writing. Int.

MUZIO CLEMENTI (1752–1832) Italy
Clementi's music is essentially classical in spirit, the result of disciplined
studies and an exceptional command of polyphonic technique and form
combined with typical nineteenth-century restlessness. His compositions
profoundly influenced Beethoven and, in many ways, foreshadowed Verdi
and Brahms. Clementi is also regarded as the originator of the proper
technique for the modern pianoforte, as distinguished from the harpsichord. His skill as a musician and teacher left a profound mark on nineteenth-century composers and pianists.
Collected Works (Br&H 1802–5, reprint Da Capo 1973) 13 vols. in
5 collections plus one fascicle of violin and flute parts and one
fascicle of cello parts. Published during the composer's lifetime, this
anthology of Clementi's accomplishments was one of the earliest
undertakings of the great Leipzig publisher, Breitkopf and Härtel.
It contains more than 100 sonatas plus a variety of other works.
Collection I (2 vols.): 12 sonatas; 9 sonatas. Collection II (2 vols.):
9 sonatas; 6 sonatas, four hands; sonata for two pianos, four hands.
Collection III (3 vols.): 17 sonatas; 7 sonatas; toccata; 2 caprices;
8 sonatas with accompaniment. Collection IV (3 vols.): 4 sonatas;
3 sonatas with accompaniment; 3 sonatas; 3 sonatas with accompaniment; 3 sonatas; 5 sonatas with accompaniment. Collection V (3
vols.): sonata and miscellaneous pieces; 4 sonatas for piano and
violin; miscellaneous other works; 11 sonatas with accompaniment.
Sonata f Op.14/3 (Sandra Rosenblum—ECS) 24pp. An outstanding study
edition based on the autograph. Listed in Alan Tyson, *Thematic*

Catalogue of the Works of Muzio Clementi (Tutzing: Hans Schneider, 1967), as Op.13/6.
Sonata A♭   1765 (P. Spada—Bèrben). Preface in Italian and English.

THE PIANO SONATAS:

It should come as no surprise to pianists that, although the piano sonatas of Muzio Clementi have been neglected for many years, they are among the most beautiful of the Classic period. Clementi's sonatas employ both virtuosity and an intense quality of expression, elements that distinguish them somewhat from the works of Haydn and Mozart and that are fore-runners of Beethoven's style. Clementi lived in England for most of his life and was head of a leading London publishing firm for some thirty years. As one might expect, the great majority of his authentic editions are indeed the English ones. Unfortunately, anyone studying Clementi's sonatas will quickly find that a problem exists with the use of different opus numbers to represent many of the sonatas. This confusing state of affairs, as Tyson puts it in his *Thematic Catalogue,* is a reflection largely of the popularity of Clementi's music throughout Europe after 1780 and of the consequent proliferation of arbitrarily numbered "Nachdrucke," or reprintings of these works. The chart below is a collation of the many opus numbers used by selected editions compared to the original order and numbering of the sonatas according to Tyson.

The editions in this collation are the incomplete "Oeuvres com-plettes" issued by Breitkopf and Härtel in 13 volumes; the Peters, edited by Ruthardt, 4 volumes; Schirmer's and Kalmus's two volumes, which are simply reprints of the first two volumes of Peters; the Ricordi, two vol-umes, edited by Cesi; and the Henle, Vol.I (No.317) edited by A. Tyson and S. Gerlach with fingering by Hans-Martin Theopold. Tyson's cata-logue lists a total of 71 published sonatas that are either for piano solo or may, as Clementi says, be performed as such. There is only one known sonata that remains unpublished (WO 13 in A♭); the manuscript is pre-served at the Bibliothèque Nationale in Paris.

SONATINAS:

6 *Sonatinas* Op.36 (6th ed.) 1820 (M. Hinson, D. Bishop—Hinshaw 1978). This sixth edition contains Clementi's fingering and many changes in the pieces, especially the use of higher octaves and the thickening of the texture at certain places. Students and teachers will be pleasantly surprised to find the "improvements" that Clementi made in this edition. Indeed, some of the changes make new pieces out of these tried but remarkably durable works. Clementi uses these pieces to focus directly on the most important aspects of piano play-ing: felicitous fingering, lucid phrasing, developing a legato touch,

Clementi's Keyboard Sonatas
as Numbered in Tyson and Five Editions

Tyson's Thematic Catalogue	Breitkopf and Härtel (Vol./No.)	Peters (Op./No.)	Schirmer and Kalmus (Op./No.)	Ricordi (Op./No.)	Henle 317 Vol.I
Op. 1/1, E♭					
1/2, G					
1/3, B♭					
1/4, F					
1/5, A					
1/6, E					
Oeuvre 1/1, F[1]	V/15				
1/2, B♭					1/2
1/3, G	V/16				
1/4, A					
1/5, a[2]					
Op. 2/2, C[3]	III/4	2/1	2/1	2/1	
2/4, A[4]	III/5				2/4
2/6, B♭	III/6				
Op. 7/1, E♭	I/11				
7/2, C	III/7				
7/3, g	I/12	7/3			7/3
Op. 8/1, g	I/8				8/1
8/2, E♭	I/9				
8/3, B♭	I/10				8/3
Op. 9/1, B♭	VI/3				
9/2, C	VI/4				
9/3, E♭	VI/5				9/3
Op. 10/1, A	VIII/2				10/1
10/2, D	VIII/3				
10/3, B♭	VIII/4				
Op. 11, E♭[5]	VI/7				
Op. 12/1, B♭	I/1	12/1	12/1		
12/2, E♭	I/2	12/2			
12/3, F	I/3				
12/4, E♭	I/4	12/4		12/4	
Op. 13/4, B♭	X/1				
13/5, F	X/2				
13/6, f	X/3				13/6
Op. 16, D[6]	XI/4				
Op. 20, C	VI/6				
Op. 23/1, E♭	I/5				
23/2, F	I/6	24/2			
23/3, E♭	I/7	24/3			
Op. 24/1, F					
24/2, B♭	VI/2	47/2	47/2	47/2	24/2
Op. 25/1, C	II/4	25/1			
25/2, G	II/5	25/2		25/2	
25/3, B♭	II/6				
25/4, A	II/1	26/1		26/1	

Tyson's Thematic Catalogue	Breitkopf and Härtel (Vol./No.)	Peters (Op./No.)	Schirmer and Kalmus (Op./No.)	Ricordi (Op./No.)	Henle 317 Vol.I
25/5, f$\sharp$	II/2	26/2	26/2	26/2	
25/6, D	II/3	26/3	26/3	26/3	
Op. 26, F	XI/8				
Op. 32/1, F[7]	VII/8				
32/2, D					
32/3, C	VII/7				
Op. 33/1, A	II/7	36/1	36/1	36/1	
33/2, F	II/8	36/2	36/2		
33/3, C	II/9	36/3	36/3		
Op. 34/1, C	V/1	34/1	34/1		34/1
34/2, g	V/2				
Op. 35/1, C[8]	XIII/9				
35/2, G	XIII/10				
35/3, D	XIII/11				
Op. 37/1, C	IX/1	39/1			
37/2, G	IX/2	39/2		39/2	
37/3, D	IX/3	39/3			
Op. 40/1, G	III/1	40/1	40/1		
40/2, b	III/2	40/2	40/2	40/2	
40/3, d & D	III/3	40/3	40/3	40/3	
Op. 41, E♭	VI/1				
Op. 46, B♭					
Op. 50/1, A					
50/2, d					
50/3, g		50/3			
WO 3, F	III/8				
WO 14, G					WO 14

1. This is the revised version of Op.1. Tyson calls this revision "Oeuvre 1" to distinguish it from the original. The revised opus preserves very little of the original material.

2. This sonata is actually a fugue.

3. Op.2/1, 3, and 5 are for harpsichord or pianoforte with an accompaniment for flute or violin. Op.2/2 was later revised as Op.30 for pianoforte or harpsichord and violin accompaniment, with an added slow movement. It was revised a third time years later using the original opus number.

4. This sonata was later revised as Op.31, with a new introduction of 32 bars, for harpsichord or pianoforte and flute accompaniment. It too was revised a third time years later using the original opus number.

5. Op.11 also contains a Toccata in B♭, which is in the Ediciones Lux edition.

6. Titled "La Chasse"; this work is actually a sonata with three movements.

7. All three sonatas of Op.32 were composed for pianoforte, flute, and violoncello and were marked "ad libitum," which would seem to indicate that they could be performed as piano solos.

8. As with Op.32, all three sonatas of Op.35 were composed for pianoforte, flute, and violoncello and were marked "ad libitum," which would seem to indicate that they too could be performed as piano solos.

(The author is indebted to Wesley Roberts for the collated chart and its related material.)

and careful dynamic control. A highly interesting addition to the basic piano repertoire. Int.

Preludes Op.43 (Dorothy Bishop—CF). 28 short technical pieces in all major and minor keys, some transposed by the editor. Variety of styles, helpful preface. Excellent Int. material.

Works for Pianoforte (Frank Dawes—Schott) 4 vols. Sonatas Op.9/3; Op.13/6; Op.34/2; Capriccio C, Op.47/2. M-D.

6 Monferrine (P. Spada—Bèrben 1972) 20pp. Preface in Italian and English. These are not part of the "Monferrinas" published in London in 1821.

Tre Pezzi (P. Spada—Bèrben). Allegro. Allegro. Finale. Int.

Sei Arie Russe e Tarantelle (P. Spada—Bèrben 1972). These six Russian Airs are harmonizations and pianistic adaptations of popular Russian tunes. Preface in English and Italian. Int.

Introduction to the Art of Playing on the Pianoforte 1801 (Sandra Rosenblum—Da Capo) 63pp. This work is among the earliest keyboard methods written specifically for the pianoforte. The most popular tutor of its day, it was published in eleven English editions by Clementi's firm and was translated into French, German, Spanish, and Italian. Designed to meet the needs of relatively inexperienced students and amateurs, this work presents a succinct introduction to the new technical skills and interpretative knowledge needed for the performance of the emerging piano literature. Varied pieces by well-known composers are used instead of the usual short practice pieces written by the author. These pieces reflect both the musical attitudes in England at the time and the taste of the compiler. A new introduction by Rosenblum discusses the *Introduction* in relation to other contemporary piano tutors and the musical practices of the times. She also deals with Clementi's use of ornamentation, tempo, pedaling, and fingering, and provides detailed bibliographic information on all known editions of the book.

Clementi's Selection of Practical Harmony for the Organ or Piano-Forte, containing voluntaries, fugues, canons, and other ingenious pieces by the most eminent composers, to which is prefixed an epitome of counterpoint by the editor (London: Clementi, Banger, Collard, Davis & Collard, 4 vols., 1803–15; reprint Forni, 1974), 145pp.

See: Joseph Bloch, "A Forgotten Clementi Sonata," PQ 79 (Fall 1972): 24–31. Facsimile of the 1803 Longman, Clementi Co. printing of the piano sonata in g, Op.8/1 (first published in 1782) with historical data about its composition and publication, formal analysis, performance suggestions, and brief discussion of Clementi's piano sonatas and his importance.

Rosemary Clark, "Clarifying Clementi—Realizing the Ornaments in Sonata Op.2/1," *Clavier,* 15 (January 1976):31.

Joseph A. Dipiazza, *The Piano Sonatas of Clementi,* DMA diss., University of Wisconsin—Madison, 1977, 115pp. Presents information on the performance-related topics of Clementi's instrument, style, teachings on technique, editions, dynamics, and articulation. The English piano and its German counterpart, the Viennese piano, are discussed for the purpose of evaluating Clementi's contributions to a new style of pianism and composition. Observations on Clementi's style in relation to texture, melody, harmony, and form are presented in addition to a discussion of his pianistic style. The contents of the composer's *Introduction to the Art of Playing on the Piano-Forte* and an analytical description of the *Gradus ad Parnassum* offer information regarding Clementi's views on technique. Accessible editions of the sonatas and a critique of the Da Capo reprint (New York, 1973) of the original *Oeuvres complettes de Muzio Clementi* published by Breitkopf and Härtel (Leipzig, 1803–19) are given. The eighteenth-century practices regarding dynamics and articulation are discussed including interpretative performance suggestions. Particularly helpful to teachers as well as students is a listing of the sonatas, which includes pertinent comments and a classification—technical, educational, or artistic—for each sonata (from author's abstract, abridged).

Leon Plantinga, "Clementi, Virtuosity and the 'German' Manner," JAMS, 25 (Fall 1972):303–30. Discusses different influences and styles of Clementi's keyboard writing with special emphasis on J. S. Bach's influence, the "German" Manner. This "German" Manner became a permanent element of his style, and his best music continued to reflect his study of J. S. Bach.

——. *Clementi: His Life and Music* (London: Oxford University Press, 1977).

VICTOR CLOWEZ (–   ) Belgium
Fantasque et Humoresque (Editions du Zéphyr   1972) 2 pieces, 7pp.

SAMUEL COLERIDGE-TAYLOR (1875–1912) Great Britain
4 Characteristic Waltzes Op.22 (Nov). 1. Valse bohémienne. 2. Valse rustique. 3. Valse de la reine. 4. Valse mauresque. Int. to M-D.
24 Negro Melodies Op.59 (OD   1905; IU) 127pp. Preface by Booker T. Washington.

GIUSEPPE CONCONE (1810–1861) Italy
Thirty Brilliant Preludes Op.37 (G. Anson—Willis   1962) 27pp. In all the major and minor keys, edited, plus 6 original preludes by the editor.

JUSTIN CONNOLLY (1933–   ) Great Britain
Sonatina in Four Studies Op.1 (Nov).
Studies in the Garden of Forking Paths (Nov).

FRANZ CONSTANT (1910–   ) Belgium
Arcanes Op.68 (CeBeDeM   1974) 12pp. 7 min.
Paysages (Metropolis   1965) 7pp. Flexible meters, motivic development, rhythmic bounce, chords in alternating hands at climax. M-D.
Pour la Jeunesse   1962 (Metropolis) 5pp. Five short pieces, MC, varied moods. Int.
Sonatine (Metropolis   1960) 7pp. Three short Impressionistic movements with the finale in toccata style. Int.

DINOS CONSTANTINIDES (1929–   ) USA
Constantinides teaches composition in the School of Music at Louisiana State University, Baton Rouge, LA.
Theme and Variations (Editions Philippe Nakas, Panepistimiou 44 Athens, Greece   1965) 18pp. Theme in 5/8 is like a Greek dance followed by 10 contrasting variations. Neoclassic, well laid out for the keyboard, metronome indications for most variations. A colorful set. M-D.
Sonata   1977 (MS available from composer) 21pp. Impressions: clusters; moves all over keyboard; some sonorities held for a given number of seconds; wide dynamic range. Madness: scherzo; fast repeated notes; great contrasts in dynamics, tempo, and mood. Dream: almost Impressionistic; widely spaced sonorities. Comedy: fast; chromatic; slower mid-section; specific figures to be repeated indicated number of times. Colorful writing. D.

JOSEPH COOPER (–   ) Great Britain
Hidden Melodies (Paxton   1975). Six improvisations, from BBC Television's "Face the Music." While Shepherds Watched Their Flocks by Night, in the style of J. S. Bach. John Peel, in the style of Mozart. Loch Lomond, in the style of Grieg. Come Landlord Fill the Flowing Bowl, in the style of Schubert. The Lincolnshire Poacher, in the style of Tchaikowsky. Yes, We Have No Bananas, in the style of Schumann. Clever, humorous characterizations with delightful cartoons. Int. to M-D.
More Hidden Melodies (Paxton) Six improvisations. Three Blind Mice, in the style of J. S. Bach. Waltzing Matilda, in the style of D. Scarlatti. When Johnny Comes Marching Home, in the style of Schubert. For He's a Jolly Good Fellow, in the style of Chopin. Londonderry Air, in the style of Brahms. I Saw Three Ships, in the style of Schumann. Clever, fun. Int. to M-D.

PAUL COOPER (1929–   ) USA
Cooper is a member of the music faculty at Rice University, Houston, TX.
Sonata (JWC   1962) 14pp. A one-movement sectionalized work. Tranquillo diventando agitato: proportional rhythmic relationships; serial; figuration increases to a *fff* level, then thins out, relaxes, and melts into a Grave with harmonics and some chords to be "half depressed."

Intensity develops, textures are reduced, and Grave section leads to a Vivace that is pointillistic and moves over keyboard. This section gives way to a Molto agitato diventando tranquillo (mf a ff ad libitum ma con bravura), which builds to an enormous climax, then fades away to a Tranquillo *pppp* closing. Large span, solid musicianship, and mature pianistic expertise required. D.

DAVID COPE (1941–   ) USA
Sonata No.1 (Seesaw).
Sonata No.2 (Seesaw).
Sonata No.3 (Seesaw).
Sonata No. 4 (Seesaw).
Three 2-Part Inventions (Seesaw).
Iceberg Meadow (CF   1976) 5pp. Facsimile edition.
Parallax (CF   1976) 17pp. Reproduced from composer's MS. Includes instructions for performance.
See: David Cope, *New Directions in Music,* 2d ed. (Dubuque: W. C. Brown Co., 1976), 271pp.

AARON COPLAND (1900–   ) USA
Our Town (Bo&H   1945). 10pp. Three piano excerpts from the film score.
In Evening Air (Bo&H   1971) 3pp. Melodic, pastoral, freely tonal around g, rather plain writing. Well fingered and pedalled. Good for teaching cantabile touch and balance of tone in chord playing. Int.
Night Thoughts (Homage to Ives) (Bo&H   1972). Commissioned by the Van Cliburn International Piano Competition, 1973. 5pp. Bell-like opening and closing; built on interval of ascending 3rd; many directions, e.g., sharp and clear, bell-like, simply sung, firmly sung, violent (on each chord), tenderly, etc.; con tutta forza mid-section; Impressionistic closing. Moody; interpretation problems but notes are not difficult to cover; changing meters and tempi; wide stretches. Copland says: "What I would hope for would be that *Night Thoughts* would bring out the essential musicality of the contestants and perhaps give the judges more to think about than technical brilliance and display features." M-D.
Midsummer Nocturne (Bo&H   1977) 2pp. "Slowly, poetically (and somewhat thoughtfully)" (from the score). Melodic, thin textures, tonal around A. Int.
See: David Burge, "Aaron Copland's Piano Variations," CK, 3 (April 1977):44.
Richard Coolidge, "Aaron Copland's Passacaglia: An Analysis," *Musical Analysis,* 2 (Summer 1974):33–36.

ROQUE CORDERO (1917–   ) Panama
See: Jerry Benjamin, "Sonatina Ritmica," 1963, IU, 9pp., for a thorough analysis of this work.

ARCANGELO CORELLI (1653–1713) Italy
24 Pieces (K). Vol.I: 3 Sarabandes; 2 Adagios; 2 Präludium; Corrente;
Largo; Gavotte; Allegro; Gigue. Vol.II: 5 Gavottes; Präludium;
Sarabande; Menuett; Corrente; Allegro; Folies d'Espagne. Over-
edited. Int.

MIGUEL ANGEL CORIA VARELA (1937–   ) Spain
Dos piezas para piano (Editorial de Música Española Contemporanea
1974) 10pp. Ravel for President. Frase.

ANGELO CORRADINI (1914–   ) Italy
Episodi: dodice pezzi per pianoforte (Carisch   1974) 18pp.
Risonanze (Carisch   1977) 7 pieces, 18pp.

SÉRGIO OLIVEIRA DE VASCONCELLOS CORRÊA (1934–   )
Brazil
Corrêa is a member of the music faculty of the University of Campinas,
São Paulo, Brazil.
Contrastes—Variações sôbre um tema popular (Ric Brazil   1969) 10pp.
4½ min. Theme and 6 variations that alternate expressive elements,
rhythms, dynamics, and agogic accents. Some contrapuntal elements
present. Opens and closes in a savage, hammered character. M-D.
Introdução e Chôros (Ric Brazil   1972) 12pp. 6 min. Introduction is a
two-part invention. Chôro I, II, and III. M-D.
Suite Infantil I (Ric Brazil). 1. Acalanto; 2. Chorinho; 3. Modinha; 4.
Moda Caipira; 5. Baião.
Suite Infantil II (Ric Brazil   1960–1) 11pp. Four movements. Int.
Tocatina (Ric Brazil   1971) 4pp. 2 min. Transfer of lines between hands.
More lyric than most tocatinas. M-D.
Variações sôbre um tema de Cana-Fita (Ric Brazil   1961) 11pp. 6 min.
Theme: canon. Var. I; Acalanto: song, two voices. Var. II, Dança.
Var. III, Modinha: popular song. Var. IV, Pregão: sad, crying mood.
Var. V, Valsa. Var. VI, Miudinho: popular dance. Var. VII, Baião:
folk dance. Thin textures, clever treatment. Int.
Moda   1972 (Gerig) 1½ min.

RAMIRO CORTÉS (1933–   ) USA
Suite (EV   1955) 14pp. Sinfonia; Capriccio; Arioso Sentimentale;
Finale. Shows a fine craft. Similar melodic and rhythmic figures are
juxtaposed in a free linear style. Chromatic, spiky metric patterns,
à la Ragtime section in finale. Requires a large span. M-D.
The Genie of the Waters (TP   1956) 3pp. Centers around F♯, evocative,
veiled, mysterious arpeggi. M-D.

GEORGE CORY (1920–   ) USA
Sonatina (Gen).

LUIZ COSTA (1879–1960) Portugal
Fiandeira (Ildefonso Alier). A MC "Spinning Song." M-D.

Poemas do Monte Op.3 (Sassetti). Pelos montes foro. Murmurios das fontes. Ecos dos vales. Campanários. Romantic character pieces. M-D.

FRED COULTER (1934–   ) USA

Coulter studied with Ross Lee Finney at the University of Michigan and is presently a member of the music faculty at the University of Miami, FL.

Variations for Agnes (Hinson—Hinshaw 1978) in collection *Twelve by Eleven*. Fresh approaches to the durable and delightful folk tune "Twinkle Twinkle, Little Star." The style is intentionally simple orally and technically. Careful attention should be paid to cross-phrasing between the voices. Int. to M-D.

JEAN COULTHARD (1908–   ) Canada

Pieces for the Present (Waterloo). 9 original pieces, MC, varied in mood and style. Int.

Variations on BACH (Nov 1972) 12pp. 10 min. No.8 in Virtuoso Series. John Ogdon, the editor, points out the meditative quality of the work with contrasting scherzando and drammatico interludes. A 16-bar theme provides a good basis for this neo-Romantic work of 7 well-contrasted and worked out variations. Chromatic; mainly slow tempi exploited. D.

FRANÇOIS COUPERIN (1688–1733) France

L'art de toucher le clavecin (The Art of Playing the Harpsichord). (Alfred 1975). This magnificent edition, edited by Margery Halford, of the great eighteenth-century treatise on keyboard playing, has much to recommend it. The French text of both the first and second versions (1716 and 1717) has been reproduced alongside a new English translation by the editor. Five beautiful facsimiles from the 1716 edition together with two portraits of Couperin add to this valuable edition. Excellent editorial introduction covers many aspects of performance. It describes the sources and deals with early traditions in music writing, the variable dot in Baroque music, notés inégales, ornamentation, fingering, phrasing and articulation, expression and style, and includes a helpful summary of Couperin's rules, and finally a bibliography. Useful footnotes throughout. Clears up the old Breitkopf and Härtel edition and Arnold Dolmetsch's transcription in a scholarly way. F and G clefs are substituted for the moveable C clefs in the original edition, and the use of lighter print for all editorial suggestions is outstanding. Also contains the eight Preludes Couperin intended to be played before each of his suites in the corresponding key. This practice should be revived.

Pièces de Clavecin (K. Gilbert—Heugel). 4 vols. Vol.I contains a facsimile of Couperin's table of ornaments; an alphabetical list of the contents of all four books; a general introduction, in which performance practice, instruments, and sources are discussed; and Couperin's preface of 1713.

Pièces de Clavecin (J. Gat—EMB). Vol.I: Ordres 1–5. Vol.II: Ordres
6–12. Vol.III: Ordres 13–19. Vol.IV: Ordres 20–27.

Couperin Album (J. Gat—EMB Z.7377) 52pp. Contains: L'Amphibie;
L'Anguille; L'Audacieuse; Les Bergeries; Les Chinois; La Florentine;
Les Jeunes Seigneurs; Les Moissonneurs; La Muse-Plantine; Passacaille; Soeur Monique; Les Timbres; La Triomphante; La Volup-
tueuse. Well fingered, especially the many ornaments. M-D.

HENRY COWELL (1897–1965) USA

Maestoso (NME   October 1940) 7pp. Three staves are used most of the
time. M-D.

Pa Jigs Them All Down (Century).

Pegleg Dance (Century).

Rhythmicana   1938 (AMP   1975) 11pp. Three untitled pieces that explore and exploit unusual rhythms, rubato feeling. This is the last and
longest of Cowell's experimental piano works. D.

Set of Four   1960 (AMP). 15½ min. For harpsichord or piano. A pseudo-
Baroque suite consisting of Rondo; Ostinato; Chorale; Fugue and
Resume. M-D.

Sinister Resonance (AMP). Violinistic treatment of the piano with muted
and stopped strings as well as pizzicato. M-D.

Three Irish Legends (Br&H   1922). New notation.

JOHANN BAPTIST CRAMER (1771–1858) Germany

21 Etüden (Hans Kann—UE   1974) xvii+43pp. Preface in German. This
edition, prepared from a copy stemming from Anton Schindler's
library, contains annotations and finger exercises by Beethoven. M-D.
See: William S. Newman, "On the Rhythmic Significance of Beethoven's Annotations in Cramer's Etudes," Kongressbericht of the International Musicological Society in Bonn, Germany, September 5–7,
1970.

La Parodie Sonate Op.43 (Schott   1913).
See: Alan Tyson, "A Feud between Clementi and Cramer," ML, 54
(1973):281–88.
Jerald C. Graue, "The Clementi–Cramer Dispute Revisited," ML, 56
(January 1975):47–54.

84 Studies (CFP; K).

PAUL CRESTON (1906–   ) USA

Creston Publications may be ordered from Box 28511 San Diego, CA
92128.

Five Dances Op.7 (Creston Publications).

Sonata Op.9 (Creston Publications).

Five 2-Part Inventions Op.14 (Seesaw   1972).

Six Preludes Op.38   1949 (MCA). Int. to M-D.

Metamorphoses (Creston Publications).

Three Narratives Op.79 (Creston Publications). About 9 min. each. Each piece is written for a different pianist (Mildred Victor, Claudette Sorel, Earl Wild). D.

Pony Rondo (Creston Publications). Int. to M-D.

Virtuoso Technique (Creston Publications). 2 vols. M-D to D.

Rhythmicon (Belwin-Mills). 10 vols. The pieces can be performed in recitals individually or in various combinations as suites. Easy to D.

See: Carol Walgren, "Paul Creston: Solo Piano Music," AMT, 24 (April–May 1975):6–9.

BAINBRIDGE CRIST (1883–1969) USA

Oriental Dances (CF). Arabian Dance. Chinese Dance. Moorish Dance. Int. to M-D.

WILLIAM CROFT (1678–1727) Great Britain

Complete Harpsichord Works (S&B 1974). 2 books. Newly transcribed and edited by Howard Ferguson and Christopher Hogwood. Includes editorial and textual notes. Vol.I: 10 suites. Vol.II: 7 suites. The suites are short and use dance forms. M-D

RANDELL CROLEY (1946–   ) USA

Quattro Espressioni (Philharmusica 1968) 4pp. Short, fleeting, expressionistic, serial, subtle dynamics. D.

ALLAN CROSSMAN (–   ) USA

Three Pantomimes (Branden Press).

GEORGE CRUMB (1929–   ) USA

Crumb teaches at the University of Pennsylvania. He is one of the most original voices in new music.

Five Piano Pieces 1962 (CFP 1973) 11pp. 8 min. Plucked strings, harmonics, stopped strings, fascinating sonorities. Includes instructions for performance. To be played as a group. D.

Dream Images (Love-Death Music) in collection *12 by 11* (Hinson—Hinshaw 1978). From Vol.I of *Makrokosmos*. Elegant sonorities are created with varied vertical and horizontal densities. Chopin's *Fantaisie-Impromptu* excerpts must enter and leave as the character directions at the beginning of the piece states: "Musingly, like the gentle caress of a faintly remembered music." Highly effective writing. M-D.

Makrokosmos I. Twelve Fantasy-Pieces (CFP 1973). For amplified piano. 14pp. 33 min. Highly eclectic style including singing, whistling, speaking, and groaning as well as playing both inside the piano and on the keyboard. Microphone should be placed near bass strings inside piano. A powerful work and a major addition to twentieth-century piano literature.

Makrokosmos II. Twelve Fantasy-Pieces after the Zodiac for amplified piano (CFP 1974) 14pp. 30 min. This completes the sequence of

24 fantasy-pieces (12 in Vol.I) inspired partially by Debussy's *24 Preludes* and Bartók's *Mikrokosmos.* As in Vol.I, each piece carries a sign of the zodiac and the initials of a person born under that sign. Some pieces are notated symbolically: No.4, "Twin Suns," has two circular staves; No.8, "A Prophecy of Nostradamus," has two opposing quarter circles surrounding a short horizontal staff, etc.

The two volumes share such musical materials as the notes A, B, and F and a great emphasis on chromatic lines. The last two pieces in Vol. II contain brief quotes from Vol.I, and the sub-titles "Genesis" and "Night-Spell" appear in both volumes. Unusual timbre and sonorities are produced by plucking and muting strings, placing paper on and sliding glass tumblers over strings, rapping the piano frame with the knuckles. Moaning, shouting, singing, and whistling are also called for by the pianist. Long pedals and electronic amplification add effectively to the pieces. In spite of the avant-garde tendencies of this work, references to Beethoven's *Hammerklavier* Sonata and Crumb's earlier *Madrigals,* plus other aspects, tie it to musical tradition. Highly effective works for the avant-garde pianist. D.

See: David Burge, "Contemporary Piano," CK, 2 (May–June 1976):48. Discusses the piano music of Crumb.

————. "Performing the piano music of George Crumb," CK, 2 (July–August 1976):20–21, 36–37. Devoted mainly to *Makrokosmos* volumes 1 and 2.

Richard Steinitz, "George Crumb," MT, 1627 (October 1978):844–45, 847.

Thomas Warburton, "New Piano Techniques for Crumb's Piano Music," PQ, 87 (Fall 1974):15–16.

PETER NORMAN CRUMP (1928–   ) Great Britain
Unum ex illorum sabbatorum (Thames   1967) 7pp. Photostat of MS. In Anglican New Music series.

IVO CRUZ (1901–   ) Portugal, born Brazil
Suite (Valentim de Carvalho   1974) 16pp. Preludio; Valsa Romantica; Marcha. Colorful, Impressionistic, attractive. M-D.

CÉSAR CUI (1855–1918) Russia
Piano Works, Selections (USSR   1975). Op.39/4; Op.20/4, 2; Op.64/16; Op.39/6; Op.31/2; Op.83/5, 1; Op.21/2; Op.22/3.
Marionette (APS). Fast, carefree, and playful. Int.

RICHARD CUMMING (1928–   ) USA, born China
24 Preludes   1968 (Bo&H) 43pp. 29 min. Written as a birthday present for John Browning, who has recorded them. Various contemporary techniques are exploited. Groupings are possible without playing all 24. Contains one Prelude for right hand only and one for left hand only. Large span required. Int. to D.

ARTHUR CUNNINGHAM (1928–   ) USA

Cunningham has written in both tonal and atonal styles, making use of both traditional Western scales and of modal and serial techniques.

Harlem Suite: Engrams (TP   1978) 11pp. 6 min. Atonal. Multisections vary between slow and fast, different thematic materials and moods. M-D.

MICHAEL G. CUNNINGHAM (1937–   ) USA

Cunningham has degrees from Wayne State University, Indiana University, and the University of Michigan. He teaches at the University of Wisconsin —Eau Claire.

Piano Suite Op.8 (Seesaw) 4 min.

Three Impressions (Seesaw   1964) 3pp. Prelude: Allegretto, chromatic. Prelude Variant: Rubato. Landscape: Slowly, chordal, Impressionistic. Int. to M-D.

Sonata Op.33 (Seesaw   1970) 10 min. Excitation: large chromatic gestures; simultaneous white and black glissandi; large span required. Highly Sustained: broad dynamic range. Fast: dry, percussive, linear, extremes in range. Thoroughly contemporary idiom. D.

American Folk Songs (Seesaw) 24pp. 30 min. Contains a total of 61 folksong settings from various states including a U.S. sea chantey. Most are short (two lines or less) and are attractively presented with the tunes easily identified; MC harmonies. Int. to M-D.

Portraits for Modern Dance   1964 (Seesaw) 17pp. *Suite Montage:* The Event; Incitement; Undertow; Lyric; Demonia; Resolvae. *Three Impressions:* Icon; Dark Vista; Improvisation on a Spiritual. *Haiku Suite:* Fujiami; Creaking Cricket; Purpling Sky; Ambling Cat. Clever, colorful, programmatic, appealing, MC. Int. to M-D.

ALVIN CURRAN (1938–   ) USA

Curran studied composition with Elliott Carter, Mel Powell, and Allen Forte. He received a Master of Music from Yale University.

First Piano Piece (CPE   1967). Directions include discussion of notation and interpretation, metered time, nonmetered time, space-time notation, nonspecified pitches, clusters, graphic notation. Duration of unstemmed notes is to be freely chosen (when enclosed in a "box" they may necessitate an exception to the 10-second maximum per system). P.10 may or may not be performed. Terribly complex writing. Avant-garde. D.

CURTIS CURTIS-SMITH (1942–   ) USA

Curtis-Smith teaches at Western Michigan University, Kalamazoo, MI 49003.

Rhapsodies   1973 (Sal). For prepared piano. I . . . a swift pure cry . . . II But wait! Low in dark middle earth. Embedded ore. III And a call, pure, long and throbbing. longindying call. IV Listen! The spiked and winding cold seahorn. Requires extensive inside-the-piano work (like bowing the strings with fishline); produces some incredible sounds. Highly original and effective. D.

See: David Burge, "Curtis Curtis-Smith's Rhapsodies," CK, 3 (May 1977): 44.

CARL CZERNY (1791–1857) Austria

Sonata A♭ Op.7 1810 (Ernst Sauter—UMKR 1971) No.99 in series, 43pp. The first movement—Andante, Allegro moderato ed espressivo —develops a main idea with the Andante section closing the movement. Prestissimo agitato in c♯ exploits a short–long figure and moves through closely related keys. Adagio espressivo e cantabile is in SA design and based on a stately marchlike rhythm. The Rondo—Allegretto is a playful romp. The fifth movement, Capriccio Fugato, is a four-voice fugue in a♭; the final four bars bring back the Andante theme of the first movement. A highly interesting work that precedes by a number of years the musical style and character we associate with late Beethoven, Mendelssohn, Schubert, and Schumann. M-D.

Bravura Variations Op.12 (Musica Obscura).

Les charmes de l'amitie sur un thème favori de Louis van Beethoven Op.55 (Heuwekemeijer 1973) 12pp.

SCHOLASTIC STUDIES:

Basic Elements of Piano Technique (O. von Irmer—GS) 97pp. 34 pieces selected to develop an advanced technique. Int. to M-D.

The School of Velocity Op.299 (Palmer—Alfred). Nos.6 C, 19 F, and 21 c have musical as well as technical interest. Int. to M-D.

The School of Legato and Staccato Op.335 (A. Ruthardt—CFP) 1974 reprint. Fingered and pedalled. Int. to M-D.

First Teacher of the Piano Op.599 (Sikorski). Int.

Preliminary School of Finger Dexterity Op.636 (Harry Dexter—Hansen House 1975). 24 progressive studies. Nos.4 B♭, 7 C, 8 a, and 13 B♭ are highly effective and musical. M-D.

24 Studies for the Left Hand Op.718 (GS). Contain some of Czerny's finest musical writing. Students enjoy these pieces. Int. to M-D.

L'Infatigable—Grand etude de Vélocité Op.779 (Eulenburg). 15pp. Long, brilliant cascades of scales, broken octaves, and arpeggi. Requires solid technique. M-D.

See: Malcolm S. Cole, "Czerny's Illustrated Description of the Rondo or Finale," MR, 36 (February 1975):5–16.

D

INGOLF DAHL (1912–1970) USA, born Germany

Hymn and Toccata (Boonin 1943–47) Hymn 7½ min. Toccata 4½ min. Hymn is chordal with big, gonglike sonorities; syncopation helps delineate melodic line. Much eighth-note figuration throughout Toccata; a slower, dramatic mid-section provides contrast before eighthnote figuration returns. Both works use chromaticism freely. D.

Pastorale Montano (Boonin 1936–43). An alpine landscape. Strong tonal organization. M-D.

Prelude and Fugue (Boonin 1935–39).

Reflections (Boonin 1967). A miniature, based on an 11-note row that suggests A, with transpositions to D and E. M-D.

Sonata Pastorale (PIC 1959). Moderato—Allegretto comodo; Elegia—Adagio ma non troppo; Scherzino—Allegretto leggiero; Fête champêtre—Allegro con brio. Infectious tunes; jazzy rhythms; movements spaced a fifth apart; variation technique combined with free association of ideas; constantly evolving phrases. M-D to D.

See: James N. Berdahl, "Ingolf Dahl: His Life and Works," Diss., University of Miami, Coral Gables, FL, 1975, 282pp.

LUIGI DALLAPICCOLA (1904–1975) Italy

Tre Episodi dal Balletto "Marsia" (Carisch 1950) 13 min. Arranged by the composer from his dramatic ballet (1942–3). 1. Angioscoso. 2. Ostinato. 3. Sereno.

See: David Burge, "Contemporary Piano," CK, 4 (April 1978):58. Contains a discussion of the *Quaderno Musicale di Annalibera*.

FRIDOLIN DALLINGER (1933–) Austria

Sonatine (Dob 1954) 9pp. Leichte bewegt; Langsam und getragen; Rondo: Sehr flüssig und bewegt. Neoclassic, some imitation. Int. to M-D.

JEAN-MICHEL DAMASE (1928–) France

Apparition (Sal). Morceau de Concours.

Movement Perpetuel Op.10 1949 (Sal). Freely chromatic, busy. M-D.

Pieces for Piano or Harp (Rideau Rouge 1972). 1. Les Charmeaux. 2. L'Insecte. 3. Promenade. 4pp. each. Published separately.

JEAN FRANÇOIS DANDRIEU (1682–1738) France

Trois Livres de Clavecin de Jeunesse   1701–13 (Brigitte François-Sappey
—Heugel). Less than ideal edition. Int. to M-D.

RAM DA-OZ (1929–   ) Israel, born Germany
Five Contrasts (IMI 618).
Movimento quasi Sonata (IMI 615).
Neun Tanzsätze (IMI 196).
Strolling gaily (IMI 665   1976) piano pieces for young people. 11pp. 9
pieces. Int.
After the Rain (IMI 666   1976) more piano pieces for young people.
12pp. 9 clever pieces. Int.

VOLFGANGS DARZINS (1906–   ) USA, born Latvia
Suite A (Kalnajs   1956) 21pp. Four movements. M-D.
Petite Suites 4, 5, 6 (Kalnajs   1960) 20pp. Three contrasting movements
in each suite. Large span required. M-D.

JOSÉ DAVID (1913–   ) France
Etude et Danse (Braun/Billaudot   1970) 6pp.

THOMAS CHRISTIAN DAVID (1925–   ) Austria
Bagatellen (Dob).
Sonate (Dob   1967) 21pp. Vivace: contains much rhythmic and harmonic
repetition. Adagio: developed with arpeggi and full chords. Allegro
assai: thin texture in constant eighth-note motion. Chromatic, neoclassic. Complex but knowledgeable writing. D.

MARIO DAVIDOVSKY (1933–   ) USA, born Argentina
Davidovsky is Associate Director of the Columbia–Princeton Electronic
Music Center and Professor of Music at the City College of New York.
His music is characterized by its breadth and concentration, a balance between craftsmanship and spontaneity of development, imagination, and,
when needed, simplicity.
Synchronisms VI for Piano and Electronic Sounds (EBM   1970) 23pp.
7½ min. "The electronic sounds in many instances modulate the
acoustical characteristics of the piano, by affecting its decay and attack
characteristics. The electronic segment should perhaps not be viewed
as an independent polyphonic line, but rather as if it were inlaid into
the piano part. A coherent musical continuum is sought while trying to
respect the idiosyncracies of each medium" (supplied by the composer). The electronic sounds do indeed modify the piano acoustics
rather than present an independent part. The piece is characterized by
skillfully integrated bursts of virtuosity and delicate lyricism. It is one
of a series of compositions for electronically synthesized sounds in
combination with the more conventional instruments. Awarded the
1971 Pulitzer Prize. M-D.

PETER MAXWELL DAVIES (1934–   ) Great Britain
Stevie's Ferry to Hoy (Bo&H   1978) 3pp. 1. Calm Water. 2. Choppy Seas.
　　3. Safe Landing. Colorful, descriptive. Easy to Int.

ALLAN DAVIS (1922–   ) USA
Razorback Reel (OUP 93.211   1963) 5pp. A good MC hoedown. Re-
　　quires strong rhythmic drive. M-D.

EMIL DEBUSMAN (1921–   ) USA
Four Sonatinas Op.27 (AME   1957). Sonatina Fanfare. Gregorian Sona-
　　tina. Chromatic Sonatina. Sonatina for a Birthday. All are short and
　　MC, and exploit various sonorities. Int.

CLAUDE DEBUSSY (1862–1918) France
With the copyright running out on many of Debussy's works, numerous
companies are presently publishing his piano compositions.

EARLY WORKS:

Danse bohémienne (CFP). Int.
Arabesque E (CFP; EBM; UMP; B&VP; Waterloo, study edition). Int.
Arabesque G (CFP; EBM; UMP; B&VP). Int.
Nocturne D♭ (Swarsenski—CFP; EBM; B&VP). Int. to M-D.
Rêverie (CFP; B&VP). Int. to M-D.
Danse (CFP; B&VP). Int. to M-D.
Valse Romantique (CFP; EBM; B&VP). Int.
Ballade (CFP; B&VP). M-D.
Mazurka f♯ (Swarsenski—CFP; EBM; B&VP). Int. to M-D.
Le Petit Negre (CFP has note in English; EBM; B&VP; Durand). Int.
Suite Bergamasque (Alfred; Demus—Ric; UMP; B&VP; Waterloo, study
　　edition). M-D.
Images (*oubliées*)   1894 (PQ 102 [Summer 1978]: 15–19, 103 [Fall
　　1978]:31–42; TP   1978). Three previously unpublished works ap-
　　pear under this collective title. The autograph of the *Images* contains
　　the dedication and the following recommendation: "These pieces
　　would fare poorly in 'les salons brillamment illuminés' where people
　　who do not like music usually congregate. They are rather 'conversa-
　　tions' between the piano and one's self; it is not forbidden furthermore
　　to apply one's small sensibility to them on nice rainy days." A few
　　annotations are sprinkled throughout the scores, à la Satie. Lent: pre-
　　ludelike; subtle harmonies; maintains a dreamlike grace in the gait of
　　its supple rhythms. In the Rhythm of a 'Sarabande': the first version
　　of the future Sarabande of the suite *Pour le piano* of 1901; interesting
　　harmonic changes compared to the final version. Nous n'irons plus au
　　bois: contains melody and figuration in alternating hands, similar to
　　the Prélude in *Pour le piano;* hand crossings; harplike sonorities;
　　duplets with triplets; *ppp* ending. M-D.

See: Arthur Hoérée, "Images (oubliées)," PQ, 102 (Summer 1978):
15. Translated by Barry S. Brook.

TRANSITIONAL WORKS :

Suite pour le piano (Swarsenski—CFP; UMP; B&VP; PWM). M-D.
D'un cahier d'esquisses (CFP; EBM).
Masques (CFP).
L'Isle joyeuse (GS; CFP; UMP; B&VP; PWM). D.

MATURE WORKS:

Estampes (CFP; B&VP; PWM).
   Available separately: Soirée dans Grenade (CFP; UMP), Jardins sous
   la pluie (EBM; UMP).
Images (1905) (CFP; UMP; PWM; B&VP). M-D.
   Available separately: Reflets dans l'eau (UMP), Mouvement
   (PWM).
Images (1907) (CFP; UMP; PWM; B&VP). M-D.
   Available separately: Poissons d'or (UMP).
Children's Corner (J. Demus—Ric; UMP; PWM; B&VP). M-D.
   Available separately: Doctor Gradus ad Parnassum (UMP; CFP;
   B&VP), Serenade for the Doll (UMP), The Little Shepherd (EMB;
   UMP), Golliwog's Cake-Walk (EMB; CFP; UMP; Waterloo, study
   edition).
Hommage à Haydn (CFP). M-D.
Élégie 1915 (TP). This brief piece is Debussy's last composition for piano
   solo—a touching and poignant elegy to the fallen French soldiers of
   World War I. M-D.
La plus que Lente (CFP; RBM; UMP; PWM; B&VP). Int. to M-D.
Préludes Book I (Marius Schweppe—B&VP; B. Woytowicz—PWM; G.
   dell'Agnola—EC 10039, preface and explanations in Italian). Int. to
   M-D.
   Available separately: Danseuses de Delphes (UMP; Ric), Des pas sur
   la neige (CFP; Ric), Voiles (CFP; EBM; J. Demus—Ric; UMP), La
   Fille aux cheveux de lin (CFP; EBM; J. Demus—Ric; UMP), La
   Sérénade interrompue (J. Demus—Ric), La Cathédral engloutie (J.
   Demus—Ric; CFP; UMP; EBM; Waterloo, study edition), Minstrels
   (J. Demus—Ric; EMB; UMP).
   See: Marion A. Guck, "Tracing Debussy's 'Des pas sur la neige,' "
   ITO, 1/8 (November 1975):4–12. Dennis Todd, "Three Preludes of
   Debussy," *Music Teacher,* 56 (April 1977):13–14, for analysis and
   discussions of Voiles, La Fille aux cheveux de lin, and La Cathédral
   engloutie. TM, Analysis of La Fille aux cheveux de lin, pp.151–63.
Préludes Book II (Marius Schweppe—B&VP; B. Woytowicz—PWM;
   UMP). M-D to D.

Available separately: Bruyères (UMP; Ric), La Puerta del Vino (Ric), Feux d'artifice (Ric; EBM).

12 Etudes (CFP; B&VP; PWM). D.

See: Richard S. Parks, "Organizational Procedures in Debussy's *Douze Etudes,*" Ph.D. diss., Catholic University, 1973, 595pp. Detailed analytical studies of each Etude.

La Boîte à Joujoux 1913 (Durand). A children's ballet inspired by Debussy's daughter. Unfinished, but piano score by Debussy is available. Charming and delightful. M-D.

See: Robert Orledge, "Another Look Inside Debussy's Toybox," MT, 1606 (December 1976):987–89.

6 Epigraphes antiques (Durand; CFP). The composer's own two-hand version. M-D.

Berceuse Héröique (Durand; CFP; B&VP). Written towards the end of 1914 as a tribute to King Albert of Belgium and his soldiers. Alfred Cortot says: "The accent of Moussorgsky speaks in its tragic simplicity, as the voice of the homely Brabançonne attains sublime powers and re-echoes as the mighty clarion of a struggling people." Int. to M-D.

COLLECTIONS:

Il mio primo Debussy (J. Demus—Ric 1975) 32pp. My First Debussy. Includes: La Fille aux cheveux de lin. 1st Arabesque. The Little Negro. The Little Shepherd. Serenade for the Doll. Page d'album. Clair de lune. Rêverie. Int. to M-D.

Album of Five Pieces (BMC). Mazurka. Ballade. Danse. Rêverie. Valse Romantique.

Three Albums (Forsyth). I. La Fille aux cheveux de lin; The Little Shepherd; Jimbo's Lullaby. II. Clair de lune; Des pas sur la neige; The Snow Is Dancing. Serenade of the Doll; La Puerta del Vino; Sarabande (from *Pour le piano*).

Piano Works (E. Klemm—CFP). Vol.I: 2 Arabesques; Suite Bergamasque; Children's Corner. Preface in German, French, and English, critical note in German. Vol.II: Préludes, Book I. Vol.III: Préludes, Book II. Vol.IV: Images. Vol.V: Etudes. Edited with preface in German, French, and English and critical note in German.

Claude Debussy—An Introduction to the Composer and His Music (Banowetz—GWM). Includes: Two Arabesques: Rêverie; Valse Romantique; Mazurka; Suite Bergamasque. Informative preface. Interpretative suggestions. M-D.

Supplementary Volume (H. Swarsenski—CFP 7250). Contains preface, chronological list, glossary of French terms, La Fille aux cheveux de lin, and color reproduction of the composer by Jacques-Emil Blanche.

Masterclasses in Debussy (Daniel Ericourt—Hinshaw 1979). Ericourt knew Debussy, heard him play, and played for him. In this unique collection of seven favorite pieces, Ericourt has described the most important aspects of these works. Includes: Deux Arabesques; Rêverie; Ballade; D'un cahier d'esquisses; Clair de lune; La Cathédral engloutie. Int. to M-D.

Piano Music (1888–1905) (Dover). Deux Arabesques; Suite Bergamasque; Rêverie; Danse; Ballade; Pour le Piano; D'un cahier d'esquisses; Estampes; Mazurka; Valse Romantique; Masques; L'Isle joyeuse; Images (first series); Reflets dans l'eau; Hommage à Rameau; Mouvement. Int. to D.

See: Gwilym Beechey, "A New Edition of Debussy's Piano Works," MO, 101 (October 1977):25–27, 35. A discussion of the C. F. Peters edition edited by H. Swarsenski.

Kenneth Geyer, "Interpretative Directions in the Piano Music of Claude Debussy," M.A. thesis, Catholic University, 1974, 83pp. An English translation of every interpretative direction in the piano works.

Roy Howat, "Debussy, Ravel and Bartók: Towards Some New Concepts of Form," M&L, 58 (July 1977):185–293. Includes a penetrating analysis of *Reflets dans l'eau*.

Virginia Raad, "Claude Debussy's Use of Piano Sonority," Part I, AMT, 26 (September–October 1976):6–9; Part II, AMT, 26 (January 1977): 7–14; Part III, AMT, 26 (April–May 1977):9–13.

Arnold Whittall, "Tonality and the Whole-Tone Scale in the Music of Claude Debussy," MR, 36 (November 1975):261–71.

RENÉ DEFOSSEZ (1905–   ) Belgium
Three Fragments in Irregular Meters (Schmitt). Unconventional time signatures; imaginative and contrasting. Int.

RENATO DE GRANDIS (1927–   ) Italy
Rosenkreuzer—Sonate (settima sonate) (SZ 1975) 17pp. 10 min.
Sonata No.8 (Tonos 1976) 16pp. First Part 1. 4. 2. 1. a. The first sound and the field of action. b. The first two sounds and their reflection. c. The three sounds united and their consequences. 4. 2. d. The "four accords" in another dimension: the variability in the self-mirrored "double" sphere. Second Part: The sounds and the luminous forces. Third Part: a. Introduction. b. The Raga Megha Mallâr and the sounds 1. 3. 4. 1. c. The three levels. Complex, aleatoric, avant-garde. D.

TON DE LEEUW, see Leeuw, Ton de

NORMAN DELLO JOIO (1913–   ) USA
Diversions (EBM 1975) 16pp. 9 min. Five pieces in a gentle modern idiom, effective as a group or as individual pieces. Preludio: solemn. Arietta: rich melody. Caccia: bright horn sounds. Chorale: based on "Good Christian Men Rejoice." Giga: brilliant closing. Int.

DAVID DEL TREDICI (1937–   ) USA
Fantasy Pieces (Bo&H   1959 60) 18pp. 6 min. 1. Adagio, Espressivo.
    2. Poco allegretto. 3. Allegro minacciando. 4. Largo, senza tempo.
    Complex; dramatic appeal; well organized; emphasis on augmented
    and diminished octaves; widely spaced textures; fragments grow into
    broader lines. Sensitive pedaling required throughout. M-D.
Soliloquy 1958 (Bo&H   1975) 10pp. 7 min. A major contribution. Great
    cohesion achieved through close motivic control. Debussy-like sonori-
    ties, freely chromatic and dissonant, pointillistic. Simultaneous lines
    require great tonal control. Large span required. D.

EDISSON WASSILJEWITSCH DENISSOW (1929–   ) USSR
Bagatellen 1960 (CFP   1971) 15pp. Fingered by Günter Philipp.

JEAN-MARIE DEPELSENAIRE (1914–   ) France
Les métamorphoses d'Arlequin (Lemoine   1972) 4pp. Theme, variations,
    et final.
Suite pimpante (Amphion) 3 min.

PAUL DESSAU (1894–   ) Germany
Fantasietta in Cis (Bo&Bo   1972) 7pp. Varied meters and tempi, broad
    gestures, expressionistic, complex notation. Extreme ranges exploited;
    a few fists are used; some improvisation required. D.
Sonatina II (Bo&Bo   1977) 7pp. Three short movements. M-D.

DUBRAVKO DETONI (1937–   ) Yugoslavia
Phonomorphia 2 (Udruzenje Kompositora Hrvatske   1968) 8pp. For
    piano and tape. Explanations in German. Avant-garde.

ROBERT NATHANIEL DETT (1882–1943) USA
Dett's music ranges from short melodic pieces to extended virtuoso works.
Although his work became more complex as he became more involved in
the craft of composition, he never broke from his strong roots in the lyricism
of the Negro spiritual.
The Collected Piano Works (SB   1973) 208pp. Informative foreword in-
    cludes a short biography and a brief analysis of the music. The music
    is a reprint of the original plates. This collection is not complete but
    contains a sizable portion of Dett's piano works. Six suites containing
    32 pieces. *Magnolia:* Magnolias; Deserted Cabin; My Lady Love;
    Mammy; The Place Where the Rainbow Ends. *In the Bottoms:* Pre-
    lude; His Song; Honey; Barcarolle; Dance (Juba). *Enchantment:* In-
    cantation; Song of the Shrine; Dance of Desire; Beyond the Dream.
    Cinnamon Grove: 1. Moderato molto grazioso; 2. Adagio cantabile;
    3. Ritmo moderato e con sentimento—Quasi Gavotte. *Tropic Winter:*
    The Daybreak Charioteer; A Bayou Garden; Pompons and Fans;
    Legend of the Atoll; To a Closed Casement; Noon Siesta; Parade of
    the Jasmine Banners. *Eight Bible Vignettes:* Father Abraham; Desert

Interlude; As His Own Soul; Barcarolle of Tears; I Am the True Vine; Martha Complained; Other Sheep; Madrigal Divine. Int. to M-D.

GODEFROID DEVREESE (1893–1972) Belgium

Danse lente (Cranz   1919).

Sixième Sonatine 1945 (CeBeDeM   1972) 20pp. 11 min. Allegro vivo (Hommage à Claude Debussy): similar techniques used by Debussy in the first movement of his *Pour le piano*. Andante (Hommage à Johannes Brahms): theme, 4 variations, return of theme. Allegro (Hommage à Paul Gilson): somewhat in the style of Poulenc. M-D.

ANTON DIABELLI (1781–1858) Austria

Variations on a Theme of Diabelli (W. Newman—Music Treasure 1973). 50 variations by various composers. Int. to M-D.

11 Sonatinas (GS).

DAVID DIAMOND (1915–   ) USA

Album for the Young (EV   1946). Ten short excellent pedagogic pieces. Easy to Int.

A Myriologue   1935, rev. 1969 (PIC) 5pp. A short, slow, funereal dance, rhythmic patterns, composed for Martha Graham. M-D.

Prelude and Fugue (Hinson—Hinshaw   1978) in collection *Twelve by Eleven*. Clearly structured, tightly knit, neoclassic. The cantando lyric lines of the Prelude go their graceful individual way and finally arrive at a colorful cadence. The three-voiced Fugue is basically tonal but uses chromaticism freely and builds to a strong emotional climax. A rhythmic subject with strong off-beat accents adds excitement to this forceful work that is constantly idiomatic for the piano. Int. to M-D.

JOSEF DICHLER (1912–   ) Austria

24 Klavierspiele (Dob   1976) 31pp. Klavierspiele für mässig Fortgeschrittene. Notes in German and English.

Six Little Pieces   1953 (Dob).

PETER DICKINSON (1934–   ) Great Britain

Dickinson is a graduate of Cambridge University. He studied composition with Bernard Wagenaar at the Juilliard School from 1958 until 1960. "Interest in the styles of Schönberg and Ives and in indeterminacy developed from his contacts with such American composers as Henry Cowell and John Cage" (BBD, 73).

Five Diversions (Nov).

Paraphrase II (Nov   1967) 14 min. Based on Dickinson's earlier motet "Mark." Here, ideas are transformed and extended from the Motet. Seven varied sections. Repeated notes, octaves, skips, solid contemporary writing, tonal. Large span required. D.

Variations Vitalitas   1957 (Nov) 15 min.

See: Roger Norrington, "Peter Dickinson," MT, 106 (1965):109–10.

EDWARD DIEMENTE (1923–   ) USA
4 Waltzes (World Library).
In a Call of Wind (World Library).
Regina Coeli   1956 (TP). Short, built on a chorale and a Gregorian chant. Int.

EMMA LOU DIEMER (1927–   ) USA
Diemer is a graduate of the Yale and Eastman schools of music and is presently professor of theory and composition at the University of California, Santa Barbara.
Four Piano Teaching Pieces (Bo&H   1962) published separately. Gavotte. Gigue. Invention. Serenade. Each emphasizes special technical problems: 5-note scale figures in both hands, 2-note slow trills, 4-note chords in each hand, staccato in one hand, legato in other, etc. Attractive. Int.
Seven Etudes (CF   1966) 16 min. Facsimile edition. Energetic; Slow; Fast; Slow (much use of tremolo); Fast "Hommage à Schönberg" (serial, disjunct); Very Slow "Hommage à Rachmaninoff"; Spirited. Well conceived for the instrument. Makes a most convincing set. M-D.
Sound Pictures (Bo&H   1971) 11pp. Ten pieces. Clusters and dots. Circles. Contraction and Expansion. Double Dots. Incline and Plateau. Parallels. Strata. Angles. Particles. Infinity. Accepted twentieth-century techniques cleverly employed. Precocious teenager would enjoy these. Int.
Four on a Row (Scribner's). In Vol.4 of the *New Scribner Music Library*.

BERNHARD VAN DIEREN (1884–1936) Great Britain, born The Netherlands
Tema con Variazione (OUP   1928) 12pp. Chromatic theme, 14 variations. Lines are polyphonically textured with the harmonies created by the part writing. Harmonics, wide dynamic range, tumultuous closing. Widely arpeggiated chords require a large span. D.

CASPAR DIETHELM (1926–   ) Switzerland
Sonate IX (Heinrichshofen 1183).
Sonate VII (Heinrichshofen 6213).

JAN VAN DIJK (1918–   ) The Netherlands
Couple (Donemus   1969) Reproduced from holograph.
Salmo (Donemus   1973) 4pp. Photostat.
Sonatina No.14 (Donemus   1969) Reproduced from holograph.

RENATO DIONISI (1910–   ) Italy
Suoni e risonanze (Ric   1971) 8pp. 5 min. Two short pieces utilizing harmonics. No meters, freely chromatic, tremolos. Difficult to unravel. D.

WIM DIRRIWACHTER (1937–   ) The Netherlands
10 Studies (Donemus   1974) 38pp. Photostat. Note in Dutch.

MILAN DLOUHY (1938–   ) Czechoslovakia
Bagately (Supraphon   1972) 11pp.

VÁCLAV DOBIAS (1909–   ) Czechoslovakia
Sonata (Panton   1940, rev.1973) 31pp.

ANDRZEJ DOBROWOLSKI (1921–   ) Poland
Dobrowolski teaches at the State College of Music in Warsaw.
Music for Magnetic Tape and Piano Solo (PWM   1971) 22pp. 11 min.
Explanations in German and English. Space is crucial to this work,
for the recording of the tape in stereo allows for transference of sound
from one side to another. Chance plays its part in the improvised
chords and runs at certain points in the work, for which the composer
has given directions. M-D.

STEPHEN DODGSON (1924–   ) Great Britain
Dodgson studied at the Royal College of Music in London.
Suite I C for clavichord (Chappell   1974) 16pp. Little Fanfare; First Air;
Plaint; Pantomime; Greater Fanfare; Second Air; Tambourin; Last
Fanfare. Freely tonal, neoclassic, short movements. M-D.
Suite II E♭ for clavichord (Chappell   1974) 15pp. Overture; First Fan-
fare; A Dream; Second Fanfare; A Fancy; Round Dance. M-D.

MARTIN DOERNBERG (1920–   ) Germany
Klaviersonate (Viewcg   1973) 12pp. Four movements. Twelve-tone; row
contains many whole tones, which produce fairly tame sonorities.
Opening of the third movement is the most imaginative section (somewhat atmospheric) of the entire sonata. M-D.

ERNST VON DOHNÁNYI (1877–1960) Hungary
4 Clavierstücke Op.2 (Dob; K).
Humoresken (in form of a suite) Op.17 (UE; Simrock). March (No.1) is
available from (Lengnick).
Suite in the Olden Style Op.24 (Lengnick). Displays high spirits with bright
clear sounds. M-D.
Ruralia Hungarica Op.32a (EMB). Nos.1 and 5 are reproduced and dis-
cussed in *Clavier,* 16 (February 1977):37–40.
Valse Boiteuse Op.39b (Lengnick). Charming. M-D.
6 Piano Pieces Op.41 (Lengnick   1947). Impromptu (No.1) is reproduced and discussed in *Clavier,* 16 (February 1977):25–28.
Dohnanyi Album I (EMB Z7464). 6 Concert Etudes Op.28. Variations on
a Hungarian Folksong Op.29. M-D.
Dohnanyi Album II (EMB Z7465). Pastorale (Hungarian Cradle Song).
Ruralia Hungarica Op.32a. M-D to D.
See: George Mintz, "Dohnányi's Piano Works," *Clavier,* 16 (February
1977). A survey of all Dohnányi's piano works that have been published. Also indicates which ones are still in print.

JACOB VAN DOMSELAER (1890–1960) The Netherlands
Variations 1951–2 (Harmonia 1974) 28pp.

GAETANO DONIZETTI (1797–1848) Italy
Donizetti left 26 pieces for piano, two hands.
Klavierwerke I (Irene Patay—Eulenburg 1974) 39pp. Guido Zavadini
has catalogued Donizetti's works. Contains: Vivace G, Z.295; Larghetto, Tema con variazioni, Z.300; Drei Walzer, Z.200 and 311;
Allegro vivace C, Z.294. These pieces were probably written between
1813 and 1821. They provide a broad sample of Donizetti's keyboard
style, which is a combination of classic figuration with Romantic harmonies. Haydn seems to be the model for most of this music. The Larghetto, Tema con variazioni is the finest piece and displays real mastery
of keyboard technique. Melodic ornamentation is Mozartian. Mistakes
noted in this edition are omitted ledger lines, incorrect notes (they are
easy to spot as they create a dissonance completely foreign to this
style), Waltz III should return to bar 19, not to the Introduction. Int.
to M-D.
Allegro f (Raymond Meylan—CFP 1971). Short preface by editor.
Fingered, Romantic figuration, miniature operatic overture with superficial brilliance. Recently discovered. M-D.
La Guiseppina (Girard). A polka-mazurka. Int. to M-D.
Tre Valzer Z.299 and 311 (Ric 1971) 15pp. Two waltzes and Invito.
Variations on a theme from Mayr's "La rosa bianca e la rosa rossa" (Ric).

JOSÉ ANTONIO DE DONOSTÍA (1886–1956) Spain
Obras musicales (Archivo Padre Donostia, Lecaroz—Harrassowitz 1972)
Vol.X, works for piano. ix+231+(x) pp.

JOSEF FRIEDRICH DOPPELBAUER (1918–   ) Austria
10 Kleine Klavierstücke (Dob 1956) 16pp. Uses such compositional devices as quartal harmony, repeated notes, staccato study. Neoclassic
orientation. Int. to M-D.

JOHN DOWD (1932–   ) USA
Sonata (MS available from composer, c/o Music Dept., Milligan College,
Milligan College, TN 37682) 15pp. Moderato pesante—Allegro;
Adagio molto uguale; Leggiero. Atonal, driving rhythms, dramatic
scalar gestures, alternation of hands, frequent tempo changes (espe-
cially in first movement), colorful sonorities, effective. M-D.

JOHN DOWNEY (1927–   ) USA
Pyramids (TP). Improvisatory; strong dissonances; flexible meters, tempos,
and dynamics. Requires a powerful percussive touch. D.

JAMES DREW (1929–   ) USA
Primero libro de referencia laberinto (TP 1974) 6pp. on 1 leaf. Directions for performer. Avant-garde writing; only for the bravest pianist.

Terribly complex, large skips, rhythmic inequalities, new notation. Certain sections to be repeated a number of times. This is probably a powerful work if it can be successfully realized. Title is appropriate. D.

JOHANNES DRIESSLER (1921–   ) Germany
Since 1946 Driessler has been a professor at the Nordwestdeutsche Musikakademie in Detmold. His style is neoclassically oriented.
Musik für Klavier Op.2/2 (Br 2541).
Aphorismen Op.7 (Br).
Three Toccatas Op.29/1 (Br 2494).
Three Sonatinas Op.29/2 (Br 2694).

MIECZYSLAW DROBNER (1912–   ) Poland
The Lane of Master Watchmakers (PWM). Eight clock pieces; musically satisfying. The Sundial; The Water Glass; The Sandglass; The Tower Clock, etc. Easy to Int.

PIERRE MAX DUBOIS (1930–   ) France
Contes de Nourrices (Leduc   1964). Fourteen short, clever, MC pieces. Int.
Pour Ma Mieux Aimée (Leduc   1956) For My Best Beloved Just So Stories. Ten pieces. Published separately and in a collection. MC. Int. to M-D.
Pour Anne (Rideau Rouge   1971) 4pp. Three small pieces.
Strepitosso 3—Toccata pour piano (ESC) 5½ min.

LOUIS DUMAS (1877–1952) France
Theme et Variations (EMT   1971) 16pp. Sixteen-bar theme in e; eight variations using triplets, 16ths, 32nds, double notes, trills, octaves. Varied moods; short coda; *pp* ending, MC. M-D.

PIERRE DURAND (1939–   ) France
22 Leçons de Lecture de rythme et d'indépendance (Rideau Rouge   1974) 22pp. Explores such contemporary techniques as unusual notation, clusters, hand independence, rhythmic problems. Performance directions in French. Int. to M-D.

LOUIS DUREY (1888–   ) France
Deux études Op.26 (Editions Françaises de Musique/Technisonor   1974) 23pp.
De l'automne 53 Op.75 (Editions Françaises de Musique/Technisonor   1974) 19pp. Six pieces.
Dix Basquaises (UMP).

ZSOLT DURKO (1934–   ) Hungary
Chance (EMB   1973) 16pp.
Dwarfs and Giants (EMB   1974) 15pp. Eight short pieces. New notation,

palm and forearm clusters, suitelike, Hungarian flavor, dissonant. Titles and descriptions in Hungarian and English. Int.

Microstructures (EMB   1973) 18pp.

JOHANN LADISLAV DUSSEK (1760–1812) Bohemia

"Dussek's significance in music history is unjustly obscured; he was a master craftsman . . . his piano writing had both brilliance and science; there are some idiomatic harmonies that presage Schumann and Brahms. He was a virtuoso at the keyboard; with Clementi he shares the honor of having introduced the 'singing touch' " (*Baker's Biographical Dictionary of Musicians*).

Collected Works (Da Capo). Twelve volumes in six with a new introduction by Orin Grossman. Vol.I: 6 Sonatas Op.9; Variations Op.10; Romance favorite. Vol.II: 4 Sonatas Opp.35, 43. Vol.III: 12 sets of Variations Opp.71, 6. Vol.IV: 12 Sonatas with accompaniment Opp. 46, 28; 3 Sonatas, 4-hands Op.67. Vol.V: 4 Sonatas Opp.44, 45. Vol. VI: 3 Sonatas with accompaniment, Op.8; La Chasse and Rondeau. Vol.VII: 3 Sonatas, 4-hands Opp.32, 48, 74. Vol.VIII: 6 Sonatas Opp.39, 47, 23; 3 Rondos. Vol.IX: Sonata Op.72; 3 Fugues, 4-hands. Vol.X: 6 Sonatas, 5 with accompaniment Opp.25, 51. Vol.XI: Fantasia and Fugue Op.55; 2 Sonatas Opp.70, 75. Vol.XII: Fantasia Op.76; 3 Sonatas with accompaniment Op.12. The sonatas are frequently loosely structured, sometimes wander, and are difficult to hold together, but they all have interest and are worth studying.

The Sufferings of the Queen of France Op.23 (Igor Kipnis—Alfred). An unusual piece of program music in ten movements that expresses the feelings of Marie Antoinette during her imprisonment. Excellent preface. Int. to M-D.

Douze Leçons par gradations Op.30   1798 (LC).

See: Heino Schwarting, "The Piano Sonatas of Johann Ladislav Dussek," PQ, 91 (Fall 1975):41–45.

JACQUES DUTILLET (1945–   ) France

Visages d'enfants (EMT   1973) 5pp. Five short MC pieces. Int.

HENRI DUTILLEUX (1916–   ) France

Dutilleux writes in a rich, expressionistic style that is balanced with classical forms and a subdued lyricism plus a perfect sense of instrumental nuance.

Au Gré des Ondes (Leduc). 6 petites pièces. 1. Prélude en berceuse. 2. Claquettes. 3. Improvisation. 4. Mouvement perpétuel. 5. Hommage à Bach. 6. Etude. Int.

ANDRZEJ DUTKIEWICZ (1942–   ) Poland

Dutkiewicz is a graduate of the State School of Music in Warsaw and also studied piano and composition at the Eastman School. He specializes in performing twentieth-century music.

Suite (AA 1973) 16pp. Preludium: freely barred; a study in thirds, double thirds, triads, full bitonal chords built of thirds. Aria: seconds and octaves are emphasized, clusters. Toccata: single notes; octaves; ninths; forearm clusters; molto crescendo plus clusters and octaves provide a tumultuous conclusion. M-D.

Toccatina (AA 1977) 12pp., 2½ min. Alternates hands with black and white keys, extension of Prokofieff "Toccata" techniques, subito *pp* ending. M-D.

ANTONÍN DVOŘÁK (1841–1904) Czechoslovakia

8 Humoresques Op.101 (SHV). Critical edition. Preface and critical note in Czech, German, English, and French. No.7 is the most familiar piece. Rhythmic originality and highly interesting pianistic textures. M-D.

Humoresque and Other Miniatures (S. Szpinalski—PWM). Humoresque Op.101/7; Furiant F Op.42/2; Furiant Op.12; Waltzes Op.54/1,4

Piano Works—Selections (Supraphon AP 569 1973) 44pp. Preface and critical note in Czech, German, English, and French. Contents: Eclogues; Album Leaves; untitled compositions; fragments. M-D.

MARIA DZIEWULSKA (1909–) Poland

Dziewulska graduated from the Warsaw Conservatoire in theory and composition. At present she is Professor and Dean of the Faculty of Composition and Theory at the State College of Music in Cracow.

Inventions (PWM 1959). Eight short polyphonic works intended to introduce young musicians to the problems of contemporary polyphony by bold treatment of horizontal chords and free rhythms, often expressed by nontraditional musical notation. M-D.

E

CHARLES EAKIN (1928–   ) USA

Eakin is a member of the College of Music, University of Colorado, Boulder, CO 80302.

Frames 1976 (MS available from composer). Opens with a "motto" that serves as a recognizable transition from one section to the next. The rest of the piece consists of a series of episodes (frames) that may be arranged in any order by the pianist. A dynamic and accessible work. D.

See: David Burge, "Contemporary Piano," CK, 4 (July 1978):58, for a discussion of this work.

PETR EBEN (1929–   ) Czechoslovakia

Small Portraits (Panton AP 1889   1968) 21pp.

HORST EBENHÖH (1930–   ) Austria

Programme 13 Op.22/2 (Dob   1975) 14pp. Many of the movements are only a page long, but of fiendish difficulty.

HELMUT EDER (1916–   ) Austria

Rhythmische Klavierstücke Op.18 (Dob   1955) 11pp.

Zwei Aphorismen um ein Nachtstück Op.52 (Bosse 341). Serial. M-D.

GEORGE EDWARDS (1943–   ) USA

Draconian Measures (Mobart   1977) 27pp. 11 min. Reproduced from holograph.

ROSS EDWARDS (1943–   ) Australia

Monos II (J. Albert 212   1970) 12pp. Facsimile of composer's MS. Pointillistic, fast changing meters and dynamics, serial, proportional rhythmic notation, expressionistic. D.

Five little piano pieces (Faber FO 423   1977).

ROBERT EHLE (1939–   ) USA

English Suite Op.17   1972 (MS available from composer: c/o Music Dept., University of Northern Colorado, Greeley, CO 80631) 15pp. Galiard; Fantazia in foure parts; Saraband; Toccata in the Locrian mode. Well written for the piano, MC and attractive sonorities. M-D.

Piano Etudes for Composers Op.33   1973 (MS available from composer) 12pp. 1. Improvisation Study (Ellington): slow jazz tempo, quartal and quintal harmony, rhythmic, slow and pensive concluding section. 2. Pedal Study (Janáček): rhythmic and accented; uses sostenuto pedal; concludes with furioso section. 3. Structures (Copland): flexible meters; moves over keyboard; dynamic extremes. 4. Rhapsodic Variations (Barber): rubato; expressive melody supported by chords; fugal; chorale texture. M-D.

Hypersonde (CF 1972) 4pp. For electronically prepared piano. Five microphones are attached close to the strings to modify the sound electronically. Contains performing directions. Written so that a particular note on the upper staff stands for a microphone placed close to the string sounding that pitch. Experimental, avant-garde. M-D.

OLEG KONSTANTINOVICH EIGES (1905–   ) USSR
Sonatas (USSR 1975) 116pp. Contains piano sonatas Nos.2–5, 8.

HANNS EISLER (1898–1962) Germany
Variations 1940 (DVFM 1973) 24pp. Full of Schoenbergisms. Rather dry and stiff; row contains two internally tonal hexachords. M-D.

JAN EKIER (1913–   ) Poland
Melodies in Color (PWM 1948) 16pp. 9½ min. Nine contrasting settings of Polish and Pomeranian folk songs, freely tonal, appealing. Int.
Toccata (PWM 1935).
20 Christmas Carols (PWM 1947).

EDWARD ELGAR (1857–1934) Great Britain
Adieu (K. Prowse).
Serenade (K. Prowse).
Two Piano Pieces (Nov 1976) 8pp. In Smyrna: gently evocative of the Middle East. Skizze: quiet; expressive allegretto requiring careful pedaling. M-D.

BRIAN ELIAS (1948–   ) Great Britain
Five Piano Pieces for Right Hand (JWC 1969) 4pp. Each piece is very short, with sparse textures, a few large chords, and rhythmic surprises; Webernesque. Pedal carefully exploited. Directions incorporated into score. To be played as a set. Pieces work just as well for the left hand alone. M-D.

HERBERT ELWELL (1898–   ) USA
Pieces for Piano (Accura Music, Box 887, Athens, OH 45701). Prelude. Cortege. Berceuse. Dance.
Three Preludes (Accura Music).
Tarantella (CF).

MAURICE EMMANUEL (1862–1938) France
See: Eleanor Anne Carlson, "Maurice Emmanuel and the Six Sonatines for Piano," DMA diss., Boston University, 1974, 209pp.

EINAR ENGLUND (1916–   ) Finland, born Sweden

Introduzione e Toccata (Fazer   1950) 11pp. 5½ min. Large chords and
   arpeggi in Introduzione; martellato touch in Toccata, plenty of driving
   rhythms, like the Prokofiev "Toccata." D.

Sonatina d (Fazer   1966).

RENAT ACHMETOWITSCH ENIKEJEW (1937–   ) USSR

Sonata (Sowjetskij Compositor   1971) 39pp. Title in Russian.

MANUEL ENRÍQUEZ (1926–   ) Mexico

Enríquez studied composition with Miguel Bernal Jiménez, Peter Mennin,
and Stefan Wolpe. He teaches composition and chamber music at the
National Conservatory of Music in Mexico City.

A Lápiz, tres apuntes para piano (Collecion Arion   1965) 11pp. Trazos—
   Molto libero: impulsive. Deleneadno—Brillante: sparkling. Figuras—
   Molto tranquillo: five short parts to be arranged by performer. Three
   short sketches containing many directions in Spanish. Dissonant;
   rhythmic and textural problems. D.

Para Alicia (PIC   1970) 3pp. Diagrammatic notation, aleatoric. Ten seg-
   mented schemes to be played in any order. Many sounds are to be
   made inside the piano: plucking; striking strings with fingernails, open
   hand, and knuckles. Explanatory notes not always clear. Sonorities
   range from brutal to delicate. Colorful. M-D.

DAVID EPSTEIN (1930–   ) USA

Epstein is professor of music at MIT. He studied with Roger Sessions.

Piano Variations 1961 (MS available from composer: c/o Music Dept.,
   Massachusetts Institute of Technology, Cambridge, MA 02139) 17pp.
   Bold and dramatic theme followed by 15 variations, some short, some
   longer. Character of some of the variations: Tranquillo, Dolce,
   Angrily, Fantasia—Molto lento e misterioso, Martial. The entire set
   is a compendium of twentieth-century techniques handled judiciously
   and musically. An impressive work that requires first-rate pianism and
   musicianship. D.

DONALD ERB (1927–   ) USA

Erb teaches at the Cleveland Institute of Music.

Summermusic (Merion   1975) 8pp. 6 min. Strings are to be plucked and
   tapped with a mallet while playing clusters. Dynamic extremes, experimental notation. Facile fingers required. D.

Correlations (Merion).

DANIEL ERICOURT (1907–   ) France

Ericourt teaches piano at the University of North Carolina, Greensboro.

Fantaisie (Leduc   1924) 8pp. Varied tempi and figuration, Impressionistic, some flamboyant writing. M-D.

EDUARDO ESCALANTE (1937–) Brazil
Escalante did extensive research on the folklore of the Ribeira River Valley in 1973–4. He teaches folklore and theoretical studies in São Paulo.
Romance 1957 (Vitale) 3 min.
Suite I 1968 (Vitale) 5 min.

RUDOLF ESCHER (1912–) The Netherlands
Arcana Musae Dona (B&VP 1944). One of the most important piano works in Dutch piano literature. Long and difficult.
Non troppo; 10 eenvoudige pianostukken (B&VP 1949).
Sonata I (B&VP 1935).
Sonatina (Alsbach 1951) 9 min.
Due voci (Bender 1950).
Due voci (B&VP 1949).

AYLTON ESCOBAR (1943–) Brazil
Escobar has conducted experiments in creativity with audience participation, particularly among young people.
Assembly (SDM 1972) for piano and tape. 2pp. 5 min. Performer must make tape according to detailed directions contained in the score (in English). Aleatoric, clusters. Piano is amplified from Structure D to the end; strings are plucked and scraped with nails; a glass is to be used to slash the central strings. Avant-garde. D.
Mini Suite das Três Máquinas (SDM 1970) 6pp. Mini-Suite for Three Machines. 1. A Máquina de Escrever ("Typewriter"): clusters, glissandi. 2. A. Caixinha de Musica ("Music Box"): blurred pedal effects, improvisation. 3. O Coração da Gente ("Your Heart!"): aleatoric; sections titled Childhood, Youth, Adult, Death (pulsating in agony with clusters). Avant-garde. D.
Quatro Pequenos Trabalhos (SDM 1968) 15pp. 1. Devancio (Nocturne). 2. Chorinho (invention for two voices and two free canons). 3. Seresta (Valsa chôro). 4. Cantos (Recitativo e coral). Highly complex writing. Canons are the most accessible. Recitativo on "Lacrimosa dies Illa." Coral in clusters. D.

AKIN EUBA (1935–) Nigeria
Euba's early training was in Lagos. He had further study in London, at UCLA, and in Legon. He is editor of the series *Ife Music Editions* published by the University of Ife Press in Nigeria.
Scenes from Traditional Life 1970 (University of Ife Press, Ile-Ife, Nigeria 1975). Three scenes "based on a 12-tone row whose notes are systematically assigned to a series of predetermined rhythmic phrases" (from the score). Displays Schönberg influence with Nigerian roots. Strong dissonance in mainly two-voice textures, some notational complexities. M-D.

FRANCO EVANGELISTI (1926–   ) Italy

Proiezioni Sonore (Tonos   1955–6) 2 folded sheets. Two pieces. Instructions in Italian and German. Clusters, pointillistic, proportional rhythmic relationships, flexible meters, new notation. M-D.

ROBERT EVETT (1922–1975) USA

Chaconne 1950 (ACA).

F

MARCO FACOLI (ca.1588) Italy

Balli d'Arpicordo 1588 (Friedrich Cerha—Dob 1975). Contains 2 pavans, 4 arias, a napolitana, 2 tedescas, and an unidentified piece. Mainly homophonic style with occasional imitation. Fresh modal harmonies and varied rhythmic treatment. Ornamentation places demands on the performer. The complete set is available in the edition by Willi Apel, Vol.II of *Corpus of Early Keyboard Music* (American Institute of Musicology).

RICHARD FAITH (1926–   ) USA

Night Songs (SP   1975) 8pp. I. Andantino. II. Andante, poco rubato, espressivo. Two expressive nocturnes that could be played separately. The second is freer in form, has lush harmonies and Romantic melodies. M-D.

Recollections (SP   1974) 16pp. Nine pieces. The Hunt. Fountains. Monastery. Masks. Autumn. Coach Ride. Reflection. Cavaliers. Sailor's Dance. MC, descriptive, attractive. Int.

Souvenir (Hinshaw   1978) in collection *Twelve by Eleven*. The title suggests a remembrance of a sad and tender nature, a recollection of something in the distant past. Bitonal shifting from a to F is colored with chromatics that add interest to the flowing melodic lines. Rich sonorities coupled with upper-register textures make for a beautiful work. Int. to M-D.

Dances (SP   1977) 8pp. Five untitled imaginative pieces. Int.

Moments in a Child's World (SP   1978) 23pp. Eighteen pieces, all one page except the last one, which is two pages. Appealing, colorful. Int.

Three Sonatinas (GS   1971). Three movements each, short, appealing. Easy to Int.

Galliard (MS available from composer: c/o School of Music, University of Arizona, Tucson, AZ 85721) 4pp. Modal, flowing, lovely. Int. to M-D.

Nocturne (MS available from composer) 7pp. Expressive, pianistic. Outer sections require a delicate and feeling approach; textural contrasts appear in mid-section. A polished performance will receive warm audience response. M-D.

JULIEN FALK (1902–   ) France

Dix études atonales, dont deux de concert, selon la technique de l'atonalisme intégral pour le piano (Leduc   1972) 29pp. Ten atonal studies: Prelude; Valse; Dactyle; Chords; Broken Chords; Prelude 2; Trills; Canon for two voices; and two concert pieces—Etude Caprice and Toccata—which are based on atonal writing. Solid technique required. M-D to D.

MANUEL DE FALLA (1876–1946) Spain

Nocturne f (UME). In the Chopin tradition, contains none of de Falla's usual accent. Tuneful, minor tonality. Int.

Vals—Capricho (UME). An early salon style pianistic snapshot. M-D.

El Sombrero de Tres Picos ("The Three-Cornered Hat") (JWC). The composer effectively transcribed the following for solo piano: Danse de la Meunière ("Miller's Wife") (Fandango); Danse du Corregidor (Neighbor): resourcefully re-creates the instrumental lines, crisp rhythms and all the native color of the orchestral version. Virtuosic piano writing. Danse du Meunier (Miller) (Farruca); Danse des Voisina; Danse Finale (Jota) abridged. Virtuosic.

El Amor Brujo ("Love the Magician") (JWC). Arranged by the composer from his brilliant and colorful ballet. Danse de la Frayeur; Danse rituelle de Feu ("Ritual Fire Dance"); Pantomime; Récit du Pêcheur ("Fisherman's Song"). All available separately.

La Vida Breve ("Life is Short") (UME). De Falla's sterling transcriptions from his only opera: Spanish Dance I a; Spanish Dance II d. Evocative sensualism permeates both pieces. M-D.

Pour le tombeau de Paul Dukas   1935 (Ric   1974) 3pp. The composer's version of his original setting for guitar. 42 bars of dark f minor harmonies with a poignant, unresolved tonic chord addition. No Spanish atmosphere. M-D.

See: Gilbert Chase, "Falla's Music for Solo Piano," *The Chesterian,* 21 (1940):43.

Ronald Crichton, *Manuel de Falla: A Descriptive Catalogue of His Works* 19–27. This piece is No.4 from the *Pièces espagnoles.*

Julio Esteban, "Andaluza, A Master Lesson," *Clavier* 15 (October 1976): (London: J. W. Chester, 1976), 80pp.

GUIDO FARINA (1903–   ) Italy

Lauda, Colloquio, Leggenda per pianoforte (Carisch). Revised by Francesco Beccalli.

CARLOS FARINAS (1934–   ) Cuba

Sones Sencillos (Tonos) 7 separate sheets. Four pieces utilizing many harmonic sixths. Freely tonal, syncopated. Imitation in No.4. M-D.

FERENC FARKAS (1905–   ) Hungary

3 Burlesques (Artia   1949). Energetic writing in Bartók idiom. Nos.1 and 3 are brilliant and vigorous, while No.2 is slower with unusual left-hand melodic figuration. D.

2 Aquarelles (EMB 1955).

Quaderno Romano 1931 (Zenmukiado 1967). Preludio. Cavatina. Dialogo. Caccia. Passeggiata. Epilogo. A fine MC suite; contrasting movements have much color. M-D.

Holiday Excursions 1975 (EMB Z7908) 12pp. Six pieces for young people.

DAVID ANDROSS FARQUHAR (1928–) New Zealand

And One Makes Ten (Price Milburn). Ten pieces that make an interesting suite. Each piece begins where the previous one concluded, therefore the end of Epilogue leads back to the beginning of the opening Prelude. Prelude; Toccata; Scherzo; Procession; Bell Dance; A Weird Waltz; Nocturne; Antiphony; Fantasy; Epilogue. Austere style with influences of Bartók and Stravinsky noted. M-D.

ARTHUR FARWELL (1872–1952) USA

American Indian Melodies 1902 (M. Hinson—Hinshaw 1977) 19pp. Approach of the Thunder God. The Old Man's Love Song. Song of the Deathless Voice. Ichibuzzhi. The Mother's Vow. Inketunga's Thunder Song. Song of the Ghost Dance. Song to the Spirit. Song of the Leader. Choral. These ten short pieces are some of Farwell's most attractive settings. Harmonized in a post-Romantic style with flexible and original Indian rhythms. Farwell's extensive preface gives background and directions for performance. Int.

See: *Guide to the Music of Arthur Farwell and to the Microfilm Collection of His Work*. Compiled by his children and issued by his estate, 5 Deer Trail, Briarcliff Manor, NY 10510.

Maurice Hinson, "Piano Solos Inspired by American Indian Melodies," *Clavier*, 17 (May–June 1978):22–23. Discusses Farwell and his *American Indian Melodies;* includes "Song of the Ghost Dance," p.21.

GABRIEL FAURÉ (1845–1924) France

Piano Works (Eberhardt Klemm—CFP P-9560a, 9560b). Vol.I: 9 Preludes Op.103; 6 Impromptus Opp.25, 31, 34, 86b, 91, 102. Vol.II: 13 Barcarolles.

Impromptu No.II Op.31 (PWM).

Fauré: An Album of Piano Pieces (I. Philipp—GS). Nine works: Romance sans Paroles Op.17/3. Barcarolles Nos.1, 4, 6. Impromptu III Op.34. Clair de lune Op.46/2. Nocturne IV Op.36. Improvisation Op.84/5. Berceuse Op.56/1. M-D.

Gabriel Fauré—His Greatest Piano Solos (Copa 1973) 191pp. A comprehensive collection of his works in their original form. Compiled by Alexander Shealy. Contains: Romance sans Paroles Op.17. Capriccio Op.84/1. Fantasia Op.84/2. Fugue a Op.84/3. Adagietto Op.84/4. Improvisation Op.84/5. Allegresse Op.84/6. Fugue Op.84/7. Barcarolles 1–5. Nocturnes 1–8. Impromptus 1–3. Theme with Variations Op.73.

Selected Pieces (Robin de Smet—Cramer). Transcriptions: Berceuse and Kitty Waltz from Dolly Suite; Romance without Words. Original works: Nocturnes II B Op.33, IV E♭ Op.36; Pavane f♯; Barcarolles IV A♭ Op.44, VI E♭ Op.70; Improvisation c♯; Fugue e. Metronome marks given; no fingering; little pedaling.

See: Gwilym Beechey, "Gabriel Fauré—His Piano Music and Songs," MO, 1165 (November 1974):61–66.

Robert Dumm, "A Fauré Improvisation," *Clavier*, 15 (April 1976):20–23. Contains an analysis of and the music for Op.84/5.

Barrie J. Jones, "The Piano and Chamber Works of Gabriel Fauré," Ph.D. diss., Cambridge University, 1973.

HANS FAZZARI (–   ) Italy
So Long, George! (EC   1970) 11pp. Three pieces.

REINHARD FEBEL (–   ) Germany
Asymptote (Döring   1974) 16pp. Photostat.

VACLAV FELIX (1928–   ) Czechoslovakia
Sonatina (Supraphon AP1836   1975) 11pp.

RAMON FEMENIA-SANCHEZ (1936–   ) Spain
Homenaje (Homage) Preludio (UME   1973) 10pp. Varied meters and tempos. Contrasting sections, whole-tone and quartal harmonies, MC. M-D.

Per Tierra de Asturias ("The Land of Asturias") (UME   1973) 4pp. Opening Andante requires a singing tone; followed by an Allegro that uses plenty of rubato. Andante returns with an accelerando to the end. Romantic writing. M-D.

Recuerdo ("Remembrance") (UME   1973) 3pp. Interval of the fourth is exploited. Bell-like sonorities at opening and closing; mid-section is nocturnelike. Some Flamenco characteristics; Romantic style. M-D.

FEDELE FENAROLI (1730–1818) Italy
Andante in Re maggiore (Carisch   1971) 6pp. Edited with preface (in Italian) by C. Z. Zecchi and H. Fazzari.

VIKTOR FENIGSTEIN (1924–   ) Switzerland
3 Hommages (Eulenburg   1974) 16pp.

BRIAN FERNEYHOUGH (1943–   ) Great Britain
Three Pieces (Hin   1971) 19pp. 15 min. Plastic ring-bound. Many different tempi, thick contrapuntal complex textures, frequent meter changes, extreme dynamic range. D.

Epigrams (CFP) 7 min.

ARMAND FERTÉ (1881–1973) France
Ferté was a well-known piano pedagogue and taught at the Paris Conservatory for many years.
Barcarolle (EMT).
Etude(EMT).
Improvisation (EMT).
Nocturne (EMT).
Pirouettes (EMT).
Pour le piano (EMT   1972) 15pp. Six short pedagogical pieces. Int.
Tarentelle (EMT).
Toccata (EMT   1971) 8pp.
24 Courtes pièces (EMT   1972) 13pp. For beginners. Two books, 12
    pieces in each. Contrapuntally oriented in two-part writing. Easy.

FRANÇOIS JOSEPH FÉTIS (1784–1871) and
IGNAZ MOSCHELES (1794–1870)
Méthode des méthodes de piano (Minkoff Reprint   1973) 54pp. Reprint
    of the Paris edition (Schlesinger   1840). Contains 18 études de per-
    fectionnement pour le piano, composées par Bénédict et al.

GEORGE FIALA (1921–   ) Canada, born USSR
Children's Suite (Waterloo   1976) 16pp. Five contrasting, MC pieces full
    of humor and clever ideas. Titles in English, French, and Russian:
    Instead of an Overture. What the Youngster Whistled Gathering
    Chestnuts in the Grass. Little Bear's Minuet. Moorish Doll Offended.
    March. Large span required. Int. to M-D.

JOHN FIELD (1782–1837) Ireland
Selected Nocturnes (PWM 80). Seven nocturnes: B♭, A♭, two in F, two
    in A, d.
Nocturne No.5 B♭ (GS; Century).
Nocturne No.10 e (Anson—Willis).
Nocturne No.18 E (APS) Nocturne characteristique.
March Triomphale (David Branson—Helicom   1975) 3pp.
See: Nicholas Temperley, "John Field and the First Nocturne," M&L, 56
    (July–October 1975):335–40.

AMADEO DE FILIPPI (1900–   ) USA, born Italy
Dance Rhythms (Gen).
Folk Melodies (Gen).
7 Easy Pieces on a Row (Gen).
3 Preludes and Fugues (Gen).

VIVIAN FINE (1913–   ) USA
Four Polyphonic Piano Pieces 1931–2 (CFE) 11pp. Moderato. Non al-
    legro, intensivo (canon). Scherzando. Vivace. Atonal; tight rhythmic

structure. Great emotional intensity expressed with an intellectualized technique. M-D.

Sinfonia and Fugato (LG   1952) 6 min. In collection *New Music for the Piano*. M-D.

REINHOLD FINKBEINER (1929–   ) Germany

Suite für Klavier (Br&H   1973) 17pp. Impressive, intellectual writing, granitic quality, somewhat ungrateful to performer and listener. M-D.

ROSS LEE FINNEY (1906–   ) USA

Medley (Hinshaw   1978). In collection *Twelve by Eleven*. Finney has dipped into American folk tunes for this piece ("Red River Valley" and "Dinah, Won't You Blow Your Horn?"). Develops naturally. Charm of sheer sound is enhanced with a harmonic translucency. Strong tonal functions support this brightly colored piece. Int.

Variations on a Theme by Alban Berg 1952 (J. Kirkpatrick—CFP 1977) 12pp. 8 min. Slow chromatic theme (the opening theme of Berg's *Violin Concerto*) followed by 7 variations. Freely tonal around g, strong pianistic figurations, *pp* closing. M-D.

MICHAEL FINNISSY (1945–   ) Great Britain

All. Fall. Down. (UE).

English Country Tunes (UE).

Jazz (UE).

EDWIN FISCHER (1886–1960) Switzerland

Klingende Wochenshau. Schnappschüsse aus alle Welt (Heinrichshofen 436).

Südlich der Alpen. Suite (Heinrichshofen 84).

Treffpunkt Wien. Ouvertüre (Heinrichshofen 85).

ALFRED FISHER (1942–   ) USA

Fisher studied composition with Douglas Moore and David Burge. He teaches in the Department of Music at the University of Western Ontario in London, Canada.

Six Aphorisms (Seesaw   1967). Contemporary techniques, i.e., clusters, nonmusical objects used. Cleverly handled. M-D.

MARIAN FISHMAN (1941–   ) USA

Vignettes (CF   1971) 4pp. Five short contrasting abstract pieces, expressionistic. M-D.

ANDOR FOLDES (1913–   ) USA, born Hungary

Introvert—Extravert (EBM).

ROBERT FLEMING (1921–1976) Canada

Bag-o-Tricks (Waterloo   1968) 9pp. Four pieces for young pianists. Short, contrasting, MC. Int.

Toccatina (Waterloo   1968) 3pp. Brisk and rhythmic; changing meters.

Two-line texture until end, where chords in left hand reinforce sonorities. Freely tonal around C. Prestissimo closing. Int.

BJORN FONGAARD (1919–   ) Norway
Peintures, Moods for Piano (Lyche).
Sonata Op.110/1 (Lyche).

JACQUELINE FONTYN (1930–   ) Belgium
Fontyn teaches at the Royal Flemish Conservatorium in Antwerp.
Ballade (CeBeDeM   1963) 21pp. 6½ min. Required piece for the Concours International Reine Elisabeth 1964. Rhapsodic, freely tonal; virtuoso technique required. D.
Capriccio (CeBeDeM   1954) 12pp. 4½ min. Chromatic, expressionistic, chords in alternating hands, varied figuration. D.
Mosaici (Metropolis   1964) 16pp. 10 min. Eight short contrasting pieces that may be performed in 13 different orders (listed in the score). Pointillistic, expressionistic, large gestures, dissonant. D.

LUKAS FOSS (1922–   ) USA, born Germany
Grotesque Dance (CF 1938). Also available in *51 Piano Pieces from the Modern Repertoire* (GS 1940).

ANTONIO FRAGOSO (1897–1918) Portugal
Composicies para Piano, Vol.2 (Valentim de Carvalho). 21pp. 2 Noturnos. Preludio. Pensées Extatiques (2 short character pieces). M-D.
Sonata em Mi Menor (Valentim de Carvalho   1971) 28pp. Muito agitado; Calmo e cantando com doçura. Post-Romantic techniques, dashing figurations. M-D.
Cancão e dança Portuguesas (Valentim de Carvalho   1912) 5pp. Contrasting, MC, and colorful. M-D.
Três Peças do Seculo XVIII (Valentim de Carvalho) 3pp. Minueto; Aria; Gavotte. Int.

JEAN FRANÇAIX (1912–   ) France
Zehn Stücke für Kinder zum Spielen und Träumen   1975 (Schott 6665). Portrays 10 stages in the development of a boy, from The Newly Born Child (Easy) to The Emancipated Young Man (D).

ARNOLD FRANCHETTI (1906–   ) USA, born Italy
Franchetti teaches at the Hartt College of Music, University of Hartford, West Hartford, CN 06117.
Sonata I (Bongiovanni   1954) 12pp. Allegrissimo: SA. Lento e dolce: ABA, pastorale quality. Fuga a tre voci: not literally three voices; leads to a quasi cadenza. Mosso e dolce: rondo. M-D.
Sonata IV (Scarlattiana) 1968 (MS available from composer). Molto mosso. Serenata I. Serenata II. Canzonetta. Fuga in Mi. M-D.
Sonata Settima   1974 (MS available from composer) 21pp. Legatissimo: opens with cadenzalike figuration; recitative; builds to strong climax;

subsides. Recitative Mesto: freely chordal; tonal; melody moves through various voices. Scherzo: fleeting chromatic figuration, folk song melody in trio. Abschied variationen: 7 variations, fughetto, affettuoso, choralelike closing. Austere writing. D.

See: Watson W. Morrison, "The Piano Sonatas of Arnold Franchetti," DMA diss., Boston University, 1971, 234pp.

CÉSAR FRANCK (1822–1890) France

Prélude, Chorale et Fugue (PWM; WH; Schott 08860½). D.

Prélude, Aria et Finale (WH; Schott 08864/5). M-D.

Prélude, Fugue et Variation Op.18 (WH). M-D.

Selected Piano Compositions (Vincent d'Indy—Dover) 138pp. This collection contains ten pieces, evenly divided between early germinal compositions and important late pieces. 3 early compositions (written at age 14); Eglogue Op.3; Premier Grand Caprice Op.5; Ballade Op.9; The Doll's Lament; Danse lente; Prelude, Chorale and Fugue; Prelude, Aria and Finale. Each work is analyzed by the editor in his Introduction. Int. to M-D.

JOHAN FRANCO (1908–   ) USA

See: Sandro Rector, "The Piano Compositions of Johan Franco," Master's thesis, Radford College, 1972.

FREDERICO DE FREITAS (1902–   ) Portugal

Dança (A. Moraes) 2pp. Short, strong rhythms, attractive. M-D.

JOHAN HENRIK FREITHOFF (1713–1767) Norway

Two Minuets (Editions Norvegica   1971) 4pp. In D and A. Light eighteenth-century style. Int.

Two Minuets (Editions Norvegica   1971) 3pp. In G and A. Flowing, simple. Int.

Gavotte (Editions Norvegica   1971) 2pp. Syncopation, accented appoggiaturas. Int.

GIROLAMO FRESCOBALDI (1583–1643) Italy

Partitas I, II (K).

Toccatas (K).

GEORGES FRIBOULET (1910–   ) France

Gestes et sentiments ("Gestures and Feelings") (Lemoine   1972) 16pp. Album of 14 pieces. M-D.

Le Pré aux Loups ("Wolves' Meadow") (Lemoine   1975) 11pp. A Romantic and descriptive suite with the following miniature movements: Wolves' Meadow; The Squirrels; On the Road to the Val-au-Cesne; Strolling in the Henry IV Forest; The Beech Grove; On the Mall at Yvetot. Int. to M-D.

Nous (Lemoine). Suite of five short contrasting pieces: Ourselves; Baroque; Phrase; Caprice; Me without You; Paris Morsang. M-D.

PETER RACINE FRICKER (1920–   ) Great Britain
Fricker teaches at the University of California, Santa Barbara, CA 93106.
Both of these pieces make use of a "mosaic" form, being built up from a
number of short sections.
Episodes I Op.51   1967–8 (MS available from the composer) 8½ min.
   Generally delicate in texture. Fragments four sections and arranges the
   pieces around a central scherzo. M-D.
Episodes II Op.58   1969 (MS available from the composer) 6 min. More
   aggressive and dramatic than *Episodes I*. Constructed from pieces of
   five sections, with the central one being a recitative. M-D.

GÉZA FRID (1904–   ) The Netherlands, born Hungary
Frid studied with Bartók and Kodály in Hungary before he went to Holland
in 1929.
Quatre études Op.12   1932 (Donemus   1976) 18pp. Photostat of MS.
Sonata per pianoforte Op.5   1929 (Donemus   1972) 17pp. Reproduc-
   tion of composer's MS.

KURT JOACHIM FRIEDEL (1921–   ) Germany
Bagatellen (Heinrichshofen   1973) 18pp. In two parts.

WITOLD FRIEMANN (1889–   ) Poland
50 Pièces Romantiques (PWM   1962) 103pp. 25 preludes and 25 mazurkas written in a post-Brahms idiom. Pianistic, colorful chromatic writing. Int. to M-D.

JOHANN JACOB FROBERGER (1616–1667) Germany
Oeuvres Completes pour Clavecin (Howard Schott—Heugel). Vol.I:
   Toccatas, capriccios, ricercari, fantasies, canzone, and suites.
Selected Keyboard Works (David Starke—Tonos   1972) xvi/85pp. Pho-
   tostat. Preface, critical note, and sources in German.
Nine Pieces (K).

SANDRO FUGA (1906–   ) Italy
Toccata (Ric   1935). Triplets juxtaposed against chords and melodies in
   varied patterns. Freely tonal with brilliant writing. M-D.
7 Studi (EC   1971) 48pp.
Valzer amorosi (EC 6886).
Sonata II (EC   1977) 25pp.

KAZUO FUKUSHIMA (1930–   ) Japan
Suien (Ongaku-No-Tomo   1972) 16pp. 6½ min. The title refers to a hazy
   mist from waterfalls. Contains performance directions. Aleatoric, fast
   arpeggi with palm and fingers of right hand; harmonics; spatial notation. Avant-garde. M-D.

ANIS FULEIHAN (1900–1970) USA, born Cyprus
Sonata No.3 (PIC   1971). Allegro: linear textures; clear sectional form;

opening theme foreshadows transparent treatment for entire movement; tonal, modal, scalar, and chordal patterns. Andantino, semplice: simple melodic accompaniment, numerous meter changes, calm, modal setting. Presto: forward moving 6/8 meter; Andantino mid-section provides contrast; imitation and pandiatonic treatment frequently used; con fuoco conclusion. M-D.

A Foot in the Door (BMC). Int.

Not for Squares (BMC). Int.

Seven Supplementary Exercises (PIC).

NORMAN FULTON (1909–   ) Great Britain

Prelude, Elegy and Toccata (Lengnick   1955) 23pp. Freely tonal; accessible to the student with enough technique to handle it but who has not had much experience with MC music. M-D.

JOHANN JOSEPH FUX (1660–1741) Germany

Fux was a daring and vital composer who could write in a lyric and highly poetic style.

Selected Works for Keyboard Instruments (Friedrich Riedel—Nag   1972) 31pp. Includes a multi-movement Capriccio; 3 Partitas; 3 Menuets. Facsimile of an ornamentation table by Gottlieb Muffat is included. Int. to M-D.

G

PIERRE GABAYE (1930–   ) France
Six Pièces "Tonales" (Technisonor   1971) 27pp.

OSSIP GABRILOWITSCH (1878–1936) Russia
Caprice-Burlesque Op.3/1 (Musica Obscura; J. Church). Short salon
    piece. Chordal, octaves, brilliant. M-D.
Intermezzo appassionata (Roszavölgyi).
Meditation (Roszavölgyi).
Melody Op.5 (J. Church).
Oriental Melody in collection *Composer–Pianists.*
Thème varié Op.4 (Zimmermann). M-D.

BOGDAN GAGIC (1931–   ) Yugoslavia
Sonata I   1966 (Društvo Hrvatskih Skladatelja) 5pp.
Sonata III   1968 (Društvo Hrvatskih Skladatelja) 5pp.
Sonata IV   1971 (Društvo Hrvatiskih Skladatelja) 6pp.

BALDASSARE GALUPPI (1706–1785) Italy
"I." stands for Hedda Illy, who is bringing out a complete edition of the
sonatas, being published by De Santis.
6 Sonatas (E. Woodcock—Galliard   1963).
Dodici sonate (I. Caruana—Zanibon   1974) 73pp. I.30, 45, 50, 1, 2, 3,
    56, 57, 60 (third movement omitted), 68, 6, 18. I.45 and I.57 are of
    fine recital quality; the others make fine teaching material. Fine edi-
    torial policy followed. Int. to M-D.
Dieci sonate (Iris Caruana—Zanibon   1972). Revised with introduction
    (in Italian and English) and transcribed into modern notation: 8
    sonatas and 2 divertimenti.
Sonate per il Cembalo (Heddy Illy—De Santis). Contains: I.7, 8, 19, 23,
    24, 32, 36–41, 49, 53, 95.
See: David E. Pullmann, "A Catalogue of the Keyboard Sonatas of Baldas-
    sare Galuppi," thesis, American University, 1972, 227pp.

JOHN GAMBOLD (1760–1795) Great Britain
Rondo ca.1788 (Moravian Music Foundation Publications No.7). Edited
    and arranged, with commentary by Karl Kroeger, c.1974. Gambold
    wrote this piece while he was teaching at the Moravian School in
    Niesky, Germany. The Rondo is designed mainly for instructional pur-

poses but its well-developed classic style and charm make it suitable for concert use. Editorial performance instructions have been added in brackets or with dotted lines. Int., but M-D up to the indicated Presto marking.

CARLTON GAMER (–   ) USA
Gamer teaches at Colorado College, Colorado Springs, CO 80903.
Piano Rāga Music (1962–70). Published in PNM, Fall–Winter 1973 and Spring–Summer 1974:191–216. "Notes on the Structure of Piano Rāga Music" by composer is found in same issue, pp.217–30. The music employs 48 set-forms. Highly organized tonal and rhythmic structures. D.

RUDOLPH GANZ (1877–1972) USA, born Switzerland
Three Rubes (Gerig) in collection *Contemporary Swiss Piano Music.*
Exercises for Piano (SB). Contemporary exercises.

JUAN GABRIEL GARCIA-ESCOBAR (1934–   ) Spain
Danzas Populares Españolas (UME   1974) 2 books, each 7pp. I. Amapolas de Castilla. II. Aromas de Levante.
Suite Popular (UME   1970) 30pp. Six Spanish dances, including Zapateado, Sequidilla, Farruca, etc. Strong rhythmic interest, MC. M-D.

PETER GARLAND (1955–   ) USA
Garland is one of the guiding lights of new music on the West Coast. MS copies are available from the composer at 1750 Arch St., Berkeley, CA 94709.
A Song   1971 (MS). Satie influence. Simple phrases are repeated until another phrase takes over.
The Fall of Quang Tri   1972 (MS). Black key clusters lend a Southeast Asian touch.
Nostalgia of the Southern Cross   1976 (MS). A waltzlike improvisation, hypnotic effect.
Two Persian Miniatures   1971 (MS). Widely spaced intervals, sustained single pitches, effective. All the above use avant-garde techniques.

JANINA GARŚCIA (1920–   ) Poland
Favorite Tunes Op.27 (PWM   1973) 23pp. 20 pieces, attractively set. Includes colorful drawings. Int.
Miniatures Op.5 (PWM   1971). 13 pieces, colorful, varied. Int.
Teasers (PWM). Easy.
Very Easy Pieces for Children Op.3 (PWM). 8 imaginative pieces, not "very easy." Int.
Winter Fun (PWM). Easy.

ODETTE GARTENLAUB (1922–   ) France
7 Short Studies for Intervals for Piano (Rideau Rouge   1974) 15pp. Each

piece focuses on one interval, i.e., seconds, thirds, fourths, fifths, sixths, sevenths, octaves. MC. Int.

IRENA GARZTECKA (1913–1963) Poland
Garztecka studied piano with N. Jacynowa at the Warsaw Conservatory and composition with K. Sikorski at the State College of music in Lodz.
Polish Dances (PWM). Six miniatures that evoke the atmosphere and rhythms of typical Polish folk dances. Mazur; Kujawiak; Krakowiak; Oberek; Zbójnicki; Polonez. Int.
Suite (PWM). Five movements, each may be performed separately. Simplicity of construction, serious, concentrated. M-D.

SERGE DE GASTYNE (1930–   ) USA, born France
Proem (EV   1958) 5pp. Flexible meters, freely tonal, thematic development from opening idea, più mosso mid-section, lyric orientation, large span required. M-D.

STEPHANOS GASULEAS (1931–   ) Greece
11 Aphorisms (UE   1961) 8pp. Vol.II in a series edited by Hanns Jelinek called *Libelli Dodecaphonic*. The preface states that all the pieces are by pupils of the editor, Gasuleas being one of them. Int. to M-D.

ROLF GEHLHAAR (1943–   ) Germany
Klavierstück 1–2 (Constellations) (Feedback Studio   1971) 17pp. For piano with pickup, electronium, synthesizer (VCS-3) tape and echo producer, etc. Explanations in German.

FRITZ GEISSLER (1921–   ) Germany
Sonata (DVFM   1968) 24pp. Individual writing up to final pages, where a thick Regerian chromatic quality emerges. D.
Zweite Klaviersonate (DVFM 8037   1976) 17pp. Sehr ruhige: no bar lines, spatial notation, serial, palm and arm clusters. Sehr lebhafte: secco style, skips, chordal tremolo, percussive; requires large span. Expressionistic, avant-garde. D.

FRANCESCO GEMINIANI (1687–1762) Italy
Pièces de clavecin, tirées des differences ouvrages de M. F. Germiniani (Bibliotheca Musica Bunoniensis, through Arnaldo Forni Editore 1975). 59pp. Originally published London 1743.
The Second Collection of Pieces for the Harpsichord (Bibliotheca Musica Bunoniensis, through Arnaldo Forni Editore). Originally published London 1752.

ARMANDO GENTILUCCI (1939–   ) Italy
Iter (Ric   1969) 7pp. 5 min. Involved figuration and chordal sonorities splashed over keyboard. Some aleatoric sections, dynamic extremes, highly percussive and dissonant. D.

HARALD GENZMER (1909–   ) Germany
Dialogues (Litolff   1963) 26pp. 22 min. Twelve contrapuntal studies of
   great ingenuity and musicality. Twentieth-century equivalents of Bach
   Inventions, one for each key. M-D.
Suite C (Schott   1951). Moderato: introductory and with full chords.
   Allegro: pseudo contrapuntal, large gestures, clever ending. Andante:
   ostinato-like. Presto: toccata style with syncopated chords. M-D.

ROBERTO GERHARD (1897–1970) Spain
Dances from Don Quixote (K. Prowse).

EDWIN GERSCHEFSKI (1909–   ) USA
Gerschefski's style contains elements of humor, rhythmic strength, and
lyricism. His harmonies tend to be rather dense and rugged.
Sonata Op.4B (after a famous 18th-century composer) (MS available from
   composer, P.O. Box 162, Hiawassee, GA 30546). 23pp. Allegro con
   spirito; Andante; Menuetto—Allegretto; Maestoso. In an eighteenth-
   century style. M-D.
Concert Minuet Op.4D (CFE) 4pp. From Classic Symphony. Neoclassic.
   Int.
Six Preludes Op.6 (CFE) 18pp. Varied sonorities and moods, MC. M-D.
   No.6 available separately (CFE) in a revised version. 6pp.
Nocturne Op.6/7 (Pioneer) 2pp. Highly independent lines. M-D.
Toccata and Fugue Op.7 (MS available from composer) 6pp. Dramatic
   gestures; exploits extreme ranges of keyboard. M-D. to D.
The Portrait of an Artist Op.13 (CFE) 4pp. Four short contrasting pieces,
   subtle sonorities. M-D.
Lament Op.13/5 (MS available from composer) 1p. Thin textures, chro-
   matic. Int.
Lullaby Op.13/6 (CFE   1934) 1p. Two-voice lines. Int.
Invention Op.13/7 (Pioneer) 1p. M-D.
Eight Variations Op.14 (CFE   1961) 8pp. Contains an especially colorful
   Recitative near the beginning and at the end. M-D.
Lullaby to a Child Unborn Op.14/9 (CFE   1965) 6pp. 5 min. Sectional-
   ized, chromatic, on quiet side. M-D.
Suite for Left Hand Alone Op.15 (CFE) 11pp. Allegro moderato; Largo;
   Allegretto. D.
Study in 7/8 Time Op.18/1; *Study in 5/8 Time* Op.18/2; *Mazurka* Op.
   18/3 (Pioneer) 3pp. Int. to M-D.
Six Waltzes Op.19 (CFE) 6pp. M-D.
Second Sonatine Op.20/2 (Pioneer   1961) 8pp. Lento ma non troppo;
   Allegro con brio. Strong independent lines, chromatic. M-D.
New Music Op.23 (Pioneer 1937) 7pp. Four pieces. All except No.4 are
   thin textured. M-D.
Two-Part Invention Op.27/3 (MS available from composer) 3pp. Freely
   tonal, linear treatment. Int.

March Op.29/1a (MS available from composer) 3pp. M-D.

2nd March Op.29/2a (MS available from composer) 4pp. "Music for a Stately Occasion." M-D.

South Carolina Waltz Op.27/4 (Pioneer) 1p. Freely tonal. Int.

Prairie Hymn Op.30/3A; *Prairie Nocturne* Op.30/3B (Pioneer) 2pp. The Nocturne is a variation of the Hymn. Int.

Waltz Nocturne Op.31/3 (CFE 1945) 3pp. Formerly titled "Schillinger Nocturne." 9/8, freely tonal around E, ends in B. M-D.

Invention Op.34/3; Teletype Etude Op.34/4 (Pioneer 1961) 4pp. Invention: chromatic, flowing lines. Etude: Presto energico, motoric in 5/8. M-D.

Seven Piano Pieces Op.47 (Pioneer 1964) 15pp. Contrasting, complementary. Would make a nice suite. M-D.

Six Piano Pieces Op.48 (CFE) 6pp. Short, two-voice textures, linear. Easy to Int.

Twelve Etudes Op.58 (Pioneer 1966) 15pp. Contrasting, craggy textures. Large span required. M-D.

Three Inventions Op.59 (CFE 1964) 9pp. Free dissonant counterpoint. M-D.

Hommage à Chopin Op.60 (CFE 1966) 28pp. Fourteen contrasting variations, each one built on techniques used by Chopin in his *Préludes*. Clever; effective; contains some pleasantly surprising results. Int. to M-D.

Sonata Op.61/2 (CFE 1968) 12pp. Allegro: 7/8. Allegretto espressione: 7/8. Scherzo: 5/8. Allegro moderato: 9/8; a set of variations with theme in the middle of the movement; the most involved movement. Neoclassic. M-D.

Six Pieces Op.65 (CFE 1969) 6pp. Short, freely tonal, varied textures. Int. to M-D.

Six Pieces Op.67 (CFE) 6pp. M-D.

Five Pieces Op.68 (CFE) 5pp. Contains metric experimentation. M-D.

GEORGE GERSHWIN (1898–1937) USA

Music by Gershwin (University Society 1975) 185pp. Includes: Rhapsody in Blue. 3 Preludes. Impromptu in 2 Keys. Two Waltzes C. 18 transcriptions of songs made by the composer. Also includes photographs of Gershwin and his circle of friends, bibliography, discography, and indexes of titles and first lines. Also includes a small 33⅓ LP of Gershwin playing the solo version of Rhapsody in Blue. A revealing performance! Int. to M-D.

Gershwin at the Keyboard (New World Music). Eighteen song hits arranged by the composer. Delightful, short. M-D.

Impromptu in Two Keys (New World Music 1973) 2pp. Jazzy melodic line over punctuated bass. M-D.

Two Waltzes C 1933 (New World Music) adapted by Saul Chaplin. Introduction, Waltz I, Waltz II, then both waltzes combined. Attractive. Int. to M-D.

Rhapsody in Blue (New World Music). This solo piano version is what Gershwin actually wrote. It stands complete on its own. M-D.

George Gershwin for Piano (Chappell   1974). Includes: Merry Andrew. Three-quarter Blues. Promenade. M-D.

See: Margory Irvin, "It's George, Not Jazz: Gershwin's Influence in Piano Music," AMT, 23 (November–December 1973):31–34.

OSWALD GERSTEL (1923–   ) Israel, born Rumania

Metacycle (Israeli Music Publications   1975) 39pp. Three sonatas for piano. D.

Notations (Israeli Music Publications   1975) 17pp. With magnetic tape ad lib. Performance notes, spatial notation, some notation not explained, unexciting choice of pitches. D.

Petite Suite (Israeli Music Publications   1975) 10pp. For harpsichord or piano.

OTTMAR GERSTER(1897–1969) Germany

Fantasie G (CFP   1970) 22pp. Fingering by Annerose Schmidt.

DINU GHEZZO (1941–   ) USA, born Romania

Ritualen (Seesaw   1975) 13pp. For prepared piano; also uses mallets. Reproduced from holograph. D.

VITTORIO GIANNINI (1903–1966) USA

See: Donald E. Bechtel, "A Bibliography of the Works of Vittorio Giannini," Master's thesis, Kent State University, 1972.

Michael L. Mark, "The Life and Works of Vittorio Giannini (1903–1966)," DMA diss., Catholic University, 1969, 170pp.

ORLANDO GIBBONS (1583–1625) Great Britain

Album (K 3470).

Courante F (Farrenc—Leduc) with 2 courantes by Crofurd. Int.

WALTER GIESEKING (1895–1956) Germany

Jazz Improvisation (Schaum Publications) in collection *Composer–Pianists*.

ANTHONY GILBERT (1934–   ) Great Britain

Little Piano Pieces Op.20B (Schott) 6 min. From *String Quartet with Piano Pieces,* Op.20. Pieces look more difficult than they are. Chance composition. M-D.

ALBERTO GINASTERA (1916–   ) Argentina

Danzas Argentinas Op.2 (Durand   1937).

Tres Piezas Op.6 (Ric Americana   1940).

Twelve American Preludes Op.12 (CF   1944).

Piezas Infantiles (GS   1942) in collection *Latin-American Art Music for the Piano.* Int. to M-D.

Suite de danza criollas Op.15 (Barry   1946).

Rondo on Argentine Children's Folk Tunes Op.19 (Bo&H   1947).

Sonata Op.22 (Barry   1952).

See: Mary Ann Hanley, CSJ, "The Solo Piano Music of Alberto Ginastera," Part I, AMT, 24 (June–July 1975):17–20; Part II, AMT, 25 (September–October 1975):6–9.

Mary Ann Hanley, CSJ. "The Solo Piano Compositions of Alberto Ginastera (1916–   )," DMA diss., University of Cincinnati, 1969, 85pp.

ALMERIGO GIROTTO (1897–   ) Italy

Sonata (Zanibon 25461   1975) 40pp. Preface in Italian.

LODOVICO GIUSTINI (18th century, flourished 1736) Italy

See. Joseph Bloch, "Lodovico Giustini and the First Published Piano Sonatas," PQ, 86 (Summer 1974):20–24. Includes the complete Sonata IV in facsimile with performance suggestions.

PEGGY GLANVILLE-HICKS (1912–   ) USA, born Australia

Glanville-Hicks studied composition with Vaughan Williams, Egon Wellesz, and Nadia Boulanger. In 1960 she moved to Greece.

Prelude for a Pensive Pupil (LG) in collection *New Music for Piano, Guide,* p.754. Flowing legato required. A few left-hand octave skips. MC. M-D.

ALEXANDER GLAZUNOV (1865–1936) USSR

Complete Piano Works (K) 2 vols.

Piano Works (USSR   1974) 194pp. Contains: Op.25; Op.22/1; Op.31/3; Op.41; Op.49; Op.54; Opp.74–75; Op.101/2, 4; Op.103; Poem-Improvisations e and g.

Deux Prelude—Improvisations (Belaieff   1976) 12pp.

La Nuit Op.31/3 (Belaieff). Melodious and flowing. M-D.

Grand Valse de Concert Op.41 (Belaieff   1889). Lilting, gracious, racing conclusion, a good encore. M-D.

The Seasons Op.67   1899 (Belaieff 318) 69pp. Piano reduction of the complete ballet by the composer. M-D to D.

Theme and Variations Op.72 (GS 7933).

Two Sonatas Opp.74, 75 (Muzyka) 79pp.

Sonata II Op.75 (GS 278).

Song of the Boatman Op.97 (Belaieff   1974).

REINHOLD GLIERE (1875–1956) Russia

Piano Works (USSR   1974) 82pp. Contains: Op.16/1; Op.19/1; Op.26/1–4; Op.31/1–12; Op.34/1, 4, 6–8, 12, 20, 22; Op.43/1, 3, 4, 7; Op.47/3.

The Bronze Horseman (USSR   1974). Ballet in four acts, eleven scenes
  with a prologue. Piano score by the composer.

MIKHAIL GLINKA (1804–1857) Russia
Selected Works for Piano (USSR   1976).
Heavy Are My Thoughts (A Prayer) (GS 291).
Nocturne (The Separation) (GS 295).
Polyphonic Notebook (GS 296).
15 Selected Pieces (Otto, Nathanson—GS 297).
Souvenir d'une Mazurka (GS 298).
Two Two-Voice Fugues (GS 299).
Variations on a Russian Folk Song "Mid Gentle Dales" (GS 301; Musica
  Obscura).
Variations on Aliabev's Song "The Nightingale" (GS 302).
11 Variations on a Theme by Glinka (AMP). A collection of eleven varia-
  tions by some of the leading Soviet composers on a theme from
  Glinka's "Vanya's Song" from the opera *Ivan Susanin*. Contains one
  variation each by Dmitri Kabalevsky, Eugen Kapp, Andrei Eshapy,
  Rodion Shchedrin, Georgi Sviridov, and Yuri Levtin; two by Vas-
  sarion Shebalin; and three by Dmitri Shostakovitch. Contains some
  brilliant and highly interesting writing. M-D.

VINKO GLOBOKAR (1934–   ) Yugoslavia
Notes (CFP P-8284   1972) 7 leaves. Performance instructions in German.
  Reproduced from holograph.

LEOPOLD GODOWSKY (1870–1938) Poland
Miniatures (CF   1920). Humoresque. Rigaudon. The Miller's Song. Pro-
  cessional March. Arabian Chant (Orientale). All are tuneful and
  colorful, but not easy. Available separately. Int. to M-D.
Meditation (Schaum Publications) in collection *Composer–Pianists*.
Moto Perpetuo (Musica Obscura).

HUGO GODRON (1900–1971) The Netherlands
24 Chansonnettes (Donemus   1973) Livres I–IV. Charming, gentle and
  elegant, jazz-oriented, many seventh chords. Some pieces in form of
  dances (gavotte, minuet, waltz, etc.). Impressionistic influences. M-D.

FRANZPETER GOEBELS (1920–   ) Germany
Bird-Boogie (Br   1974) 12pp. For harpsichord or piano.

ALEXANDER F. GOEDICKE (1877–1957) USSR
Goedicke is mainly remembered for his melodious instructional piano
pieces.
Sechzig Klavierstücke Op.36 (CFP) Book I: 30 pieces consisting of Etudes,
  Russian Songs, Dances, Cradle Song, Polka, etc. Essential fingering
  indicated. Easy. Book II: carefully graded; more difficult than Book I.
  Easy-Int.

ALEXANDER GOEHR (1932–   ) Great Britain, born Germany
Nonomiya Op.27 (Schott   1973) 13pp. A Noh play in which the main
  character presents an aria in the first part, reappears as a ghost in the
  second, and finally dances before leaving. Exotic decoration in the
  first part, dance elements in the second part. Subtle sonorities, repeated harmonic gestures. D.

RICHARD FRANKO GOLDMAN (1910–   ) USA
Etude on White Notes (Bo&H   1973) 4pp. Groups of 4 eighth notes
  against groups of 3 eighth notes, flowing thirds, cantabile and molto
  rubato mid-section, subito large *ff* chords, strongly accented closing,
  much dissonance. M-D.

FRIEDRICH GOLDMANN (1941–   ) Germany
Klavierstücke 4 (CFP   1973) 11pp. Reproduced from holograph.

JÜRGEN GOLLE (1942–   ) Germany
Miniaturen (CFP   1970) 18 small pieces. Lyrical, tonal, neo-Hindemith-
  ian. Int.
Sonata Fugata (DVFM   1968) 17pp.

FRANÇOIS GOSSEC (1734–1829) France, born Belgium
Tambourin (De Smet—Br&H).

LOUIS MOREAU GOTTSCHALK (1829–1869) USA
Compositions for Pianoforte (Amiram Rigai—Chappell 1972). Ten
  pieces: The Banjo. La Scintilla. Souvenir de Porto Rico. Morte!!
  Marche Funèbre. Bamboula. Minuit à Séville. Ballade, Op.6. Tournament Galop. Pasquinade. Also contains notes about the composer's
  life and works. M-D to D.
Gottschalk Album (K). Le Banjo. Pasquinade. Valse Poetique. Pastorella
  e Cavalhere. Tremolo. M-D.
Piano Music (Dover) 301pp. Edited with an Introduction by Richard Jack-
  son. Divided into four categories: I. United States Ethnic and Patriotic
  Music: Bamboula; Le Bananier; The Banjo; La Savane; Ballade Cre-
  ole; Union. II.Music from Spain: La Jota Aragonesa; Manchega;
  Minuit à Séville; Souvenirs d'Andalousie. III.West Indian Souvenirs:
  Danza; La Gallina; Le Mancenillier; O, Ma Charmante, Epargnez
  Moi!; Ojos Criollos; Souvenir de la Havane; Souvenir de Porto Rico;
  Suis Moi!. IV.Concert and Salon Music: Sixième Ballade; Berceuse;
  The Dying Poet; Grand Scherzo; The Last Hope; Morte!!; Pasquinade;
  Ses Yeux; Tournament Galop. M-D to D.
Creole and Caribbean Piano Pieces (Eberhardt Klemm—CFP 1974)
  74pp. Preface in German, French, and English; critical notes in Ger-
  man. Contains: Bamboula. La Savane. Le Bananier. Le Banjo. Souve-
  nir de Porto Rico. Les Yeux Creoles. Souvenir de la Havane. Pasquinade. M-D.

Le Bananier (CFP P-7185).

Cradle Song (APS).

Orfa Grande Polka (OD).

The Little Book of Louis Moreau Gottschalk (Richard Jackson, Neil Rat-
liff—Continuo Music Press   1975). A performing edition based on
materials at the New York Public Library. Preface by Gilbert Chase.
Includes: Romance. Ballade. Polka B♭. Chanson du gitano. Polka A♭.
Mazurk. Ynes. Also includes the manuscripts in facsimile. These are
all previously unpublished works and form what could be called a suite
of songs and dances. They are well balanced and have great variety
and mood contrast. A fine introduction with notes about each piece
makes for interesting reading. The Mazurk is a real find! M-D.

MORTON GOULD (1913–   ) USA

Abby Variations (Chappell   1964). Theme and 12 variations. Int.

Pavanne (Belwin-Mills). Easy moving, needs loose wrists. Int.

Prelude and Toccata (Belwin-Mills).

Rag—Blues—Rag (LG) in collection *New Music for the Piano, Guide,*
p.754.

ULF GRAHN (1942–   ) Sweden

Snapshots (Frank   1975) 11pp. Eight pieces. Includes performance directions, introduction and contemporary techniques, optical and graphic
notation. Aleatoric, improvisatory, clusters, multiple activity. Avant-
garde. M-D.

To Barbo (Frank). Short contemporary character piece. Int.

PERCY GRAINGER (1892–1961) Australia

The Grainger Museum at the University of Melbourne, Parkville, Victoria
3052, Australia, publishes a catalogue of its holdings.

The Young Pianist's Grainger (R. Stevenson—Schott   1967) available
through (GS) in the USA.

See: Teresa Balough, *A Complete Catalogue of the Works of Percy Grain-
ger* (Nedlands, W. A.: Department of Music, University of Western
Australia, 1975), 258pp. Available in USA from Theodore Front
Musical Literature.

ENRIQUE GRANADOS (1867–1916) Spain

Danza Caracteristica (UME   1973) Op. posth. 4pp. Three contrasting
sections. Large span required. M-D.

2 Danses caractéristiques (Sal).

Danza Lenta Op.37/1 (UME). Probably one of Granados' last works.

Dos (2) Gavotas (UME   1973). Op. posth.

El Pelele (GS). The Dummy. Based on music from the opening scene of
the opera *Goyescas*. Lively and strongly rhythmic, depicting the "man
of straw" being tossed in the air by the "Majas." Although composed

last, it is really a kind of introduction to the piano suite *Goyescas*. M-D.

Escenas Poéticas Libro de Horas (UME 1923) Segunda Serie. Recuerdo de paises lejanos. El Angel de los claustros. Cancion de Margarita. Suenos del poeta. Colorful miniatures. Int.

Escenas Romanticas (IMC 1973). This suite of six "Romantic Scenes" is not as Spanish-sounding as most of the other piano works but they are as pianistic as Chopin's. Mazurka. Berceuse. Lento con estasi. Allegretto. Allegro appassionata. Epilogo. Int. to M-D.

Estudio (UME 1973). Op. posth.

Goyescas 1911 (K).

Jácara (UME 1973) 4pp.

Los soldados de carton ("The Cardboard Soldiers") (UME 1973). Op. posth. 4pp. Shifts from minor to parallel major. Int. to M-D.

Mazurla alla polacca Op.2 (UME) 3pp. Chopin-inspired, tuneful, and rhythmic. Int.

Oriental. Cancion variada, intermedio y final (UME 1973) 12pp.

12 Spanish Dances (CF). No.6, *Playera* available separately (BMC).

7 Valses Poeticos with Prelude and Postlude 1887 (UME). Succinct writing that casts a glance toward Ravel. Similar in length and structure to Ravel's set *Valses Nobles et Sentimentales,* composed 24 years later. Moods range from gaiety to melancholy. M-D.

6 Pieces on Spanish Folk Songs (UME). An expansive set. D.

Reverie—Improvisation 1916 (published in *Clavier,* 6 [October 1967]: 29–33). Recorded by Granados when he was in USA and notated by Henry Levine and Samuel Randlett. Romantic, attractive, easily accessible. Int. to M-D.

JOHANN CHRISTOPH GRAUPNER (1683–1760) Germany

8 Partitas (Albert Küster—Möseler).

Monatliche Klavierfrüchte (A. Küster—Möseler). Consists of allemandes, courantes, sarabandes, minuets, and gigues. M-D.

HAROLD BELLMAN GREEN (1921–) USA

Green is a staff member of the theory department of the Wisconsin College of Music, Milwaukee, WI.

The Diabolic Fiddler (Schroeder & Gunther 1975) 3pp. Many fifths, rhythmic, MC, *pppp* ending. Int.

Summer Sketch Book (Providence Music Press 1974) 12pp. Six short colorful pieces. Int.

Three Old Rhymes and Three French Folk Tunes (Waterloo 1968) 8pp. London Bridge. Tom, Tom the Piper's Son. Hickory, Dickory Dock. Frère Jacques. Sur le pont d'Avignon. Pierrot. Clever; colorful MC settings; familiar melodies embellished with delicate sounds. Int.

Variations in Phrygian (Providence Music Press 1970) 16pp. Theme in

Phrygian mode and twelve variations, mostly short, well-contrasted, and contrapuntal, with individual titles. Final variation is a toccata. Brilliant and effective for recitals. M-D.

RAY GREEN (1908–   ) USA
Prelude Blues (AME   1973). From "Dedications." Dedicated to George Gershwin.
See: Sidney Richard Vise, "Ray Green: His Life and Stylistic Elements of His Music from 1935 to 1962," diss., University of Missouri—Kansas City, 1975.

ARTHUR GREENE (–   ) USA
7 Wild Mushrooms and a Waltz (Galaxy). Easy pieces for prepared piano. These ingenious little pieces by a young West Coast composer will make the experience easy and memorable. A rubber eraser and some wood screws are required. They will not hurt the piano. The resulting percussion sounds will generate much interest in the young student. Int.

MAURICE GREENE (1695–1755) Great Britain
A Collection of Lessons for the Harpsichord (S&B 1977) 73pp. A facsimile of the original edition with an introduction by Davitt Moroney. Contains 48 pieces, first published in 1750, arranged in groupings by keys, 7 groups on either side of a central Aria con Variationi in d. Suite and sonata characteristics are present. Int. to M-D.
See: Harry Diack Johnstone, "The Life and Work of Maurice Greene (1695–1755)," diss., Oxford University, 1968.

ALEXANDER GRETCHANINOFF (1864–1956) Russia
Brimborions (Galaxy). Brimborions means "knick-knacks" in French. There are delights for everyone in this charming suite. Int.
Eight Pastels Op.61 (K).
Historiettes Op.118 (Leduc   1930). 12 pieces. Int.
Kinder-Album (CFP). Fifteen short, varied pieces. Not graded progressively; little fingering given. Int.
Little Beads Op.123 (GS).
Suite Miniature Op.145 (Leduc   1948). Ten pieces. Int.

EDVARD GRIEG (1843–1907) Norway
Complete Works (CFP) edited by the Edvard Grieg Committee under the auspices of the Institute of Musicology, University of Oslo. Piano Solo: 1. Lyric Pieces I–X. 2. Other original compositions. 3. Arrangements of Norwegian Folk Music. 4. Arrangements of own works.
Lyric Pieces (CFP) in *Complete Works*. Preface indicates that Grieg's *Lyric Pieces* comprise 66 pieces for piano two-hands, which were published in ten sets between 1867 and 1901 with the opus numbers 12, 38, 43, 47, 54, 57, 62, 65, 68, and 71. Opp.12 and 38 each

contain eight pieces; Opp.43 and 71 seven pieces each; all other sets six each.

Available separately: Books 1, 2, and 3 (Supraphon). *Notturno* from Op.54 (Anson—Willis).

See: Brian Schlotel, "Grieg's Lyric Pieces: Teaching Material and So Piano Student," *Music Teacher,* 55 (February 1976):12–13.

————. "Grieg's Other Piano Music—A Mine of Interest for the Piano Student," *Music Teacher,* 55 (February 1976):12–13.

OTHER SMALLER SETS:

6 Poetic Tone-Pictures Op.3   1863 (CFP; WH). The spirit of the smaller Schumann piano pieces is evident here, especially in No.4. Int. to M-D.

Moods Op.73   1905 (CFP). 1. Resignation. 2. Scherzo—Impromptu. 3. A Ride at Night. 4. Popular Air. 5. Hommage à Chopin. 6. Student's Serenade. 7. The Mountaineers Song. Int. to M-D.

Improvisations on 2 Norwegian Folk Songs Op.29   1878 (CFP). A kind of Grieg version of Liszt's *Hungarian Rhapsodies.* M-D.

Slätter Op.72   1902 (CFP). These are the most original pieces based on Norwegian folk music. Int. to M-D.

LARGER WORKS:

Sonata e Op.7   1865 (PWM).

See: Wadham Sutton, "Grieg: Sonata in E Minor, Op.7," *Music Teacher,* 52 (May 1973):13–14.

Ballad g Op.24   1875 (GS) Grieg's most difficult solo piano work. D.

COLLECTIONS:

38 Pieces (A. Morrison—ABRSM) Vol.I: Easy to Int. Vol.II: M-D.

Grieg—An Introduction to His Piano Works (M. Halford—Alfred). 22 pieces in progressive order. Informative foreword. The editor suggests playing most of the ornaments on the beat, an instruction that might be questioned. Some of the unusual pieces are: A King Rules in the East, Op.66/3; Bell-Ringing, Op.54/6. Int. to M-D.

Selected Works (H. Levine—Alfred 1974) 144pp. 44 of the shorter works. Contains fine biographical information. Editorial additions shown in light print.

Selected Piano Works (Bo&H). Includes selections from Peer Gynt suites and the Norwegian Dances.

45 Selected Compositions (GS) 2 books.

Il mio primo Grieg (Pozzoli—Ric ER 2600) 12pp. Contains: National Song, Op.12/8. Popular Melody. Waltz, Op.12/2. Arietta Op.12/1. Dance of the Nymphs, Op.12/4. The Lonely Wanderer Op.43/2. Little Bird, Op.43/4. Int. to M-D.

Grieg, the First Book for Young Pianists (M. Halford—Alfred   1977)
24pp.

CHARLES TOMLINSON GRIFFES (1884–1920) USA

De Profundis 1915 (Donna Anderson—CFP 6647   1978) 8pp. 6 min.
The editor suggests Tempo rubato throughout. Changing meters.
Broken-chord and arpeggi figuration in left hand supports chords;
melody in right hand. Contains some dissonant and quartal harmonies. Style is similar to Griffes's *Piano Sonata*. M-D.

ROMUALD GRINBLAT (1930–   ) USSR

Sonata (T. Front   1973) 13pp. In the style of Stockhausen. D.

RENATO GRISONI (–   ) Italy

Tregenda Op.3 (EC   1976) 12pp.

Aforismi in modo misolidio Op.51, *e in modo dorico* Op.52 (EC   1974)
38pp.

COR DE GROOT (1914–   ) The Netherlands

Canzone d'après une melodie de Hans Krieg (Donemus   1975) 7pp. Photostat.

C—D—G—Wals (Donemus   1974) 6pp. Photostat.

Cloches dans la martin (Donemus   1972). Bell sonorities, pedal study,
5/4 meter, Impressionistic. Int.

In Any Direction (Donemus   1974) 4pp. A poem for the right hand only,
uses two pedals.

It's a Long 'Lòng' Way—Waltz (Donemus   1974) 11pp. Photostat.

GABRIEL GROVLEZ (1879–1944) France

2 Impressions (Heugel). Nostalgique. Joyeuse.

Le Royaume Puérii (Heugel). Eight pieces for children. Easy to Int.

LOUIS GRUENBERG (1884–1964) USA, born Russia

Jazzberries Op.25 (UE). 1. Fox-trot. 2. Blues. 3. Waltz. 4. Syncopep.

Polychromatics (UE   1924). An effective light suite, wittily conceived if
not strikingly original. Adroit and brilliant piano writing. M-D.

See: Robert F. Nisbett, "Louis Gruenberg: A Forgotten Figure of American
Music," *Current Musicology,* 18 (1974):90–95.

ODD GRÜNER-HEGGE (1899–   ) Norway

From Early Years (NMO 7943) Book I, 8pp.: From My Diary (1915);
Arietta (1917); Humoreske (1918); Elegi (1918). Book II, 11pp.:
Intermezzo (1918); Capriccio (1917); Novelette (1918). Post-Ro-
mantic style. Int. to M-D.

JEAN-JACQUES GRÜNEWALD (1911–   ) France

Partita (Rideau Rouge   1971) 12pp.

CAMARGO GUARNIERI (1907–   ) Brazil

"To be a Brazilian composer" was Guarnieri's motto from the beginning of
his career. Through his "Open Letter to the Musicians and Critics of

Brazil" (1950), Guarnieri exerted decisive influence on the development of Brazilian music; in this letter he asked for the preservation of national values. Many Brazilian composers of the last generation went through his "school," which was founded at that time and has been active for many years. Guarnieri founded the Coral Paulistano and the Academia Brasileira de Musica, whose president he was. He was conductor of the Municipal Symphony Orchestra of São Paulo, and since 1975 has been chief conductor of the orchestra of the University of São Paulo. Guarnieri has many other piano compositions in MS. He can be contacted about them at Rua Pamplona, 825 Apt. 83, 01–405 São Paulo (SP) Brazil.

Toada (K 1929) 3 min. Opening and closing sections a warm con muita saudade. Mid-section is a nemm rhythmado; dancelike. M-D.

Preludio e Fuga (MS 1929).

Canção Sertaneja (Ric 1928). Emotional, subtle syncopation. M-D.

Sonatina I (Ric 1928). 5 min.

Sonatina II (Ric 1934). 5 min.

Sonatina III (Ric 1937). 12 min. Three movements.

Sonatina IV (AMP 1958) 19pp. 14 min. Com Alegria; Melancolio; Gracioso. No key signatures, many accidentals, asymmetrical rhythms, uniform figurations. Concluding flowing movement with polyrhythms and countermelodies is most effective. M-D.

Sonatina VI (AMP) 14 min. A major work, a sonata in content and length. Represents some of Guarnieri's most involved thinking. Recalls some of the ideas presented in the *Estudos*. Gracioso: SA; intense; angular lines; left hand has much thematic activity. Etéreo: ABA, bitonal, much use of thirds. Humoristico, molto ritmato: a two-voice fugue; Etéreo theme of second movement returns at climax of fugue; fugue subject returns for a majestic closing. D.

Sonatina VII (Ric 1971) Copy of MS.

Improviso 1 (Ric Brazil 1957) 4pp. 3 min. A calm, wistful, Brazilian "Song Without Words." M-D. Nos.2, 3, 4 (Ric 1970).

Acalanto (Ric Brazil 1957) 2 min. Two-voice texture; lovely expressive little lullaby. From Suite IV Centario 1954. Uses only treble clef. Int.

As Tres Gracas (Ric Brazil 1963–71) 3 min. 1. Acalanto para Tânia. 2. Tanguinho para Miriam. 3. Toada para Daniel Paulo. A short suite in linear design. Folk elements seemingly permeate the pieces with a melancholy Spanish character, but no folk tunes are quoted. Int.

Valsas 1–5 (Ric Brazil 1962). 1. Lentemente. 2. Preguicoso. 3. Com Molesa. 4. Calmo e Saudoso. 5. Calmo. Published together. M-D.

Valsa 6 (Ric Brazil 1949) 3 min. Lento.

Valsa 7 (Ric Brazil 1954) 3 min. Saudoso.

Valsa 8 (Ric Brazil 1954) 3 min. Calmo.

Valsa 9 (Ric Brazil 1957) 3 min. Calmo.

Valsa 10 (Ric Brazil 1958) 4 min. Chorôso.

5 Estudos, Vol.II, 6–10 (Ric Brazil 1962) 12 min. 6. Impetuoso:

ABABA; much unison writing two octaves apart; preference for melodic interval of fourth; moves over most of keyboard in angular lines; atonal. 7. Sem Pressa (expressivo): 2 with 3 in same and both hands; polymeters; melodic; chain phrases repeated in groups; right-hand legato is vital. 8. Comodo: ABABA; left-hand study; highly chromatic; varied textures; enormous conclusion; mirror writing in final measures; large span required. 9. Furioso: ABA; 16th-note figures; bitonal; flexible meters are imperceptible; parallel motion between hands a ninth apart. 10. Movido: ABA; melody in left hand with conflicting rhythmic groupings in each hand. Well-written pieces. M-D to D. Vol.III, 11–15, 1968–70, pending.

Sonata V   1972 (MS available from composer) 21pp. Tenso; Amarqurado; Triunfante—Energico (Fuga a 3 partes). Three large virtuoso movements; thoroughly contemporary; Fuga returns to the Triunfante to conclude this brilliant sonata. D.

Sonata (Ric   1971) copy of MS.

Toada Triste (GS 1936) in collection *Latin American Art Music*. 5 min.

See: David Appleby, "Capturing Brazilian Flavor," *Clavier,* 16 (January 1977):19–20. Discusses the "Ponteios" and has a lesson on No.18.

Sister Marion Verhaalen, "The Solo Piano Music of Francisco Mignone and Camargo Guarnieri," diss., Columbia University, 1971.

————. "Guarnieri—Brazilian Nationalist," *Clavier,* 16 (January 1977): 18–19.

SOFIYA GUBAYDULINA (1931–   ) USSR

Sonata (AMP   1977). Published in collection *Two Piano Sonatas* by Young Soviet Composers. 43pp.

PELLE GUDMUNDSEN-HOLMGREEN (1932–   ) Denmark

Udstillingsbilleder (WH   1968) 13pp. Seven short pieces are contained in this "Picture Gallery." Clusters and contemporary compositional techniques are used. A large hand span plus adroit pedal techniques are requirements. D.

JEAN-PIERRE GUEZEC (1934–1971) France

Pièces pour piano (Sal   1960).

JEAN GUILLOU (1930–   ) France

Guillou completed his studies at the Paris Conservatory as a pupil of Marcel Dupré, Maurice Duruflé, and Olivier Messiaen. He is presently organist at Saint-Eustache in Paris.

Sonata I (Amphion   1974) 36pp. One unwinding movement that builds to an enormous climax. The final section unleashes blazing sonorities all over the keyboard. Strong dissonances. D.

Toccata (Leduc   c.1971) 16pp. 9 min. Some writing spread over four staves, triple trills, widely spaced, chromatic. D.

FRIEDRICH GULDA (1930–   ) Austria
Gulda is best known as an international concert pianist.
Introduction and Scherzo (Papageno   1973) 8pp.
Klavier-Kompositionen (Papageno   1971) 112pp. Play Piano Play (10
     Ubungestücke für Yuko); Sonatine; Prelude and Fugue; Variationen
     über Light My Fire; The Air from Other Planets; Variations. Introduc-
     tion by the composer.
Vier Konzertstücke (Papageno   1968) 49pp. Preface by the composer.

JESÚS GURIDI (1886–1961) Spain
Guridi studied with d'Indy and Joseph Jongen.
Ocho Apuntes (UME   1954) 19pp. Amanecer. Cancion Vasca. Danza
     Rustica. Canto de Arriero. Romanza. Cortejo Funebre. Rumor de
     Agua. Marcha Humoristica. Eight short, varied pieces written in a late
     nineteenth-century style. Int.
10 Melodias Vascas (UME).
Tres Piezas Breves 1910 (UME   1956) 11pp. Amanecer: written-out
     trills with melody embedded in the line. Nostalgia: 6/8 in right hand
     with 2/4 in left; Romantic harmonies. Serenata: dancelike, alternating
     hands, colorful. Int.
Vasconia (UME). Three pieces on popular Basque themes.

CORNELIUS GURLITT (1820–1901) Germany
A First Book (K 3497).
The Classicality Op.115 (Augener). Variations on "Ach, du lieber Augus-
     tin" in the style of various composers.
First Lessons Op.117 (K 3498).
O Sanctissima Op.135/1 (Kuhlstrom—Augener). Variations on a Sicilian
     Air.
Album for the Young Op.140 (Alfred).
Six Sonatinas (Alfred).
Musical Sketches Op.182 (Ashdown).

GENE GUTCHE (1907–   ) USA, born Germany
Piano Sonata Op.32/2 (Highgate   1973). 23pp. 18 min. One movement,
     intriguing sonorities, virtuoso writing. D.

H

POLO DE HAAS (1933–) The Netherlands
Pinos (Donemus 1973) 5 leaves.

ALOIS HÁBA (1893–1973) Czechoslovakia
Sest Nálad (Sechs Stimmungen) Op.102 (Artia 1817 1971).

YOSHIO HACHIMURA (1938–) Japan
Improvisation (Ongaku-No-Tomo 1964) 8pp. Five short pieces (sections) with variable meters, some "senza tempo." Pointillistic, harmonics, clusters, dynamic extremes. M-D.

ALEXEI HAIEFF (1914–) USA, born Siberia
Saint's Wheel (Gen).

ANDRÉ HAJDU (1932–) Israel, born Hungary
Journal from Sidi-Bou-Said (IMI 204) 10pp. 4 min. Composed in 1960 during "an intense and malevolent moment of my life" (from note in score). Short, fragmentary, strong and intense writing, complex rhythms, harmonics, pointillistic. M-D.

TALIB RASUL HAKIM (1940–) USA
Sound-Gone 1967 (Bo&Bo 22669 1976) 6pp. 10 min.

ERNESTO HALFFTER (1905–) Spain
Preludio y danza (UME 1974) 8pp.

RODOLFO HALFFTER (1900–) Mexico, born Spain
Dos Sonatas de El Escorial Op.2 (UME 1930). Reflects the spirit of D. Scarlatti and Soler with piquant bitonal vocabulary. M-D.
　　See: L. E. Powell, Jr., "Rodolfo Halffter, Domenico Scarlatti, and Kirkpatrick's Crux," AMT, 26 (June–July 1976):4–7. A discussion of the "Dos Sonatas de El Escorial" and the "Danza de Avila."
Homenaje a Arturo Rubinstein. Nocturno Op.36 (UME 1974) 14pp.
Labertino Op.34 (Coleccion Arion 1972) 19pp. Labyrinth, Four Attempts to Locate the Exit. One page of symbol descriptions; also uses conventional notation. Aleatoric, disjunct, harmonics. Same basic material used throughout but disguised. D.
Tercera Sonata Op.30 (Coleccion Arion 1968) 22pp. Allegro; Moderato cantabile; Liberamente—Lento molto espressivo; Impetuoso. Twelve-tone, indeterminate note values, clusters, some avant-garde notation, good introduction to duodecaphonic technique. D.

RICHARD HALL (1903–   ) Great Britain
Hall is a former composition teacher of the concert pianist John Ogdon.
Suite (Nov) No.7 in Virtuoso series. Prelude; Ostinato; Intermezzo;
Scherzo (with two trios); Second Ostinato; Recitative and Chorale.
"In the best sense neo-classical and suffused with a deeply-felt mysti-
cism" (John Ogdon, editor of the series). M-D.

HANS PETER HALLER (1929–   ) Germany
Sonata (Heinrichshofen 8672).

HERMANN HALLER (1914–   ) Switzerland
Elf Kleine Klavierstücke Op.26 (Hug   1961) 15pp. Short, varied charac-
ter pieces. Large span required. Int.
Sonata (Heinrichshofen/Sirius   1972) 24pp.

SHOJI HAMAGUCHI (1899–   ) Japan
Hamaguchi worked with Emmanuel Metter and studied in the USA, Germany, and France.
Autumn (Japan Federation of Composers) 5pp. Koto-inspired, melancholy, triadic with some quartal harmonies, slow opening, increased
tempo from middle of the work. M-D.

IAIN HAMILTON (1922–   ) Scotland
Piano Sonata I (TP   1973) 24pp. Originally published by Schott in 1951
as Op.13. Three movements. Rhythmic and contrapuntal motives com-
bined in a swirling chromatic texture, Bartók influence. D.
Piano Sonata II (TP   1976) 20pp. 12 min. Five short continuous sections: Placido; Con bravura; Sospeso; Espansivo; Moto perpetuo.
Elaborate, dazzling; combines florid figuration with driving rhythms.
Strong dissonances, clusters, brilliant cadenza. Large span required. D.
Palinodes 1972 (TP   1975) 22pp. Seven imaginative studies after lines
of Rimbaud (1854–1891), the famous French poet. A quotation from
Rimbaud precedes each work. Some of the music seems to be program-
matically connected to the poems and contains wild images, dreams,
etc. Strong complex writing involving clusters, pointillistic treatment,
pliable rhythms, glissandi, fast atonal figuration. Highly original
pieces. Require virtuoso technique and superb musicianship. D.
See: David Burge, "Five New Pieces," CK, 3 (December 1977):66.
Discusses "Palinodes."

GEORGE FREDERIC HANDEL (1685–1759) Germany
Hallischer Händel-Ausgabe (Br) Series IV, Vol.IV. 37 miscellaneous key-
board pieces known only from contemporary MS copies, including
the Aylesford pieces. Introduction in German. No.19, Air, is very
lovely, and No.34, Courante, is as fine as any in the "Eight Great"
Suites. No.30, Air, is delightful. Int. to M-D.
Vol.17, II: *Miscellaneous Suites and Pieces* (Peter Northway—Br).
Excellent preface; scholarly. Seven suites, one prelude, and two cha-

connes, originally published in 1733. Varied style. Int. to M-D. III: *Miscellaneous Suites and Pieces* (Terence Best—Br). Shorter pieces such as Preludes, Sonatas, Suites. Excellent preface and edition. Int. to M-D.

Sixteen Suites (K 3508, 3509) Vols.I, II.

Suite No.3 d (James Erber—CFP 7215). Erber includes notes and a table of ornaments with realizations. Improvisatory Prelude leads to Allegro (fuga), Allemand, Courante, Air with 5 Doubles, Presto. The Air is a rare case where Handel wrote out the full ornamented line. Florid passagework; not for small hands. M-D.

23 Easy Dances and Pieces (Pfeiffer—CFP 5019).

6 Fughettas (PWM).

16 Small Pieces (Lajos Hernadi—EMB). Embellishments realized, well edited. Int.

Handel—An Introduction to His Keyboard Works (G. Lucktenberg—Alfred). Contains in addition to the music, biographical information, bibliography, hints on interpretation, and information about Handel's instruments. Most of the pieces in the first half of the collection are taken from the Aylesford MSS and represent Handel's teaching pieces in a variety of moods and types. From p.28 to the end of the book, pieces are grouped according to key so that they may be played in sequence as "suites" of two or more movements if desired, in accordance with eighteenth-century practice. Easy to M-D.

A Handel Album (E. C. Scholz—UE 1959) 17 short, well-edited, easy pieces.

Handel—A First Book (K 3507) 25pp. Corrente F. Menuetto I and II. Sonatina B♭. Sarabanda d and variation. Giga d. Sonata C. Gavotta C. Air G. Allemande g. Gavotta con (5) Variazioni G. Corrente G. Int.

Il Mio Primo Handel (Pozzoli—Ric E. R. 1954) 19pp. Menuets F, F. Sonatine B♭. Corrente F. Sarabanda g. Gigue B♭. Fughetta C. Sarabanda d with variations. Fughetta D. Preludio G. Allegro g. Allemande g. Int. to M-D.

Handel, The First Book for Young Pianists (G. Lucktenberg—Alfred 1977) 24pp.

Easy Graded Handel (J. Ching—K. Prowse) 32pp. Air G from Suite No.14. Allegro d from Suite No.10. Allegro F from Suite No.2. Allemande f from Suite No.8. Chaconne G with Variations. Courante G from Suite No.14. Gavotte G. Gigue e from Suite No.4. Minuet d from Suite No.11. Minuet I F, and II F from "Seven Pieces." Prelude G from "Seven Pieces." Sarabande d with Variations from Suite 11. Highly edited. Int. to M-D.

Concerto in "Judas Maccabaeus" (Frederick Hudson—Br 6212) for organ, harpsichord, or piano. First edition. In his preface the editor provides a detailed account of the sources, history, and background of the various stages of the Concerto as summarized in the essay "Das 'Concerto' in Judas Maccabaeus identifiziert," *Händel–Jahrbuch* 1974–75.

Handel Album Vol.I (EMB 6990): Corrente e due menuetti F. Fantaisie C. Fugues a, G. Praeludium a, D. Sonata C. Suites G, G. Vol.II (EMB 6991): Chaconne G. Fugues b, B♭, c. Suites B♭, C, g. Clear, unencumbered edition. Int. to M-D.

See: Robert Dumm, "Performer's Analysis of a Handel Capriccio," *Clavier,* 14 (November 1975):24–28. Includes score.

Franklin B. Zimmerman, *G. F. Handel: Index of Themes, Titles and First-Lines* (Pennsylvania Pro Musica, 4816 Beaumont Ave., Philadelphia, PA 19143, 1976).

HOWARD HANSON (1896–   ) USA

For the First Time (CF) 31pp. A suite of twelve evocative pieces written in varied style with diverse tonal vocabulary. Includes commentary on the pieces. Int. to M-D.

HIROSHI HARA (1933–   ) Japan

21 Etudes (Ongaku-No-Tomo 1967) 69pp. Each etude is titled: Boîte à musique; Berceuse de Blanche Neige; Pinocchio; March pour Don Quichotte; Valse pour la Traviata; Le fils d' "Erlkönig"; etc. Programmatic, thin textures, tonal, special technical emphasis and treatment in each etude. Int. to M-D.

Toccata (Zen-On 301 1971) 8pp. Strong rhythms; freely chromatic around a. M-D.

LOU HARRISON (1917–   ) USA

Homage to Milhaud (Hinshaw 1978) in collection *Twelve by Eleven.* Flexible meters, simple flowing lines, motivic extension, tonal, thin textures. Int.

Reel, Homage to Henry Cowell (Hinshaw 1978) in collection *Twelve by Eleven.* A fine Irish-like tune is treated with all black keys in right hand, white keys in left hand, except where indicated. 16th-note palm and arm clusters. Thin textures contrast with thick clusters. Cowell would have approved of this piece. Int. to M-D.

Gigue and Musette 1941 (MS available from composer, 7163 View Point Rd., Aptos, CA 95003) 2pp. Gigue: arpeggi in triplets juxtaposed against longer melodic line, harmonic ninths in left hand. Musette: diatonic lines, nimble rhythms. Int.

Ground in E Minor 1936, rev.1970 (MS available from composer) 1p. Two-voiced syncopated lines, seven-bar ground heard five times. Perhaps more effective on harpsichord but also comes off well on the piano. Int.

Third Piano Sonata 1938, edited 1970 (MS available from composer) 8pp. Slowish and singing: freely chromatic with dramatic one-bar opening; builds to expressive rhapsodic surges; many harmonic major seconds;

pp closing. Fast and rugged: syncopated octotonic lines interspersed with punctuated chords; large leaps. Very slow, very solemn and singing: lyric octaves in right hand duplicated two octaves below in left hand. Narrow dynamic range *pp–f;* subtle and sensitive. M-D.

Western Dance 1947 (MS available from composer) 4pp. Strong rhythms, thin textures, freely tonal around e, short *ff* dramatic closing. Alto clef used for part of this piece. M-D.

Largo Ostinato 1937, rev.1970 (MS available from composer) 4pp. A subtly sensuous ostinato in alternating harmonic sixths provides the support for the development of a lyric line of powerful simplicity. A highly original work. M-D.

Prelude and Sarabande (NME   July 1938). Octotonic, dramatic. Large chords, plucked strings, harmonics. M-D.

Six Sonatas (PIC). Reprint of the 1943 NME publication.

WALTER S. HARTLEY (1927–   ) USA
3 Moods for Piano (EBM   1975).

KARL AMADEUS HARTMANN (1905–1963) Germany
Jazz-Toccata and Fugue (Schott   1928) 19pp. Toccata opens with a boogie ostinato; fugal-coda in the Charleston concludes fugue. Hindemith-oriented. M-D.

Sonatine (Schott   1931) 12pp. One short, atonal movement. Percussive, Stravinsky-oriented. Glissandi, tremolando effects, changing meters. D.

JONATHAN HARVEY (1939–   ) Great Britain
Four Images after Yeats (Nov   1969) 25 min. Also available from Blackwell's in microfiche.

Piano Sonata (Blackwell's). 58pp. Available with the above work in microfiche.

HANS LEO HASSLER (1564–1612) Germany
Ausgewählte Werke für Orgel (Cembalo) (Georges Kiss—Schott   1971) 70pp. "The pieces of our collection come from a previously unknown ms written between 1637 and 1640 probably for the Fugger family" (from the preface). Toccata e fuga noni toni; Ricercar del secondo toni; Ricercar a; Fuga a; Fantasia ut re mi fa sol la; Magnificat quarti toni; Canzon; Canzon. Most of these pieces sound well on the piano. M-D.

Ich gieng einmal spatieren (G. Kiss—Schott   1971) 39pp. Variations.

JOHANN WILHELM HÄSSLER (1746–1822) Germany
Fantasia I c (Farrenc—Leduc) 7pp. Allegro–Presto–Andante. M-D.

Fantasia II E♭ (Farrenc—Leduc) 4pp. Allegretto moderato; Minuetto. Int.

2 Solos (Farrenc—Leduc) in e, F. Each is three movements; could have been titled sonatas. M-D.

Sonata A (Farrenc—Leduc). Untitled first movement; Adagio; Allegro. M-D.

ROMAN HAUBENSTOCK-RAMATI (1919–   ) Austria, born Poland

Catch 2 (UE   1968). For one or two pianos. Ten loose leaves.
Chordophonie I (WH) for keyboard.
Chordophonie II (WH) for keyboard.

CHARLES HAUBIEL (1892–   ) USA

Madonna (Composer's Press). The madonna and child are paid musical
    homage. Large span required. M-D.
Metamorphoses (Composer's Press). Variations on a theme of Stephen
    Foster. The tune is subjected to a series of treatments in medieval,
    Romantic, post-Romantic, twentieth-century, experimentalist, and,
    finally, American jazz style. D.
Snowflakes (Composer's Press). Serene, Romantic-style pedal study. M-D.

JOSEF MATTHIAS HAUER (1883–1959) Germany

Hauer was an early exponent of tone-row composition and wrote several
books on the subject.
Nomos Op.19   1919 (Dob   1976) 18pp. Twelve-tone; row unwinds in
    numerous guises but not always strictly. Complete metronomic details
    are listed. M-D.

LUKAS HAUG (1921–   ) Germany

Diatonisch—Dodekaphonisch (Noetzel   1972) 10pp. 2 × 4 easy studies
    for youth. Four pieces in diatonic writing. Four pieces in 12-tone writ-
    ing. Good introduction to easy 12-tone writing. Int.
Spielbuch für Martina (Noetzel   1973) 35pp.
Spielbuch für Wiltrud (Noetzel   1973) 38pp.

MITSUAKI HAYAMA (1932–   ) Japan

Piano Sonata (Ongaku-No-Tomo   1960) 32pp. 18 min. Allegro assai;
    Lento; Allegro molto. Large dramatic gestures, freely chromatic, big
    chordal skips, virtuoso character. D.

AZUSA HAYASHI (1936–   ) Japan

Preludes (Japan Federation of Composers   1972) "Mai" (Movement)
    71pp. Seven extensive pieces written in an improvisational, Impres-
    sionistic, modal style. MS is beautiful and easy to read. M-D.
Suite (Japan Federation of Composers   1967) 39pp. Playing a Ball;
    Whirling a Pinwheel; Song of a Turtledove; Tag; Tune of a Straw-
    pipe. Based on children's songs. Similar to a five-movement sonatine.
    MC. M-D.

HIKARU HAYASHI (1931–   ) Japan

Hayashi studied composition with Hisatada Otaka and Tomojiro Ikenouchi.
Sonata (Ongaku-No-Tomo   1965) 15pp. Fluid motivic development in
    each movement, freely chromatic. Andante: extreme dynamic range.
    Allegro: much rhythmic drive. Sostenuto e pesante: sonorous, free
    metric usage, many octaves. D.

FRANZ JOSEPH HAYDN (1732–1809) Austria

Sonatas (Georg Feder—Henle). Vol.I, 1971; Vols.II and III, 1972. Henle now has all the sonatas available in three volumes. Fingering has been added by Hans-Martin Theopold. Preface is in German, French, and English. This is the same edition as the sonatas in the Complete Edition of the Haydn Works, Series XVIII, vols.1, 2, and 3. See chart below for identification of sonatas in individual volumes.

Selected Sonatas (Sliwinski—PWM 1974) Contains Sonata D, H.XVI: 19; Sonata C, H.XVI:20; Sonata F, H.XVI:23; Sonata E♭, H.XVI: 28; Sonata b, H.XVI:32; Sonata A♭, H.XVI:43; Sonata G, H.XVI: 40; Sonata E♭, H.XVI:49. Includes notes on sources, ornamentation, and articulation. Ornaments are frequently realized, and alternate readings from other sources are shown. Essential fingering given. M-D. Available separately: (Martienssen—CFP). Sonata D, H.XVI:19. Sonata c, H.XVI:20. Sonata F, H.XVI:23. Sonata e, H.XVI:34. Sonata C, H.XVI:35. Sonata c♯, H.XVI:36. Sonata D, H.XVI:37. Sonata E♭, H.XVI:38. Sonata G, H.XVI:39. Sonata A♭, H.XVI:46. Sonata C, H.XVI:48. Sonata E♭, H.XVI:49. Sonata E♭, H.XVI:52.

The Easiest Original Haydn Pieces for the Piano (A. Rowley—Hin 4) 22pp. Divertimento D, H.XVI:4; Minuet and Finale from Sonata A, H.XVI:26; Minuetto from Sonata B♭, H.XVI:2; Arietta con Variazioni E♭, H.XVII:3; Adagio from Sonata G, H.XVI:6; Finale from Sonata D, H.XVI:24. Int. to M-D.

Sonatinas (R. Dumm—BMC) 28pp. Six of the early Divertimenti dating from around 1760. The editor has realized ornaments in a most tasteful manner. Also includes a helpful foreword and editorial notes. No.I G, H.XVI:8. No.II G, H.XVI:11. No.III C, H.XVI:7. No.IV F, H.XVI:9. No.V C, H.XVI:10. No.VI D, XVI:4. Int.

Six Sonatinas (Palmer—Alfred).

Six Divertimenti (Sonatinas) (CFP 4443).

14 Dances and Pieces (CFP 5004).

12 Short Pieces (CFP 1120).

12 Minuets (Nana Krieger—UE). Based on early editions and autographs. Short. Easy to Int.

Il mio primo Haydn ("My First Haydn") (Rattalino—Ric) 21pp. Based on MS and first editions; no editing except fingering. Hoboken numbers given. Quadrille C, H.IX:29/6. Country Dance B♭, H.IX:29/2. 3 German Dances, H.IX:10/8–10. Gypsy Dance D, H.IX:28/3. Gypsy Dance d, H.IX:28/4. Minuet E♭, H.IX:3/7. Minuet D, H.IX:3/5. Minuet D, H.IX:8/5. 12 New German Dances, H.IX:12. Contains mainly dances. Provides an excellent approach to the composer for the young pianist. More suitable for an introduction to Haydn than are the Sonatas and Variations. Easy to Int.

A Digest of Short Piano Works (P. Zeitlin, D. Goldberger—BMC 1972)

Haydn's Keyboard Sonatas
As Numbered in Hoboken Catalogue and Nine Editions

Key	Universal (Vienna Urtext) (C. Landon)	Haydn Urtext (Feder) Vol.I	Breitkopf & Härtel (Päsler)	Schirmer (Klee and Lebert) and Presser	Peters (Martienssen)	Breitkopf & Härtel (Zilcher)	Universal (Rauch)	Associated (Raymar)	Augener (Pauer)	Hoboken Catalogue
G	1	I	8		D.4					XVI: 8
C	2	I	7		D.5					XVI: 7
F	3	I	9		D.6	42				XVI: 9
G	4	I App. mvts. 2, 3								XVI: G1
G	5	I	11		11	31				XVI: 11
C	6	I	10		43					XVI: 10
D	7	I								XVII: D1
A	8	I	5		23	41				XVI: 5
D	9	I	4		D.3					XVI: 4
C	10	I	1		D.1					XVI: 1
Bb	11	I	2		22	40		3		XVI: 2
A	12	I	12		29	28	5		11	XVI: 12
G	13	I	6		37	36	22		15	XVI: 6
C	14	I	3		D.2					XVI: 3
E	15	I	13	17	18	18	4		7	XVI: 13

145

Concordance of Haydn piano sonata numberings (keys and catalogue numbers):

Key	Universal (Vienna Urtext) (C. Landon)	Haydn Urtext I (Feder)	Breitkopf & Härtel 14 (Päsler)	Schirmer 14 (Klee and Lebert) and Presser	Peters 15 (Martienssen)	Breitkopf & Härtel 15 (Zilcher)	Universal 3 (Rauch)	Associated 2 (Raymar)	Augener 4 (Pauer)	Hoboken Catalogue
D	16	I								XVI: 14
E♭	17	I								XVI: 47ii, iii, iv
E♭	18	I	18	18	19	19	28		8	XVI: 18
E	19	I								
B♭	20	I App.								XVI: 2a lost
d	21	I App.								XVI: 2b lost
A	22	I App.								XVI: 2c lost
B	23	I App.								XVI: 2d lost
B♭	24	I App.								XVI: 2e lost
e	25	I App.								XVI: 2g lost
C	26	I App.								XVI: 2h lost
A	27	I								
D	28	I						8		XVI: 5 fragment survives
E♭	29	I	45		26	25	30		21	XVI: 45
D	30	I	19	9	9	9	16		20	XVI: 19
A♭	31	I	46	8	8	8	31		28	XVI: 46
g	32	I	44	4	4	4	33		23	XVI: 44
c	33	II	20		25	24	26		27	XVI: 20
D	34	III	33	19	20	20	11		9	XVI: 33
A♭	35	III	43	15	41	11				XVI: 43
C	36	II	21		16	16	23		5	XVI: 21
E	37	II	22		40	39	19		26	XVI: 22

147

32pp. Fourteen original pieces and pieces based on Haydn's transcriptions of movements from his symphonies and string quartets. Unfamiliar and familiar works. Outstanding preface. Int.

A First Haydn Book (K 3523) 12pp. 6 German Dances; 6 pieces from "12 Easy Pieces"; Arietta con Variazioni E♭ (only the Arietta); Finale from Sonata C; Arietta con Variazioni A (Arietta and Var.2). Easy—Int.

The Young Pianist's Guide to Haydn (Y. Novik—Studio P/R 1978) 24pp. Includes 6 German Dances; 2 Minuets; and 2 Prestos, a Scherzo, and Andante movements from various sonatas. Edited for the piano tastefully. Record of the contents included. Int.

Easy Graded Haydn (J. Ching—K. Prowse) 32pp. Air and Variations (La Roxolane); Allegro from Sonata C; Allegro from Sonata e; Allegro from Sonata G; Arietta e♭; Finale from Sonata D; Larghetto from Sonata F; 2 Minuets C; Theme and Variations from Sonata A. Int. to M-D.

Haydn (H. Ferguson—OUP 1972) 62pp. Part of the Oxford Keyboard Classics series. Includes: Variations f, H.XVII:6; Fantasia C, H.XVII:4; Sonatas c, H.XVI:20 and A, H.XVI:26; and a few shorter pieces, i.e., Divertimento G, H.XVI:8; Adagio, H.XVI:6; Allegretto, H.XVI:40; and Menuet, H.XIX:9. Discusses instruments of the period as well as dynamics, pedaling, phrasing, and articulation. Includes comments on the specific works. Int. to M-D.

Original Compositions (Soldan—CFP 4392). Arietta con Variazioni A; Arietta con Variazioni E♭; Capriccio G; Fantasia C; Tema con Variazioni C; Variations (Andante Variée f). M-D.

Piano Pieces (VU UT50047). Edited from autographs, MS copies, and first editions. Fingering added by Franz Eibner and Gerschon Jarecki. Informative preface and critical notes. This is the largest collection of Haydn piano pieces so far, including transcriptions as well as original works. Contents: Capriccio G, H.XVII:1; Fantasia C, H.XVII:4; 20 Variations G, H.XVII:2; Arietta I E♭, H.XVII:3; Arietta II a, H.XVII:2; 6 Easy Variations C, H.XVII:5; Andante con Variazioni f, H.XVII:6; Variations on "Gott erhalte" after H.III:77[II]; Adagio F, H.XVII:9; Adagio G, H.XV:22[II]; Allegretto G, H.XVII:10; Allegretto G, H.III:41[IV]; Il Maestro e Scolare (Sonata for 4 hands) H.XVIIa:1; piano setting of song "Gott erhalte" H.XXVIa:43. A superb volume in spite of some curious editorial policies. Int. to M-D.

Anson Introduces Haydn (Willis). Twelve German Dances, all in binary form. Int.

Andante B♭ with (4)Variations (Robert Taylor—TP 1974). Based on an 1870 edition. Attributed to Haydn. Charming classical style with ornamentation and running figuration. Helpful editorial notes by the editor. H.XVII:12. Int. to M-D.

Variations (Z. Sliwiński—PWM   1976).

See: A. Peter Brown, "A Re-Introduction to Joseph Haydn's Keyboard Works," PQ, 79 (Fall 1972):42–47. Recent research and editions of works from Hoboken's groups XIV, XV, XVI, XVII, and XVIIa are reviewed. Two tables collate the numberings of the solo sonatas and piano trios in the Hoboken catalogue and major editions.

————. "Problems of Authenticity in two Haydn Keyboard Works" (H.XVI:47 and H.XVI:7), JAMS, 25 (Spring 1972):85–97.

————. "The Structure of the Expositions in Haydn's Keyboard Sonatas," MR, 36 (May 1975):102–29.

Paul Henry Lang, "Haydn at the Keyboard," HF (January 1977):106–108. A most perceptive review of recordings of the piano sonatas.

Egon Willfort, "Haydn's Compositions for Mechanical Instruments," MT, 63 (1932):510.

MICHAEL HAYDN (1737–1806) Austria

Leichte Spielstücke (Peter Heilbut—Hug   1973) 12pp. Preface in German. Easy variations.

JACK HAWES (1916–   ) Great Britain

Toccata (CF). Lively and attractive "toccata" writing in traditional techniques. Rapid octaves, full chords. A technically rewarding excursion that "sounds" and will dazzle an audience. M-D.

ROBERTO HAZON (1930–   ) Italy

Preludi alla notte (EC   1974) 82pp. Preface by Mario Delli Ponti, introduction by Lorenzo Arruga in Italian. Contents: Lontanaza. Assenza. Cammino. Ricordo. Dimora. Corale. Soltanto una Voce. Strade. Quasi fuga. Sbarre. Pianura. Accettazione.

CHRISTOPHER HEADINGTON (1930–   ) Great Britain

Piano Sonatas 1, 2 (Blackwell's) 59pp. Microfiche.

5 Preludes   1953 (JWC).

Toccata   1962 (JWC).

ANTHONY HEDGES (1931–   ) Great Britain

Hedges received his education at Oxford University and the Royal Scottish Academy of Music. He is presently Senior Lecturer in Music at Hull University.

Five Preludes Op.5 (Roberton   1959).

Four Pieces Op.20 (Chappell   1966). Serial; sonatalike characteristics. M-D.

Masquerade (UE   1961). Album of 14 educational pieces.

Playground (UE   1959). Album of 15 educational pieces.

Scherzetto (Ric   1963).

Sonata (Chappell).

See: Ernest Bradbury, "Anthony Hedges," MT, 1555 (September 1972): 858–61.

MAGNE GUNNAR HEGDAL (1944–   ) Norway
Three Prunes   1972 (NMO 8947   1977) 6pp. Salon music for piano.

WERNER HEIDER (1930–   ) Germany
Fauststück (Gerig   1970).
Landschaftspartitur (Litolff   1968) 10 leaves. 6 min. Explanations of symbols in English and German. Stockhausen influence, traditional piano techniques, unusual construction and musical content. Avant-garde. D.
Modi (Ahn & Simrock   1959).

PETER HEILBUT (1920–   ) Germany
Sonatinas E, G (Heinrichshofen   1976) 15pp.

PAAVO HEININEN (1938–   ) Finland
Toccata Op.1 (Finnish Music Centre   1956) 10pp. 4 min. Constant eighth-note motion. Harmonic interval of fourth is present by itself and in many chordal structures. Freely tonal and centers around C. Martial quality in some sections, changing meters, effective. D.
Sonatine Op.2 (Westerlund   1957) 15pp. 9 min. Allegro; Largo lugubre; Presto. Freely chromatic, no time signatures, large chords plus octotonic writing, atonal, M-D.
Libretto della primavera Op.28 (Finnish Music Centre   1971). Op.28a: Sonatine della primavera: 11 min. Five contrasting movements, serial, thin textures, linear, atonal, pointillistic. D. Op.28b: Due danze della primavera: 6 min. Op.28c: Piccola poesia della primavera: 5 min.

ANTON PHILIP HEINRICH (1781–1861) USA, born Bohemia.
Called the "Beethoven of America," Heinrich was completely untrained musically, but wrote some of the most original music of his day. In many ways Heinrich's accomplishments can be equated with those of Charles Ives.
The Dawning of Music in Kentucky, or the Pleasures of Harmony in the Solitudes of Nature (opera prima); *The Western Minstrel* (opera secunda) (Da Capo) Earlier Music Series, Vol.10, edited by H. Wiley Hitchcock. Both works were originally printed in Philadelphia in 1820. Surely the most daring first opus ever written. The pieces range all the way from simple tunes set at about Int. level to virtuoso settings. Deserves more investigation.
Song Without Words   1850 (Hinshaw) in collection *Piano Music in Nineteenth Century America,* Vol.I. Written in honor of Jenny Lind's first tour of the USA. Charming, elegant, and hauntingly beautiful. Int. to M-D.
The Debarkation March (A-R Editions) in collection *Anthology of Early American Keyboard Music 1787–1830.*

Toccatina capriciosa (A-R Editions) in collection *Anthology of Early American Keyboard Music 1787–1830*.

JOHN HEISS (1938–) USA

Heiss teaches theory, chamber music, and music literature at the New England Conservatory. He has a degree in mathematics from Lehigh University and an MM from Princeton University.

Four Short Pieces (Bo&H 1975). One page each. Schönberg idiom. Tightly compressed writing, slow tempi. Interpretive problems require mature pianism. Would make a good preparatory study for the Schönberg Op.19. M-D.

WALTER HEKSTER (1937–) Netherlands

Hekster studied composition with Gardner Read at Boston University.

Derivations (Donemus 1965) 9pp. 7 min. Reproduction of the composer's poor MS. Seven pieces, avant-garde, musical content questionable.

Pinoa (Donemus 1971) 15 min.

Sonata (Donemus 1966) 15pp. Reproduction of composer's MS.

Studies in Spatial Notation (Donemus 1970) 8pp. 6 min. Reproduction of MS. Notes only in English. Play; Soundings; Clusters; Night Play; Robust. Written "as an introduction to a new kind of free notation. Ordinary note values are disregarded and instead a new system has been developed. . . . Time is measured visually, that is, the distance between notes varies depending on the amount of space between them." This is not new and has been around since the early 1950s. D.

HALLGRIMUR HELGASON (1914–) Iceland

Sonata II (Edition Gigjan, P.O. Box 121, Reykjavik, Iceland) 16pp. Allegro arctico: freely tonal, nineteenth-century figuration, contrasting ideas, big conclusion. Adagio non troppo: melody treated in various guises; fast harmonic rhythm. Rondo: contrasted sections in 4/4, 6/8, 2/4. Folk-tune element present. M-D.

Rondo Islanda (Edition Gigjan 1954) 7pp. A jiglike dance, flexible meters, freely tonal, folk-like tunes. Int. to M-D.

STEPHEN HELLER (1813–1888) France, born Hungary

Heller Rediscovered (Alec Rowley—Lengnick) Book 1, Miniatures. Book 2, Preludes. Book 3, Mood Pictures. Book 4, Dances. Book 5, Nature Sketches. Selected from the best of the composer's entire works. The pianist who dips into these attractive collections, whether in the course of study or merely for recreation, has a real treat in store. Heller's music is ageless. Freedom from sentimentality, impeccable workmanship, and refinement and simplicity of outlook go to the making of a miniaturist whose sole object was to perpetuate beauty. Int.

56 Studies and Pieces (A. Alexander—ABRSM) Vol.I. Easy to Int. Vol. II. M-D.

See: Hippolyte Barbedette, *Stephen Heller: His Life and Works,* trans.
Robert Brown-Borthwick (Reprint of the first English ed. [London,
1877], Detroit: Information Coordinators), 89pp.

DAVID HELLEWELL (1932–   ) Hungary
Zongoradarab (EMB   1976) 8pp.

ROBERT HELPS (1928–   ) USA
Music for Left Hand (AMP   1976) 13pp. 8½ min. Three etudes. Contrasting. D.

Nocturne (CFP   1973) 16pp. 9 min. "All expressive indications, including tempo, dynamics and pedal, are to be viewed freely; rubato is
hardly indicated but should be allowed extensively. The printed page
suggests only one possibility, approximately notated" (from notes in
score). Varied tempi, moods, and meters; climaxes; colorful pedal
effects; complex; wide keyboard range; triplet followed by duplet figuration gives "rocking" motion; chromatic; rhythm treated flexibly
throughout. D.
See: David Burge, "New Pieces, Part II," CK, 4 (January 1978):50.

Quartet   1962 (CFP   1972) 22pp. 20 min. Prelude: Lento; intervals
gradually increase from a unison to a ninth; hypnotic effect. Confron-
tation: Con passione, dramatic sweeping gestures, pointillistic, chromatic, syncopation, ostinati. Intermezzo: Tempo rubato; quiet; interval of second exploited. Postlude: Andante; wide-skipping right hand
over chordal left hand; mid-section more expressionistically treated;
four staves required to notate last three pages, which include some
highly refined sonorities. D.

Trois Hommages (CFP   1975) 17pp. 9 min. Hommage à Fauré; Hommage à Rachmaninoff; Hommage à Ravel. Written in each composer's
style, slightly modernized by Helps. An eminently attractive pianistic
group. M-D.

OSCAR VAN HEMEL (1892–   ) The Netherlands
Fantasia; 10 pianostukjes (Alsbach).
Humoresque (B&VP   1942) 3 min.
Kleine suite   1936 (Donemus).
2me Sonate   1945 (Heuwekemeijer).
Tema con variazioni   1955 (Donemus) 10 min.
Vier oorlogspreludes   1945 (B&VP).

CARLO HEMMERLING (1903–1967) Switzerland
Petite Suite (Foetisch 7560) 11pp. Marchette; Arietta; Valsette; Polkette;
Giguette. Each piece is based on the name of the student association
of the Lausanne Conservatory, ADAEDC. Romantic harmonies. Int.

GERALD HENGEVELD (1910–   ) The Netherlands
A la maniere de Monsieur Erik Satie (B&VP 1289).

Partita Rhythmique (B&VP 1145   1974). Prelude; Allemande; Courante; Sarabande; Gavotte; Musette; Gigue. Looks like and inspired by Bach, but the syncopation and stress signs clearly give it a later sound. M-D.

MICHAEL HENNAGIN (1936–   ) USA
Hennagin teaches at the University of Oklahoma.
Sonata (Walton Music Corp.   1977) 20pp. One movement of solid contemporary writing. Wide skips, jazz influence, frantic movement around the keyboard, quiet closing. Displays a strong compositional talent. Virtuoso demands are made on the performer, and the results provide a fine new work for the repertoire. D.

ADOLF HENSELT (1814–1889) Germany
24 Preludes (Musica Obscura). Short pieces, some only one line long. M-D.
Chanson de Printemps (Century).
Four Romances Op.18 (Musica Obscura).
See: Raymond Lewenthal, "Henselt—A Look at a Fantastic Romanticist," *Clavier,* 13 (April 1974):17–20. The piano pieces *La Fontaine* Op. 6/2 and *Petite Valse* Op.28/1 are contained in this issue.

LOUIS JOSEPH FERDINAND HEROLD (1791–1833) France
Rondeau turc facile et brillant Op.47 (Heuwekemeijer   1971). 9pp. Reprint of original edition.

HUGO HERRMANN (1896–1967) Germany
Cherubinische Sonate (Sikorski 396   1956) 11pp. Toccata epiphania: short introduction; rest of movement based on choral "Veni creator"; single line with parallel chords; freely centered around G. Choralvariationen: theme based on Advent song "O Heiland reiss den Himmel auf"; followed by six short contrasting variations; big chordal conclusion. Festiva resurrectionis: based on an Easter alleluia; octotonic; parallel chords; freely tonal around e-E; neoclassic. M-D.
Liturgische Fantasien (Tonos   1966) 14pp. 13 min. Litanei. Offertorium. Credo. Flagellation. Mette. Abendmahl. Gloria. Freely tonal, quartal and quintal harmonies, colorful contrasts. Large span required. M-D.

PETER HERRMANN (1941–   ) Germany
Toccata and Fugue (CFP   1974) 9pp.

HENRI HERZ (1803–1888) Germany
Variations brillantes sur "The Last Rose of Summer" Op.159 (Musica Obscura).

HEINRICH VON HERZOGENBERG (1843–1900) Austria
Eight Variations Op.3 (UWKR 41   1975) 15pp. Similar in character and design to the Brahms "Variations on an Original Theme" Op. 21/1. M-D.
Variations on the Minuet from Don Giovanni Op.58 (J. Rieter—Bieder-

mann 1889) 19pp. Independent style; fades out quietly with a hauntingly beautiful coda. A remarkable set, well able to stand among other
similar masterpieces from this period. M-D.

Capricien Op.107 (J. Rieter—Biedermann 1900) 17pp. A set of variations based on a theme formed from the initials of a friend's name.
Ends with a fugue similar to a Reger double fugue. M-D to D.

WILLY HESS (1906–   ) Switzerland

Theme mit Variationen Op.18 (Eulenburg 1974) 16pp. A ten-bar theme
is followed by ten contrasted variations. Romantic themes and harmonies; final variation is the most extended. M-D.

Suite B♭ Op.45 (Hug 1956) 9pp. Praeludium; Siziliano; Intermezzo I;
Menuett I, II; Intermezzo II; Gavotte; Gigue. Neobaroque. Int. to
M-D.

KURT HESSENBERG (1908–   ) Germany

Eight Inventions Op.1 (Müller 1930). Some two-, some three-part. Hindemith-oriented. M-D.

Sieben kleine Klavierstücke Op.12 (Schott 1941).

Sonatine Op.17 (Müller). M-D.

Kleine Hausmusik für Klavier. 14 Bagatellen Op.24 (Schott 1942). Int.

Zehn kleine Präludien für klavier oder Clavichord Op.35 (Schott 1949).
Int.

Sonata I Op.78 (WH).

Sonata II Op.79 (WH).

JAMES HEWITT (1770–1827) USA, born Great Britain

Hewitt was a leader of the Court Orchestra of George III before coming to
America in 1792. He was active in New York as a music publisher, concert
violinist, director of theater orchestras, and organist of Trinity Church.

The Battle of Trenton (E. Power Biggs—Merion 1974). Arranged for
the organ. Dedicated to George Washington. This piece was originally
written for solo piano, and this arrangement could easily be played
on the piano. Pictorial subtitles (à la Satie) indicate the musical intention for the various sections. M-D. Also found in abbreviated form
in collection *Music from the Days of George Washington* (AMS
Press).

Mark My Alfred With Variations in *A Collection of Early American Keyboard Music* (Willis). Printed in New York in 1808; based on the tune
we know as "Twinkle, Twinkle, Little Star," the same tune used by
Mozart for his famous set, K.265. Both sets are full of charm and
childlike humor. The Hewitt set contains ten variations. Int. to M-D.

JACKSON HILL (1941–   ) USA

Hill studied composition with Iain Hamilton and received his Ph.D. from
the University of North Carolina at Chapel Hill.

Three Fantasies 1965 (MS available from composer: c/o Music Department, Bucknell University, Lewisburg, PA 17837) 6pp. Dolente: atonal, spread-out sonorities, clusters, serial influence. Lirico: long pedals add to dense dissonance; expressive opening and closing. Pezzato: expressionistic, pointillistic, short. M-D.

Three Pieces for Children 1967 (MS available from composer). Gremlin. Nocturne. March. Clever, appealing for sophisticated children. Int.

LEJAREN HILLER (1924–   ) USA

Sonata I 1946, rev. 1968 (MS available from composer: c/o Music Department, State University of New York, Buffalo, NY 14214) 20 min. Four movements.

Sonata II 1947, rev. 1953 (MS available from composer) 20 min. Three movements.

Seven Artifacts 1948, rev.1972 (MS available from composer). Seven pieces to be played as a unit. String of Pearls; Palindrome; Plinth; Filigree; Clockwork; Blue Triangle; Ormolu. Investigates novel scales, structures and harmonic systems. String of Pearls: written entirely in the three "string-of-pearls" scales that consist of alternating half-tone and whole-tone steps. Palindrome: can be read frontwards or backwards, based on a tritone transposition at its midpoint, which produces inversion symmetry as well as front-to-back symmetry. Plinth: a short piece also based on harmonic symmetry based on the tritone; the melodic line is built on five-beat phrase groups that skip out of coordination to a harmonic structure based upon four-beat periods. The other pieces need no explanations. M-D.

Children's Suite 1949 (MS available from composer). 13 min. Seven movements.

Sonata III 1950 (MS available from composer) 12 min. Four movements.

Sonata IV 1950 (MS available from composer) 57pp. Each movement is based on a different pianistic style: late Romanticism in the first (Andante), blues in the second (Andante–Allegretto), sprightly mock seriousness in the third (Alla marcia), and a tarantella in the fourth (Prestissimo). D.

Twelve-Tone Variations for Piano 1954 (TP 1971) 63pp. Six different rows are worked out in five movements. The theme is based on a combination of the six rows followed by a variation based on one row, a variation based on two rows, etc. Copious analytical and performance notes by the composer point up the row construction and utilization in each variation. D.

Scherzo 1958 (TP 1973) 30pp. Opens with a slow Prologue followed by an Epilogue, the Prologue in retrograde. The Scherzo proper is a series of nine scherzi with eight interlacing trios. Scherzo II employs only the odd-numbered bars of Scherzo I, and the compression idea continues until the last Scherzo is one measure long. Clever inventive atonal writing. D.

Sonata V 1961 (MS available from composer) 31pp. Allegro Tranquillo; Interlude—Lentissimo; Rondo—Presto; Finale—Allegro moderato ma accelerando poco a poco alla fermata. Third movement takes 12½ minutes and uses the upper register of the piano throughout. Abstract, serial, but improvisatory; long over-elaboration of ideas. D.

Sonata VI "Rage over the Lost Beethoven" 1972 (MS available from the composer). Programmatic, can be played as a solo composition, in three movements: Rage over the Lost Composer (24 min.); Rage over the Lost Artifacts (7 min.); Rage over the Lost Spirit (22 min.). The music is also designed to be performed as part of the "museum piece" *Rage over the Lost Beethoven* by Frank Parman. A fascinating experience that incorporates much material from Beethoven's own piano music into the texture of the movements but never as overt quotations or crude collage. D.

Two Theater Pieces for Piano 1956 (MS available from composer) 4pp. I. Aria, for Act II of Pirandello's *Right You Are If You Think You Are:* cantabile melody supported with Romantic harmonic chords, in the style of Paisello. II. Chords and Wild Dance, for Act IV of Ibsen's *Hedda Gabler:* Allegro moderato introduction to a Presto flowing melody; concludes with an Agitato and Precipitato section and two wild final chords. Written to be played off-stage at theater productions. M-D.

PAUL HINDEMITH (1895–1963) Germany

Sonata No.2 (Schott).

See: Felix Salzer, *Structural Analysis,* Vol.II (New York: Charles Boni, 1952), pp.298–305 for an analysis.

Sonata No.3 (Schott). Modeled after Beethoven's Sonata Op.110?

DAVID HINDLEY (1933–   ) Great Britain

The Cuckoo's Nest (Nov 1972). A suite of thirty pieces published in two separate books—19 pieces in Book I, 11 in Book II. The pieces take the form of very free variations of English Morris and Country Dance tunes, and are arranged in progressive order of difficulty. Original titles of the tunes have been preserved. Int.

KOZABURO Y. HIRAI (1910–   ) Japan

Variations on the Theme of "Kojo No Tsuki" (Zen-On 296 1957) 11pp. Pentatonic theme, 8 variations, virtuoso writing. D.

Sakura-Sakura (Zen-On 297 1971) 4pp. A fantasy for piano. Introduction, varied short sections, tonal, nineteenth-century gestures. M-D.

TAKEICHIRO HIRAI (1937–   ) Japan

Hirai studied piano and composition with his father, Kozabura Hirai. He studied cello with Pablo Casals and has won a number of competitions.

Poem for Piano Solo (Japan Federation of Composers   1971) 11pp. "This piece . . . is a hymn to nature and some fine traditions which Japan is actually losing. The work is composed rather free in form. After the energetic introduction with a characteristic rhythm, comes the theme quietly. This theme, as it later on appears several times with little changes, should be played each time with some different expression. While in D major, it is essential that the performer sings fully with refined tone, and at Grandioso before the ending, it is required to be played in a dignified manner but with emotion" (the composer discussing the work in *Contemporary Japanese Composers* [Japanese Federation of Composers, 1971]. Effective colorful contemporary writing requiring fully developed technique. D.

JUNICHI HIRANO (1947–   ) Japan
Hirano graduated from the High School for the Blind (Tokyo University of Education) and Nihon University. He studied composition with Hidetake Tsutsui, Kan Ishii, and Kiyohiko Kijima.
Three Movements (Japan Federation of Composers   1971) 19pp. Three contrasting movements in a highly chromatic, individual style that requires complete pianistic equipment. D.

KISHIO HIRAO (1907–1953) Japan
Sonate pour piano 1948 (Ongaku-No-Tomo   1965) 38pp. 20 min. Poco lento—Allegro molto; Lento; Allegro assai. Freely tonal, based on traditional forms, short motivic figuration. M-D.

MIROSLAV HLAVÁČ (1923–   ) Czechoslovakia
Stenograms, 9 Studies of Performance for Piano (Supraphon   1973) 29pp. Mostly written in twelve-tone technique, each piece tackles a particular problem and exploits it. No bar lines, no meters, many pedal marks. Musical throughout. M-D.
Musica Carnevalesca (GS   1977) 16pp. Rondo for piano. A catalog of varied expressionistic pianistic figuration. Requires strength and stamina. D.

THEODORE HLOUSCHEK (1923–   ) Czechoslovakia, born Germany
Suite Giocosa (Br&H   1975) 27pp. Toccatina; Intermezzo marciale; Theme and (5) Variations; Rondo. Witty and contrasting movements; MC; pianistic; brisk atonal writing. D.

ANATOLI HOD (–   ) Israel, born Russia
Seven Movements on a Single Theme (Israeli Music Publications). Simple theme; contrasted variations; final one is complex and virtuosic but ends quietly. Contemporary treatment. M-D.

ALUN HODDINOTT (1929–   ) Wales
Sonata No.6 Op.78/3 (OUP   1974) 15pp. 10 min. One movement, strong dissonance in bitonal setting, large dynamic contrasts, fierce rhythmic

treatment, cadenza, colorful closing of soft sad chords. Virtuosic and effective writing. D.

RICHARD HOFFMAN (1831–1909) USA, born Great Britain
Hoffman came to the USA as a lad of sixteen after having reportedly studied with Liszt, Moscheles, Rubinstein, and Thalberg. He settled in New York and made an outstanding contribution to the musical life of that city. He was a close personal friend of Louis Moreau Gottschalk.

In Memoriam LMG in collection *Piano Music in Nineteenth Century America,* Vol.I (Hinson—Hinshaw). Written in 1869 on the occasion of Gottschalk's death. A nocturne in style; effective; one of the better pieces from this decade. M-D.

Rigoletto Fantasy (copy in the British Museum). D.

See: Richard Hoffman, *Some Musical Recollections of Fifty Years* (New York: Charles Scribner's Sons, 1910; reprint, Detroit: Detroit Reprints in Music, 1975).

LEE HOIBY (1926–   ) USA
5 Preludes Op.7 rev. ed. (A. Broude   1977) 22pp. Andante con moto; Allegro vivo; Moderato con moto; Allegro; Allegro ma non troppo. Not harsh on the ears or too hard on the hands. Large span required. M-D.

JAN HOLCMAN (1922–   ) USA, born Poland
Three Echoes (TP   1973). Like a Polish Folksong; Almost Classical; Somewhat jazzy. Wry contemporary harmonies; straightforward rhythms; three different styles reflected. Int.

KARL HÖLLER (1907–   ) Germany
Suite Op.2 (Müller). M-D.
Sonatine Op.29 (Leuckart). M-D.
Drei kleine Sonaten Op.41 (Sikorski 113, 114, 115   1950). Available separately. Op.41/1 d, 15pp.: Allegro molto; Un poco vivace; Andante con espressione; Molto Allegro. Op.41/2 G, 19pp: Un poco Allegro amabile; Molto vivace; Andante con espressione; Allegro con spirito. Op.41/3 b, 15pp.: Allegro moderato, Vivo e leggiero; Un poco lento; Allegro molto. All three sonatas are neoclassic in style, show a preference for thin textures, and are freely tonal with a few Impressionistic techniques (parallel chords, unresolved dissonances). M-D.
Tessiner Klavierbuch Op.57 (Schott   1962). M-D.
Sonatine I, II Op.58 (Schott   1963) Int. to M-D.

MANFRED HOLLMANN (1928–   ) Germany
Suite (DVFM   1968) 20pp. Six pieces to be performed as a group. Introduction (slow and solemn); March Grotesque (staccato, dissonant); Intermezzo I (quiet); Scherzo (flexible meters, jesting idea); Intermezzo II (quiet, unusual rhythmic patterns); Toccata (brilliant and dashing). M-D.

VAGN HOLMBOE (1909–   ) Denmark, born Africa
See: Paul Rapoport, *Vagn Holmboe: A Catalogue of His Music, Discography, Bibliographical Essays* (London: Triad Press, 1975).

GUSTAV HOLST (1874–1934) Great Britain
2 Folksong Fragments Op.46/2, 3 (OUP) 3 min. No.1. O! I hae seen the roses blaw. No.2. The Shoemakker. Imaginative vitality in No.2. Int.

SIMEON TEN HOLT (1923–   ) The Netherlands
Composition I, II, III, IV   1958 (Donemus).
Diagonaal Suite   1957 (Donemus).
Five Etudes   1961 (Donemus).
Five Pieces (Donemus   1972). Explanations in English only.
Music for Pieter   1958 (Donemus) seven little pieces.
Soloduiveldans   1959 (Donemus) 5 min. Solo devil's dance.
Twenty Bagatellen (Donemus   1954). Composer's MS reproduced.

ARTHUR HONEGGER (1892–1955) Switzerland, born France
La Neige sur Rome   1925 (Sal) 2pp. Arranged by Honegger from the Incidental Music score for *L'Impératrice aux Rochers*. Lent et doux. M-D.
Sarabande   1920 (ESC) No.2 in the *Album des Six pour Piano*. M-D.
Trois Pièces   1910 (Desforges). Scherzo. Humoresque. Adagio espressivo.

JAMES HOOK (1746–1827) Great Britain
A James Hook Album (Eve Barsham—Elkin   1975) 29pp. 22 easy pieces from "Guida di Musica." A graded selection from the 52 pieces contained in Op.37 and Op.81. Admirable teaching material, well fingered. Easy to Int.

ANTHONY HOPKINS (1921–   ) Great Britain
For Talented Beginners (OUP) 2 vols. Displays a highly creative approach to basic keyboard skills. Easy.
Sonatine (OUP   1970) 11pp. Allegro assai: fresh melodies and harmonies. Quasi adagio: Impressionistic chordal sonorities. Capriccioso: introduction to an alla marcia, delightful. Int. to M-D.

BILL HOPKINS (1943–   ) USA
Studies, Row-wise (Schott   1969).

ZOLTAN HORUSITZKY (1903–   ) Hungary
Horusitzky studied composition with Zoltán Kodály. Since 1946 he has been professor of piano at the Academy of Music in Budapest.
Piano Pieces for Children (Rózsavölgyi   1935).
Sonata (EMB   1968) 26pp.

ALAN HOVHANESS (1911–   ) USA
Toccata and Fugue Op.6 (CFP   1971). The Toccata has many repeated notes that create a shimmering effect. The Fugue relies on much use of dynamics. M-D.

Mystic Flute Op.22 (CFP). 7/8 meter, open fifths, melodic augmented
seconds, hypnotic. Int.

Farewell to the Mountains Op.55/2 (CFP). Rapid, like an Oud, flexible
meters, repeated notes and rhythms. M-D.

Macedonian Mountain Dance Op. 144b/1 (CFP). Restless, simple harmonies, big climax. M-D.

Visionary Landscapes (CFP). A group of descriptive pieces. "Midnight
Bell" uses extra-keyboard sonorities. Int.

Komachi Op.240 (CFP) 11 min. Seven short descriptive pieces in a suite
that honors Kamachi, the great Japanese woman poet. Impressionistic,
pentatonic, melodic with many arpeggiated chords. Adept pedaling
required. The notes are easy but beautiful imagery makes them appealing to a mature performer. See especially No.5, Flight of Dawn Birds,
and No.7, Moon Harp. M-D.

MARY HOWE (1882–1964) USA

Stars (Composer's Press 1938) 3pp. Sonorous, Impressionistic, large climax, *ppp* closing. M-D.

Whimsy (Composer's Press 1938) 2pp. Clever, staccato touch, a few
fast octaves, abrupt *fff* ending. Int.

HERBERT HOWELLS (1892–) Great Britain

Sonatina (ABRSM). Vivo-inquieto: lively, wide dynamic contrasts. Quasi
adagio, serioso ma teneramente: in a cantabile style. Finale: requires
agility and verve. Large span necessary. M-D.

Howells' Clavichord 1961 (Nov 10022807). 20 pieces for clavichord or
piano. Previously published as two sets. Displays a splendid craftsman-
like style. M-D.

See: Larry Palmer, "Herbert Howells' 'Lambert's clavichord,' " *Diapason*,
66 (December 1974):7–8. Describes the twelve character pieces.

ALEXANDRU HRISANIDE (1936–) Rumania

Piano Piece No.8 (Gerig) 12pp. 4½ min. A toccata using clusters and
numerous contemporary techniques. Great facility required. D.

Sonata No.2 (Gerig 1959) 19pp. Sonata piccola.

TSANG-HOUEI HSU (1929–) China

Hsu graduated from the National Taiwan Normal University and pursued
further studies in Paris with Jacques Chailley and André Jolivet. He is presently a member of the music faculty at Soochow University, Taipei, Taiwan.

Un jour chez Mademoiselle Hellene Op.9 ("One Day when I Was at
Eilena's") (MS available from the composer) 22pp. Written between
1960 and 1962 after the composer's return from Paris to Taiwan. The
piece is a delicate blend of contemporary Europe and traditional
China. "Although the sound of Chinese gongs appears in the Prelude
of the first movement, the whole movement actually exemplifies the

composer's experience with contemporary Western European music. In spite of the fact that the theme of the fugue is based on the pentatonic scale, the second movement is derived from the French Impressionistic School. On the contrary, in the third movement (Fugue et Toccata), the composer seems to have discovered his own self in traditional Chinese music. The fugue of the Adagio conveys the lyrical mood of ancient Chinese Chin music. In the Toccata, the composer uses the techniques of Chinese lute, Pi-Pa, on the piano to express simple but strong Chinese flavor" (from the score). Contains some effective writing. M-D.

Sound of Autumn Op.25 (MS available from composer) 4pp. Suite of three movements: Love Song in the Moonlight; Autumn Breeze; Grief in Autumn. More tonal than Op.9. Int. to M-D.

WEN YING HSU (–   ) China
Sonata I (Wen Ying Studio, Taipei 1972) 17pp. LC has a copy, LC M23II 874 No.1.

ERIC HUDES (1920–   ) Great Britain
Variations for Piano (Thames Publishing   1972) 15 min. Forced serial style, overly long. D.
Nine Variants for Piano (Thames Publishing) 10 min. More interesting than the Variations; sections contrasting. Some cumbersome piano writing but contains a good sense of movement. M-D.

KEITH HUMBLE (1927–   ) Australia
Arcade II (UE   1969) 4 loose sheets. Includes instructions for performance. Four sections, produced on four separate sheets A–D. Material was derived from a computer research program. Boulez-inspired. D.

BERTOLD HUMMEL (1925–   ) Germany
Invocation 52 (Simrock   1972) 6pp. Much tremolo, large gestures of fleet passagework, extensive dynamic and keyboard range, carefully pedaled. D.

JOHANN N. HUMMEL (1778–1837) Germany
Complete Piano Sonatas (Musica Rara   1975). Long and informative introduction by Harold Truscott. Vol.I, 89pp: Sonatas Op.2/3 C; Op. 13 E♭; Op.20 f; Op.38 C. Vol.II, 91pp: Sonatas Op.81 f♯; Op.106 D; VII G, VIII A♭, IX C. These last three works are more like sonatinas. The Opp.81 and 106 Sonatas display Hummel's pianistic skills admirably. All of these works are important documents in the history of the form and in the evolution of Romantic piano music. They display both classical and Romantic characteristics, with florid runs and glittering figurations. Also available in 2 vols. (Hänssler 41.813, 41.814). M-D to D.
Rondo E♭ Op.11 (PWM). Scales, octaves, and broken thirds. M-D.

God Save the King, Air Varie (Musica Obscura).

Preambules dans tous les tons Op.67 (Musica Obscura).

Scherzo A (Zen-On 114) 2pp. An effective little study. Int.

See: Rita A. Muffolett, "The Pianoforte Works of Johann Nepomuk Hummel (1778–1837)," MA thesis, Catholic University, 1961, 81pp.

Joel Sachs, *Kapellmeister Hummel in England and France* (Detroit: Information Coordinators, 1978).

ANDRZEJ HUNDZIAK (1927–   ) Poland

A Circus (PWM). Five musical sketches in contemporary astringent idiom. Unusual rhythmic interest. Easy to Int.

CONRAD F. HURLEBUSCH (1696–1765) Germany

See: Bess Karp, "The Keyboard Suites and Sonatas of Conrad Friedrich Hurlebusch," master's thesis, University of California, Los Angeles, 1969.

KAREL HUSA (1921–   ) USA, born Czechoslovakia

Working from within an essentially classical orientation, Husa compounds elements of the past and present, using his own distinctly individual recipe.

Elegy 1957 (Leduc 1968) 2pp. 4½ min. Simple opening grows to great intensity, quiet opening and closing, agitato and dramatic mid-section. M-D.

Sonatina Op.1 1943 (AMP 7709) 23pp. 12 min. Allegretto moderato; Andante cantabile; Allegretto marciale. Classical sonatina form, delightful and remarkably fresh. M-D.

Sonata II 1975 (AMP 1977) 18 min. 3 movements.

JERE HUTCHESON (1938–   ) USA

Hutcheson is a member of the music faculty at Michigan State University.

Electrons 1966 (MS available from composer: c/o Music Department, Michigan State University, East Lansing, MI 48823) 8pp. Six short pieces, flexible meters, pointillistic, atonal, extreme registers exploited, dramatic gestures. Large span required. M-D.

Fantaisie-Impromptu 1974 (Seesaw) 12 min. Virtuosic writing requiring virtuosic performance. D.

WARNER HUTCHISON (1930–   ) USA

Hutchison is a member of the music faculty, New Mexico State University, Las Cruces, NM 88001.

Mass for Abraham Lincoln (Tempo Music 1975) for amplified/prepared piano, and tape. 40 min. Requires two performers. Nine movements.

Monday Music (Seesaw 1975) for piano and synthesizer. 6 min.

Six Preparations (MS available from composer) 7 min. For prepared piano.

ANSELM HÜTTENBRENNER (1794–1868) Austria

Klaviersonate F Op.10 (Krenn 1969) 27pp. From *Musik aus der Steiermark,* edited by the Streiricher Tonkünstlerbund, under the direction of Konrad Stekl, Wolfgang Suppan, Ernst Ludwig Uray, and Otto Zettl. Reihe I: Vol.53.

CARL-THEODOR HÜTTEROTT (–   ) Germany
Spiel mit neun Achteln in zwölf Tönen (Möseler   1976) 8pp. Hausmusik 152.

I

MICHAEL A. IATAURO (–   ) USA
Children's Pieces for Adults (PIC   1975). A charming and whimsical set
of seven pieces with unusual titles such as "A Stuffed Lion Called
Jonathan," "The Toy Donkey." MC and freely dissonant, clever. M-D.

JACQUES IBERT (1890–1962) France
Histoires (Leduc).
   Available separately: *Le petit ane blanc* (EBM); *A Giddy Girl*
   (EBM).
Toccata sur le nom d'Albert Roussel   1929 (Leduc   1961) 2pp.
Noël en Picardie (Heugel   1914).
Escales (Leduc). Arranged by the composer. 1. Rome-Palerme. 2. Tunis-
Nefta. 3. Valencia.

TOSHI ICHIYANAGI (1933–   ) Japan
Piano Media (Zen-On 370   1972) 16pp. Constant buildup of unbarred
eighth notes (=1/9 second or faster) from beginning to end. A tour
de force for performer and listener. D.

CARLO DE INCONTRERA (1937–   ) Italy
. . . Und in sich hinein (Ric   1972) 3pp. For piano and the external noise
of the hall in which it is performed. Contains only sounds from *p* to
ppppp. Strict pedal indications. To be played very freely and very
slowly. Approximate rhythmic notation. In Cage tradition, many symbols explained. Preface in Italian, English, and German. Only for the
adventurous. D.
Piano piece for Fred Dosek (Ric 131383).

MANUEL INFANTE (1883–1958) Spain
Poachades Andalouses (Leduc). 1. Canto flamenco. 2. Danse gitane.

DÉSIRÉE-ÉMIL INGHELBRECHT (1880–1965) France
Paysages (JWC). Five impressionistic pieces. M-D.

YANNIS IOANNIDIS (1930–   ) Greece
Three Studies (Gerig   1975). Notes in English.

JOHN IRELAND (1879–1962) Great Britain
The Collected Piano Works of John Ireland (S&B) 315pp. Five books with
50 some pieces that reveal Ireland in all aspects as a fine keyboard

composer. Vol.I: In Those Days: Daydream, Meridian. A Sea Idyll. The Almond Trees. Decorations: The Island Spell, Moonglade, The Scarlet Ceremonies. Three Dances: Gipsy Dance, Country Dance, Reapers' Dance. Preludes: The Undertone, Obsession, The Holy Boy, Fire of Spring. Rhapsody. Vol.II: London Pieces: Chelsea Reach, Ragamuffin, Soho Forenoons. Leaves from A Child's Sketchbook: By the Mere, In the Meadow, The Hunt's Up. Merry Andrew. The Towering-Path. Summer Evening. The Darkened Valley. Two Pieces: For Remembrance (perhaps the best work in all 5 vols.), Amberley Wild Brooks. Equinox. On a Birthday Morning. Solioquy. Vol.III: Prelude in Eb. Two Pieces: April, Bergomask. Sonatina. Spring Will Not Wait. Ballade. Two Pieces: February's Child. Aubade. Ballade of London Nights. Vol.IV: Month's Mind. Greenways: The Cherry Tree, Cypress, The Palm and May. Sarnia: Le Catioroc, In a May Morning, Song of the Springtides. Three Pastels: A Grecian Lad, The Boy Bishop, Puck's Birthday. Columbine. Vol.V: Piano Sonata.

Amberley Wild Brooks (Galliard).

April (Galliard).

Bergomask (Galliard).

The Darkened Valley (Galliard).

February's Child (Schott).

Merry Andrew (Ascherberg).

Month's Mind (Galliard).

On A Birthday Morning (Galliard).

Prelude Eb (Galliard).

Puck's Birthday (Galliard).

Sarnia, An Island Sequence (Bo&H 1940). Sarnia is the Roman name for the Island of Guernsey. Ireland is at his most colorful in this splashing and ebullient suite. M-D.

Sonatina (OUP). 15pp. Three movements.

Spring Will Not Wait (OUP 1927). The final part of Ireland's song cycle "We'll to the Woods No More." Full, rich chords and long, sustained phrases are its main characteristics. Impressionistic. A large span and ability to bring out inside melodies are necessary. No fingering or pedaling. M-D.

Summer Evening (Ascherberg).

The Towering-Path (Galliard).

See: Eric Parkin, "John Ireland and the Piano," *Music Teacher,* 53 (1974) June:11–12; July:15–16; August:12–13; September:13.

Donald W. Rankin, "The Solo Piano Music of John Ireland," diss., Boston University, 1970.

MAKI ISHII (1936–   ) Japan

Aphorismen II (Ongaku-No-Tomo   1972) 8 loose leaves, explanation of symbols. The seven parts are performed in whatever order the player chooses. Glockenspiel, tam tam, maracas, and claves needed for special percussive effects. Avant-garde notation, pointillistic, clusters. D.

PIERRE ISRAEL-MEYER (1933–   ) France
Requiem pour une sonatine. Humoresque pour piano (Editions Françaises de Musique/Technisonor   1974) 13pp.

RYUTA ITO (1922–   ) Japan
Petite Suite pour Piano (Zen-On 323   1968) 8pp. Prelude. Nocturne. Toccata. Bitonal, Impressionistic, some oriental flavor. Int. to M-D.

CHARLES IVES (1874–1954) USA
First Piano Sonata   1902–10 (PIC) 50pp. 42 min. D.
Second Piano Sonata "Concord, Mass., 1840–1860" 1909–1915 (Arrow). D.
> See: Sondra Rae Sholder Clark, "The Evolving *Concord Sonata:* A Study of Choices and Variants in the Music of Charles Ives," diss., Stanford University, 1972; "The Element of Choice in Ives *Concord Sonata,"* MQ, 60 (April 1974):167–86. Fred Fischer, "Ives Concord Sonata," PQ, 92 (Winter 1975–76):23–27.
Three-Page Sonata   1905 (J. Kirkpatrick—Mer). Includes extensive editorial notes. Uses the BACH motive over 40 times. Large span required. D.
Etude No.22   1912 (J. Kirkpatrick—Merion   1973). Three-part structure, witty B section. M-D.
> See: Robert Dumm, "Performer's Analysis of an Ives Piano Piece," *Clavier,* 13 (October 1974):21–25.
Five Piano Pieces (Merion   1925). Contains: Varied Air and Variations. Study No.22. The Antiabolitionist Riots. Three-Page Sonata. Some South Paw Pitching. Includes photographs, illustrations, and biographical information. No musicological notes are included here, although the single publications, especially the *Varied Air and Variations,* have extensive notes. D.
Varied Air and Variations (J. Kirkpatrick, Garry Clarke—Merion   1971). 92 bars subtitled "Study No.2 for Ears or Aural and Mental Exercise." Contains valuable musicological notes.

The Ives Society has commissioned editions of the following compositions, and editorial work on them is proceeding:
Waltz—Rondo (J. Kirkpatrick, Jerrold Cox—GS).
Five Take-Off's for Piano (J. Kirkpatrick—PIC).
Study No.20 (J. Kirkpatrick—TP).
London Bridge Is Falling Down (Singleton—PIC).
Improvisations X, Y, and Z (J. Dapogny—AMP).
Four Transcriptions from "Emerson" (J. Kirkpatrick—AMP).
The Celestial Railroad (J. Kirkpatrick—AMP).

Piano Marches Nos.1–6 (Kirkpatrick, Singleton—AMP/PIC).

See: James M. Burke, "Ives Innovations in Piano Music," *Clavier,* 13 (October 1974):14–16.

Sondra Rae Clark, "Ives and the Assistant Soloist," *Clavier,* 13 (October 1974):17–20.

Maurice Hinson, "The Solo Piano Music of Charles Ives," PQ, 88 (Winter, 1974–75):32–35.

H. Wiley Hitchcock, *Ives,* Oxford Studies of Composers, 14 (London: Oxford University Press, 1977), 95pp.

Elizabeth McCrae, "The Piano Music (of Charles Ives)," *MENC Journal,* 61 (October 1974):53–57.

Jane E. Rasmussen, "Charles Ives's Music for Piano," *Student Musicologists at Minnesota,* 6:201–17. Capsule analyses of many of Ives's pieces for piano, both published and unpublished.

Guy S. Wuellner, "The Smaller Piano Works of Charles Ives," AMT, 22 (April–May 1973):14–16.

JEAN EICHELBERGER IVEY (1923–   ) USA

Skaniadaryo (CF   1973) 14pp. 11 min. Facsimile edition. For piano and tape. Contains performance directions and explanation of symbols for special effects. Tape plays continuously from the beginning of the piece to the end. "Skaniadaryo (Handsome Lake) was a Seneca Indian who lived in western New York from about 1749 to 1815. Inspired by visions, and mingling old and new elements, he founded a reformed version of the traditional Iroquois religion, which became widespread among his people, and persists today among the Iroquois. To me Skaniadaryo symbolizes New York's heroic past—the times celebrated, for instance, in the novels of James Fenimore Cooper—as well as the mingling of two heritages, and a way of life more intimate with nature. In this composition, which in its way also blends new and traditional elements, and suggests sounds of nature with pure electronics, I have tried to convey some of this complex of feelings" (from the score). Pointillistic, long pedal effects, proportional rhythmic relationships, sudden dynamic extremes, many harmonic seconds, clusterlike sonorities, glissandi, harmonics, strings damped at one place. Guided improvisation required. Piano and tape sonorities well blended. M-D.

J

HANLEY JACKSON (1939–   ) USA

Jackson teaches at Kansas State University, Manhattan, KS 66506.

Tangents (SP 1974) 11pp. 4½ min. For piano and prerecorded tape. The piano score notates tape sounds. Tape, which contains both electronic and piano sounds, is in two versions: tape part by itself, tape in a performance with Margaret Walker, pianist. Divided sections: Very slow —Slow—Rhythmic. Colorful, rhythmic, octotonic, pointillistic. M-D.

The Elements 1973 (MS available from composer) for piano and tape. Earth. Air. Fire. Water.

GORDON JACOB (1895–   ) Great Britain

Jacob studied composition with Charles Stanford and Herbert Howells. He teaches at the Royal College of Music in London.

Sonata 1957 (Belwin-Mills) 20 min.

Sonatina (Chappell 1975) for harpsichord or piano. Allegro con spirito; Adagio semplice; Allegro non troppo. Highly chromatic, melodic emphasis contrasted with more exploratory passages. M-D.

Three Pieces 1929 (Belwin-Mills).

The Frogs 1958 (OUP).

Suite for the Virginal 1960–1 (OUP) 10 min.

MAURICE JACOBSON (1896–   ) Great Britain

Carousal (Lengnick 1946) 16pp. A colorful tone poem. Freely tonal. Highly attractive Alla Musette mid-section. M-D.

Romantic Theme and Variations (Lengnick 1946) 18pp. Theme dates from 1910, variations from 1944. Six well-constructed and developed variations that have an MC flavor reminiscent of Rachmaninoff. Effective. M-D.

MICHAEL JACQUES (1944–   ) Great Britain

Five Piece Suite (Roberton 5514 1974) 12pp. 7 min. Fanfare. Elegy. Scherzo. Aria. Toccata. Well put together, MC. Int.

EMILE JACQUES-DALCROZE (1865–1950) Switzerland

Dix Miniatures (Foetisch 1958) 12pp. Ten short, colorful, contrasting pieces; traditional harmonies. Int.

Esquisses Rythmiques (Foetisch 1528, 1536) 2 vols., 16 pieces in each. MC with Impressionistic sonorities, rhythmically oriented. Int. to M-D.

Six Danses Romandes Op.32 (Foetisch 411) 16pp. Rhythmic pieces for piano. Varied, Impressionistic tonal style. See No.2, Allegro moderato, especially. Int.

THOMAS JAMES (1937–   ) USA
Variations (Boelke-Bomart   1974) 6 min.

LEOŠ JANÁČEK (1854–1928) Czechoslovakia
The Overgrown Path (Artia) 53pp. 22 min. Ten pieces. Inspired by memories of childhood. Int. to M-D.
In the Mist   1912 (Hudební Matice   1938) 21pp. 14 min. 1. Andante. 2. Molto adagio. 3. Andantino. 4. Presto. More concentrated and more concise in motif and mood than *The Overgrown Path*. Uses the whole-tone scale. Veiled in Impressionistic floating chords of mystical beauty. Some of Janáček's finest piano writing. All four pieces are pervaded by a melancholy mood, clear-cut form. Each has a contrasting middle section. M-D.
Complete Works, Vol.I, Piano Works (Edition Supraphon and Bi, available in USA through European American Music Distributors). 160pp. Clothbound.

ARTHUR JANNERY (1932–   ) USA
Jannery studied at Boston University and Washington University. He teaches at Radford College, Radford, VA 24141.
Pensive Pentad—Va 73 (MS available from composer) 23pp. Huntin: very fast, toccata-like, alternating hands. Prayin: chordal accompaniment to folk-like tune. Funnin: giocoso, catchy rhythms, light and bouncy. Weepin: lento, spread-out sonorities, important inner lines. Dancin: allegretto, oohm-pah-pah bounce, repeated chords and octaves, glissando conclusion. M-D.
Pensive Pentad—Va 76 Op.48 (MS available from composer). Contains: Lord Thomas and fair Elinor; Come All You fair and tender Ladies; The Tree in the Wood; Jack Went A-Sailing; Brennan on the Moor. Each is freely based on an English/Irish/Scottish folk tune from Botetourt County, VA, and represents manifestations of the English, Irish, and Scottish heritage. Date back to revolutionary times. Clever, attractive, MC settings. Int. to M-D.

ALFRED JANSON (1937–   ) Norway
Janson is both concert pianist and composer. He studied at Darmstadt and Stockholm.
November 1962 (WH). Tremolo, much use of damper pedal, a few clusters, no clefs. D.

ZOLTÁN JENEY (1943–   ) Hungary
Végjáték ("End Game") (EMB   1975) 7pp.

DONALD JENNI (1937–   ) USA

Jenni studied at Alverno College, De Paul University, and Stanford University. He teaches at the University of Iowa.

A Game of Dates   1974 (AMP). For Dancer. For Conductor. For Percussionist. For Composer. An interrelated set of character pieces; birthday presents to four of the composer's friends. Each piece is a brilliant musical portrait. Much dissonance, convincing, pianistic. Large span required. M-D.

JAKOB JEŽ (1928–   ) Yugoslavia
Drei Etüden (Gerig   1970) 8pp. Three studies.

KAREL JIRÁK (1891–1972) Czechoslovakia
See: Alice Tischler, *Karel Boleslav Jirák: A Catalogue of His Works* (Detroit: Detroit Information Coordinators, 1975), 32pp.

IVAN JIRJO (1926–   ) Czechoslovakia
Sonata (Statni Nakladatelstvi Krasne Literatury   1956) 47pp.
Sonata II ("Elegie Disharmonique") (Supraphon AP 1850   1975) 31pp.
Variace na téma Johannes Brahms (Panton   1964   1973) 19pp.

MAGNÚS BLÖNDAL JÓHANNSSON (1925–   ) Iceland
Jóhannsson studied at the Reykjavík School of Music, and at the Juilliard School with Bernard Wagenaar and Marion Bauer.
Four Abstractions (Iceland Music Centre   1955). Twelve-tone, short, contrasted. Int. to M-D.

BENGT EMIL JOHNSON (1936–   ) Sweden
Disappearances (Reimers   1975) 8pp. For piano and tape. Explanations in English and German.

HARRIETT JOHNSON (–   ) USA
Johnson is music critic for the *New York Post*.
Questions I, II, III (CF   1972) 7pp. 4 min. A pleasantly modern suite in three contrasting movements. To be played as a group. M-D.

LOCKREM JOHNSON (1924–1977) USA
Chaconne Op.29   1948 (Mer) 6 min.
Impromptu Op.48   1957 (MS copy available from M. Hinson) 6pp. Quasi improvisando style, flowing lines, Adagio, quasi cadenza, freely tonal, calm nostalgic character of closing section. M-D.
Two Sonatinas Op.49 (Puget Music Publications).

ROBERT SHERLAW JOHNSON (1932–   ) Great Britain
Asterogenesis (OUP   1974) 19pp. Explanations in English. Used as a test piece in the 1975 Leeds International Piano Competition. Astrological significance; influence of Varèse and Messiaen felt; clear architectural lines missing. Exploits keyboard alone; no inside-piano techniques as in Johnson's earlier works. Makes use of extended bass range of the Bösendorfer piano but can be adapted for performance on a regular

concert grand. Vigorous atonal melody, complex rhythms, clusters, extensive dynamic range. D.

Sonata III (OUP   1978) 12 min. Based on a more traditional tonal and metrical scheme than is *Asterogenesis,* with individual notes used as tonal centers. Four clearly defined sections are played continuously, with the most intriguing being the second, in which a richly colored sea of sound rides above a series of sustained bass pedal points. D.

TOM JOHNSON (–   ) USA

Septapede (AMP   1969) 7pp. 159 fragments to be arranged by the performer in an aleatory manner. Each fragment may be repeated as many times as performer wishes. Performance should sound improvised and no two performances should ever sound alike. Pianist will need to plan some arrangement until confidence is attained. Avant-garde. M-D to D.

See: David Burge, "Five New Pieces," CK, 3 (December 1977):66.

Spaces (AMP   1975) 10pp. 12 min. Varied types of music are combined. No meters, bar lines, or key signatures. Slow opening with highly dissonant chords that lead to almost inaudible figurations that become more obvious. Dynamics and pedalling are vitally important. Demanding and diverting. Ives and Feldman influence. M-D.

BENJAMIN JOHNSTON (1926–   ) USA

Since 1951 Johnston has taught at the University of Illinois.

Celebration (Orchesis) (McGinnis & Marx).

BETSY JOLAS (1926–   ) France, born USA

Jolas is a pupil of Messiaen and a protegé of Pierre Boulez.

B for Sonata (Heugel   1973) 30pp. 20 min. One movement of diverse material well laid out over the keyboard, with octaves used in an interesting manner. Momentum is lost about half way through, and the piece tends to drift to a conclusion. Study in sonorities, no relationship to sonata form. Three pages of directions in French, German, and English. Some sections require four staves to notate. Avant-garde. D.

Chanson d'approche (Heugel   1972) 11pp. 8½ min. Avant-garde notation; bars are measured in seconds of duration. Numerous pedal markings including half-pedals. Strong contrasts, silently depressed clusters. Instrument's sonorities exploited. D.

Mon Ami   1974 (Heugel) 4pp. For a singer-pianist who is either a woman or a child. The performer sings a simple, folklike melody in French and must accompany herself some of the time (easy passages) and play solo passages at other times (not easy!). Jolas has arranged five versions of the piece in different lengths. Performed with taste the work will surprise you. Contains some exquisite sonorities. M-D.

See: David Burge, "Five New Pieces," CK, 3 (December 1977):66.

ANDRÉ JOLIVET (1905–1974) France
3 Temps 1931 (Sal). Invention. Air. Rondeau. M-D.
Chansons Naïves 1951 (P. Noël). Six children's pieces. Int.

RICHARD JONES (before 1730–1744) Great Britain
Pièces de clavecin 1732 (Stoddard Lincoln—Heugel 1974) 79pp. Six
suits or sets of lessons for harpsichord or spinnet. Consisting of a great
variety of movements, such as preludes, aires, toccats, all'mands, jiggs,
corrents, borre's, sarabands, gavots, minuets. Preface in French, English, and German. One of the most attractive collections among the
repertoire of English harpsichord music but still little known. Most of
the pieces sound well on the piano. Int. to M-D.

JOSEPH JONGEN (1873–1953) Belgium
Serenade Op.19 (Sal 1901) 7pp. Lyric, contrasting sections, quiet. M-D.
Deux Rondes Wallonnes Op.40 (Durand).
Toccata Op.91 1929 (CeBeDeM 1972) 8pp. 5 min.

SCOTT JOPLIN (1868–1917) USA
Joplin's works are an original contribution to American piano literature.
This gifted American has told our story in a certain age as no one else could.
The Collected Works of Scott Joplin for Solo Piano (Vera Brodsky Law-
rence—New York Public Library 1971 through Belwin-Mills) 352
pages. Contains 51 works—rags, marches, waltzes—pieces written in
collaboration with other composers, and the *School of Ragtime*. Also
included are a rollography and a discography of 78 rpm recordings of
Joplin compositions.
Original works: Antoinette—March and Two-Step (1906), Augustan
Club Waltz (1901), Bethena—A Concert Waltz (1905), Binks' Waltz
(1905), The Cascades—A Rag (1904), Breeze from Alabama, A—A
Ragtime Two Step (1902), The Chrysanthemum—An Afro-Inter-
mezzo (1904), Cleopha—March and Two Step (1902), Combination
March (1896), Country Club—Rag Time Two-Step (1909), The
Easy Winners—A Ragtime Two Step (1901), Elite Syncopations
(1902), The Entertainer—A Ragtime Two Step (1902), Eugenia
(1905), Euphonic Sounds—A Syncopated Novelty (1909), The
Favorite—Ragtime Two Step (1904), Gladiolus Rag (1907), Great
Crush Collision—March (1896), Harmony Club Waltz (1896), Leola
—Two Step (1905), Magnetic Rag (1914), Maple Leaf Rag (1899),
March Majestic (1902), Nonpareil (None to Equal) (1907), Original
Rags (arranged by Charles N. Daniels) (1899), Palm Leaf Rag—A
Slow Drag (1903), Paragon Rag (1909), Peacherine Rag (1901),
Pine Apple Rag (1908), Pleasant Moments—Ragtime Waltz (1909),
The Ragtime Dance (1906), Reflection Rag—Syncopated Musings
(1917), Rosebud—Two-Step (1905), Scott Joplin's New Rag
(1912), Solace—A Mexican Serenade (1909), Stoptime Rag (1910),

The Strenuous Life—A Ragtime Two Step (1902), Sugar Cane—A Ragtime Classic Two-Step (1908), The Sycamore—A Concert Rag (1904), Wall Street Rag (1909), Weeping Willow—Ragtime Two Step (1903).

Collaborative Works: Felicity Rag (with Scott Hayden) (1911), Heliotrope Bouquet—A Slow Drag Two-Step (with Louis Chauvin) (1907), Kismet Rag (with Scott Hayden) (1913), Lily Queen—A Ragtime Two-Step (with Arthur Marshall) (1907), Something Doing —Cake Walk March (with Scott Hayden) (1903), Sunflower Slow Drag—A Rag Time Two Step (with Scott Hayden) (1901), Swipesy —Cake Walk (with Arthur Marshall) (1900).

Miscellaneous Works: School of Ragtime—6 Exercises for Piano (1908), Sensation—A Rag (by Joseph F. Lamb, arranged by Scott Joplin) (1908), Silver Swan Rag (attributed to Scott Joplin) (1971). Most all of these works are M-D.

Scott Joplin Piano Rags (Paxton   1974) 32pp. Vol.I: Maple Leaf Rag; The Entertainer; Ragtime Dance; Gladiolus Rag; Fig Leaf Rag; Scott Joplin's New Rag; Euphonic Sounds; Magnetic Rag. Some pieces are fingered and have pedal indications. M-D. Vol.II: Elite Syncopations; Eugenia; Leola; Rose Leaf Rag; Bethena (a concert waltz); Paragon Rag; Solace; Pine Apple Rag. M-D. Vol.III: Original Rags; Weeping Willow; The Cascades; The Chrysanthemum; Sugar Cane; The Nonpareil: Country Club; Stoptime Rag. M-D.

The Missouri Rags (Max Morath—GS   1975) 66pp. Seventeen rags written while Joplin lived in Missouri. Unedited, helpful preface. Maple Leaf; Original Rags; Peacherine; Easy Winners; A Breeze from Alabama; Elite Syncopations; Strenuous Life; Entertainer; Weeping Willow; Palm Leaf; The Favorite; The Chrysanthemum; The Sycamore; The Cascades; Bethena; Eugenia; Ragtime Dance. M-D.

Complete Ragtime Piano Solos (C. Hansen) 177pp. Includes waltzes, marches, songs, and a vocal and original piano solo of The Entertainer. M-D.

Scott Joplin, King of Ragtime (Compiled by Albert Gamse—Lewis Music Publishing Co.   1972) 159pp. Piano solos and songs.

Gladiolus Rag (EBM).

Pineapple Rag (Belwin-Mills).

Solace (MCA). A very slow march. M-D.

An Adventure in Ragtime (M. Hinson, D. C. Glover—Belwin-Mills) 32pp. Gay Ninety Rag; The Entertainer; "The Story of Scott Joplin"; Maple Leaf Rag; The Strenuous Life; The Easy Winner; Cascades (encore duet). An informative picture about Ragtime; features the music of Joplin. Easy to Int.

Rags by Scott Joplin (Jerry Vogel Music Co. 112 West 44th St., New York, N.Y. 10036). Rose Leaf Rag; Fig Leaf Rag; Search Light Rag. These

Rags are not contained in the New York Public Library edition of *The Collected Works of Scott Joplin for Solo Piano* (Vera Brodsky Lawrence).

Ragtimes for Piano (E. Klemm—CFP P9678a). The first volume of a new critical urtext edition.

MIHAIL JORA (1891–1971) Rumania

Poze Si . . . Pozne ("Pictures and Pranks") (Editura Muzicala a Uniunii Compozitorilor　1964). 3 vols. 22 pieces. Clever colorful settings of scenes in the life of a child. Easy to Int.

WILFRED JOSEPHS (1927–　　) Great Britain

Pièces pour ma belle-mere Op.18　1958–9 (Bo&H　1974) 7 min. Three short pieces. Int.

29 Preludes Op.70　1969 (Nov) 26 min.

JOHN JOUBERT (1927–　　) Union of South Africa

Sonata II Op.71 (Nov 10023009　1977) 49pp. 20 min. Moderato—Poco Allegro: chromatic, trills, triplets, 8/8 divided 3+3+2/8, full chords, Bartók influence, *ppp* closing; large span required. Presto: octotonic, freely tonal, poco lento mid-section more chordal. Poco lento: secco *pp* octaves and tremolo open the movement; repeated chords; broken chordal figuration; leads to an Allegro Vivace section in bravura style followed by a tranquillo section; Lento and serene *ppp* closing. Solid and exciting contemporary writing. D.

K

DMITRI KABALEVSKY (1904–   ) USSR
Four Preludes Op.5 (GS).
Sonata I Op.6(CFP).
Sonatinas C, g Op.13 (Palmer—Alfred). The Sonatina in C is overplayed, while many teachers do not know the very tuneful one in g, which is of the same difficulty. Int.
Three Rondos from the opera *Colas Breugnon* Op.30 (Sikorski). New version 1969.
24 Little Pieces Op.39 (Sikorski).
Sonata III Op.46 (Bo&H).
5 Easy Sets of Variations Op.51 (Ric).
Spring Games and Dances Op.81 (CFP; GS; Sikorski).
Recitative and Rondo Op.84 1967 (Sikorski).
6 Pieces Op.88 (Soviet Composer   1973; Sikorski). From series 10, Piano Music for Children and Young People.
35 Easy Pieces Op.89 (Soviet Composer   1974; Sikorski). From series 10, Piano Music for Children and Young People.
Piano Music for Children and Young People, Series 3 (GS 4696).
Kabalevsky for the Young Pianist (D. Goldberger—GS). 21 pieces from Opp.14, 27, 39, 51. Fingered and pedaled. Int.
Kabalevsky for the Young (EBM). 25 pieces from Op.27, books 1 and 2, and Op.39. Easy to Int.
30 Pieces for Children (GS).
Kabalevsky—An Introduction to his Piano Works (Palmer—Alfred) 64pp. Selections from Opp.27, 39, and 40. Comments on each piece. Int.
Young Pianist's Guide to Kabalevsky (Y. Novik—Studio P/R) 24pp. with recording. 14 of the easier teaching pieces. Tastefully edited. Easy to Int.
22 Pieces for Children (A. Gretchaninoff—Ric   1971).
See: John P. Adams, "A Study of the Kabalevsky Preludes, Op.38," DM diss., Indiana University, 1976, 59pp. Each prelude is analyzed from a theoretical and a pianistic point of view.
Mervyn Coles, "Kabalevsky's Piano Music," *Music Teacher,* 57 (July 1978):22.

PÁL KADOSA (1903–   ) Hungary
Suite I Op.1/1 (EMB) 11pp. 4 contrasting movements. Intricate rhythms and sonorities. M-D.
Suite II Op.1/2 (EMB). Based on Hungarian folk elements, driving rhythms. M-D.
Suite III Op.1/3 (EMB 1972) 4pp. Three short movements, introspective. Fourths and fifths exploited in last movement, Allegro giusto. M-D.
3 Easy Sonatinas Op.18A (EMB).
Folksong Suite Op.21 (EMB 1933) 11pp. In Bartók style. M-D.
Five Studies Op.23F (EMB). Each study is devoted to a particular problem. Int. to M-D.
Snapshots Op.69 (EMB 1971) 7pp. Five short pieces. Clashing dissonance and cimbalon effects. Good hand span required. Int. to M-D.
12 Short Pieces for Children (EMB).
Sonatina on a Hungarian Folk Song (EMB).

MAURICIO KAGEL (1931–   ) Germany, born Argentina
Metapiece (Mimetics) (UE 1961). 13 pages folded into one long accordion-like page. Detailed explanation; can be performed as solo, by two pianos, as piano duet, or with other instruments. Diagrammatic notation in part. Stones can be placed on the strings and/or on the keyboard. Many clusters and pointillistic figurations. More interesting for performer than listener. Avant-garde. D.

FRIEDRICH KALKBRENNER (1785–1849) Germany
Traité d'harmonie du pianiste Op.185 (Heuwekemeijer 1970). Reprint of 1849 Paris edition. Contains etudes, fugues, and preludes with an introduction by the composer.
La femme du Marin (Zanibon).
The Musical Box (Rondo in C) (Banks).
Sonata for Left Hand Op.40 (Musica Obscura).
Variations on 'Rule Britannica' from Alfred—Dr. Arne Op.52 (Musica Obscura.

LÁSZLÓ KALMAR (1931–   ) Hungary
Invenzioni (EMB 1976) 19pp.

DENNIS KAM (1942–   ) USA
Several Times 1970–1 (MS available from composer: 1204 W. Stoughton, Apt. 22, Urbana, IL 61801) 6pp. I. Steady with motion: sustaining pedal is held throughout, repeated 16th-note figuration in right hand, single punctuated notes in left hand, narrow dynamic range. II. Smooth and relaxed: long pedals; subtle sonorities; "Aggressively" section with many repeated triplet g♯'s closes this piece. III. Driving but controlled and connected: repeated chromatic chords; builds to dramatic closing. M-D.

HANS KANN (1927–   ) Austria, born Japan
Zehn Klavierstücke ohne Bassschlüssel (Dob   1971) 15pp. Ten short
   pieces without bass clef. Close proximity of hands, varied styles. M-D.

PÁL KÁROLYI (1934–   ) Hungary
Accenti (EMB   1972) 14pp. Explanations in Hungarian and English.
24 Piano Pieces for Children (EMB). Hungarian flavor. Easy to Int.
4 Studies (EMB   1972) 8pp. Explanations in Hungarian and English.

UDO KASEMETS (1919–   ) Canada, born Estonia
10 Pieces on Well-Known Songs (BMI). Familiar tunes with new sounds.
   Easy.

LUCJAN M. KASZYCKI (1932–   ) Poland
Children's Variations (PWM   1952).
Sonatina (PMP   1954) 13pp. Allegro risoluto; Romanza; Allegro vivo
   marciale. Folk tune style, freely tonal, somewhat Impressionistic,
   bitonal, strong conclusion. Int.

HERMAN KATIMS (1904–   ) USA
Caprice and Fuge (Lyric   1968) 10pp. Caprice is freely tonal, with strong
   rhythms. Fuge works to broad climax, subsides, and builds to ending.
   M-D.
Chaconne (Providence Music Press   1971) 16pp. A concert transcription
   loosely based on a chaconne by Tommaso A. Vitali, well developed,
   strong pianistic figurations, tonal. M-D.
Chant d'Amour Op.1/3 (Lyric   1953) 7pp.
Humoresque (Providence Music Press   1972) 4pp. Clever rhythms, sud-
   den dynamic changes, chromatic lines, surprise ending. Int. to M-D.
Legend (Lyric   1958) 2pp. Cantabile melody supported by Romantic
   harmonies, quasi cadenza, quiet ending. Int.
Melody in D Flat Op.4 (Lyric   1962) 8pp. Large character piece, in style
   of Sibelius *Romance*. M-D.
Sonatina (Providence Music Press   1971). Pedagogic piece. Easy.
Waltz in C-sharp Minor (Lyric   1978) 5pp. Sectionalized, key changes,
   nineteenth-century style. Int. to M-D.

ULYSSES KAY (1917–   ) USA
Kay is Professor of Music at Herbert H. Lehman College.
First Nocturne (MCA   1974) 11pp. 6 min. A tone row is heard at the
   opening and closing. Cantabile melodic treatment, meter changes, dissonant harmonies, uneasy rhythms, ostinati. M-D.

ROLAND KAYN (1933–   ) Germany
Quanten   1957 (SZ 6667).

LEIF KAYSER (1919–   ) Denmark
Bagatelle (Engstrom & Sodring) for 2 or 4 hands.

VASIL IVANOV KAZANDZHIEV (1934–   ) Bulgaria
Jugend-Album (Nauka i Izkustvo   1973) 40pp.

DONALD KEATS (1929–   ) USA
Keats studied composition with Quincy Porter, Paul Hindemith, Otto Luening, Douglas Moore, and Henry Cowell. He teaches at the University of Denver.
Sonata (Bo&H   1960) 28pp. Comfortably flowing: gentle, widely spaced, contrapuntal middle voices. Fast and precise: toccatalike, some hemiola, driving rhythms. Slow, in a free style: atmospheric, effective pedaling, wide registers, *pp* closing. Very fast and with vigor: Prokofiev style, percussive, energetic. Written in a freely tonal style; serial influence; powerful; large-scale, eclectic nature. D.
Theme and Variations (MS available from composer, c/o Lamont School of Music, University of Denver, University Park, Denver, CO 80210) 13pp. Theme, five variations, and coda. Neoclassic, structural clarity, strong motivic construction, flowing lines. Contains a few pianistic challenges but is not of great difficulty. M-D.

ALFRED KELLER (1907–   ) Switzerland
Drei Klavierstücke (Hug). Melancholericon: choralelike. Consolation. Omaggio: based on the motive B E B♭ E L (a). M-D.

BRYAN KELLY (1934–   ) Great Britain
Sonata for Piano   1971 (Nov) 20pp. 13 min. Three movements, FSF. Traditional writing, thin textures. Large span required. M-D.

WALTER KEMP (1938–   ) Canada
Five Latvian Folk Pieces (Waterloo   1971) 11pp. In addition to containing particular technical problems, these pieces introduce the pianist to the rich, but relatively unfamiliar, heritage of Latvian folk song. Each song is identified. Modal, lyric, attractive. Int.

TALIVALDIS KENINS (1919–   ) Canada, born Latvia
Toccata—Dance (F. Harris   1971) 2pp. MC. Int.
The Juggler/Sad Clown (Bo&H). Original children's pieces. Easy to Int.

KENT KENNAN (1913–   ) USA
Kennan teaches at the University of Texas at Austin.
Three Preludes (GS   1938) 9pp. Allegro scherzando: chromatic, arpeggio gestures, flexible meters, sudden *ff* ending. Lento, nello stile di un Chorale: freely tonal around e♭, four subtle phrases, thick textures. Allegro con fuoco: driving rhythms, repeated octaves in ostinatolike patterns, dramatic gestures, effective conclusion. Deservedly one of the most popular sets by a contemporary American composer. M-D.
Two Preludes (LG   1951) in collection *New Music for the Piano*. Rather freely; with a feeling of yearning and unrest: neo-Romantic, frequent motivic repetition, strong melodies. Massive and vigorous: two-part counterpoint punctuated with chords, contrary motion. M-D.

LOUIS KENTNER (1905–   ) Great Britain
Sonatinas No.1 F, No.2 C, No.3 G (OUP   1939) published separately.
All three Sonatinas are freely tonal and eminently pianistic and display a fine craft. M-D.

WILLEM KERSTERS (1929–   ) Belgium
Bagatelle IV (Metropolis   1956) 4pp. Contrasting, ABA design, secco style, MC, bitonal influence. Int. to M-D.
Three Preludes Op.56 (CeBeDeM   1971) 26pp. 11 min.

GEERT VAN KEULEN (1943–   ) The Netherlands
Music for Her (Donemus   1975) 11pp. Photostat.

NELSON KEYES (1928–   ) USA
Keyes teaches in the School of Music at the University of Louisville.
Three Love Songs for Piano Solo 1968 (Hinshaw) in collection *Twelve by Eleven*. Gently, Johnny, My Jingalo: gently swinging, modal, four repetitions with varied treatment. Shenandoah: expressive melody accompanied by moving sixths; changing meters; requires large span. Lolly Too Dum: open-fifth accompaniment, bitonal, more development in this piece than in the other two, clever coda. An appealing set. Int. to M-D.

ARAM KHATCHATURIAN (1903–1978) USSR
Album for Children (Ric   1971).
Children's Album (K).
Poem   1927 (MCA; K) 7½ min.
Recitatives and Fugues (Sikorski   1974) 50pp.
Sonatina (G. Sandor—GS   1976) 23pp.
Sonata (L. Vosgerchian—GS   1976) 47pp.
Two Dances from "Spartacus" (CFP 4777).
Ten Pieces for the Young Pianist (GS).
Three Dances from "The Maskerade" (K 9493). Waltz; Mazurka; Galop.
Colorful, attractive; would make a fine group. Large span required; facility necessary, especially in the Galop. M-D.

TIKHON KHRENNIKOV (1913–   ) USSR
Khrennikov studied with Mikhail Gnessin at the Gnessin Music School and at the Moscow Conservatory. Since 1948 he has been first secretary of the Union of Soviet Composers. His music derives from the concert-music tradition of eighteenth- and nineteenth-century Russia and from Russian folk music.
Three Pieces Op.5 (GS 398).
Twenty Selected Pieces (GS 3039).

DIMITUR IORDANOV KHRISTOV (1933–   ) Bulgaria
Sonate (Nauka i Izkustvo   1962) 12pp.
Miniatures Concertantes (Nauka i Izkustvo   1973) 28pp.

BRUNO KIEFER (1923–   ) Brazil, born Germany
Sonata I 1958 (Ric Brazil   1973) 17pp. 10 min. Com Energia; Saudoso; Fuga e Toccata. Preference for thin textures, subtle syncopation; neoclassic in conception. M-D.
Sonata II (SDM   1959) 19pp. 10 min. Three movements, the last of which is a set of variations. A logical sequel to *Sonata I*. Similar techniques used but with a surer hand. M-D.
Tríptico 1969 (Editora Vozes Ltda. Riachuelo, 1280 Porto Alegre—RS, Brazil) 10 min.

OLAV KIELLAND (1901–   ) Norway
5 Small Pieces Op.10 (NMO).
Marcia nostrale Op.11 (NMO).
Tjølstul Blesterbakken Op.12 (NMO).
Villarkorn Op.13 (NMO). 20 pieces.
Toccata Op.16 (NMO).
Two Moods (NMO). 1. Serenade 2. Romance.

WILHELM KILLMAYER (1927–   ) Germany
An John Field—Nocturnes (Schott 6688   1976) 27pp. Freely tonal, tremolo in inner voices, large left-hand skips, fast repeated chords and octaves, varied and contrasted figuration. M-D to D.

EARL KIM (1920–   ) USA
Kim studied composition with Arnold Schönberg and Roger Sessions. He teaches at Harvard University.
Two Bagatelles (LG). See Anthologies and Collections U.S.A., *New Music for the Piano, Guide,* pp.753–54. I. Allegro scherzando (1950): bold gestures, tremolando, expressionistic. M-D. II. Andante sostenuto (1948): expressive, changing meters not noticeable. M-D.

YON-JIN KIM (1930–   ) Korea
Three Short Pieces (Seoul, University Printing Center   1973) 18pp.
Three Short Pieces (Seesaw). May be the same as entry above.

LEON KIRCHNER (1919–   ) USA
Kirchner is a vital force in American music.
See: Nelita True, "Style Analysis of the Published Solo Piano Music of Leon Kirchner," DMA diss., Peabody Conservatory, 1976.

THEODOR KIRCHNER (1823–1903) Germany
Sketches Op.11 (Hug   1977) 20pp.

JOHANN PHILIPP KIRNBERGER (1721–1783) Gergany
Acht Fugen für cembalo oder orgel (Ruf, Bemmann—Schott 6501). Eight thinly textured fugues preceded by a short Prelude C. The three "jig" fugues are the most attractive. No editing. Int.

STEFAN KISIELEWSKI (1911–   ) Poland
Kisielewski studied composition at the Warsaw Conservatoire and then in

Paris. A prominent writer and music critic, he is the author of a number of books. From 1945 to 1949 he was a professor at the State College of Music in Cracow.

Danse Vive (PWM   1939) 16pp. Vivacissimo; groups of notes alternate between hands; extreme registers exploited; freely tonal around F; syncopated rhythms; brilliant octaves at conclusion. M-D.

Prelude and Fugue (PWM   1943). The fast four-part fugue ends with a recitativo cadenza. D.

Toccata (PWM   1943). Short, brilliant, much passagelike figuration. D.

Serenada 1945 (PWM   1973) 8pp. 4½ min. Descending staccato notes, arpeggio gestures, chordal melody, recitative section, closing like opening. M-D.

Suite (PWM   1955) Melodic, uncomplicated texture. M-D.

Berceuse (PWM   1968) 11pp. 4 min. Allegretto moderato, fast chromatic figuration, 4 with 3, changing meters, trills in low register, many starts and stops, *ppp* ending. M-D.

YASUJI KIYOSE (1900–   ) Japan

Piano Works (Ongaku-No-Tomo   1958) 53pp. 4 Preludes. 8 Piano Compositions (various titles). Ryuku Dances (3). Ballad. Colorful, MC. Int. to M-D.

ARNLJOT KJELDAAS (1916–   ) Norway

Av Min Poesibok ("From My Poetrybook") (NMO   1947) 16pp. Solitude. Evening on the Randsfjord. Hopscotch. Cross Country Ride. The Trolls Pass By. Saturday Eve of the Trolls. The Wood Goblins Dance. Colorful character sketches; large span required. Int. to M-D.

GISELHER KLEBE (1925–   ) Germany

Nine Piano Pieces for Sonja Op.76 (Br 6195   1977).

RICHARD RUDOLF KLEIN (1921–   ) Germany

Sech Sonatinen für Klavier (Noetzel   1970) 27pp. Neoclassic, mostly three contrasted movements each, thin textures preferred. Int.

Capriccio (Möseler   1973) 16pp.

JAN KLEINBUSSINK (1946–   ) The Netherlands

Variazioni (Donemus   1971) 12pp., 8 min. Explanations in English. Reproduction of the composer's MS. Based on a 24-note "theme" frequently treated chordally. Metered and proportional notation. D.

ERNST GERNOT KLUSSMANN (1901–   ) Germany

Xenien Op.27 (Sikorski 201   1951) 11pp. Six short contrasting pieces, thin textures, neoclassic. No.5, Invention, is Hindemithlike in gesture and style. Int.

ROLF KNAP (1937–   ) The Netherlands

Harmonische Reflecties (Donemus   1976) 3pp. Photostat of MS.

PETER KNAUER (–   ) Germany
Canadian Dance Suite (Sikorski 509   1960) 15pp. Introduktion: strong
    syncopation, lyric mid-section. Schnell: scherzo-like; requires large
    span. Ruhig, fliessend: diatonic melody, chromatic accompaniment.
    Lebhaft: has characteristics of opening movement. Requires a strong
    rhythmic drive. M-D.

FREDERICK KOCH (1924–   ) USA
Koch is a product of the Cleveland Institute of Music, Case Western Re-
serve University, and the Eastman School of Music. He studied composition
with Arthur Shepherd, Herbert Elwell, Henry Cowell, and Bernard Rogers.
Sonatina (Seesaw).
Five Children's Sketches (Seesaw).
Toccatina (BMC).
Babette Piano Book (Gen   1969) 10pp. Five fresh sounding pieces. Int.
Five Memories (CF). Five short contrasting pieces (graceful, lively, folk
    dance, gentle, etc.), Romantic. Int.

JOHN KOCH (1928–   ) USA
From the Country (Gen   1971) 10pp. Five Pictures for the Young Pianist.
    A Beautiful Morning. The Moon Rises. Little Boot Dance. Snow Fall-
    ing (Impressionistic pedal study). Rondino for a Quacking Duck.
    Short, MC. Int.
Suite for Piano (Gen   1968). Impromptu: contrasted neoclassic figura-
    tion. Andante and Scherzo: like a two- and three-part invention.
    Finale Gaudioso: thin textures, bright, moves over keyboard. M-D.

GÜNTER KOCHAN (1930–   ) Germany
Fünf Klavierstücke (CFP   1971) 11pp.
Sieben leichte Klavierstücke (CFP   1971) 8pp. One-page pieces, no key
    signatures, attractive, tuneful. Each one exploits a certain technique,
    e.g., melody and accompaniment, staccato and legato, and cantabile
    style. No fingering. Easy to Int.

MIKLÓS KOCSÁR (1933–   ) Hungary
Improvisazioni 1972–3 (EMB) 16pp. Improvisatory, full of contrasting
    dynamics, no bar lines, great skips, aleatory sections, strong disso-
    nance, effective climax. Much experience is necessary to "bring off"
    this work. D.

ZOLTÁN KODÁLY (1882–1967) Hungary
12 Little Pieces (Bo&H   1973) 5pp. Nos.1–4 are to be played a half step
    lower and No.6 is to be played a half step higher, all on black keys.
    Also suitable for rote teaching. Easy.
See: Ylda Novik, "Gyorgy Sandor Plays and Discusses Kodály," PQ, 88
    (Winter 1974–5):14, 16. Prompted by Sandor's recording of the com-
    plete piano pieces of Kodály.

CHARLES KOECHLIN (1867–1951) France
Cinq Sonatines Op.59   1915–6 (Sal). Represents a microcosm of Koechlin's writing. Int. to M-D.
10 Petites Pièces faciles (Sal). Nos.2–7 available separately.
L'Ecole du Jeu lié (Sal).
Sarabande Op.205 (Sal).
See: Thomas H. McGuire, "Charles Koechlin," AMT, 25 (January 1976): 19–22.

GOTTFRIED MICHAEL KOENIG (1926–   ) Germany
Zwei Klavierstücke (Tonos   1961) I. 15pp. II. 15pp. Performance directions in German and English. Atonal, pointillistic, flexible meters, long pedals, harmonics, clusters, avant-garde. Large span required. D.

LOUIS KÖHLER (1820–1886) Germany
Easiest Studies Op.151 (K 3590).
Children's Album Op.210 (K 3588).
Children's Exercises Op.218 (K 3591).
Short School of Velocity (Alfred).
12 Easy Studies (Alfred).

KARL KOHN (1926–   ) USA, born Austria
Kohn teaches at Pomona College.
5 Bagatelles   1961 (CF). Contrasting colors and figurations. M-D.
Bits and Pieces   1973 (CF   1977) 10pp. 12½ min. Largo; Allegro giusto; Lento; Largo. M-D.
Exercise for Bill   1972 (CF) 2½ min.
Partita 1963–4 (CF   1972). Reproduced from composer's MS. Aleatoric; extensive diagram and directions are given so the performer can chart the course. Expressionistic style, avant-garde. D.
Second (Hungarian) Rhapsody   1971 (CF) 12 min.

JOONAS KOKKONEN (1921–   ) Finland
Five Bagatelles 1968–9 (Fazer) 17pp. 13½ min. Praembulum. Intermezzo. Aves. Elegiaco. Arbores. Contrasted pieces in a thoroughly contemporary idiom. M-D.
Sonatine (Fazer   1953) 11pp. 8½ min. Adagio; Allegro; Adagio–Allegro. Repeated chromatic chords, ornate cantabile melody, octotonic. Good octave technique required. M-D.

NICOLAU KOKRON (1936–   ) Brazil, born Hungary
Kokron teaches composition in the music department at the University of Brasilia.
Study I (Slaves of Jó) (Ric BR). More difficult than *Study II*.
Study II (Seresta) (Ric BR NMB 11   1969) 5pp. Tuneful, sectionalized, MC. M-D.

BARBARA KOLB (1939–   ) USA

Solitaire (CFP) 13½ min. For piano and tape. Dreamy, subtle coloristic contrasts. M-D.

Appello (Bo&H). Serial influence; makes a strong impact by both the coherence of contrasting structures and a "furia," which exploits virtuoso pianistic percussion techniques; cascades of sound pour forth. D.

MIECZYSLAW KOLINSKI (1901–   ) Poland

Sonata (Hargail   1972) 29pp. Lydian Theme and Variations: appealing and distinctive theme followed by seven contrasting variations. Chaconne: 13 short sections, variation treatment. Minuet: short, quiet. Rondo quasi Tarantella: metrical pattern based on three plus two, rousing concluding movement with propulsive forward motion. Traditional structures and musical treatment but a fresh, novel approach plus an inherent understanding of the piano's sonorities produces a first-class work of spontaneity and excitement. D.

First Suite for Piano   1976 (Berandol).

Second Suite for Piano   1976 (Berandol).

Third Suite for Piano   1976 (Berandol).

Fourth Suite for Piano   1976 (Berandol).

JO KONDO (1947–   ) Japan

Click Crack (Zen-On 381   1975) 11pp. Serial, harmonics, proportional rhythmic notation, avant-garde. D.

GEORGIJ EDUARDOWITSCH KONJUS (1862–1933) USSR

Deux Morceau Op.10 (Forberg) 11pp. Reprinted 1971.

IWAO KONKO (1933–   ) Japan

Klaviersonate II (Ongaku No Tomo Sha   1968) 32pp. Allegro energico; Lentissimo; Vivace. Varied ideas, contemporary techniques throughout, Schönberg influence. D.

PAUL KONT (1920–   ) Austria

Divertissement (Dob).

Diwan (Dob).

Egegh. Klavierstück (Dob   1957).

Klaviermusik für Kinder (Dob).

Kleine Salonmusik (Dob).

Sonatine An Sophie (Dob).

Tanze (Dob   1975) 19pp.

Tanzstück (Dob).

Trip for Piano (Dob   1975) 11pp. Five short pieces. Frankfurt Airport. Nella pergola. O Santa Cecilia. Jumping back to Goethe. Mozart Express, terminal Vienna.

12 Walzer mit Koda "Valses noires et lamentables (Dob   1971) 26pp. Inspired by Schubert and Ravel. Twelve varied Valses in a mixture of neoclassic and Impressionistic style. Int. to M-D.

FRANZ KORINGER (1921–   ) Austria
Südosteuropäische Bauerntänze für Klavier ("Southeast European Peasants Dance") (Dob   1974) 12pp.

GREGORY W. KOSTECK (1937–   ) USA
Cantilena (MS available from composer, c/o Music Department, East Carolina College, Greenville, NC 27834) 12pp. A large free-form work in eight sections. Serial, expressionistic, harmonics, recitative-like. D.

ANDRZEJ KOSZEWSKI (1922–   ) Poland
Pyzystroje (AA   1973) 6 min.
Sonata Breve (AA   1973) 11 min.

KIYOSHIGE KOYAMA (1914–   ) Japan
Kagome Variations (Zen-On 316   1972) 6pp. Theme, 8 variations, and coda. Theme appears to be a Japanese folk song. Pentatonic usage throughout, attractive set. Int. to M-D.

LEO KRAFT (1922–   ) USA
Kraft studied composition with Karol Rathaus at Queens College, where he received his B.A. degree, and with Randall Thompson at Princeton for his Master of Fine Arts. He is professor of music at Queens College.
Allegro Giocoso (LG   1957). See Anthologies and Collections, U.S.A. *New Music for the Piano, Guide,* pp.553–54. Changing rhythmic usage, syncopation, fun to play. M-D.
Partita I (Gen). Strong craft, lyrical, polished writing. M-D.
Short Sonata (Gen   1968) 6pp. For harpsichord or piano.
Ten Short Pieces: for young pianists (Gen   1976) 14pp.

JONATHAN D. KRAMER (1942–   ) USA
Kramer studied at Harvard and the University of California at Berkeley. His composition teachers have included Richard Felciano, Arnold Franchetti, Andrew Imbrie, Leon Kirchner, Roger Sessions, and Karlheinz Stockhausen. He presently teaches theory at Yale University.
Music for Piano I   1966 (MS available from composer, Yale University, New Haven, CT 06520) 4pp. 3½ min. Pointillistic, serial including dynamics, harmonics, clusters. D.
Music for Piano II   1967 (MS available from composer) 10pp. 10½ min. Flexible meters, rhythmic proportional relationships, rugged textures, forearm clusters. D.
Music for Piano III   1968 (MS available from composer) 12pp. 10½ min. This piece has similar characteristics to those of Nos.I and II but develops a greater intensity and is more complex. D.
Two Tunes   1970 (MS available from composer) 8pp. Zetta's Tune: bitonal, freely chromatic, strong syncopations. Wilma's Tune: slow, lyric, more tonal than Zetta's Tune. M-D.
Music for Piano IV   1969–72 (MS available from composer) 18pp. 15

min. "This piece deals with contrasting styles and methods of composition . . . . several bracketed terms appear in the score. These terms suggest appropriate playing styles or gestures . . . the passages marked <ULTRARATIONAL> are to be played in a style appropriate to highly precompositionally ordered (e.g., totally serialized) music, although they may, in fact, not be so constructed" (from note in score). Other terms used include: expressionistic, scherzo, blues, ragtime, fantasia, waltz, minuet, Impressionistic, jazz, atonal, transition. An involved work with some complex parts. D.

ZYGMUNT KRAUZE (1938–   ) Poland

Krauze studied composition with Kazimierz Sikorski and piano with Maria Wilkomirska at the State College of Music in Warsaw. Further studies were with Nadia Boulanger in Paris. As a pianist, he specializes in contemporary and avant-garde music.

Piec Kompozycji Unistycznych (PWM). Five Unitary Piano Pieces. An experimental work. Avant-garde.

Triptych (PWM   1964) 9½ min. Employs a compositional notation that designates the precise tone and tempo but gives the performer an option of one of 24 versions. The idea for the design of the notation comes from the Gothic triptych. Contains one central panel and two moving side wings. During performance the pianist may connect the central panel with the side wings by opening or closing them. The parts may be connected in four ways, thereby providing 24 different versions depending on the order in which the connections are made. Avant-garde. D.

ERNST KRENEK (1900–   ) Austria

See: Ernst Krenek, *Horizons Circled: Reflections on My Music* (Berkeley: University of California Press, 1975), 167pp.

EDINO KRIEGER (1928–   ) Brazil

Preludio (Cantilena) e Fuga (Marcha-rancho) (SDM   1954) 8pp. Colorful writing showing more nationalistic flavor than most of Krieger's other works. D.

3 Miniaturas (SDM   1952) 8pp. I. Moderato. II. Andante. III. Andante moderato. Skillful handling of pianistic techniques. Pieces are complementary and require mature pianism. D.

Sonata I (SDM   1953–4) 27pp. Andante–Allegro enérgico; Seresta— Lento (Homenàgem a Villa-Lobos); Variaçoes e Presto. Bravura writing requiring advanced pianistic equipment. D.

Sonata II (SDM   1956) 26pp. 18 min.

Sonatina (Vitale   1971) 13pp. Moderato; Allegro. Contemporary treatment of Alberti bass, neoclassic style. Second subject of first movement is well contrasted with the first by being more rhythmic. M-D.

RAFAEL KUBELIK (1914–   ) Czechoslovakia

Sonatina für Klavier   1957 (Litolff   1970) 20pp. Allegro: uses a double exposition. Arietta: expressive. Vivace: scherzo-like. Toccata and Chorale: Toccata is percussive; repeated notes and chords. Classical forms and disciplined writing. M-D.

JULIASZ KUCIUK (–   ) Poland
Children's Improvisations (PWM). Careful guidance will help young pianists enjoy these avant-garde pieces. Int.

FRIEDRICH KUHLAU (1786–1832) Germany
Three Sonatinas Op.20 (Laubach—Augener) C, G, F. (GS) has Sonatina C. Int.
Six Sonatinas Op.55 (GS; TP; Century). C, G, C, F, D, C. (GS) has Nos.1 and 3 separately. Int.
Three Sonatinas Op.59 (GS; TP; Century). A, F, C.
Sonatina Op.60/2 (GS).
Four Sonatinas Op.88. Available separately: No.1 (Delrieu); No.2 (Harris); No.3 (GS).
Sonatinas I Opp.20, 55, 59 (CFP; GS; K 3599).
Sonatinas II Opp.60, 88 (CFP; GS; K 3600). These seven sonatinas are all fine pieces for this level. Int.

MAX KUHN (1896–   ) Switzerland
Fünf Klavierstücke (Hug   1969) 12pp. Andante. Presto. Lento. Moderato. Allegro agitato. Expressionistic, freely dissonant, strong contrasts in No.4. M-D.

JOHANN KUHNAU (1660–1722) Germany
Musicalische Vorstellung einiger Biblischer Historien in *6 Sonaten* 1700. (CFP   1973) has a facsimile of the original 1700 edition with Kuhnau's preface and description of the pieces elegantly translated into English by Michael Talbot.
Sonata I C: The Battle between David and Goliath (M. Halford—Alfred).
Sonata II g: Saul Cured through Music by David (PWM).

FELICITAS KUKUCK (1914–   ) Germany
Die Brucke über den Main: Klaviervariationen (Möseler   1976) 7pp.

FRANZ KULLAK (1844–1913) Germany
Son of Theodore.
Scenes from Childhood (K 3596). Int.

THEODORE KULLAK (1818–1882) Germany
Scenes from Childhood Opp.62, 81 (CFP; Klauser—GS L365). 24 characteristic pieces. Int.

JOS KUNST (1936–   ) The Netherlands
Solo Identity II (Donemus   1973) 9pp. Photostat of the composer's MS.
Glass Music (CFP 7142   1977) 19pp. Includes notes for performers in English, Dutch, French, and German. Proportional notation; extreme

ranges of keyboard and dynamics exploited; clusters; staccato sonorities suggest glasses tinkling; avant-garde. M-D.

ALFRED KUNZ (1929–   ) Canada
Music to Do Things By (Waterloo   1969) Vol.I: 7 short pieces. A collection of diverse pieces for all minutes, hours, days, seasons, and moods. Vol.II: 8 short pieces. Both volumes are written in a MC style with provocative titles, e.g., What to do till the Doctor comes; I Wonder?; Music to play when sad or in doubt; The strange people one meets when going for a walk. Int.

MEYER KUPFERMAN (1926–   ) USA
Second Thoughts (Gen).
Short Suite (Gen   1968). Prelude; Close-up; March; Canvas; Game. M-D.
14 Canonic Inventions for Young Composers (Gen   1966). Short contrapuntal models with analytical material. Can be used by student "to compose a set of his own original canons based on these models" (from the preface). Int.

YOSHIMITSU KUROKAMI (1933–   ) Japan
Suite for Piano—12 Folk Songs in Southern Japan (Japan Federation of Composers   1969) 20pp. Merry Dance. Elegy. Rice Planting Song. Festival. Cradle Song. Among the Mountains. Barcarole. Rest. Ballad. Humming Song. Harvest Song. Fox Fire. Each piece uses harmonies based on pentatonic melodies. Requires an easy octave span. Int.

EUGENE KURTZ (1923–   ) USA
Kurtz received his Master's degree from the Eastman School of Music, and studied at Tanglewood with Darius Milhaud and at Darlington, England with Aaron Copland. He presently teaches composition at the University of Michigan.
Four Movements (Jobert   1951). Prélude; Capriccio; Interlude; Allegro Martellato. M-D.
Le Capricorne (Jobert   1952, rev. 1970). Suite for Piano in Three Movements. Introduction; Intermezzo; Toccata.
Motivations (Jobert). Book I (1963). Book II (1965).
Animations (Jobert   1968). Reproduction of MS, easy to read. Résonances: many avant-garde techniques, numerous special effects called for. "The performer will have to decide whether or not he will need some sort of protection for his wrists" (from description of special effects). D.
Rag: (*à la mémoire de Scott Joplin*). Ragtime rhythms in a contemporary harmonic setting. Cleverly changing meters. M-D.

KEI KUSAGAWA (1919–   ) Japan
Kusagawa graduated from the Tokyo College of Music. He has written a great deal of music for films.

Nine Pieces (Japan Federation of Composers 1970) 31pp. "I started writing these pieces in 1964. Feeling the change of seasons and observing nature in the neighborhood green foliage, I wrote these. These are to me a diary or essays" (from the composer's note). Prelude. Tiny Shock. Nocturne. Marianna. 1st Sonnet. Breezes. 2nd Sonnet. A Stir. To Pretend. Colorful, contrasted, some quartal harmony, extremes in ranges exploited. Int. to M-D.

JOHANN KVANDAL (1919–   ) Norway

Fem Sma Klaverstykker Op.1 (NMO 7194) 5pp. Five small pieces, MC. Would make a fine little suite. Int.

Fantasy Op.2 (NMO). Sounds like a nordic Brahms. M-D.

Lyric Pieces Op.5/4–7 (NMO 1976) 18pp. 2 Intermezzi, Capriccio, Scherzino. M-D.

Fantasia Op.8 (NMO 8979 1977) 7pp.

Tre Slätterfantasier Op.31 (NMO 1970) 14pp. Three pieces based on Norwegian folk songs. Jew's Harp Slätt: Lydian mode, strong rhythms. Langleik Improvisation: Mixolydian melody. Springleik for Fiddle: mixture of major and minor, irregular periodic construction. *Slätt* is the Norwegian word for peasant dance. M-D.

TROND KVERNO (–   ) Norway

Gradus ad Parnassum: polyfone undervisningsstykker for klaver 1970–73 (NMO) 16pp.

RYSZARD KWIATKOWSKI (1931–   ) Poland

Seven Moon Pictures (AA 1973) 28pp. Notes in Polish and English.

L

FELIX LABUŃSKI (1892–   ) Poland
Miniatures (PWM). Easy.

WIKTOR LABUŃSKI (1895–1974) USA, born Poland
Easy Compositions (PWM). Four colorful miniatures. Int.
Second Impromptu (Century).

OSVALDO LACERDA (1927–   ) Brazil
Lacerda is a disciple of Camargo Guarnieri and lives in São Paulo.

Brasiliana No.1 (Vitale   1965). The *Brasiliani* are suites based on native
   Brazilian tunes and dances. Dobrado: a Brazilian march. Modinha: a
   love song treated linearly. Mazurca: with a Brazilian rhythmic twist.
   Marcha de Rancho: somewhat slow and sentimental. Contains a number of "wrong note" sounds. Int. to M-D.

Brasiliana No.2 (Vitale   1966). Romance: theme and four variations.
   Chote: Schottisch in ABA form. Moda: ABA. Côco: like a folk song.
   Int. to M-D.

Brasiliana No.3 (Vitale   1967) 6½ min. Cururú. Rancheira. Acalanto.
   Quadrilha.

Brasiliana No.4 (Vitale   1968) 6½ min. Dobrado. Embolada. Seresta.
   Candomblé.

Brasiliana No.5 (Vitale   1969) 4½ min. Desafio: two-voice fugue. Valsa:
   ABA. Lundu: ABA. (The Lundu was originally a rather lascivious
   dance in which the dancers touched belly buttons. It is a parent form
   of a number of other Brazilian dances and songs.) Cana-verde: green
   sugar cane dance, ABA. Int. to M-D.

Brasiliana No.6 (Vitale   1971) 7 min. Roda. Ponto. Toada. Baiao.

Estudos (Vitale   1969) Book I:1–4; Book II:5–8. Each piece deals with
   certain pianistic problems and compositional techniques. 1. Melody
   and accompaniment in same hand. 2. Staccato and melodic playing.
   3. Free, runs. 4. Divided between hands. 5. Intervallic study. 6. Broken
   octaves. 7. Tremolo. 8. Chromaticism. D.

Cinco Invenções a Duas Vozes (Ric Brazil 2701   1958) 13pp. Freely
   tonal, linear, some flexible meters. M-D.

Ponteio I (Ric Brazil   1955) 3pp. A Ponteio is kind of a Prelude in Brazilian style. Flowing melody, weaving accompaniment, freely tonal
   around d. M-D.

Ponteio II (Ric Brazil   1956) 2½ min.

Ponteio III (Ric Brazil   1964) 3 min. Flexible rhythms, big climax, subsides to *pp* closing, colorful. M-D.

Ponteio IV (Ric Brazil   1968) 2 min.

Ponteio V (Ric Brazil   1968) 2½ min. Linear, mostly thin textures, freely dissonant. M-D.

Ponteio VII (Ric Brazil   1971) 2 min.

Suite Miniatura (Ric Brazil   1960) 5½ min. Chorinho. Toada. Valsa. Modinha. Cana verde. Influenced by Brazilian folk and popular music. M-D.

Variações sobre "Mulher Rendeira" (Vitale   1953) 12 min. Folk song theme followed by twelve variations that work to a strong closing. M-D.

HELMUT LACHENMANN (1935–   ) Germany

Wiegenmusik ("Cradle Music") 1963 (Gerig   1974) 7pp. Explanations in German.

Fünf Variationen über ein Thema von Franz Schubert (Gerig   1973) 11pp. Theme is from Schubert's *Deutscher Tanz, D.643.*

Echo Andante (Verlag Herbert Post Presse   1962) New notation. Avant-garde. D.

THÉODORE LACK (1846–1921) France

Sonate pastorale Op.253 (B&VP   1972) 8pp. Revised by Mary Metz.

Trois sonatines Op.257 (B&VP   1972) 23pp. Revised by Mary Metz.

EZRA LADERMAN (1924–   ) USA

Momenti   1976 (OUP) 8 min. Eight "moments." Varied moods, colorful performance instructions, dissonant and freely chromatic. Each "moment" is strongly characterized. Large span required; much use of clusters. D.

PAUL LADMIRAULT (1877–1944) France

2 Breton Folk-Dances (OUP). Allegro moderato. Kerzomp!

4 Esquisses (Demets). 1. Le chemin creux. 2. Valse mélancolique. 3. Vers l'église dans le soir. 4. Minuit dans les clairicres.

Hommage à Gabriel Fauré (Revue Musicale   1922).

Ronde (Rowley—Schott   1936).

SZYMON LAKS (1901–   ) Poland

Suite dans le goût ancien 1966 (PWM   1973) 15pp. 12 min. Allemande; Menuet; Gavotte; Sarabande; Gigue. MC, freely tonal around a–A, neoclassic. Gigue is an imitation of the Gigue from *French Suite* No.5 of J. S. Bach. Int. to M-D.

DOMING LAM (–   ) China

Lam is a graduate of the Toronto Conservatory and the University of Southern California. He lives in Hong Kong.

"Uncle" Suite Op.5   1960 (VPAD Corporation, P.O. Box 7, 3 Taipei, Taiwan R.O.C.) 7pp. Dedicated to the composer's five nephews. 1. Count the Stars: atonal. 2. Fountain in the Rain: bitonal. 3. Little Soldier's March: prolonged procession of thirds and fifths. 4. Story Time: varied patterns and combinations of rhythms, whole-tone scale. 5. Catching Butterflies: canonic with traditional Chinese flavor, subtle contrapuntal writing. A simple introduction to contemporary techniques. Int. to M-D.

CONSTANT LAMBERT (1905–1951) Great Britain

Sonata 1928–9 (OUP). Three movements, based on jazz rhythms but a highly serious work. Ravellian in its harmonic richness and brilliant pianistic virtuosity. D.

Elegiac Blues (JWC).

JOHN LA MONTAINE (1920–   ) USA

Questioning (OUP).

JACQUES LAMY (1910–   ) France

Premier mazurka a (Lemoine   1972) 6pp.

SERGE LANCEN (1922–   ) France

Domino-Suite Fantasque (Hin 57   1952) 15pp. Entree. Tango. Guinguette. Fumisterie. Music Hall. "This Suite is intended to be light and diverting in the French style. The title *Domino* was chosen to suggest that the music has no pretension to seriousness, for in addition to the actual game of Domino, the word itself also suggests a masquerade" (from the score). Each movement is briefly discussed. MC. Requires a large span. M-D.

Fantaisen sur un thème ancien (Hin 1904   1959) 8pp. 7 min. Modal theme treated in various ways, freely tonal, quiet ending. Requires large span. M-D.

Moins Que Rien ("Less Than Nothing") (Hin 1901   1955) 4pp. A short MC character piece with a contrasting trio. Int.

Trois Impromptus (Hin 373   1953) 12pp. Written in a style reminiscent of Fauré with a bit more use of chromaticism. M-D.

Zwiefache (Folk Dances) (Hin 1902   1957) 19pp. A la mémoire de Franz Schubert. Six ländler-like pieces that use multiple meters (3/4 2/4), freely tonal, delightful. Int. to M-D.

ISTVAN LANG (1933–   ) Hungary

Intermezzi (EMB) 12pp. 10 min. Ten short contrasting pieces in MC idiom. Impetuous opening, subdued effects in No.4. Clusters, tremolandos, all add variety. M-D.

WALTER LANG (1896–1966) Switzerland

Miniatures Op.17 (Hug   1927). Ten short alluring pieces. Int.

Variations Op.35 (Hug) 11pp. Introduction, theme, two variations, coda. Requires a fine octave technique. M-D.

10 Klavier-Etüden Op.74 (Hug   1964) 16pp. Trill Study. Canon. Scales. For the Right Hand alone. For the Left Hand alone. Fughetto. Basso Ostinato. 2 Against 3. Staccato. Legato. All written for two voices. Int.

Sonata III Op.75 (Hug   1965) 14pp. Praeludium; Sarabande; Finale. Continues the neoclassic style found in *Sonata II;* freely tonal with a very expressive slow movement. M-D.

JOSEPH LANNER (1801–1843) Austria
Werke für klavier (BB). 8 vols.
Valses Viennoises (GS) transcribed by Wanda Landowska.
8 Waltzes (CFP 1382a).

PAUL LANSKY (1944–   ) USA
Lansky studied composition with George Perle, Milton Babbitt, and Hugo Weisgall, among others. Since 1969 he has taught at Princeton University.
Modal Fantasy (Kings Crown Music Press   1970) 20pp. In three sections: Prelude (thick textures); Ludus (complex writing with corky rhythmic problems); Postlude (solemn, quiet). D.
Dance Suite   1977 (MS available from the composer: c/o Dept. of Music, Princeton University, Princeton, NJ 08540). Preambulum; Courante; Galliarde; Sarabande; Air; Pavane; Capriccio. D.

ALCIDES LANZA (1929–   ) Argentina
Plectros I (1962) (Barry) 5½ min. For 1 or 2 pianos.
Plectros II (1966) (Bo&H) 5 min. For piano and tape.
Toccata (Ric   1957) 5 min.

ANDRÉ LAPORTE (1931–   ) Belgium
Ascension (Tonos   1967) 8pp. Pointillistic, atonal, dynamic extremes, proportional rhythmic notation, aleatoric, clusters, contrary motion glissandi, plucked strings, changing meters, avant-garde. D.

LARS-ERIK LARSSON (1908–   ) Sweden
Latta spelstycken Op.56 (GM).
Pianostycken Op.57 (GM).
7 Fughette con Preludi in modo antico Op.58 (GM).

JOAN LAST (1908–   ) Great Britain
Time Twisters (OUP   1972) 8pp. Five contrapuntal pieces, each with a rhythmic twist. Int.
Notes and Notions (OUP   1974). Eight short pieces. Int.

LAURIDS LAURIDSEN (1882–1946) Denmark
Fra min drommeverden (D. Fog   1971) 15pp. Suite: Sogeren; Syrink; Kirkegärden; Humoresque. M-D.

MARIO LAVISTA (1943–   ) Mexico
Pieza para Un(a) Pianista Y un Piano (Collecion Arion   1970) 3 pages folded as one. Piece for one pianist and one piano. Performer decides the order of the seven musical events. Tempi indicated quantitatively

(in seconds) or qualitatively (grave, very slow, vivo, etc.), clusters, harmonics. Avant-garde. M-D.

PETER LAWSON (1951–   ) Great Britain

Momenta 94 (CFP   1970) 14pp. 94 three-bar "moments" all evolve from the first moment. Varied sonorities in extreme registers, nonmusical objects used to pluck, brush strings, etc. Detailed instructions for performer. Composer states in the score that "there are no rules governing the relationship between movements." Avant-garde.

HENRI LAZAROF (1932–   ) USA, born Bulgaria

Lazarof composes in a full-blooded and highly international style. He is professor of music at the University of California at Los Angeles.

Cadence IV   1970 (AMP) 9pp. Uses a notation that leaves nothing to chance. With the exception of some dramatic plucked and hand-damped notes played directly on the strings, its technical context is conceived in a traditional way. This piece shares distinct thematic kinship with another Lazarof work, *Textures* (1971), for piano and 24 instruments. D.

ERNESTO LECUONA (1896–1963) Cuba

Andalucia Suite (EBM).

Diary of a Child (EBM).

Mazurka Glissando (EBM).

Tres Miniaturas (EBM).

Malagueña (EBM). Surely this is Lecuona's most popular piano work. M-D.

JACQUES LEDUC (1932–   ) Belgium

Apostrophes Op.35 (CeBeDeM   1971) 14pp. Joyeuse; Inquiète; Vehemente.

NOËL LEE (1924–   ) USA

Sonatine (OUP   1959) 5½ min. Allegretto; Song; Rondo—Presto. Neoclassic style, Impressionist influences especially in Song (molto lento ed espressivo). M-D.

Sonata (1955, rev. 1956, 1968. MS available from composer, 4 Villa Laugier, 75017 Paris, France) 10pp. In one movement. Lento introduction is chordal and sustained; requires a large span. Leads to a Moderato with many triplets that exploit the tritone; flexible meters and varied key signatures. Coda rounds off the work using ideas from the introduction. M-D.

Four Etudes Series I (Billaudot   1961) 20pp. 11 min. Explanations in French, German, and English. On a Rhythm of Bartók. With Varied Sonorities (includes special explanation). With Acute Sounds. For Grave, Serious Sounds. Technical studies that explore different sonorities, including playing inside the piano. Much melodic and rhythmic interest, thoroughly contemporary, imaginative and colorful. M-D to D.

Four Etudes Series II (MS available from composer) 24pp. For Legato Playing. Using Sonorous Effects. For Velocity. On Chords from Charles Ives. Calls for harmonics, playing inside the piano by plucking and damping strings, highly pianistic, pointillistic, clusters. Strong personality comes through. Requires large span. D.

NORMAN LEE (1895–   ) USA

Temple Song (MS available from the composer: 360 Forest Avenue, Palo Alto, CA 94301) 16pp. Quartal, quintal harmonies, much parallel motion, chromatic, extensive use of 16th-note figuration, Impressionistic, communicative, oriental sonorities. The harmonies, while incorporating musical ideas of the past, also become more chromatic and dissonant in the exploration of spiritual unrest. M-D.

Temple Song II (MS available from composer) 6pp. Chromatic, repeated chords, 3 with 2. M-D.

Fantasia d (MS available from composer) 19pp. Freely tonal around d, arpeggio figures, alternating 16th notes between hands, nineteenth-century pianistic gestures, slower mid-section, fast octaves in both hands together, brilliant ending. M-D.

Variations 1964 (MS available from the composer) 10pp. Repeated notes and octaves, dramatic scale gestures, well-contrasted variation techniques, freely tonal. M-D.

BENJAMIN LEES (1924–   ) USA, born China

Odyssey 1970 (Bo&H) 12pp. Full resources of keyboard exploited; strong rhythms in this neo-Romantic ballade. Opens with "slow with strange foreboding." Accelerandi, leads to Tempo I with indication "from here to the end the feeling should be almost surrealistic." Ends with violent palm clusters. Pianistically grateful writing. D.

TON DE LEEUW (1926–   ) The Netherlands

De Leeuw is director of the Conservatory in Amsterdam.

Cinq Etudes pour le piano (Donemus 1951) 7 min. Pour les notes répétées. Pour l'unisson. Pour le main gauche. Pour les mains croisées. Pour l'agilité. These pieces are de Leeuw's most successful works for piano. M-D.

Variations sur une chanson populaire française (Donemus 1950). 7pp. For piano or harpsichord.

NICOLA LEFANU (1947–   ) Great Britain

LeFanu is the daughter of the well-known English composer Elizabeth Maconchy. She studied with Egon Wellesz and Goffredo Petrassi, and spent one year at the Royal College of Music.

Chiaroscuro (Novello 1969) 12½ min. Seven short diversified sections (pieces) whose titles refer to pictorial art that emphasizes light and shade: Exultate; Refrain; Sound and Silence; Epithalamion; Reflection and Cadenza; Refrain; Scherzo—Epilogue. MS reproduction but easy to read. Interpretative directions, rhythmic difficulties, sharp characterization and definition of musical ideas. Effective sonorities cleverly juxtaposed; variation concept permeates entire work. M-D.

See: Richard Cooke, "Nicola LeFanu," MT, 1593 (November 1975): 961–63, for a discussion of the composer's works and career.

VICTOR LEGLEY (1915–   ) Belgium
Brindilles Op.80 (CeBeDeM   1974) 20pp. 18 min. 18 short pieces. Int. to M-D.
Sonata II Op.84/1 D♭ (CeBeDeM   1974) 10pp. 5½ min.

HANS ULRICH LEHMANN (1937–   ) Switzerland
Lehmann teaches cello at the Basel Musik-Akademie in Switzerland.
Instants (Ars Viva   1968) 5pp. Seven sections cover a 3-page fold out. Performer decides on order of the sections as well as the dynamics, tempi, etc. D.
Keys (Gerig   1972) 8pp. Explanations in German.

FRANZ X. LEHNER (1904–   ) Germany
For Piano (Orlando   1974) 13pp. Photostat.

NACHMANN LEIB (1905–   ) Rumania
Studii de virtuozitate Nos.1–12 (Editura Muzicala a Uniunii Compozitorilor).

ALAN ROBERT LEICHTLING (1947–   ) USA
Sonata II Op.63   1975 (Seesaw) 31 min. 4 movements. D.

JÓN LEIFS (1899–1968) Iceland
Leifs studied music in Leipzig from 1916 to 1922 and lived in Germany for about thirty years. He founded the Union of Icelandic Artists in 1928, the Society of Icelandic Composers in 1945, and the Performing Rights Society in 1948. He was active as a conductor and a collector of Icelandic folk songs.
Torrek Op.1/2 (Islandia Edition   1919). A dramatic Intermezzo, chromatic mid-section that builds to great climax, sonorous ending. M-D.
Icelandic Dances Op.11 (Islandia   1950). Four separate dances. Changing meters, rhythmic, tuneful. Sections can be combined freely. Int. to M-D.
Neue Island-Tänze Op.14 (Islandia   1931). Two separate dances, sections freely combined, similar to Op.11. M-D.

KENNETH LEIGHTON (1929–   ) Great Britain
Nine Variations Op.36   1959 (Nov) 15 min.
Conflicts Op.51 (Nov   1971) 19 min. Fantasy on Two Themes. Variation

principle subtly at work, passacaglia organization, strongly contrasted moods, virtuoso contemporary writing of the highest order. D.

Six Studies Op.56 (Nov   1971) 37pp. 18 min. These study variations are percussive and strongly dissonant and require a well-developed pianism. Expanded pitch phrases are tied to strong pedal points that create much tension. D.

AUBERT LEMELAND (1932–   ) France
Cinq épisodes Op.6 (Billaudot   1965) 11pp.

PEDRO LERMA (–   ) Spain
Impromptus (UME   1971) 13pp. Short, Romantic style. Int. to M-D.
Preludios (UME   1971) 13pp. Short, accessible rhythmic usage. Int. to M-D.

THEODORE LESCHETIZKY (1830–1915) Poland
Deux Alouettes ("Two Larks") Op.2 (GS; Cen).
Two Mazurkas Op.8 (Leuckart) 1. D♭, 2. f.
Andante Finale de "Lucia di Lammermoor" Op.13 (GS; Cen). For left hand alone. M-D.
Mazurka Op. 24/2 (Cen).
4 Morceaux Op.36 (Rahter). 1. Aria. 2. Gigue (canon à deux voix). 3. Humoresque. 4. "La Source" etude.
Valse-Caprice Op.37 (Rahter).
Souvenirs d'Italie Op.39 (Bo&Bo). 1. Barcarola (Venezia). 4. Mandolinata (Roma). 5. Tarantella (Napoli). M-D.
Intermezzo in Octaves Op.44/4 (GS). A delicious musical study. M-D.
Two Arabesques Op.45. 1. Arabesque en forme d'un etude (GS; Cen). 2. À la tarentelle (Bo&Bo).
Trois Morceaux Op.48 (Bo&Bo). Prélude humoresque. Intermezzo scherzando. Etude Héroïque: a fine right-hand arpeggio study. M-D.
Deux Préludes Op.49 (Bo&Bo). Chant du soir-Prélude. Valse-Prélude.

JOHN LESSARD (1920–   ) USA
New Worlds for the Young Pianist (Gen   1966) Vol.I: 24 pieces, is "likened to the exploration of the new worlds still to be found in our old world." Vol.II: 16 pieces, is "a modest attempt at seeking out the planets" (from the score). MC sounds and idioms. Easy to Int.
Mask (Gen).

FRANCISZEK LESSEL (1780–1838) Poland
3 Sonaty Op.2 (PWP   1970) 65pp. Vol.IV in *Sonaty polskie*.

JEFFREY LEVINE (1942–   ) Great Britain
Cadenza (SZ   1974) 13pp.

BURT LEVY (1936–   ) USA
Levy received his DMA in composition from the University of Illinois.
Six Moments (Smith Publications   1976) 8 min.

GILBERT LEVY (1942–   ) France
Pièces caracteristiques (Delrieu   1975) 7pp.

ERNST LÉVY (1895–   ) USA, born Switzerland
7 Piano Pieces   1954 (Bo&H).

MALCOLM LEWIS (1925–   ) USA
Three Short Pieces   1970 (MS available from composer: c/o Music Department, Ithaca College, Ithaca, NY 14850) 6pp. I. Slowly and sustained: strong melodic emphasis, chromatic accompaniment. II. Moving: flowing, dancelike lines. III. Fast and rhythmic: syncopation, sudden dynamic changes, active figuration, mildly dissonant, pianissimo conclusion. M-D.

PETER TOD LEWIS (1932–   ) USA
Sweets for Piano (TP   1965). Ten short pieces, freely twelve-tone, strong on color and dynamic contrasts, pointillistic textures. Various sized noteheads used to indicate dynamic range. Some serial technique (in No.3), same material used in outer movements. Metronome required for Sweet 3. Harmonics, clusters. M-D.
3 Bagatelles (ACA).
Black Sabbath (ACA).
6 Chips off the Old Block (ACA).
7 Chips—1969 (ACA).
Innerkip (ACA).
Perpetuum Mobile (ACA).
Sestina (ACA).
Sonata   1957 (ACA).
9 Spanish Chips (ACA).
10 Short Pieces (ACA).

ROBERT HALL LEWIS (1926–   ) USA
Five Movements (Seesaw   1960).

ANATOL LIADOFF (Liadov) (1855–1914) Russia
Novellette Op.20 (Belaieff).
On the Prairie Op.23 (Belaieff).
Marionnettes Op.29 (Belaieff).
Variations on a Theme of Glinka Op.35 (Belaieff).
Barcarolle Op.44 (Belaieff).
8 Russian Folk Songs Op.58 (Belaieff).
30 Selected Pieces (C. Hellmundt—CFP 9193). Prefatory notes by the editor in German and English. Contains: Op.2/1, 2, 5, 6, 8; Op.3/4; Op.4/4; Op. 7/2; Op.10/2; Op.11/1, 2; Op.15/2; Op.17/1, 2; Op.21; Op.26; Op.27/1; Op.31/2; Op.32; Op.40/1, 3; Op.44; Op.46/4; Op.57/1–3; Op.64/1–4. These pieces demonstrate nationalistic influence mixed with characteristics of Brahms, Chopin, Schumann, and

Scriabin. Technically demanding. M-D.
Prelude b♭ (Century).

SERGEI LIAPUNOFF (1859–1924) Russia
Two Pieces (GS 469). Canon. Allegretto.
See: David Kaiserman, "The Piano Works of S. M. Liapunov (1859–1924)," JALS, 3 (June 1978), 25–26.

ELIO LIGUORI (1933–   ) Italy
Preludio, intermezzo e fuga (EC   1972) 10pp.

DOUGLAS LILBURN (1915–   ) New Zealand
Chaconne 1946 (University of Otago Press   1972) 23pp. 18 min. Reproduced from holograph. Chaconne in f♯ is stated and followed by thirty variations. Final return same as beginning. MC style. Requires a large technique. D.
Nine Short Pieces (J. Albert 1965–6) 10pp. 12 min. Contrasting, atonal, free dissonant counterpoint, flexible meters, pointillistic. Int. to M-D.
Occasional Pieces for Piano (Price Milburn Music   1975) 20 pieces. 4 short Preludes (1942–44); 2 Christmas Pieces in a (1949); 4 Preludes (1948–60); other untitled pieces. Int. to M-D.
Two Sonatinas 1946   1962 (A. Kalmus). Sophisticated writing. Neo-Romantic conception in No.I. More dissonant harmonies in No.II, with its three linked sections. M-D.

TOMÁS DE LIMA (–   ) Portugal
Caminheiro Saudoso do Lar Op.30/2 (Sassetti   1959) 5pp. Melancholy, melodic, Impressionistic. Includes a brief cadenza. M-D.
Imagens Romanticas (Sassetti). Three Romantic character pieces. Resignação Op.7/2. Danca nobre do Seculo XVI Op.32/2. A Ermida no Mar Op.30/1. M-D.
Minuete Antigo Op.6 (Sassetti   1946) 5pp. Neoclassic, sectional. M-D.
Visão Op.37 (Sassetti) 9pp. A colorful Portuguese "rhapsody." M-D.

LITA LIPSCHUTZ (–   ) USA
Three Episodes (CF   1953) 9pp. 4 min. Presto: toccata-like, two voices, octotonic. Adagio espressivo: freely contrapuntal, lyric. Vivace: much contrary motion, clever, MC. Int.

RAINER LISCHKA (1942–   ) Germany
Allez Hopp! (CFP   1973) 19pp. illustrations. Sixteen short pieces. Descriptive titles such as "Entry of the Lions," with an appropriate roar, and "The Little Monkeys," which will develop a good staccato. Jaunty tunes with much appeal. No fingering. Easy.

FRANZ LISZT (1811–1886) Hungary
Interest in the works of Liszt continues to grow. The American Liszt Society (Professor Fernando Laires, President, Peabody Conservatory of

Music, Baltimore, MD 21202) has helped stimulate interest in this great Romantic personality.

EDITIONS:

Arrangements and Paraphrases of Wagner (Gregg Press).

Arrangements of Beethoven Symphonies (Belwin-Mills). Vol.I:1–5; Vol. II:6–9.

New Edition of the Complete Works (Br and EMB, available through TP). The following volumes are now available:

Vol.I (1970), *Studies I:* 12 Etudes d'exécution transcendante.

Vol.II (1971), *Studies II:* 3 Etudes de Concert, Ab irato, 2 Concert Studies, 6 Grandes Etudes de Paganini.

Vol.III (1972), *Hungarian Rhapsodies I:* 9 Hungarian Rhapsodies, including *Le Carnaval de Pesth.*

Vol.IV (1973), *Hungarian Rhapsodies II:* 10 Hungarian Rhapsodies, including *Rákóczi-Marsch.*

Vol.V (1974), *Années de Pèlerinage I:* Première Année—Suiss; Appendix, including three pieces from *Impressions et poésies* and 9 pieces from *Fleurs mélodiques des Alpes.*

Vol.VI (1975), *Années de Pèlerinage II:* Deuxième Année—Italie; Supplement of three pieces; Appendix of four pieces from *Venezia e Napoli* (1st version).

Vol.VII (1976), *Années de Pèlerinage III:* Troisième Année.

Available separately (BR and EMB, through TP): Après une Lecture de Dante; Au Bord d'une Source; Au Lac de Wallenstadt—Pastorale; Aux Cypres de la Ville d'Este I; Aux Cypres de la Ville d'Este II; Chapelle de Guillaume Tell; Chasse-neige; Les Cloches de Genève; Églogue—Le Mal du Pays; Eroica; 3 Études de Concert; Étude a; Étude f; Feux Follets; Grandes Études de Paganini; Harmonies du Soir; Les Jeux d'Eau à la Villa d'Este; Mazeppa; Orage; Il Penseroso —Canzonetta del Salvatore Rosa; Preludio—Paysage; Rhapsodies Hongroises I, II, III, IV, V, VII, X, XVI, XVII, XVIII, XIX (each individually); Ricordanza; Sposalizio; Sunt Lacrymae Rerum— Marche Funèbre; Tre Sonetti di Petrarca; Vallée d'Overmann; Venezia e Napoli; Vision; Wilde Jagd; Zwei Konzertetuden.

Complete Piano Works, Vol.6 (GS 7733). This is the USSR edition.

12 Studi Op.1 (L. P. Giacchino—EC 1976) 40pp. Introduction in Italian and French. D.

Années de Pèlerinage. Three albums of sensitive tone paintings, kind of a musical scrapbook.

Première année: Suisse (E. Herttrich—Henle 173). Available separately :Au bord d'une source (Cortot—Sal).

Deuxième année: Italie (E. Herttrich—Henle 174). Available separately: Venezia e Napoli (Cortot—Sal); Après une lecture de Dante (J. Milstein—USSR).

Troisième année (listed above). Available separately: Les jeux d'eau
à la Villa d'Este (Cortot—Sal).
See: F. E. Kirby, "Liszt's Pilgrimage," PQ, 89 (Spring 1975):17–21.
Walter Robert, "Après une lecture de Dante," PQ, 89 (Spring 1975):
22–27.
Sharon Winklhofer, "Liszt, Marie d'Agoult and the 'Dante' Sonate,"
19th Century Music, 1 (July 1977).
Consolations (Schmid-Lindner—Br&H).
See: John Diercks, "The Consolations: 'delightful things hidden
away,'" JALS, 3 (June 1978):19–24.
Two Csárdás (Prostakoff—GS). Csárdás obstiné; Csárdás macabre. Excel-
lent for budding virtuosi. M-D.
Concert Etude No.3 D♭ (Busoni, da Motta—Br&H). M-D.
Die Zelle in Nommenwerth 1843. Reproduced with an article about the
piece by Joseph Bloch in PQ, 81 (Spring 1973):4–11. M-D.
Impromptu 1877 (JALS 3 [June 1978]:46–49). Known as the Gort-
schakoff Impromptu, this charming work is bathed in an atmosphere
of Impressionism. M-D.
Two Legends: St. François d'Assise. No.1 *La prédication aux oiseaux* and
No.2 *St. François de Paule marchant sur les flots* (Sauer—CFP).
Available separately: No.2 (Irme—EMB).
Lyon (Galaxy). This piece was originally part of the first book of *Années
de Pèlerinage*, but it has disappeared from all subsequent editions.
Liszt wrote this work in tribute to the silkworkers of Lyon, the
"canuts," following the Lyon Revolution of 1834.
Miniatures (Prostakoff—GS). Contains 5 Hungarian Folk Songs, 4 Little
Pieces, and 3 pieces from the later years. Int.
3 Nocturnes (Cortot—Sal).
Romance Oubliée (Musica Obscura). Three versions, 1848 to 1880, Searle
169, 309A, 527.
Rhapsodie Zingarese 1885 (Kreutzer—BMC). Original title was *Puszta
—Wehmut*, which means "Longing for the Plains." A kind of miniature *Hungarian Rhapsody*. Int.
Sonata b (E. Herttrich—Henle 273). A beautiful urtext edition. (Henle)
also has a magnificent facsimile edition in five colors that shows connected shorter passages and crossed-out sections followed by numerous
pages with extensive revisions. Of special interest is the conclusion of
the work: the original imposing conclusion of 25 bars rising to *fff* was
replaced by an ending 32 bars longer, which gradually fades away to
ppp. Claudio Arrau adds "Some Final Thoughts" to this unusual facsimile edition. (J. Milstein—USSR). D.
See: Ray Longyear, "The Text of Liszt's B Minor Sonata," MQ, 60
(July 1974):435–50.
————. "Liszt's B Minor Sonata—Precedents for a Structural Analysis," MR, 34 (August 1973):198–209.

Wadham Sutton, "Liszt: Piano Sonata in B Minor," *Music Teacher,* 52 (September 1973):16–17.

Valses Oubliées. Available separately: No.1   1881 (Bo&Bo; Schott; Philipp—Heugel; CF; Durand). No.2   1882 (Bo&Bo; Schott). No.3 1883 (Bo&Bo; Schott). Nos.2 and 3 (Liszt Society Publications, Vol.4). No.4   1885 (TP).

Hexameron Variations on the March from Bellini's I Puritani   1837 (K, with a short introduction by Eugene List; Paragon). Liszt, Thalberg, Pixis, Herz, Czerny, and Chopin each wrote one variation. Liszt also wrote the Introduction, several interludes, and the Finale. One of the grandest of the Romantic extravaganzas. D.

SONG TRANSCRIPTIONS:

Hark! Hark! the Lark (Schubert) (APS). M-D.

On Wings of Song (Mendelssohn) (APS) M-D.

Chant Polonais I & II (APS). Two songs from Chopin's Op.74. Includes analysis.

6 Chants Polonais (Chopin, Op.74) (Galaxy). Includes the famous Maiden's Wish Waltz.

The Love of Nature (JALS 1, June 1977). No.5 from *Six Songs of Gellert,* set by Beethoven. Int.

Prayer (JALS 2, December 1977). No.2 from *Six Songs of Gellert.* Int.

OPERA TRANSCRIPTIONS:

Paraphrase from Verdi's Aida   1879 (CFP D-2802). Sacred dance and final duet. This late work is beautifully realized for the keyboard. D.

La Regata Veneziana (Rossini) (Heinrichshofen 550).

OTHER TRANSCRIPTIONS:

Battle of the Huns (GS 6015). Symphonic Poem No.11.

Hamlet (USSR   1975) 18pp. Symphonic Poem arranged for piano. D.

Hungaria (GS 7937). Symphonic Poem No.9.

Transcriptions (USSR   1970) 219pp. Transcriptions of work by other composers. Arcadelt: *Ave Marie.* Mozart: *Miserere d'Allegri et ave verum corpus.* J. S. Bach: 6 Preludes and Fugues for organ (a, C, c, C in 9/8, e, b); Fantasie and Fugue g for organ. Mozart: "Confutatis maledictis" and "Lacrymosa" from *Requiem.* "La Marseillaise." Beethoven: Septet, Op.20; *Adelaide,* Op.46; *Six Songs of Gellert,* Op.48; 6 Lieder ("Mignon"; "Mit einem gernalten Bande"; "Freudvoll und Leidvoll" from Goethe's *Egmont;* "Es was einmal ein König" from Goethe's *Faust;* "Wonne der Wehmut"; "Die Trommel gerühret" from Goethe's *Egmont;* "An die Ferne Geliebte," Op.98). Int. to D.

Easy Operatic Transcriptions (GS 6273).

Twenty Piano Transcriptions (August Spanuth—OD   1903) 156pp. Alabieff: *The Nightingale*. Chopin: *The Maiden's Wish*, Op.74/1 (Chant Polonais); *The Ringlet*, Op.74/14 (Chant Polonais). Robert Franz: *The Messenger*, Op.8/1, 3. Gounod: Berceuse from *The Queen of Sheba*. Mendelssohn: *On Wings of Music*, Op.34/2. Paganini: *La Campanella*. Rossini: *La Ragatta Veneziana* (Notturno); Barcarole G ("La Gita in Gondola"). Schubert: *Faith in Spring*, Op.20/2; *Hark, Hark! the Lark; My Peace Thou Art*, Op.59/3; Valse-Caprice D♭ No.4 from *Soirées de Vienne;* Valse Caprice No.6 from *Soirées de Vienne*. Schumann: *Widmung*, Op.25/1; *Frühlingsnacht*, Op.39/12. Verdi: *Rigoletto Paraphrase* on the Quartet, Act III. Wagner: "Spinning Song" from *The Flying Dutchman;* "O Thou Sublime, Sweet Evening Star"; "Elsa's Bridal Procession." M-D to D.

COLLECTIONS:

Il mio primo Liszt (Rattalino—Ric ER2702) 18pp. Andantino and Adagio, from *Four Little Pieces*. The Shepherds at the Crib, from the *Christmas Tree*. Consolation I. Lassan, Allegretto, Lassan, from *Five Hungarian Folk Songs*. Cradle Song. Sadness of the Puszta (Little Hungarian Rhapsody). Int.

Selected Works (Margaret Gresh—GS 1977) 159pp. Five Hungarian Folk Songs. Four Little Piano Pieces. Nuages gris. Abschied. En rêve. Csárdás obstiné. Csárdás macabre. Consolations 1–6. Liebesträume. *Années de Pèlerinage, 2. année:* Sonetto 47 del Petrarca; Sonetto 104 del Petrarca; Sonetto 123 del Petrarca. Two concert etudes: *Waldesrauschen; Gnomenreigen*. Two legends: *St. François d'Assise. La prédication aux oiseaux; St. François de Paule marchant sur les flots*. Int. to D.

Liszt (Gordon Green—OUP 1973) 63pp. Part of the *Oxford Keyboard Classics* series. Includes: Variation on a Waltz by Diabelli, S.147 (S. refers to Humphrey Searle's thematic catalogue in his book, *The Music of Liszt*, 2d ed., New York: Dover, 1966); Funeral March and Cavatina, S.398 from Donizetti's *Lucia di Lammermoor;* Chant Polonais V: Nocturne, S.480/5 (Chopin–Liszt); Consolation V, S.172/5; La Chasse, S.141/5 (Paganini–Liszt); Hungarian Rhapsody III, S.244/3; Églogue, S.160/7; Hungarian Folksong, S.245/2; Andantino, S.192/4; Elegy II, S.197; Nuages gris, S.199. The introduction discusses Liszt as pianist, his attitude to his texts, playing Liszt today, Liszt's style of playing, his piano music, his achievement, the pedal, the una corda pedal, ornamentation, this edition. Notes on individual pieces. Int. to M-D.

Waltzes (USSR 1967) Vol.IV 121pp. Grand Valse di Bravura (1st version 1836); Bravura Waltz (2d version 1850); Valse Mélancolique (1st version 1839); Valse Mélancolique (2d version 1852); Ländler A♭ (1843); Petit Valse Favorite (1842); Valse–Impromptu (1850);

Première Valse Oubliée (1881); Deuxième Valse Oubliée (1882); Troisième Valse Oubliée (1883); Quatrième Valse Oubliée (1885). M-D.

Unfamiliar Piano Works (Schott 11298). Liszt Society Publications Vol.7. Magyar Dallok Nos.1, 2, 3, 6, 8, 9, 10; Sancta Dorothea; In Festo Transfigurationis Domini Nostri Jesu Christi; Piano Piece F♯; Romance e; Romance Oubliée; Die Zelle in Nonnenwerth (final version); Vive Henri IV (first publication); La Romanesca (first and second versions). M-D to D.

Franz Liszt, a Highlight Collection of His Best-Loved Original Works (C. Hansen 1972). Abschied; Au lac de Wallenstadt; Canzonetta del Salvator Rosa; Chapelle de Guillaume Tell; Consolations; En rêve; Hungarian Folk Song; Hungarian Rhapsody No.2; Il Penseroso; La lugubre gondola; Liebesträume; Little Piano Pieces; Mephisto Waltz; Nuages gris; Soirées de Vienne; Sonata; Sposalizio; Unstern.

Franz Liszt—An Introduction to the Composer and His Music (Joseph Banowetz—GWM 1973). Includes biography, pedagogical aids, and unusual photographs. Editing printed in red. Contains: Carrousel de Madame Pelet-Narbonne; Sancta Dorothea; Wiegenlied; En Rêve; Five Hungarian Folk Songs; Abschied; Album Leaf; Album Leaf in the Form of a Waltz; Four Small Piano Pieces; Sospiri!; Ancient Provençal Christmas Carol; The Shepherds at the Manger; Etudes Op.1/4 d, 1/9 A♭; Variations on a Waltz Tune of Diabelli; Toccata. An outstanding broad introduction to Liszt's piano works. Int. to M-D.

The Twilight of Ferenc Liszt by Bence Szabolcsi. Reprint, Boston: Crescendo Publishers. Piano works (1880–1886) include: Abschied; Csárdás obstiné; László Teleki; Trübe Wolken; Unstern.

Liszt Album (EMB Z.4545) 67pp. Contains: Chant polonais (Chopin): Souhait d'une jeune fille (Op.47) R.145 (R stands for Peter Raabe, *Franz Liszt: Leben und Schaffen,* Stuttgart, 1931). Consolations Nos.3 and 4, R.12. La Pastorella dell'Alpa: G. Rossini Soirées Musicales No.6, R.236. La Regatta Veneziana: G. Rossini Soirées Musicales No.2, R.236. Rhapsodie Hongroise II, R.106 (transposed to C minor by Fr. Bendel). Soirées de Vienne No.6: Schubert: Wiener Abendgesellschaften, R.252. Trois Valses Oubliées I, R.66/b. Valse Impromptu, R.36.

Liszt Technical Exercises (J. Esteban—Alfred 1971).
See: Julio Esteban, "On Liszt's Technical Exercises," JALS, 1 (June 1977):17–19.

The Liszt Studies (E. Mach—AMP). This collection and the Esteban edition contain selections from the original 12-volume set.

See: Joseph Banowetz, "A Liszt Sonetto: Sonnet 47 of Petrarch," *Clavier,* 17 (March 1978):12–21, including the music.

Alfred Brendel, *Musical Thoughts and Afterthoughts* (Princeton: Princeton

University Press, 1976) pp.84–87, offers penetrating insights on the Hungarian Rhapsodies.

Elise Braun Barnett, "An Annotated Translation of Moriz Rosenthal's 'Franz Liszt, Memories and Reflections,'" *Current Musicology,* 13 (1972):29–37.

Linda W. Claus, "An Aspect of Liszt's Late Style: The Composer's Revisions for *Historische, Ungarische Portraits,*" JALS, 3 (June 1978): 3–18.

Maurice Hinson, "The Present State of Liszt Studies Relating to His Piano Works—A Selected Bibliographic Survey," PQ, 89 (Spring 1975): 50–56. Lists the most important bibliographic materials in English dealing with the large body of piano works. Also reprinted in *The Liszt Society Journal* (London), 2 (Summer 1977):27–29.

Istvan Kecskeméti, "Two Liszt Discoveries: 1. An Unknown Piano Piece; 2. An Unknown Song," MT, 1578, 1579 (August, September 1974): 646–48; 743–44. Contains a careful description of the MS of *Siegesmarsch,* a piano work virtually unknown until now, dated at about 1870 or later. Contains stylistic characteristics such as open fifths, ostinato structure, and extreme changes of register.

The Piano Quarterly, 89 (Spring 1975). A special issue devoted to Liszt.

Mark Wait, "Liszt, Scriabin, and Boulez: Considerations of Form," JALS, 1 (June 1977):9–16.

Alan Walker, "Liszt and the Keyboard," MT, 1615 (September 1977): 717, 719–21. Deals mainly with the *Transcendental Etudes.*

Konrad Wolff, "Beethovenian Dissonances in Liszt's Piano Works," JALS, 1 (June 1977):4–8.

MATTHEW LOCKE (ca.1622–1677) Great Britain
Suites (T. Dart—S&B). Contains all the known keyboard pieces by Locke: Five suites, eleven other short pieces for harpsichord, and seven organ voluntaries. Int. to M-D.

THEO LOEVENDIE (1930–   ) The Netherlands
Strides (Donemus   1976) 14pp. Photostat.

FRED LOHSE (1908–   ) Germany
Mouvements (CFP   1971) 21pp. Five concert etudes. D.

LUCA LOMBARDI (1945–   ) Italian
Albumblätter (Moeck   1967–8) 12pp. Reproduced from holograph. Explanations in Italian, German, and English.
Wiederkehr (Moeck   1971) 28pp. Reproduced from holograph. Explanations in Italian, German, and English.

ROBERT LOMBARDO (1932–   ) USA
12 Contemporary Pieces for Children (PIC). Nontriadic, linear counterpoint, twelve-tone suggestion. Easy to Int.

TOM LONG (–   ) USA

Alea: Music by Chance (Canyon Press   1974) 19pp. Includes instructions
   for performance. Melogic; Durations; Deceiving; Modulation; Maze;
   Random Density; Circulation; Contour. Eight aleatoric, or chance,
   music designs, introducing even the youngest students to creativity at
   the piano, using aleatoric experience. Easy to Int.

HEINZ MARTIN LONQUICH (1937–   ) Germany

Neun kleine Klavierstücke (Gerig   1964–71) 12pp. Reproduced from the
   composer's MS.

BENT LORENTZEN (1935–   ) Denmark

Five Easy Piano Pieces (WH   1971) 11pp. Explanations in English.
   Avant-garde notation, fist and forearm clusters. Look more difficult
   than they actually are. Int. to M-D.

GIOVANNI LOSAVIO (1872–1956) Italy

Invocazione e danza (EC   1971) 8pp.

Estro e vita—Valzer brillante and *Novalis—Valzer lento* (EC   1972)
   12pp.

HANS-GEORG LOTZ (1934–   ) Germany

Klavierspiele (Möseler   1972) 22pp. Sixteen short musical pieces introducing twelve-tone technique. Preface and annotations by the composer in German. Some fingerings given. Series used is printed at top
   of each piece as is first inversion, when used. Int. to M-D.

JEAN LOUËL (1914–   ) Belgium

Toccata (CeBeDeM   1972) 33pp. 10 min.

JACQUES LOUSSIER (1934–   ) France

En col roulé (Rideau Rouge   1971) 4pp.

ALAIN LOUVIER (1945–   ) France

Etudes pour Agresseurs, Vols.I and II (Leduc   1969). Seven etudes in
   each volume. "These studies have been conceived for the training of
   pianists in view of the modern aggressive approach to the keyboard.
   We have at command a maximum of 16 'aggressors' (10 fingers, 2
   palms, 2 fists, 2 forearms), individually treated" (from the Foreword).
   Traditional and avant-garde notation. Contains some clever, impressive and wild sonorities. D.

Etudes pour Agresseurs, Vol.III (Leduc   1971) Four Etudes for 14 aggressors for harpsichord.

Quatre Préludes pour Cordes (Pour les cordes du piano) (Leduc) 9pp.
   10 min. For one or more pianos. Two pages each, four folded loose
   leaves in cover. Detailed instructions. Avant-garde. D.

Etude No.37 for Piano for Left Hand (Leduc   1973) 11 min. For 5
   fingers, 1 palm, 1 fist, and 1 arm. Contains a chart of notations. Time
   changes in each bar. M-D.

Etudes pour Agresseurs No.38 (Choudens   1976) 6pp. Explanation in
French. Pour 16 agresseurs apprivoises. D.

Trois gymnopédies automatiques (Leduc   1976) 4pp. 4 min. These pieces
were written using a chart of numbers, a pocket computer, and a 1974
telephone directory. They are based on the pianistic style of Erik
Satie, to whom they are dedicated. M-D. Int.

VINCENT LÜBECK (1654–1740) Germany
Prelude and Fugue a, Suite g (CFP 4478).

JULIUSZ LUCIUK (1927–   ) Poland
Luciuk studied musicology at the Jagiellonian University and composition
with S. Wiechowicz at the State College of Music in Cracow. He continued
his studies in Paris with Nadia Boulanger and Max Deutsch.

Improvisations for Children (PWM   1962). Eight miniatures. Experimental work; aleatoric technique employed where improvisation on the
given materials is called for. Provides a good introduction to music of
our time. Many young pupils are more ready for this type of music than
are their teachers. Int.

Lirica di timbri (PWM   1963). Five compositions for prepared piano.
The composer says: "In this composition the substance of sound is
derived directly from the strings with all kinds of drum sticks and without the use of the keyboard. The perpendicular line of the notations
gives a faithful picture of the movement of the sticks, in that the range
of the strings set in vibration in a given register is not given precisely.
Every performance may, therefore, bring certain variations in sound
and in individual accenting. Two colors are used: red to denote the
RH and green to denote the LH. The scale of the piano strings is divided into four registers which correspond to the metal frames that
extend through the length of the piano. These are: registro basso,
medio, alto and superiore" (from the score). Somewhat similar to
Henry Cowell's *The Banshee*. Avant-garde. D.

4 Sonatine (PWM   1966–69) 30pp. I. 3 movements, freely tonal. Int. II.
3 movements, more chromatic than No.1. Int. III. 3 movements, more
extensive and complex writing, dissonant, closer to M-D. IV. 3 movements, clusters, extreme ranges exploited, short sections, experimental.
M-D.

Passacaglia (PWM   1968) 14pp. Reproduced from holograph. Explanations in Polish and English. M-D.

WOLFGANG LUDEWIG (1926–   ) Germany
Klavierstücke (Bo&Bo   1966) 15pp. 1. Exercises—seven short atonal
pieces. 10pp. 2. Meditation: atonal. 5pp.

OTTO LUENING (1900–   ) USA
Eight Piano Pieces (Galaxy   1952) 15pp. 1. Intermezzo (free in time).

2. Intermezzo. 3. Chorale. 4. Humoresque. 5. Prelude Starlight. 6. Prelude . . . The Philosopher. 7. Prelude . . . Introspection. 8. Prelude . . . To the Warriors. Varied sonorities but chordal preference is strong. M-D.

Five Intermezzos (Galaxy) 11pp. Allegro moderato: varied textures, exciting mid-section, flowing arpeggiated chords in coda. Andante: flowing thirds, Romantic harmonies. Stars: two 16th-note figures in alternating hands, fleeting. Birds: decorative lines. Swans: moving triplets plus chordal closing. A very attractive set. M-D.

Four Preludes (Galaxy   1952) 7pp. Slow; Moderato; Andante; Andante. Freely tonal, motivic figures evolve, sensitive writing. M-D.

Two Preludes (Galaxy   1963) I. 2pp. Freely tonal in E♭, sixths and thirds in right hand, broken chord accompaniment in left hand. II. 4pp. Built on the half-step; free dissonant counterpoint; varied rhythms; concludes in F. M-D.

Dance Sonata for Piano (Highgate   1952) 10pp. Grave; Alla breve; Andante; Allegro energico. Chordal, rhythmic, freely tonal. M-D.

Sonata in Memoriam Ferruccio Busoni (Highgate) 20 min. Eclectic, engaging. A first-rate work; conventional material used in unexpected and original ways; splashing virtuoso demands. Offers a fascinating play of a twentieth-century mind on nineteenth-century ideas. "In my *Sonata* I have attempted to assimilate and follow style he [Busoni] was interested in but without using direct quotes" (from jacket of recording of this work, CRI SD334). D.

First Short Sonata (Highgate   1958) 9pp. Allegro giusto: mainly linear, thickens at coda. Grave: chordal, builds to large climax. Vivace: contrasted with Andante section. M-D.

Third Short Sonata (Highgate   1966) 10pp. "Entertainment, That Glorious Science." Moderato un poco allegro; Molto moderato; eighth note equals 144–160; Allegro moderato. Delightful, witty, clever. M-D.

Fourth Short Sonata (Highgate) 10pp. Allegro moderato: flexible meters, clusters, varied textures. Adagio: built on same motive as first movement. Allegro: repeated notes, large span required. Allegro moderato: varied tempi, clusters, octotonic perpetual motion closing. M-D.

Phantasy (Highgate   1958) 8pp. Freely tonal; sections flow freely; chords alternate with contrary motion runs; quartal and quintal harmony. M-D.

2 Bagatelles (Highgate   1962) 5pp. Maestoso; Allegro. Fetching figurations. M-D.

Andante (Highgate   1958) 4pp. A freely tonal character piece that works to a large climax. M-D.

Music for Piano (A Contrapuntal Study) (CFE) 7pp. Requires fleet but expressive fingers. M-D.

6 Short and Easy Pieces (Highgate) 5pp. Linear, thin textures. Int.

STANLEY LUNETTA (1937–   ) USA
Piano Music (CPE).

MOSHE LUSTIG (1922–1958) Israel
Two Bagatelles (IMI   1946) 7pp. 3 min. Thorny, not for the amateur.
M-D.

WITOLD LUTOSLAWSKI (1913–   ) Poland
Album of Piano Pieces (PWM   1975) 51pp. Contains: 2 etiudy (1940–
1); Melodie ludowe (1945); Bukoliki (1952); 3 utwory dla mlodziezy
(1953); Inwencja (1968). Epilogue in Polish, English, and German.
Illustrations, portrait. These 23 pieces of varying difficulty are the
complete piano works of this eminent contemporary Polish composer.
All the pieces are fingered and have pedal indications.
Available separately: *Two Studies* (PWM). Inspired by Chopin but
display the composer's style even though they are early works. No.1
is very similar in figuration to the Chopin Etude Op.10/1. Both make
use of all the instrument's potential and are full of accidentals. M-D.
Three Pieces for Young Performers (PWM). 1. Four Finger Exercise. 2.
An Air. 3. March. Int.
Invention (PWM   1968) in *Album of Piano Pieces* discussed above.
Atonal, changing metrical units. M-D.

ELIZABETH LUTYENS (1906–   ) Great Britain
Five Bagatelles Op.49 (Schott   1962). M-D.

GUY-PHILIPPE LUYPAERTS (–   ) Belgium
Frenetika (Schott Frères   1971) 8pp. Concours national de musique pro
civitate. Jazz-influenced, dissonant, mixture of styles. D.

M

JOHN MCCABE (1939–   ) Great Britain

McCabe uses the "Study" series to explore different aspects of contemporary piano writing.

Sostenuto   1969 (Nov) 8pp. Study No.2. Widely spread sonorities, harmonics, varied figurations, extremes of keyboard used. Impressionistic. Evaporates "a niente." M-D.

Gaudi (Nov   1970) 25pp. 15 min. Study No.3. A tribute to the Spanish architect Antonio Gaudi. Sounds of bells and gongs; complex; highly contrasted sections; strong Messiaen influence; repeated cluster chords, irregular rhythms; flamboyant writing. D.

Aubade (Nov   1970) 8pp. 7 min. Study No.4. Slow, extended use of arpeggio figures and appoggiaturas; formally fairly free; concentrated thematic material; intended to conjure up the moment of stillness before dawn. Brief fragments of melodies are heard, but as if in recollection. Impressionistic. Requires an elegant legato. D.

Couples (Nov   1976) 2pp. Theme music from the Thames Television Series. Broad sweeping melody; seventh chords and octaves. Int.

Intermezzi   1968 (Nov) 16pp. 9 min. Five contrasted movements are linked by the opening fanfare-like passage, which appears again during the course of the piece and from which many of the themes derive. Each section presents problems of musicianship (e.g., phrasing and pedaling); all require careful rhythmic control. Eclectic, idiomatic style. M-D.

EDWARD MACDOWELL (1861–1908) USA

Forgotten Fairy Tales Op.4   1897 (Hinson—Hinshaw   1975). 1. Sung outside the Prince's Door. 2. Of a Tailor and a Bear. 3. Beauty in the Rose-Garden. 4. From Dwarf-land. Int.

Six Fancies Op.7   1897 (Hinson—Hinshaw   1975). 1. A Tin Soldier's Love. 2. To a Humming Bird. 3. Summer Song. 4. Across Fields. 5. Bluette. 6. An Elfin Round. These pieces and the Op.4 set are endowed with sparkle and a charming Romantic atmosphere. Int.

First Modern Suite Op.10   1883. Prelude (Podolsky—SP; AMP). M-D.

Two Fantastic Pieces Op.17   1884 (Century).

Two Pieces Op.18   1884. No.1, Barcarolle (GS).

Moonlight Op.28/3 (Hinson—Hinshaw) in Vol.II of *Piano Music in Nine-*

teenth Century America (Anson—Willis). A Romantic American nocturne.

Four Pieces Op.24 1887. No.4, Czardas (GS).

Marionettes Op.38 1901 (Hinson—Hinshaw 1979). 1. Prologue. 2. Soubrette. 3. Lover. 4. Witch. 5. Clown. 6. Villain. 7. Sweetheart. 8. Epilogue. In their original form (1888) this charming set contained only six pieces. MacDowell afterward revised them extensively, rearranged their order, and added the Prologue and Epilogue. He uses descriptive English words rather than the usual Italian musical terms. This album comprises one of MacDowell's most interesting portrayals of everyday human nature camouflaged in the form of marionettes. Int.

Twelve Studies (For the Development of Technique and Style) Op.39 1890 (GS). Romance available separately (BMC). Int. to M-D.

Twelve Virtuoso Studies Op.46 (AMP). Nos.1, 2, 4, 7, 11, 12 also available separately.

Ten Woodland Sketches Op.51 1896 (Ashley). This collection contains much variety and uses the piano delicately and opulently. Int. to M-D.

Piano Pieces Opp.51, 55, 61, 62 (Da Capo). Part of the Earlier American Music series. A reprint of the first editions.

MacDowell Masterpieces (Schaum Publications 1973). Contents: Bluette; Of a Tailor and a Bear; The Eagle; Improvisation; To a Wild Rose; In Autumn; From an Indian Lodge; To a Water Lily; Starlight. Int. to M-D.

ROMAN MACIEJEWSKI (1910–   ) USA, born Poland

Maciejewski's early works showed much Polish folklore influence. Later his compositions were affected by Impressionistic influences, and since the early 1950s he has written in a completely individual contemporary idiom.

Cradle Song (PWM).

Four Mazurkas (PWM 1952). Problems of form and construction are solved in a highly individual style. M-D.

Triptych (PWM 1948). Virtuoso treatment of the instrument. D.

DONALD MACINNIS (1923–   ) USA

Toccata for Piano and Two-channel Tape (EBM). Also published in Vol. III of American Society of University Composers Journal of Musical Scores (J. Boonin) 6pp. 8 min. Serial; dramatic octaves at opening; linear. The pianist is invited to respond to the sound events on the tape by improvising, from time to time, from a number of given tone rows and short phrases. Some may be executed either at the keyboard or inside the piano (plucked strings, strumming, rapping with the knuckles on resonant parts of the frame, etc.). Opens and closes on B♭. Avant-garde. D.

NEIL MCKAY (1924–   ) USA, born Canada

Four Miniatures (SP 1975) 7pp. Dance; March; Lullaby; Caprice. Appealing, MC, not easy, programmatic. Int. to M-D.

ELIZABETH MACONCHY (1907–   ) Great Britain
Economy of thematic material characterizes Maconchy's work.
Impromptu 1938 (Hin) 3 min.
Sonatina (Lengnick   1972) 14pp. 6 min. Four movements. For a two-
  manual harpsichord although the work sounds remarkably well on the
  piano. Questionable use of dynamics (e.g., quick accents and sforzan-
  dos) for harpsichord style. Many repeated patterns, short phrases,
  linear, forceful rhythmic treatment. Effective arpeggiando and legatissimo writing. M-D.

IVÁN MADARASZ (–   ) Hungary
Ludi (EMB Z7249   1975) 7pp.
Metamorphosis (EMB   1971) 8pp.

BOGUSLAW MADEY (1932–   ) Poland
Madey studied at the State College of Music in Poznan and at the Guildhall
School of Music in London. At present he is professor at the State College
of Music in Warsaw and conductor of the Warsaw Opera.
Sonatina (PWM   1952) 14pp. Allegro; Andante quasi rubato; Moderato–
  Allegro assai. Freely tonal, more interpretative problems than tech-
  nical. Left-hand skips, thin textures. M-D.
5 Preludes (AA) 10 min.

JEF MAES (1905–   ) Belgium
Divertimento 1970 (CeBeDeM) 8pp.
Oefening (Exercise)   1977 (CeBeDeM) 8pp.

JOSIP MAGDIC (1937–   ) Yugoslavia
Mali zoo (Udruženje kompozitora Bosne i Hercegovine   1972) 7pp.
Ritmičke ekspresije za klavir (Udruženje kompozitora Bosne i Hercegovine
  1972) 15pp.

MARY MAGEAU (1934–   ) USA
Australia's Animals (GS 19090   1978) 5pp. Sleepy Koala. Wandering
  Wombat. Ponderous Platypus. Silver Swan. Capering Kangaroo. Elegant Emu. Colorful and clever descriptive pieces. Excellent introduction to contemporary techniques. Int.

MILOSZ MAGIN (1929–   ) France
Images d'enfants (Durand   1970). Seven short, clever, colorful movements. Int. to M-D.
Sonate (Durand   1972) 35pp. Four contrasting movements with the slow
  one the most successful. Long pedal points underlie changing Ravelian
  harmonic treatment. M-D.

ERNST MAHLE (1929–   ) Brazil, born Germany
Mahle is founder and director of the Escola Livre de Música of Piracicaba
in the state of São Paulo.

As Melodias da Cecilia (Vitale   1971) 54pp. Forty short harmonizations of children's folk songs. Easy to Int.

As Músicas da Cecilia (Ric Brazil   1969) 8pp. Six short harmonizations of children's songs. Colorful, contrasted. No.6, O Gatinho Pega O Ratinho, is the trickiest. Int.

7 Pecas sôbre uma e duas notas só 1954 (Ric Brazil   1969) 7pp. Seven pieces, all on one or two notes each. Dynamic range exploited, pointillistic, harmonics, Webernesque. M-D.

Sonatina (Ric Brazil   1956) 6pp. A one-movement work with much driving rhythm in open fifths. A short Lento mid-section uses chordal sonorities. Driving rhythms return; a short reference to the Lento section appears before the final rhythmic conclusion. M-D.

MESIAS MAIGUASHCA (1938–   ) Ecuador
Maiguashca lives in Cologne, where he serves as an assistant in the Radio Electronic Music Studio and works independently as a composer.
Solo (FSV   1971) 16 min.

SAMUIL M. MAIKAPAR (1867–1938) USSR
Kleine Geschichten Op.8 (Forberg/Jurgenson   1973) 50pp.

Pedal Preludes (SB). Romantic-flavored pieces designed to develop pedal technique. Mechanical action of pedals is discussed. Attractive recital pieces. Int.

18 Selected Pieces (A. Mirovitch—MCA   1956) 32pp. Genuinely fine and imaginative music for the early years of study. Annotations by the editor. Int.

Variations on a Russian Theme (JWC).

Trifles Op.28 (GS) 26 short pieces. Int.

MARTIN MAILMAN (1932–   ) USA
Martha's Vineyard Op.48 (TP   1971) 8pp. Lazy Circles. Short Parade. Breezes. Walk on the Beach. Invention. Inside and Out. Sand Dance. Short, dissonant, clusters, contemporary techniques. Int. to M-D.

Petite Partita (Belwin-Mills). Prelude. Invention. Arietta. Toccatina. Chorale. Dance. Short, strong works. Int. to M-D.

JERZY MAKSYMIUK (1936–   ) Poland
Drops and Droplets (PWM   1976) 28pp. Colored illustrations.

ARTUR MALAWSKI (1904–1957) Poland
Malawski studied in Cracow and Warsaw. From 1948 to 1951 he was president of the Polish Section of the International Society of Contemporary Music. He lectured in composition and conducting at the State College of Music in Cracow.

Miniatures (PWM   1946). Folk-music idiom crafted in a terse, witty style. M-D.

Toccata and Fugue in the Form of a Variation (PWM). Opens with a theme of four bars and nine short variations that form an introduction to a broadly developed fugue. Colorful harmony, lively rhythms. D.

GIAN FRANCESCO MALIPIERO (1882–1973) Italy
6 Pezzi 1907 (Carisch 1975) published separately. Short. Int. to M-D.
Arménia (Sal).
3 Danze Antiche (Rahter 1910). Gavotta. Minuetto. Giga. M-D.
Impressioni (Zanibon). Madrigale; Una processione a mezzanotte. M-D.

RICCARDO MALIPIERO (1914–   ) Italy
Le rondini di Alessandro (SZ 1971). 7 easy pieces.

MICHIO MAMIYA (1929–   ) Japan
Three Preludes (Ongaku-No-Tomo 1972) 20pp. Can be played in any order. Proportional rhythmic notation, time differential left to performer, four staves used for some parts. Pointillistic, expressionistic. D.

KI-LU MANA-ZUCCA (1887–   ) USA
Piano Sonata III (Congress Music Publications 1973) 34pp.

CHRISTIAN MANEN (1934–   ) France
Manen is a professor at the National Conservatory in Paris.
Cortège (Lemoine).
Danse (CFP C393).
Les contes de grand-mère (Lemoine) 2 vols. Twenty short progressive pieces, ten in each volume. Int.

VINCENZO MANFREDINI (1737–1799) Italy
Sei Sonate (Anna Maria Pernafelli—SZ 1975) 55pp. Well edited from the first edition of 1765. Preface in Italian, French, German, and an awkward English translation. These six sonatas have real melodic charm and include a bit of dissonance from time to time. M-D.

FRANCO MANNINO (1924–   ) Italy
Adolescenza (EC 1972) 28pp. Ideas, images, sensations in a collection of sixteen short pieces for piano, written when the composer was between 8 and 14 years of age.
Sonata II Op.69 (EC 1972) 24pp. First movement: an eight-bar theme worked out in a short set of eight variations. Lento: broad gestures, unbarred, large dynamic range (*pppp* to *fff*). Allegro: lengthy, demanding, driving rhythms in compound quadruple meter. D.
Sonata III (EC 1977) 19pp. Nuova collana di musica contemporanea.
Il primo concerto Op.76 (EC 1972) 7pp. Six pieces for the first years of study. Easy-Int.
Sei esercizi dodecafonica da concerto Op.77 (Carisch 1972) 11pp. 7 min.

ROBERT P. MANOOKIN (1918–   ) USA
Little Sonata (MS available from composer, c/o Music Department, Brigham Young University, Provo UT 84601) 14pp. Rather light and

capricious, not too fast: many harmonic sevenths, flowing lines, octotonic, mildly chromatic. Very slowly, with expression: ornaments are
to be played on the beat somewhat leisurely; Ravel-like. Vigorously:
varied figuration, choralelike mid-section, many harmonic major and
minor thirds. A highly effective piece. M-D.

PHILIPPE MANOURY (1952–   ) France
Cryptophonos (Editions Rideau Rouge   1975) 20 leaves. Can be played
on a Steinway D model only. Avant-garde. D.

GIACOMO MANZONI (1932–   ) Italy
Klavieralbum 1956 (SZ   1971) 9pp. 6½ min.

MYRIAM MARBE (1931–   ) Rumania
Sonata (Editura Muzicalà   1956) 18pp.

BENEDETTO MARCELLO (1686–1739) Italy
Sonates pour clavecin (L. Bianconi, L. Sgrizzi—Heugel). Twelve sonatas
in an urtext edition. Contains helpful performance suggestions and historical background. M-D.

ERICH MARCKHL (1902–   ) Austria
Gespräche Sonate (Dob). Intense emotions. Shadows of Bartók, Berg, and
Hindemith are present. M-D.
Sonata E (Dob   1945) 15pp.
Sonata (Dob   1973).

CZESLAW MAREK (1891–   ) Switzerland, born Poland
Mala Suita (PWM   1949) 12pp. Invencja; Marsz; Piosenka; Rondo;
Taniec; Toccata. M-D.
Variations on an Original Theme Op.3 (Amadeus) 22pp. Twelve variations
on a choralelike Romantic theme. Variations alternate between quick
and slow, calm and vigorous, brilliant and less involved. Last variation
is powerful and effective. Whole work is basically Romantic in conception. D.

FRANCO MARGOLA (1908–   ) Italy
15 pezzi facili per gióvani pianisti (Ric). Good for small hands. Easy to
Int.
Another 15 Easy Pieces for the Young Pianist (Ric). Well fingered; contrasted in style and keys. Easy to Int.

WLADYSLAWA MARIEWICZOWNA (1900–   ) Poland
Pictures in Colour (PWM   1947). Six easy attractive pieces. Last composi-
tion, Butterfly Dance, is more difficult than rest of collection. Easy to
Int.
Sonatina (PWM   1956) 13pp. 6 min. Allegro; Lento funèbre; Vivace leg-
giero. Artistic pedagogic material. MC. Int.
Tema con variazioni (PWM   1965) 11pp. 5½ min. Theme and six varia-
tions. Serial, contrasted, thin textures. M-D.

RUDOLF MAROS (1917–   ) Czechoslovakia
Maros studied with Albert Siklós, Zoltán Kodály, and Alois Hába. He is
presently professor at the Academy of Music in Prague, teaching music theory and chamber music for wind instruments.
East European Folksong Suite (PIC   1971) 11pp. Nine short movements
based on folklike material: Slovakian 1 and 2; Austrian; Hungarian;
Croatian 1 and 2; Rumanian; Ruthenian [a province of Czechoslo-
vakia] 1 and 2. Effective. Int.

FRANK MARTIN (1890–1974) Switzerland
Rhythmical Study (Gerig) in collection *Contemporary Swiss Piano Music.*
M-D.
Guitare. Four Short Pieces for Piano 1933 (UE 15041). Dedicated to
Segovia, these pieces were originally written for guitar. Prelude: b.
Air: slow, rhythmic, arabesques, flamenco influence. Plainte: widely
spread chordal figures, repeated notes, Spanish influence. Gigue: cross
rhythms. Musically interesting, sound well on piano. Not as difficult
technically as the *Eight Preludes*. Large span required. M-D.
Fantasie sur des rythmes flamenco   1973 (UE 15042) 17pp. Rumba
lente–Rumba rapide–Soleares–Petenera. ". . . one day I stumbled on
a series of chords which evoked sufficiently well the dreamy spirit of
the romantics and immediately took on the slow rhythm of the rumba.
The special character of this beginning informs the whole of the first
part of the fantasia. The rhythm gets progressively faster until it bursts
into the frenzy of a flamenco rumba. At its climax it breaks off
abruptly. After a prolonged silence a different dance form appears—a
'Soleares.' Like most of the flamenco dances the 'Soleares' is based on
an ostinato rhythm which has its complete exposition at the beginning
of the dance. . . . The work ends with another dance, called the
'Petenera,' which is similarly based on a completely traditional, imper-
turbable rhythm. . . . the music, based on its traditional rhythms, expresses the character of flamenco without speaking the same musical
language" (from the preface by the composer). Contains strong
rhythms, trills, glissandi, fast repeating chords in alternating hands.
Requires large span. M-D.

PADRE GIAMBATTISTA MARTINI (1706–1784) Italy
Sette composizioni inedite per il clavicembalo (Gabriele de Toma—Zanibon   1976) 16pp. Seven fluent, short, graceful pieces, but not the best
of Martini. Preludio F; Rondeau; Sonatas in C, e, C, F, G. The title
"Sonatas" was given by the editor; each sonata has only one movement. Excellent introduction; editorial additions carefully noted. One
page in facsimile. M-D.

DONALD MARTINO (1931–   ) USA
Pianissimo (A Sonata for the Piano)   1970 (ECS   1977) 43pp. 30 min.

Four continuous movements. A solo sonata of Lisztian scope. As diverse in its expressivity as in its virtuosity. D.

Seven Piano Pieces (ECS).

Impromptu for Roger 1978 (Dantalian, Inc., 11 Pembroke St., Newton, MA 02158) 2½ min. For Roger Sessions at 80. Advanced contemporary style, expressively varied, lyrical, fantastical. M-D.

BOHUSLAV MARTINŮ (1890–1959) USA, born Czechoslovakia

Borová: 7 Czech Dances 1931 (Leduc). Borová was the name of Martinů's home town. Acerbic harmonic idiom. M-D.

Christmas (Le Noël) 1927 (Karel Solc—Artia). 1. Sledding. 2. A Child's Lullaby. 3. Christmas Carol. Int. to M-D.

Dumka 1941 (ESC 1970). Easy flowing. Int.

Trois Esquisses 1927 (ESC) 6 min. Debussy style, especially in the second piece, which reminds one of "La Puerta del vino." M-D.

Klavirni skladby ("Piano Compositions") (Panton 1970) 21pp. Preface by Miloslav Nedbal. Contains: The Cats' Procession in the Solstice Night; Dumka; A Composition for Little Elves; Adagio; Prelude; Piece without Title. Int. to M-D.

Kleine Klavierwerke (Věra Zouharová—Panton AP2197 1974). Seven pieces written between 1913 and 1936. Preface by editor, in part translated into Russian, German, and English. Int.

See: B. J. Large, *Martinu* (New York: Holmes and Meier, 1975), 198pp.

TAUNO MARTTINEN (1912–   ) Finland

16 Inventiota (Fazer).

Sonata Op.52 (Fazer) 8 min.

Taara Op.34 (Finnish Music Information Centre 1967) 14pp. 12 min. Virran aania; Taaran lähde; Metsässa tuulee. Twelve-tone orientation, flowing chromatic lines. First and third movements are fast, while the middle movement is slow and melodically treated. M-D.

JAN MASSEUS (1913–   ) The Netherlands

Pentatude Op.46 (Donemus 1974) 12pp. Five concert etudes. Reproduced from holograph. D.

WILLIAM MASON (1829–1908) USA

Mason's compositions are classical in form and refined in style and treatment.

Dance Antique (Hinshaw 1975) in collection *Piano Music In Nineteenth Century America,* Vol.I. Contains some clever canonic writing. M-D.

Silver Spring (Century) M-D.

Spring Dawn (Century) M-D.

EDUARDO MATA (1942–   ) Mexico

Mata is conductor of the Dallas Symphony Orchestra.

Sonata (EMM 1960) 12pp. Serial, rhythmic proportional relationships, pointillistic, atonal, flexible meters, numerous dynamics and tempo changes, harmonics. D.

WILLIAM MATHIAS (1934–   ) Great Britain
See: Malcolm Boyd, *William Mathias* (Cardiff: University of Wales Press, 1978). Available in USA from Lawrence Verry, Inc., P.O. Box 98, Mystic, CT 06355.
Charles Henderson, "An Interview with William Mathias—Welsh Composer," M&M, 9 (July 1975):28–30.
Hugh Ottaway, "Some Thoughts on William Mathias—and Some of His Own," M&M, 26 (June 1978):28–30.

JANEZ MATICIC (1926–   ) Yugoslavia
Intermittences (DSS   1967) 9pp. Explanations in Yugoslav and French.
Nocturne 1952 (DSS   1975) 7pp.
Palpitations (DSS   1971) 8pp., plastic ring binder. Explanations in Croatian, English, and French.

YORIAKI MATSUDAIRA (1931–   ) Japan
Allotropy (SZ   1971) 9pp.

YORITSUNE MATSUDAIRA (1907–   ) Japan
Matsudaira studied composition with H. Werkmeister and A. Tcherepnin, and piano with Lautrup and Gil-Marchex. He is professor at Ueno Gakuen College.
Koromoi-uta (SZ   1972) 16pp. Twelve pieces based on popular tunes. Easy to Int.
Pièces de piano pour les enfants (Ongaku No Tomo Sha   1969) 47pp. 32 short pieces based on Japanese children's songs and folk songs. Oriental harmonizations. Arranged by progressive difficulty. Easy to Int.
Souvenirs d'Enfance I, II, III (Zen-On 317, 318, 329) published separately. I: Berceuse; Boîte à Musique. II: Poissons rouges; Mauvais rêve; Cheval de bois. III: Bulles de savon; Marche. MC. Int.
6 Préludes pour piano en Forme de Thème et Variations (Ongaku-No-Tomo   1976) 32pp. The player may begin the performance with any prelude and play the six pieces in any order. Inexact rhythmic notation, pointillistic, avant-garde. D.

TAMINOSUKE MATSUMOTO (1914–   ) Japan
Album—for Piano (Zen-On   1969) 87pp.+16pp. on 9 loose leaves. Preface and explanations in Japanese. German translation by Kurt Opiolka. Contains: Piano Poems 1–10; Piano Suites 1, 2; Sonatines 1, 2. Int. to M-D.

NAOMICHI MATSUNGA (1920–   ) Japan
Piano Sonata (Japan Federation of Composers   1971) 10pp. Allegro con

moto: SA, traditional harmonies. Allegro con brio: ABA design, "B" part pentatonic. Int.

SHIN-ICHI MATSUSHITA (1922–   ) Japan

Spectre IV (Ongaku-No-Tomo   1971) 4 loose leaves. Extensive directions for performance. Aleatoric, pointillistic, dynamic extremes, clusters, diagrammatic notation, avant-garde. D.

Trois mouvements pour piano—Temps mesurable et temps topologique (Ongaku-No-Tomo   1962) 15pp. Pointillistic, broad contrasting gestures, expressionistic. D.

COLIN MATTHEWS (1947–   ) Great Britain

Five Studies for Piano (Faber   1977) 14pp. Available separately.

SIEGFRIED MATTHUS (1934–   ) Germany

Variationen 1958 (DVFM   1973) 11pp. Expressionistic Lento theme and seven short variations based on dance forms, from ancient to modern —minuet, waltz, polka, tango, fox-trot to boogie woogie. A final Epilogue recalls theme. Clever rhythmic usage. M-D.

WILLIAM R. MAYER (1925–   ) USA

Trains and Things (TP   1971). Suite of four pieces, also available separately. Subway in the Sunlight: ostinato-like bass; crisp, rhythmic melody; attractive. Distance Times, Distance Places: 1. The Aging Troubadour: melody in left hand, bitonal, flowing lines. 2. Cold of the Moon: recitative-like; short figures that press forward; long sustained chords; large span required. A Most Important Train: heavy chords alternate between hands; repeated octaves; arpeggi figures; repetitious left-hand figures give suggestion of moving train; large span required. Int. to M-D.

Toccata   1972 (MS available from composer: 735 Ladd Rd., New York, NY 10471). Flexible meters; varied rhythms, textures, and figures; not like a toccata in the usual sense. Freely chromatic, brilliant conclusion. Requires large span. M-D.

NICHOLAS MAW (1935–   ) Great Britain

Personae (Bo&H   1973) 13 min.

See: Arnold Whittall, "Maw's 'Personae,' Chromaticism and Tonal Allusion," *Tempo,* 125 (June 1978):2–5, for a complete analysis of the piece.

SAMUEL MAYKAPAR. See Samuil M. Maikapar

RICHARD MEALE (1932–   ) Australia

Coruscations (UE 29033   1971) 15pp. One page of explanations in English and German. Oblong format, five basic notations for fast figurations. The notation is the most difficult part of the piece. Pointillistic, extreme dynamic ranges, chordal ideas, varied tempi, Boulez-inspired, virtuoso writing, avant-garde. D.

KIRKE MECHEM (1925–   ) USA
Mechem studied with Walter Piston at Harvard University. He is composer-in-residence at the combined music department of San Francisco College for Women and the University of San Francisco.
Suite Op.5 (ECS). Overture: cheerful, pompous. Elegy: cantabile, contrasting middle section in octaves. Scherzo: spirited. Nocturne: Chopin style. Finale: a brilliant presto, frequent meter changes. MC. M-D to D.
Sonata Op.26 (ECS). Three contrasted movements in traditional form. Neo-Romantic style. M-D.
Whims Op.31 (ECS   1972) 23pp. Fifteen short varied pieces in a neo-Romantic style, strongly rhythmic. Cryptic titles, such as The Happy Drunken Organ Grinder, Impertinence. Int.

TILO MEDEK (1940–   ) Yugoslavia
Adventskalender (CFP 9657   1967–73) 39pp. 24 pieces. Reproduced from holograph. German text only, varied difficulty. Some of the titles are: Hunt Fanfare; Nameless; Evergreen; Nikolaus; I Am Sad; Weigenstück; Birthday Presents; Ostinato; Holy Eve. Contemporary techniques used throughout. Int. to M-D.
Kaminstücke (CFP   1968–70) 63pp.
Meine kleine Nostalgie (CFP   1974) 14pp. Seven character pieces. Reproduced from holograph.
Miszellen I (Gerig   1965) 8pp.

NICHOLAS MEDTNER (1880–1951) Russia
8 Mood Pictures Op.1   1902 (Forberg   1973; Jurgenson) 30pp.
Sonata Op.5 (Belaieff). Revised edition.
3 Arabesques Op.7   1905. No.1, An Idyll (EBM).
3 Fairy Tales Op.9   1906. No.1 (Forberg   1973) 8pp. Large span required for chord and octave passages. M-D.
3 Dithyrambs Op.10   1906. No.1 (Forberg   1973; Jurgenson). No.1 is written in Brahmsian style, rich harmonies, full chords and octaves. M-D.
2 Fairy Tales Op.14   1908 (Forberg   1973) 12pp. (EBM) separately. M-D.
4 Fairy Tales Op.26   1913 (EBM). Nos.1, 3, 4 (EBM) separately. Int. to M-D.
3 Pieces Op.31   1915. No.2, Funeral March (EBM).
4 Fairy Tales Op.34. No.2 (EBM). M-D.
6 Fairy Tales Op.51   1929 (Zimmermann) available separately. M-D.
See: Henry S. Gerstle, "The Piano Music of Nicolas Medtner," MQ, 10 (October 1924):500–10.
    Sidney Miller, "Medtner's Piano Music," MT, 82 (October–November 1941):361–63, 393–95.

LOUIS DE MEESTER (1904–   ) Belgium
Mimes (CeBeDeM   1975) 18pp. 10 min.
Petite Suite (Metropolis   1965) 8pp. Moderato; Vivace; Lento; Scherzando; Presto. Chromatic, moves over keyboard, MC, thin textures. Int. to M-D.
Sonatina (CeBeDeM   1964) 30pp. 12 min.

JACQUELINE MEFANO (–   ) France
Jeu de Durées (Jobert).

KARL MEISTER (1903–   ) Germany
Berg op Zoom Op.78 (Möseler   1975) 16pp. Klaviervariationen über ein altes niederlandisches Siegeslied.

WILFRID MELLERS (1914–   ) Great Britain
Cat Charms   1965 (Nov) 11pp. Three times three pieces for piano. Morning: 1st charm—for walking to; 2nd charm—for hunting to; 3rd charm —for weaving to (at lunch time); 4th charm—for washing to; 5th charm—for dancing to in sunlight; 6th charm—for purring to at night; 7th charm—for keeping still in the dark to; 8th charm—for dancing to by midnight; 9th charm—for falling asleep to. Clever contemporary writing. These pieces could be mimed and danced to by a group of children. Suggested improvised added percussion is listed for such an occasion. Int.

FELIX MENDELSSOHN-BARTHOLDY (1809–1847) Germany
Complete Works for Pianoforte Solo (Julius Rietz—Dover) Reprint of the Br&H 1874–77 edition. Vol.I: Capriccio f♯ (1825); Sonata E (1826); Seven Characteristic Pieces; Rondo Capriccioso E (1824); Fantasy on "The Last Rose of Summer"; Three Fantasies or Caprices (1829); Scherzo b; Gondola Song A (1837); Scherzo a Capriccio f♯; Three Caprices (1833–35); Six Preludes and Fugues (1827–35); Variations Sérieuses d (1841); Fantasy f (1833); Andante cantabile e Presto agitato B (1838); Etude f (1836); Six Pieces for Children (ca.1842); Variations E♭ (1841); Variations B♭. Vol.II: Three Preludes (1836); Three Etudes (1834–38); Sonata g (1821); Sonata B♭ (1827); Album Leaf (Song without Words) e; Capriccio E/e (1837); Perpetuum Mobile C; Prelude and Fugue e (1827, 1841); Two Pieces; Songs Without Words (48 pieces in 8 books).
Songs Without Words (EMB). (Cortot—Sal) has a volume including Op. 19/1, 3; Op.53/4; Op.62/3, 6; Op.67/4, 6.
Capriccio f♯ Op.5 (Cortot—Sal).
Andante and Rondo Capriccioso Op.14 (Sylvia Haas—Henle; Cortot— Sal).
Six Preludes and Fugues Op.35 (Cortot—Sal).
Variations Sérieuses Op.54 (Cortot—Sal).

Kinderstücke Op.72 (Kovats Gabor—EMB Z7812; H. O. Hiekel—Henle 221; PWM 274). The Henle edition is based on an earlier version. Pieces are well suited to the young pianist. An Andante E♭ is included here for the first time. Int.

Variations E♭ Op.82 (Cortot—Sal; Kullak—CFP).

Three Etudes Op.104a (Cortot—Sal) No.2.

See: Thomas Schumacher, "Performance Lesson on a Mendelssohn Etude," *Clavier,* 14 (February 1975):19–23. Discusses No.3 in a.

Selected Works for the Piano (Eric Werner—Henle). Contains: Op.7; Op. 35; Op.54; Op.106; Songs Without Words Op.19/6, Op.30/4, Op. 38/6, Op.53/3, 6, Op.62/1, 3, 6, Op.67/3.

Il mio primo Mendelssohn (Pozzoli—Ric ER2447) 21pp. Contains: 6 pieces from Op.72; Andante sostenuto E♭; Andante con moto D; Allegretto G; Allegro non troppo G; Allegro assai g; Vivace F; 5 Songs Without Words: Venetian Barcarolle, Op.19/6; Op.30/3, 6; Op.85/2; Op.102/3. Int. to M-D.

The Young Pianist's Mendelssohn (Harry Dexter—Hansen House 1972) 33pp. A collection of the easier piano works in their original form. Int. to M-D.

See: Joscelyn Godwin, "Early Mendelssohn and Late Beethoven," M&L, 55 (July 1974):272–85. Discusses Mendelssohn's Sonata E Op.6 and Fantasies for piano f♯ Op.28 and E Op.15 and their inspiration drawn from Beethoven.

GILBERTO MENDES (1922–   ) Brazil

Prelúdio IV 1952 (Ric BR2548) 2pp. Hemiola accompaniment, wistful expressive melody, attractive. Int. to M-D.

USKO MERILÄINEN (1930–   ) Finland

Riviravi 1962 (Fazer) 15pp. Small pieces, sophisticated, clever and tricky. Int.

Sonata II (Weinberger 1966) 16pp. 17 min. A tempo variable lento— mosso; Lento; Presto. A major work that uses clusters and experimental techniques in sounding harmonics, atonal. D.

Sonata III 1972 (Fazer).

Sonata IV (Fazer 1975) 24pp. Epyllion II. Includes a table of notational devices. Strings are to be plucked. Four movements; only the third is slow; the others are full of pianistic acrobatics. Requires virtuoso technique. D.

Sonatina (Fazer 1958) 4 min.

Tre notturni (Fazer) 6 min. Expressionistic. D.

MICHEL MERLET (1939–   ) France

Jeu de quartes (Leduc 1973) 9pp. 4½ min. This "Play of Fourths" is constructed on fourths in every conceivable way. Atonal, dynamic extremes, harmonics. Large span required. D.

OLIVIER MESSIAEN (1908–   ) France

Les Offrandes Oubliées   1930 (Durand) 8pp. A transcription by Messiaen of an orchestral work. The middle section shows the influence of Dukas both rhythmically and harmonically, but the language is still highly personal. A very pianistic transcription. M-D.

Rondeau   1943 (Leduc) 5pp. Vif et gai. Chromatic, many seconds, triads, trills, rubato, effective. M-D.

Vingt Regards sur l'Enfant Jésus ("Twenty Contemplations of Looking at the Christ Child")   1944 (Durand). This pianistic marathon requires 1¾ hours to perform the complete work.
Available separately (Durand): VI. Par lui tout a été fait. X. Regard de l'Esprit de joie. XI. Premiére communion de la Vierge. XV. Le baiser de l'enfant Jésus. XVII. Regard du Silence. D.

Quatre Etudes de Rythme   1949 (Durand). Contains unusual sonorities such as drum, bell, and bird sounds and tunes from India and New Guinea, plus a rhapsodic grandeur. D.
See: John M. Lee, "Harmonic Structure in the *Quatre études de Rythme* of Olivier Messiaen," diss., Florida State University, 1972.

La Fauvette des Jardin ("The Golden Warbler") (Leduc   1972) 55pp. Introduction in French. Belongs in style to the *Catalogue d'oiseaux*. D.
See: Andrew Porter, "Messiaen's Wonderful World of Birds," HF, 23 (September 1973):79–80.
Robert Sherlaw Johnson, *Messiaen* (London: Dent, 1975).

ANTONIO MESTRES (18th century) Spain

Doce Piezas (Francisco Civil—UME). Twelve pieces, most of them called Toccatas. No suggestions for performance. Mainly two-part textures, da capo form, syncopated rhythms, triplet figures. Appealing, colorful. Int.

FRIEDRICH METZLER (1910–   ) Germany

Sonatine (Möseler   1972) 6pp. Opening march leads to a 3/4 andantino, in which tied notes need special care. Opening idea returns to conclude the final 24 bars. Int.

ERNST HERMANN MEYER (1905–   ) Germany

Toccata appassionata (Br&H   1966) 19pp. Facsimile of the autograph. Preface by the composer in German. Introduction evolves to a driving Allegro, followed by a slower Romanza section; Allegro idea returns. Involved, strong, contemporary linear writing of restless energy. Fugal motive heard at opening unifies the piece. Freely tonal, changing tempi, somewhat labored. D.

KRZYSZTOF MEYER (1943–   ) Poland

Meyer studied composition at the State College of Music in Cracow with K. Penderecki. He has also studied with Nadia Boulanger.

Sonata I Op.5 (PWM).

Sonata II Op.7 (PWM 1962). Traditional notation combined with a
    series of original symbols. D.

Four Piano Sonatas (PWM 1974) 88pp. Op.5 (1962), Op.7 (1963),
    Op.13 (1966), Op.22 (1968). Explanations in Polish and English.

Sonata V 1975 (Polish Composers Union Library) 16 min.

NIKOLAI MIASKOVSKY (1881–1950) USSR

Complete Piano Sonatas (GS 6279).

Yellowed Pages Op.31 (GS 532). Two short bagatelles, both poetic. Int.

4 Easy Pieces in Polyphonic Style Op.43, Book 2 (GS).

4 Little Fugues Opp.43, 78 (K). Fugues in c, F, d, g. Excellent pedagogic
    material. Int.

2 Fugues Op.43 (GS 3760).

2 Fugues Op.78 (GS 522).

Polyphonic Sketches Op.78, Book 2 (GS 523).

Simple Variations (Lyric Suite) Op.43/3 (GS 525).

Sonata II Op.13 (GS 528).

Song and Rhapsody Op.58 (GS 529).

Whims; Memories; Yellow Borders (GS 6322).

Two Fugues (Sentimental Mood; Hunting Call) (GS 7909).

PAUL-BAUDOUIN MICHEL (1930–   ) Belgium
Michel graduated from the Royal Conservatory of Mons and studied for
three years with Jean Absil at the Chapell Musicale Reine Elisabeth de
Belgique. Until 1963 his works were mainly atonal, but after several visits
to Darmstadt, elements of total serialization as well as aleatory characteristics have found their way into his music.

Cinq postludes poétiques (CeBeDeM 1965–67) 7pp. 6½ min. Serial, ex-
    pressionistic, pointillistic; aleatoric elements present. M-D to D.

Orbe (CeBeDeM 1972) 8pp. 5 minutes.

Piano, mon ami (Ouvrières 1973) Vol.I, 17pp. Vol.II, 19pp. Trente et
    une études progressives et récréatives.

Variations concentriques (CeBeDeM 1971) 11pp. 8 minutes. Oeuvre im-
    posée at the Concours Musical International Reine Elisabeth 1973.
    Variation V, IV, III, II, I, Theme, I, II, III, IV, V. Expressionistic
    writing demanding virtuoso technique. D.

ROBERT MIDDLETON (1920–   ) USA

Due Variazioni (MS available from composer, c/o Music Department, Vas-
    sar College, Poughkeepsie, NY 12601) 6pp. Contains performance
    directions. Notes are placed on the page without rhythmic arrange-
    ment. The player improvises or "realizes" the given pitches into me-
    lodic parts, accompaniment material, etc. Aleatoric, avant-garde.
    M-D.

Inventions on the Twelve Notes 1963 (MS available from composer)

45pp. Each invention is titled. Among the most attractive is a Toccata somewhat in the style of Prokofieff, and a dashing Capriccio. Thoroughly contemporary writing. D.

Notebooks of Designs (MS available from composer) 12 Realizations, 12 Gravitations, 7 Crystallizations. Contains performance directions. Realizations and Crystallizations are serially organized while Gravitations are not. Realizations may be played in random order. Aleatoric, avant-garde. M-D to D.

Ossiano Improvviste—Notebooks of Designs (Supplement) (MS available from composer) 22pp. "The order results from the tracing of geometric designs amongst the number within a magic square" (from score). Contains extensive performance directions. Aleatoric, avant-garde. M-D.

Sonata 1957 (MS available from composer) 25pp. Largo–Allegro; Andante; Allegro. A skillful work, solid and logical in a contemporary harmonic structure. In the canonic Andante it is fascinating to hear the manner in which a pure musical form is given a gripping and unearthly mood. Strong melodic writing throughout. D.

PETER MIEG (1906–   ) Switzerland

Sonata IV 1975 (Amadeus) 23pp. Four contrasting movements in Romantic style. Virtuoso technique required. D.

Lettres à Goldoni 1971 (Henn).

FRANCISCO MIGNONE (1897–   ) Brazil

Mignone is considered the dean of living Brazilian composers.

Quarto peças brasileiras 1930 (Ric BT 1976) 7 min. 1. Maroca; 2. Maxixando; 3. Nazareth; 4. Toada.

Noche granadina 1931 (Mangione) 2 min.

El retablo del Alcázar 1931 (Mangione) 1½ min.

Tango 1931 (Mangione) 2½ min.

Valsa em Sol maior 1931 (Mangione) 2 min.

Cucumbizinho 1931 (Wehrs) 2 min.

Cateretê 1931 (Wehrs) 2½ min.

Quebradinho 1931 (Wehrs) 2 min.

Lenda sertaneja 7 1932 (Wehrs) 3 min.

Quando eu era pequenino 1932 (Ric) 2 min.

Serenata humoristica 1932 (Mangione) 2 min.

Lenda sertaneja 8 1938 (Wehrs) 2 min.

Valsa de esquina 1 1938 (Mangione) 3 min.

Valsa de esquina 2–12 (Mangione) published separately.

Puladinho 1938 (Wehrs) 2 min.

Caixinha de brinquedos 1939 (Napoleao; EBM 1958) 5 min. Seven pieces.

Modinha 1939 (Mangione) 3 min.

Dança do botucudo   1940 (Mangione) 3 min.

Lenda sertaneja 9   1940 (EBM) 2 min.

Quase modinha   1940 (EBM) 2½ min.

Três prelúdios sobre temas canadenses   1943 (SDM) 5 min. 1. Marianne s'en va-t-au moulin; 2. Sainte Marguerite, veillez ma petite!; 3. A la claire fontaine.

Doçura de manhãzinha fresca   1944 (Mangione) 3 min.

No fundo do meu quintal   1945 (Ric BR) 2 min.

O pobre e o rico   1945 (Ric BR) 1½ min.

Valsa-choro 1–12 (Ric BR) published separately.

Pequena valsa de esquina   1947 (Editora Musical Brasileira) 1 min.

Valsinha   1947 (Editora Musical Brasileira) 1 min.

Lundu (em forma de rondó)   1947 (Todamerica) 2 min.

Toccatina   1947 (Todamerica) 2 min.

Narizinho   1948 (Ric BR) 4 min. Four movements.

Seis pequenas valsas de esquina   1964 (Mangione) 9 min.

E o piano canta também   1969 (Fermata) 2 min.

Valsa brasileira 3   1975 (Fermata) 3 min.

Peças fáceis   1976 (Fermata) 18 min. Eight easy pieces.

Cinco peças para piano   1976 (Musicália, Rua Conselheiro Nébias, 1136, 01–203 São Paulo (SP) Brasil) 6½ min.

Nazarethiana (5 peças)   1977 (Fermata) 15 min.

Trê choros   1977 (Fermata) 10 min.

Microbinho (K 3684).

Seven Piano Pieces for Children (EBM). Little Japanese Toy and Butterflies at Play are available separately. Int.

6½ Preludes 1971–2 (MS available from composer: Rua Pompeu Loureiro 148 20.000 Rio de Janeiro, R.J. Brazil; Gerig in collection *New Brazilian Piano Music*). In Mignone's new atonal style. Sure handling of this technique. M-D.

Sonata II   1962 (SDM) 19pp. 20 min. Three movements. Mignone's first attempt at atonal writing for the piano. All thematic ideas lean heavily on the interval of the third. Serialized melodies but not developed serially. D.

Sonata III   1964 (SDM) 15pp. 19 min. Four separate movements thematically related. Atonal, fragmentary texture, serial techniques. D.

Sonata IV   1964 (Mangione) 15 min. One continuous atonal work in four sections. Texture is more cohesive than in Sonatas II and III. Different from any other Mignone work; displays an integrated maturity not always seen in his other sonatas. D.

Twelve Studies (Columbia Music Co.) 2 vols. Recital pieces. M-D.

See: Sister Marion Verhaalen, "The Solo Piano Music of Francisco Mignone and Camargo Guarnieri," diss., Columbia University, 1971.

MARCEL MIHALOVICI (1898–   ) France, born Rumania
Sonate Op.90   1965 (Leduc) 18pp. 16 min. Allegretto piacevole; Lento,
improvisando; Allegro giocoso. Special signs are explained. Written in
a style that is developed from Enesco, Bartók, neoclassic Stravinsky,
and Les Six. Large span required along with virtuoso technique. D.

PAVEL MIHELCIC (1937–   ) Yugoslavia
Limita (Gerig).

LECH MIKLASZEWSKI (1910–   ) Poland
Four Sonatinas (PWM   1960) 24pp. C, e, G, F. A popular collection of
well-written easy pieces for beginner to intermediate level.

DARIUS MILHAUD (1892–1974) France
La Libertadora (Ahn & Simrock) 7 min. A set of five pieces. Light, deft,
some fancy writing with some performing problems. Folk-like tunes
and samba rhythms used. Originally for two pianos, this arrangement
is by the composer. M-D.
Polka   1929 (Heugel) 5pp. No.7 from *L'eventail de Jeanne,* a ballet by
Ravel, Ferroud, Ibert, Roland-Manuel, Delanney, Roussel, Milhaud,
Poulenc, Auric, and Schmitt. M-D.

THOMAS MIRANTE (1931–   ) USA
Mirante studied composition with Earl George and David Diamond. At
present he is teaching in the Oneida, N.Y. schools.
Eight Recital Encores (PIC   1972). Attractive contrasting pieces, MC.
Easy to Int.

FRANCIS MIROGLIO (1924–   ) Italy
Soliels (SZ   1966). New notation. Avant-garde. M-D.

SHUKICHI MITSUKURI (1895–   ) Japan
Klavierwerke (Ongaku No Tomo Sha   1958) 23pp. Mazurka Op.3/1 and
Tarantella Op.3/4 from *Romantische Suite*. Gavotte Op.4/2 and Men-
uette Op.4/3 from *Klassische Suite*. Sakura-Sakura Op.16/2. Es ist
März, der Frühling Op.16/3. Traditional harmonic, rhythmic, and
melodic treatment. Int. to M-D.

HARUNA MIYAKE (1942–   ) Japan
Miyake graduated from the Juilliard School and studied composition with
Vincent Persichetti and Vittorio Giannini.
Piano Sonata III   1964 (Ongaku-No-Tomo) 7pp. One movement. Flexi-
ble meters, constant dynamic and tempo fluctuation, expressionistic,
thin textures, atonal. M-D.

AKIRA MIYOSHI (1933–   ) Japan
Sonate   1958 (Ongaku No Tomo Sha) 34pp. 24 min. Allegro; Andante;
Presto. This nontonal work requires virtuoso technique and mature

musicianship. Big chords, fluid arpeggi passages, large skips, strong rhythmic drive, and a subtle sonority palette display a well-developed compositional talent. D.

SHUKO MIZUNO (1934–   ) Japan
Provisional Color   1967 (Ongaku No Tomo Sha) 15pp. 15 min. Includes performance directions: "both hands should not touch the keys at the same time but tone overlapping is preferable," etc. Short phrases, pointillistic, subtle sonorities, avant-garde. M-D.

ROBERT MOEVS (1920–   ) USA
Moeves teaches at Rutgers University.
Phoenix   1971 (EBM1199). Notated on three staves throughout. Serial, pointillistic, expressionistic, sensitive lyricism. Builds to dramatic intensity, fades away. M-D to D.
See: David Burge, "New Pieces, Part II," CK, 4 (January 1978):50 for a discussion of this work.

JÉRÔME JOSEPH MOMIGNY (1762–1842) France
Momigny is best known today for his theoretical writings, such as *Cours complet d'harmonie et de composition,* and his publishing activities.
Three Sonatas Op.7 (Albert Palm—Amadeus/Päuler 1973) 19pp. One page of notes. Sonatas in C, G, D, each two movements. Short, naive, charming classical style; similar to Clementi Sonatinas Op.36. Int.

FEDERICO MOMPOU (1893–   ) Spain
Scènes d'enfants (Sal 1915). Five short, colorful descriptive pieces. No.5, Jeunes filles au Jardin, was a favorite encore of Gina Bachauer. Int.
Cancion y Danza   1921–2. 1–4 (UME); 5, 7 (EBM); 5–12 (Sal). Includes some of the most beautiful folk tunes of Spain. M-D.
Musica Callada   1959 (Sal). Book 1 and 2, nine pieces: chromatic. Book 3 (Sal), seven pieces. Book 4 (Sal), seven pieces: somewhat Impressionistic, dedicated to Alicia de Larrocha. Int.
Variations on a Theme by Chopin   1961 (Sal). Quotes from the *Fantaisie-Impromptu.* M-D.
Pessebres   1914–16 (UME). 1. Danza; 2. L'Ermitage (The Hermitage); 3. El Pastor (The Shepherd). Int. to M-D.
Souvenirs de l'Exposition   1937 (ESC) in collection *Parc d'Attractions.* 1. untitled; 2. Tableaux de Statistiques; 3. Le Planétaire; 4. Pavillon de l'Elégance. M-D.
Dialogues 3 and 4 1941, 1944 (ESC).
Paysages No.3 (Sal). Carros de Galicia (Carts of Galicia).
Chanson de Berceau (P. Noël 1962) in collection *Les Contemporains.*
See: Dean Elder, "Federico Mompou, Poet of the Soul's Music," *Clavier,* 17 (December 1978):14–20.

JOAQUIN MONTERO (before 1790–after 1796) Spain

Diez minuets (UME   1973) 9pp. For harpsichord or piano. Realized by Antonio Ruiz-Pipó. Int.

Seis Sonatas (UME). Six sonatas, two movements in each (slow and fast), movements in binary form. Style is a mixture of baroque (Scarlatti) and classic (early Mozart). Int. to M-D.

ARMANDO MONTIEL-OLVERA (–   ) Mexico
Cuatro Danzas Mexicanas   1946 (EMM) 10pp. Allegretto: sixths, thirds, syncopation, clever use of eighth-note triplets. Gaio: 6/8 versus 2/4, crashing chords at closing. Allegretto cantabile: freely chromatic first half, more tonal in second half. Gaio: 8/8 (6/8+2/8), clever. An attractive set. M-D.

XAVIER MONTSALVATGE (1912–   ) Spain
Sonatine pour Yvette   1962 (Sal) 9½ min. Vivo e spiritoso: lighthearted fluency. Moderato molto: expressive. Allegretto: vivacious rondo based on a popular theme. Virtuoso character. D.

DOROTHY RUDD MOORE (–   ) USA
Dream and Variations   1973 (Rudmor Publishers, 33 Riverside Drive, New York, NY 10023) 18 min. Commissioned by Ludwig Olshansky.

TIMOTHY MOORE (1922–   ) Great Britain
Three Two-Part Inventions (Schott 10156   1950) 8pp. About the same difficulty as the J. S. Bach *Sinfonias,* but more Romantic tonal vocabulary. Int. to M-D.

OSCAR MORAWETZ (1917–   ) Canada, born Czechoslovakia
Scherzino (F. Harris   1975) 2pp. MC, changing moods and meters. Fleet fingers required. M-D.

MAKOTO MOROI (1930–   ) Japan
Eight Parables   1967 (Ongaku No Tomo Sha) 10pp. These are based on the first eight letters of the Japanese alphabet and are related to old proverbs. Preface gives background. Pages can be rearranged in any order. Pointillistic, harmonics, clusters. Int. to M-D.

Alpha und Beta Op.12   1953–4 (Ongaku No Tomo Sha) 18pp. 13 min. A little sonata. Alpha: chromatic, dissonant, varied figurations. Beta: theme and twelve variations. Complex. D.

Klavierstück Op.14   1956 (Ongaku No Tomo Sha) 9pp. 7 min. In one volume with *Alpha und Beta.* Strong Schönberg influence, involved, serial. D.

FINN MORTENSEN (1922–   ) Norway
Sonatina II Op.2   1949 (NMO rev. 1952) 14pp. 9 min. Three movements. M-D.

12 kleine Zwölftonstücke für Kinder Op.22   1961, 1964 (NMO) 12pp. For sophisticated children. Explanations in German. Int.

Piano Piece Op.28 (NMO). D.

IGNAZ MOSCHELES (1794–1870) Bohemia

Canon à la Septième (Musica Obscura). Published with Amy Fay-Deppe Exercises.

La Carina (Banks). Rondino B♭.

Recollections of Scotland Op.80 (Musica Obscura).

LAWRENCE MOSS (1927–   ) USA

Moss is a member of the music faculty at the University of Maryland.

Four Scenes for Piano   1961 (Seesaw) 10pp. 6½ min. Reproduction of composer's score. Allegro tempestoso; Adagio sostenuto; Allegro scorrevole; Epilogo. Closely related pieces. Linear, changing meters. Liquid sound required in legato flowing counterpoint. Somewhat similar in style to Leon Kirchner's music. M-D.

Fantasy for Piano (EV   1973). 20pp. 11½ min. I. Very slowly and reflectively: Impressionistic. II. Adagio—as if still. III. Delicately, cloudlike. IV. Allegro ritmico: toccatalike. Written in a free serialistic style; subtly shaded; great delicacy; cascades from beginning to end. Reproduced from MS and not easy to read. A major new work. D.

MORITZ MOSZKOWSKI (1854–1925) Poland

Spanish Dances Op.12. Nos.1, 2, 4, 5 are available separately (Century).

Serenata Op.15/1 (Century).

From Foreign Parts Op.23 (K 9231).

En Autonne Op.36/4 (Century).

Etincelles Op.36/6 (APS; Century). M-D.

Tarantelle Op.77/6 (Schott 09722).

Carmen Fantasy (Musica Obscura).

Etude Melodique (APS). Annotations by the composer. M-D.

Valse Brillante (Century).

KRYSTYNA MOSZUMANSKA-NAZAR (1924–   ) Poland

Bagatelles   1971 (PWM) 17pp. Explanations in Polish and English.

Konstellationen für Klavier (Tonos   1972) 8pp. Explanations in Polish and German. Strings are strummed and plucked. Clusters, pointillistic, aleatoric, avant-garde. D.

JOSÉ VIANNA DA MOTTA (1868–1948) Portugal

Danca da Roda Op.15/1 (Sassetti).

Adeus Minha Terra Op.15/2 (Sassetti).

Chula do Douro Op.15/3 (Sassetti).

LÉON MOURAVIEFF (1905–   ) Germany

Strophe, Antistrophe und Epode (Belaieff   1973) 27pp.

FRANZ XAVIER MOZART (1791–1844) Austria

W. A. Mozart's younger son.

Four Polonaises Melancoliques Op.22 (OUP   1975) 7pp. A facsimile of the first edition with a valuable introduction by Stoddard Lincoln. Somewhat representative of the earlier Romantic period, these pieces have something in common with Hummel, Schubert, and Weber and point stylistically to early Chopin. Graceful and charming. Similar in proportions to the W. F. Bach Polonaises. Int.

LEOPOLD MOZART (1719–1787) Germany

Notebook for Nannerl (E. Valentin—Br) 72 pieces, text. (H. Kann—Zen-On) 41 pieces. Int.

Piano Pieces (Keller—CFP). Three suites from the Notebook for Wolfgang. Int.

12 Musikstücke für das Clavier (K. H. Taubert—R&E   1971). Preface and annotations in German. One short, charming, programmatic piece for each month in the year. Int. to M-D.

Der Morgen und der Abend (Franz Haselböck—Dob   1974) 15pp. Twelve short pieces, one for each month of the year: five by Eberlin; six by Mozart; and one anonymous, with variations by Mozart. Originally written in 1759 for the mechanical organ or horn-work that played every morning and evening from the heights of Salzburg Castle. Int.

WOLFGANG AMADEUS MOZART (1756–1791) Austria

EDITIONS OF THE SONATAS:

(Herttrich—Henle   1976) 18 sonatas in 2 vols. A comprehensive critical edition with suggestions for performance of ornaments; fingered; critical notes in French, German, and English.

(Füssl, Scholz—VU   1973) 18 sonatas in 2 vols. Critical notes in German and English. Information about two or more traditional readings of the text is given. Conclusions are made on the basis of analogy, and musical quality sometimes substitutes for documentary evidence.

(Bartók—K) 1 vol. (Bartók—EMB) 2 vols. Interesting edition but contains excessive pedal markings.

SEPARATE SONATAS:

Sonata G K 283 (Stanley Sadie—ABRSM). Careful edition.
　　See: TM, Analysis of first movement, 108–19.
Sonata F K 332 (Lampe—Henle).
Sonata B♭ (Ichthys Verlag) has facsimile of the autograph.
Sonata c K 457.
　　See: William S. Newman, "K 457 and Op.13—Two Related Masterpieces in C Minor," PQ, 57 (Fall 1966):11–15; also extended article in MR 28 (1967):38–44.
Sonata C K 545.

See: Ilse Gerda Wunsch, "Mozart's Sonata Facile—How Facile?" *Piano Guild Notes,* 24 (May–June 1975):14, 48–50.

See: M. Hinson, "Three Editions of the Mozart Piano Sonatas," PQ, 95 (Fall 1976):33–35. Compares the Broder (TP), Henle, and Vienna Urtext editions.

Antony Hopkins, *Guide to the Interpretation of Piano Classics* (Nov. 87000208), music and cassette: Mozart Sonatas K 282 E♭, 545 C.

VIENNESE SONATINAS:

(Hans Kann—VU). After a contemporary arrangement of the wind divertimentos K 439B.

EDITIONS OF THE VARIATIONS:

(Müller, Seemann—VU   1973) Vol.I: K 24, 25, 180, 179, 354, 265, 353. II: K 264, 352, 398, 455, 500, 573, 613. Preface and critical notes and suggestions for interpretation in German and English.

SEPARATE SETS OF VARIATIONS:

12 Variations C on "Ah, vous dirai-je, Maman" K 265 (CFP 273b).

9 Variations D on a Minuet of Duport K 573 (Zimmermann—Henle 190).

EDITIONS OF THE MISCELLANEOUS WORKS:

Mozart at Eight—The Chelsea Notebook (Zalic Jacobs—TP   1972). Historical introduction by Paul Glass. Twenty short compositions selected from the original forty-three. Written during 1764–5, when Mozart was in London. Charming and surprising works for an 8-year-old, especially No.14. Unusual understanding of contrapuntal and harmonic techniques. Fingering included. (Henle) has the complete London Notebook in Mozart: *Klavierstücke.* Easy to Int.

London Musical Notebook (Ric   1975) 51pp. Contains K 15a–z, K 15aa–mm, K 1500–qq. Preface in Italian, English, and German.

Mozart als achjähriger Komponist (Br&H   1972, reprint of 1909 edition). Includes piano works K 15a–ss. Preface and critical note in German. Easy.

London Musical Notebook (R. Risaliti—Ric   1975) 51pp. 39 pieces.

Prelude (EMB   1977) without K number. Preface by Imre Sulyok in German, English, and Hungarian. Facsimile edition of this modulating piano prelude of Mozart. "According to Wolfgang Plath, and judging by the writing, the MS might have originated around 1776–77. Up till now the prelude was unknown to research and thus it is not included in the Köchel list" (from the preface).

Mozart: Selected Works for Piano Solo (Margaret Gresh—GS   1977) 160pp. Includes: Fantasias I K 397, II K 396, III K 394; Rondos I K 485, II K 577, III K 494, edited by G. Buonamici. Sonatas K 189f, K

189d, K 547a, K 300d, K 576, K 475; Fantasia and Sonata K 457; edited by Richard Epstein. M-D.

London Sketchbook (PWM 82).

The Easiest Original Mozart Pieces for the Piano (A. Rowley—Hin 5) 26pp. Minuet and Trio (*London Notebook*); Two Short Pieces (*London Notebook*); Two Minuets (1762); Ah! Vous dirai-je Maman (Theme with Variations) K 265; Andante Cantabile from Sonata C, K 330; Rondo D (1786); Romance A♭ (Mozart's authorship is not established); Minuet from *Don Giovanni*. Easy to Int.

Leichte Klavierstücke aus dem Londoner Skizzenbuch de achtjährigen Mozart (Br&H 6711). Nine short varied pieces. Easy to Int.

W. A. Mozart—An Introduction to His Keyboard Works (W. Palmer—Alfred). Excellent preface; fine, varied selection of pieces. Easy to M-D.

Mozart Easy Piano (Alfred). 14 pieces including short dances, arrangements of familiar opera arias and brief orchestral works, and two movements from an easy sonata. The short biography and notes on each piece are helpful. Easy to Int.

Mozart—Favorite Piano (Alfred). 24 pieces with eleven duplications in the above album. Fantasia d, K 397; Rondo D. Short biography and notes on each piece. Int. to M-D.

Easy Graded Mozart (J. Ching—K. Prowse) 32pp. Adagios C, D; Alla Gavotta; Allegrettos A, B♭; Allegro B♭; Minuet G; Minuettos from Sonata E♭, K 282; Minuettos A, B♭, C, C; Polonaise F; Rondo C; Theme and Variations from Sonata A, K 331; Waltz D. Highly edited. Int. to M-D.

Eight Minuets with Trios K 315a (B. Paumgartner—UE). Written in Salzburg, probably early in 1779. Attractive, clean editing. (Henle) Easy to Int.

W. A. Mozart—Piano Selections (Albert Kranz—Oberursel). Revised by Günther Hinz. Contains: K 1–5; 7; 15hh; 94; 109b/1, 2, 9; 150; 236; 265; 355; 545. Int. to M-D.

Klavierstücke (Müller, Kann—VU). Contains: K 395, 394, 397, 485, 511, 540. Six of the more extensive pieces Mozart wrote partly for his sister and partly for his pupils. M-D.

Drei Klavierstücke (Karl Marguerre—Ichthys) 16pp. Allegro B♭, K 400; Allegro g, K 590d; Romanze B♭, K Anh. 205.

Musik für Klavier (Otto von Irmer—Br). Easy to M-D.

Easy Piano Pieces (Doflein—Br). The aim of this collection is to make Mozart's charming and noble music loved and known by every child. This first book contains a selection of pieces that Mozart composed when he was six to eight years old. Easy.

Fantasie d, K 397 (Wallner—Henle). Fingering by W. Lampe. (APS 692). Highly edited. M-D.

Zwei Divertimenti K 487 (Br&H 6712). I. Allegro; Menuetto; Polonaise.

II. Andante; Menuetto; Allegro. A delightful set. Int.

Country Dances K 606 (CF). Transcribed by Wanda Landowska.

Due Valzer (Berben) from K 600. F, E♭. Int.

Andante F, K 616 (Wallner—Henle). Fingered by W. Lampe. A waltz written for a small mechanical organ. Very mature Mozart. M-D.

Zwei Rondos (Hans Gal—UE). Facsimile reproductions of K 485 D and K 511 a. (CFP) has a facsimile of K 511. M-D.

Rondo D, K 485 (Henle 53).

Rondo a, K 511 (Henle 54).

Selected Pieces for the Piano (Henle 133).

Adagio b, 540 (Henle 137).

Young Pianist's Guide to Mozart (Y. Novik—Studio P/R 1977) 24pp. Includes 5 minuets, Allegro, Air, Little March, Burlesque (by Leopold), Country Dance, Polonaise, Allegretto, Presto, Adagio, Rondo, Andantino. Tastefully edited for the piano. Record of the contents included. Int.

See: Malcolm Bilsom, "Some General Thoughts on Ornamentation in Mozart's Keyboard Works," PQ, 95 (Fall 1976):26–28.

Betty C. Museus, "Mozart's Fantasia in C Minor, K 475," AMT, 26 (November–December 1976):31–32.

Jörg Demus, "Two Fantasies—Mozart's Fantasy in C Minor (K.475) and Schubert's Fantasy in C Minor (D.993)," PQ, 104: (Winter 1978–79):9–11. A perceptive comparison of these two works.

HENRIQUE DE CURITIBA MOZOROWICZ (1934–   ) Brazil
Since 1976 Mozorowicz has coordinated the graduate music curriculum of the Federal University of Paraná. He has been professor and artist at the International Music Courses of Paraná since 1966, and has also been active throughout Brazil as pianist and organist.

Três estudos breves 1958 (Ric BR 1970) 8 min.

Três prelúdios melancólicos 1958 (EMBAP: Biblioteca da Escola de Musica e Belas Artes do Paraná, Rua Emiliano Perneta, 197, 80.000 Curitiba (PR) Brazil) 5 min. 1. Rubato e molto espressivo. 2. Lento e triste. 3. Moderado.

Pequena Suite 1960 (Ric BR) 5 min. Four movements.

Variações Ingênuas 1960 (EMBAP) 12 min.

4 Pequenos estudos 1966 (EMBAP) 5 min.

8 Pequenos prelúdios e fugas 1969 (EMBAP) 40 min.

Pour Martina 1972 (Gerig) 4 min.

ALBERTO MOZZATI (1917–   ) Italy
Diapositive musicali (Ric 1971). Fascicle I, 16pp. Fascicle II, 18pp.

ROBERT MUCZYNSKI (1929–   ) USA
First Piano Sonata Op.9 (SP). Two contrasting movements, brilliant figuration, imitation, effective dissonances, climactic conclusion. D.

Seven Op.30 (GS) 23pp. Seven untitled contrasted pieces, varied styles, all technically well conceived, astringent dissonances coupled with lyric charm. The last piece requires a fine octave technique and provides a stunning conclusion to this fine suite. Rewarding. M-D.

Third Sonata Op.35 1973–4 (TP) 29pp. Allegro moderato: evolves from short opening fragment; great climax reached in coda before subsiding. Allegro grazioso: a happy 5/8 movement that has many delightful moments. Andante sostenuto: lyric and expressive, leads to a subito allegro to conclude the movement. Atonal, Prokofieff influence, powerful. D.

See: David Burge, "Five New Pieces," CK, 3 (December 1977):66. Discusses the Third Sonata.

Maverick Pieces (GS).

GOTTLIEB MUFFAT (1690–1770) Germany
12 Toccatas and 72 Versets (Upmeyer—Br).

AUGUST EBERHARD MÜLLER (1767–1817) Germany
Andante avec variations par W. A. Mozart (Heuwekemeijer 1970). Variations on the Andante grazioso from Mozart's Divertimento K 271ʰ (287), which is a set of variations on the folksong "Heissa hurtig, ich bin Hans und bin ohne Sorge." M-D.

PAUL MÜLLER (1898–) Switzerland
4 Miniaturen (Foetisch 1971) 7pp.

HERMANN MÜLLICH (1943–) Germany
3 Kontroversen 1972 (R&E) 10pp.

THEA MUSGRAVE (1928–) Great Britain
Monologue for Piano (JWC 1960) 16pp. 5 min. Variations and fugue. Theme is twelve-tone. Variations are highly concentrated and have an intensifying, culminating effect. Influenced by French Music. Rhythms and contours must be strongly etched. D.

Piano Sonata II 1956 (JWC) 14 min.
See: Susan Bradshaw, "Thea Musgrave," MT, 105 (December 1963):866–68.

MODEST MUSSORGSKY (1839–1881) Russia
Pictures at an Exhibition (Emiliia Lazarevna, V. Vladimirovicha—USSR 1975) 6 color plates. In cloth slipcase. One of the most beautifully produced facsimile editions, including the Viktor Hartman paintings that inspired the music and an analysis and history of the work in English. The colored facsimile is reproduced from the MS in the Saltykov-Shchedrin Library in Leningrad. (EBM).

Cinq pièces "Souvenir d'enfance (Forbert reprint 1974) 24pp.

Ein Kinderscherz ("A Children's Jest") (Rahter, Elite Edition 1228). Int.

Mussorgsky Album (György Balla—EMB Z.7017) 60pp. Contains: Bydlo (excerpt from *Pictures at an Exhibition*); Capriccio "On the Southern Shore of the Crimea," No.2; Childhood Memory; Children's Games (Scherzo); First Punishment, from *Memories of Childhood*, No.1; Gurzuf "On the Southern Shore of the Crimea," No.1; Hopak (from the opera *Sorochintsy Fair*) arranged by the composer; Impromptu passionné; Meditation; Nurse and I from *Memories of Childhood*, No.1; Reverie; The Seamstress; Scherzo; Tear. A fine survey with some highly interesting pieces. Int. to M-D.

Compositions for Piano (Forberg   1971) 2 vols. I: En Crimée (Notes de voyage); Méditation; Une larme. II: La couturière; En Crimée; Au village. Int. to M-D.

Selected Piano Pieces (GS 6324).

7 Selected Pieces (Yegorov—GS 561) Book 2.

Operatic Choruses Transcribed for Piano (GS 7970).

ZYGMUNT MYCIELSKI (1907–   ) Poland

Mycielski studied composition in Paris at l'Ecole Normale de Musique with Paul Dukas and Nadia Boulanger. He is a well-known writer of articles and essays on music. In 1960 he became the chief editor of the periodical *Ruch Muzyczny*.

Five Preludes —Piano quintet (PWM   1973) 16pp.

Six Preludes (PWM). Heavy demands are made on the performer regarding interpretation of the mood, subtle color and complex rhythmic textures. D.

N

NICOLAS NABOKOV (1903–   ) USA, born Russia
Sonata I   1926 (Rouart-Larolle).
Sonata II   1940 (Bo&H).

ZVI NAGAN (1912–   ) Israel, born Germany
Five Bagatelles (Israeli Music Publications 195   1964) 7pp. A Town Is
    Awakening. Strolling on the Boulevard. The Grasshopper. Boating.
    Quarrel and Reconciliation. Provides an introduction to contemporary
    techniques. Int.

YOSHINO NAKADA (1923–   ) Japan
Nakada graduated from the Tokyo Academy School of Music. He is pro-
fessor at the Felix Woman's College and director of the Japanese Society
of Rights of Authors and Composers.
Time   1952 (Ongaku No Tomo Sha). Prelude. Harpsichord. Piano: Schu-
    mannesque. Etude: Chopinesque. Romanticist: in style of Gershwin.
    Toyopet: in a perpetual-motion Prokofieff style. The first two move-
    ments are for harpsichord. Int. to M-D.
Light and Shadow   1957 (Ongaku No Tomo Sha). Published with the
    suite above. Highlight; A Story of Ocean; The Girl Playing the Koto;
    Electronic Calculator; Dirge; Labor. Tonal, modal, and atonal writing.
    Int. to M-D.
Sonata   1956 (Japanese Society of Rights & Composers) 32pp. Moderato
    gioviale; Agitato; Allegro ma non troppo. Full resources of the instru-
    ment are used in this freely chromatic, rhythmically driving work. D.
Piano Pieces for Little Hands (Ongaku No Tomo Sha   1976) 30pp.
    Covers a broad range of difficulty. Easy to M-D.
Piano Pieces for Children (Ongaku No Tomo Sha   1976) 29pp. Int. to
    M-D.

CONLON NANCARROW (1912–   ) USA
Rhythm Study I for Player Piano (NME   1951) 22pp. This piece has been
    recorded by the composer on a piano roll by punching accurately
    spaced holes. In this way he is able to achieve rhythmic combinations
    that otherwise would be practically unplayable. Highly complicated
    rhythms. D.
Sonatina (MS available from composer: Apartado 20–550 Mexico City,

237

D.F. Mexico) 12pp. Presto: thin textures; freely tonal; large span required. Moderato: melody accompanied by chords, added-note technique. Allegro molto: toccatalike; flexible meters; builds to large climax at conclusion. M-D.

Conlon Nancarrow: Selected Studies for Player Piano 1977 (available from 1750 Arch Street Records, Berkeley CA 94709) 300pp. Contains numerous scores written for the player piano. There is some remarkably powerful and beautiful music embedded in these works. Complex rhythms, changing tempi, fast moving lines. Also contains valuable essays on Nancarrow by Jim Tenney, Roger Reynolds, Gordon Mumma, and John Cage.

ROBERT NASVELD (1955–   ) The Netherlands
Registers 1974 (Donemus) 7pp. Explanations in Dutch and English.

YVES NAT (1890–1956) France
Berceuse pour un nénuphar (Rideau Rouge 1971) 4pp.
Clown (Sal).
Six Préludes (Sal) published separately. 1. b; 2. B♭; 3. F♯; 4. Le Bucharon; 5. Le Tempete; 6. Préludes à l'Automne.

SHOKO NATSUDA (1916–   ) Japan
Stories of Female Convicts 1955 (Dance Suite for Piano) (Japan Federation of Composers 1970) 15pp. Four contrasting movements. Moderato: bitonal, flowing. Presto: brief introduction; syncopated left hand; slower Dolce contrasting section; returns to Tempo I. Adagio espresso: melodic, sustained. Allegro moderato: rhythmic, contrasting closing section. Originally a ballet suite. M-D.

VACLAV NELHYBEL (1919–   ) USA, born Czechoslovakia
Kaleidoscope (Gen 1968) 2 vols. 103 short pieces that introduce the young pianist to contemporary compositional techniques such as modal writing, changing meters, atonality, percussive usage, Bartókian style. Easy to Int.
Russian Folk Songs (E. C. Kerby 1972) 11 pp. Black Beaver; Birch Tree; Glory to God; Christka; Luli, Lula; Christ Is Risen; The Volga Boatman; Kalinka. Easy to Int.
Four Pieces (Gen 321).

FRIEDRICH NEUMANN (1925–   ) Germany
Spiel-Sachen (Möseler 1972) 25pp. 16 small "play-things." Intellectual writing, strongly rhythmic. Int.

DIKA NEWLIN (1923–   ) USA
Newlin received her doctorate from Columbia University and worked privately with Roger Sessions and Arnold Schönberg. She is a member of the music faculty at North Texas State University.
Fantasy on a Row (ACA).

Fido Flew Away (ACA).

Lhazebur (ACA).

Old Dog Tweetie (ACA).

Sinfonia (ACA).

STEFAN NICULESCU (1927–   ) Rumania

Tastenspiel (Gerig   1972) Choice of 1–6 loose leaves. 5–7 min. Explanations in German and English.

CARL NIELSEN (1865–1931) Denmark

Theme and Variations Op.40   1916 (WH) 27pp. Theme is somber and choralelike. The 15 variations represent a wide diversity of moods, tempi, and styles. Counterpoint, contrasting tonalities and modes, and a great variety of textures and articulations are devices that add interest to this large-scale set. D.

See: Arne Skjold-Rasmussen, "The Piano Works," in *Carl Nielsen, Centenary Essays,* edited by Jürgen Balzer (Copenhagen: Nyt Nordisk Forlag Arnold Busck, 1965), pp.57–67.

RICCARDO NIELSEN (1908–   ) Italy

Cromonomie (Ric   1969) 11pp. 10 min. Broad gestures, pointillistic, performance directions in Italian, English, and German. Avant-garde. D.

Sonatina in Signo Magni Arnold (Bongiovanni 2401).

Sonatina Perbrevis ad usum Petri et Karoli Mariae (Bongiovanni 2402).

ALFRED NIEMAN (1913–   ) Great Britain

Nieman studied composition with Benjamin Dale and piano with York Bowen and Claude Pollard at the Royal Academy of Music. He is professor of composition at the Guildhall School of Music in London.

Enchanted Trumpet   1955 (Lengnick) 8 min.

Five Adventures (Bo&H   1973) 8pp.

Sonata II (Gen   1975) 42pp. 23 min. Fantasy; Passacaglia; Music of Changes. A large, three-movement introverted work in a neo-expressionistic vein. Clusters, polychords, thick textures contrasted with thin ones. One section requires holding the pedal down for five pages. Some serial usage, pointillistic. Stockhausen influence. D.

Two Serenades (Nov) 7½ min. Part of Virtuoso Series edited by John Ogdon. Colombine and Pierrot. Two miniatures that employ delicate, free atonal writing. "Nieman is concerned to express not only the differences, but also the identity of the two characters from the renaissance 'Commedia dell' Arte.' The serenades are elegantly laid out for the piano and are not too difficult" (from editorial note by John Ogdon). M-D to D.

Suite   1955 (Lengnick) 25 min.

Variations and Finale   1962 (Galliard) 12 min.

Arie Fantasie (Nov   1978). Displays constructional devices used by Stockhausen. M-D to D.

WALTER NIEMANN (1876–1953) Germany
Ancient China Op.62 (CFP 3723). Five colorful pieces. M-D.
Barrel Organ Op.107/9 (CFP 3864B). Grotesquely out of tune. An encore piece, greatly indebted to Verdi. The tunes are very well known; the barrel organ effect is unmistakable. Int. to M-D.
Christmas Bells Op.129 (CFP 4272A). Eight little variations on an old English melody. Int. to M-D.
Garden Music Op.117 (CFP 3867). M-D.
Gardens in Spring Op.112/6 (CFP 3864D). M-D to D.
Hamburg Op.107 (CFP 3856). Thirteen characteristic pieces. Int. to M-D.
In Children's Land Op.46 (CFP 3507). 19 pieces. Int. to M-D.
Janmaaten Op.136 (CFP 4277). Two Humoresques from the Port of Hamburg. M-D.
12 Kocheler Ländler Op.135 (CFP 4276) Int. to M-D.
2 Sonatinas Op.152 (CFP 4471). Int. to M-D.
Yule Slumber Lilt Op.143 (CFP 4279). Six easy Christmas pieces. Int.

SERGE NIGG (1924–   ) France
Strepitoso (Jobert).
Variations (Jobert   1964) 9pp. 10 min. Serial, lyric lines. D.

TOLIA NIKIPROWETZY (1916–   ) France, born Russia
Treize Etudes (Bo&H   1973) 31pp. Each of these thirteen pieces deals with some problem of contemporary music. Some are highly dissonant. New symbols are used for pedal markings: full pedal, half pedal, combinations of both. Directions in French. Nos.1, 3, 5, and 11 are well balanced between form and content and display ingeniously developed rhythmic ideas. Somewhat reminiscent of Scriabin *Etudes*.

ANDRZEJ NIKODEMOWICZ (1925–   ) Poland
Sonorità   1966 (PWM) 7pp. Explanations in Polish and English.

VLASTIMIR NIKOLOVSKI (1925–   ) Yugoslavia
Jugendalbum (CFP   1971) 19pp. Youth album with a biographic note in German, French, and English. Reprint of the Skopje edition 1961. Int.

JOAQUÍN NIN-CULMELL (1908–   ) Cuba, born Germany
Tonadas (Rongwen   1957–59) 4 vols. 48 short evocative pieces; colorful, pianistic. Based on folk songs and dances from many regions of Spain. Int.

MARLOS NOBRE (1939–   ) Brazil
Nobre studied with C. Guarnieri and A. Ginastera. In his present position as artistic director of the Ministry of Culture and Education, Radio Service of Rio de Janeiro, Nobre has made Brazilians aware of the wealth of music being written through regular broadcast performances of contemporary works. Nobre is very active as a composer. He writes in a free serialistic

style, and his works display aleatoric structures and indigenous Afro-Brazilian influences.

Nazarethiana Op.2   1960 (Vitale) 4pp. 3 min. Written in the style of Ernesto Nazareth. Light, popular, and classical. M-D.

1º Ciclo Nordestino Op.5   1960 (Vitale) 7pp. 6 min. A suite of five pieces based on folk materials from northeast Brazil. 1. Samba Matuto; 2. Cantiga; 3. E Lamp; 4. Gavião; 5. Martelo. Clever; contrapuntal style. Tonal and modal combinations. Int. to M-D.

Tema e Variações Op.7   1961 (Vitale) 11pp. 4 min. Theme and six variations. Folklike theme with contrasted variations; thoroughly contemporary treatment. M-D.

16 Variações sôbre un tema de Frutuoso Vianna Op.8   1962 (Ric Brazil 1973) 19pp. 11 min. Vianna is a contemporary Brazilian composer. A large, thoroughly contemporary work. Highly pianistic. D.

Tocatina, Ponteio e Final Op.12   1963 (Vitale) 10pp. 4 min. Fast, Slow, Fast. Quasi expressionistic treatment. M-D.

2º Ciclo Nordestino Op.13   1963 (Vitale) 10pp. 6 min. Five folklike dances from northeast Brazil. 1. Batuque; 2. Praiana; 3. Carretilha; 4. Sêca; 5. Xenhenhém. Pedal instructions. The music of northeastern Brazil contains a mixture of African and Gregorian elements. Int.

3º Ciclo Nordestino Op.22   1966 (Vitale) 10pp. 5 min. 1. Capoeira; 2. Côco I; 3. Cantiga de Cego; 4. Côco II; 5. Candomblé. Special notation for clusters. Right hand taps different rhythm from what left hand plays. M-D.

Sonata Breve Op.24   1966 (Tonos) 13 min.

Homenagem a Arthur Rubinstein Op.40 (Tonos   1973) 11pp. Free 32nd-note Presto con fuoco figuration alternates with slower Violento sections. Flexible meters; recitativelike Lento section with long pedals. Con fuoco–più vivo–prestissimo conclusion. Notational peculiarities. D.

TERUYUKI NODA (1940–   ) Japan

Trois Développements pour Piano (Zen-On 383   1974) 12pp. 6½ min. Four different kinds of attack, clusters, pointillistic, proportional rhythmic notation, many tempo changes. Avant-garde. D.

Berceuses Op.6b (Ongaku No Tomo Sha) D.

Fantasiestück (published in same volume with Berceuses). Abstruse, chromatic, changing meters, broad gestures. D.

Märchen   1964 (published in same volume with Berceuses). Same characteristics and qualities as the Fantasiestück. Complex writing. D.

GIORDANO NOFERINI (1934–   ) Italy

Dièci [10] *Miniature* (EC   1975) 10pp.

A. THEODORO NOGUEIRA (1928–   ) Brazil

9 Danças Brasileiras (Ric BR 1497   1973) 28pp. 17 min. Maxixe; Maracatu; Lundu; Samba; Baião; Cateretê; Marcha Carnavalesca; Jongo; Frevo. Contrasting, colorful, chromatic, strong syncopation. All require a well-developed technique and a rhythmic drive. M-D.

10 Serestas 1944–70 (Ric BR 3114) 22 min.

Competições atléticas 1963 (Ric BR) 13 min. Six Scherzos.

12 Valsa-Choros 1940–70 (Ric BR 2898) 28 min.

LUIGI NONO (1924–   ) Italy
Sofferte onde serene (Ric   1977) 14pp. For piano and tape. Reproduced from holograph.

PEHR HENRIK NORDGREN (1944–   ) Finland
Nordgren studied at Helsinki University and in 1970–73 at Tokyo University of Arts and Music. Though he does make use of twelve-tone technique, free application of both clusters and traditional harmonies are also found in his music.
Hoichi the Earless Op.17   1972 (Fazer) 7pp. 9 min. Clusters, widely spread gestures, dynamic extremes, involved rhythms. D.

ARNE NORDHEIM (1931–   ) Norway
Since 1968 Nordheim has been interested in experimental music, particularly music that is to be performed outside a concert hall.
Listen (WH   1971) 4pp. 10 min.

IB NORHOLM (1931–   ) Denmark
Signatures from a Province   1971 (WH) 42pp.

JAN NOVAK (1921–   ) Germany
Inventions (Edition Modern   1960). For harpsichord or other keyboard instruments. 25pp.

25 Exercises for Piano on Moravian Folk Songs (Zanibon 5388   1974). 46pp. Titles in English. Varied, MC, attractive. Int. to M-D.

Rondini (Zanibon   1970). Eight short rondos. Int.

Puerilia (Zanibon   1970). Ten easy pieces. Easy.

Rustica musa, 24 esercizi per pianoforte su canzoni populari morave (Zanibon   1974) 46pp.

VÍTĚZSLAV NOVÁK (1870–1949) Czechoslovakia
Mein Mai Op.20 (Br).

Exotikon Op.45 (Supraphon). A suite.

EMMANUEL NUNES (1941–   )   France
Litanies du Feu et de la Mer (Jobert   1972) 2 separate sheets, 4pp. each. 25 min. A full page of directions is included. Aleatoric, extremes in dynamics and range, clusters, some unusual notation. D.

O

MAURICE OHANA (1914–   ) France

Ohana is one of France's most respected composers, a musician of Spanish extraction who has created a highly personal style rooted in the mysteries of folk music and bathed by the Mediterranean sun and sands.

24 Préludes (Jobert   1974) 47pp. 42 min. Performance directions in French. Clusters, harmonics, careful pedal indications, mostly unmetered, black- and white-key glissandi together. These pieces are conceived as a unit with immediate attacas. Some improvisation is called for. Wide variety of rhythmic patterns; dynamics and range exploitation evident. Double-note percussive effects are highly effective in No.13. Some of the pieces are very short (No.23 is 1⅓ lines). Only a pianist with highly developed technique and interpretive powers could bring these off in performance. D.

Sonatine Monodique (Billaudot   1945) 17pp. 12 min. Allegretto con motto: unisons, chromatic, thin textures, uses wide ranges. Vif: 5-flat signature; scampering 16ths broken up by Lento sections; moves to three sharps, concludes by cancelling all. Andante: single-line introduction leads to thicker textures and faster tempi, *fff* climax. Animé: shifting tempi; slow, sonorous, cadenzalike section; returns to opening textures; drives to final climax. D.

Three Caprices (Billaudot)

HAJIME OKUMURA (1925–   ) Japan

Japanese Children's Songs for Piano   1964 (Ongaku No Tomo Sha) 27pp. 14 charming songs; original flavor and sentiments retained. Includes information about each song as well as an English translation. Easy to Int.

Japanese Folk Songs   1964 (Ongaku No Tomo Sha) 2 vols. Int. to M-D.

Odori   1961 (Ongaku No Tomo Sha) 2 min. Bound with *Sonatine IV*. A short dance. Changing meters, octotonic lines juxtaposed with repeated chromatic chords, più lento mid-section. M-D.

Sonatine III   1961 (Ongaku No Tomo Sha) 7 min.

Sonatine IV   1961 (Ongaku No Tomo Sha) 8 min.

Toccata under Construction (Zen-On 307 1972) 13pp. Energetic rhythms, contrasting sections, fast alternating hands, clusterlike chords, bitonal. M-D to D.

Preludes to Three Flowers (Zen-On 287   1971) 8pp. Anemone. Hyacinth.
Tulip. Clever, colorful characterizations. Int. to M-D.
Dance Impromptu (Zen-On 277   1970) 7pp. Brilliant, glissandi, appeal-
ing. M-D.
Capriccio (Zen-On 270   1969) 10pp. Broken-chord figuration, octaves,
punctuated syncopation. M-D.

FERNANDO CORRÊA DE OLIVEIRA (1921–   ) Portugal
O Principe do Cavalo Branco ("The Prince of the White Horse") Op.6
(Parnaso) 22pp. 16 short colorful pieces. Clusters, galloping effects,
effective. Int. to M-D.
50 Peças para os 5 Dedos ("50 pieces for 5 fingers") Op.7 (Parnaso) 62pp.
Composed in the author's harmonic system, called "Symmetric Harmony," which has a new nomenclature for intervals; black keys are
indicated by oblique crosses. Short, a kind of contemporary "Album
for the Young." Easy to Int.
Variações classicas Incompletas Op.10 (Parnaso) 9pp. Theme and 13 contrasting variations. Modal. M-D.
20 Peças em Contraponto Simétrico Op.15 (Parnaso) 24pp. MC, linear,
twentieth-century inventions. Int.
Sete Estudos de Pequena Virtuosidade Op.18 (Parnaso) 22pp. Each study
emphasizes particular pianistic problems. M-D.

WILLY CORREA DE OLIVEIRA (1938–   ) Brazil
Oliveira is resident composer at the University of São Paulo. He is presently
working on musical structures at the levels of syntax and semantics. Aleatory processes occur in his works though always under the control of all
parameters.
Cinco Kitschs 1967–8 (Ric BR) 12pp. 14 minutes. 1. Back-ground. 2.
Nocturne. 3. Make It Yourself. 4. Jazztime: uses a drummer for assistance. 5. Narcisus: to be taped; the pianist is to sit in the audience and
applaud himself! Avant-garde writing aptly named (*Kitsch*=trash, or
trifle, a doo-dad). Problematical concepts with each kitsch built on a
series. Detailed directions. D.
Impromptu para Marta   1971 (Ric BR) 4pp. 4 min. New notation. Basically in two parts. Aleatoric, form left to performer. Extensive instructions for pianist. Improvisation required. The piece can never be played
as it is written. D.
Two Intermezzos (Ric BR   1973) 5pp. 3 min. New notation. Intermezzo
I: predetermined intensity levels, such as right hand piano, left hand
mezzo forte; square black notes performed at forte level; other gradations are to be developed from these intensities. Intermezzo II: re-
volves around rhythm and meter problems. D.
Prelúdio I   1975 (Ric BR) 3 min.
Prelúdio II   1975 (Ric BR) 3 min.

HAROLD OLIVER (1942–   ) USA

Oliver was trained at the Peabody Conservatory and at Yale and Princeton universities.

Piano Etude (CF   1969) 8pp. Reproduced from holograph. Varied moods, tempi, pointillistic, broad gestures, expressionistic. Wide span required. D.

SPARRE OLSEN (1903–   ) Norway

Norwegian Folk Songs (NMO   1946) 15pp. 19 folk songs from Gudbrandsdal. Winsome and racy tunes, whimsical and touching poems. Much expressed in little. Foreword by Percy Grainger. Easy to Int.

FRANCO OPPO (1935–   ) Italy

Five Pieces (Ric   1970) 11pp. Explanations in Italian, English, and German.

JULIÁN ORBÓN (1925–   ) Cuba, born Spain

Toccata (PIC   1944).

BEN-ZION ORGAD (1926–   ) Israel, born Germany

Variationen über C (IMI 165).

LEO ORNSTEIN (1892–   ) USA, born Russia

Dwarf Suite Op.11 (Schott).

Suite Russe Op.12 (WH   1914). Seven pieces.

Impressions de la Tamise Op.13/1 (Schott   1920).

Poems of 1917 Op.41 (CF   1918) 10 movements. Requires brute force. Strong hypnotic element. Written as a reaction to the horrors of World War I. Martha Graham choreographed and danced to some of these pieces. D.

Six Tragic Sketches Op.48 (Br&H).

Six Watercolors Op.80 (CF   1921).

In the Country (GS   1924). Five children's pieces.

Memories from Childhood (GS   1925). Eight children's pieces.

Musings of a Piano (GS   1924). Four children's pieces.

Sonata IV (GS   1924). Photocopy. Moderato con moto; Simplice; Lento; Vivo. Russian-oriental flavor. D.

Piano Sketch Book (EV   1939) 2 vols. for beginners.

9 Miniatures (CF).

Cossack Impressions (WH   1914) 2 vols.

See: Vivian Perlis, "The Futurist Music of Leo Ornstein," *Notes,* 31 (June 1975):735–50.

BUXTON ORR (1924–   ) Great Britain

Bagatelles   1952 (Eulenberg   1973) 24pp. MS. reproduction. Four contrasted pieces. Light style, complexities infused with numerous unison passages. Effective when played as a group; engaging and usable. M-D.

JUAN ORREGO-SALAS (1919–   ) USA, born Chile

Sonata Op.60   1967 (PIC) 21pp. Libero e mesto; Maestoso; Prestissimo; Violento e cangiante. Twelve-tone, atonal, thoroughly authoritative contemporary writing. Moderate length. D.

LEON ORTHEL (1905–   ) The Netherlands

3 Kleine Preludes Op.60 (Donemus   1975) 9pp. Photostat of MS.

Sonatina No.6 Op.70 (Donemus) 14pp. 12 min. Photostat of MS.

Uit 1920 en 1922. Sonatine 7 Op.73 (Donemus   1975) 13pp. Photostat of MS.

Sonatina No.8 (Donemus   1975) 10pp. Photostat of MS.

Sonatina Brevissima (Donemus). Three movements.

HANS OSIECK (1910–   ) The Netherlands

Sonatina No.3 (Donemus   1972) 13pp. Photostat of the composer's poor MS.

JENS-PETER OSTENDORF (1944–   ) Germany

Transkription für Klavier (Sikorski   1970) 7pp. Tonal, large skipping chords, fast octaves, flexible tempi and meters, tremolando, waltz section, Liszt-like. M-D.

HISATADA OTAKA (1911–1951) Japan

Sonatine Op.13 (Ongaku No Tomo Sha   1965) 20pp. 10 min. Allegretto moderato; Adagio recitativo; Allegro vivace. Colorful and expressive, toccatalike finale in Ravellian style. M-D.

ROBERT OWENS (1930–   ) USA

California Sonata Op.6 (Sikorski 565   1958) 13pp. Allegro cantabile: flowing melodies accompanied by leggiero broken seventh chords; an Andante espressivo mid-section is more chordal and returns at end of movement like a coda. Andante: chordal and octotonic; più mosso section more melodic. Vivace: ostinato-like left-hand figure supports right-hand melody. The whole sonata is freely tonal and displays Impressionistic influence. M-D.

Carnival Op.7 (Sikorski 661   1962) 25pp. Arrival; Merry-Go-Round; Roller-Coaster; Clowns; Valse; Promenade; Trapeze Artists; Acrobats. This MC, freely tonal suite is attractive and well written for the instrument. Programmatically conceived. M-D.

P

IGNACE JAN PADEREWSKI (1860–1941) Poland
Mélodie Op.8/3 (Century).
Menuet Op.14/1 (TP; CF).
Caprice à la Scarlatti Op.14/3 (EBM). Sparkling salon pianism required.
   M-D.
Cracovienne fantastique Op.14/6 (PWM; H. Ries—BMC).
Theme and Variations Op.16/3 (GS; Schott).
Nocturne B♭ Op.16/4 (Anson—Willis). Rich Romantic sonorities. M-D.
Sonata e♭ Op.21 (Bo&Bo) 33 min. Overt Romantic writing. D.
   See: Bryce Morrison, "Paderewski's Sonata," M&M, 23 (July 1975):
   18.
Variations and Fugue e♭ Op.23 (Bo&Bo) 26 min. D.
Album per pianoforti (Z. Sliwinski—PWM 1973) 67pp. Krakowiak E;
   Mazurek; Krakowiak B♭, Op.5/1–3; Album de Mai, Op.10/2;
   Op.14/1, the famous Menuet; Cracovienne fantastique, Op.14/6;
   Op.16/1. Légende, 2. Mélodie, 3. Thème varie, 4. Nocturne, 6.
   Moment musical. These pieces were composed between 1880 and
   1890. Pedaling and some fingering are indicated. Also contains a
   photograph of Paderewski and editorial notes. Int. to M-D.

JOHN KNOWLES PAINE (1839–1906) USA
A Christmas Gift Op.45 1889 (Hinson—Hinshaw) in collection *Piano
   Music in Nineteenth Century America,* Vol.II. This piece was written
   for Paine's sister. Shows thorough workmanship. A delightful scherzo
   feeling permeates its entirety and gives it a kinship with Mendelssohn. M-D.

GIOVANNI PAISIELLO (1740–1816) Italy
See: Jno L. Hunt, "The Keyboard Works of Giovanni Paisiello," MQ, 61
   (April 1975):212–32.
———. "The Life and Keyboard Works of Giovanni Paisiello (1740–
   1816)." Diss., University of Michigan, 1973, 381pp.

FRANÇOIS PAITA (–   ) France
Ballade du Lac Blanc (ESC).
Danza espanola I Op.22 (ESC).
Nocturne II b (ESC).

247

MANUEL PALAU (1893–   ) Spain
Campanas (UME   1971) 4pp.
Evocation de Andalucia ((UME).
Homenaje a Debussy (UME   1957) 7pp. Romantic style interlaced with
   a few dissonances. Tuneful, showy. M-D.
Marcha burlesca (UME   1960) 13pp. Requires plenty of rhythmic con-
   trol. M-D.
Ritmo de Habanera (UME   1955) 4pp.
Toccata e (UME).

JÓZSEF PÁLFALVI (1928–   ) Hungary
Four Pieces for Piano (EMB   1974) 9pp. Lullaby; March; Air; Waltz.
   Technical demands are minimal. Music has much to recommend it.
   Int.

PIERO PALLENBERG (–   ) Italy
Fantasia (Berben). Flexible meters and tempi; augmented triads form
   basis of piece; thick textures. D.

ROBERT PALMER (1915–   ) USA
Epigrams IV–VII 1959 (MS available from composer: c/o Music Department, Cornell University, Ithaca, NY 14850) 8pp. IV. Andante
   con moto: rocking chromatic lines, large chords. V. Vivace e scherzando: uses four types of accents, motivic. VI. Andantino: Romantic,
   bimodal. VII. Allegro vivace e scherzando: 3 with 2, large chords,
   voicing problems, meter fluctuation. M-D.
Second Piano Sonata 1942 and 1948 (MS available from composer) 12pp.
   Edited by John Kirkpatrick. Andante con moto tranquillo: flowing,
   quartal harmony, melody-oriented, freely tonal. Allegro agitato:
   octotonic, flexible meters, chordal development; large span required.
   D.

SELIM PALMGREN (1878–1951) Finland
24 Preludes Op.17 (Fazer   1976) 52pp.
5 Sketches from Finland Op.31 (BMC). Karelian Dance. Minuet. A Guilty
   Conscience Waltz. Finlandish Dance. Int. to M-D.
Sonatine Op.93 (GM).
Sonatine Op.113/34 (GM).
Palmgren Album (BMC). Twelve pieces including: Prelude; Dalliance;
   Intermezzo; Waltz; Berceuse; Humoresque; Gavotte and Musette;
   Sarabande; The Dragon-fly; The Sea; May-night. Int. to M-D.
See: Anne Christiansen, "Palmgren, the Finnish Impressionist," *Clavier,*
   17 (January 1978):12.

ROBERT PALMIERI (1928–   ) USA
Palmieri is chairman of the piano department at Kent State University.
Twenty Piano Exercises (OUP   1971) 21pp. "Problems of bi-rhythms

in one hand, legato-staccato, two-note patterns played as triplets or three-note patterns played as quadruplets are some of the difficulties involved" (from the score). Highly musical. Would make fine recital pieces. Int. to M-D.

GUIDO PANNAIN (1891–) Italy
Sonata (Curci 1973) 40pp.

MARCELLO PANNI (1940–) Italy
Appunto 8.68 (SZ 1972) 3pp. For right hand only.
Tristezza 1968 (SZ 1973) 3pp. Based on Chopin Etude Op.10/3.

ANDRZEJ PANUFNIK (1914–) Poland
Reflections (Bo&H 1971) 12pp. 12 min. Improvisatory, no bar lines, pointillistic, atonal, mixture of Impressionist and MC style, echo phrases, *pp* opening and closing, sparse textures. A three-note cell is subjected to varied treatment. Avant-garde. D.
See: Andrzej Panufnik, *Impulse and Design in My Music* (London: Boosey & Hawkes, 1974), 27pp., for brief descriptions of Panufnik's works.

JEAN PAPINEAU-COUTURE (1916–) Canada
Complementarite 1971 (CMC) 25pp. Clusters, harmonics, plucked strings, half pedals, un-metered. Extreme ranges and dynamics exploited; many avant-garde techniques creatively explored. D.

YORAM PAPORISZ (1944–) Israel, born Poland
Horla, nach einer Novelle von Maupassant 1970 (Moeck) 8 min.
Metamorphosen 1970 (Noetzel) 14pp.
Pianist im Märchenland (IMI 632).

LÁJOS PAPP (1935–) Hungary
Improvvisazione 1965 (EMB 6383). Five short contrasted colorful sections; moves over keyboard. M-D.
Skizze 1971 (EMB 7085) 7pp.
Three Piano Pieces (EMB 5703). Two Burlesques and a theme with five variations. Bartók- and Kodály-inspired. M-D.

PIETRO DOMENICO PARADIES (Paradisi) (1707–1791) Italy
Five Sonatas (Farrenc—Leduc). In E, c, F, A, B♭. M-D.
Gigue B♭ (Ashdown; Banks).
Toccata A (Schott; GS; Durand; Br).

IAN PARROTT (1916–) Great Britain
Theme and Six Variants 1945 (Lengnick) 23pp. 12½ min. Well-developed and contrasted variations. Requires fine pianistic equipment. M-D to D.
Westerham 1940 (Lengnick) 7pp. 4 min. A freely tonal colorful rhapsody. Large span required. M-D.

OEDOEN PARTOS (1907–1977) Israel, born Hungary

Metamorphoses 1971 (IMI) 12pp. 8 min. Includes biographical and program notes in Hebrew and English. Motives expand and contract; proportional rhythmic notation; expressionistic. D.

CLAUDE PASCAL (1921–   ) France

Douze Dechiffrages 1963–9 (Durand) first part. Twelve pieces. Varied moods, MC, appealing. Int.

Suite 1970 (Durand) 13½ min. Prélude; Fugue; Interlude; Canon; Finale. Neobaroque. D.

THOMAS PASATIERI (1945–   ) USA

Pasatieri's music is all highly dissonant and intense and reveals a unique compositional personality.

Cameos (Belwin-Mills 1975). Six short pieces. Contrasting moods and tempi. M-D to D.

Sonata I 1969 (Belwin-Mills 1975) Allegro: broad, builds to huge climax. Lento: slow, cantabile, strong conclusion. Third movement: motoric, driving, toccatalike, double octage passagework. Moderato: moderate opening, ends slowly. Employs a repeated-note figure throughout; strong rhythmic drive, complex polyrhythms. D.

Sonata II 1974 (Belwin-Mills). Opening movement is agitated; middle movement is scherzo- and toccata-like; finale opens in a dark brooding mood but closes with a dramatic climax. M-D.

YVES-MARIE PASQUET (1946–   ) France

Tropes (EMT 1973) 17pp.

BERNARDO PASQUINI (1637–1710) Italy

Opera per cembalo e organo, Vol.I. (Transcribed and revised by Hedda Illy—Edizioni de Santis 1971) 90pp. Introduction in English and Italian. 15 selections: Fantasia; canzone francese; ricercari; variations; and a few dance movements including a charming and rhythmically unusual Bergomasca. M-D.

Otto pezzi per instrumenti a tastiera di compositori della scuola di Bernardo Pasquini (Gerhard Doderer—SZ 1973).

Complete Keyboard Works (Hänssler) 7 vols.

BORIS PASTERNAK (1890–1960) Russia

Prelude g♯ 1906 (*Tempo,* 121:20–25). Early in his life Pasternak had planned to be a musician. He was close friends with Alexander Scriabin and this Prelude shows that influence strongly along with a few Wagnerisms. M-D.

See: Christopher Barnes, "Pasternak as Composer and Scriabin-Disciple," *Tempo* 121 (June 1977):13–19. Discusses the Prelude and surviving piano pieces and fragments of Pasternak.

FRITZ PAUER (–   ) Germany
Meditationen (Papageno 1972) 11pp. Preface in German by Friedrich Gulda.

JIŘÍ PAUER (1919–   ) Czechoslovakia
Bagately (Supraphon).

BERTHOLD PAUL (1948–   ) Germany
Klavierstück 68 Op.10 (Sikorski 1968) 11pp. 8 min. No.18 in Exempla Nova. Improvisational, pointillistic, clusters, dynamics on almost every note. D.

ANTHONY PAYNE (1936–   ) Great Britain
Paean 1971 (JWC) 15pp. 10½ min. Eloquent; explosive; variation procedures; rapidly evolving ideas with a considerable degree of conscious numerical manipulation. This conscious control is not inhibiting but is used as a dramatic device. D.
See: Susan Bradshaw and Richard Rodney Bennett, "Anthony Payne and His 'Paean,' " *Tempo*, 100 (Spring 1972):40–44.

RUSSELL PECK (1945–   ) USA
Suspended Sentence (Jobert 1973) 12pp. In part graphic notation; aleatoric. Notation carefully explained in French and English. Numerous sonorities and keyboard effects investigated, including: black and white chromatic clusters, sometimes rolled with both hands and arms; extreme dynamic treatment; glissandi in various speeds; rhythmic figuration, sometimes free sometimes strict. All over keyboard. D.

JOSÉ ENRIQUE PEDEIRA (1904–   ) Puerto Rico
Ensueno de Marta (EBM). Dance. M-D.
Ritmo (Zapateado) (EBM). M-D.
Súplica (EBM). Dance. M-D.

FLOR PEETERS (1901–   ) Belgium
12 Chorale Preludes Op.114 1966 (CFP) 2 vols. MC treatment of twelve fairly well known chorales in three and four parts. Includes: A Mighty Fortress is Our God; O Sacred Head; O God Thou Faithful God; Wake, Awake for Night is Flying. Int. to M-D.
20 Divertimenti Op.121 1974 (Lemoine). Conservative idiom with some Impressionistic influences. Int. to M-D.

GUERRA PEIXE (1914–   ) Brazil
Peixe has studied Brazilian music all his life. His compositions use folk music materials as the basis for much of his inspiration. Sonatinas I and II and Sonata I are based on nationalistic styles employing folk materials.
Musica II 1942 (SDM) 9pp. I. Allegro. II. Largo. Serial, harmonics. M-D.

Sonatina I   1951 (SDM) 22pp. Three movements. D.

Sonatina II   1969 (SDM) 17pp. Three movements. D.

Sonata I   1950 (SDM) 27pp. Three movements. D.

Sonata II   1967 (SDM) 34pp. Vivace: ostinatolike left hand, driving chordal figuration in right hand, contrasting second tonal area in brillantissimo treatment of coda. Largo: calm; melodic; chordal usage in mid-section rises to climax; concludes *pp*. Allegro: in a quasi march style, à la Prokofieff; bravura passages; Vivace coda. D.

Suite II Nordestina   1954 (Ric BR) 27pp. 1. Violeiro (The Guitar Player): ostinatolike left-hand syncopated accompaniment; color chords in right hand decorate melody. 2. Cabocolinhos (The Little Half-Breed): burlesque, vigorous melody, repeated chords. 3. Pedinte (The Beggar): diatonic melody, chordal accompaniment, bravura return of opening section. 4. Polaca (Polka): graceful; works to climax and recedes to *pp* closing. 5. Frêvo (Brazilian Dance): vigorous, rhythmic, dashing climax. This suite displays Peixe's maturity in using folk materials for his inspiration. M-D to D.

Suite II Paulista   1954 (Ric BR2257) 28pp. 1. Catereté. 2. Jongo. 3. Canto-de-Trabalho. 4. Tambu. Nationalistic style based on native materials. Requires a big technique with strong rhythmic drive. D.

JOSÉ PENALVA (1924–   ) Brazil

Sonata I (Seresta e Desafio)   1970 (Ric BR3186) 7pp. 5 min. A one-movement work, Moderademente: twelve-tone with row given at the opening. Clusters, long trills, toccatalike passages, lento, *ppp* ethereal closing. M-D.

3 Versetos   1963 (Ric BR   1969) 2½ min. Twelve-tone.

Mini-Suite 1   1968 (Ric BR) 2½ min. Twelve-tone.

Mini-Suite 2   1969 (Ric BR) 2½ min. Twelve-tone.

Mini-Suite 3   1971 (Gerig) in collection *New Brazilian Piano Music*. 2 min.

JOSEPH PENNA (1925–   ) USA, born Italy

Six Modations (J. Boonin   1977) 8pp. Eclogue. Faubourdon. Density. Chorale. Dialogue. Icicles. Short, MC, varied, sophisticated. Large span required. Int. to M-D.

BARBARA PENTLAND (1912–   ) Canada

Maze-Puzzle (Waterloo   1969). Two short, freely chromatic pieces with shifting five-finger positions. Int.

Music of Now (Waterloo   1970) 3 vols. Based on contemporary techniques. 1. Intervals; tapping rhythms; student should try to feel the shape of the music and express it with gestures. 2. More black keys used; dotted notes and tone clusters. 3. Simple part playing introduced; triads; use of damper pedal. Main concern in all three volumes is the development of a sensitivity to rhythm and line. Easy to Int.

Shadows (Waterloo 1964) 3pp. Long pedals, serial, pointillistic, subtle sonorities. M-D.

Space Studies (Waterloo 1968) 7pp. 1. Frolic: study in use of wide compass (moving over keyboard). 2. From Outer Space: 1. In Space (study in use of pedal connecting widely spaced melody and of vibration of overtones to enrich harmony); 2. Beeps (rhythm study); 3. Quest (contrapuntal phrasing); 4. Balancing Act (rhythm study). Int.

Angelus–Spectra–Whales 1977 (Ephemera 1, 2, and 3) (CMC).

CLERMONT PÉPIN (1926–) Canada

Trois Pièces pour la Legende Dorée (Leeds Canada). Three short pieces based on the legend of an early French pirate: Prelude; Interlude; Toccata. MC. Int.

RONALD PERERA (1941–) USA

Piano Suite 1966 (ECS 1973) 12pp. Three atonal pieces to be played together. Prelude: mood contrasts, meter and tempo changes. Nocturne: mainly quiet but contains quick figuration near end. Toccata: free, some brilliant and driving effects, harmonics. D.

GEORGE PERLE (1915–) USA

Fantasy-Variations 1971 (MS available from composer: 114 82nd Rd., Kew Gardens, NY 11415) 13pp. 6½ min. Based on a system that "creates a hierarchy among the notes of the chromatic scale so that they are all referentially related to one or two pitches which then function as a tonic note or chord in tonality" (DCM 568). Various serial procedures, twelve-tone modal system. Includes pedal directions. D.

Suite in C 1970 (MS available from composer) 22pp. 18 min. Introduction; Cycles; Chinese Puzzle; Improvisation; Nocturne; Etude. Freely chromatic, twelve-tone modal system, tritone exploited, octotonic, rhythmic proportional relationships, flexible meters, melodically generated tone centers. Requires large span. M-D.

Toccata 1969 (TP) 19pp. 6 min. Bristling intellectuality that displays changing meters, a few slower contrasting sections, restless qualities, and a soft and tonal conclusion. Based on two sets of inversional chromatic scales. Toccatalike figuration. Opening material is most interesting. D.

Six Etudes 1973–76 (Margun 1977) 26pp.

VINCENT PERSICHETTI (1915–) USA

Parable for Piano Op.134 1976 (EV) 10½ min. (Parable XIX). Uses thematic ideas from three folk songs: Waillie, Waillie; Who Will Shoe Your Pretty Little Foot?; De Blues Ain Nothing. Flexible tempi and meters, improvisatory, changing moods, Impressionistic. Interpretive problems, pointillistic melody in alternating hands, hypnotic effects. M-D to D.

See: Vincent Persichetti, "The Modal Sonatina," *Staff Notes,* 13 (Holiday Edition 1974):2–5. A discussion of Sonatina No.3.

MORRIS PERT (1947–   ) Great Britain

Voyage in Space (J. Weinberger   1978) 38pp. Twenty pieces. "This collection of miniature pieces is intended to introduce some of the freedoms of contemporary notation, expression and sound production to the adventurous and imaginative piano student. The most important aspect of each piece is its evocative and sonic nature and the player must be primarily concerned with quality of sound and the creation of atmosphere. In addition to performance of the complete collection, suites of varying length can be drawn from the set for concert purposes" (from the score). Easy to M-D.

WILHELM PETERSEN (1890–1957) Germany

Suite II c Op.53 (Süddeutscher Musikverlag   1976) 13pp.

Variationen über ein Lied des Königs Thibaut von Navarra (1201–1253) Op.50 (Süddeutscher Musikverlag   1973) 16pp.

GOFFREDO PETRASSI (1904–   ) Italy

See: Olga Stone, "Goffredo Petrassi's Eight Inventions for Pianoforte," MR, 33 (August 1972):210–17.

————."Goffredo Petrassi's Toccata for Pianoforte: A Study of Twentieth-Century Toccata Style," MR, 37 (February 1976):45–51.

ROMANO PEZZATA (1939–   ) Italy

Immagine   1971 (SZ) 6pp. Explanations in Italian.

IRENA PFEIFFER (1912–   ) Poland

Let Us Hasten to the Stable (PWM   1972) 29pp. Twenty short attractive Christmas carols and pastorals, MC. Int.

HUGO PFISTER (1914–1969) Switzerland

Sonatine bitonale (Eulenburg   1973) 15pp. Different key signatures for each hand. First movement exploits E♭ major in right hand against d minor in left hand. Slow expressive movement juxtaposes c in right hand with c♯ in left hand. Finale (Rondo) has E♭ fighting with D. Obvious material, unimaginative rhythms. In spite of the title, true bitonality never seems to exist. M-D.

NICOLE PHILIBA (1937–   ) France

Jubilé (Billaudot   1975) 8pp. 4½ min. Vivacious opening; then moves to a toccata style full of octaves and unison figuration. Brilliant with some dissonance. D.

Quatre mouvements successifs (EMT   1973) 14pp.

Six Pièces (Billaudot). Vol.I: Prélude; Mouvement; Marche; Andante; Valse; Final. Easy. Vol.II: more difficult than Vol.I. MC. Int.

Evocations (Lemoine). 2 vols. Second volume more difficult than the first. Easy to Int.

MICHEL PHILIPPOT (1925–   ) France

Sonate II (Sal   1973) 18pp. 15 min. One movement. No metric directions, pointillistic, dynamics for almost every note. Exploits full range of keyboard. Avant-garde. D.

ISIDOR PHILIPP (1863–1958) France, born Hungary

An Isidor Philipp Archive and Memorial Library have been established by The American Liszt Society at the School of Music, University of Louisville, Louisville, KY 40222. The Archive and Memorial Library welcome any memorabilia related to Philipp. Further information can be obtained from Marion Korda, Librarian, Dwight Anderson Memorial Music Library, University of Louisville.

Deux Etudes d'après Fr. Chopin Op.25/6 (Leduc). No.1 is based on chromatic sixths in the right hand. No.2 inverts the hands as contained in the original Chopin. D.

See: Maurice Hinson, "Isidor Philipp—An Appreciation," PQ, 88 (Winter 1974–5):20.

Isidor Philipp, "Some Reflections on Piano Playing," PQ, 88 (Winter 1974–5):21–28.

KARL-HEINZ PICK (1929–   ) Germany

Kleine Märchensuite für Klavier (CFP   1973) 19pp. Seven lively and varied titles from fairy tales. Folklike tunes with sudden harmonic twists. Frequent use of augmented fourths. Int.

Trois pièces (CFP   1973) 26pp.

RICCARDO PICK-MANGIAGALLI (1882–1949) Italy

Toccata Op.7 (Carisch   1930).

Prelude e Toccata Op.27 (Ric) 4 min.

2 Lunaires Op.33 (Ric   1916). Colloque au clair de lune: a sensuous nocturne. La danse d'Olaf: a difficult but rewarding piece. M-D.

Capriccio Op.65 (Carisch   1941).

Silhouettes de Carnaval (Ric   1905). 1. Mascarades. 2. Chanson—Sérénade à Columbine. 3. Et Pierrette Dansait. 4. La ronde des Arlequins.

Il Carillon Magico ("The Magic Chime"): mime-symphonic comedy (Ric 1919).

ALEXANDRA PIERCE (1934–   ) USA

Pierce was educated at the University of Michigan, New England Conservatory, and Radcliffe College, and has a doctorate from Brandeis University. She is a member of the music faculty at the University of Redlands.

Blending Stumps 1976 (Seesaw) 10pp. 11 min. For prepared piano. Preparation materials require: 7 bamboo wedges, 19 blending stumps (blending stumps, or tortillions, are made in France and consist of tightly wound paper in the shape of short pencils), 1 brass shoulder hook, 1 thin rubber washer, 1 Faber-Castell "Magic-Rub" eraser. Includes careful preparation directions. Plucked strings, pedal effects, harmonics, pointillistic, chromatic coloring in a basically diatonic idiom. D.

Coming to Standing   1975 (Seesaw) 11pp. 8 min. Performance directions include: "use abundant pedal, keep melody notes clear, ad lib unless otherwise shown; legato ½ pedal, clearing incompletely." Thin textures are increased to thicker ones. "During a sensory awareness workshop with Charles Brooks and Charlotte Selver I was struck by their frequent use of the direction, 'Come to standing.' They never discussed the expression, yet it was richly suggestive in the context of their work. It meant to me . . . bring oneself to the full presence of the process of one's own simple actions—standing, sitting, etc." (from a letter to the author, July 7, 1977). M-D.

Dry Rot (Seesaw   1977) 17pp. 15½ min. For prepared piano. Includes 4 pages of directions and preparation instructions. Preparations include: Magic Rub erasers, bamboo stalk, large hook screw, rubber tuning damper. Marimba mallet is used to strike strings. No bar lines, pointillistic. "There is a quote from Virgil which almost seems a paraphrase of 'Dry Rot': 'The wound unuttered lives deep within the heart' " (from a letter to the author, November 13, 1977). M-D.

Greycastle   1974 (Seesaw) 13pp. 8½ min. For prepared piano. Preparation materials require 4 piano tuner's rubber wedge mutes, 8 bamboo wedges, 3 pencil erasers, screws, 6 pennies, 2 dimes. Careful preparation instructions included. Repeated notes, pointillistic, trills, effective pedal usage, fast dynamic changes, thin textures. M-D.

Orb   1976 (Seesaw) 13pp. 9 min. For prepared piano. Preparation materials required: 1 piano tuner's rubber mute, 7 wooden clothespin halves, 6 rubber plumbing washers, 2 screws, 1 brass shoulder hook. Careful preparation instructions included. Ideas and fragments are repeated and expanded; no meters indicated; thin textures; varied pedal effects; subtle sonorities emerge from trills. Highly effective. M-D.

Spectres   1976 (Seesaw) 12pp. 8 min. For piano with five easy eraser preparations. Includes careful preparation instructions. A study in repeated notes; very few bar lines; much use of alternating hands; subtle pedal effects; MS easy to read. M-D.

Transverse Process (Seesaw   1977) 13pp. 11 min. No bar lines; varied textures; harmonics; freely expressionistic; sumptuous sonorities. Virtuoso pedaling requires flutter, ½, ¼, blurred releases. M-D.

ALOIS PIÑOS (1925–   ) Czechoslovakia

Tři Skladby (Panton   1968) 16pp. Three pieces. Preface in Czech, Russian, German, and English. Critical notes in Czech and German.

PANAIOT PIPKOV (1904–) Bulgaria
Piesi za piano (Nauka i Izkustvo 1971) 47pp.

GEORG PIRCKMAYER (1918–) Austria
Transitionen für Anfänger (Dob 1973) 12pp. Five pieces, each notated twice: once to show what is done at the keyboard; once to show the musical results when the pedal is used. Interpretive problems. Int.
Transitionen (Dob 1972) 27pp. Book III. Five "Transitions" in twelve-tone writing. Requires full resources of the keyboard; includes thorough pedal indications. Individual handling of dodecaphonic technique. M-D.

FILIPE PIRES (1934–) Portugal
Figurazioni II 1969 (Curci 1975) 3pp. 4½ min. Photograph of MS. The thirteen sections are arranged in any order the player wishes and then repeated in a different chain. Pointillistic, serial, dynamic extremes, one-arm cluster, quartal harmony. Large span required. M-D.

FRANCO PIVA (1936–) Italy
Episodi (Olschki 1960). *Frammenti* (Olschki 1962) 18pp. In one volume.

ILDEBRANDO PIZZETTI (1880–1968) Italy
Three Pieces 1911 (Joseph Williams). Da un autunno gia lontano: 1. Sole mattutino sul prato del roccolo; 2. In una giornata piovosa nel bosco; 3. Al fontanino. Lyrical throughout. M-D.
Sonata 1942 (Curci) 21 min. First movement: lengthy; some Arioso style. Adagio: thick chordal writing: arpeggi. Turbinoso: many octaves; variety of mood. D.
Canti di ricordanza, variations on a theme from *Fra Gherardo* 1943 (SZ).

GIOVANNI BENEDETTO PLATTI (1697–1763) Italy
Sonata No.11 c (G. Scotese—GS 1975) 14pp. Adagio; Allegro; Allegro. Each movement is in binary form. Ornaments are realized. A very beautiful work. M-D.

RAOUL PLESKOW (1931–) USA, born Austria
Pleskow studied at The Juilliard School, Queens College, Columbia University, and privately with Stefan Wolpe. He is chairman of the music department at C. W. Post College of Long Island University.
Piece for Piano (ACA).
Three Bagatelles 1969 (CFE) 8pp. Harmonics, stopped strings. Tightly knit. Keyboard exploited elastically from bottom to top. D.
Pentimento 1974 (Gen) 9pp. In five movements. Pointillistic, serial influence, changing meters and tempi, expressionistic, wide dynamic range, strong in statement. Radical restatement in final two movements of material from first three movements. D.

CLAIRE POLIN (1926–   ) USA

Polin was trained at the Philadelphia Conservatory and studied composition with Vincent Persichetti, Peter Mennin, Lukas Foss, and Roger Sessions.

Out of Childhood (Seesaw   1973) 8pp. Variations on Russian-Turkish folk songs. The Six Kings of Turkey. The Orchard. Rocking Chair Song. Sing, Birdie, Sing. The Rooster. A Gypsy Song. The Sleigh. Chromatic, freely dissonant. For adults thinking back on their childhood. Int. to M-D.

Laissez sonner   1975–6 (Seesaw) 12pp. 15 min. This piano sonata displays strong writing throughout. Inventio: chromatic; expressionistic; glissandi. Fabula: for prepared piano; subtle, misterioso; arpeggi gestures; remove preparation at conclusion of this movement. Parodia: rhythmic; flexible tempi at places; staccato style; thin textures.

ROBERT POLLOCK (1946–   ) USA

Bridgeforms   1972 (Boelke-Bomart) 35pp. 17 min. Eight pieces. Serial, complex and thorny, pointillistic, contrasting tempi and dynamics, involved, expressionistic. D.

Departure for Piano   1975 (Boelke-Bomart) 7 min. Facsimile edition.

Seven Preludes   1975 (Boelke-Bomart) 12 min.

Three Works (Mobart   1977) 26pp. Rhapsody 1969. Ballade 1975. Departure 1975. 5 min.; 3 min.; 7 min. Reproduced from holograph.

NIKOLAI N. POLYNSKII (1928–   ) USSR

Preludes Op.10 (Soviet Composer 402   1975) 46pp. Nos.17–33. Book 2.

MANUEL M. PONCE (1886–1948) Mexico

Quatre pièces (Senart).

LUCTOR PONSE (1914–   ) The Netherlands, born Switzerland

Etudes   1974 (Donemus) 61pp. Photostat of MS. Nos.1–10.

MARCEL POOT (1901–   ) Belgium

Alla Marcia et Barcarolle   1975 (Schott Frères) 4pp.

Deuxième Sonatine   1975 (ESC) 16pp. 10 min.

ANTONIO PORTUGAL (1762–1830) Portugal

Sonata y variaciones (A. E. Lemmon—UME   1976) 24pp.

See: William S. Newman, SCE, pp.305–306 for a discussion of this work.

FRANCIS POULENC (1899–1963) France

Huit Nocturnes 1929–38 (Heugel). Nos.4, 5, 6, and 8 are available separately (Heugel).

Les Biches   1923 (Heugel). Ouverture; Rondeau; Adagietto; Andantino. Based on popular French songs and transcribed by Poulenc. See especially Adagietto. M-D.

Valse—Improvisation sur le nom de Bach 1932 (Sal). Waltzlike, witty, Gallic charm, exciting conclusion. M-D.

Villageoises (Sal 1975). Edited and fingered by Martin Canin. Int.

Presto B♭ (Sal 1975). Written for Vladimir Horowitz. New edition by Martin Canin with fingering and pedal suggestions. M-D.

Bourrée au Pavillon d'Auverne (Sal 1975). Separate from the album *A l'Exposition,* in which it first appeared. M-D.

Histoire de Babar (Le Petit éléphant) (JWC 1940). Excellent musical vaudeville. M-D.

Pièce Brève sur le nom d'Albert Roussel 1929 (Leduc).

See: Laurence Davies, "The Piano Music of Poulenc," MR, 33 (August 1972):195–203.

W. Kent Werner, "The Piano Music of Francis Poulenc," *Clavier,* 9 (March 1970):17–19.

HENRI POUSSEUR (1929–) Belgium

Apostrophe et 6 Réfléxions 1964–6 (UE 894). Apostrophe is a collection of themes (structural motives) in a neo-Impressionistic vein that is full of potential development. Each Réfléxion (variation) is built on a complete fragment from Apostrophe. See especially the variations "Sur le phrase," "Sur le toucher," and "Sur les octaves." Avant-garde. D.

Mnemosyne II (SZ 7661 1977) 6pp. Realized by Pierre Bartholomée.

JOHN POWELL (1882–1963) USA

At the Fair (John Powell Foundation 1912, Box 37711, Richmond, VA 23211) 35pp. Hoochee-Coochee Dance. Circassian Beauty. Merry-Go-Round. Clowns. Snake-Charmer. Banjo-Picker. These sketches of American fun are delightful and develop from the Gottschalk and MacDowell tradition. Folklike tunes permeate the pieces, and color from the old South is apparent on every page. Also available separately. M-D.

In the South Op.16 (John Powell Foundation 1910) 25pp. Humming Birds: fast-moving chromatic and diatonic lines. Love Poem: Romantic harmonies, dramatic mid-section in ragtime style. Negro Elegy: "My Mother's dead and gone" is the theme; mid-section dreams of the past; then opening section returns. Pioneer Dance: based on tune "Howdy Stranger," which is similar to "The Arkansas Traveler"; mid-section based on "Over the Fence." This brilliant piece requires virtuoso octave technique. M-D to D.

Sonata Noble Op.21 1907 (GS 1921) 37pp. Inscribed with a quotation from the poet Sidney Lanier, "Vainly might Plato's head revolve it, Plainly the heart of a child could solve it." Displays a sophisticated contrapuntal technique and a disarming simplicity. Allegro moderato: based on folk tunes or melodies suggested by folk tunes in the mountain areas of western Virginia, West Virginia, Tennessee, and Kentucky; SA. Theme and (7) Variations: in Var. 5 the spirit of the dead returns. Minuetto—Allegretto sostenuto: this is the most intimate and contrapuntal movement. M-D.

Sonata Teutonica Op.24   1913, redaction by Roy Hamlin Johnson, 1977 (MS available from Johnson, 6804 Dartmouth Ave., College Park, MD 20740) 94pp. The text for CRI (Records) 368. D.

See: Roy Hamlin Johnson, "John Powell's Sonata Teutonica," AMT, 28 (November–December 1978):34–36.

JOHN POZDRO (1923–   ) USA

Pozdro is a graduate of Northwestern University and the Eastman School of Music. At present he is chairman of the Theory and Composition Department in the School of Music, University of Kansas, Lawrence, KN 66044.

Four Preludes   1972 (MS available from composer) 12pp. Slowly, pensively: freely tonal; flowing melody accompanied by broken or solid chords; ABA; large span required. Fast: preference for melodic and harmonic seconds; motivic figuration. Freely thoughtfully, warmly: rich harmonies. Fast, but not too fast: thin textures; asterisks represent repetitions of the figurations at the discretion of the performer. M-D.

Sonata II   1963 (MS available from composer) 22pp. Moderato e rubato; Adagio; Allegro molto. Flexible meters; rhythmic drive in outer movements; nontonal arpeggi, chords, and scales. M-D.

Sonata III 1964 (MS available from composer) 20pp. Andante–Presto e legato; Moderato; Vivo e energico. Uses techniques similar to those in *Sonata II* but thematic material is more finely chiseled. Enriched chordal structure, sensuous sonorities. D.

ETTORE POZZOLI (1873–1957) Italy

Pozzoli's style is highly attractive, and his pieces for younger students contain sterling qualities.

Berceuse (Ric 128153).

Easy Sonatina in the Classic Style (Ric 129753). One movement in SA design. Int.

5 Easy Sonatinas in the Classic Style (Ric 2278).

15 Easy Pieces (Ric 436). Delightful, charming. Easy.

Pinocchio Suite (Ric 129061).

Riflessi del mare (Ric 121108). Three characteristic pieces.

Suono il pianoforte (Ric 129754) 19 Little Pieces.

Impressions (Ric 127900) Book I. (Ric 127177) Book II.

See: Maestro Riccordo Castagnone, "Ettore Pozzoli," PQ, 82 (Summer 1973):34–36.

ALMEIDA PRADO (1943–   ) Brazil
Prado is associated with the music vanguard in Brazil. Along with other young composers, he left behind the nationalist school of Camargo Guarnieri and his disciple Osvaldo Lacerda. Prado has studied with Dinora de Carvalho, Camargo Guarnieri, Olivier Messiaen, and Nadia Boulanger.
Variações sobre o tema "Aeroplano Jahu"   1963 (Vitale) 8 min.
Toccata   1964 (Vitale) 5 min.
Sonata I   1965 (Tonos) 22pp. 14 min. Luminoso, Solar; Improvizando; Energico (Fuga). Strong Schönberg and Villa-Lobos influence. D.
Sonatina I   1966 (Ric BR) 7 min.
Variações, Recitativo e Fuga   1967 (Vitale) 11 min.
VI Momentos   1969 Book II (Ric BR) 14pp. 10 min. 1. Two types of motion: a. rapid fluid motion; b. slow dense motion; uses a series throughout this piece. 2. Pedal changed on each chord. 3. Free repetitions, unusual metrical notation, clusters. 4. Nocturnal: exploits soft sonorities, night sounds. 5. Primitivo: imitation of a native instrument. 6. Tenso, heróico: dramatic, harmonics. D.
Taaroá   1971 (Tonos) 12pp. 7 min. Theme and (5) Magic Variations. Theme is divided into chords (thème d'accords) and single line (thème mélodique), flexible meters. Taaroá II ends the piece. Complex writing, involved organization, avant-garde. D.
Ad Laudes Matutinas   1972 (Gerig) 5 min.
Ilhas   1973 (Tonos) 23pp. 13 min. Six pages of explanation; a catalogue of avant-garde techniques full of dense and explosive volcanic sonorities. D.
VI Momentos   1973 Book III (Tonos) 8 min.
VII Momentos   1974 Book IV (Tonos) 12 min.
Cartas celestes ("Celestial Charts")   1974 (Tonos) 15 min. Pieces are: Doors of Sunset; Night-Milky Way; Nebulae and Constellations; Milky-Way; Doors of Dawn. The work was originally composed to accompany a show at the São Paulo Planetarium, and was later developed into a concert work. The sky is depicted during the Brazilian springtime (September to November). There are twenty-four different chords, each related to a letter of the Greek alphabet, which is utilized for the classification of stars, constellations, galaxies, and nebulae. The celestial bodies of the Southern Hemisphere are musically interpreted through the combination of the chords. The piano language is deliberately luminous and brilliant, with emphasis on resonance and on the complexity of several simultaneous "clusters"; these generate both vertiginous brightness and thick sonoric vagueness. The musical structure is very free, "like a promenade through the skies in Brazil." There are, however, certain fixed elements, the repetition of which results in the punctuation of the musical text.
Rios 1975–6 (Tonos) 38pp. 20 min. Three movements. Includes three

pages of notes, thematic indexes, and explanation. Very involved and complex rhythmic structures, strong Messiaen influence. A catalogue of avant-garde techniques; virtuoso technique required. D.

Itinerário Idílico e Amoroso, ou o livro de Helenice 1976 (Tonos) 15 min. 1. Estação das Amenidades. 2. As terras do Coração. 3. As Colinas Imaginárias. 4. O Jardim Secreto e a Polifonia dos perfumes. 5. Estação das Densidades. 6. Os Ventos do Amor e da Paixão. 7. Os Rios da Memória.

ANDRÉ PREVIN (1929–   ) USA, born Germany
Five Pages from My Calendar 1976 (Bo&H). "The dates which form these five preludes are the birthdates of my five children. The pieces are in no way meant as portraits of their complex personalities; rather they are simply birthday greetings from me to them" (from the score). Contrasted, chromatic, jazz influence, sophisticated. D.

Paraphrase on a Theme by William Walton 1971 (Nov) 8pp. 4 min. No.10 in Virtuoso series, editorial note by John Ogdon. Based on a theme from Act 2 of *Troilus and Cressida*. "Pianistically, the *Paraphrase* is very sharply etched and needs for its performance the staccato effects . . . almost a stencilled style, which Gershwin asked for in his music" (editorial note). Contains much dissonance, but basically the piece is a lyric and tonal arabesque. Debussy influence is noted toward the conclusion in consecutive sevenths and other chordal structures. M-D.

The Invisible Drummer (Bo&H). Written for Vladimir Ashkenazy. Five preludes in an improvisatory jazz dissonant style. Polyrhythms, large leaps, rich harmonies. Title implies an invisible drummer is necessary at all times to maintain absolutely steady tempi. Dazzling pieces of concert jazz for the more advanced pianist. M-D to D.

MARIA TERESA PRIETO (–   ) Mexico
24 Variaciones (EMM 1964) 30pp. Consists of twelve tonal variations (one each in twelve different keys) and twelve serial variations. The tonal set seems to unfold more naturally. Concludes with an exciting fugue. M-D to D.

SERGIO PRODIGO (1949–   ) Italy
Bagatelles Op.14, Op.23 (Zanibon 1975) 8pp. Collezione di musiche contemporàneo.

SERGE PROKOFIEFF (1891–1953) USSR
Four Pieces Op.3 1907–11 (Rahter).
Four Pieces Op.4 1910–11. No.4 Suggestion diabolique (EBM).
Ten Pieces Op.12 1913. Marche (EBM); Gavotte (EBM); Prelude A (EBM).
Sarcasms Op.17 1912–13 (Bo&H).

Visions fugitives Op.22 1915–17 (Goldberger—GS). Twenty short aphoristic pieces. M-D.

Music for Children Op.65   1935 (Ric).

Peter and the Wolf Op.67   1936 (CFP 5730). English translation by Walter Bergmann of the engaging narrative. M-D.

Sonata No.6 Op.82 A   1939–40 (Sikorski).

Sonata No.7 Op.83 B♭   1939–42 (Sikorski).

Sonata No.8 Op.84 B♭   1939–44 (Sikorski).

Three Pieces Op.95 (CFP   1977) 16pp. From ballet *Cinderella*. M-D.

Sonata No.9 Op.103 C   1947 (Sikorski).

Album (K).

Album of Prokofieff Masterpieces (EBM). Includes original works for piano: Etude Op.2/4; Conte Op.3/1; Devilish Inspiration Op.4/4; Marche Op.12/1; Gavotte Op.12/2; Prelude Op.12/7; Sarcasms Op.17/3, 5; and transcriptions from Opp.25, 33, 48, 67, and 75. Int. to M-D.

Six Pieces for Piano (GS   1978) 23pp. Specially edited by Prokofieff. Includes: Etude c Op.2/4; March Op.12/1; Gavotte Op.12/2; Prélude Op.12/7; Sarcasme Op.17/3; Vision Fugitive, Op.22/16. M-D.

See: Lawrence Chaikin, "The Prokofieff Sonatas: A Psychograph," PQ, 86 (Summer 1974):9–19.

CARLO PROSPERI (1921–   ) Italy

Fantasia   1973 (SZ) 11pp.

Intervalli (SZ   1971) 9pp.

Sonatina profana (SZ   1971) 15pp.

JOSEPH PROSTAKOFF (1911–   ) USA, born Asia

Prostakoff studied piano with Abby Whiteside and composition with Mark Brunswick and Karol Rathaus. He is a private teacher and free-lance editor in New York.

Two Bagatelles (LG) in collection *New Music for the Piano*. I. Adagio molto e espressivo: twelve-tone, quiet, meanders. II. Con moto: changing meters, twelve-tone, much 16th-note figuration. M-D.

SERGEJ PROTOPOPOW (–   ) USSR

Sonata II Op.5 (UE   1924) reprint 1971. 23pp. One movement, numerous short, highly contrasted sections. Broad dynamic range, dissonant, interesting pedal instructions. Directions in Italian and Russian. D.

KAZIMIERZ B. PRZYBYLSKI (1941–   ) Poland

Tema con variazioni (PWM   1964) 11pp. Chromatic theme, seven contrasting variations. 1. Contrapuntal. 2. Lyric and free. 3. Fast, light, chromatic skips and runs. 4. Heavy syncopated chords; stems without notes denote repetition of the last note or chord. 5. March, imitative octaves. 6. Harmonics. 7. Theme heard forward, backward, inverted, etc. M-D.

HENRY PURCELL (ca.1659–1695) Great Britain

Eight Suites (H. Ferguson—S&B 1964) 2 vols. Superb edition.
See: Arthur Steiger, "Purcell Called His Suite a Lesson," *Clavier,* 14 (November 1975):21–23. Suite I G is analyzed. Music included. Int. to M-D.

Eight Suites and Various Pieces (K 3808). Int. to M-D.

Trente-Cinq Pièces (Farrenc—Leduc) I. 15 pieces: Suites in G, g, G, a. II. 20 pieces: Suites in C, D, d, F; 3 marches in C; Chaconne g. Int. to M-D.

Purcell—Easy Piano Pieces (Keller—CFP 5071). 18 pieces. Int.

See: Franklin B. Zimmermann, *Henry Purcell (1659–1695): A Thematic Index to his Complete Works* (Philadelphia: Pennsylvania Pro Musica, 4816 Beaumont Avenue, Philadelphia, PA 19143).

EDUARD PÜTZ (1911–   ) Germany

Sonate (Tonos 1965) 19pp. 14 min. Three untitled movements. Atonal; pointillistic; exploits extremes of keyboard; harmonics; percussive treatment. Large span required. D.

Q

MARCEL QUINET (1915–   ) Belgium

Quinet teaches at the Brussels Conservatory.

Enfantines   1959 (CeBeDeM   1973) 15pp.

Badineries (Zephyr   1975) 15pp.

Tableautins (CeBeDeM   1975) 13pp. 9 min. Marche. Un peu triste. Rengaine. Fileuse. Chromatisme. Tarantelle.

Trois Préludes (CeBeDeM   1970) 17pp. 10 min. 1. Somewhat Impressionistic, spread over wide range of keyboard. 2. Broken-seventh figuration, perpetual motion, upper register exploited. 3. Broken figurations accompany upper register chords; eighth-note motion maintained. M-D.

HECTOR QUINTANAR (1936–   ) Mexico

Sonidos für Klavier   1970 (Tonos) 6pp. Explanations for performance in Spanish and English. Plucked strings, clusters, metallic comb and ruler used on strings, aleatoric, avant-garde. M-D.

R

JAN RÄÄTS (1932–   ) Estonia
Rääts graduated from the Tallinn Conservatory, where he is now a professor. He is also musical director of Estonian Television.
Toccata (GS   1977) 14pp. Fast repeated thin textures grow into fast repeated chords. Clusters, glissandi, cadenza. ABA, exciting close. Prokofieff influence, but more contemporary sounding. M-D.

SERGEI RACHMANINOFF (1873–1943) Russia
Complete Piano Works (USSR). Vol.I: Opp.3, 16, 23, 32. Vol.II: Opp.33, 39, 22, 42, 3/3 (2nd version, 1940), Polka V.R.
Three Nocturnes 1887 (Sorel—EBM 1973). First American edition of these early works. 1. f♯: longest, dramatic. 2. F: melodically oriented. 3. c: mid-section resembles early c♯ Prelude. Slavic melancholy; hint at Rachmaninoff's later style. Large span required. M-D.
7 Pieces Op.10 (Anson—Willis; Century).
6 Moments musicaux Op.16 (M. Frey—Simrock Elite ed. 3170). Written in a full-blown late-Romantic style. M-D to D.
Sonata I Op.28 (K).
13 Preludes Op.32 (Belwin-Mills). E, F, f, available separately.
    See: Morton Estrin, "Playing the Preludes, Op.32," *Clavier,* 12 (October 1973):19–20, 30.
24 Preludes (USSR).
6 Etudes-Tableaux Op.33 (Belwin-Mills) C, E♭ available separately.
Prelude 1917 (Belwin-Mills) 3pp. This beautiful posthumous work (Andante ma non troppo) has many characteristics of other works composed at this time. It is full of rich harmonies, cantabile melodies, and somber sonorities. M-D.
Variations on a Theme of Corelli Op.42 1932 (Belwin-Mills). Rachmaninoff erroneously attributed the "La Folia" tune to Corelli.
Polka de W. R. (Bo&H). Written for Wassili Rachmaninoff, Sergei's father, an amateur pianist. M-D.
Italian Polka (Bo&H). M-D.
Sergei Rachmaninoff; a highlight collection of his best-loved original Works (C. Hansen Educational Music and Books   1973). Notes on the life and times of Rachmaninoff by H. Dexter. Includes: Op.3/1,

2, 3, 4, 5; Op.10/2, 3; Op.23; Op.32; Op.33; Second Piano Concerto arranged for piano solo.

A Commemorative Collection—Original Works and Transcriptions (Belwin-Mills 1973) 115pp. A centennial edition. Original works include: Fragments; Humoresque Op.10/5; Mélodie Op.3/3; Polichinelle Op.3/4; Oriental Sketch; Prelude (Posthumous). Transcriptions include: J. S. Bach, Suite from Partita E for violin (Preludio, Gavotte, Gigue); Bizet, Minuet from *L'Arlesienne Suite;* Mendelssohn, Scherzo from *A Midsummer Night's Dream;* Mussorgsky, Hopak; Rimsky-Korsakoff, The Bumblebee; Schubert, The Brooklet; Tchaikowsky, Lullaby. Most of these transcriptions are available separately (Belwin-Mills). M-D to D.

See: Francis Crociata, "The Piano Music of Sergei Wassilievitch Rachmaninoff," PQ, 82 (Summer 1973):27–33.

Geoffrey Norris, "Rachmaninoff's Second Thoughts," MT, 114 (April 1973):364–68. Discusses Rachmaninoff's revisions to the Second Piano Sonata, the first and fourth piano concertos, and several other works.

HANS-KARSTEN RAECKE (1941–   ) Germany
Sonata D   1965 (DVFM 8013   1975). Three short contrasting movements in MC idiomatic writing. M-D.

ERHARD RAGWITZ (1933–   ) Germany
Sonate Op.19 (DVFM   1968). Grave: built on springy, dissonant figuration; lyrical episodes. Allegro con fuoco: much use of triplet figure; leads to marcato section with melody in bass; triplet figure returns and leads to clashing conclusion. Hindemith influence. D.

PRIAULX RAINIER (1903–   ) Great Britain, born Africa
Rainier studied harmony and violin at the South African College of Music in Cape Town, and at the Royal Academy of Music in London. She also worked with Nadia Boulanger. Since 1942 Rainier has taught at the Royal Academy of Music.
Barbaric Dance Suite (Schott   1950) 12 min.
Five Pieces for Keyboard   1952 (MS available from composer: 75 Ladbroke Grove, London W.112PD, England) 16 min. Some pieces are for the piano, others for the harpsichord.

BRANKO RAKIJAS (1911–   ) Yugoslavia
Piano Suite (Drustvo Hrvatskih Skladatelja   1973) 12pp.

JEAN-PHILIPPE RAMEAU (1683–1764) France
Complete Works for Keyboard (Kenneth Gilbert—Heugel) Le Pupitre series L.P. 59. Based on a comparison of all the early printings. Resolves the disputed question of Rameau's ornament changes. Ra-

meau's own settings for harpsichord of dances from *Les Indes Galantes* are printed here for the first time since the eighteenth century.
Pièces de Clavecin, Books One and Two (Farrenc—Leduc).
Selected Works (Mariassy Istvan—EMB 1977) 52pp. Notes in Hungarian and English.
Pièces Choisies (Heugel).
Elegy (L. Podolsky—SP). Freely transcribed by L. Godowsky. Effective. M-D.
Les Indes Galantes (EV). First suite.

PHILIP RAMEY (1939–   ) USA
Leningrad Rag 1972 (EBM) Mutations on Scott Joplin. 7pp. 5 min. Freely based on Joplin's *Gladiolus Rag.* The two might be performed together. Bitonal, biting dissonances, in true rag style. D.
Piano Fantasy 1969–72 (MS available from composer: 307 East 60 St., New York, NY 10022) 19pp. 13 min. Constructed rather strictly on the principle of cumulative variation. Motivic manipulation, declamatory, dense harmonic masses. Strong dramatic gestures have some affinity with the piano music of Liszt; piano writing has an orchestral quality although it is idiomatically conceived for the piano. D.
Sonata IV 1968 (MS available from composer) 10pp. 9½ min. In one movement, slow and measured. Atonal, free-form and nondevelopmental, clangorous bell-like effects, no pianistic display; sonorities conceived in an orchestral manner. D.

SHULAMIT RAN (1947–   ) Israel
Ran is a member of the music faculty at the University of Chicago.
Hyperbole (IMI 6070) 12pp. 7 min. This was the required piece at the second Arthur Rubinstein International Piano Master Competition in Israel in 1977. The first few bars supply the material for the entire piece. Uses a few avant-garde notational signs.

BERNARD RANDS (1935–   ) Great Britain
Espressione Va 1969–70 (UE) 5–15 min.
Espressione Vb 1969–70 (UE) 5–15 min.

GYÖRGY RANKI (1907–   ) Hungary
Easy Piano Pieces on Melodies from Viet Nam 1973 (EMB).
Easy Variations on a Hungarian Folk Song (EMB).

SAM RAPHLING (1910–   ) USA
Passacaglia Ebraica 1973 (Gen) 9pp. Varied moods, colored with Hebraic influences. A few involved rhythms, flexible tempos. M-D.
Six Tiny Sonatas (Gen 1971) 13pp. Each short sonata has three or four movements. MC, clever. Not as easy as they look. Int.

KARL AAGE RASMUSSEN (1947–   ) Finland
Min forars dagbok ("My Spring Diary") (WH 1975) 15pp. Vol.2.
Explanations in Danish and English. Depicts the progress of the day
from afternoon to night. Nine pieces, contemporary notation. Vol.1
is a set of duets with the same title. Int. to M-D.

EINOJUHANI RAUTAVAARA (1928–   ) Finland
Rautavaara studied at the University of Helsinki and the Sibelius Academy,
and in New York, Tanglewood, and Switzerland. At present he is lecturer
on the theory of music at the Sibelius Academy. His works reveal not only
a discriminating control of technical resources but also the effects of a
personal struggle for artistic expression, as in his solutions to the problems of form and in his intelligent organization of symbolistic devices.
In spite of his conscious modernism Rautavaara's output up to now is
also marked by an adherence to conservative principles, which is reflected in his scores primarily by a cultivated taste.
Pelimannit ("Fiddles," or "Folk Musicians") Op.1 1952 (Fazer) 11pp.
8 min. Six free fantasies based on dances written by an eighteenth-
century Finnish fiddler, Samuel Rinda-Nickola. A colorful set that
begins with a procession and concludes with a stamping, jumping
dance. M-D.
Ikonit ("Icons") Op.6 1956 (Fazer) 13pp. 12 min. The Death of the
Mother of God; Two Village Saints; The Black Madonna of Blaker-
naya; The Baptism of Christ; The Holy Women at the Sepulchre;
Archangel Michael Fighting the Antichrist. Notes in the score describe the background of each icon (piece). Full sonorities, many
texture contrasts, freely chromatic, an impressive suite. M-D.
Seven Preludes Op. 7 1957 (Fazer) 11pp. 11 min. Elastically Hammer-
ing. Slowly Enough. Nervously But in Rhythm. Choral and Variation. Fugato. Shivering. Alla Finale. Strong gestures, dissonant, free
rhythms. M-D.
Three Symmetric Preludes Op.14 1949 (Fazer 1972) 7pp. 6 min. 1.
Contrary chromatic lines; tremolo; large span required. 2. Syncopated chords, hand crossings, broken-chord figures. 3. Contrary
motion figuration, mixture of styles. M-D.
Partita Op.34 1958 (Fazer 1967) 5pp. 5 min. Three short contrasting
movements. Freely chromatic, mild dissonance. M-D.
Etudes Op.42 1969 (Fazer) 19pp. 13 min. 1. Thirds, broken and solid,
chromatic and diatonic. 2. Sevenths, melodic treatment. 3. Tritones.
4. Fourths, arpeggi, and chords. 5. Seconds, harmonic treatment.
Freely dissonant. M-D.
Sonata I "Christus und die Fischer" Op.54 1969 (Fazer) 8pp. 13 min.
1. Based on three contrasting tempi with contrasting ideas and fig-

uration; clusters; large span required. 2. Cluster sonorities in changing meters, frequent alternation of hands, harmonics. 3. Chromatic chords, different meters for each hand, freely dissonant counterpoint. M-D.

Sonata II "The Fire Sermon" Op.64   1970 (Fazer) 15pp. Molto allegro: 8/8 divided into groups of 3+2+3, freely chromatic, fast alternation of hands, clusters. Andante assai: quiet melodic opening; appassionato mid-section made of arpeggi and chords; clusters; quiet opening returns and then concludes with clusters. Allegro brutale: fuguelike opening, parallel chords, driving rhythms, crushing clusters at conclusion. Individual idiomatic writing. D.

MATTI RAUTIO (1922–   ) Finland
Suita per piano   1951 (Fazer). Int. to M-D.
Hanoniana. Jeux pianistiques sur les touches blanches   1971 (Fazer) 13pp.
Der frohe Musikant ("The Jolly Musician") (Fazer). Fifty short piano pieces. Int.

MAURICE RAVEL (1875–1937) France
Ravel's pianistic textures display a tapestry-like beauty. His chordal harmonies usually play a subordinate role to line and rhythm.
Sérénade grotesque   1893 (Sal). Guitar sounds, Chabrier influence. The guitarlike pizzicatissimo chords of the opening bars and the alternation of triads between the hands foreshadow *Alborado del gracioso.* The nascent fantastic irony found in the *Sérénade grotesque* appears later in the "Scarbo" from *Gaspard de la Nuit.* M-D.
Menuet antique   1895 (K).
Pavane pour une Infante défunte   1899 (EBM).
Jeux d'Eau   1901 (EBM; K 3839).
Sonatine f♯   1905 (K 3838).
    See: Saul Dorfman, "Ravel's Sonatine—A New Edition," *Clavier,* 16 (October 1977):16–22. Includes the first and second movements; the third movement is contained in the November 1977 issue. Careful fingering, pedaling, and redistribution of parts are included since Ravel indicated practically nothing in these areas. M-D to D.
    Edwin Smith, "Ravel: Sonatine," *Music Teacher,* 55 (March 1976): 13–15. An analysis of the work.
Miroirs   1905. All five movements are available separately from (EBM).
    See: Roy Howat, "Debussy, Ravel and Bartók: Towards Some New Concepts of Form," *M&L,* 58 (July 1977):285–94. Contains a penetrating analysis of "Oiseaux tristes."
    Dean Elder, "According to Gieseking—A Master Lesson on 'La vallée des cloches,' " *Clavier,* 14 (October 1975):29–33.
Valses nobles et sentimentales   1911 (Durand). More chordally oriented

than most of Ravel's works. M-D.

See: Natalie M. Pepin, "Dance and Jazz Elements in the Piano Music of Maurice Ravel," diss., Boston University, 1972. Analyzes the *Valses nobles et sentimentales* as an instance of sonata form within a waltz type.

Elizabeth McCrae, "Ravel's Valses nobles et sentimentales: Analysis, Stylistic Considerations, Performance Problems," DMA diss., Boston University, 1974, 196pp. A detailed analysis of thematic, rhythmic, motivic, tonal, and formal elements.

La Valse 1920 (Durand). Ravel's own solo version. Highly effective but requires virtuoso technique. D.

Ravel Album (K 3826). Miroirs, Sonatine, Jeux d'eau.

See: *Clavier,* 14 (October 1975). A special issue devoted to Ravel.

Marguerite Long, *At the Piano with Ravel* (London: Dent, 1974).

Arbie Orenstein, "Scorography: The Music of Ravel," *Musical Newsletter,* 5 (Summer 1975):10–12. Includes a list of corrections for most of the piano works. Especially helpful for *Gaspard de la nuit.*

ALAN RAWSTHORNE (1905–1971) Great Britain

Theme and Four Studies (OUP 1973) 15pp. 9 min. The fourteen-bar theme in C major is in 5/4 and is simple and haunting. It is followed by four contrasted variations with a quiet closing. The second study occupies the center of the work. Recalls the style of the earlier *4 Bagatelles.* M-D.

See: Edwin Smith, "Rawsthorne: Bagatelles," *Music Teacher,* 55 (January 1976):13–14.

MARTIN CHRISTOPH REDEL (1947–) Germany

Evolution 1974 (Bo&Bo 22639) 18pp.

MAX REGER (1873–1916) Germany

7 Waltzes Op.11 1891 (Schott; Augener) 29 min.

10 Little Instructional Pieces Op.44 (UE). Int.

Variationen und Fuge über ein Thema von Telemann Op.134 (CFP) 32 min. Contains some very beautiful music with extraordinarily fine craft and poetic sensibility. D.

Vier Klavierstücke (O. Junne 1966) 15pp. Romanza. Improvisation. Nachtstück. Perpetuum mobile. M-D.

GUY REIBEL. (1936–) France

Melisonance (Heugel 1977) 4pp. For piano and tape.

ANTON REICHA (1770–1836) Bohemia

Selected Works for Piano (Dana Zahn—Henle 254). Fingering by Hans-Martin Theopold. Edited after the first editions. Contains: Sonata E♭ Op.43; L'Art de varier ou 57 variations F Op.57; Fantaisie E Op.61. Representative works from three genres cultivated by Reicha. M-D.

36 Fugues Op.36   ca.1805 (V. J. Sykora—Br). Book I: Fugues 1–13.
    Book II: Fugues 14–24. Book III: Fugues 25–36. Preface in French,
    German, and English. Bold writing for the period. Makes high de-
    mands on the pianist's interpretive powers. Kind of a later *Well-
    Tempered Clavier*. Some fugues are based on subjects by other com-
    posers, such as J. S. Bach, Mozart, Haydn, and Scarlatti. Excellent
    urtext–performing edition. M-D.

PAUL REIF (1910–   ) USA, born Czechoslovakia
Pentagram   1970 (Bo&H) 18pp. Fast. Calmly. Slow. Fast. Fairly Fast.
    Five pieces in contemporary idiom to be played without a break.
    Free in style; includes improvised cadenzas. Large span required. D.

ARIBERT REIMANN (1936–   ) Germany
Spektren   1967 (Ars Viva) 19pp. 9 min. Unbarred, pointillistic, flashy
    piano writing, a-thematic, antirhythmic. Mainly on three staves ex-
    cept for final climax, which calls for four. Some notational problems.
    Avant-garde. D.

ALEXANDER REINAGLE (1756–1809) USA, born Scotland
Six Scots Tunes (Krauss, Hinson—Hinshaw   1975) 19pp. 1. Lee Rigg. 2.
    East Nook of Fife. 3. Malt Man. 4. Black Jock (Gypsy Laddie). 5.
    Laddie Lie Near Me. 6. Steer Her Up and Had Her Gawn. Thin tex-
    tures, unusual modulations, strong Scottish flavor. Int. to M-D.
Twenty-Four Short and Easy Pieces Op.1 (Krauss, Hinson—Hinshaw
    1975) 19pp. Short pieces used by Reinagle in his teaching. Simple
    classic style, highly attractive writing for this level. Easy.
The Philadelphia Sonatas   ca.1790 (Robert Hopkins—A-R Editions
    1978) 84pp. Sonata I D; Sonata II E; Sonata III C; Sonata IV F.
    Scholarly edition, extensive preface, sources identified. Reinagle com-
    posed these sonatas after he arrived in the U.S. They "may well be
    the first real piano music, as well as the first sonatas for any instru-
    ment, written in the United States" (from the preface).
See: Ross Wesley Ellison, "The Piano Sonatas of Alexander Reinagle,"
    AMT, 25 (April–May 1976):23.
Anne McClenny Krauss, "More Music by Reinagle," *Clavier,* 15 (May–
    June 1976):17–20. Includes "Lee Rigg" and excerpts from *24 Short
    and Easy Pieces.*
Katherine Hines Mahan, "Hopkinson and Reinagle: Patriot–Musicians of
    Washington's Time," *Music Educators Journal,* 62 (April 1976):
    40–50.
John F. Strauss, "Alexander Reinagle—Pianist—Composer—Impresario
    in Federalist America," *Clavier,* 15 (May–June 1976):14–16. Pp.
    25–27 contain the final movement of the F major Sonata.
———. "An Annotated Edition of Two Pianoforte Sonatas by Alexander
    Reinagle," diss., University of Texas at Austin, 1976. The D and F
    sonatas.

HUGO REINHOLD (1854–1935) Austria
Hungarian Dance (GS; Willis). Int.
Impromptu c♯ Op.28/3 (GS; TP). Int.

ALFONSO RENDANO (1853–1931) Italy
Rendano composed primarily for the piano and invented the "pedale independente," which was worked by the heel. Rendano was praised by Rossini.
Composizioni per pianoforte (Rodolfo Caporali—Curci 1975) Vol.I. 115pp.

PAOLO RENOSTO (1935–) Italy
Per Marisa T, Pianista (Ric 1970). Contains a certain number of sound events arranged on 7 loose leaves. 16 min. Explanations in Italian, English, and German. Aleatoric, clusters, pointillistic, "memorized" chords. Avant-garde. D.

OTTORINO RESPIGHI (1879–1936) Italy
Notturno (Anson—Willis).

JULIUS REUBKE (1834–1858) Germany
Grosse Sonate b (G. Cotta'sche 1926) 55pp. There is a copy in the New York Public Library. This work provides a striking example of originality through metamorphosis and contains interesting anticipations of Mahler and Reger. D.

VERNE REYNOLDS (1926–) USA
Sonata 1972 (MS available from composer: c/o Eastman School of Music, 26 Gibbs St., Rochester, NY 14604) 31pp. Fantasy: twelve-tone; many short fast–slower sections; large gestures; clusterlike sonorities; generally thin textures; forearm clusters; sound decay leads to soft bass sonorities; agitation moves to a Presto coda with harmonics; large span required. Calm: long pedals; "*pp* and soft pedal throughout, with slight rhythmic and dynamic nuances" (from score); unbarred. Motion: contrapuntal; varied meters; works to large climax; subsides; *pp* ending. Patterns: opens with a quasi cadenza; octotonic; fast repeated notes in one hand with long figures in the other; slight jazz feeling; alternating octaves, brilliant conclusion. Virtuoso writing. D.

RHENÉ-BATON (1879–1940) France
En Bretagne Op.13 (Durand). Six picturesque movements. M-D.
Ballade A♭ Op.22 (Durand 1921).
Au Pardon de Rumengol Op.25 (Durand 1922). Six movements.
Album Rose (ESC) Six easy pieces, published separately. Petite melodie. Bluette. Intermezzo. Petit choral. Vieille romance. Musette. Int.
Prelude d (ESC).

ANTAL RIBARI (1924–) Hungary

All' Antica (Gen   1969) 11pp. A MC suite with contrasting (slow and fast) movements, varied meters. M-D.

Six Etudes   1970 (Gen) 7pp. L'indifference. Grotesque. Tristesse. Burlesque. Silence. Cloches. Contrasting moods, short, MC. M-D.

Sonata (Gen   1973) 12pp.

FERDINAND TOBIAS RICHTER (1649–1711) Austria

Suite D (C. David Harris—W. C. Brown) in *Notations and Editions,* pp.146–53. Entreé; A; C; M; S; B; G. Attractive writing with less technical demand than the virtuosity usually ascribed to Richter and found in certain of his other works for keyboard. Int.

See: C. David Harris, "Problems in Editing Harpsichord Music: *Suite in D* by Ferdinand Tobias Richter (1649–1711)," *Notations and Editions* (Dubuque, Iowa: W. C. Brown), pp:142–45, for a discussion of the problems in editing the above suite.

CARLOS RIESCO GREZ (1925–   ) Chile

Sonata (Universidad de Chile, Facultad de Ciencias y Artes Musicales y de la Representacion   1975) 21pp.

VITTORIO RIETI (1898–   ) Italy, born Egypt; USA since 1950

Sei Pezzi Brevi   1932 (Gen). Six short pieces. M-D.

Chironomos (Gen   1975). Preludio. Allegro volante. Intermezzo. Mazurka. Improvviso. Epilogo.

Five Pieces for Young Pianists   1948 (Gen). Canon. Prelude. Valsette. Silly Polka. Tarantella. Int.

WOLFGANG RIHM (1952–   ) Germany

Klavierstück II Op.8b (Br&H   1971) 18pp. Photostat of MS.

DENNIS RILEY (1943–   ) USA

Riley studied with George Crumb.

Six Canonic Variations: Piano Piece I Op.2a (CFP   1963) 4pp. Serial, expressive, short, Webern influence. M-D.

Five Little Movements: Piano Piece II Op.2b (CFP   1963). Short, serial, pointillistic, contrasted moods and dynamics. Evocative of Schönberg's Op.19. Firm rhythmic control necessary. M-D.

NICOLAS RIMSKY-KORSAKOV (1844–1908) Russia

Four Pieces Op.11 (Belaieff   1974). Impromptu. Novelette. Scherzino. Etude. Make an effective recital set. M-D.

Radio City Album (EBM).

JEAN RIVIER (1896–   ) France

Alternances (EMT   1975) 8pp. 5½ min. An exciting contemporary work in freely chromatic style. Highly sectionalized, each section dealing with a single idea. Written for the Marguerite Long and Jacques Thibauld Concours International 1975. D.

Quatre fantasmes 1971 (Billaudot). Lianes. Méandres. Ombres. Flammes.

Sonate en cinq mouvements 1969 (EMT) 21 min. Fluide: chromatic, octaves, skips. Incisif: scherzolike, many dynamic changes. Concentré: imitative; large span required in left hand. Souple: syncopated; fast-moving full chords. Violent: frenetic, toccatalike, glissandi. Facile, colorful writing. D.

ANTÓN ROCH (1915–   ) Spain
Roch is a pseudonym for Antonio Garcia Rubio.

Consonantes (UME   1973) 8pp. Four bagatelles to be played together. Each one short and effective in performance. Nos.1 and 3 are Impressionistic; No.2 is highly rhythmic; and No.4 is brilliant and in Spanish style. Wide dynamic contrast. D.

Labyrinthus (UME   1973) 8pp.

GEORGE ROCHBERG (1918–   ) USA

Arioso 1959 (TP) 3 min. Tender, Italianate, three-voiced, modified Phrygian mode. Int.

12 Bagatelles 1952 (TP). Intense serial writing. A significant work. D.
   See: Steven D. Jones, "The 12 Bagatelles of George Rochberg," thesis, Indiana University, 1974, 101pp.

Bartókiana 1959 (TP) 1½ min. Joyous, Lydian and Mixolydian modes, mixed meter. M-D.

Carnival Music 1971 (TP   1975) 39pp. Fanfares and March; Blues; Largo Doloroso; Sfumato; Toccata—Rag. Amalgamates original music and quotations from other music in a hallmark of Rochberg's extroverted style. Multilayered. D.

Nach Bach (After Bach) Fantasy for Harpsichord or Piano (TP). Updated classicism. M-D.

Partita Variations 1976 (TP). 13 continuous sections, extreme ecleticism, tonal and atonal juxtaposed with contrapuntal and homophonic styles, summation in final section. A *tour de force*. D.

Prelude on "Happy Birthday" 1969 (TP) 3pp. (For almost two pianos). Big sound, great fun. Uses another piano if available (playing different music at the same time) and possibly a radio. Large span required. M-D.

Sonata—Fantasia 1958 (TP) 23 min. Intricate structure, wide range of mood and expression. D.

JOAQUIN RODRIGO (1902–   ) Spain

Berceuse d'Automne (Sal).

Berceuse de Printemps (Sal).

Danza de la Amapola ("Dance of the Poppy") (UME) 5pp. A lively 3/8 dance, excellent for fast fingers and small hands. Int.

A l'ombre de "Torre Bermeja" (Sal).

Prelude au coq matinal (Sal).

Sarabande Lointaine (ESC).

Suite pour Piano (Sal). Prélude; Sicilienne; Bourrée; Menuet; Rigaudon. M-D.

El Album de Cecilia (UME). Six pieces in treble clef.

BENJAMIN ROGERS (1614–1698) Great Britain

Rogers was known mainly for consort music during his day. Some of his church music is still performed today.

Complete Keyboard Works (Richard Rastall—S&B 1973) 15pp. Fifteen dance pieces including corants, sarabands, almains, and a jig as well as the four pieces from *Musicks Hand-Maide*. In Purcellian cantabile style. A four-movement Suite C is especially interesting as well as a facsimile of two pages of a Voluntary C. Editorial notes and commentary as well as metronome marks are included. Int. to M-D.

JENS ROHWER (1914–   ) Germany

Kleine Webmuster (Möseler 1971) Vol.I. 20pp. Fifteen two-part pieces in easy to more complex tonalities. Easy to M-D. Vol.II. 32pp. Twenty Easy to M-D two- and three-part pieces in elementary to advanced tonalities.

Grosse Webstücke (Möseler 1972) 43pp. Seven two-part fugues with preludes. Seventh fugue has an optional part for flute or violin. May also be played on the organ or harpsichord. M-D.

Sonate (Möseler 1958) 16pp.

Variationen über ein eigenes Weihnachtslied (Heinrichshofen 421).

CLAUDE ROBERT ROLAND (1935–   ) Belgium

Sonance II Op.22 1960 (CeBeDeM 1974) 12pp. 10 min. Variations. Lent. Fugue.

Préludes Op.28 1961–2 (CeBeDeM 1975) 8pp. Book I.

AMADEO ROLDÁN (1900–1939) Cuba

Preludio cubano (PIC 1967).

NED ROREM (1923–   ) USA

Eight Etudes 1976 (Bo&H) 35pp. 20 min. An outstanding set of virtuoso studies, written in an Impressionistic idiom that has interest melodically, rhythmically, and texturally. Conceived as a suite. Each study focuses on a different technical problem. D.

HILDING ROSENBERG (1892–1962) Sweden

Plastic Scenes 1921 (NMS). Eight pieces.

Sonata No. 4 1927 (NMS).

MANUEL ROSENTHAL (1904–   ) France

Sérénade (Heugel). Four pieces.

Six Caprices (Heugel).

FRANZ ANTON ROSETTI (1746–1792) Germany

12 Easy Piano Pieces (Bernhard Pauler—Eulenburg GM 244 1975) 19pp. Attractive, somewhat in the style of W. A. Mozart. Some of the pieces are titled—e.g., Schleifer, Scherzo, Capriccio, Romanze— while others have only character indications. Int.

WALTER ROSS (1936–) USA

Dances for Small Spaces 1972 (MS available from composer: c/o Music Department, University of Virginia, Charlottesville, VA 22903) 14pp. For piano, tape, and dancer. Five short pieces that employ clusters, plucking of strings, harmonics, and muted notes created by damping strings. Each line of the score equals twenty seconds. Pianist must improvise and play fast random notes, following, in general, the melodic shape indicated. Chromatic, arpeggi gestures, exciting tape. Effective without dancer. Avant-garde. M-D.

Prelude, Nocturne and Dance (Bo&H 1974) 5pp. Nontonal and non-measured pieces. D.

GIOACCHINO A. ROSSINI (1792–1868) Italy

Ten Selections (Fondazione Rossini 1975) Preface in Italian by Bruno Cagli, rev. by Sergio Cafaro. Contains: Prélude blaguer; Des tritons s'il vous plaît (Montée–Descente); Petite pensée; Une bagatelle; (Mélodie italienne–Descente), une bagatelle: In nomine patris; Canzonetta "La Venitienne"; Une réjouissance (pour album); Encore un peu de blague (Montée–Descente); Tourniquet sur la gamme chromatique (Ascendante et descendante); Ritournelle gothique. M-D.

Five Pieces for Piano (Marcello Abbado—Ric). Introduction in French, German, and English. Une caresse à ma femme; Un petit train de plaisir; Momento homo; Petite [*sic*] caprice; Marche et réminiscenses pour mon dernier voyage. In the last piece Rossini quotes fragments from some of his operas. M-D.

Original Piano Pieces (P. Zeitlin—TP 1976). Six pieces from *Les Riens* and *Pièces Diverses,* including Bagatelles in A♭ and E♭; Entr'acte; Waltz E♭; Regret; and Austrian Waltz. Int. to M-D.

Complete Works (UE) Vol.17: Piano Pieces. Vol.19: Quatre Mendiants; Quatre hors d'oeuvres.

6 Pezzi (Fondazione Rossini). From *Album de château.* Preface by Alfredo Bonaccorsi. Vol.12 of Quaderni Rossiniani.

FRÉDÉRIC VAN ROSSUM (1939–) Belgium

Van Rossum is a graduate of the Royal Conservatory in Brussels. He has received numerous prizes in piano and composition.

Adagio Op.4 (CeBeDeM 1962) 12pp. 11 min. Sonorous, arpeggiated accompaniment, chromatic. Builds to large climax, then subsides. M-D.

Douze Miniatures Op.10 (GS 1974) 32pp. Twelve miniatures that use

many contemporary techniques in very musical settings. Prélude;
Cantilène; Psaume; Capriccio; Arioso; Scherzo; Pastorale; Pierrot;
Toccata; Marche; Elegie; Finale. Int. to M-D.

Egogue et Conte bleu Op.24 (Schott Frères 1972) 6pp. Eglogue:
mainly three-voiced, accompanied syncopated melody, expressive.
Conte bleu: chromatic, mainly four-voiced chords, rocking quality,
careful pedal indications, MC. M-D.

NINO ROTA (1911–   ) Italy
Variazioni e fuga nei dodici toni sul nome di Bach (Carisch 1972) 31pp.

POUL ROVSING-OLSEN (1922–   ) Denmark
Olsen studied at the Copenhagen Conservatory and also with Nadia
Boulanger. He later studied ethnomusicology.

Images Op.51 (Moeck 1965) 13 min. Explanations in French, German,
and English.

Many Happy Returns Op.70 (WH 1974) 12pp.

Nocturnes Op.21 1951 (WH 29397 1977) 13pp. For Debussy. For
Ali Akbar Khan. For Chopin. Styles match titles. D.

ALEC ROWLEY (1892–1958) Great Britain
Twelve Little Fantasy Studies Op.13 (Bo&H 1917). For the first year.
Attractive, five-finger studies, trill study, easy arpeggi, chord study,
etc. Easy.

From My Sketch Book Op.39 (CFP 4367A).

18 Studies Op.42 (CFP).

12 Studies Op.43 (CFP 4383B).

EDWIN ROXBURGH (1937–   ) Great Britain
Roxburgh was educated at Liverpool Cathedral, the Liverpool Matthay
School of Music, the Royal College of Music, and Cambridge. He is the
director of The 20th Century Ensemble of London.

Labyrinth 1970 (UMP) 12pp. A quick-witted fantasy that contains
some sensuous piano sonorities with many patterns and clusters. Precise directions given for speed, notation, and pedal. Extended lower
keyboard required (only an Imperial Bösendorfer has it!). Moves
through numerous textural changes. Outbursts are interspersed with
moments of graceful, almost Impressionistic sonorities. D.

MIKLÓS RÓZSA (1907–   ) USA, born Hungary
The Vintner's Daughter Op.23 (BB 1953) 15 min. Twelve variations
on a French folk song, each of which is related to a verse of the text.
Tonal but freely chromatic. Hungarian folk element gently permeates
the work. M-D.

See: Christopher Palmer, *Miklós Rózsa: A Sketch of His Life and Works*
(Wiesbaden: Brietkopf & Härtel, 1974), 80pp.

EDMUND RUBBRA (1901–   ) Great Britain
Studies Op.74/1–9 (Lengnick).
Studies Op.139/1–4 (Lengnick).

MARCEL RUBIN (1905–   ) Austria
Sonata II 1927 (Dob 1973) 21pp. 15 min.

ANTON RUBINSTEIN (1829–1894) Russia
Five Barcarolles (I. Philipp—Heugel).
Two Pieces (GS 694). Nocturne Op.69; Barcarolle I Op.30. M-D.
Three Pieces (GS 696). Impromptu Op.16/1; Nocturne I Op.28; Romance Op.44/1. M-D.
Waltz-Caprice (GS 697). M-D.
Ten Selected Pieces (GS 4217).
12 Preludes for Piano Op.24 (GS 8069). M-D.
Selected Piano Pieces (GS 8073). M-D.
See: Ernest Lubin, "The Other Rubinstein—Anton," *Clavier*, 16 (April 1977):14-17.

POUL RUDERS (1949–   ) Denmark
Tre Breve dra den ukendte soldat ("Three Letters from the Unknown Soldier") (Engstrom & Sodring 1973) 6pp. Explanations in English and German. March: brutal; primitive force required with some impossible muting effects. Bells: tension of the piano's lowest strings is changed by pushing with thumb or pulling with fingers of one hand while other hand plays on the keyboard. Prayer: chromatic scale in major seconds *pppp;* concludes with a cluster played "tutta forza" seven times! D.

DANE RUDHYAR (1895–   ) USA, born France
In some ways Rudhyar's works anticipate Messiaen, and he is a spiritual confrère of Scriabin in their mutual mystical interests.
Granites (Merion). Published with *Three Paeans.* Five sketches in different moods. Granitic dissonances, dynamic extremes. Writhes in quartal-quintal harmonic structures. Large span required. D.
Three Paeans (Merion 1927). Three hymns, Scriabin-like ideology, lofty works, panchromatic. Requires virtuoso technique. D.
Pentagrams One and Two (Columbia University Press 1974) 24pp. No. 1: The Summons. No.2: Enfoldment. Anachronistic and naive writing, static rhythms. Poetic fantasy in the directions, but instructions are impossible to incorporate into the music. D.
Pentagrams Three and Four (Columbia University Press 1974) 34pp. No.3 (Release): Gates, The Gift of Blood, Pentecost, Stars, Sunburst. Intriguing harmonic and timbral spectrum. No.4 (The Human Way): Pomp, Yearning, Irony, Overcoming, Peace. These poems are strongly dissonant and display complex writing at every turn. D.

WILLIAM R. RUDOLPH (–   ) USA
Music for Piano (Li Debco   1977) 15pp. Sonatina. Nocturne. Invention.
Suite. "These pieces were first conceived as musical compositions
aimed at meeting the needs of the college music major, minoring in
piano, e.g., the trombonist, cellist, vocalist, etc. This folio, in addition to its college use, will be suitable material for the not-so-ad-
vanced pianist who is looking for interesting and expressive music"
(from the score). Also contains notes and directions for studying
each piece. Well-written MC repertoire. Int. to almost M-D.

WITOLD RUDZINSKI (1913–   ) Poland
Proverbia Latina (AA) for clavichord. 10 min.

ZBIGNIEW RUDZINSKI (1935–   ) Poland
Sonata   1975 (AA   1977) 21pp. 20 min.

CARL RUGGLES (1876–1971) USA
See: Dave R. Harman, "The Musical Language of Carl Ruggles (1876–
1971)," AMT, 25 (April–May 1976):25–27, 31.

WIM DE RUITER (1943–   ) The Netherlands
Solo (Donemus   1970) 7pp. Reproduction of MS. Explanations in
Dutch. Strings strummed with a triangle beater. Avant-garde.

LOREN RUSH (1935–   ) USA
Rush taught for a while at the San Francisco Conservatory.
Oh, Susanna (Jobert   1970) 10 min. Amusing treatment of material
tucked in with complex rhythmic and harmonic usage. Refers to
Susanna in Mozart's opera *Marriage of Figaro*. Upper range of the
keyboard is exploited in a pointillistic manner. ¼ pedal is required
throughout. Cool, unpretentious avant-garde writing played *p*
throughout. Ends with quotation from "Look What They Have Done
To My Song, Ma" in an innocent C major. M-D to D.

FRIEDRICH WILHELM RUST (1739–1796) Germany
Sonata f♯ (Podolsky—CF) in *Classic Sonatas for Piano* IV. Also available separately (CF).

GIOVANNI RUTINI (1723–1797) Italy
Sei sonate per cembalo Op.8 (Forni Editore   1969). Facsimile of the
first edition, Firenze 1774.
See: Bess Hieronymous, "Rutini, the Composer of Pianoforte Sonatas,
Together with Thematic Index of the Sonatas," thesis, Smith College,
1948. Thematic index only for Opp.1, 2, 3, 5, 6, 7, 13.

PETER RUZICKA (1948–   ) Germany
Ruzicka studied at the Conservatory of Music in Hamburg. He also
worked in composition with Hans Werner Henze in Rome and with Hans
Otte in Bremen.

Ausgeweidet die Zeit . . . Drei Nachtstücke für Klavier (Sikorski   1969) No.16 in Exempla Nova. 8 min. Based on poems from the cycle *Glühende Rätsel* by Nelly Sachs (1891–1970). 1. Molto calmo, quasi meditativo: clusters, dynamic range *ppppp* to *sfff,* plucked strings. 2. Molto agitato: wide dynamic range, pointillistic, free rhythms, dramatic gestures. 3. Elegiaco: complex metrical patterns, tiny bits from Beethoven Op.110 (III) and Schönberg Op.19 (VI). Pedal directions are carefully notated. Avant-garde. D.

Movimenti (Sikorski 1969–70).

FELIKS RYBICKI (1899–   ) Poland
Rybicki studied at the Warsaw Conservatory, where he also taught. In 1952 he was awarded the Prime Minister's Prize for his works for young people.

I Begin to Play Op.20 (PWM   1946) 35pp. 26 short pieces, many in five-finger position. Titles in Polish, English, and German. Clever illustrations. Easy.

I Am Already Playing Op.21 (PWM). 18 pieces. Provides ample opportunity for developing musical and pianistic abilities. Easy to Int.

The Young Modernist Op.23 (PWM   1947) 25pp. 15 MC pieces with colorful illustrations. Easy to Int.

Folk Songs Op.46 (PWM). 16 miniatures that introduce basic piano problems. Easy to Int.

Etudes for the Left Hand Op.54 (PWM). Three books, ranging from easy to difficult. There are few comparable collections in the available pedagogical literature for piano. Skillful use of a number of technical problems.

This is Our Garden-Fair Op.58 (PWM   1971) 17 Czech and Slovak folk songs attractively arranged for piano. Easy to Int.

I Can Play Anything (PWM). 14 varied pieces, fingered and pedalled. Int.

S

HARALD SAEVERUD (1897–   ) Norway
Siljuslatten Op.17 (NMO). M-D.
Birdcall—Variations Op.36 (EMH).

KETIL SAEVERUD (1939–   ) Norway
Rondo con Variazioni 1970 (Lysche 1973) 14pp. Theme, rondo,
  theme repeated, three variations, finale. Chromatic, sudden dynamic
  changes, fast alternating hands, expressionistic. Theme played backward ends the piece. M-D to D.

TORMOD SAEVERUD (1938–   ) Norway
Saeverud is the son of Harald Saeverud.
Five Small Tone Poems (NMO 1969). Short attractive settings. Easy
  to Int.
Three Novelettes (NMO). Capriccio. Elegi. Humoreske. Freely disso-
  nant, neoclassic. M-D.
Tide Rhythm (NMO). Race. Tune. Springtime. Footprints in the Sand.
  Happy Lovers. Tide Rhythm. Jazz influences, freely tonal. M-D.

MICHEL DE SAINT-LAMBERT (–   ) France
Les principes du clavecin (Minkoff Reprints 1972). Reprint of the
  Paris edition of 1702. One of the earliest and best-organized methods
  on playing the harpsichord. Based mainly on the works of Chambonnières, Le Bègue, and d'Anglebert. The chapter on ornamentation
  is excellent.

CAMILLE SAINT-SAËNS (1835–1921) France
Carnival of the Animals (Durand). All fourteen numbers are also avail-
  able separately (Durand).
Fantaisie sur l'Hymne National Russe in collection *Manuscrits Auto-
  graphes.*
Marche-scherzo Op.2 (Durand).
Romance sans Paroles (Century).
Piano Works (Rolf-Dieter Arens—CFP 9295) 104pp. Contains: 6 Baga-
  telles Op.3; Allegro appassionato Op.70; Album pour piano Op.72
  (six separate pieces); Les cloches du soir Op.85; Suite pour piano
  Op.90 (four separate pieces). Preface by Reiner Zimmerman in
  German, French, and English; critical note in German.
Rhapsodie D'Auvergne Op.73 (Durand).

TAKEO SAITO (1904–   ) Japan
Shukaku-Ondo (Japan Federation of Composers 1972) 9pp. A dance expressing joy for an abundant harvest. ABA, left hand ostinato. In the mid-section the dance reaches a climax, and the dancers grow very lively. Gradually they disappear until the music ends. M-D.

AULIS SALLINEN (1935–   ) Finland
Notturno 1966 (Fazer) 2pp. 3 min. Misterioso, dark sonorities, changing meters, freely chromatic and dissonant. M-D.

ERKKI SALMENHAARA (1941–   ) Finland
Sonata I e♭ 1965–66 (Fazer) 27pp.
17 Small Pieces (Fazer).

FRANZ SALMHOFER (1900–   ) Austria
All these pieces show Salmhofer's music to be firmly rooted in the traditions of the Viennese Romantics. "His work may be defined as an attempt to modernize the style of Schubert by exploiting the achievements of Bruckner" (GD, VII, 380).
Klavierstück in Quarten Op.3 (UE 7140).
Scherzo Op.4 (UE 7141).
Sonata C (UE 12129).

KAREL SALMON (1897–   ) Israel
Suite on Greek Themes (IMI 1943) 35pp. 18 min. Syrtos Thrakikos; Theme and Variations; Intermezzo: The Lemon Tree; Finale: Horra Hellenica. Also available for two pianos, four hands. M-D.
Israel lebt (IMI 103).

PIERRE SANCAN (1916–   ) France, born Morocco
Petites Mains (Rideau Rouge). Six pieces. No.1 is the easiest. All are suitable for small hands. Int. to M-D.

WIAROSLAW SANDELEWSKI (1913–   ) Poland
Miniature per giovani pianisti (EC).
2 Danze Polacche (EC 1970) 10pp.

PETER SANDER (1933–   ) Great Britain, born Hungary
Birds' Quarrel (Schmitt 1974) 2pp. Rapid pianistic figurations alternate between hands. Descriptive, skillful, freely tonal. M-D.
Moonflakes (Schmitt 1974). Impressionistic. A lovely transparency emerges through effective pedalling and rubato. M-D.
Toccatina (Schmitt). Strong rhythmic intensity. Dissonance, bravura style. M-D.

PEDRO SANJUAN (1886–   ) USA, born Spain
Toccata (Mercury 1949) 10pp. Lyric passages alternate with toccata ideas. Freely tonal, exciting, brilliant conclusion. M-D.

RODRIGO A. DE SANTIAGO (1907–   ) Spain
Rincones Coruneses. Suite para piano (UME 1973) 26pp.

CLAUDIO SANTORO (1919–   ) Germany, born Brazil

Sonata 1942 (Edição Savart) 12 min. Lento; Alegre, bricando e gracioso; Muito lento.

Pequena Toccata 1942 (Edição Savart) 1 min.

4 Pequena Invenções a 2 vozes 1942 (Edição Savart) 5 min.

4 Peças (1st series) 1943 (Edição Savart) 5 min. 1. Lento. 2. Lento. 3. Vivo grotesco. 4. Moderato.

Sonata I 1945 (Edição Savart) 12 min. Lento; Allegretto; Andante-allegro.

Sonatina infantil 1946 (Edição Savart) 4 min. Allegro; Lento; Allegro.

6 Peças (2nd series) 1946 (Edição Savart) 5 min. 1. Lento. 2. Espressivo. 3. Allegro–lento–allegro. 4. Muito lento. 5. Lento–allegro. 6. Andante–presto.

Prelúdio I (1st series) 1946 (Edição Savart) 2½ min.

Prelúdio II (1st series) 1947 (Edição Savart) 1½ min. Incencao a 2 vozes.

Prelúdio III (1st series) 1948 (Edição Savart) 2 min.

Prelúdio IV (1st series) 1948 (Edição Savart) 3 min.

Sonatina I 1948 (Edição Savart) 8 min. Allegretto; Adagio; Presto. M-D.

Sonatina II 1948 (Edição Savart) 12 min. Allegro; Lento (espressivo); Allegro vivo. M-D.

Batucada 1948 (Edição Savart) 3 min.

Prelúdio V (1st series) 1950 (Edição Savart) 1½ min.

Dança 1950 (Edição Savart) 2½ min.

Miniatura 1950 (Edição Savart) 2 min.

9 Peças infantis 1952 (Ric BR) 18 min. Int.

Frevo 1953 (Ric BR 1601) 6pp. 3 min. Syncopated octaves and chords, sixteenth-note figuration. An exciting dance. Large span required. M-D.

7 Paulistanas 1953 (Vitale) 21 min. Seven short pieces with rhythmic elements characteristic of São Paulo dances. Int. to M-D.

22 Prelúdios 1957–63 (2nd series) (Edição Savart) available separately.

Sonatine II 1964 (Tonos) 6pp. 6 min. Allegretto moderato; Andante; Vivo. MC, neoclassic. Int.

Intermitencias I (Jobert 1967) 4pp. 4 min. Explanations in French and German.

Mutationen III (Tonos 1970) 8pp. For piano and tape. Extensive explanations in English. Preface in German. Study score. Clusters, non-traditional notation. Avant-garde. D.

Balada 1976 (Edição Savart) 10 min.

Sonata IV (fantasia) 1957 (Tonos) 20pp. 16 min. Allegro deciso; Andante; Allegro molto. Well crafted, serially oriented. Allegro molto contains highly effective toccatalike writing. D.

VASSILY SAPELLNIKOFF (1868–1941) Russia

Valse E♭ Op.1 (Zimmermann).

Dance of the Elves Op.3 (Musica Obscura). This was a favorite of Ossip Gabrilowitsch, who played it with great success. A bravura piece requiring nimble fingers. M-D.

Chanson Melancolique Op.4/3 (André).

Gavotte E Op.4/2 (André).

Gavotte D Op.5/2 (André). Also contained in collection *Twenty-Six Romantic and Contemporary Piano Pieces* (GS).

Solitude Op.12 (Zimmermann).

JÓZSEF SÁRI (1935–   ) Hungary

Episodi (EMB   1968) 10pp. Serial, strongly contrasted moods, hammered repetitions, wide skips. M-D.

6 Pezzi (EMB   1971) 10pp. Six pieces.

LÁSZLÓ SARY (1940–   ) Hungary

Collage 1974 (EMB   1977) 12pp.

ERIK SATIE (1866–1925) France

Fun seemed to be the essence of Satie's aesthetic. Most of his works present no great difficulties, but they must be played almost perfectly or they run the strong risk of failure. His compositions clearly reveal the early development of twentieth-century French music.

Deux Oeuvres de Jeunesse: Valse-Ballet Op.62 and *Fantaisie-valse* 1885 (Sal). Satie's first compositions for piano. Salon style. Romantic, graceful. Int.

Trois Gymnopédies 1888 (B&VP). Gymnopédies are ceremonial dances performed at ancient Greek festivals. Each of these three pieces is a different approach to the same idea, sad and languorous. Int.

Trois Gnossiennes, Book I, Nos.1–3   1890 (GS). "Gnossienne" is most likely a vague allusion to Gnossos, an ancient city on the island of Crete—the site of the mythical King Minos. Repeated melody, basic bass rhythm.

Trois Gnossiennes, Book II, Nos.4–6 (B&VP   1968). Each has a different mood. Int.

Available separately: Nos.1–6 (Sal).

Chorals ca.1906 (Sal   1968). Twelve small chorals. Int. to M-D.

Première Pensée Rose-Croix (Sal). Plodding, mystical, dull. Int.

Danses gothiques 1893 (Sal). Nine pieces. Int. to M-D.

Le fils des étoiles 1892 (Sal   1972) 8pp. Preludes for piano. Wagnérie Kaldéenne du Sar Péladan.

Musique intimes et secrètes (Sal   1968). Nostalgie—Froide Sogerie. Fâcheux Exemple.

Poudre d'or (Sal). Valse.

Rêverie du Pauvre (Sal; B&VP).

3 Valses du Précieux Dégoûté (Sal).

Rag-Time Parade (Sal). From ballet *Parade*.

2 Rêverie Nocturnes (Sal). Simple, restful. Int.

The Dreaming Fish (Sal).

Le Piccadilly 1904 (Sal 1975). A march, similar to a cake-walk, rhythmic, would make a good substitute for the Debussy *Le Petit Negre*. Int.

Pièces froides 1897 (Sal). Available separately. 1. Airs à faire fuir ("Three Airs Put to Flight"). 2. Danses de travers ("Crooked Dances"). Barless notation. Basic ideas viewed differently. M-D.

Nouvelles pièces froides (Sal). Sur un mur. Sur un arbre. Sur un pont. Simple and strong. Int.

Véritables préludes flasques 1912 (ESC). Four "flabby preludes"; terse, bony, and highly contrapuntal. M-D.

Déscriptions automatiques 1913 (ESC). Fun; lively and naughty. M-D.

Croquis et agaceries d'un gros bonhomme en bois ("Sketchings and Provocations of a Big Wooden Boob") 1913 (ESC). Three lively parodies of Mozart, Chabrier, and Debussy. M-D.

Chapitres tournés en tous sens ("Chapters Turned Every Which Way") 1913 (ESC).

Vieux Séquins et Vielles Cuirasses ("Old Sequins and Breast-Plates") 1914 (ESC). M-D.

Ogives (Sikorski 1970) 4pp.

Trois nouvelles enfantines (ESC 1972). Le vilain petit vaurien; Berceuse; La gentille toute petite fille. Int.

Heures séculaires et instantanées ("Old Age and Instantaneous Moments") 1914 (ESC). M-D.

Caresse (Sal 1968).

Carnet de Croquis et d'esquisses (Sal). 20 pieces.

Danse de Travers (Sal). Avant-premièrs en forme d'Air à faire fuir.

Les Pantins Dansent ("The Puppets Dance") 1913 (Sal).

12 Petits Chorales (Sal).

Petite Ouverture à Danser (Sal; B&VP 1288). Dull exercises.

6 Pièces de la Période 1906–13 (B&VP). Desespoir agréable. Effronterie. Poésie. Prélude canin. Profundeur. Songe creux. Int. to M-D.

Trois Valses distinguées d'un précieux dégoûté ("Three Distinguished Waltzes of a Disgusted Dandy") 1914 (Sal). 1. His Waist. 2. His Spectacles. 3. His Legs. Ingenious, delightful. Int. to M-D.

Sports et Divertissements 1914 (Sal; Cramer 1977). The Sal edition has an English translation by Virgil Thomson. According to Satie's wish, the texts are to be read between the pieces, and not during their performance. The summation of Satie's piano music. Int. to M-D.

Avant-dernières Pensées ("Three Next-to-Last Thoughts") 1915 (Sal). M-D.

2 Nocturnes and a Minuet 1919 (ESC). Published together. Two of

Satie's best works. M-D.

Sonatine bureaucratique (Consortium; EV; B&VP; Sal). Three colorful movements. The (Sal) edition has the commentary translated into English. Int.

Le Piège de Méduse ("Medusa's Snare") (Sal). Seven short delicious pieces based on an operetta of the same name (1913), for which Satie also wrote the libretto. Quadrille; Valse; Pas vite; Mazurka; Un peu vif; Polka; Quadrille (different from the first one). Modal, no key signatures or bar lines, added-note chords, varied textures. Anticipates Dada. Int.

Children's Pieces for Piano (Nov 1976) 16pp. Nine pieces for beginners published for the first time as a complete collection. Contains: Menus propos enfantines ("Children's Chatter"); Enfantillages pittoresque ("Child's Play"); Peccadilles importunes ("Silly Pranks"). Easy.

Piano Music Vol.I (Sal). Selected works 1887–94: Sarabandes 1, 2, 3; Gymnopédies 1, 2, 3; Gnossiennes 1, 2, 3; Les fils des étoiles—preludes; Sonneries de la rose e croix; Prélude de la porte héroïque du ciel. Int. to M-D.

Piano Music Vol.II (Sal). Selected works 1897–1919. Pièces froides; Airs à faire fuir; Danses de travers; Je te veux; Poudre d'or; 3 Valses distinguées du précieux dégoûté; Avant-dernières pensées; 3 Nocturnes. Int. to M-D.

Piano Music Vol.III (Sal). Sports et Divertissiments. Int. to M-D.

Piano Works Vol.I (Maurice Rogers—Cramer) 75pp. Contains 34 works including: 3 Gymnopédies; 3 Gnossiennes; Embryons Desséches; 3 Sarabandes; 5 Nocturnes; Sonatine Bureaucratique; Véritables préludes flasques. Int. to M-D.

Piano Works Vol.II (M. Rogers—Cramer). Croquis et agaceries d'un gros bonhomme en bois; Chapitres tournés en tous sens; Vieux séquins et veilles cuirasses; Heures séculaires et instantées; Les trois valses distinguées du précieux dégoûté; Valse-Ballet; Fantaisie-Valse Op.62; Premier Menuet. Contains an erudite introduction. Int. to M-D.

A Satie Entertainment (D. Ratcliffe—Nov 1976). Contains three piano pieces Satie used in the nightclub where he was pianist and three short love songs accompanied by chromatic harmonies. Other piano solos include 3 Sarabandes; 3 Gymnopédies; 3 Gnossiennes; Airs à faire fuir from Piéces froides. The three nightclub piano pieces are Je te veux; Poudre d'or; Le Piccadilly. Editorial additions given in square brackets. Int. to M-D.

See: Marcelle Vernazza, "Erik Satie's Music for Children," *Clavier,* 18 (January 1979):39–40.

KEIJIRO SATOH (1927–   ) Japan

Calligraphy (Ongaku no Tomo Sha 1957–60) 12pp. Performance directions in English and Japanese. Harmonics; notation indicated by seconds, with eighth note=56; pointillistic; frequent dynamic changes, proportional rhythmic notation; dense textures contrast with thin ones. Avant-garde. D.

DOMENICO SCARLATTI (1685–1757) Spain, born Italy

Scarlatti composed more than 550 keyboard sonatas for the musically gifted Portuguese Princess Maria Barbara. For nearly ten years he served as her music teacher, and upon her marriage in 1729 to the heir of the Spanish throne, he moved with her court to Spain, where he spent the rest of his life. Most of these sonatas were collected toward the end of his life in a series of volumes for his former pupil, now Queen of Spain. Evidence indicates that more than half of them were composed when Scarlatti was between the ages of 67 and 72. In these sonatas, which show a constantly developing style and an abundance of creativity, Scarlatti gave the binary form a variety and expressive range that has never been surpassed by any other composer.

Complete Edition of the Sonatas (Alessandro Longo—K 1978) 545 sonatas in 11 volumes. This American reprint makes easily available a series first published in the early part of this century. Highly edited. See p.552 in *Guide* for contents of each volume. Also available from (K) is a complete thematic index to the entire series.

200 Sonatas (Gyorgy Balla—EMB) 4 vols. This exciting new urtext edition contains 50 sonatas in each volume. Helpful performance suggestions in English, German, and Hungarian; convenient thematic index. Critical note in German. English translation of the preface is awkward, but the information is helpful. Excellent fingering provided. Vol.I (1977): K.1, 9, 11, 20, 24–27, 29, 30, 37, 43, 51–53, 55, 64, 69, 72, 78, 82, 96, 98, 102, 103, 106, 107, 113, 114, 119, 120, 121, 122, 124, 125, 129, 132, 133, 140, 141, 145, 146, 148, 149, 150, 151, 154, 155, 158, 159.

36 Sonatas (Leon Kartun—Les Éditions Ouvrières). Book I: L.488, 366, 338, 370, 104, 487, 449, 415, 224, 8, 486, 462, 429, 374, 407, 390, 158, 416. Book II: L.413, 475, 465, 499, 48, 383, 171, 241, 375, 33, 461, 391, 14, 32, Supplement 26 (K.337), Supplement 40 (K.172), 382, 345. Edited for the piano in good taste.

Scarlatti Album I (Zbigniev Drzewiecki—PWM). Contains: K.1, 2, 9, 19, 20, 33, 125, 132, 159, 259, 377, 380, 430, 533. Clean edition.

Complete Keyboard Works (Johnson Reprint Corporation) 18 volumes in facsimile from the Parma manuscript and printed sources, compiled and annotated by Ralph Kirkpatrick. Each volume contains a preface, notes on sources, notes on texts, catalogue of sonatas, table of sonatas in the order of Longo's edition, listing of sonatas in the order of tonalities and time signatures. Vol.I: Sonatas K.1–42 (1–30 are the thirty *Essercizi* [1738–9] and 31–42 are the twelve sonatas that Thomas Roseingrave added in his 1739 printing of forty-two sonatas). Vol.II: Sonatas K.43–68, Appendix of K.8, 31, 33, 37, 41. Vol.III: Sonatas K.69–97, Appendix with variants of K.52, 53. Vol.IV: Sonatas K.98–123. Vol.V: Sonatas 124–47. Vol. VI: Sonatas K.148–76. Vol.VII: Sonatas K.177–205. Vol.VIII: Sonatas K.206–35. Vol.IX: Sonatas K.236–65. Vol.X: Sonatas K.266–95. Vol.XI: Sonatas K.296–325. Vol.XII: Sonatas K.326–57. Vol.XIII: Sonatas K.358–87. Vol.XIV: Sonatas K.388–417. Vol.XV: Sonatas K.418–53. Vol.XVI: Sonatas K.454–83. Vol.XVII: Sonatas K.484–513. Vol.XVIII: Sonatas K.514–55.

See: William S. Newman, "Kirkpatrick's facsimile Edition of Scarlatti's Keyboard Sonatas," PQ, 79 (Fall 1972):18–21.

Complete Keyboard Works (Kenneth Gilbert—Heugel) 11 vols. Preface in English, French, and German. Critical note in French. This scrupulous new edition has much to recommend it. Based on the Venice manuscripts. Vol.1: Sonatas K.1–52. Vol.2: Sonatas K.53–103. Vol.3: Sonatas K.104–55. Vol.4: Sonatas K.156–205. Vol.5: Sonatas K.206–55; Vol.6: Sonatas K.256–305. Vol.7: Sonatas K.306–57. Vol.8: Sonatas K.358–407. Vol.9: Sonatas K.408–57. Vol.10: Sonatas K.458–506. Vol.11: Sonatas K.507–55.

100 Sonatas (Eiji Hashimoto—Zen-On 1975) 3 vols. Contains a six-page preface and seven pages of textual notes in an English translation, as well as two pages of facsimiles. No fingering. Vol.1: Sonatas K.6, 9, 24, 25, 26, 30, 49, 87, 99, 100, 104, 113, 114, 123, 126, 127, 128, 141, 147, 173, 179, 180, 181, 182, 183, 184, 201, 211, 212, 213, 214, 225, 226. Vol.2: Sonatas K.232, 233, 240, 241, 246, 247, 248, 249, 261, 262, 298, 299, 318, 319, 320, 321, 347, 348, 364, 365, 368, 369, 380, 381, 424, 425, 430, 434, 435, 436, 437, 438, 443, 444. Vol.3: Sonatas K.445, 446, 447, 448, 454, 455, 466, 467, 468, 469, 474, 475, 478, 479, 485, 486, 487, 497, 498, 499, 500, 511, 512, 520, 521, 526, 527, 532, 533, 546, 547, 550, 551.

27 Selected Sonatas (BMC). L.201, 286, 268, 249, 262, 24, 6, 15, 10, 11, 3, 481, 496, 457, 302, 406, 126, 127, 187, 383, 366, 378, 390, 385, 360, 263, 376. Edited.

5 Pairs of Sonatas (S. Rosenblum—ECS). The excellent preface includes a discussion of stylistic considerations. L.24, 61, 64, 88, 93, 95, 322, 359, 454, 483. A careful and clean edition. Int. to M-D.

Scarlatti—An Introduction to His Keyboard Works (Margery Halford—Alfred 1974). Includes a discussion of the manuscripts, style and form, interpretation, ornamentation, rhythmic alterations, phrasing, articulation and fingering, dynamics, pedal, figured bass. Includes:

K.32, 63, 77b, 80, 83b, 391, 44e, 40, 42, 73b, 73c, 415, 81d, 88c, 90d, 431, 89b, 34, and a thematic index. A most useful volume. Int. to M-D.

Domenico Scarlatti—An Introduction to the Composer and His Music (J. Banowetz—GWM 1978) 80pp. Highly informative preface with discussion of the sources used for this edition, Scarlatti's Grouping of the Sonatas, Playing Scarlatti on the Piano, Ornamentation, and other topics. Includes Sonatas: K.63 G L.84; K.64 d L.58; K.78 F L.75; K.178 D L.162; K.208 A L.238; K.274 F L.297; K.275 F L.328; K.277 D L.183; K.322 A L.483; K.323 A L.95; K.330 C L.55; K.391 G L.79; K.393 B♭ L.74; K.431 G L.83; K.440 B♭ L.97; K.453 A (no L no.); K.481 f L.187. Also includes notes for each sonata. An exemplary edition with all editorial marks in red. Int. to M-D.

37 Pieces and Sonatas (Arnold Goldsbrough—ABRSM 1962). Vol.1: Pieces K.80, 40, 34, 32, 42, 81, 88, 83, 163, 322, 377, 95, 74, 88 (another part), 512, 471, 63. Vol.2: Sonatas K.389, 342, 123, 278, 67, 102, 537, 25, 427, 11. Vol.3: Sonatas K.9, 481, 535, 436, 140, 525, 4, 380, 8, 38. Includes source identification, fingering, and a preface that discusses ornamentation, tempi, and touch. The three volumes are graded and range from Easy to Int. in Vol.1 to M-D in Vol.3.

Il mio primo Scarlatti ("My first Scarlatti") (R. Risaliti—Ric 1976) 21pp. Includes: K.32 D L.423. K.34 d L.S.7. K.40 c L.357. K.42 B♭ L.S.36. K.78 F L.75. K.80 G. K.94 F. K.95 C L.358. K.332 A L.483. K.391 G L.79. K.431 G. L.83. K.440 B♭ L.97. K.453 A. Int.

A Scarlatti Notebook (Christina Emra—McAfee 1977) 2 vols. Sixty of the easier sonatas.

Scarlatti, the First Book for Young Pianists (M. Halford—Alfred 1977) 24pp.

2 Sonatas (E. Hashimoto—Zen-On 221). K.380; 381 (L.23; 225).

2 Sonatas (E. Hashimoto—Zen-On 222). K.499; 500 (L.193; 492).

10 Selected Sonatas (Wouters—Zephyr 1975) 32pp. L.213, 345, 358, 375, 388, 413, 461, 486, 495, 499.

2 Sonatas (APS). K.34, 42. Highly edited. Int.

Album for Keyboard (Alfred A. Kalmus). 14 sonatas with editorial additions of fingering, dynamics, and interpretation of ornaments. Also contains an account of Scarlatti's life, his contribution to the repertoire, and his technique of composition.

20 Sonate brillanti (T. Alati—Carisch).

5 Klaviersonaten (W. Gerstenberg—Gustave Bosse 1933). K.452, 453, 204a, 204b, 357.

See: Robert Dumm, "A Performer's Analysis—A Scarlatti Sonata," *Clavier,* 14 (February 1975):27–30. Discusses the "Pastorale Sonata d," K.9.

Edwin Smith, "Four Scarlatti Sonatas," *Music Teacher,* 53 (June 1974): 20–21. Discusses K.113, 159, 426, 96.

R. MURRAY SCHAFFER (1933–   ) Canada
Since 1965 Schaffer has served on the staff of Simon Fraser University.
Polytonality (Berandol 1648   1974). The left hand seldom varies the pattern of a G/a broken chord figure, kind of a hillbilly accompaniment. The right hand has a clever melody. No fingering, key signature, time signature, or tempo indications. A cheerful work, would be excellent for an encore. M-D.

BOGUSLAW SCHÄFFER (1929–   ) Poland
aSa 1975 (AA) 10pp. 12 min. For clavichord.
Model No.7   1971 (AA) 7 min.

PETER SCHICKELE (1935–   ) USA P.D.Q. Bach (1807–1742)?
In My Nine Lives (EV).
Four Pieces   1957 (ACA).
Little Suite for Josie   1957 (ACA).
Sequence   1961 (ACA).
Serenade   1961 (ACA).
Three Folk Settings (EV   1963) 7pp. Henry Martin; Turtle Dove; Old Joe Clark. Octotonic, modal, thin textures, attractive. Int.
The Household Moose   1965 (EV   1975) 9pp. Written in tribute to Darius Milhaud, especially for his piano suite *The Household Muse.* Seven colorful, inventive pieces, MC. Suitable for sophisticated young players as well as for more advanced pianists. Int. to M-D.
Presents I (EV   1974) 4pp. Celebration; Peaslee Porridge Hot; Crab Game; Song for Susan; Remembrance; Berceuse; Notes from Underground. Atonal, serial, pointillistic, contrasted. M-D.
Presents II   1972 (EV).
A Garland of Rags   1973 (ACA).
Notebook for Betty Sue Bach S.13 going on 14 (TP   1973) 23pp. Written in P.D.Q. Bach's most gingerly style—great fun! Contains: Allemande Left; Corrate; Oh! Courante!; Two-Part Contraption; Three-Part Contraption; Andre Gigue; Traumarie; Capriccio Espagnole for Charles III, "The Reign in Spain." Int.
Three Piano Sonatinas (EV   1974) 16pp. Three movements each, in contemporary idiom. Sonatina II is the shortest and easiest. Dissonance, wide leaps, and changing meters require good pianistic equipment. Some bitonality used. Sonatina III is based on poems by American poets. Large span required for all three. M-D.

LALO SCHIFRIN (1932–   ) USA, born Argentina
Schifrin studied composition with Juan Carlos Paz in Argentina and later with Olivier Messiaen at the Paris Conservatory. He came to the USA in 1957 and has made his biggest reputation in writing for films and television.

Jazz Sonata (MJQ).

Mima (EBM 1958). A progressive jazz suite in five movements. El
Jefe; Mima; Buenos Aires Minuit; Blues for Berger; Silvia. Each
movement is short. Int. to M-D.

HENRYK SCHILLER (1931–   ) Poland
Sonata (AA) 7 min.

GUSTAV ADOLF SCHLEMM (1902–   ) Germany
Fünf Klavierstücke (Tonos 7002 1968) 17pp. 15 min. Präludium.
Ciaconnetta. Nächtliche Vision. Impression. Impromptu. Freely tonal,
neoclassic. M-D.

Sieben Klavierstücke nach Albrecht Dürer's Kupferstich-Passion (Tonos
1954, rev.1974) 11pp. Christus als Schmerzensmann. Jesus in
Gethsemane. Die Gefangennahme. Die Geisselung. Die Kreuztragung.
Die Kreuzigung (a three-voice fugue). Die Beweinung. Chromatic,
somewhat in Frank Martin's early style, full chords, octaves, flexible
meters. M-D.

YVES RUDNER SCHMIDT (1933–   ) Brazil
Batuque 1952 (Vitale) 2½ min.
Matéria e Espirito 1952 (Ric BR) 3½ min.
Zóinho (sambinha) 1953 (Vitale 1977) 1½ min.
Dois Ponteios 1954–5 (Vitale) 9pp. 1. Groups of five notes in broken
chordal figuration serve as accompaniment to left-hand melody. 2.
Ideas are inverted so left hand has broken chordal figuration. Post-
Romantic sonorities. M-D.
Toada II 1954 (Vitale 1975) 2pp. Brazilian rhythms and melodies.
Int.
Oração 1955 (Ric BR 1965) 2 min.
Dança Crioula 1955 (Vitale 1968) 3 min.
De Profundis 1956 (Vitale 1972) 1½ min. From series *Expressões*.
Canto Nostálgico 1957 (Ric BR 1965) 2½ min.
Acalanto 1957 (Ric BR) 1 min. From series *Três temas brasileiros*.
Zangarreio 1957 (Ric BR) 2½ min.
Balanco de rede 1958 (Ric BR) 1 min. From series *Três temas brasi-
leiros*.
Cochilo 1958 (Ric BR) 1 min. From series *Três temas brasileiros*.
Überfall, Norder Strasse No.46 1959 (Ric BR) 2 min. From series
Impressões Européias.
Mágoa—Suchkind 1959 (Vitale) 1½ min. From series *Espressões*.
Bola de sabão 1960 (Cembra) 2 min.
Walzer 1960 (Ric BR) 1½ min. From series *Impressões Européias*.
Damrak 1960 (Ric BR) 1½ min. From series *Impressões Européias*.
Die Mauer 1962 (Ric BR) 2½ min.
Quartier Latin 1962 (Ric BR) 1½ min.

Ibéria I   1962 (Ric BR) 2 min.
Ibéria II   1962 (Ric BR) 1½ min.
5 Ensaio Ritmico   1964 (Ric BR) published separately.
Devoção   1964 (Vitale) 1 min.
As aulas do Visconde de Sabugosa   1964 (Vitale) 2 min.
História de tia Nastácia   1964 (Vitale) 1 min.
Diálogo triste   1965 (Ric BR   1973) 2 min. Unusual chromatic ostinato treatment. M-D.
Reinações de Narizinho Arrebitado   1965 (Vitale) 1 min.
O triunfo de Dona Benta   1965 (Vitale) 1 min.
Recreação   1965 (Ric BR) 2½ min.
Súplica   1966 (Vitale) 1½ min.
O sonho de Emilia   1966 (Vitale) 1½ min.
Jeca Tatu   1966 (Vitale) 1 min.
Travessuras de Pedrinho   1967 (Vitale) 1 min.
O Marquês de Rabicó   1967 (Vitale) 1 min.
Hoje eu mesmo, amanhã o mundo ("Today, I Myself, Tomorrow the World")   1967 (Ric BR) 4pp. 2 min. National Brazilian influences mixed with an international style. Sonorities are explored by playing with all the fingers, the arms, and the palms; and finally the pianist sits on the keyboard with a fermata! Traditional notation. D.
Desamor   1974 (Vitale) 1½ min.
Impressões Européias 1959–62 (Ric BR   1971) 17pp. Published together. M-D.

FLORENT SCHMITT (1870–1958) France
Ballade de la Neige Op.6   1896 (Sal).
Brises (Sal).
Cortège des Adorateurs du Feu (Sal).
Danse des Milliards (Sal).
Feuilles mortes (Sal).
Homage sur le nom de Gabriel Fauré Op.72 (Durand   1922).
Menuet vif (Sal).
Prelude . . . . pour une suite à venir   1948 (EFM 1815).
Ritournelles Op.2/11 (Sal).
Tombeau de Paul Dukas Op.86/6 (*Revue Musicale* May–June 1936).

ARTUR SCHNABEL (1882–1951) Germany
Valse Mignnone (Schaum Publications) in collection *Composer–Pianists*.

OTHMAR SCHOECK (1886–1957) Switzerland
Ritornelle und Fughetten Op.68 1953–55 (Hug). Neobaroque; scholarly and academic exercises; idiomatic and ultraconservative writing. M-D.

ROBERT SCHOLLUM (1913–   ) Austria
Sonata III (Pastorale) Op.46/3 1952–63 (Dob   1975). In three move-

ments. Nontonal. Flowing opening movement with dancelike figuration. Second movement is a Lied: contains a few meter changes, short. The quick finale displays active octave passages; fast fingers and a strong rhythmic drive are required. M-D to D.

15 Etudes Op.89 (Dob 1974) 29pp.

ERWIN CHRISTIAN SCHOLZ (1910–   ) Austria

Die moderne Studie (Dob). Three graded books. The art of performance technique in new piano music. Text in German.

Romantische Studie ("Erwartung") (Dob).

ARNOLD SCHÖNBERG (1874–1951) Austria

Drei Klavierstücke 1896 (Belmont). Early Schönberg with strong Brahms influence. The first piece has a 3/8 pulse but is notated throughout in a 2/4 meter. More interesting than effective, and yet there are some lovely sonorities in all three pieces. M-D.

Piano Piece Op.33b (UE).

See: Elaine Barkin, "A View of Schoenberg's Op.23/1," PNM (Fall–Winter 1973, Spring–Summer 1974):99–127.

Robert Blash, "An Interpretive Analysis of the Suite for Piano, Op.25 by Arnold Schönberg," diss., Columbia University, 1971.

Eric Graebner, "An Analysis of Schoenberg's *Klavierstück* Op.33a," PNM (Fall–Winter 1973, Spring–Summer 1974):128–40.

Hugo Leichtentritt, "Schönberg and Tonality," MM, 5 (May–June 1928): 3–10. Contains an analysis of Op.19.

Adriane Van Bergen, "The Stylistic Evolution of Schoenberg's Piano Music," Master's thesis, Brigham Young University, 1966.

RUTH SCHONTHAL (1924–   ) USA, born Germany

Potpourri (CF). Ten short, bright pieces, MC. Int.

Sonata Breve (OUP 1976) 8pp. 7½ min. Fresh harmonies; silent clusters add unusual harmonics; chromatic. Interesting recital possibilities. M-D.

Variations in Search of a Theme (OUP) 16 min. 15 individual and contrasting sections. Careful performance directions. M-D.

Near and Far (CF). Thirteen musical scenes. For the more sensitive student. Int.

KEES SCHOONENBEEK (1947–   ) The Netherlands

Toccata 1972 (Donemus) 10pp. Photostat.

HERMANN SCHROEDER (1904–   ) Germany

Sonata Piccola (Gerig 1974) 18pp.

Sonatina No.3 C (Simrock 1972) 11pp.

HEINZ SCHRÖTER (1907–1974) Germany

Four Pieces for Three (Bo&Bo 1970). Published separately. Cadenza for cello and piano. Capriccio for violin and piano. Monogram, for

piano solo. Elegy, for violin, cello, and piano.
Reflections   1973 (Gerig) 28pp. 17 min.

WLADIMIR WLADIMIROWITSCH SCHTSCHERBATSCHJOW (1889–1952) USSR

Sonata II Op.7 (Sowjetskij Kompositor   1972) 39pp. Title and preface in Russian.

FRANZ SCHUBERT (1797–1828) Austria

According to Walther Dürr (MT, 1619 [January 1978]:68), in Schubert's autographs *decrescendo* means "getting gradually softer," while *diminuendo* means "getting gradually softer and slower," the latter indication customarily being followed by *a tempo*.

Complete Piano Music (Dover). Reprint of Vol.V of the critical edition of 1884–97 (Epstein—Br&H). Now divided into: *Complete Sonatas* and *Shorter Works for Pianoforte Solo* (34 pieces).

DANCES:

Dances for Piano (P. Zeitlin—TP   1976) 19pp. Original dances through the twelve major keys with an introduction and finale in minor keys (fourteen dances in all). Int.

Dances (GS L1537). German dances and écossaises Op.33; Ländler Opp. 67, 171, and posthumous; Last Waltzes from Op.127; Minuets (posthumous); Trio E; Valse nobles, Op.77; Valses sentimentales from Op.50; Waltzes, Opp.9a, 9b, 91a; Waltzes and écossaises from Op. 18a. Int. to M-D.

Ländler and Other Dances (Bauer—GS).

3 Waltzes (GS).

16 German Dances and 2 Ecossaises Op.33 D.783 (P. Mies—Henle 179).

Complete Dances for the Piano (A. Weinmann, H. Kann—VU   1973) Preface, critical notes, and sources in English and German. Vol.I: works published during Schubert's lifetime or shortly thereafter. Vol.II: later sets and smaller individual pieces. Some dynamic and phrasing marks are found in parentheses with no explanation. Few critical notes. Remarks on musical details contained in footnotes at bottom of page. Int. to M-D.

Dances and Waltzes (K 3878).

Ecossaises (K 3879).

The Easier Schubert (Eve Barsham—Elkin). 45 pieces, mainly écossaises, minuets, ländler, waltzes, and other dances. Serves as an excellent introduction to Schubert. Fingering and pedaling as well as some dynamics have been added. Concise and helpful preface on the dance forms. Int.

Leichte Spielstücke für Klavier (Hug).

Chain of Ländler (Br&H; Gutheil). Transcribed by Wanda Landowska.

12 Ländler Op.171 (Cortot—Sal).

Il mio primo Schubert (Pozzoli—Ric 1956) 17pp. 2 Scottish Dances
G, B♭; Little Waltz D; Ländler A; Waltzes Op.9/2, 3, 11, 12; Op.
67/15; Sentimental Waltzes Op.50/3, 11, 13, 17; Dance A♭; Moment musical Op.94/3. Int.

PIANO PIECES:

Four Impromptus Op.90 D.899 (Badura-Skoda—VU 50001). M-D.
Four Impromptus Op.143 D.935 (Badura-Skoda—VU 50001). M-D.
Klavierstücke 1827 (Dob 1978) 24pp. facsimile. No.805 in Diletto
musicale series. Preface in German and English, critical note in
German; edited by Otto Brusatti. No.1, D.916B in C, and No.2,
D.916C in c. Published here for the first time.
Six Moments musicaux Op.94 D.780 (Badura-Skoda—VU 50006). Also
published with the Eight Impromptus in VU 50001.
Fantasia C Op.15 D.760 "Wanderer Fantasia" (Herttrich—Henle 282).
Fingering added by H.-M. Theopold. A critical urtext edition.
See: Elaine Brody, "Mirror of His Soul—Schubert's Fantasy in C
(D.760)," PQ, 104 (Winter 1978–79):23–24, 26, 28, 30–31.
Tedd Joselson, "Schubert's Wanderer Fantasy," CK, 4 (December
1978):63. Examines the Adagio movement from a performer's
point of view.
Fantasy c, Largo, D.993 (J. Demus—TP 1979) also available in PQ,
104: (Winter 1978–79):12–17. 4½ min. This first publication com-
memorates the 150th anniversary of Schubert's death. It is of major
interest in that it represents a rare composition for the keyboard from
Schubert's mid-teens (ca.1812). Listed in the Schubert Foundation
catalogue as "Largo for Clavicembalo." The editor, Jörg Demus, has
titled the piece *Fantasy,* because of its resemblance to the famous
Mozart C-minor *Fantasy* (K.475). The Schubert work is a three-
part song form Largo–Andantino–Largo. Motives evolve into melodies; fluctuating tonalities; third-relationships. M-D.
See: Jörg Demus, "Two Fantasies—Mozart's Fantasy in C Minor
(K.475) and Schubert's Fantasy in C Minor (D.993)," PQ, 104
(Winter 1978–79):9–11. A perceptive comparison of these two
works.

EDITIONS OF THE SONATAS:

(Henle) 3 vols. Vol.I (Mies, Theopold—Henle 146): Sonatas A Op.
posth. 120 D.664; a Op.42 D.845; a Op. posth. 143 D.784; a Op.
posth. 164 D.537; D Op.53 D.850; E♭ Op. posth. 122 D.568; B
Op. posth. 147 D.575. Based on autographs and first editions.
M-D to D. Vol.II (Mies, Theopold—Henle 148): Sonatas G Op.

78 D.894; c, A, B, D.958–60. Based on autographs and first editions. Vol.III (P. Badura-Skoda, Theopold—Henle 150): Contains the early and unfinished sonatas: Sonatas A♭, D.557; C, D.279/346; C, D.613/612; C ("Reliquie") D.840; D♭, D.567; E, D.157; E (5 Klavierstücke) D.459; e, D.566/506; f, D.625/505; f♯ D.571/604/570; and Appendix containing early sketches for D.154, D.157, D.279. Preface in German, French, and English. Critical note in German and English. Badura-Skoda has completed the movements of the incomplete works for practical use, basing his work on available fragments. Based on autographs and first editions.

Noël Lee has also completed the unfinished sonatas. His completions can be obtained from him at 4 Villa Laugier, 75017 Paris, France.

Sonatas (Howard Ferguson—ABRSM). Vol.I 1978. Vols.II and III forthcoming 1979.

Sonatas (W. Weismann, G. Erber—CFP 1974) 2 vols.

Sonata E♭ Op.122 D.568 (H. Swarsenski—CFP). Originally written in D♭ (D.567).

See: Harold Truscott, "The Two Versions of Schubert's Op.122," MR, 14 (May 1953):89–106.

Sonata A Op.120 D.664 (Henle 157).

Sonata a Op.42 D.845 (Henle 156).

See: Brian Newbould, "A Schubert Sonata," *Music Teacher,* 56 (November 1977):14–16, for discussion and analysis of Op.42.

See: Arthur Satz, "Alfred Brendel: The Playing of Schubert Sonatas Is a New Art," *Musical America,* 23 (August 1973):12–13.

Robert Simpson, "Schubert. Pianoforte Sonata in c minor, edited by Kathleen Dale," MR, X (May 1949):147–48. Discusses D.566.

Adele Marcus, "Performance Hints on a Schubert Sonata," *Clavier,* 15 (March 1976):27–29. Discusses *Sonata* A D.959.

Martin Chusid, "Cyclicism in Schubert's Piano Sonata in A Major (D.959)," PQ, 104 (Winter 1978–79):38–40.

Konrad Wolff, "Observations on the Scherzo of Schubert's B♭ Sonata Op. posth. D.960," PQ, 92 (Winter 1975–76):28–29.

COLLECTIONS:

Schubert—An Introduction to His Piano Works (Margery Halford—Alfred 1977) 64pp. Includes: facsimile of an Album Leaf; Allegretto D.915; Andante D.29; 8 Ecossaises; 2 German Dances Op. 33/2, 15; Impromptu Op.142/2; Ländler, from 17 Ländler No.13; Moments Musicaux Op.94/3, 5; Scherzo I & II D.593; Scherzo con Trio from Five Pieces, No.4; Variations on a Theme by Anselm Huttenbrenner D.935 (7 variations omitted); 4 Waltzes. Subjects discussed in the foreword include Schubert's biography, style and interpretation, ornamentation, origin and sources. An altogether excellent contribution. Int. to M-D.

Various Pieces (K 3885).

An Easy Album (K 3876).

3 Piano Pieces 1828 (Walter Niemann—CFP P7091).

6 Popular Pieces (CFP1825a). Theme from B♭ Impromptu Op.142/3; Scherzo Op. posth.; Moment Musical Op.94/3; Andante from Sonata A Op.120; 2 Waltzes from Op.9a; 6 German Dances from Op.33. Int. to M-D.

Schubert (Stephen Bishop—OUP 1972) 58pp. Part of the *Oxford Keyboard Classics* series. Includes: Sonata D♭ D.567; two movements from unfinished Sonata C ("Reliquie") D.840; Variation c (on the Diabelli waltz) D.719; Allegretto c, D.915; Valse sentimentale A, D.779/13. Also includes notes on interpretation, including instruments of the period, dynamics, pedaling, ornamentation. Int. to M-D.

Schubert. The First Book for Young Pianists (M. Halford—Alfred 1977) 24pp. Many of the selections included are taken from *Schubert—An Introduction to His Piano Works*. Contains 3 Ländler; 3 Menuets and Trios; 7 Ecossaises; 2 German Dances; 4 Waltzes. Int.

See: Paul Badura-Skoda, "Textual Problems in Schubert—Discrepancies Between Text and Intention," PQ, 104 (Winter 1978–79):49–55.

Malcolm Bilson, "Schubert's Piano Music and the Pianos of His Time," PQ, 104 (Winter 1978–79):56–61.

Alfred Brendel, "Schubert's Piano Sonatas, 1822–1828," in *Musical Thoughts and Afterthoughts* (Princeton: Princeton University Press, 1976), pp.57–74.

Maurice J. E. Brown, "Schubert's Piano Sonatas," MT, 1592 (October 1975):873–75.

Stewart Gordon, "Anniversary Reflections on Schubert's Solo Keyboard Music," AMT, 28 (November–December 1978):20, 22.

Maurice Hinson and F. E. Kirby, "A Schubert Bibliography," PQ, 104 (Winter 1978–79):63–64.

Reinhard van Hoorickx, "Thematic Catalogue of Schubert's Works: New Additions, Corrections and Notes," *Revue Belge Musicologie*, 28–30 (1974–76):136–71. Deals with more than 100 new additions—either omitted previously or discovered since the Deutsch Catalogue appeared in 1951—with corrections and additional notes.

Walter Schenkman, "Impromptu Thoughts on a Schubert Anniversary," *Clavier*, 17 (October 1978):24–33. Includes "A Lesson on a Schubert Impromptu" (Op.90/2).

Miriam K. Whaples, "Styles in Schubert's Piano Music from 1817 to 1818," MR, 35 (1974):260–80. Discusses the "Graz" Fantasy and the eight piano sonatas of these years.

————. "Schubert's Piano Sonatas of 1817–1818," PQ, 104 (Winter 1978–79):34–37.

ZENON SCHUBERT (1934–   ) Poland
Metamorphoses 1963 (PWM   1975) 9pp.

PETER SCHULTHORPE (1929–   ) Australia, born Tasmania
Schulthorpe is a major force in creating a truly Australian contemporary musical language.
Night Pieces (Faber   1973) 4½ min. 1. Snow, Moon and Flowers: delicate; ephemeral; black-key glissando. 2. Night: quiet, languorous, short. 3. Stars: dart about in calmness. Mysterious and subtle sonorities; should be played directly on the strings; harplike textures. Exact sense of timing required for these short, descriptive, and evocative little pieces. Int. to M-D.
Sonatina 1954 (Leeds) 7½ min. Fast, ritualistic, nonmelodic and non-harmonic textures and slow harmonically static melodies. In place of developing ideas, there are many repetitive variational patterns and taut miniature forms. M-D.

SVEND SIMON SCHULTZ (1913–   ) Denmark
Moments musicaux (Musikhøjskolens   1971) 15pp.

CLARA SCHUMANN (1819–1896) Germany
Premier Concert pour le pianoforte avec accompagnement d'orchestra, Op.7 (arranged for solo piano). Reprint of the original Hofmeister edition (Musica Revindicata   1970, available from Front) 28pp.
Selected Piano Music (Da Capo   1979). Introduction by Pamela Süss-kind.
Variations on a Theme by Robert Schumann Op.20 (Süddeutscher). Based on the first of the five *Albumblätter* Op.99. Brahms used this same theme for his *Variations on a Theme by Schumann* Op.9. Clara elaborates the theme considerably as the basis for her set with varied harmonies. Pianistically imaginative. M-D.
See: Donald Bea Isaak, "Clara Schumann as a Composer," *Clavier,* 15 (February 1976):22–24. Also includes Prelude and Fugue B♭ Op. 16/2.
Pamela G. Süsskind, "Clara Wieck Schumann as Pianist and Composer: A Study of Her Life and Works," Ph.D. diss., University of California, Berkeley, 1977. Vol.1: Literary text, 306pp. Vol.2: Music, 277pp.

REINHARD SCHUMANN (1938–   ) Germany
Kleine Stücke (Möseler   1970) 16pp. Fifteen little pieces for piano.

ROBERT SCHUMANN (1810–1856) Germany
Henle has almost finished its complete edition of the piano works, based on the latest research.

Piano Solos Vol.1 (W. Boetticher, W. Lampe—Henle 108): Scenes from Childhood Op.15; Album for the Young Op.68; Colored Leaves Op.99; Album Leaves Op.124. Vol.II (W. Boetticher, W. Lampe— Henle 110): Abegg-Variations Op.1; Fantasy Pieces Op.12; Arabesque Op.18; Flower Pieces Op.19; Novelettes Op.21; Night Pieces Op.23; 3 Romances Op.28; Forest Scenes Op.82; 3 Fantasy Pieces Op.111. Vol.III (W. Boetticher, H.-M. Theopold—Henle 112): Papillons Op.2; Intermezzi Op.4; Davidsbündlertänze Op.6; Carnaval Op.9; Symphonic Etudes Op.13; Kreisleriana Op.16; Carnaval Prank from Vienna Op.26. Vol.IV (W. Boetticher, H.-M. Theopold—Henle 114): Toccata Op.7: Sonatas Opp.11 and 22; Fantasie Op.17; Concerto without Orchestra Op.14. All four volumes are based on autographs and early editions.
Available separately: Opp.1, 2, 4, 6, 7, 9, 12, 13, 15, 16, 17, 18, 19, 21, 23, 26, 28, 68, 68 with 15, 82, 99, 111, 124 (Henle). Opp.1, 2, 6, 9, 15 with 68, 16, 18 and 19, 99 and 124 (Hans Joachim Köhler— CFP), with detailed critical commentaries in English, German, and French. Opp.16, 17 (Cortot—Sal). Opp.2, 12, 15, 18, 19 (VU). Opp.1, 2, 6, 7, 9, 11, 12, 13, 15, 16, 17, 18, 20, 21, 22, 26, 28, 32, 68, 82 (Carlo Zecchi—EC).

Exercises (Beethoven-Etüden) 1833 (Robert Münster—Henle 298 1976) 15pp. Seven studies based on the theme in a from Beethoven's Seventh Symphony (second movement). These pieces reveal a marked affinity to the *Symphonic Etudes* Op.13, a very close relationship existing between Op.13/6 and study No.3 of the *Exercises*. The character of the *Exercises* is more pianistic than that of variation techniques. Schumann adheres closely to Beethoven's theme. An excellent preface and critical notes in French, German, and English provide great detail. D.

Variations on the name Abegg Op.1 (Henle; CFP; EC).

Papillons Op.2 (Henle; EC).

Intermezzi Op.4 (Henle; EC).

Davidsbündlertänze Op.6 (Henle; CFP).

Toccata Op.7 (Henle; EC).

Carnaval Op.9 (Henle; EC).

Sonata f♯ Op.11 (EC).

Fantasiestücke Op.12 (Henle; VU; EC).

Etudes en forme de variations Op.13 (Henle; EC).
See: John L. Kollen, "Tema, Op.13, Robert Alexander Schumann (1810–1856)," in *Notations and Editions* (Dubuque, Wm. C. Brown; 1974, reprint, New York: Da Capo Press, 1977), pp.163–71.

Sonata f Op.14.
See: Linda Correll Roesner, "The Autographs of Schumann's Piano Sonata in F Minor, Op.14," *MQ*, 61 (January 1975):98–130.

Kinderszenen Op.15 (Henle; CFP; EC; VU; Heugel).
> See: MT, (February 1974):146 for a review of the VU edition and a comparison with the Clara Schumann edition.
> Robert Polansky, "The Rejected *Kinderszenen* of Robert Schumann's Opus 15, JAMS, 31 (Spring 1978):126–31.

Kreisleriana Op.16 (Henle; CFP; EC).

Arabesque Op.18 (Henle; VU, with Op.19; EC; CFP 9508).

Blumenstück Op.19 (Henle; VU; CFP 9508; EC).

Humoresque Op.20 (EC).

Noveletten Op.21 (Henle; EC).

Sonata g Op.22 (EC).
> See: Wadham Sutton, "Schumann: Piano Sonata in G Minor, Op.22," *Music Teacher*, 52 (April 1973):14–15.
> Linda Correll Roesner, "Schumann's Revisions in the First Movement of the Piano Sonata in G Minor, Op.22," *19th Century Music*, I (November 1977):97–109.

Nachtstücke Op.23 (Henle).

Faschingschwank aus Wien Op.26 (Henle; EC).

Three Romances Op.28 (Henle; EC).

Scherzo, Gigue, Romanze and Fughetta Op.32 (EC).

Waldszenen Op.82 (Henle; EC).

Bunte Blätter Op.99 (Henle).

Fantasiestücke Op.111 (Henle).

Album Blätter Op.124 (Henle; CFP 9505).

Seven Pieces in Fughetta Form Op.126 (CFP 7222).

EASIER COMPOSITIONS:

Album for the Young Op.68 (Banowetz—GWM). Contains 26 pieces plus the *Scenes from Childhood* Op.15.

Unpublished Pieces from Album for the Young Op.68 (J. Demus—Ric). Contains 17 pieces originally intended for Op.68. Some are surprisingly fine while others are not up to the standards of those included in the original collection. Require a good hand span. Easy to Int.
> See: Eric Sams, MT (June 1974):488.

COLLECTIONS:

The Easiest Original Pieces for the Piano (A. Rowley—Hin 7) 19pp. A Little Cradle Song Op.124/6; Album Leaf Op.99/4; Solitary Flowers Op.82/3; Waltz Op.124/4; A Country Dance Op.124/7; Fantastic Dance Op.124/5; Grief's Forebodings Op.124/2; Album Leaf Op.99/8; Gipsy Dance from Op.118; To a Flower from Op. 19; Fughetta Op.126/1; Canon from Op.118. Int. to M-D.

Schumann—An Introduction to his Piano Works (Palmer—Alfred

1976) 63pp. Selections from Opp.68, 124, 15, 82, 99, 118a. Excellent choice of repertoire. A most helpful preface includes a brief biography, comments about the music, identification of sources, and discussion of ornamentation, pedaling, and metronome markings. Int.

Schumann Easy Piano (Alfred). 18 pieces, mainly from *Album for the Young;* plus three from *Scenes from Childhood* and two from other works. Includes a short biography and a note about each work. Easy to Int.

Schumann—Favorite Piano (Alfred). 29 pieces, some of which duplicate selections in *Schumann Easy Piano.* Also includes four pieces from *Carnaval, Arabesque, Forest Scenes,* as well as pieces from *Album for the Young* and *Scenes from Childhood.* Biography and notes on each piece. Int. to M-D.

Piano Works—Selections (J. Antal—EMB 1974) Book I, 56pp. Book II (EMB 1976) 59pp. Contains works from Opp.21, 22, 26, 28, 82, 99, 111, 118, 124.

Young Pianist's Guide to Schumann (Y. Novik—Studio P/R 1978) 31pp. Includes 13 easy works from Opp.15, 68, 99, 124. Tastefully edited for the piano. Record of the contents included. Int.

The Solo Piano Music of Robert Schumann (C. Schumann—Dover) Vol.I: Opp.1, 2, 3, 6, 7, 8, 9, 10, 11, 12, 14, 15, 16, 18, 19. Vol. II: Opp.20, 21, 22, 23, 26, 68, 72, 82, 99, 118.

See: Wolfgang Boetticher, *Robert Schumanns Klavierwerke. Neue biographische und textkritische Untersuchungen. Teil I, Opus 1–6* (Quellenkataloge zur Musikgeschichte, Bd. 9) (Wilhelmshaven: Heinrichshofen, 1976), 208pp., 15 plates. Presents all data pertinent to the compositional history of the individual works, and also serves as a critical apparatus to Boetticher's edition of Schumann's piano music published by G. Henle Verlag (Urtext-Ausgabe, Neue Revision, 1974ff.).

GERARD SCHÜRMANN (1928–   ) Great Britain, born Indonesia
Bagatelles   1946 (Lengnick) 8 min.
Contrasts (Nov   1975) 28pp. 15 min. A colorful suite that displays both Liszt and Ravel pianistic influence. 1. Cumulonimbus: many sevenths, dramatic, driving rhythms, majestic opening. 2. Summer Rain: capricious, long melodic lines punctuated by scalar interjections, clever pedal effects. 3. Becalmed: expressive, slow-moving, chromatic; rises to furioso climax and then subsides. 4. Undersun: similar to opening movement in rhythmic treatment; chordal tremolos; dashing arpeggi figures; a ma flessibile mid-section leads to a toccatalike coda. Keyboard fully explored. D.
Leotaurus   1975 (Nov 12022110) 23pp. 15 min. Theme and ten varia-

tions. A prickly eight-bar introduction leads to a tranquillo dolcissimo cantabile theme that is freely tonal around b. Contrasted variations range from simple textures (No.5) to Allegro toccatalike (No.10) with a crashing conclusion. Neoclassic orientation. M-D.

EDUARD SCHÜTT (1856–1933) Austria, born Russia
Etude mignonne D Op.16/1 (GS). M-D.
Canzonetta D Op.28/2 (GS). Int.
Prelude A♭ Op.35/4 (GS). Int.
Carnaval mignonne (Simrock). M-D.
A la bien-animée. Valse Op.59/2 (GS).
Paraphrases on "Die Fledermaus" (Cranz). Schütt wrote paraphrases on many other Strauss waltzes as well as innumerable other salon pieces of good quality.

KURT SCHWAEN (1909–   ) Germany
Leichte Variationen für Klavier (Neue Musik 1972). Variations on a children's song. 23pp.

ELLIOTT SCHWARTZ (1936–   ) USA
Music for Prince Albert on his 150th Birthday (Bowdoin 1971) 13pp. Two pre-recorded tapes come with the score. D.
Mirrors 1973 (CF) 12pp. 7 min. For piano and two-channel tape. Tape is prepared by the pianist. Pointillistic; some improvisation required. Mallet used to strike different parts inside the piano; plucked and strummed strings; harmonics; fist clusters; drum-stick is to be thrust into piano lower register; keyboard cover is slammed; pianist must hum at conclusion. Aleatoric. Avant-garde notation is similar to *Music for Prince Albert.* D.

SALVATORE SCIARRINO (1947–   ) Italy
De la nuit; alla candida anima di Federico Chopin, da giovane (Ric 1971) 29pp. Scurries dissonantly all over the keyboard; very quiet; wanders; requires enormous control. D.
Esercizio (Ric 132305 1975) 5pp.
Prima sonata (Ric 1977) 65pp.

EDOUARD SCIORTINO (1893–   ) France
Hommage à Albeniz Op.7 (Philippo & Combre).
Ibère Berbère Op.8 (Philippo & Combre).
Diaphonies en opposition automatiques Op.11 (Philippo & Combre 1975) 8pp. Deux études.
Ludes Op.12 (Philippo & Combre 1975) 16pp.
Shamrock: ou trefle à quarter Op.13 (Philippo & Combre 1975) 7pp. Pièce breve pour piano.

CYRIL SCOTT (1879–1970) Great Britain
Egypt (Schott 1436 1913) 21pp. An album of five impressions. In

the Temple of Memphis. By the Waters of the Nile. Egyptian Boat
Song. Funeral March of the Great Ramses. Song of the Nile. Colorful, Impressionistic. Large span required. M-D.

For My Young Friends (Elkin). Ten separate attractive pieces. Int.

Indian Suite 1922 (Schott). The Snake Charmer. Juggernaut. Indian
Serenade. Dancing girls. M-D.

Lento and Allegro (GS   1907) 16pp. From two Pierrot Pieces. Int.

ALEXANDER SCRIABIN (1872–1915) Russia

Selected Piano Works (Günter Philipp—CFP). Vol.IV: Mazurkas Opp.
3, 25, 40 (21 mazurkas). Vol.V: Sonatas Nos.1–5. Vol.VI: Sonatas
Nos.6–10.

The Complete Preludes and Etudes (Dover   1973). Reprint of Moscow
1966, 1967 editions. Opp.8, 11, 33, 42, 48, 65, 74, and the Preludes and Etudes from Opp.2, 9, 13, 15, 16, 17, 22, 27, 31, 35, 37,
49, 51, 56, 59, 67. 108 pieces in all. Editorial marks in English.
Presents a complete spectrum of Scriabin's work.

33 Selected Piano Pieces (CFP). Preludes, Poems, Mazurkas, and other
pieces from Opp.9 (for left hand), 11, 13, 16, 25, 27, 31, 33, 37,
40, 44, 45, 46, 47, 48, 51, 56.

Selected Works (Murray Baylor—Alfred   1974). Contains 30 pieces
including: 6 etudes; 11 preludes; 2 Poems Op.32/1, 2; Mazurka Op.
40/1; 4th Sonata Op.30; Quasi valse Op.47; Album Leaf Op.45/1;
Winged Poem Op.51/3; Languorous Dance Op.51/4; Ironies Op.
56/2; Nuances Op.56/3; Desire Op.57; Strangeness Op.63/2; Gar-
lands Op.73/1. Includes discussions of the music and the playing of
Scriabin, and photographs. Contains some of the technically easiest
pieces. An excellent introductory anthology. Int. to M-D.

SEPARATE WORKS (listed numerically by opus numbers):

Twelve Studies Op.8 (G. Philipp—CFP). Preface in German, French, and
English. Glittering virtuosity required in most of these pieces. M-D
to D.

Two Pieces for the Left Hand Op.9.
See: Samuel Randlett, "Scriabin's Prelude for the Left Hand,"
Clavier, 17 (April 1978):23–29.

Twenty-four Preludes Op.11 (G. Philipp—CFP). Nos.2 and 4 available
separately (APS).

Ten Preludes Opp.15, 74 (K9492).

Seven Preludes Op.17 (Belaieff). M-D.

Concert Allegro Op.18 b♭ (USSR). A showy concert piece. M-D.

Sonata Fantasy Op.19/2 (K9502).

Four Preludes Op.22 (Beliaeff).

Sonata No.3 Op.23 (G. Philipp—CFP).

Two Preludes Op.27 (Belaieff).
Fantasia Op.28 (Belaieff; K9491).
Two Poems Opp.32, 61 (K9490).
Four Preludes Op.33 (Belaieff).
Three Preludes Op.35 (Belaieff).
Four Preludes Op.37 (Belaieff).
Four Preludes Op.39 (Belaieff).
Two Mazurkas Op.40 (Belaieff; CFP).
Poem Op.41 (Belaieff).
Two Poems Op.44 (Belaieff).
Three Pieces Op.45 (Belaieff; K9503).
Three Pieces Op.49 (Belaieff). Full chords; large span required. M-D.
Sonata No.5 Op.53 (G. Philipp—CFP).
Deux morceaux Op.57 (Belaieff).
Sonata No.6 Op.62 (Bo&H).
Two Preludes Op.67 (Rahter).
Two Poems Op.71 (Rahter).
Poem vers la flamme Op.72 (G. Philipp—CFP).
Two Dances Op.73 (Rahter).

COLLECTIONS:

Etudes (K 3941). Includes Op.2/1; Op.8/1–12; Op.49/1; Op.56/4; Op.65/1, 2.
Selected Piano Pieces (GS 8089). Set 2.
See: Hilda Somer, "Scriabin's Complete Preludes and Etudes," PQ, 94 (Summer 1976):46–47.

RUTH CRAWFORD SEEGER (1901–1953) USA
Seeger was one of America's finest women composers.
Etude in Mixed Accents 1930 (NME) 14pp. Somewhat similar in style and difficulty to the Bartók *Etude* Op.18/3. M-D to D.
Four Preludes 1927–8 (NME) 4pp. Shows equal influence of Scriabin and Schönberg. Meritorious in craft and style. There are five other preludes in MS at the Library of Congress. M-D.
See: Maurice Hinson, "Remember Ruth Crawford," *Clavier*, 15 (December 1976):29. Also includes *Prelude* VI, pp.26–28.

LEIF SEGERSTAM (1944–   ) Finland
Three Meditations 1965 (Busch   1973) 7pp.
Three Sketches 1964 (Busch   1973) 7pp.

RÜDIGER SEITZ (1927–   ) Austria
Aperçus 12 transparent Stücke. Epigramme (Dob   1974) 15pp. Lucid, fresh style in Hindemith idiom. M-D.
Epigramme (Dob   1974) 11pp. Ten pieces. Similar to the *Aperçus*. M-D.
9 Bagatellen (Dob   1971) 15pp.

Sonatine 1955 (Dob) 7pp. Alla marcia; Scherzo; Espressivo; Rondo: especially attractive. Four short playable movements influenced by Hindemith, some counterpoint. Int. to M-D.

JULES SEMLER-COLLERY (1902–   ) France
Prélude (ESC   1971) 4pp.

JOSÉ SEREBRIER (1938–   ) USA, born Uruguay
Sonata 1957 (PIC). Allegro molto vivace: animated, meter changes, percussive. Andante: tender, expressive, large dynamic range. Moto perpetuo: driving Presto with much two-part texture. Effective tonal writing in three contrasting movements. M-D.

TIBOR SERLY (1900–   ) USA, born Hungary
Sonata in Modus Lascivus 1973 (PIC) 26pp. 15 min. Three movements, MC, many accidentals. Modus Lascivus is a system of composition Serly has developed over a period of years. D.

KAZIMIERZ SEROCKI (1922–   ) Poland
Krasnoludki (The Gnomes)   1953 (PWM). Seven miniatures in a freely tonal style. Int.

JUAN DE SESSÉ Y BALAGUER (1736–1801) Spain
Seis fugas (Almonte Howell—UME 22159   1976) 40pp. For keyboard instruments. Preface in Spanish and English. Sonorities varied through freely voiced changes of register and texture. Capricious and good-humored writing. M-D.

ROGER SESSIONS (1896–   ) USA
Five Pieces 1974–5 (Merion   1976) 23pp. Atonal, contrasting (slow, fiery, light, agitated, very slow), require thorough pianism and mature musicianship. Written in memory of Luigi Dallapiccola. D.

KILZA SETTI (1932–   ) Brazil
Setti is a member of the music faculty of the Conservatorio Musical Brooklin Paulista. She is also on the Santa Marcelina Music Faculty.
8 Variações Sobre um tema popular "Onde Vais, Helena" (Ric BR 1972) 19pp. 15 min. Eight variations in individualistic style, strongly contrasted. Fondness for chromaticism noted. M-D.
Valsa (Ric BR   1970) 9pp. 5 min. Calmo: chromatic; thin textures; builds to climax in mid-section; ends *ppp*. M-D.

DÉODAT DE SÉVÉRAC (1873–1921) France
Peppermint—Get (Sal   1907). A valse brillante de concert, salon style, full of Gallic charm although not very brilliant. Three contrasting sections. Int. to M-D.

STEPHEN K. SHAO (–   ) China
Chinese Folk Songs for the Young Pianist (EBM   1973) 32pp. 14 folk songs skillfully arranged by retaining an Eastern flavor of melodic

development with simple harmonic accompaniment, striking rhythms. Int.

RALPH SHAPEY (1921–   ) USA

Mutations No. 2 1966 (MS available from composer, c/o Music Department, University of Chicago, 5835 S. University Ave., Chicago, IL 60637). 1. Of majestic passion—of designs, movements and forces—of majestic passion—of peace and quiet, of majestic passion—of singing tenderness, of majestic passion—of passion and fury, of majestic breadth—of majestic passion, of majestic breadth. 2. With furious wildness, intensity, brilliance and sound—of majestic passion—of majestic breadth. D.

ARNOLD SHAW (1909–   ) USA

A Whirl of Waltzes (TP   1974). Seven MC waltzes with attractive titles, e.g., The Waltzing Walrus, Waltz for a Piano Teacher, A Waltz in Space. Int.

Mobiles (Tp   1966). Ten graphic impressions. Short, imaginative, written in a jazz style. Int. to M-D.

Plabiles (TP   1971) 23pp. Twelve Songs without Words composed to help develop phrasing and a singing line. Pieces are linked, with each new selection taking off from the terminal notes of the preceding piece. Int.

Stabiles (TP   1968). Twelve Images.

The Mod Moppet (TP   1974) 16pp. Seven Nursery Rip-Offs. For the playful and young-in-heart. Seven familiar tunes with different titles. Clever, sophisticated. Int.

RODION SHCHEDRIN (1932–   ) USSR

Piano Works (USSR MK 1700423   1976). 3 vols. Book II, 127pp.: Pocm   1954; Four pieces from the *Humpbacked Horse* ballet 1955; Humoresque   1957; À la Albeniz   1959; Troika   1959; Two Polyphonic Pieces 1961; Sonata   1962; The Polyphonic Book 1972. M-D to D.

Humoresque (Chant du Monde   1971) 4pp.

6 Piano Pieces (CFP).

Polyphonic Notebook (Sikorski) 58pp. 25 polyphonic preludes for piano. M-D.

Sonata   1962 (GS). Three movements of strong dissonant writing. The second movement is a set of contrapuntal variations. D.

Sonata   1975 (USSR) 32pp.

MINAO SHIBATA (1916–   ) Japan

Improvisation for Piano No.2 (Ongaku No Tomo Sha   1968). One large sheet folded into 8pp. Performance directions in English. Aleatoric; note values only approximations; clusters; avant-garde. M-D.

SEYMOUR SHIFRIN (1926–   ) USA, born Austria

Responses 1973 (MS available from composer, c/o Music Department, Brandeis University, Waltham, MA 01830).

MAKOTO SHINOHARA (1931–   ) Japan

Tendance 1962–69 (Moeck).

MUTSUO SHISHIDO (1929–   ) Japan

Toccata 1966 (Ongaku No Tomo Sha) 16pp. 4½ min. A moderato introduction leads to Vif, with alternating hands, strong accents, rapid figuration, full-chord tremolo, and extreme registers exploited. Moderato idea returns briefly, then alternating hands are used until a short chordal coda concludes. Freely tonal around a. M-D.

DMITRI SHOSTAKOVITCH (1906–1975) USSR

3 Fantastic Dances Op.1 (Bo&H; EBM; Sikorski). Int.

Aphorisms Op.13 (MCA; GS). Highly experimental, adventurous harmonies. M-D.

Sonata No.1 Op.12 (Sikorski; USSR) 14 min.

Sonata No.2 Op.64 (USSR).

24 Preludes Op. 34 (Sandor—GS; BMC). Nos.14 and 24 available together (MCA).

24 Preludes and Fugues Op.87 (Sikorski). (J. Musafia—MCA) has a revised edition in one volume. M-D.
> Available separately: Op.87/5 (CFP 7214); Op.87/11 (CFP 7221). See: Dean Elder, "Lesson on Performance of a Shostakovitch Prelude and Fugue (No.17 of Op.87)," *Clavier,* 13 (September 1974): 25–33.

5 Preludes (Sikorski).

A Childhood Notebook (Ric). Six easy pieces.

Easy Pieces for Piano (Prostakoff—GS 1972). Excerpts from films, ballets, and operettas, transcribed in simplified versions. Also includes two pieces for piano duet. Easy.

Dmitri Shostakovitch, Igor Stravinsky, Alexander Scriabin: Their Greatest Piano Works (Copa 1973). See under "Collections."

Selected Preludes (EBM). Op.34/13, 16, 17, 24. Published together as a set. M-D.

Piano Compositions (CFP 5717). Three Fantastic Dances Op.1; Aphorisms Op.13; Five Preludes, without opus number. Int. to M-D.

Shostakovitch Album I (K). 3 Fantastic Dances; 4 Preludes Op.34/13, 16, 17, 24; 24 Preludes and Fugues Op.87/1–5, 6–9; Sonata No.I.

JAN SIBELIUS (1865–1957) Finland

Five Christmas Songs Op.1 (Fazer).

Six Impromptus Op.5 (Br&H).

Sonata F Op.12 (Br&H). Allegro molto; Andantino; Vivacissimo. D.

Romance Op.24/4 (Br&H). Published with *Valse* Op.24/5 (British & Continental 1972).

Ten Pieces Op.34. Published separately (Fazer): 1. Waltz, 5. Drollery, 7. Danse pastorale, 8. The Harper, 9. Reconnaissance, 10. Souvenir. Int. to M-D.

Pensées Lyriques Op.40 (Fazer). 1. Valsette; 2. Chant sans paroles; 3. Humoresque; 4. Minuetto; 5. Berceuse; 8. Scherzando; 9. Petite sérenade; 10. Polonaise. Int. to M-D.

Kyllikki Op.41 (Br&H). Three lyric pieces based on *Kalevala* legends: Largamente; Andantino; Commodo. M-D.
See: Glenn Gould, "Sibelius and the Post-Romantic Piano Style," PQ, 99 (Fall 1977):22–24. Includes the Andantino Op.41/2 and a discussion of this work and other piano works of Sibelius.

Three Sonatinas Op.67 f♯, E, b♭ (Fazer).
See: Cedric T. Davie, "Sibelius's Piano Sonatinas," *Tempo,* 10 (March 1945).

Five Pieces Op.75. Published separately (Fazer). Pleasant if not strikingly individual. Int. to M-D.

13 Pieces Op.76. Published separately (Fazer): 2. Etude; 5. Consolation; 6. Romanzetta; 8. Pièce enfantine. Int. to M-D.

Six Pieces Op.94. Published separately (Fazer): 1. Danse; 2. Nouvellette; 3. Sonnette. Int. to M-D.

Six Bagatelles Op.97. Published separately (Fazer): 1. Humoreske; 2. Lied; 3. Little Waltz. Int.

Eight Short Pieces Op.99. Published separately (Fazer): 1. Pièce humoristique; 2. Esquisse; 3. Souvenir; 4. Impromptu; 5. Couplet; 6. Animoso; 7. Moment de Valse; 8. Petite marche. Int.

Esquisses Op.114 (Fazer 1973). Five pieces available separately. Landscape. Winter Scene. Forest Lake. Song in the Forest. Spring Vision. M-D.
See: Eric Blom, "The Piano Music," in *Sibelius, A Symposium,* ed. G. Abraham (New York: Norton, 1947; reprint, New York: Da Capo Press, 1975), pp.97–107.
Alec Rowley, "The Pianoforte Works of Jan Sibelius," *Musical Mirror,* May 1929:121.

THORKELL SIGURBJÖRNSSON (1938–) Iceland
Sigurbjörnsson studied at the Reykjavik School of Music. He took further studies at the University of Illinois, with Kenneth Gaburo and Lejaren Hiller, and at Darmstadt. He has been active as a teacher, pianist, conductor, and music critic and for a time was president of the Musica Nova in Reykjavik.

Eight Songs from Apaspil (Iceland Music Information Centre). A Happy Monkey; The Animal Trainer; In the School; The Animal Trainer

Comes; The Monkey Begs to Be Set Free I; The Law Books; The Monkey Begs to Be Set Free II; A Happy Ending. Folklike, treated in a MC style. Int.

Der Wohltemperierte Pianist (Iceland Music Information Centre).

So (Iceland Music Information Centre).

TOMASZ SIKORSKI (1939–   ) Poland

Sonant (PWM). The elementary levels of attack and decay (action and consequence) are repeated until they become confused in the listener's mind. M-D.

Two Preludes (PWM). Short, contrasting character. M-D.

View from the Window in a Distracted Mood (AA   1973).

Zerstreutes Hinausschauen (Moeck   1971) 4pp. 4½ to 11 min. Aleatoric.

JEAN CLAUDE SILLAMY (1932–   ) France

Musique contemporaine sur des modes bibliques (Dactylo-Sorbonne 1971). Reproduced from MS. Biographical note in French. Contains: Promenade dans le parc; Le réveil de la mer; Chant de peuple exterminé; Le chant des hirondelles; Gloire aux morts d'Auschwitz. M-D.

ADELAIDE PEREIRA DA SILVA (1938–   ) Brazil

Da Silva is lecturer in composition at the Ecola Superior de Música Santa Marcelina, in literature and structure of music at the Faculdade de Música Marcelo Tupinamba, both in São Paulo, and in composition at the Faculdade Santa Cecília in Pindamonhangaba (SP). She studied with Osvaldo Lacerda and Camargo Guarnieri.

Ponteio 1   1962 (Ric BR   1966) 1½ min.

Ponteio 2   1962 (Ric BR   1965) 1½ min.

Valsa choro 1   1962 (Ric BR) 1½ min.

Valsa choro 2   1963 (Ric BR) 1½ min.

Ponteio 4   1963 (Ric BR) 2 min.

Suite I   1965 (Ric BR   1966) 6 min. Arrasta-pé. Modinha. Polka. Valsa. Cataretê.

Ponteio 5   1965 (Ric BR) 1½ min.

Ponteio 3   1966 (Ric BR) 2 min.

Suite II   1966 (Vitale). Dobrado. Ciranda. Chorinho. Baião.

Cantiga ingênua   1970 (Vitale) 1 min.

Suite Caleidoscópio   1973 (Fermata) 5 min. De rosa e azul. Vitraes. Um punhado de cores.

CONSTANTIN SILVESTRI (1913–1969) Rumania

Selection of Piano Works (Editura Muzicala a Uniunii Compozitorilor 1973) 89pp. Contents: Suite I Op.3/1; Suite II Op.3/2; Sonatina Op.3/3; Suite III Op.6/1; Rumanian Folk Dances from Transylvania Op.4/1. Preface in Rumanian only.

JEAN-MARIE SIMONIS (1931–   ) Belgium
Historiettes Op.24   1972 (CeBeDeM) 40pp. 14 min.
Evocations Op.29 (CeBeDeM   1975) 19pp. 6 min.
2 Pastourelles (Zephyr 1973) 5pp.
Notturno Op.33   1977 (CeBeDeM) 16pp.

NETTY SIMONS (1913–   ) USA
Night Sounds (TP). Evening Haze. Thinking of Past Things. Stars on the
Pond. The Rain Beats on the Rain. Short, atonal pieces that are
evocative and contain sensitive harmonic, dynamic, and rhythmic
colorations as well as dissonant counterpoint. M-D.

LARRY SITSKY (1934–   ) Australia, born China
Sitsky describes his style as "expressionistic (i.e., dealing with extreme
emotional states), and influenced by the music of Bartók, Berg, and
Bloch and by the esthetics of Busoni, on whom he has done extensive
research" (DCM, 684).
Bagatelles for Petra (Ric). 17 contemporary pieces for young pianists to
introduce them to contemporary signs and sounds. Elbow clusters,
boxed ostinato figures, free notation, and continuous pedal are some
of the devices encountered. Int. to M-D.
Fantasia in Memory of Egon Petri   1962 (Ric). Sitsky studied with Petri
from 1959 to 1961.
Little Suite   1958 (Allans 1062) 6pp. Improvisation (Jazz Waltz).
Folk Song. Nocturne. Two-Part Invention on a Name. Elegy. Clever,
clusterlike chords, attractive. Int.
Sonatina Formalis   1960 (Allans 9038) 5pp. Melody with Accompaniment. Canon at the Tritone. Preludio. Fuga (on the name Egon
Petri). MC, effective fugue. Int. to M-D.

EMIL SJÖGREN (1853–1918) Sweden
Sjögren's purity of style, warmth of feeling, and refinement of his in-
strumental works entitle him to a place of distinction.
Erotikon Op.10 (NMS). 1. Allegro agitato. 2. Allegretto. 3. Vivacissimo
(Au bord d'une source). 4. Andantino. 5. Andante tranquillo: noc-
turne. Int. to M-D.
Stemninger Op.20 (WH 20471). Eight pieces.
Sonata Op.35 e (WH 13266) 15 min.
3 Klavierstücke Op.41 (WH).
Thema med variationer Op.48 (WH 14371).
Svenska Kungssanger: Syv variationer Op.64 (WH 16284).
Valse Caprice (WH 18838).
Klaverstykker (Per Winge—WH15897). Includes: Erotikon Op.10/4;
Morgonvandring Op.15/1; Stämnigar Op.20/3,4.

HOWARD SKEMPTON (1947–   ) Great Britain
Piano Pieces   1967–73 (Faber   1974) 12pp. Short repetitive sound
patterns in a contemporary style. Easy.

LUCIJAN MARIJA SKERJANC (1900–1973) Yugoslavia
Six Pieces for One Hand Alone (Slovenska Akademija   1952).

DANE SKERL (1931–   ) Yugoslavia
Sest klavirskih skladb (Društvo Slovenskih Skladateljev   1971)   21pp.
   Six piano compositions.

KLEMENT SLAVICKÝ (1910–   ) Czechoslovakia
Edudy a eseje   1965 (Panton) 49pp.

WLADYSLAS SLOWINSKI (1930–   ) Poland
Miniatury   1967 (PWM) 15pp.
Sonatina (AA   1973) 24pp.

LUBOS SLUKA (1928–   ) Czechoslovakia
Sonata   1970 (Rev. Petr Messiereur—Panton).

ROGER SMALLEY (1943–   ) Great Britain
Missa Parodia I   1967 (Faber)   16 min.
Monody   1972 (Faber) 10pp. 12 min. For piano and electronic modulation (1 player). Includes notes for performer. Like a fantasy,
   some unusual harmonic effects created by a ring modulator. Grave,
   fiercely embellished, strong character. In 21 short sections, uses
   four different types of material, strong rhythmic patterns. Some percussion: 4 triangles, 2 congas, 2 large bongos or timbales. D.

BEDŘICH SMETANA (1842–1884) Czechoslovakia
Smetana treated the Czech national dance form the way Chopin treated
the mazurka. All of Smetana's polkas are an important and too much
neglected part of the nationalistic piano repertoire.
Album Leaf No.2 B♭ (Faber). Op.5/7 and Op.5/22 (GS).
Six Bohemian Dances (K 3980; CFP 4435).
Bohemian Dance No.2 "The Little Pullet" (CFP 4435A).
10 Polkas (CFP 4455).
Selected Pieces (CFP 4642).
Selected Piano Works (D. Baloghová—Panton   1974) 68pp.

LEO SMIT (1921–   ) USA
For Matushka (CF) 3 min.
Martha through the Looking Glass 1974 (CF). 5 min. Three pieces.
Two Alchemy Pieces   1975 (CF) 3½ min.

HALE SMITH (1925–   ) USA
Faces of Jazz   1968 (EBM) 16pp. Twelve short pieces, each titled;
   clever and effective. Int.
See: Malcolm Joseph Breda, "Hale Smith: A Biographical and Analytical
   Study of the Man and His Music," diss., University of Southern
   Mississippi, 1975, 240pp.

JOHN CHRISTOPHER SMITH (1712–1795) Great Britain

Suite I C (Farrenc—Leduc) 7pp. Prélude; Allegro; Allemande; Allegro; Air; Gigue. In Handelian style. M-D. There are eight other suites by Smith (G. F. Handel's treasurer) in *Le Trésor des Pianistes*.

See: Gwilym Beechey, "The Keyboard Suites of John Christopher Smith (1712–1795)," *Revue Belge Musicologie*, 24 (1970):52–80. The four collections of six suites for harpsichord (1732–57) by J. C. Smith (Johann Christoph Schmidt) are similar to Handel's. The fifth collection (1765) contains twelve sonatas and shows the influence of the *style galant*.

JULIA SMITH (1911–) USA

Characteristic Suite (TP 1967) 16pp. 10 min. Canon; Waltz; Passacaglia (with 5 variations and coda); March; Toccata. MC. M-D.

Prelude (TP).

Sonatine C (TP).

LELAND SMITH (1925–) USA

Intermezzo and Capriccio (ACA).

Six Bagatelles 1965 (San Andreas Press) 6pp. Graphic realization by POP 10 computer. Strong voice-leading, contrapuntal textures, freely tonal, short, expert craft displayed. Expressionistic, careful and unusual notation used for pedal indications. M-D.

MICHAEL SMOLANOFF (–) USA

Smolanoff teaches in the School of Music at Rutgers University.

Children's Suite Op.44 1972 (Seesaw) 4pp. Five very short pieces: A Song; Canon; Dialogue; Dance; Prayer. Stringent harmonies, involved phrasing. Not for children, or perhaps for very precocious ones. Int. to M-D.

Preludes (Belwin-Mills 20565).

Piano Sonata I Op.59 (Li Debco 1977) 12pp. 12 min. In one movement with several sections. Opening section is free and unbarred and uses harmonics and fast repeated notes. "Moderately" is tempo marking of two other sections. Pointillistic, expressionistic. Large span required. D.

Variations for Piano (Seesaw).

PAUL GUTAMA SOEGIJO (1934–) Indonesia

Klavierstudie I (Bo&Bo 1968) 14pp.

NARESH SOHAL (1939–) Great Britain, born India

Sohal studied science and mathematics at Punjab University. He came to England in 1962, as his interests lay in composing Western music. He has worked with Alexander Goehr.

Mirage 1974 (Nov) 12 min.

SUZANNE SOHET-BOULNOIS (–) France

Petite Suite espagnole (Lemoine) 10pp. Six easy, attractive pieces. Int.

Musique pour Bibiche (Lemoine. Ten progressive pieces in one volume. Easy to Int.

Pour les enfants sages (Lemoine). Twelve easy pieces.

Trois petites histoires (Lemoine). 1. De pompiers. 2. En forme de legende. 3. Pour s'endormir. Int.

JOSÉ SANCHEZ SOLA (1930–   ) Spain

Ternura (UME   1970) 4pp. Tendresse.

JOSEP SOLER (1935–   ) Spain

Soler studied composition with Cristofor Taltabull in Barcelona.

Tres Peçes per a piano (PIC   1970) 5pp. Lentisimo: frequent tempo and dynamic changes. Tranquilo: terse. Rápido: extremes in register exploited. Expressionistic, complex writing. D.

PADRE ANTONIO SOLER (1729–1783) Spain

Soler wrote many sonatas in a one-movement design similar to those of Domenico Scarlatti. Later in his career he wrote sonatas in three and four movements. Frederick Marvin, in a letter to the author, stated that, "My belief is that he [Soler] was not a pupil [of Domenico Scarlatti]. He admired Scarlatti greatly (quoting him in his book *Key to Modulation* but does not in this book refer to him as his teacher). He does however mention his other teachers. His contact with Scarlatti would have been limited to a few weeks a year when the Royal family visited Escorial."

Fandango M.1a (Frederick Marvin—A. Broude; UME).

Sonatas, Complete edition (S. Rubio—UME) 120 sonatas in 7 vols. Vol.7: Sonatas 100–120.

Sonatas Vols.I–VI (F. Marvin—A. Broude). M=Marvin Catalogue number. Vol.I: Sonata c M.1; Sonata c M.2; Sonata g M.3; Sonata c M.4; Sonata C M.5; Sonata e M.6; Sonata f M.7; Sonata d M.8; Sonata 9 M.9. Vol.II: Sonata C M.10; Sonata c M.11; Sonata c M.12; Sonata B♭ M.13; Sonata E♭ M.14; Sonata D♭ M.15; Sonata b M.16; Sonata e M.17; Sonata F♯ M.18; Sonata f♯ M.19; Sonata g M.20; Sonata g M.21. Vol.III: Sonata g M.22; Sonata c M.23; Sonata c M.24; Sonata B♭ M.25; Sonata B♭ M.26; Sonata F M.27; Sonata a M.28; Sonata F M.29; Sonata D M.30; Sonata a M.31; Sonata G M.32; Sonata f♯ M.33; Sonata D M.34. Vol.IV: Sonata G M.35; Rondo e M.36; Sonata F♯ M.37; Sonata g M.38; Sonata F M.39; Sonata f M.40; Sonata A M.41. Vol.V: Sonata B♭ M.42 (four movements). Vol.VI: Sonata F M.43; Sonata c M.44. Vol.VII: Sonata C M.45 (four movements). Vol.VIII: Sonata (Rondo) G M.46; Sonata D♭ M.47.

Sonaten für Tasteninstrum (Kastner—Schott 4637).

See: Richard S. Hill, *Notes,* 16 (December 1958):155–57 for a review that compared all editions available at that time.

Frederick Marvin, "On the Trail of Padre Antonio Soler," PQ, 80 (Winter   1972–73):17–19.

Reah Sadowsky, "Antonio Soler: Creator of Spain's Fifth Century of Musical Genius," AMT, 28 (September–October 1978):10, 12, 14–15. Contains an excellent discussion of the sonatas and the *Fandango*.

OISTEIN SOMMERFELDT (1919–   )Norway

3 Sma Valser Op.17 (NMO 1971) 7pp. Three small, freely tonal waltzes. Int.

Sonatina IV Op.20 (NMO 1970) 15pp. Largo–Allegretto; Adagio; Presto. Clear, linear, and attractive writing. M-D.

Sonatina V Op.31 (NMO 1972) 11pp. Allegretto grazioso; Adagio cantabile; Presto scherzando. Colorful, unusual harmonic progressions, thin textures in outer movements. M-D.

3 Lyric Pieces Op.32 (NMO 1972) 5pp. Lyric Fragment. Miniature Waltz. Little Folk Tune Elegy. Int.

Norske religiose folketoner Op.35 (NMO 8904 1976) 15pp. Eleven pieces. Preface and commentary in Norwegian.

Short Seasonal Suite Op.49 (NMO). Four contrasting movements, each representing a season. Int. to M-D.

RAYMOND SONGAYLLO (–   ) USA

Ten Short Piano Pieces (OUP 93 814 1975) 8 min. For the third year of study. Clever, well thought out, good introduction to contemporary techniques. Int.

JÓZSEF SOPRONI (1930–   ) Hungary

Incrustations 1973 (EMB) 12pp. Freely dissonant and chromatic, pointillistic, proportional rhythmic relationships, much use of rubato, improvisational. Large span required. D.

Invenzioni sul B-A-C-H 1971 (EMB) 18pp. Six short pieces. Pointillistic, fast repeated notes, highly organized, clusters, strong dissonance. D.

Ot (EMB). (5) kis negykezes zongoradarab.

Note Pages (EMB) Book I 1974, 25pp. Explanations in Hungarian and English. Book II 1975, 20pp. Explanations in Hungarian and English.

KAIKHOSRU SHAPURJI SORABJI (1892–   ) Great Britain

In 1977 Sorabji lifted the ban on the performance of his works. In 1977 he completed his Sixth Symphony (*Sinfonia Magna*) for piano solo but it is not yet published. He has also recently finished *Sinfonia Notturno* (also unpublished) for Yonty Solomon (the pianist allowed to perform Sorabji's works), which is supposed to be of epic dimensions!

Three Piano Sonatas (OUP). The Third Sonata lasts about 1½ hours. It is totally athematic and defies analysis! D.

Pastiche on the Minute Waltz of Chopin (Music Treasure Publishers 1969). 5 min. D.

Le Jardin Parfumé (OUP) 15–20 min. A tropical nocturne, exotic and richly creative. D.

Fantaisie Espagnole (OUP). Brilliant, virtuoso piece on the grand scale. D.

Two Piano Pieces (OUP). In the Hothouse; Toccata (OUP). Debussy and Scriabin influences. A fine introduction to Sorabji's work. D.

Prelude, Interlude, and Fugue 1920 (OUP) 20 min. D.

Valse Fantaisie—Homage to Johann Strauss (OUP). 15 min. D.

Gulistan 1940 (OUP). Inspired by a thirteenth-century literary source. Oriental melodic and rhythmic complexities vie with its luxuriant occidental harmony. Shimmering colors and pianistic writing owe much to Ravel and Szymanowski. Rich chromatic harmony interwoven polyphonically and polyrhythmically with flowing arabesques. D.

St. Bertrand de Comminges: "He was laughing in the tower" 1941 (OUP). Based on a ghost story by M. R. James. Events in the piece "describe" the developing story. Stream-of-consciousness style reminds one of the Ives piano sonatas. Violent changes of mood, wild and virtuoso pianism required. D.

See: Paul Rapoport, "Sorabji Returns?" MT, 1606 (December 1976): 995. Sorabji allowed the pianist Yonty Solomon to play three of his works in London in December 1976.

CLAUDETTE SOREL (1934–   ) USA

Fifteen Smorgasbord Piano Solos (EBM 1974). Music plus recipes! Pieces are MC and introduce varied rhythmic and melodic ideas. The Hungarian recipes sound delicious. Int.

ENRIQUE SORO (1884–1954) Chile

The Spinner. Etude (GS) in collection *51 Pieces from the Modern Repertoire.* M-D.

JOÃO SOUZA LIMA (1898–   ) Brazil

Souza Lima studied piano with Isidor Philipp, Marguerite Long, and Egon Petri. He is considered one of the outstanding personalities in piano teaching in Brazil.

Canção infantil 1918 (Vitale 1970) 3 min.

Valsa amorosa 1927 (A. Napoleão 1973) 4 min.

Brincando de jazz 1930 (Ric BR) 4 min.

Toccatina 1940 (Ric BR) 2 min.

Primeira valsa brasileira 1942 (Ric BR) 5 min.

Improvisação I 1950 (Ric BR) 6 min.

Prelúdios, 1.ª série 1954 (Vitale) 25pp. 14 min. Five preludes. Colorful post-Romantic writing. No.2 Humoristicamente is especially attractive. M-D.

Brincando 1957 (Vitale) 1 min.

Rolando na areia 1957 (Vitale) 1 min.

Improvisação II 1959 (Ric BR) 6 min.
Peças infantis 1959 (Vitale) 10 min.
Suite infantil 1966 (Vitale) 12 min.
Peças românticas 1968–73 (Vitale) 44 min. Eight pieces.
Segunda valsa brasileira 1969 (Vitale) 5 min.
Danza 1970 (Vitale) 3 min.
Prelúdios, 2.ª série 1972 (Vitale) 12 min.
Valsa chorosa 1973 (A. Napoleão) 5 min.

LEO SOWERBY (1895–1968) USA
Burnt Rock—Pool (BMC).
Fisherman's Tune (Hinshaw 1975) 5pp. A sophisticated rag. M-D.
The Irish Washerwoman (BMC 1920). Varied harmonizations and treatment of the tune, a fine concert set. M-D.
The Lonely Fiddle-Maker (BMC).
The Two Lovers (BMC).

AURELIA SPAGNOLO (–) Italy
12 Studietti (EC 1973) 32pp.

CLAUDIO SPIES (1925–) USA, born Chile
Spies teaches at Princeton University.
Bagatelle (Bo&H 1970) 4pp. Twelve-tone. Extensive directions for all three pedals. Fluid meters, pointillistic, quiet and cantabile. Carefully realized dynamics will reveal imbedded rows. Large span required. D.
Impromptu (EV 1963) 2pp. Twelve-tone, changing meters, dynamic range *p–ppp*, sophisticated writing. M-D.
Three Intermezzi 1950–54 (EV) 11pp. I. Quarter note=66: varied textures, inner lines, freely tonal. II. Non troppo adagio: delicate cantando lines, three staffs used to notate ⅔ of piece. III. Allegretto capriccioso: octotonic, repeated chords, secco style, big conclusion. M-D.
See: Paul Lansky, "The Music of Claudio Spies—An Introduction," *Tempo,* 103 (1972):38–44.

LOUIS SPOHR (1784–1859) Germany
Sonata A♭ Op.125 1843 (Ric) L'Arte antica e moderna, scelta di composizioni per pianoforte, 21 vols., Vol.IV, pp.180ff. Allegro moderato: chromatic suspensions, harmonic flow in triple meter, well organized, some surprising harmony, unpianistic—written more in quartet style. Romanze: cloying chromaticism. Scherzo: most successful movement. Finale: refined writing but melodic ideas are weak; hints at Weber in the figuration; well-designed form. M-D.

ALOJZ SREBOTNJAK (1931–) Yugoslavia
Macedonian Dances (GS 1975) 20pp. Five elaborate transcriptions of

Macedonian folk tunes à la Bartók. Interesting rhythms and sonorities, modal, repeated notes. M-D.

FERDINAND STAES (1748–1809) Belgium
Three Sonatinas F, C, D, (Metropolis EM4720) 16pp. Similar in style and length to the Kuhlau *Sonatinas* Op.55. Int. Published with a *Sonatine* G by P. J. van den Bosch (1736–1803).

ALPHONSE STALLAERT (1920–   ) The Netherlands
John Blot Variations (Editions Françaises de Musique) 15pp. Photostat of MS.

PATRIC STANDFORD (1939–   ) Great Britain
Variations Op.23   1969 (Nov) 8pp. Reproduction of MS, not easy to read. Style is based on the nineteenth century. Well-etched theme is always present (in different guises) in the varied variations. No meter indications, some double octaves. M-D.

ROBERT STARER (1924–   ) USA, born Austria
Evanescents   1975 (MCA) 19pp. An extensive, unfolding piece, like a fantasy. Expressionistic, contrasting sections and character, difficult to hold together. Requires large span. D.
   See: David Burge, "New Pieces, Part II," CK, 4 (January 1978):50.
Fantasie (Noetzel).
Sketches in Color (MCA) Book II. Seven pieces, more advanced technically and musically than the first book. Int. to M-D.
12 Pieces for 10 Fingers (S. Fox).

FJÖLNIR STEFÁNSSON (1930–   ) Iceland
Stefánsson studied at the Reykjavík School of Music and with Matyás Seiber in England from 1954 to 1958. He is the headmaster of the Music School of Kópavogur.
Five Sketches   1958 (Iceland Music Information Centre). Twelve-tone, short, contrasted, moves over keyboard. M-D.

WOLFGANG STEFFEN (1923–   ) Germany
Les Spirales Op.36 (Bo&Bo).

WALTER STEFFENS (1934–   ) Germany
Sonata Op.21 (Bo&Bo).
Pluie de Feu Op.22 (PIC   1970). One folded leaf. Based on a fire-graphic by B. Aubertin. "Touch durations are schematically fixed; note entries are freely interpretable. Definitely fixed notes within the fire centre should be regarded as central tones" (from the score). Avant-garde. M-D.

JACQUES STEHMAN (1912–1975) Belgium
Burlesque en six formes   1973 (Zephyr) 7pp. Six delightfully contrasted pieces. M-D.

Le tombeau de Ravel   1949 (CeBeDeM) 36pp. 24 min. A suite.
Promenade   1975 (CeBeDeM) 8pp.

GREG A. STEINKE (1942–   ) USA
Steinke received his training at Oberlin Conservatory, Michigan State University, and the University of Iowa. He is a member of the music faculty at California State University, Northridge.
Six Pieces   1964 (Seesaw   1972) 20pp. Lento interotto. Andante con moto e linea. Quieto e tranquillo. Allegro martellato. Adagio con frase larga. Allegro. Flexible meters, atonal, four staves required for some notation, harmonics, dynamic extremes, clusters. Contains some very subtle and compelling sonorities, an effective set. D.

WILHELM STENHAMMAR (1871–1927) Sweden
Tre Fantasien Op.11   1895 (NMS   1971). M-D.
Nights of Late Summer Op.33   1914 (WH). Five Romantic piano pieces that depict late-summer Scandinavian evenings. D.

JOSEPH ANTON ŠTĚPÁN (Steffan) (1726–1797) Bohemia
Capricci (A. Weinmann—Henle 227). Five pieces. Rhapsodic fantasy style. Based on earliest sources. M-D.

JOHANN FRANZ XAVER STERKEL (1750–1817) Germany
Ausgewählte stücke für Klavier (Walter Frickert—Hug 1971) 16pp. M; Arioso; Vivace; P; Adagio–Allegro; Marsch.

BERNARD STEVENS (1916–   ) Great Britain
Theme and Variations Op.2   1942 (Bo&H) 11 min.
Five Inventions Op.14 (Lengnick   1950) 13pp. Contrasting, freely tonal, thin textures except for No.4 (Adagio), neoclassic. M-D.
Ballad Op.17 (Lengnick   1953) 13pp. 12 min. Laid out in a post-Brahms pianism with MC harmonies. Arrives at a dramatic climax before concluding *pp* in G♭. M-D to D.
Fantasia on "Giles Farnaby's Dreame" Op.22 (Lengnick   1953) 14pp. 13 min. Variation treatment, quasi cadenza, fugal conclusion, Romantic harmonies. M-D.
Sonata in One Movement Op.25   1954 (Lengnick) 13 min.

HALSEY STEVENS (1908–   ) USA
Intrada 1949–54 (ACA) 3½ min. An adagio 4/8 meter using dotted rhythms begins quietly in the lower register of the piano, works to climax with dramatic arpeggi gestures in upper register, subsides briefly and returns to climactic treatment before returning to a calm conclusion in lower register of piano. This would make an excellent opening recital number. M-D.
Preludes (First Series)   1952 (ACA). Written for Lillian Steuber. 1. Poco lento: legato; inner voices require careful balance; works to a suonando climax assisted by sostenuto pedal; mid-section uses

left hand to provide a contemporary Alberti bass for the right hand; cantando melody; effective chordal ending. 2. Andante con moto, quasi menuetto: long, semi-contrapuntal lines between the hands treated in a highly expressive manner is the basis for this 80-bar piece. 3. Allegro, in modo burlando: a driving, well-accented 5/8 rhythm opens this Prelude; at bar 20 a cantando espressivo melody takes over; these two elements treated in various guises make up the piece; brilliant coda in octaves and a dashing arpeggio conclude the work. M-D.

Preludes (Second Series) 1952–56 (ACA). 4. Moderato: legato octaves interspersed with well-articulated broken chromatic chordal figures work to a *ff* climax at bar 54; music quickly subsides and concludes with the broken chordal figure in the lower register. 5. Andante con moto: accompanied melody in left hand is reversed at bar 18; mainly a very sustained work; accompaniment rocks back and forth between small and large intervals. 6. Andante quasi allegretto: broken fourths in left hand accompany an expressive right-hand melody; figuration becomes more chromatic and dramatic, is extended over a broad area of the keyboard, and leads to a dashing close. All M-D.

Nepdalszvit, Zongorára 1950 (ACA) Eight Magyar Folk Songs. Based on melodies collected by Bartók and Péczely. Short, original, and fresh sounding. Could be played as a complete group or a selection could be made from them. Mode for each piece is listed. Int. to M-D.

Piano Music Vol.I 1948–49 (ACA). Toccata: shifting meters, chromatic textured melodic writing, tonal orientation. M-D. Inventions 1, 2, 3: two-voiced; display attractive contrapuntal chromatic writing; notes not difficult but solid pianism and sensitive interpretative equipment are required. Int. to M-D. Improvisation: Andante, giusto e con moto: very lyric and expressive; builds to *ff* climax; concludes *pp* in lower register. M-D. Scherzo: Quasi presto tagliente: a bouncing light diatonic figure evolves into punctuated octaves; both ideas cleverly treated in this lively short setting. M-D.

Four Improvisations on Javanese Themes 1951 (ACA) 4pp. 4 min. "Closely akin to the children's songs are the dongèng-songs; they are very ancient ditties, usually containing only a few tones, and intoned every now and then during dongèng (i.e., the telling of fairy-tales) . . . . According to Radèn Kodrat (this song) No.1 (which occurs in a story that strongly reminds one of 'Hop o' me thumb'), is neither sléndro nor pelóg—although perhaps tending toward the latter . . ." (from the score). 1. Poco andante: based on four notes only—b, c♯, d, f♯; melody in octaves in mid-section. 2. Allegro: pentatonic; lacks fourth and seventh; has much rhythmic vitality, melody in left hand in mid-section. 3. Andante: pentatonic; charming setting with melody treated between hands as well as given to right hand; unique harmonizations. 4. Quasi parlando: based on five notes—e, f, g, b, c; melody treated octotonically and in octaves over low pedal open fifths; recitative-like. Colorful treatment of all four pieces. Strong oriental flavor. Would make a highly effective and unusual recital group. Int. to M-D.

Ah! Mon Beau Château 1959 (MS available from composer: 9631 Second Avenue, Inglewood, CA 90305) 1p. Attractive setting of a French popular tune in a lively tempo. Melody moves between hands. Int.

Moto Perpetuo 1961 (MS available from composer) 1p. Continuous 16th-note motion (broken thirds interspersed with chromatic elements) throughout mainly in right hand. Left hand punctuates with open fourths, fifths, sevenths, and single notes. The main body of the work (up to the coda) may be repeated more than once. *Pp* closing on a partial cluster. M-D.

Notturno "Bellagio Adagio" 1971 (Hinshaw) in collection *Twelve by Eleven.* 2pp. 3 min. ABA, expressive and chromatic, short motives, transfer of line between hands, a beautiful work. Notes not difficult but piece requires mature musicianship. M-D.

3 Ukrainian Folk Songs 1960 (ACA) 2 min. All three are short and modal. Nos.1 and 2 are slow and linear with melody in left hand some of the time. Control of inner voices in No.2 is important. No.3 is quick and rhythmic and uses harmonic seconds, thirds, fourths, and fifths; alternating hands with left-hand octaves. Int.

Fantasia 1961 (Helios) 4 min. Grows from opening motif e, f, d. Varied figuration; treatment held together by subtle permeation of motif; spread over keyboard. Fine octave technique required. M-D.

Study in Irregular Rhythms (Helios) 2 min. Flexible meters, hands work close together, octotonic. Requires strict time. M-D.

Sonatina I (ACA) 6 min.

Sonatina II (Helios 1975) 7 min. Allegro moderato; Canon; Rondo. Int. for notes, M-D for interpretive problems.

Sonatina III 1950 (ACA) 9 min. Allegretto semplice: thin textures thicken during second tonal area; some contrapuntal writing; centers around E. Lento, parlando (Elegy) in memory of Bartók: molto espressivo writing, chromatic coloration, poignant treatment. M-D.

Sonatina V (ACA) 7 min.

Sonatina VI (ACA) 7 min.

Music for Ann 1954 (Helios) 5½ min. Modal elements combined with traditional harmonic functions. Int. to M-D.

Ritratti per pianoforte 1959–60 (Helios).

4 Bagatelles 1960 (Helios) 8pp. 5 min. MC, short, contrasting. M-D.

See: Maurice Hinson, "The Piano Music of Halsey Stevens," PQ, 96 (Winter 1976–77):32–34.

RONALD STEVENSON (1928–   ) Scotland

Peter Grimes Fantasy (Bo&H   1972) 12pp. 6½ min. On themes from
Benjamin Britten's opera. This powerful operatic transcription follows in miniature form the design of the opera. Full sonorities,
bravura octaves, and arpeggi passages; some Impressionistic effects;
eclectic style. Free recitativo middle section, more strict outer sections. Effective calm ending. Requires virtuoso technique. D.

FRANK GRAHAM STEWART (1920–   ) USA

Stewart is a graduate of the Eastman School of Music and Michigan State
University.

Suite for Piano based on American Indian Songs   1949 (Seesaw) 8 min.
Mojave-Apache Medicine Song. Hopi Lullaby. Cheyenne and
Arapaho. He-Hea Katzina Song (Hopi Rain Dance). Colorful, con-
trasting. Int. to M-D.

WILLIAM GRANT STILL (1895–1978) USA

Marionette (MCA) in collection *U.S.A. 1946*. 1 min. Int.

Quit dat fool'nish (Belwin-Mills   1938) 3pp. 2 min. Rapid 16th-note
figuration accomplished by staccato chords, alternating hands. M-D.

KARLHEINZ STOCKHAUSEN (1928–   ) Germany

From the Seven Days (UE 14790).

Spiral (UE 14957).

Zodiac (UE). Twelve movements named after the signs of the Zodiac.
The upper register of the piano is exploited. In Virgo the right and
left hands outline two clear tonal centers. D.

See: David Burge, "Contemporary Piano—Karlheinz Stockhausen," CK,
4 (May 1978):58. Includes a discussion of *Klavierstück X*.

William C. Pflugradt, "Continuity and Discontinuity in the Piano Music of
Karlheinz Stockhausen," Master's thesis, Indiana University, 1972,
92pp.

Jonathan Harvey, *The Music of Stockhausen* (Berkeley: University of
California Press, 1976), 143pp. The analysis of Stockhausen's piano
pieces and his work with electronic composition will be of the most
interest to pianists.

SIMON STOCKHAUSEN (1967–   ) Germany

Musik für Junge 1974–76 (Stockhausen Verlag). Twelve charming and
imaginative pieces for piano and/or melody instrument written by
Karlheinz Stockhausen's son when he was 7 or 8 years old. Int.

WOLFGANG STOCKMEIER (1931–   ) Germany

2 Sonatinen   1954 (Möseler   1974) 9pp.

Suite II (Möseler   1970) 9pp.

RICHARD STOKER (1938–   ) Great Britain

Stoker studied with Lennox Berkeley at the Royal Academy and with

Nadia Boulanger in Paris. Since 1962 he has been professor of composition
at the Royal Academy of Music in London.

A Poet's Notebook 1969 (MCA). Six pieces. Neoclassic style, no key
signatures, bitonally flavored. Int.

The Fairground (Ashdown). Six easy pieces.

Fireworks 1970 (Ashdown). Six little pieces. Triads with superimposed
fourths, bitonal implications. Int.

From an Artist's Sketchbook (Hin). Six pieces.

The Little Giraffe (Ashdown). Twelve easy pieces.

Piano Sonata I Op.26 1966 (CFP   1973) 11pp. 12 min. Ritmico: *pp*
to explosive *fffs*, much impetuosity, big gestures. Reposo: varied
meters, broader mid-section with widely spaced chords, octave passages. M-D.

Zodiac Variations 1963 (Ashdown) 10 min. Twelve pieces. Theme and
11 simple transformations, all of which retain the thematic melodic
shape. Some rhythmic, register, touch, mood, and meter changes. A
fine suite for student recitals. Int. to M-D.

See: "Richard Stoker Talks to Christopher Norris," M&M, 23 (February
1975):16, 18, 20, 22.

IAKOV EFIMOVICH STOLLIAR (1890–1962) USSR

Isbrannye fortepiannye proizvedeniia (Sovetskii Kompozitor   1972) 23
pp. Selected piano works including: Sonata Op.2, edited by I. Nei-
mark; Two Poems Op.5. Title in Russian only.

ALAN STOUT (1932–   ) USA

Stout is a member of the music faculty at Northwestern University.

Music for Good Friday Op.24   1955–58 (ACA). Five movements. Abstruse, complex writing. Some sections are spread over four staves. D.

Communio Op.30b (ACA).

Partita Op.27 (ACA).

For Prepared Piano Op.23 (ACA).

Variations for Piano Op.41 (ACA).

Invention Op.41a (ACA).

Sonata Op.45/1 (ACA).

Sonata Op.45/2 (ACA).

Fantasy Op.62/2 (ACA).

Elegy Op.75/4 (ACA).

Toccata Op.76 (ACA).

Varianti (ACA).

JOEP STRAESSER (1934–   ) The Netherlands

Straesser teaches theory at Utrecht Conservatory.

Intersections III   1971 (Donemus) 6pp. "Hommage à Bach; if it were
a fantasia and fugue." Facsimile of the composer's MS. Two dis-

similar movements. I: chromatic groupings evolve into clusters. II: performer may vary interpretation. Avant-garde. M-D.

See: Daan Manneke, "About Joep Straesser's Intersections III for Piano," *Sonorum Speculum,* 53 (1973):24–36.

Five Close-ups 1960–1, rev. 1973 (Donemus) 4 min. Based on a twelve-tone row by Pierre Boulez.

ULRICH STRANZ (1946–   ) Germany
Anabasis 1971 (Orlando) 13pp. Photostat. Musik unserer Zeit—Junge Komponisten.

HERMAN STRATEGIER (1912–   ) The Netherlands
6 Etuden 1974 (Donemus) 15pp. 20 min. Photostat.
Drie Speelmuziekjes 1974 (Donemus).
Suite 1937 (Donemus   1973). For piano or harpsichord.

JOSEPH STRAUSS (1827–1870) Austria
Brother of Johann Strauss.
Selected Dances for the Piano (BB   1971, reprint of 1901 edition). Six volumes in two. Int. to M-D.

RICHARD STRAUSS (1864–1949) Germany
Enoch Arden Op.38 (Forberg) 63 min. Recitation with piano. With German and English words. Based on Tennyson's "Enoch Arden." Could be performed by solo piano. M-D.

IGOR STRAVINSKY (1882–1971) USA, born Russia
Four Etudes Op.7 (Bo&H) in collection *The Short Piano Pieces.* No.4 F♯ (EBM). Effective and strong post-Romantic studies in poly-rhythms. M-D.

Scherzo   1902 (Faber) 7pp. One of Stravinsky's earliest surviving com-positions, along with *Sonata* f♯. Helpful preface by Eric White. A kind of a salon piece; coda is most interesting part. M-D.

Sonata f♯ 1903–4 (Faber) 42pp. Allegro: melody in dotted rhythms with accompanying left-hand octaves. Scherzo: quiet and fast, clever syncopation. Andante: Romantic, in D, leads to Allegro: F♯, op-posing D and F♯ sonorities. The entire work is something of a mix-ture of Beethoven, Liszt, Brahms, and Rachmaninoff. Displays a fine grasp of idiomatic piano writing. An excellent example of late Russian Romanticism and a document of emerging creativity. D.

Valse pour les enfants   1917. Published in *Le Figaro* in 1922. Contained in Eric Walter White's book *Stravinsky* and in *The Short Piano Pieces,* listed below.

Ragtime   1919 (JWC). Originally written for instrumental ensemble. Transcribed for piano by Stravinsky. M-D.

Les cinq doigts   1921 (K).

Trois mouvements de Petrouchka   1921 (Bo&H).

See: Charles Leonard Fugo, "A Comparison of Stravinsky's *Trois mouvements de Petrouchka* with the Original Orchestral Version," diss., Indiana University, 1973, 98pp.

Tango   1940 (Mercury).

Circus Polka   1942 (AMP).

The Short Piano Pieces (Soulima Stravinsky—Bo&H   1977) 55pp. Includes: Piano Rag Music   1919; Tango   1940; The Five Fingers   1920–21; Valse and Polka   1915; Valse pour les enfants   1917; Four Etudes Op.7   1908. Foreword by the editor includes background information on the works. This edition differs in some minor respects from other printed versions in performance suggestions since the editor had personal advice from his father regarding some of the works. Easy to M-D.

See: Susan Hull Foster, "The Solo Piano Works of Igor Stravinsky," Master's thesis, Indiana University, 1972, 117pp.

Charles M. Joseph, "Igor Stravinsky—The Composer and the Piano," AMT, 25 (April–May 1976):16–17, 21.

Joan Purswell, "Stravinsky's Piano Music," *Clavier,* 18 (January 1979): 24–31, 51. Also includes Valse pour les enfantes and Les cinq doigts.

AUREL STROE (1932–   ) Rumania

Sonate   1972 (Sal) 28pp. Moderato: changing meters, chromatic, quartal and quintal harmonies, main subject identified, serial-like. Andante: quintal harmony emphasized; chromatic arpeggi-like figuration; cadenza with trills; glissando; opening section returns; large span required. Fuga—Allegro energico: changing meters; marcato handling of subject; one statement of subject in octaves accompanied by clusterlike chords; same compositional techniques as in first movement utilized; tranquillo closing without rallentando. M-D.

FOLKE STRÖMHOLM (1941–   ) Norway

Etude Fantastique   1964 (NMO   1971) 6pp. Molto presto: alternating hands with harmonic seconds, full chords, glissandi, strong driving rhythms, freely tonal. M-D.

10 Sma Pianostykker for Barn og Ungdom Op.17 (NMO 8674   1970) 11pp. Varied short pieces, contemporary techniques. Duggdräper has left hand on all black keys, right hand on white keys. Not easy. Int.

Sonatina Op.25 (NMO   1977) 14pp. Two movements, harmonics, delightful melodic and rhythmic material used. M-D.

Water = Vann: A Phenomenological Study for Piano (NMO 1977) 4pp. Explanations in English.

GEORGE TEMPLETON STRONG (1856–1948) USA

Ballade II Op.34 (Jost & Sander   1888) 11pp.

JOACHIM STUTSCHEWSKY (1891–   ) Israel, born Russia
Quatre Inattendues 1967 (IMI 329) 11pp. Allegro; Allegro ritmico; Andante con espressione; Maestoso. Neoclassic, freely tonal, well varied. Large span required. M-D.
Drei Stücke (IMI 183).
Hassidic Dance (IMI 624).
Kleine Marsch (IMI 184).
Rikkud (IMI 182).
Skizzen aus Israel (IMI 179).
Vier jüdische Tänze (IMI 181).
Zwölf Bagatellen (IMI 180).

MORTON SUBOTNICK (1933–   ) USA
Prelude No.3 for Piano and Electronic Sounds 1964 (MCA). 2 scores, 7pp. each. Aleatoric in part, many clusters, avant-garde. D.

DIA SUCCARI (–   ) Syria
Suite Syrienne 1976 (Jobert) 28pp. Nida; Samah; Dabké. Colorful and intriguing music based on Syrian tunes, complex rhythms, recurring motif. Dabké ends with a brilliant and driving climax. May be played individually or as a suite. D.

ROBERT SUDERBURG (1936–   ) USA
Suderburg is Chancellor of the North Carolina School of the Arts in Winston-Salem.
Six Moments for Piano 1966 (TP) 3pp. Six brief sketches. Atonal, pointillistic, contrasts in mood and tempo, flexible rhythmic flow. D.

REZSÖ SUGÁR (1919–   ) Hungary
Hungarian Children's Songs (Bo&H). 25 short pieces. Various moods and keys with melodic and rhythmic interest, varied harmonizations. Contains sources from which the folk material is taken. Handsomely illustrated, expertly written. Int.

PETER SUITNER (1928–   ) Germany
Toccata Op.34 (Löffler 1972) 6pp.
Drei Klavierstücke Op.35 (Löffler 1972) 6pp.
Variations Op.37 (Löffler 1973) 9pp.
Stücke Op.45 (Löffler 1973) 6pp.

TOSHIYA SUKEGAWA (1930–   ) Japan
Two Pieces from "Little Poems of Four Seasons" (Zen-On 315 1970) 3pp. Short, thin textures, MC, oriental flavor. Int.
Sonatina (Zen-On 213 1975) 17pp. Poems in Blue. Three contrasting movements, contemporary writing, serial influence. M-D.

ARTHUR SULLIVAN (1842–1900) Great Britain
Sullivan Piano Music (Chappell 1976) 55pp. Ten short pieces. Edited

with an introduction and notes by John Parry and Peter Joslin. Contains: Thoughts I and II; Day Dreams 1–4; Allegro risoluto; Twilight. Shows both Mendelssohn and Schumann influences; charming if shallow. Contains an introduction and a few photographs. Int. to M-D.

FERNANDO SULPIZI (1936–   ) Italy
Epigrammati Op.10 (Edicioni Casimiri).
Album per Daniela Op.15 (Berben). Eleven easy pieces.
Album secondo per Daniela 1975 (Berben) 9pp. Seven contemporary pieces. The last two (one for each hand) are unmetered and contrapuntal. Notes are easy but interpretive problems abound. Int. to M-D.
Epigrammata Alia Op.21 (Berben) 12pp. Five sonority studies. 1. Webernesque. 2. Continuous motion, pointillistic. 3. Three layers of contrasting textures. 4. Heavy chordal outer sections, toccatalike midsection with alternating hands. 5. Study in trills, frequently punctuated with punched chords. D.

ROBERT SUTER (1919–   ) Switzerland
Suite I 1943 (Heinrichshofen) 12pp.
Suite II 1945 (Heinrichshofen) 13pp.

RUDOLF SUTHOFF-GROSS (1930–   ) Germany
Drei Miniaturen (Möseler 1972) 9pp.

SVEINBJÖRN SVEINBÖRNSSON (1847–1927) Iceland
Idylle (Islandia Edition 1924) 4pp. Romantic character piece in the style of Grieg. M-D.
Vikivaki Dance (Islandia Edition 1924) 4pp. Marchlike; nineteenth-century harmonies. M-D.

LUCILE BURNHOPE SWENSON (–   ) USA
Preludes and Nocturnes (TP 1973) 28pp. Five preludes and two nocturnes written in a generally Romantic style. Fine pedal studies. Int.

RICHARD SWIFT (1927–   ) USA
Summer Notes. Printed in PNM, 15 (Spring–Summer 1977):97–114.
See: Thomas Stauffer, "Richard Swift's *Summer Notes,*" PNM, 15 (Spring–Summer 1977):115–21. A thorough analysis and discussion of the work.

GEORGIJ WASSILJEWITSCH SWIRIDOW (1915–   ) USSR
Works for Piano (USSR 1970) 115pp. Preface and titles in Russian. Partita f 1947; Partita e 1947; Sonata 1944; Children's Album 1948.

HENRY SYMONDS (ca.1650–   ) Great Britain
Six Sets of Lessons for the Harpsichord (Heuwekemeijer 1970) 53pp. First published in London in 1734.

WITOLD SZALONEK (1927–   ) Poland

Szalonek teaches in the Department of Composition at the State College of Music in Katowice. He is also secretary of the Katowice Circle of the Union of Polish Composers.

Mutanza   1968 (JWC) 9pp. 18 min. For prepared piano. Precise explanation of diagrammatic notation. Strings to be struck with nonmusical objects (4 steel rods, 30 steel balls, 20 sticks of plasticene, etc.). Score is reproduction of MS. Sound is only that made by dropping, brushing, rolling objects inside the piano. Avant-garde. D.

ENDRE SZÉKELY (1912–   ) Hungary

Sonata III   1971 (EMB   1976) 16pp. 10 min. Explanations in Hungarian and English.

ERZSEBET SZÖNYI (1924–   ) Hungary

Musical Tales, The Stubborn Princess (EMB).

MARIA SZYMANOWSKA (1789–1831) Poland

Five Dances (PWM   1975). Contredanse: has a march, *Jean of Paris,* in the mid-section. Anglaises in B♭, E♭, A♭. Quadrille: lively, attractive, simple. All are tuneful and are about the scope of Schubert's waltzes. The collection contains a delightful portrait of the young composer. Int.

KAROL SZYMANOWSKI (1882–1937) Poland

Study b♭ Op.4/3 (PWM) separately. Szymanowski's most popular piano work. Int. to M-D.

Métopes Op.29 (PWM). Late Scriabin influence noted. D.

Masques Op.34 (PWM).

Twenty Mazurkas Op.50 (UE 15972). Varied in style and tonality. Dedicated to Arthur Rubinstein. M-D. to D.

Two Mazurkas Op.62   1935 (ESC).

Romantic Waltz (PWM 89). Recently found. Int. to M-D.

Piano Works I (PWM) from the *Works of Karol Szymanowski,* Vol.XIV. Sonata c Op.8; Sonata A Op.21; Sonata III Op.36. Edited and with preface by W. Kedra. D.

Piano Works II (PWM) from the *Works of Karol Szymanowski,* Vol.XV. Métopes Op.29; Masques Op.34.

Some Polish Songs (PWM). Nine Polish folk and popular songs arranged for piano (lyrics written in). Commentary and notes by M. Tomaszewski.

T

MICHEL TABACHNIK (1942–   ) Switzerland
Frise   1969 (Nov) 25 min. Triglyphes 1-A, 2-A, 1-B, 2-B, 1-C, 2-C, and Métope are to be played in various orders suggested by the composer, who says, "The title of this work (and its construction) is based upon architectural terminology." Written in a similar vein to that of the Boulez *Third Piano Sonata*. Sometimes spread out over four staves. Contrast lacking. Avant-garde. D.
Eclipses (Ric 1974) 33pp. 3 pédales obligatoires. Performance instructions in Italian, French, and German.

RICARDO TACUCHIAN (1939–   ) Brazil
Tacuchian studied composition with José Siquera, Francisco Mignone, and Claudio Santoro. He teaches at the Music Department of the Federal University of Rio de Janeiro. In 1971 he co-founded the Conjunto Ars Contemporânea, an ensemble that specializes in twentieth-century music.
Primeira Sonata   1966 (SDM) 18 min.
Segunda Sonata   1966 (SDM) 13 min.

HUNG-HSUEN TAI (1942–   ) China
Tai teaches music theory at the National Academy of Arts in Taipei, Taiwan.
Well-Tempered Piano Album I   1971 Op.6 (Yo-Fu Music Publishers Co., Taipei, Taiwan) 31pp. Two preludes and fugues. "The rhythm and dynamics of these pieces should be played mechanically and with perfect accuracy. With this, the composer wants to show the materialistic view of music" (from the score). Thin textures alternate with thicker ones. Bitonal, clusterlike chords, MC. M-D.

YOSHIHISA TAIRA (1938–   ) Japan
Sonomorphie I   1971 (Rideau Rogue) 29pp. One movement divided into two contrasting parts. Résonances: static; slow; builds to a massive climax distributed over the entire keyboard. Elans: a fast and violent rondo that finally subsides into immobility. A well-developed large work with material that is not distinctive. D.

JENÖ TAKÁCS (1902–   ) Hungary
Sonatina   1923 (Dob). Lively first movement in f♯ with a strong melody. Second movement a short nocturne, Lento dolente. Finale is a rondo

with a series of shifting fifths for the left hand and a folklike melody in the right hand. M-D.

Twilight Music Op.92 (Dob   1973) 8pp. 9½ min.

Sounds and Colours Op.95 (Dob   1977) 20pp. Notes in German and English.

When the Frog Wandering Goes (Dob   1970). Six pieces with clever titles. MC and not easy. Int. to M-D.

YUJI TAKAHASHI (1938–   ) Japan

Three Poems of Mao-tse Tung (Zen-On 404   1976) 6pp. Tapoti. Ode to the Plum Tree. Reply to Corirade Kuo Mo-Jo. English translation of poems included. Barless; arpeggiated chords; ideas inspired by poems. M-D.

SABURO TAKATA (1913–   ) Japan

Preludes 1947 (Ongaku No Tomo Sha   1964) 22pp. 16 min. Colorful titles, e.g., By the Dark-blue Marsh; The Sunlight Dances in the Wind; The Wild Pigeon; Down in the Blue Valley; Mountains Fading into the Twilight. The composer hopes "that one does not become overly conscious of these titles as they merely function as a sort of key to the music" (from the score). Freely tonal; fondness for seconds, fourths, and fifths; Impressionistic. M-D.

TORU TAKEMITSU (1930–   ) Japan

Takemitsu has perhaps emerged as Japan's leading avant-garde composer. His music reminds this writer of a Buddhist rock garden. It has floating, static, and sonorous qualities that suggest Morton Feldman's music.

Pause Ininterrompue ("Uninterrupted Rest")   1952–60 (Sal). Three short atonal pieces: Slowly, sadly and as if to converse with; Quietly and with a cruel reverberation; A song of love. To be played as a group. Dynamics attached to almost every note. Great contrast of sounds from brutal to genial. Fascinating sonorities. D.

Piano Distance   1961 (Sal). Many interpretative problems and strong dissonances but extraordinarily beautiful. Precise dynamic and pedal indications. A note in the score suggests this piece "could be interpreted as expressing the various and multiple tones of the piano."

For Away   1973 (Sal). The composer talks about "inner, personal" qualities, about "nature," about not being afraid of the past, about the unknown, about East and West, about new freedoms. Maybe that is what this piece is all about. Musically it makes great use of all three pedals. The dynamic range leans more to the quieter side. Pointillistic delicate treatment, serene, great metric freedom. Many passages have a dynamic mark for each note. D.

See: David Burge, "Oriental Composers," CK, 4 (December 1978).

KOJI TAKU (1904–   ) Japan

Three Pieces (Ongaku No Tomo Sha 1968) 20pp. Eventail Rouge: pentatonic. Rondo: moves over keyboard, freely tonal, large chords. Rustic Five: in 5/8, varied ideas, strongly rhythmic. M-D.

LOUISE TALMA (1906–   ) USA
Six Etudes (GS 1954). Ravel and Stravinsky influences. D.
Pastoral Prelude 1952 (CF) Quiet three pages, ABA, conjunct motion and wide leaps, pentatonic mid-section. Would make a good combination with this composer's *Alleluia*. M-D.
Sonata No.2 1944–55 (CF 1977) 17pp. 16 min. Neoclassical with serial elements. D.

TŌRU TAMURA (1938–   ) Japan
Fudoki 1969 (Zen-On). 23pp. plus 1 loose leaf. Preface and explanations in Japanese. German translation by Kurt Opiolka. Contains: Sato-Kagura; Komori-Uta; Saimon; Dengaku-Mai; Warabe-Uta. M-D.

HIDEKO TANIFUJI (–   ) Japan
Piano Album Vol.I. (Ongaku No Tomo Sha). Most pieces are chromatic and show a preference for use of the half step, both melodically and harmonically. *Sonatine* 1954: Moderato grazioso; Andantino soave; Rondo agevole. *Three Piano Pieces to Wild Plants* I 1953: Cosmos; Wild Camomile; Spring Horsetail. 2pp. each. M-D. *Three Piano Pieces to Wild Plants* II 1956: Rape Flowers; Giant Knotweed; Water Lilies. D. *Ten Preludes Based on Issa's 17-Syllable Poems:* most are Impressionistic. M-D. *Thema and Variations To Children Bereaved of their Fathers and Mothers* 1953: theme and ten variations. D.

ALEXANDRE TANSMAN (1897–   ) Poland
Three Ballades (AMP).
Hommage à Arthur Rubinstein (ESC 1973) 9pp. 7 min.
10 Diversions for the Young Pianist (AMP).
Etude (ESC).
Je joue pour Maman (ESC). Twelve easy pieces available separately.
Je joue pour Papa (ESC). Twelve easy pieces available separately.
15 Moderately Easy Pieces for the Young Pianist (Barth—ESC). Available separately.
2 Pièces hébraiques 1956 (ESC).
4 Polish Dances 1931 (ESC).
Preludes (ESC). 2 vols.
Rhapsody hébraique 1938 (ESC).
Sonata No.4 1941 (ESC).
Suite dans le style ancien (ESC).
Tempo Americano from "Symphonie Concertante" (ESC).
Le Tour du Monde en Miniature (ESC).

PHYLLIS TATE (1911–   ) Great Britain

Explorations Around: A Troubadour Song for Piano Solo   1976 (OUP)
47pp. 20 min. The theme is "Chevalier, mult este guariz" (1147).
Intrada; Antiphon; Impromptu; Canzonetta; Epitome. Variation
treatment. In the first and last movements the pianist must place a
small drum between his knees. Photographed MS is not easy to
read. M-D.

CARL TAUSIG (1841–1871) Germany, born Poland

Zwei Konzertetüden Op.1 (H. M. C. Linden—Eulenburg 1975) 20pp.
Published separately during Tausig's lifetime under the titles *Im-
promptu* and *das Geisterschiff*. The former contains many repeated
notes, while the latter is built on arpeggi and is rhythmically flexible.
Both breathe more Chopin influence than Liszt and are eminently
worthy of performance. M-D to D.
Available separately: *Das Geisterschiff* (Musica Obscura).
Ballade (Musica Obscura).
Reminiscences de Halka—Moniuszko Op.2 (Musica Obscura). A glitter-
ing virtuoso work. D.

COLIN TAYLOR (1880–1973) Great Britain

3 Fables   1939 (Bo&H   1973) 9pp. Easy to Int.
Whimsies (Bo&H   1973) 2 sets. 14pp. Four miniatures in each set.
Inventive and captivating writing although fairly traditional. Int.

RAYNOR TAYLOR (1747–1825) USA, born Great Britain

Taylor arrived from England in 1792 and was active along the East
Coast. He was one of the most important eighteenth-century American
musicians.

Rondo   1794 (Willis) in *A Collection of Early American Keyboard Music*.
Many characteristics of light, eighteenth-century opera can be found
in this piece. The graceful rondo theme employs imitation, a technique rarely used in American works of this period. M-D.
Variations to Adeste Fidelis (Hinson, McClenny—Hinshaw   1978). A
simple, naive, and charming setting of the familiar tune with two
variations and a Largo andante coda. Int.

ANDRÉ TCHAIKOWSKY (1935–   ) Great Britain

Inventions Op.2   1961–2 (Nov   1975) 36pp. 20 min. Ten pieces.
Dedicated to fellow concert pianists Peter Feuchtwanger, Fou Ts'ong,
Stefan Ashkenazy, Tomás Vasary, Ilona Kabos, and others. Varied
styles and moods. Astringent harmonies, atonal. Large span required. M-D to D.

PETER ILICH TCHAIKOWSKY (1840–1893) Russia

Aveu Passioné (GS 794). A transcription by the composer of the love
theme from his symphonic ballad *The Voyevode*, Op.79. M-D.

Album for the Young Op.39 (Y. Novik—Alfred). Carefully edited. Based on the first edition. Contains information about the composer and the music. Int.

Nocturne Op.19/4 (Anson—Willis). Interesting inner voices, surging melodies. M-D.

Dumka Op.59 (Forberg).

Il mio primo Ciaikovski (Pozzoli—Ric 2599) 14pp. Pieces from *Album for the Young,* Op.39: Morning Prayer; The Sighing Doll; The New Doll; The Mother; Soldier's March; Mazurka; Waltz; Song of the Lark; Popular Russian Dance. Int.

Selected Piano Works, Vol.3 (GS 819); Vol.5 (GS 820).

Children's Album (GS 8030).

ALEXANDRE TCHEREPNIN (1899–1977) USA, born Russia

"A fecund and expert composer internationally successful in classical forms and also theatrically. Initially inspired by the Russian Romantic masters, he developed in France from medieval sources an original approach to modality and rhythm, later in East Asia was influenced by classical Chinese music. His work has at all periods been filled with poetry and bravura" (Virgil Thomson, *American Music since 1910* [New York: Holt, Rinehart and Winston, 1971], p.177).

Toccata No.1 Op.1   1921 (Belaieff) 6 min. M-D to D.

Nocturne g♯ Op.2/1   1919 (Belaieff) 5 min. M-D.

Dance Op.2/2   1919 (Belaieff) 4 min. Interlocking hand technique. M-D to D.

Scherzo Op.3   1917 (Durand   1927) 3 min. Chordal, double notes. M-D to D.

Sonatine Romantique Op.4   1918 (Durand) 11 min. Uses a nine-step scale, in cyclic form. Main theme is similar to Russian chant for the dead. M-D to D.

Bagatelles Op.5 1913 18 (Heugel; GS; MCA; TP; IMC) 12 min.
   See: Guy Wuellner, "A. Tcherepnin's Bagatelles, Op.5" PQ, 99 (Fall 1977):46–48.

Episodes   1912–20 (Heugel) 12 min. Int.

Petite Suite Op.6   1918–19 (Durand). Six concert pieces: March; Chant sans paroles; Berceuse; Scherzo; Badinage; Humoresque. Int. to M-D.

Pièces sans titres   1915–19 (Durand   1925) 12pp. Eight short character pieces exploiting various pianistic devices: staccato chords in fifths in No.1; arpeggi in bass register accompanying single-note right-hand melody in No.3; chromatic runs in No.5; inner voices in No.6. Int. to M-D.

Nocturne Op.8/1   1919 (Durand). A concert piece, full sonorities. M-D to D.

Danse Op.8/2   1919 (I. Philipp–Durand) 4 min. Toccatalike figuration with interwoven melody. Brilliant arpeggi and octave passages lead to a cadenza. *Pp,* grave, chordal conclusion. Large span required in both hands. M-D to D.

8 Preludes Op.9   1919–20 (Heugel) 8 min. Chromatic, subtle style. Good concert pieces. M-D.

Feuilles libres Op.10   1920–24 (Durand) 9 min. Four short concert pieces. D.

5 Arabesques Op.11   1920–21 (Heugel) 6 min. Similar to subtle chromatic style found in Op.9. Nos.1–4 for piano solo; No.5 for piano and violin. M-D to D.

9 Inventions Op.13   1920–21 (ESC) 8 min. Freely chromatic, clear textures, short. M-D.

Etude de Concert b   1920 (Hamelle). Virtuosic, arpeggi, perpetual motion idea. D.

10 Etudes Op.18   1915–20 (Heugel) 25 min. More character pieces than studies. M-D to D.

2 Novelettes Op.19   1921–22 (Heugel). Large concert pieces. M-D to D.

Toccata No.2 Op.20   1922 (Simrock) 6 min. New edition (1974) revised by the composer. Wide stretches and skips are prevalent. Good concert piece. D.

Six Etudes de travail Op.21   1922–23 (Heugel) 12 min. Each etude exploits a specific aspect of piano technique. Also good as recital pieces. D.

Sonata No.1 Op.22   1918 (Heugel) 16 min. Allegro commodo; Andante; Allegro; Grave. Cyclic form, dark sonorities, unusual quiet closing movement. M-D to D.

4 Nostalgic Preludes Op.23   1922 (Heugel) 6½ min. One work in free form consisting of four movements. Effective improvisational style. M-D.

4 Préludes Op.24   1922–23 (Durand). One work in free form made up of four movements. Polyphonic textures. M-D to D.

Transcriptions Slaves Op.27   1924 (Heugel) 12½ min. Five effective concert pieces: Les Bateliers du Volga: paraphrases "Song of the Volga Boatmen." Chanson pour la chérie: tune stated seven times; textures thicken during repetitions. Chanson-granderussienne: tune in different registers, repeated chords. Le Long du Volga: shortest of the set. Chanson Tchèque: Slovakian tune, off-beat rhythms. M-D to D.

Canzona Op.28   1924 (Simrock) 5 min. Based on a nine-step scale, style similar to Op.13 and Preludes of Opp.23 and 24. Subdued, extreme registers used. M-D.

4 Romances Op.31   1924 (UE). Four movements. Good concert piece. M-D to D.

Histoire de la petit Thérèse de l'Enfant Jésus Op.36 bis   1925 (Durand). A set of thirteen pieces that survey the saint's life. Like a suite. Good for recital. Int.

Message Op.39   1926 (UE). Has the dimensions of a sonata in a free, one-movement form. D.

Voeux (Prayers) Op.39 bis   1926 (Durand). Six small concert pieces. No.4, "Pour le bonheur bourgeois," is best known. Like a suite. Good for recital. M-D.

Entretiens (Conversations) Op.46   1930 (Durand). Ten short pieces, experimental harmonies. M-D.

Etude de Piano sur la gamme pentatonique Op.51   1934–35 (Heugel). 3 sets. The last set of twelve short pieces (Bagatelles Chinoises) is the best known. Easy to Int. Opp.51, 52, and 53 could be called a "Chinese Mikrokosmos" (Wuellner, diss., p.223; see reference given at end of Tcherepnin listing).

5 Etudes de Concert Op.52   1934–36 (Schott). Varied textures and sonorities. Nos.2 and 3 draw upon Chinese instruments (the lute for No.2, Pi-Pa for No.3). Nos.1 and 4 draw upon Chinese folk character music. Like a suite. Good concert pieces. D.

Technical Studies on the Five-Note Scale Op.53   1934–36 (CFP). Based on pentatonic scale. Explores many aspects of piano technique. M-D.

Autour des montages russes 1937 (ESC) 1 piece: Le guichet; Les "on dit"; Le Swing; Et voilà. Int.

Sept Etudes Op.56 1938 (Belaieff) 14 min. Some reveal an interest in oriental music. Good recital pieces. M-D to D.

Pour petits et grands Op.65 1940 (Durand) 26 min. 2 volumes. 12 student character pieces. Also good for recital. Int.

Chant et Refrain Op.66   1940 (Durand) 7 min. Chant: homophonic. Refrain: polyphonic. Both pieces are unified by one tonal center. Large concert piece. D.

Badinage   1941 (CFP; Harald Lyche). Effective encore. M-D.

Polka   1944 (SP) 2 min. Effective encore. M-D.

Le Monde en Vitrine (Showcase) Op.75   1946 (Bo&H). Romantic character pieces. Like a suite. Good for recital. D.

La Quatrième 1948–49 (Heugel) 3 min. "Title alludes to the Fourth Republic of France and the difficulties which followed World War II" (Wuellner, diss., p.223; see citation below).

Expressions Op.81 1951 (MCA). Ten short character pieces, transparent writing. Like a suite. Good for recital. M-D to D.

Songs without Words Op.82   1949–51 (CFP). Five fine recital pieces. In the form of a suite. M-D to D.

12 Preludes Op.85   1952–53 (EBM; new edition revised by composer, Belaieff) 25 min. Chromatic, complex harmonies, rhythms, extreme registers used. Good for recital. D.

8 Pieces Op.88   1954–55 (TP). Like a suite. Good for recital. D.

Contemporary Piano Literature 1954 (SB) 17 easy pieces for the Francis Clark series. Easy to Int.

Sonata No.2 Op.94   1961 (Bo&H). Three connected movements, highly chromatic. D.

Rondo à la Russe   1946 (Gerig   1975) 7pp. M-D to D.

Sunny Day (Bagatelle Oubliée)   1915 (TP   1977). Also published in PQ, 100 (Winter 1977–78):34–35. Easy.

See: Gerry Wallerstein, "Happy Birthday to A. Tcherepnin," *Clavier*, 13 (January 1974):10–17. An interview with the composer.

Guy Wuellner, "Alexandre Tcherepnin 1899–1977," PQ, 100 (Winter 1977–78):29–33.

————. "The Complete Piano Music of Alexandre Tcherepnin: An Essay together with a Comprehensive Project in Piano Performance," DMA diss., University of Iowa, 1974, 487pp.

————. "The Theory of Interpoint," AMT, 27 (January 1978):24–28.

Special appreciation goes to Wuellner for his help with this section.

ALEC TEMPLETON (1910–1963) USA, born Wales

Big Ben Bounce (SP).

Flights of Fancy (SP).

Four Character Studies (SP). M-D.

Prelude C (SP).

Mendelssohn Mows 'Em Down (Big Three).

Springtime in the Village in collection *Composer—Pianists* (Schaum).

NICHOLAS TGETTIS (1933–   ) USA

Sonatina 1970 (Branden Press) 21pp. Allegro; Andante; Allegro. Good formal structure, active melodies, freely tonal, dramatic closing. M-D.

SIGSMOND THALBERG (1812–1871) Austria, born Switzerland

Grazioso—Romance sans Paroles (Musica Obscura). M-D.

Fantaisie sur les Huguenots—Meyerbeer Op.20 (Musica Obscura).

Tre Giorni, Air de Pergolesi (Musical Scope).

Home! Sweet Home! Fantasia Op.72 (Musical Obscura).

SIEGFRIED THIELE (1934–   ) Germany

Sonata alla Toccata   1969 (CFP) 16pp.

JOHANNES PAUL THILMAN (1906–1973) Germany

Thilman studied with Hindemith and Grabner.

5 Präludien 1970 (Br&H) 12pp. Improvisatory, contrapuntal, lean textures, mild dissonance. M-D.

Sonatina patetica Op.39 (Süddeutscher).

KURT THOMAS (1904–1973) Germany

Sechs zweistimmige Inventionen Op.16a (Br&H   1931) 13pp.

Fünf dreistimmige Inventionen Op.16b (Br&H   1932) 13pp.

VIRGIL THOMSON (1896–   ) USA

Ten Etudes 1943–44 (CF). Practicable and engaging, wonderfully imaginative. M-D.

Edges. A musical portrait of Robert Indiana   1966 (GS) 5pp. Opposing harmonies move over keyboard; much use of chromatic seconds; mirror effects between hands. M-D.

Nine Portraits (PIC   1974). More of Thomson's friends depicted by musical portraits. M-D.

Ten Easy Pieces and a Coda   1926 (PIC   1972) 8pp. Clever introduction to contemporary styles. Easy to Int.

Man of Iron (GS   1978). A musical portrait of Willy Eisenhart. Dissonant, frenetic arpeggi. M-D.

HEINZ TIESSEN (1887–1971) Germany
6 Piano Pieces Op.37 (UE 9687).
3 Tanzcapricen Op.61 (Leuckart   1973) 13pp.

MICHAEL TIPPETT (1905–   ) Great Britain
Sonata No.3   1973 (Schott 11162) 42pp. 25 min. A large but taut work in three movements. Allegro: changing meters, three opening ideas, close imitation, extremes in range exploited. Lento: shifting chords evolve into fascinating patterns. Allegro vivace: a virtuoso rondo. A valuable and important addition to the repertoire. D.

HEUWELL TIRCUIT (1931–   ) USA
Bartók Variations, Set II   1976 (GS) 25pp.

BORIS I. TISHCHENKO (1939–   ) USSR
Sonata III Op.32   1965 (Sovetskii Kompozitor   1974) 62pp. Dissonant writing that reflects dark, harsh colors. Freely tonal, flexible rhythms, violent, jagged conclusion. D.
Sonata IV Op.53   1972 (Panton) 30pp.

ANTOINE TISNE (1932–   ) France
Cimaise (Billaudot).
Cristaux de Feu (EMT   1975) 8pp. For harpsichord but a piano is needed for the dynamics (crescendo, decrescendo) requirements. Pointillistic, large arpeggiated chords, expressionistic, long crescendi and decrescendi, clusterlike sonorities, some avant-garde notation. D.
Epigraphe pour une stèle (Billaudot).
Soliels noirs (Billaudot).
Sonate (Billaudot).

LORIS TJEKNAVORIAN (1937–   ) Iran
Tjeknavorian is an Iranian-Armenian composer and conductor who holds a place of honor in Iran. He is also well known in Great Britain.
3 Armenian Dances (Dob).
Sonatine I Op.7 (Dob).
Sring-Athre Op.9 (Dob).
Sonatine II Op.10 (Dob).
Armenian Miniatures   1975 (Nov). Nine pieces based on Armenian

folk and dance melodies, free arrangements. Unusual key signatures, contemporary idiom, modal. Look more difficult than they are. M-D.

Armenian Sketches (Novello 1975) 32pp. 26 short, pleasant pieces illustrating traditional Armenian rhythms and modes. Wide variety of keys, modes, time signatures, and difficulty. Interesting lyric quality. Mainly cast in two-part texture. Unusual rhythms will perhaps be a problem. Fine for small hands; outstanding for developing rhythmic independence. Int. to M-D.

See: Denby Richards, "Loris Tjeknavorian," MO, 100 (December 1976): 135–36.

AMALI TLIL (1928–   ) France

Métamorphoses (Editions françaises de musique 1973) 2 vols.

KUNIO TODA (1915–   ) Japan

Fantaisie sur les sons de "koto" pour piano (Japan Federation of Composers 1970) 11pp. The title of this work means "Fantasy based on according to the traditional tuning of 'koto,' the term 'fantasy' being used, as in the Baroque era, nothing but 'Prelude and 'Fugue' " (from composer's note). Serial. M-D.

CAMILLO TOGNI (1922–   ) Italy

Quattro capricci 1969 (SZ 1974) 12pp. Similar to some of the frantic and seemingly unorganized passages in Boulez's *Third Sonata*. D.

DMITRII ALEKSEEVICH TOLSTOI (1923–   ) USSR

Sonata V Op.49 1971 (USSR 1976) 27pp.

JOHANN WENZEL TOMÁSCHEK (1774–1850) Bohemia

Eclogues Vol.I (MAB Vol.73); Vol.II (MAB Vol.74). Vol.II contains Opp.63, 66, 83. Preface and editorial notes in Czech, English, and German.

Ausgewälte Klavierwerke (Dana Zahn—Henle 260). Fingering by Hans-Martin Theopold. Preface in German, English, and French. Contains: Variations on an Unknown Theme G Op.16; 6 Eclogues Op.35; 3 Ditirambi Op.65; 3 Allegri Capricciosi de Bravura Op.84. All of these works were composed between 1805 and 1818. Excellent urtext edition. Int. to M-D.

Sonatina (Huber—Heinrichshofen 3219).

TRYGVE TORJUSSEN (1885–   ) Norway

To the Rising Sun (Volkwein 1976).

CHARLES TOURNEMIRE (1870–1939) France

Ballade Fantastique (Philippo & Combre).

Ballade Triste (Philippo & Combre).

Danse du Finistère (Philippo & Combre).

Douze Préludes-Poèmes Op.58 (Heugel 1932) 86pp. Untitled; some require four staves to notate; virtuoso figuration; avant-garde for its day. D.

Improvisation (Philippo & Combre).

Lied (Philippo & Combre).

Mélancolie (Philippo & Combre).

Petite Rapsodie Bretonne (Philippo & Combre).

Scherzo (Philippo & Combre).

EINAR TRAERUP-SARK (1921–   ) Denmark

Lette klaverstykker Op.5a (WH). Eight little pieces.

Cathédrale de Verre (Musikhojskolens   1972). Chaconne pour piano.

La déesse du printemps (Musikhojskolens   1973) 15pp.

Tamfutsak Op.25 (D. Fog   1973) 11pp. 6 min. A suite.

Visages du temps (Musikhojskolens   1973) 14pp.

ROY TRAVIS (1922–   ) USA

Travis teaches at UCLA, where he has drawn inspiration from African music at the Institute of Ethnomusicology.

African Sonata (Sonata II)   1966 (University of California [Berkeley] Press   1973) 44pp. Sikyi: a coquettish and attractive Ashanti dance, SA design. Bambara Dance-Song: intricate rhythms, chromatic major second runs. Sohu: an Ewe dance, scherzo-like, many perfect augmented fourths. Adowa: an Ashanti funeral party dance. Introduction followed by 15 variations. Based on rhythms, melodic motives, and sonorities derived from traditional West African dances. Because it is difficult for the piano to sound like the original sources, much musical content has been lost, but this is still an unusual and stimulating work. D.

Five Preludes (TP   1966) 9pp. Marcato. Andante sostenuto. Grazioso. Barcarola. Con fuoco. Freely tonal; each piece develops one main idea; borders on the expressionistic. Large span required. M-D.

ARKADY TREBINSKY (1897–   ) France

Suite française Op.20 (EMT   1971) 14pp. Gavotte: mainly two voices, chromatic coloration, witty. Gigue: thin textures, detached touch. Sarabande: sustained, accompanied melody, more tonal than first two movements. Bourrée: kind of a perpetual motion idea, some melodic emphasis with arpeggio accompanimental style. Int. to M-D.

Preludes Op.28 (EMT).

YNGVE JAN TREDE (1933–   ) Denmark

Stykker 69 (Engström & Södring   1971) 14pp.

GILLES TREMBLAY (1932–   ) USA, born Canada

Deux Pièces 1956–58 (Berandol) 8 min. All directions in French. Phases: short, slow, brutally dissonant. Réseaux: more involved, longer, changing tempi, extremes of keyboard used, very contemporary-sounding (this title might be translated as "tangles" or "webs"). D.

GILBERT TRYTHALL (1930–   ) USA

Trythall is head of the music department of George Peabody College, Nashville, TN 37203.

Coincidences (MS available from composer). Written in a kind of Stock-hausen serialism. Exciting writing; intensity increases as density of notes increases. D.

GAJANEH M. TSCHEBOTARJAN (1918–   ) USSR

Praeludium II (Sikorski 2133) 4pp. Allegro grazioso: freely modal around g, thin textures, lyric, motivic development. Int.

NIKOLAJ P. TSCHERWINSKIJ (–   ) USSR

Tri etjuda 1971 (Sowjetskii Kompositor) 19pp. Titles in Russian. Three studies, concert repertoire. D.

EISEI TSUJII (1933–   ) Japan

Hallucination 1965 (Ongaku No Tomo Sha) 8pp. 3 min. Performance directions in French and Japanese. Clusters, harmonics, pointil-listic, careful pedal indications, expressionistic, atonal, proportional rhythmic relationships. M-D.

JOAQUIN TURÍNA (1882–1949) Spain

Sevilla Op.2 (Schott   1909). Suite pittoresque.

Sonata romantica (sur un thème espagnol) Op.3 (ESC   1910). Theme and variations; Scherzo; Final. M-D.

Coins de Séville Op.5   1911 (Schott) 1st suite. 1. Soir d'été sur la terrasse. 2. Rondes d'enfants. 3. Danse des seises dans la cathédrale. 4. A los toros.

Tres danzas andaluzas Op.8   1912 (Sal). Petenera. Tango. Zapateado.

Album de Viaje Op.15   1916 (UME). Five pieces.

Mujeres españolas (Femmes d'Espagne) Op.17   1917 (Sal) Set I, three portraits.

Cuentos de España Op.20   1918 (Sal) Set I, seven pieces.

Niñerias Op.21   1919 (Sal). Set I, eight pieces.

Danzas Fantásticas ("Imaginary Dances") Op.22 (UME). Pictorial ex-cerpts from the Spanish poet José Más are used to preface each of the three dances. Exaltación ("Ecstasy"): "It seems as if the figures in that incomparable picture were moving like the calix of a flower." Ensueño ("Daydream"): "The guitar strings, when struck, sounded like the lament of a soul that could no longer bear the weight of bitterness." Orgía ("Revel"): "The perfume of flowers, mingled with the fragrance of mansanilla, and the lees of a splendid wine, was like an incense that inspired joy."

Sanlúcar de Barrameda (Sonata pintoresca) Op.24   1922 (UME).

Three movements: En la torre del castillo ("In the Tower of the Citadel"); Siluetas de la calzada ("Portrait of a Woman in Shoes"); Los pescadores en Bajo de Guia ("The Fisherman of Bajo de Guia"). Sanlúcar de Barrameda is a fortified seaport near Cádiz made picturesque by its ancient Moorish citadel and colorful fishing fleets. Turina spent his summer vacations there. This work, one of his most ambitious, describes the atmosphere of the town. The third and fourth scenes make up the third movement, an Impressionistic prelude and fugue. M-D to D.

See: Linton Powell, "Cyclical Form in a Forgotten Sonata of J. Turina (1882–1949)," AMT, 27 (September–October 1977):23–25.

El Cristo de la Calavers, leyenda becqueriana Op.30 (UME   1924).

Jardines de Andalousie Op.31 (Sal   1924). Three pieces.

La venta de los gatos Op.32   1925 (UME).

El Barrio de Santa Cruz Op.33   1925 (Sal). Rhythmic variations for piano. Theme and seven variations. M-D.

La leyenda de la Giralda Op.40 (UME   1927). Four pieces.

Dos danzas sobre temas populares españoles Op.41 (OUP   1927). 1. Cadena de Seguidillas. 2. El arbol de Guernica. M-D.

Verbena madrileña Op.42 (Sal   1927). Five pieces.

Mallorca Op.44 (Sal   1928). Suite of four pieces.

Evocaciones Op.46 (UME   1929). 1. Paisaje. 2. Mar. 3. Sardaña.

Cuentos de España Op.47   1928 (Sal). Set II, seven pieces.

Souvenirs de l'ancienne Espagne Op.48   1929 (Sal). Four pieces.

Viaje maritimo Op.49 (Schott   1930). Voyage maritime suite, three pieces.

Ciclo pianistico 1930–31 (UME). Published separately. Tocata y fuga Op.50. Partita Op.57. Pieza romántica Op.64. El castillo de Almodovar Op.65.

Miniatures Op.52 (Schott   1930). Eight pieces.

Danzas Gitanas Op.55 (Sal   1930). Set I, five pieces based on gypsy themes.

Niñerias Op.56 (Sal). Set II, eight pieces.

Tarjetas Postales (Cartes postales) Op.58 (Schott   1931). Five pieces.

Sonata Fantasía Op.59 (UME   1930).

Radio Madrid Op.62 (Schott   1931). Prologue and three Retransmissions.

Jardins d'Enfants ("The Playground") Op.63 (Sal   1931). Eight pieces.

The Circus Op.68 (Schott   1932). Seven attractive pieces: Hans Sachs; The Marquise's Silken Slippers; The Peasant's Boots; Greek Sandals; The Shoes of the Ballet Dancer; The Dainty Shoes of Her Ladyship; Shoes of a Toreador. Int.

Silhouettes Op.70 (Sal   1932). Five pieces.

Mujeres españolas (Femmes d'Espagne) Op.73 (Sal   1932). Five portraits.

Fantasía Italiana Op.75 (UME   1933).

Trilogia: El poema infinito Op.77 (UME   1933); Ofrenda Op.85 (UME 1934); Hipócrates Op.86 (UME   1934).

Rincones de Sanlúcar Op.78   1933 (UME). Four pieces.

Bailete Op.79   1933 (Sal). Suite de danzas del siglo XIX. Entrada; Tirana; Bolero; Danza de corte; Fandango.

Preludes Op.80 (UME   1933). Five pieces.

Fantasia sobre cinco notas ("Arbos") Op.83 (UME   1934). Preludio; Toccata y fuga; Coral con variaciones.

Danzas Gitanas Op.84 (Sal   1934). Five pieces based on gypsy themes. Int. to M-D.

Concierto sin orquesta Op.88   1935 (UME).

Las Musas de Andalucía Op.93 (UME). Nine pieces in all, but only three for solo piano: No.1 Clio; No.7 Urania; No.8 Terpsicore.

Por las calles de Sevilla Op.96 (UME). Three pieces.

Rincon Magico Op.97 (UME   1946). Desfile en forma de sonata.

Poema Fantástico Op.98 (UME   1951). Four sections.

Contemplación Op.99 (UME   1945). Three impressions.

Linterna Mágica Op.101 (UME).

Fantasia Cinematografica Op.103 (UME). En forma de Rondo.

Desde mi terraza Op.104 (UME). Three pieces.

See: Linton Powell, "Joaquin Turina. Another of the Spanish Nationalists," *Clavier,* 17 (October 1976):29–30.

————. "The Influence of Dance Rhythms on the Piano Music of Joaquin Turina," MR, 37 (May 1976):143–51.

————. "The Piano Music of Spain (Joaquin Turina)," PQ, 98 (Summer 1977):45–48.

PAUL TUROK (1929–   ) USA

Little Suite Op.9 (GS). Prelude; Arabesque; Toccata. Effective dissonant writing. M-D.

Passacaglia Op.10 (A. Broude   1977) 4pp. Contemporary look at a baroque form. Essentially lyrical. Explores basic piano sonorities, dissonant, bitonal influence. M-D.

GEIRR TVEITT (1908–   ) Norway

Twelve Two-part Inventions Op.2 (NMO).

Danse du Dieu Soleil ("Dance of the Sun God") Op.91/15 (NMO   1952) 16pp. Ornate figures develop into strong rhythms and full chords; thick textures; tonal. D.

50 Hardanger Op.150/50 (NMO   1951) 7pp. The final piece in a set of fifty popular Norwegian tunes developed into varied character pieces. Full chords, fast repeated notes, clusters. M-D.

Going a 'wooing. The Alleged Father. The Mountain Girl. Op.150/3, 38, 43 (NMO   1951) 10pp. Published together. Similar to style of Op. 150/50. M-D.

ROMUALD TWARDOWSKI (1930–   ) Poland

Twardowski studied at the Warsaw State College of Music. He also worked with Nadia Boulanger in Paris.

Capricci (PWM   1967) 24pp. Five separate pieces, in sections. Similar to sonatinas with two or three movements each, modal, MC. Easy to Int.

Mala Sonata   1959 (PWM).

U

ERNST LUDWIG URAY (1906–   ) Austria

Sonata breve No.3 F   1973 (Dob   1975) 12pp.

ILHAN USMANBAS (1921–   ) Turkey

Six Preludes (TP   1945) 12pp. Toccata. Siciliano. Praeludia Canonica.
    Due Liriche (Madrigale and Blues). Quarter note=138. Alla francese.
    Freely tonal, octotonic, changing meters, some Middle Eastern in-
    fluence. M-D.

V

HENRY VACHEY (1930–   ) France
Printanière (Leduc   1973) 3pp. Folklike, thin textures. Int.
Three Variations on "Cadet Rousselle" (Delrieu).

TOMÁŠ VACKAR (1945–1963) Czechoslovakia
Perspektivy pro klavír 1961–63 (Panton) 45pp. Preface in Czech and
    German

EDGAR VALCÁRCEL (1932–   ) Peru
Dicotomías I y II 1966 (Ediciones Anacrusa) 7 min.
Variaciones sobre un coral India 1963 (PIC) 7 min.

JACQUES VALLIER (1922–   ) France
Sonatine (Chappell   1973) 9pp. Collection Enseignement musical.

MAX VANDERMAESBRUGGE (1933–   ) Belgium
Caractères Op.26   1975 (CeBeDeM) 15pp.
Etude: Son et rythme Op.17   1965 (CeBeDeM   1977) 14pp.

DAVID VAN VACTOR (1906–   ) USA
Van Vactor was for many years conductor of the Knoxville, Tennessee,
Symphony.
Suite 1962 (Roger Rhodes) 10 min. Five movements.

SÁNDOR VERESS (1907–   ) Hungary
Fingerlarks (SZ   1969). 88 pianistic studies. Preface in French, German,
    and English.

TIHOMIL VIDOSIC (1902–   ) Yugoslavia
Etuda za klavir (Društvo Hrvatskih Skladatelja   1972) 10pp.

ANATOL VIERU (1926–   ) Rumania
Nautilos 1968 (Sal) for piano and tape (tape on rental) 9pp. 9½ min.
    Divided into five sections, scrupulously notated with performance
    instructions in French only. Requires normal keyboard playing as
    well as the use of a plastic stick, a small heavy glass, keys and other
    metal objects on the strings; clusters, glissandi, striking with the fist,
    etc. The tape is used in the fourth section. Dynamic marks for each
    note, pointillistic, some improvisatory sections. Timings in seconds
    are coordinated with the tape. D.

HEITOR VILLA-LOBOS (1887–1959) Brazil

A Fiandeira (Napoleão   1926). 9pp.

A Lenda do Caboclo (Napoleão   1920) 5pp. Syncopated chordal accompaniment, gently flowing melody, lush harmonies. M-D.

Chôros No.2 (Napoleão   1924). Originally for flute and clarinet, arranged by the composer for solo piano.

Cirandinhas ("Little Round Dance") (ESC). Suite of twelve moderately easy pieces based on popular children's themes.

Valsa da Dor ("Waltz of Sadness") (ESC   1932). 5pp. 5½ min. Luxuriant Romantic style. Published posthumously. M-D.

Valsa Scherzo Op.17. (Napoleão   1925) 19pp.

The Piano Music of Heitor Villa-Lobos (Consolidated   1972) 166pp. Music for Millions, vol.62. Contains a broad range of Villa-Lobos's music.

See: David Appleby, "A Visit to the Villa-Lobos Museum," AMT, 25 (June–July 1976):24.

Laurence Morton, "Villa-Lobos: Brazilian Pioneer," *Clavier,* 16 (January 1977):29–32. Contains pieces from Guia Practica Nos.8, 97, and 137.

GIULOI VIOZZI (1912–   ) Italy

Spleen (Berben). Dissonant, violent outbursts, chromatic. M-D.

NICOLETTA VIRGILIO (–   ) Italy

Cinque Brevi Impressioni (Berben   1972). Grazioso; Comodo; Giogioso; Mesto; Vivo. Contemporary techniques. Each piece is short, with basically one idea exploited. Contrasted, some imitation used. Int.

JÁNOS VISKI (1906–1961) Hungary

Sirfelirat (EMB   1960) 3pp.

BERTHE DI VITO-DELVAUX (1915–   ) Belgium

Sonatina III Op.110   1966 (CeBeDeM   1974) 8pp.

ROMAN VLAD (1919–   ) Italy, born Rumania

Sognando il sogno; variazioni su di una variazione per pianoforte (Ric 1973) 22pp. Subtitled "Variations on the First Variation." The first variation uses a twelve-note row whose first seven pitches make up the F-major scale. This allows for a varied version of Schumann's "Träumerei" for the second variation. Final variation is effective, but the whole piece involves many double sharps and flats, making for difficult reading. D.

SOTIREES VLAHOPOULOS (1926–   ) USA

Vlahopoulos is a graduate of the American Conservatory of Music and of Indiana University. He has also studied with Roy Harris and Virgil Thomson. MSS available from the composer: c/o Music Department, Rosary

Hill College, Buffalo, NY 14226. These pieces display a fine talent, expert pianistic writing.

Ballade 1958 7pp. Opening ideas are woven together in a refreshing woof. Flexible meters, fleeting tonal centers, sensuous sonorities. M-D.

Epilogue 1960 6pp. Theme and ostinato alternate, shifting thematic figures, expressive, haunting and lyric. M-D.

Invention 1961 5pp. Baroque contrapuntal techniques, malleable motifs, alternating vigorous and lyric passages, well-developed, tightly controlled. M-D.

Portrait 1964 4pp. Three-part theme reappears in various textural constructions; poignant harmonic undulations. M-D.

Prelude and Fugue 1966 9pp. Contrapuntal style using somewhat Impressionistic harmonies, three-voice fugue, homophonic coda. M-D.

Prologue 1954 3pp. Built on a delineated melodic line that is embedded in the harmonic structure, motivic fragments, nontonal. M-D.

Suite: Three French Dances 1962 12pp. Loure: ostinato, small motifs, rustic and pastoral. Sarabande: solemn theme sounds at top of chordal figures. Boutade: playful, sequences, motive altered and extended. In an MC folk idiom. M-D.

Toccata 1951 rev. 1966 17pp. Contrasts tempestuous virtuosity with rhapsodic elements. Strong toccata motif with elliptical rhythm, two contrasting sections, very exciting virtuosic coda. D.

ERNST VOGEL (1926–   ) Austria

Motivation I–V 1972 (Dob) 13pp. 9 min. Mildly dissonant, varied meters. M-D.

HANS VOGT (1911–   ) Germany

Sonata alla toccata (Bo&Bo 1971) 20pp. 13½ min. Molto allegro: broad gestures, contrasted moods, sudden closing. Andante: suggested pedal points. Presto: brilliant secco writing. Neoclassic orientation. M-D to D.

JOOP VOORN (1932–   ) The Netherlands

Voorn teaches theory at the Brabant Conservatoire, Tilburg, Holland.

Ludi ed Interludi 1969 (Donemus) 15pp. Reproduction of the composer's MS.

JAN VRIEND (1938–   ) The Netherlands

Variaties 1961 (Donemus) 5pp. Reproduction of composer's MS. Seven serial variations. D.

KLAAS PIETER DE VRIES (1944–   ) The Netherlands

Chain of Changes 1968 (Donemus) 5pp. Reproduction of composer's MS.

W

GEORG CHRISTOPH WAGENSEIL (1715–1777) Germany
Wagenseil is one of the most important influences to have shaped the
Viennese classical keyboard sonata.
Six Divertimenti Op.1   1753 (Helga Scholz-Michelitsch—Dob   1975)
   Vol.I: Nos.1–3. Vol.II: Nos.4–6. Preface in German and English.
   Charming and unpretentious rococo three- or four-movement works
   in expanded binary form. Int. to M-D.
Six Easy Lessons for the Harpsichord or Pianoforte Op.3   ca.1775
   (Heuwekemeijer   1970) 25pp.

RICHARD WAGNER (1813–1883) Germany
Sonata B♭ Op.1 (Br&H; Musica Obscura) 25 min.
Grosse Sonata A Op.4 (Gerig   1960) 22 min.
Complete Works, Piano Works Vol.19, Series A. (Dahlhaus—Schott
   1970). Sonata B♭; Polonaise D for four hands; Fantasia f♯; Grosse
   Sonate A; Albumblatt für Ernst Benedikt Lietz (Lied ohne Wortes);
   Polka G; Eine Sonate für das Album von Frau M. W.; Züricher
   Vielliebchen—Walzer; In das Album der Fürstin M; Ankunft bei den
   schwarzen Schwänen; Albumblatt für Betty Schott.
Polonaise D   1831 (A. D. Walker—Nov   1973). A sketch for the
   Polonaise D for four hands. Has much vitality, octaves, chording.
   Would make a good encore. Int.
   See: R. S. Furness and A. D. Walker, "A Wagner Polonaise," MT,
   114 (January 1973):26, with the *Polonaise* printed on p.27.
See: Charles W. Timbrell, "Wagner's Piano Music," Part I, AMT, 23
   (April–May 1974):5–9; Part II, AMT, 23 (June–July 1974):6–9.

RUDOLF WAGNER-RÉGNEY (1903–1969) Germany
The Collected Piano Works (Tilo Medek—DVFM). Foreword and commentary in German. Contains all the piano music, including many
   short pieces, suites, sonatinas and fugues. Much use is made of flexible
   meters. Int. to M-D.
Spinettmusik   1934 (UE). Six pieces in a contrapuntal idiom. Int.

ADAM WALACINSKI (1928–   ) Poland
Walacinski studied violin at the State College of Music in Cracow with
E. Uminska and later studied composition privately with S. Kisielewski.

He belongs to the artistic society Grupa Krakowska and is also active as a critic.

Allaloa (PWM 1970). 6 loose leaves in cover. Explanations in Polish and English. Avant-garde.

GEORGE WALKER (1922–) USA

Walker is a graduate of Oberlin College and Curtis Institute. He presently teaches at Rutgers University.

Prelude and Caprice 1941 (Gen 1975) 7pp. 8 min. Prelude: lyric, freely tonal, flowing. Caprice: flexible meters, syncopation, fast octaves in both hands required in coda. A fine combination. M-D.

Sonata I 1953 (Gen 1972) 27pp. 15 min. Three contrasting movements of virtuosic and dissonant writing. Allegro energico. Moderato: a theme and six variations built more on intervals and timbres than on melodic lines. Allegro con brio: sensationally exciting. An ambitious and deserving work tinged with classical touches of Ravel and Prokofieff. D.

Sonata II 1957 (Galaxy) 19pp. 10 min. Adagio non troppo: four-bar theme and ten short contrasting variations inventively manipulated. Presto: rhythmic two- and three-voice textured scherzo; exploits opening two-bar staccato figure. Adagio: changing meters; builds to dramatic climax; *ppp* close; perhaps the finest movement. Allegretto tranquillo: requires fine left-hand octave technique; most technically difficult of all movements. Written in a biting contemporary idiom, freely tonal. D.

See: Wilfrid J. Delphin, "A Comparative Analysis of Two Sonatas by George Walker: Sonata I and Sonata II," DMA diss., University of Southern Mississippi, 1976, 118pp.

D. Maxine Sims, "An Analysis and Comparison of Piano Sonatas by George Walker and Howard Swanson," *The Black Perspective in Music,* 4 (Spring 1976):70–81.

Spatials 1961 (Gen) 7pp. 4 min. Six variations, serial, flexible meters, expressive. M-D.

Spektra 1971 (Gen) 12pp. 7 min. Serial, pointillistic. Five staves required for some notation; rhythmic proportional relationships. D.

Sonata III 1976 (Gen) 13pp. 12 min. Fantoms: rhapsodic, surging sonorities. Bell: a widely spread dissonant chord is repeated seventeen times in contrasting dynamics and note values. Chorale and Fughetta: gyrating gymnastics, bristling figurations, dissonant. D.

See: David Burge, "New Pieces, Part II," CK, 4 (January 1978):50.

DAVID WARD-STEINMAN (1936–) USA

Latter-day Lullabies (EBM 1972) 7pp. 7 min. Jenna—Matthew—David —Meredith—Karen. Contemporary sounds including clusters produced by using a twelve-inch ruler. M-D.

PETER WARLOCK (1894–1930) Great Britain

5 Folk Song Preludes (Augener   1923) 9½ min. Convincing writing but does not lie well under the hands. M-D.

Valses Rêves d'Isolde   1917 (Thames Publishing   1976) 6pp. A parody on Wagner's *Tristan und Isolde.* "These slow valses hit off to a nicety the characteristic Valse de Salon at its most glutinous" (from the preface). Large chords and plenty of octaves require a large span. A fine encore. M-D.

BRUNO WASSIL (1920–   ) Italy

Dodici preludi (EC   1971) 34pp. Twelve preludes.

SCOTT WATSON (–   ) USA

Seven Variations on a Theme by Haydn   1956 (GS) 5pp. Clever variations on the famous theme from the *Surprise Symphony.* Delightful. Int.

JOHN WATTS (1930–   ) USA

Watts studied composition with Cecil Effinger, Roy Harris, John Krueger, Robert Palmer, Burrill Phillips, and David Van Vactor while attending a number of universities. He has been a member of the faculty of the New School for Social Research, in New York City, since 1969.

Sonata   1955–58, rev. 1960 (Joshua) 16 min. Allegretto leggiero: mild dissonances, Impressionistic harmonies. Andante sostenuto: fugal; concludes with great climax; classical textures; large span required. Andante semplice: Romantic-sounding harmonies; careful voicing needed. Allegrò giojoso: eighth-note ostinato bass effectively unfolds; final six bars have direction "Pound the hell out of it!"; large span required. Solid technical equipment necessary for entire sonata. D.

DONALD WAXMAN (1925–   ) USA

Fifty Etudes (Galaxy   1976) (Book 1, 1–14, Int. Book 2, 15–27, upper Int. Book 3, 28–39, M-D. Book 4, 40–50, D. An outstanding set of contemporary pedagogical etudes, each focusing on a particular problem or problems of technique related to conservative twentieth-century literature. Expressive titles. Those listed below are available separately.

Etude of Sixths in Wrist Staccato (Galaxy). The subtitle, "Motto: II—Greetings to Loeschhorn" pays homage to this composer of piano studies. Staccato sixths are used throughout. Int. to M-D.

Etude in Octaves (Galaxy). "Motto: IV—Greetings to Concone." Brilliant and bravura playing required in this strong rhythmic study. D.

Etude of Alternating Double Notes (Galaxy). This "Confetti" is light and fast. Various intervals in double notes are tossed between hands. Bright and sprightly. M-D.

ALAIN WEBER (1930–   ) France

Etudes acrostiches 1973 (Leduc) 33pp. 34 min. Explanations in French, German, and English. In the form of variations. Possibilities of a fragmentary performance set up by the composer on the third preliminary page. Contents: Choral et variation; Acrostiche 1; Résonance 1; Acrostiche 2; Mouvement perpétuel; Acrostiche 3; Résonance 2; Acrostiche 4; Mobile. Fiery rhetoric alternates with steamy Impressionism. Musical acrostic construction and solution are at their best in these difficult contemporary settings. D.

BEN WEBER (1916–   ) USA
5 Bagatelles Op.2 1938 (TP). Short and amiable pieces in clear twelve-tone technique. These were the first published American works for piano in a serial style. M-D.
3 Piano Pieces Op.23 1946 (Bomart) 11pp. Written in a serious, Bergian style. Problem lies in following every melodic line through its entire trajectory. D.
Fantasia Op.25 1946 (EBM). Expressionistic, complex textures, full of personality. D.
Humoresque Op.49 1963 (LG) in collection *New Music for the Piano*. 2 min. Economical use of material, poignant wistfulness, lyrical with some wryness. M-D.

CARL MARIA VON WEBER (1786–1826) Germany
Perpetuum mobile Op.24 (Simrock). Original and arrangements by Brahms and Tchaikowsky. Original available separately (Schott 0790½).
Rondo Brillante Op.62. (Zanibon N-309).
Concert Piece Op.79 (CFP 2899).
Master Series for the Young (Hughes—GS). Andante with variations; Andantino; March; Mazurka; Minuet; Original theme; Rondo; Sonatina; Theme from *Invitation to the Dance;* Theme from Sonata Op.70; 3 Waltzes. Int.
See: John P. Adams, "A Study of the Piano Sonatas of Carl Maria von Weber," DM diss., Indiana University, 1976, 112pp. Each sonata is analyzed from a theoretical and a pianistic point of view.

ANTON VON WEBERN (1883–1945) Austria
See: Kathryn Bailey, "The Evolution of Variation Form in the Music of Webern," *Current Musicology,* 16 (1973):55–70.
Mary E. Fiore, "Webern's Use of Motives in the Piano Variations," in *The Computer and Music* (Ithaca and London: Cornell University Press, 1970), pp.115–22.

KARL WEIGL (1881–1949) Austria
5 Nachtphantasien Op.13 (Joshua 1977) 25pp.

STANLEY WEINER (1925–   ) Belgium, born USA
Sonata Op.5 (MCA   1972) 26pp. Allegro: SA; opens with a tranquil
6/8; freely tonal; broken octave and chordal figuration; octotonic;
chromatic cadenza. Un poco lento: ABA; active melodic line; A
tempo con brio mid-section works to large climax. Presto: running
two-voice octotonic opening punctuated with chromatic chords; left-
hand skips; changing meters. M-D to D.

LOUIS WEINGARDEN (1943–   ) USA
Triptych 1969 (Bo&H   1974).

ALBIN WEINGERL (1923–   ) Yugoslavia
Sest (6) miniatur 1969 (Društvo Slovenskih Skladateljev) 10pp.

FLEMMING WEIS (1898–   ) Denmark
Limitationes (Engström & Södring   1971) 8pp. A suite.
Limitationes II (Engström & Södring   1974) 11pp. A suite.

HUGO WEISGALL (1912–   ) USA, born Czechoslovakia
Weisgall studied composition with Roger Sessions. He is president of the
American Music Center and teaches at Queens College of the City Univer-
sity of New York.
Sine Nomine (TP   1968). Graven Images No.3. Int.
Two Improvisations (TP   1969) Graven Images No.6. Serial, short.
    Large span required. M-D.
See: Bruce Saylor, "The Music of Hugo Weisgall," MQ, 59 (April 1973):
    239–62.

WILHELM WEISMANN (1900–   ) Germany
Kleine Präludien, Tänze und Stücke (CFP   1972). 24 short pieces.

DANIEL WELCHER (1948–   ) USA
Welcher is a member of the music faculty of the University of Texas at
Austin, Austin, TX 78712.
Sonatina 1972 (TP   1979) 14pp. Vigoroso; Lento; Presto. Care-
    fully balanced between linear and homophonic writing. Shows a
    fondness for octotonic techniques. Freely tonal, shifting meters, excit-
    ing and brilliant conclusion, effective gestures. M-D.
Dance Variations 1979 (MS available from composer) 20 min. Five
    movements, common leitmotif, virtuosic. Exploits different aspects of
    the dance. D.

EGON WELLESZ (1885–1974) Austria
Der Abend Op.4 1909–10 (Dob   1971) 19pp. A cycle of four im-
    pressions. M-D.

FREDERICK WERLE (1914–   ) USA
Six Fancies (A. Broude   1977). Short pieces to relieve a young pianist's
    doldrums, Romantic and contemporary sonorities. Int.
Sarabande (CF). A stately pedal study. Slow, sustained chords support
    a flowing melody. Int.

JEAN-JACQUES WERNER (1935–   ) France
Chansons-rêves (EMT   1971) 10pp.
3 Mouvements circulaires (Centre d'Art National Français   1971) 7pp.
Première Sonate (EMT   1962) 15pp. Allegro Moderato: tonal, freely
    chromatic; large span required. Adagio: dissonant cantabile writing.
    Allegro con moto: rhythmic, repeated notes and chords; large span re-
    quired. M-D.
Printanières (Billaudot).

FRANCIS B. WESTBROOK (1903–   ) Great Britain
Toccata "Hommage à Ravel" (Hin   1973) 15pp.

JOHANNES WEYRAUCH (1897–1977) Germany
Fünf kleine Klavierstücke (CFP   1969). Five simple pieces, somewhat
    dated, neoclassic oriented. Int.

CHARLES WHITTENBERG (1927–   ) USA
Whittenberg teaches at the University of Connecticut.
Three Compositions for Piano (CFP   1972). Short, contrasting, varied
    meters, pointillistic. These pieces show the composer's interest in
    twelve-tone classicism within the strict application of the twelve-
    pitch class systems. Babbitt influence noted. D.

ERNST WIDMER (1927–   ) Brazil, born Switzerland
Widmer studied composition under Willy Burkhard, piano with Walter
Frey, and conducting with Paul Mueller. Since 1956 he has been working
in Brazil, and in 1967 he became a Brazilian citizen. He is Dean of the
School of Music and Performing Arts of the Federal University of Bahia.
Ludus Brasiliensis Op.37 (Ric BR 1965–66) 2 hours 10 min. Vol.I:
    Nos.1–55. Vol.II: Nos.56–95. Vol.III: Nos.96–125. Vol.IV: Nos.
    126–53. Vol. V: Nos.154–62. Progressive pieces of pedagogical char-
    acter. Similar to Bartók's *Mikrokosmos*. Includes objectives for the
    series, pieces for sight-reading and instructions for sight-reading,
    pieces for improvisation and directions on how to improvise. Also
    contains observations for the teacher, explanation of pieces on three
    staves (ensemble pieces for teacher and student). Some pieces are
    very contemporary-sounding, and a few employ avant-garde tech-
    niques and notation. Easy to M-D.
Rondmobile Op.54   1968 (Gerig   1974) 6 min.
Suite Mirim Op.101   1977 (UFBA) 11 min. 1. Sol. 2. Lufa-Lufa. 3.
    Ressonâncias. 4. Firmamento. 5. Relax.

ALEC WILDER (1907–   ) USA
Pieces for Young Pianists (Margum   1978). Vols.I and II.
Suite for Piano (Margum) 14 min. Imaginative contemporary writing that
    includes a fugue and a passacaglia. M-D.

RAYMOND WILDING-WHITE (1922–   ) USA, born England
Wilding-White is a graduate of the New England Conservatory and Boston

University. He also spent three years studying chemical engineering at MIT and two more years at the Radio Research Laboratories (airborne radar) at Harvard University. This background comes through in his writing. He has written a number of theater pieces that involve the piano but are not basically piano pieces: e.g., *The Children's Corner,* for any number of keyboard instruments and special electric cueing systems. Wilding-White's manuscripts are available from the composer, c/o Dept. of Music, De Paul University, 25 East Jackson Blvd., Chicago, IL 60604, where he teaches and also directs LOOP GROUP, a multimedia performing ensemble.

Character Sketches—Study Pieces (Galaxy) in collection *Piano Music for the Young,* Book 2. Jacques Tati; Inspector Lestrade; Miss Prism; Truman Capote; Leonide Massine; Uriah Heep; Cesar Romero; Erik von Stroheim; Nobody at All; Stuart Little; Mack Sennett. Clever characterizations. Int.

Monte Carlo Suite II (MS). 48 short preludes for piano. The title refers to the Monte Carlo Technique for obtaining random numbers from a computer. The pieces may be played in any sequence. Most of the pieces are five–ten measures in length. Int. to M-D.

Piano Sonata 1950 (MS) 10 min. Dedicated to Irwin Freundlich. Allegretto; Andante con moto; Schrtzo [*sic*] Allegretto; Allegro vivace. Neoclassical orientation. M-D.

Whatzit III for Nancy Voigt 1968 (MS) for piano with two prerecorded parts, or three pianos. Forearm clusters, aleatoric. Timpani mallets to be struck on bottom of piano, flat of hand on strings, table kife [*sic*] bounced on strings, wire brush on strings, hands tapped. Some directions given. D.

Whatzit V 1969 (MS) for piano with two prerecorded parts. Requires a small bell and brass wind chimes. Clusters; durations of sounds not exactly alike; careful synchronization of prerecorded parts absolutely necessary. M-D.

HEALEY WILLAN (1880–1968) Canada, born Great Britain

3 Character Sketches of Old London (F. Harris). The Policeman. The Flower Girl. The Whistling Errand Boy. Int.

Peter's Book (F. Harris 1936) 14pp. Written for the composer's son. Peter's Tune. Peter's Donkey "Jenny." Peter Learns His Five-Finger Exercises. Peter Enjoys a Swing. Peter Goes Riding. Peter's Musical Box. Peter Goes to Sleep. MC. Easy.

RALPH VAUGHAN WILLIAMS (1872–1958) Great Britain

Piano Concerto (OUP). Original version for one piano dates from 1933. Joseph Cooper, in collaboration with the composer, made a two-piano version in 1946. This score includes both versions. Toccata: animated. Romanza: lyric. Fuga chromatica con finale alla Tedesca: chromatic; Romantic; cadenza precedes Tedesca. M-D.

Fantasia on "Greensleeves"   1936 (OUP). Adapted from the opera *Sir John in Love,* arranged by the composer. M-D.

MALCOLM WILLIAMSON (1931–   ) Great Britain
The Bridge that Van Gogh Painted (EBM   1976). Nine moods of southern France inspired by impressions of the French Camargue region, where Van Gogh frequently worked. Impressionistic; MC sonorities; descriptions add interest to the imaginative titles. Int.
Haifa Watercolors (EBM). Ten short descriptive pieces with playing and technical suggestions. Composer gives notes about each piece. Well fingered. Int.
Piano Impressions of New York (EBM). Six descriptive pieces. Part of the series Travel Diaries. Int.
5 Preludes (Bo&H). Ships; Towers; Domes; Theaters; Temples.
Sonata No.2   1958 (Weinberger) 20pp. Rev. 1970–71. 16 min. Quasi lento; Poco Adagio; Allegro assai. Contrasting movements. Severe, deeply expressive, dark coloration, intense. A work of major proportions; large span required. D.

RICHARD WILSON (1941–   ) USA
Wilson is a member of the music faculty of Vassar College.
Eclogue   1974 (Bo&H) 12 min. Won first prize in a competition devoted exclusively to unpublished piano music by composers from North America (1978). "Unpredictable in a stimulating way, its form emerges clearly and convincingly as the work progresses; the use of keyboard timbres is extraordinary throughout; the dramatic impact is unusually strong. . . . it is a very difficult piece requiring agility, power, and subtlety. I would compare its demands to those of Ravel's *Gaspard de la nuit*" (David Burge, "Contemporary Piano—Composition Contest Winner," CK, 5 [January 1979]). The contest and composition are discussed further in this article.

ROBERT BARCLAY WILSON (1913–   ) Great Britain
Sonata (Cramer). The first movement is restless. The second, Interlude, is slow and expressive with poignant dissonances. The finale, an Allegro giocoso in rondo form, pulls together the previous thematic ideas. M-D.

THOMAS WILSON (1927–   ) Great Britain, born USA
Piano Sonata   1959, rev. 1964 (S&B) 14pp. 20 min. Reproduction of composer's score. Two movements: Adagio introduction leads to a taut Allegro, which is a set of variations on a free ground-bass. D.
Sonatina   1954 (Chappell) 10 min.

PHILIP WINSOR (1938–   ) USA
Schema (CF   1977) 5 leaves. Facsimile edition. Chance composition. Performance instructions.

DAG WIRÉN (1905–) Sweden
Liten pianosvit Op.43 (GM 1971).

BRUCE WISE (1929–) USA
Wise is a member of the music faculty at the University of Wisconsin, Oshkosh.
Four Piano Pieces (Hinson—Hinshaw 1978) in collection *Twelve by Eleven*. The pieces use a four-note motive as the basis of the work: G, F♯, E, and F. Each piece has its own tempo and mood as well as its own treatment of the basic musical idea. As the music unfolds, a twelve-tone series is arrived at in the fourth piece. Every voice participates in the texture of these short and pointillistically conceived pieces. M-D.

JOSEPH WOELFL (1773–1812) Austria
In his day Woelfl was one of Europe's most acclaimed musicians. As a concert pianist he was a rival of Beethoven. All three sonatas listed below are enjoyable and well worth performing, and have real charm and personality.
Sonata Op.25 c (W. Newman—UNC) in collection *Thirteen Keyboard Sonatas of the 18th and 19th Centuries*. Similar to Mozart's K.475 and Beethoven's Op.13 in that it opens with an Introduction. Includes a four-voice fugue. M-D.
Sonata Op.33/2 d (LC). Juxtaposition of lyric and dramatic seem to be presaging Schubert. Keyboard figuration also suggests Schubert. M-D.
Sonata Op.33/3 E (LC). Color, finesse of style, and lyricism are a part of the success of this piece. M-D.
See: SCE, 562–64.

HUGO WOLF (1860–1903) Austria
Klavierkompositionen (Hans Jancik—Musikwissenschaftlicher Verlag 1974, through AMP). Sämtliche Werke, Vol.18. v + 143pp. Critical Edition. Published by the International Hugo Wolf-Gesellschaft. Preface in German and English, critical notes in German. Variationen Op.2 1875: Viennese classic influence here and in Op.8. Sonate G Op.8 1876: last leaf is lost. Rondo capriccioso Op.15 1876: Mendelssohn influence. Humoreske 1877: Schumannesque. *Aus der Kinderzeit:* Schlummerlied 1878, Scherz und Spiel 1878. Paraphrase über *Die Meistersinger von Nürnberg* ca.1880. Paraphrase über *Die Walküre* ca.1880. Albumblatt 1880. Kanon 1882. Contains all of Wolf's complete piano works, which are mainly early pieces and provided the distillation necessary to arrive at Wolf's lied style.

ERMANNO WOLF-FERRARI (1876–1948) Italy
Impromptus Op.13 (Elite Ed.3458/D Rahter). 1: D♭, Andante, suave melody. 2: B♭, Romantic, much rubato required, chordal. 3: F♯, impassioned, interval of sixth exploited. Some pedalling included. M-D.

Three Piano Pieces Op.14 (Elite Ed.3459/D Rahter). Melodie: f♯, left hand accompanies sweeping, decorated melody. Capriccio: b♭, scherzo section requires nimble fingers and control of leaps. Romanze: E, cantabile style, requires careful pedalling. M-D.

CHRISTIAN WOLFF (1934–   ) USA, born France
Accompaniments (CFP 66318).
Bread and Roses (CFP 66751) 5pp. Reproduced from MS. Based on the 1912 work song.
For Pianist (CFP 6496 1965) 2pp., 9 leaves. Reproduced from MS. Chance composition. Includes instructions for performance.
For Piano II (CFP 6498 1967) 8pp.
Suite I (CFP 6500) for prepared piano.
Tilbury 2 and 3 (CFP).

DARWIN WOLFORD (1936–   ) USA
Wolford studied composition with Ned Rorem and John La Montaine, and did his doctoral work at the University of Utah. He is professor of music at Ricks College, Rexford, ID.
Suite à la mode (Bo&H 1976) 19pp. Fourteen fresh and original-sounding pieces that demonstrate the various modes. Interesting titles include: Witches' Hoedown; To an African Violet; To and Fro; Fanfare for Trumpets and Tuba; Shindig. Int.

STEFAN WOLPE (1902–1972) Germany
Form 1959 (Tonos).
See: Martin Brody, "Sensibility Defined: Set Projection in Stefan Wolpe's *Form* for Piano," PNM, 15 (Spring–Summer 1977):3–22.
Form IV: Broken Sequences 1969 (CFP). Compact, great structural continuity. Opening chord in quarter notes A♭–F–B♭–A–G–E provides basis of the work. Many augmentations and diminutions. D.
Four Studies on Basic Rows 1935–36 (Merion 1974) 76pp. Study of Tritones. Study of Thirds. Presto Furioso: expanding and contrasting intervals. Passacaglia: highly complex study on all-interval row in conjunction with eleven basic rows. Almost a tone-row textbook. Pieces are probably better played separately or in sets of two. Complex and difficult writing, but overall structural drama, exciting pacing, and inherent sense of sonorities are always present. D.

HUGH WOOD (1932–   ) Great Britain
Wood worked in composition with Lloyd Webber, Iain Hamilton, Anthony Milner, and Matyas Seiber. Since 1971 he has been a lecturer at the University of Liverpool.
Variations revised 1959 (UE) 12 min.
3 Piano Pieces 1960–63 (UE) 10 min.
See: Leo Black, "The Music of Hugh Wood," MT, 1572 (February 1974): 115–17.

WILLIAM B. WORDSWORTH (1908–   ) Great Britain
Sonata Op.13 d   1946 (Lengnick) 25½ min.
Cheesecombe Suite Op.27   1948 (Lengnick) 14 min. Prelude. Scherzo.
Nocturne. Fughetta.
Ballade Op.41   1949 (Lengnick) 5 min.
Children's Pieces (A. Rowley—Lengnick   1952). Eight pieces.

WLADIMIR WORONOFF (1903–   ) Belgium
Sonnet pour Dallapiccola (NME   April 1950) 10pp. In four sections
with subdivisions. Serial; notes marked with an asterisk form the
bell motif from *Parsifal;* flexible meters. D.

JOHANN HUGO WORŽISCHEK (Voříšek) (1791–1825) Bohemia
Selected Pieces of Piano Music (Dana Zahn—Henle 278). Based on the
earliest sources, critical edition. Excellent preface. Contains: Im-
promptu B♭; 6 Impromptus Op.7; Fantaisie Op.12; 6 Variations Op.
19; Sonata Quasi una Fantasia Op.20. Appendix: Adagio b♭, which
in the autograph was between the first and second movements of
Sonata Op.20. A valuable anthology of a most interesting composer.
M-D.
See: Ates Orga, "Schubert's Bohemian Contemporary," M&M 21
(February 1973):30–40. Outlines Woržischek's career; Rondo C,
Op.18, given on pp.42–45.
Six Impromptus Op.7 (Artia). No.4 especially demonstrates an original
style. M-D.
Fantasy Op.12 (Artia). Vol.20 in MAB. Follows the first edition. One
of Woržischek's most impressive works. M-D.

BOLESLAW WOYTOWICZ (1899–   ) Poland
Twelve Studies (PWM   1948). Book I: Nos.1–6. Book II: Nos.7–12.
Musical content closely connected with various technical problems. D.

GERHARD WUENSCH (1925–   ) Canada, born Germany
A Merry Suite for Harpsichord or Piano Op.26   1972 (Waterloo) 11pp.
6½ min. Preludio. Invenzione. Menuetto. Gavotta. Giga. Postludio.
Neoclassic style, more effective on harpsichord. Int. to M-D.
A Winter Foursome Op.39   1972 (Waterloo) 7pp. 3 min. Frosted Win-
dows: slow, chordal, atmospheric. Walking on Ice: "very carefully—
oops . . . not again." Icycles: thin textures, high register, long pedal
at end. Blizzard: chromatic, furioso, tremolo, driving rhythms. First
three pieces are Int.; Blizzard is M-D.
12 Glimpses into 20th Century Idioms (MCA). Twelve short pieces, each
demonstrating a different contemporary technique with an explanation of the devices used. Int.
Six Little Etudes   1969 (Waterloo) 15pp. An introduction to technical
and musical problems encountered in contemporary music: Four

against Three. Study in Rhythm. For Passing the Thumb. Alternating Fingers. For Divided Passages. Pastorale. Int.

Mini Suite I (MCA).

Spectrum (MCA).

Sonatina   1977 (CMC).

CHARLES WUORINEN (1938–   ) USA

Wuorinen is a recognized innovator whose works provide constantly fascinating sound experiences. He represents all that is avant-garde: distinctive individualism, atonalism, and electronics, while seeking to generate the most musical material, values, and traditions as he works.

Sonata   1969 (CFP) 41pp. 20 min. In two large parts. Highly complex and only for the most adventurous pianist, uncompromisingly abstract. Based on eleven intervals in a series. Each section is twice subdivided by the same intervals. Dense textures, opening rhythmic figuration appears at end of piece to be performed "out of time." A major work that does not easily give up its secrets. D.

Second Piano Sonata   1976 (CFP   1979). This work is a Triple Discourse, containing a Prelude, three movements intermixed, a Pause, the same resumed, and the whole completed with a Postlude. D.

WALTER WURZBURGER (–   ) Germany

Klavierstück (Thames   1973) 13pp.

YEHUDI WYNER (1929–   ) USA, born Canada

Partita   1952 (AMP   1976) 24pp. Overture; Aria; Allemande; Minuet; Gigue. Derivative but highly successful neo-Bachian writing. The suite is infused with charm, grandeur, and lyric beauty. M-D.

Three Short Fantasies   1963, 1966, 1971 (AMP   1973) 11pp. 6 min. Serial, contrasted, highly melodic, much repetition, ostinato-like motives, improvisatory, successful miniatures. To be played together. Large span required. D.

IVAN WYSHNEGRADSKY (1893–   ) USSR

Deux Préludes Op.2   1917 (Belaieff) 3½ min. Strong Tchaikowsky influence. M-D.

Etude sur le Carré magique sonore Op.40   1956 (Belaieff) 9 min. Based on ultrachromatic scales (quarter-tones, sixth-tones, etc.). The principle of nonoctavian spaces (a system of control over the extremes of ultrachromaticism as well as sixth and twelfth tones) is at work in this piece. D.

JÜRG WYTTENBACH (1935–   ) Switzerland

Drei Klavierstücke (Ars Viva   1969) 7pp. Short pieces. Directions (in German) explain notation. Harmonics, strings stroked with a wooden hammer. Avant-garde. M-D.

X

IANNIS XENAKIS (1922–   ) Greece, born Rumania; now residing in France

Herma—"Musique symbolique" 1960–61 (Bo&H). The rhythm is stochastic: that is, the notation is only an approximation. A dazzling diffusion of notes. D.

Evryali 1971 (Sal) 28pp. Literal accuracy is almost impossible because of the required speed. Notes are scattered all over the keyboard. Super-Lisztian virtuosity and an acrobatic performer are required. When "brought off," there will be plenty of dazzled listeners; otherwise it could sound like a lot of primitive banging. Contains a dense, rapid-fire series of chord combinations. The rhythm is deterministic, the evenness of attacks being the decisive factor to achieve the continuity. Extravagantly difficult.

See: Peter Hill, "Xenakis and the Performer," *Tempo,* 112 (March 1975): 12–22. Contains helpful discussions of both *Herma* and *Evryali*.

Y

TADASI YAMANOUCHI (1935–   ) Japan
Yamanouchi is a graduate of Tokyo University.
Métamorphose   1971 (Japan Federation of Composers) 15pp. Moderato:
presents main idea and its development in two parts. Andante: continued harmonic development of main ideas, ternary form. Presto:
melodic development of main ideas, sonata-rondo form. Same thematic material varied throughout piece, contemporary treatment.
M-D.

RICHARD YARDUMIAN (1917–   ) USA
Danse (EV). 3½ min.
Songs and Dances from "Armenian Suite" (EV) 8 min. Arranged by
John Ogdon.

AKIO YASHIRO (1929–1977) Japan
Yashiro was one of the most brilliant young Japanese composers.
Sonate   1960 (Ongaku No Tomo Sha) 25pp. 17 min. Agitato: numerous
slow–fast tempo changes. Toccata: fast alternation of hands, pointillistic, octaves and repeated chords. Thème et Variations: chordal
chromatic theme, large climax, subsides, closes *ppp*. D.

YIP WAI HONG (1931–   ) China
Yip studied at Yen-Ching University and the Peking Central Conservatory.
He is a graduate of the School of Church Music of the Southern Baptist
Theological Seminary, and is head of the Music and Fine Arts De-
partment of Hong Kong Baptist College and director of the Hong Kong
Children's Choir.
Memories of Childhood (printed score available from composer, c/o Hong
Kong Baptist College, 224 Waterloo Road, Kowloon, Hong Kong)
13pp. A suite of six movements: Morning Haze; Having Fun; The
Voice of Old Grandmother; Dance of the Puppets; Afternoon Nap;
Picnicking. Impressionistic expressivity, clever, contrasting, some
pentatonic influence, MC. Requires subtleties. Int.

JOJI YUASA (1929–   ) Japan
On the Keyboard. Projection Topologic. Cosmos Haptic (Ongaku No
Tomo Sha   1973) 26pp. Bound in one volume. Strongly avant-garde
throughout. Requires virtuoso technique and an inquiring mind. D.

ISANG YUN (1917–   ) Germany, born Korea

Yun studied at the Paris Conservatory and with Boris Blacher and Josef Rufer in Berlin. He now lives in Berlin.

Fünf Stücke   1958 (Bo&Bo). Displays strong Schönberg and Berg influence; fluctuating meters; extreme ranges exploited. D.

See: David Burge, "Contemporary Piano—Oriental Composers," CK, 4 (December 1978):60.

AKIRA YUYAMA (1932–   ) Japan

Children's Land (Ongaku No Tomo Sha 1967) 46pp. Twenty pieces for small hands, no octaves. Provides a good introduction to contemporary piano sonorities. Int.

Sunday Sonatina   1969 (Ongaku No Tomo Sha) 55pp. Consists of a Prelude and a series of sonatinas from Sunday to Saturday. Saturday Sonatina is the most difficult. Linking each piece with a day of the week has no special meaning. Bitonal, alternating hands, freely tonal, Impressionistic sonorities. Each sonatina contains two or three movements. Int. to M-D.

Z

HAROLD ZABRACK (1929–   ) USA

Cathedral Bells (MS available from composer, 155 West 68 St., New York, NY 10023) 2pp. A contemporary "Prelude in c♯ minor." Colorful, effective, harmonics at conclusion. M-D.

Dreaming (MS available from composer) 2pp. A gentle rocking melody is accompanied by quartal harmonies (solid or broken), MC. Int. to M-D.

Eight Piano Contours (Kenyon 1978). M-D to D.

Scherzo (MS available from composer) 4pp. Neoclassic; contains a number of starts and stops; chords accompany a perky melody; subtle pedal sonorities. M-D.

Sonata I 1965 (Kenyon 1978). Allegro con brio: percussive, virtuosic. Adagio espressivo: atonal, calm. Interlude. Finale: impetuous, changing tempi, atonal, brilliant closing. A bravura work of demanding proportions. D.

Song without Words (MS available from composer) 2pp. Expressive cantilena, Alberti bass, lovely, MC. Int.

The Orchestra (MS available from composer) 1p. Marchlike. Various orchestral instruments imitated, contrasting registers, clever. Int.

Toccata (MS available from composer) 9pp. Notes and chords in alternating hands, motoric. First two lines accelerate to Tempo I, freely tonal, extremes of registers exploited, brilliant conclusion. Highly effective with the proper virtuoso technique. D.

All these pieces are beautifully conceived for the piano.

LUIGI ZANINELLI (1932–   ) USA

Fantasia (EV 1973) 9pp. Brilliant writing, requires first-rate pianist to bring it off. Toccatalike passages contrasted with freer, recitative-like sections, freely tonal. M-D.

JULIUSZ ZAREBSKI (1854–1885) Poland

Album per pianoforte (Zbigniew Drzewiecki—PWM 1974) 104pp. Selections from Zarebski's piano works, Opp.3, 6, 13, 14, 16, 25, 27. Epilogue in Polish and English by Stanislaw Haraschin. Illustrations, portrait, five facsimiles. Musical ideas not strong; recalls style of Moszkowski and Scharwenka. *Suite Polonaise,* Op.16, consisting of five Polish dances, is the finest work. Brilliant pianistic virtuosity required. M-D.

JULIEN-FRANÇOIS ZBINDEN (1917–   ) Switzerland
Suite Brève C Op.1   1937 (Hug; Foetisch   1976).

RUTH ZECHLIN (1926–   ) Germany
Zechlin teaches at the Academy of Art in Berlin. She has studied with Karl Straube, Günther Ramin, and Johann N. David.
Kontrapunkte 1969–70 (Deutscher Verlag) 8pp. For harpsichord or piano. Biographic note in German. Consists of a preludium, four inventions (mainly two-part), and postludium. Hindemith influence. M-D.

ERIC ZEISL (1905–1959) USA, born Austria
Pieces for Barbara (Dob 01374).

ISTVÁN ZELENKA (1936–   ) Hungary
Sonatine (Edition Modern   1961) 5 min.

ALEXANDER VON ZEMLINSKY (1872–1942) Austria
Zemlinsky was Arnold Schönberg's teacher, and his sister married Schönberg.
Fantasien Op.9 (Dob). Actually four "songs without words" inspired by texts by Dehmel. Written in the German Romantic character-piece tradition (Richard Strauss, Franz Schreker), they are rewarding to perform. M-D.

BERND-ALOIS ZIMMERMANN (1918–1970) Germany
Extemporale 1943 (Gerig   1950) 16pp. Sarabande: quiet, chordal. Invention: quick, two-part. Siciliano: contrasted character, sweet with harsh. Bolero: mostly left-hand rhythmic figuration. Finale: gains in intensity to closing heavy chords. Large span required. D.
Capriccio (Schwann   1947). Improvisations on folk songs and nursery rhymes.

DOMENICO ZIPOLI (1688–1726) Italy
Pieces Op.1 (Farrenc—Leduc). Book I: Toccata, 9 Versos, 2 Canzonas. Book II: Suite b: Preludio, Corrente, Aria, Gavotte; Suite g: Preludio, Corrente, Sarabande, Giga; Suite C: Preludio, Sarabanda, Gavotta. M-D.
Toccata (A. Ginastera—Bo&H). The editor has "re-created" this work. Zipoli, who died in Argentina, "was the first composer to visit our country and link us both materially and spiritually with Europe" (from the score, by Ginastera). M-D.
See: Susan E. Erickson-Bloch, "The Keyboard Music of Domenico Zipoli (1688–1726)," PhD. diss., Cornell University, 1975, 303pp.

FRIEDRICH ZIPP (1914–   ) Germany
Sonatina (HV).
Zwei Intermezzi (HV).

Variationen über "Knecht Ruprecht aus dem Walde" von Cesar Bresgen (Heinrichshofen 3306).

FELIX ZRNO (1890–   ) Czechoslovakia
Balada ve formě variaci 1958 (Panton 1975) 22pp.

BOGUSLAW ZUBRZYCKI (1929–   ) Poland
Szkice (Sketches) 1974 (PWM) 14pp. Explanations in Polish.

WAWRZYNIEC ZULAWSKI (1916–1957) Poland
Sonatina 1954 (PWM 1970) 13pp. Allegro; Andante molto cantabile; Allegretto mosso; Allegro. Neoclassic, MC in a freely tonal style, thin textures except in third movement. Int. to M-D.

RAMON ZUPKO (1932–   ) USA
Zupko is director of the Laboratory for Experimental and Electronic Music at Western Michigan University, Kalamazoo, MI 49001.
Emulations 1969 for piano and tape (MS and tape available from composer) 15pp. 12 min. Includes performance directions and attack positions. Metal beater, wood block, flat stick, brush, etc., required to play on strings. The tape is stopped for two improvisations and restarted at the pianist's cue. Pointillistic, long pedals, clusters, proportional notation. Avant-garde. D.
Winter '64 (MS available from composer) 13pp. 10 min. Performance directions. Clusters reduced and added to by chromatic subtraction and addition. Harmonics, proportional notation, pointillistic. Simultaneous contrary-motion black- and white-key glissandi. Avant-garde. D.

Part II

Anthologies
and Collections

Anthologies and collections are listed alphabetically by title. Initial articles and Arabic numerals (e.g., *A, An, Das, Der, I, Le, Les, The, 15, 24, 30*) are ignored in alphabetization.

Album I (Metropolis E.M. 4269) 15pp. Contemporary Belgian Music. Richard de Guide: Nocturne. Louis de Meester: Toccata. R. Van der Velden: Andante espressivo. Willem Pelemans: Allegro flamenco. All pieces require well-developed technique. M-D to D.

An Album of Spanish Composers (K). Includes: Albeniz: Triana and Fête-Dieu à Seville, from *Iberia;* Suite Española (Granada, Cataluna, Sevilla, Cadiz, Asturias). Granados: Spanish Dances 1–6, 10. Turina: Coins de Seville (No.I). M-D.

The America Book for Piano (William Deguire—Galaxy 1975). Contains original piano compositions, vocal and choral works transcribed for piano, and well-known tunes of traditional music freely arranged for piano by the editor. Solo piano works include: Benjamin Carr, Sonata I (from *A New Assistant for the Pianoforte or Harpsichord,* 1796). Philip Phile: The President's March. Raynor Taylor: The Subject from "Adeste Fidelis." William Mason: Lullaby Op.10 (1857). Stephen Foster: Soiree Polka (1850). John Knowles Paine: The Shepherd's Lament Op.26/4 (1875). George Chadwick: The Cricket and the Bumble Bee (1903). Arthur Foote: Prelude e Op.52/ 10 (1903). Amy Beach: Waltz Op.36/3 (1897). W. Iucho: The Arkansas Traveller (1879). Ethelbert Nevin: Narcissus Op.13/4 (1891). Edward MacDowell: To a Wild Rose Op.51/1 (1896). Harvey W. Loomis: Prayer to Wakonda; Offering of the Sacred Pipe Op.76, Book 2, No.1 (1904). Int. to M-D.

American Composers of the Twentieth Century (Schaum Publications 1969). Twelve compositions in their original form: Samuel Barber: Love Song. Cecil Burleigh: Mazurka. Abram Chasins: Prelude c. Zez Confrey: After Theater Tango. James Francis Cooke: Twilight at Carcassonne. James P. Dunn: Bewitched. Howard Hanson: Impromptu. Edward B. Hill: March of the Mountains. Alan Hovhaness: Fire Dance. Henry H. Huss: Gipsy Dance. A. Walter Kramer: Silhouette. Nicolas Slonimsky: Dreams and Drums. Int.

American Sonatinas (Schaum Publications 1963) 31pp. Six original sonatinas by six American composers. Edward Holst (1843–1899): Pilgrim Sonatina. Hans Engelmann (1872–1914): Colonial Sonatina Op.372/12. Frank Lynes (1858–1914): Spirit of '76 Sonatina Op. 39/1. Frank Addison Porter (1859–1911): New England Sonatina. William Dawson Armstrong (1868–1936): Rustic Sonatina. Frederick N. Shackley (1868–1937): Spinning Wheel Sonatina. Also contains brief information on the background of each composer. Int.

Anthology of Early American Keyboard Music 1787–1830 (J. Bunker Clark—A-R Editions   1977) 2 vols. Vol.I: William Brown: Rondo III. Benjamin Carr: The Siege of Tripoli, an Historical Naval Sonata; Sonata VI; Voluntary for the Organ; The Maid of Lodi with Variations. Charles Gilfert: Ah! What is the Bosom's Commotion with Variations. James Hewitt: The New Federal Overture; Sonatina III; Theme with 30 Variations; Yankee Doodle with Variations; Trip to Nahant. T. L. Holden: The Copenhagen Waltz. John Christopher Moller: Meddley; Rondo. Eliza Crawly Murden: March. Mr. Newman: Sonata III. Stephen Sicard: The President of the United States' March. Vol.II: Arthur Clifton: An Original Air with Variations. Frederick A. Getze: Saxon Rondo. James F. Hance: 2d Grand Fantasie. Anthony Philip Heinrich: The Debarkation March; Toccatina Capriciosa. Charles F. Hupfield: A Favorite Waltz with Variations. Francis Johnson: Honour to the Brave; Johnson's New Cotillions. Christopher Meineke: Divertimento; Variations to the favourite air Au clair de la lune. Julius Metz: Petit Pot Pourri. Peter K. Moran: A Fantasia; Moran's Favorite Variations to the Suabian Air. Oliver Shaw: Welcome the Nation's Guest. William Taylor: Clinton's Triumph. Charles Thibault: L'Adieu à Rondo. Charles Zeuner: Grand Centennial March. Contains a most helpful preface, biographical notes on each composer, and sometimes a discussion of the pieces. Int. to M-D.

Aus Alten Spielbüchern (Anna Speckner—Schott). 32 pieces and dances from the sixteenth and seventeenth centuries for keyboard instruments. More than half the pieces are by English composers. Provides a fine introduction to harpsichord playing. Clean editing, suggested registration. Int. to M-D.

The Baroque Era—An Introduction to the Keyboard Music (W. Palmer and M. Halford—Alfred   1976) 64pp. Foreword discusses such subjects as the Baroque era, ornamentation, free ornamentation, "good taste," the theory of affects, pedaling, keyboard instruments of the Baroque era, and time signatures. Pieces from the Italian Baroque include works by Salvator Rosa, A. Scarlatti, Pasquini, and D. Scarlatti; from the English Baroque, works by John Blow, Henry Purcell, and Jeremiah Clark; from the French Baroque, works by L. Couperin, Chambonnières (and a section on inequality), Rameau, M. Corrette, and F. Couperin; from the German Baroque, works by Pachelbel, Telemann, Böhm, Handel, and J. S. Bach. A fine compendium with much useful information. Easy to Int.

Beethoven and His Circle: An Anthology of Music by Beethoven and His Contemporaries (Ernest Lubin—Amsco Music   1974) 160pp. Annotations by the compiler. Bibliography. Contains: C. G. Neefe: Sonata XI. Beethoven: Sonatina f, first movement; German Song and

Romanza from the *Ritterballett;* Variations on a theme by Count Waldstein; 10 Variations on the theme "La stessa, la stessissima," from the opera *Falstaff* by Salieri (for piano duet); Largo from Sonata E♭ Op.7. D. Steibelt: Romance from Sonata G. L. Cherubini: Overture from *The Water Carrier* (for piano duet). J. Wölfl: Introduction and Allegro c. J. N. Hummel: Un scherzo all'antico from Sonata D Op.106. Beethoven: Sonata Op.54, first movement. C. Czerny: Toccata C Op. 92. Variations on Diabelli, Waltz C, by Hummel, Moscheles, Schubert, Liszt. Beethoven: Variations on a theme by Diabelli (excerpts); Bagatelles, Op.126. Int. to M-D.

The Bicentennial Collection of American Keyboard Music (Edward Gold—McAfee 1975). Covers the period from 1790 to 1900 and represents a wide variety of styles. Alexander Reinagle: La Chasse. James Hewitt: Yankee Doodle with Variations. Frederick Damish: President Adams Grand March and Quick Step. Anthony P. Heinrich: The Maiden's Dirge. Charles Grobe: Variations on My Old Kentucky Home Op. 385. Stephen C. Foster: Holiday Schottish. H. A. Wollenhaupt: Etude A♭ Op.22/1. Louis M. Gottschalk: The Dying Swan RO 76. Richard Hoffman: Chi-ci Pipi Nini (Cuban Dance). Frederick Brandeis: Still Life Op.85/2. George W. Chadwick: Caprice No.2. Edward MacDowell: A.D. 1620 Op.55/3; Starlight Op.55/4. Ethelbert Nevin: Alba (Dawn) Op.25/1. Harvey W. Loomis: Music of the Calument Op.76/1. Mrs. H. H. A. Beach: Schottish Legend Op.54/1. Scott Joplin: The Easy Winners. Arthur Farwell: Dawn Op.12. Also contains notes on the composers and the individual pieces. Int. to M-D.

The Bicentennial Collection of American Music Vol.I, 1698–1800 (Compiled by Elwyn A. Wienandt—Hope 1974) 240pp. William Brown: Rondo III G (1787). Alexander Reinagle: Federal March (1788). Raynor Taylor: An Easy and Familiar Lesson for Two Performers on One Piano Forte (1793?) consisting of a Menuetto, Gavotta and Fandango. Franz Kotzwara: The Battle of Prague (1793) (incomplete). Francis Linley: Two Selections (Tempo di Gavotta, Tempo di Minuetto) from *A New Assistant for the Piano-Forte* (1796), the first piano instruction book printed in America. James Hewitt: The Battle of Trenton (1798) (incomplete, 249 bars omitted). Commentary by the compiler. Int. to M-D.

The Birds in Piano Music (PWM 5564) 40pp. A collection of pieces that include the name of a bird in the title. F. Couperin: Le Rossignol en amour. L. C. Daquin: Le Coucou; L'Hirondelle. B. Pasquini: Toccata con lo Scherzo del Cuculo. J. P. Rameau: La Poule. A clever and interesting collection. Int. to M-D.

Bitonal Etudes by Contemporary Polish Composers (Z. Romaszkowa—PWM). This selection of etudes calls for advanced technique and a certain freedom of interpretation. M-D to D.

John Blow's Anthology (T. Dart—S&B). One of the last editions prepared by the late Thurston Dart. A discerning selection of keyboard music by the German masters Froberger, J. K. F. Fischer, and Strungk. It was copied by Blow around 1700 and concludes with his own magnificent Ground in e. M-D.

Blumen für Lenin—Zehn leichte Klavierstücke von Komponisten der Deutschen Demokratischen Republik (CFP   1972) 31pp. Works by: Ernst Hermann Meyer, Gerhard Rosenfeld, Gerhard Wohlgemuth, Siegfried Matthus, Kurt Schwaen, Andre Asriel, Karl Dietrich, Ruth Zechlin, Johannes Paul Thilman, Siegfried Köhler.

Butterflies Greet the Spring (Nguyen van Thuong—CFP P-5497). Sixteen Vietnamese airs and dances, arranged for piano by the editor. Easy to Int.

Celebri composizioni per pianoforte (Ric). Book I. A varied collection of favorite classics in chronological order ranging from Albinoni, Adagio g; D. Scarlatti, Sonata C, L.104; J. S. Bach, Jesu Joy; Paganini-Liszt, Capriccio E; to a little-known work by Giuseppe Martucci (1856–1909), Nocturne G♭ Op.70/1. Also contains short works by Haydn, Mozart, Schumann, Grieg, and Rachmaninoff. Int. to M-D. Book II. Works by Alberti, Beethoven, Casella, Chopin, Dvořák, Paradisi, Rameau, Rossini-Liszt, Scarlatti, Schubert, Schumann. M-D.

Chopin and His Circle (Ernest Lubin—Amsco   1975) 159pp. An anthology of music by Chopin and his contemporaries. A perspective of the time, with works by composers who influenced him and by composers Chopin influenced. Includes works by Chopin, J. Field, J. N. Hummel, J. Elsner, F. Liszt, S. Thalberg, H. Herz, F. Kalkbrenner, J. Kessler, R. Schumann, F. Mendelssohn, I. Moscheles, and A. Scriabin. Annotations by Lubin. Bibliography. Better editions of some of the pieces are available. Int. to D.

Classic Piano Rags (Dover   1973) selected and with an introduction by Rudi Blesh. 364pp. Contains 81 piano rags by Scott Joplin, James Scott, Joseph Francis Lamb (50 pieces by these three composers), Charles Hunter, Percy Wenrich, Thomas Turpin, Arthur Marshall, Artie Mathers, and several others. Provides a wide and diverse selection of rags from the earliest period of ragtime, when it was associated with folk songs and dance, to its later classical period. Contains the original covers on the sheet music. M-D.

The Classical Era—An Introduction to the Keyboard Music (Palmer—Alfred   1977) 64pp. A foreword covers subjects such as the classical era; classicism in architecture, art, and music; the new classical performer; and ornamentation. Includes works by W. A. Mozart: Two Minuets (with suggested ornamentation); Divertimento from Viennese Sonatina I. J. C. Bach: Minuetto from Sonata II in D. C. P. E. Bach: Arioso C from *Sonatas with Varied Reprises*. Domenico Alberti: Theme and Variations from Sonata F Op.1/7. G. C. Wagenseil: Sonatina C, Allegro. F. J. Haydn: Air; Sonata C, Moderato; Menuet;

Finale. M. Clementi: Sonatina D Op.36/6, Allegro con spirito. Beethoven: Bagatelle D Op.33/6; Sonata G Op.49/2, Allegro ma non
troppo. An excellent introduction to the period. Int.

Classics for the Young Pianist (Grace Lankford—GS). Two books of unusual and lesser-known pieces for young players. Book I: 26 pieces for
early grades. Works by J. S. Bach, Beethoven, Blow, Böhm, Corelli,
Eccles, Handel, Haydn, Loeillet, Leopold Mozart, W. A. Mozart,
Daniel Purcell, Henry Purcell, A. Scarlatti. Book II: 21 pieces for intermediate grades. Works by J. S. Bach, Beethoven, Exaudet, Handel,
Haydn, Hook, Hullmandel, Kirnberger, Kuhnau, Leo, Marais, Leopold Mozart, W. A. Mozart, Paradisi, A. Scarlatti, Türk, and an anonymous composer.

Clavecinistes Italiens des 17ᵉ et 18ᵉ siècles (Schott Frères 1953) 47pp.
Selected pieces collected and annotated by G. Piccioli. Works by
B. Galuppi, F. Gasparini, G. B. Grazioli, B. Marcello, G. B. Martini,
P. T. Paradisi, G. B. Pesetti, and G. Rutini. Int. to M-D.

Clavierbuch einer schwäbischen Herzogin 1697 (Kurt Herrmann—Schott
1942). A collection of short pieces: Arias, Gigues, Rondeaus, Men-
uetts, Bourrées, Marches, Sarabandes, Rigaudon. Fresh and little-
known works. Int.

Composer–Pianists (J. Schaum 1971) 32pp. Ten compositions in their
original form. Eugen d'Albert: Blues. Ossip Gabrilowitsch: Oriental
Melody. Walter Gieseking: Jazz Improvisation. Leopold Godowsky:
Meditation. Wanda Landowska: En Route. Gustav Mahler: I Walk
with Joy through the Green Forest. Tobias Matthay: Movement Musical. Emil Sauer: Petite Etude. Arthur Schnabel: Valse Mignonne. Alec
Templeton: Springtime in the Village. Contains some interesting and
unusual pieces. Int. to M-D.

Concert Etudes (Erno Balogh—GS 1972). 21 seldom-heard concert
etudes by composers from different countries. Composers represented
include: Blumenfield, Brahms, Dohnanyi, Goedicke, Henselt, Liadov,
MacDowell, Mendelssohn, Ponce, Prokofieff, Raff, Respighi, A. Rubinstein, Saint-Saëns, Schlözer, Schumann, Schütt, Scriabin, I. Stravinsky, Szymanowsky. Brief biographical information. All these pieces
merit more attention. D.

Concert Pieces by Soviet Composers (Valery Strukov—CFP 5738 1975)
80pp. Works by Aleksssandr Pirumov, Aleksssandr Baltin, Arno Babad-
zhanian, Jaan Rääts, Konstantin Sorokin, Merab Partskhaladze, Gen-
nan Okunev, Andrei Eshpai, and Vytautas Barkauskas.

Contemporary Composers (Schaum Publications 1976) 31pp. Twelve
compositions in their original form. Granville Bantock: Chanticleer.
Eric Coates: By the Sleepy Lagoon. Claude Debussy: Album Leaf.
Eugene Goossens: Tugboat. Arthur Honegger: Study in Cacophony.
John Ireland: Reapers' Dance. Leoš Janáček: Moravian Dances.
Zoltán Kodály: Furioso Op.3/5. Vladimir Rebikov: Dervish. Erik

Satie: Gymnopedie. Florent Schmitt: Petit Musique Op.33/8. Cyril Scott: Lento. Int. to M-D.

Contemporary Israeli Piano Music (Peter Gradenwitz—Gerig 1976). 2 vols. Preface and biographical notes in English and German. Contains works by Menahem Avidom, Paul Ben-Haim, Yehuda ben Cohen, Abraham Daus, Ram Da-Oz, Sergiu Shapira, Yoram Paporisz, Verdina Shlonsky, Habib Hassan Tourna, Erich Walter Sternberg, and Joachim Stutschewsky.

Contemporary Music and the Pianist (Alice Canady—Alfred 1974). Examples of some of the best contemporary music arranged in graded order. Includes a list of valuable source books and a graded list of other recommended contemporary music. It is as its subtitle claims, "A Guidebook of Resources and Materials." Some of the composers include Hindemith, Schönberg, Krenek, Dello Joio, Finney, La Montaine, and Helps. Six grading levels. Level 1 is not for a beginner, and level 6 would be material for an advanced high school student who had studied 8–10 years.

Contemporary Piano Repertoire (Hinson, Glover—Belwin-Mills 1971) Level 5. Bartók: Let's Dance; Peasant Dance; The Fox; Scaredy Cat! Gretchaninoff: Trumpets; Out for a Stroll; Secrets. Kabalevsky: Guessing Game; Happy Times; Miniature Waltz; Little Toccata. Rebikov: The Tin Soldier; Oriental; The Grumpy Bear. Also contains biographies aimed at their piano works. Int.

Contemporary Piano Repertoire (Hinson, Glover—Belwin-Mills 1971) Level 6. Khachaturian: Horseman's Gallop; Scampering. Prokofiev: Promenade; Fairy Tale. Shostakovitch: Gavotte; Waltz; Tricks. Stravinsky: Pastoral; In the Garden. Also contains biographies pertinent to these piano works. Int.

Contemporary Rumanian Piano Music (Alexandre Hrisanide—Gerig 1971). 2 vols. Techniques and styles range from late Romantic to avant-garde. Introduction and biographical sketches in English. Vol.I is easier than Vol.II. Vol.I: Ludovic Feldman (1893–   ): The Stubborn One; Catch as Catch Can. Vasile Spătărelu (1939–   ): Rubato. Nina Cassian (1930–   ): Scherzo. Nicolae Brânduş (1935–   ): Klavierstücke I. Anatol Vieru (1926–   ): The Chinese Bird; Taboo!; The Monkeys. Myriam Marbe (1931–   ): Allegro. Vasile Herman (1929–   ): Birds in the Meadow. Liviu Comes (1918–   ): Melopee. Sandu Albu (1897–   ): Valse pour Alice. Sigismund Toduţă (1908–   ): Trenia. Dan Constantinescu (1931–   ): Nocturne. Zoltán Aladar (1929–   ): Làhaut le sommet. Int. to M-D. Vol.II: Nicolae Coman (1936–   ): The Ancient Clock. Zeno Vancea (1900–   ): Fuga. Horaţiu Rădulescu (1942–   ): Cradle to Abysses. Ştefan Zorzor (1932–   ): Acuta. Iancu Dumitrescu (1942–   ): Diacronies II. Tudor

Ciortea (1903–   ): Weihnachtslied. Cornel Țăranu (1932–   ):
Dialogues II. Liviu Dandara (1933–   ): Structura I . . . Quasi preludio. Adrian Rațiu (1928–   ): Mónosonata I. Eugen Wendel
(1934–   ): Per pianoforte I. M-D.

Contemporary Swiss Piano Music (Charles Dobler—Gerig   1973). 2 vols.
In the introduction the editor gives a good background of the development of Swiss music, which did not develop any great individuality
until around 1800. A short biographical note is included on each composer. None of these pieces have been published before. Stylistically
they range from the Romantic to post-serial techniques. To some
extent they are arranged progressively according to degree of difficulty
and style. Vol.I: Willy Burkard (1900–1955): Intermezzo. Martin
Wendel (1925–   ): Lullaby. Peter Mieg (1906–   ): At Mont-
souris Park. Othmar Schoeck (1886–1957): Piano Piece. Henri Ga-
gnebin (1886–1960): The Two Gossips. Rudolph Ganz (1887–1972):
Three Rubes. Roger Vuataz (1898–   ): Question—Answer. Richard Sturzenegger (1905–   ): Hommage à Paul Sacher. Hugo
Pfister (1914–1969): Crystallisations. Raffaele d'Alessandro (1911–
1959): Vision III. Albert Moeschinger (1897–   ): Implacable.
Rudolf Kelterborn (1931–   ): The Little Mirror. Wladimir Vogel
(1896–   ): Loneliness Falling in Drops. Hans Eugen Frischknecht
(1939–   ): Music for Piano. Vol.II: Hermann Haller (1914–
    ): Intermezzo. Alban Roetschi (1922–   ): Lasolfation. Julien-
François Zbinden (1917–   ): Pianostinato. Frank Martin (1890–
1974): Rhythmical Study. Alfred Keller (1907–   ): Flageolett.
Edward Staempfli (1908–   ): Sonority Study. Robert Suter (1919–
    ): White and Black. Jacques Wildberger (1922–   ): Vision
Fugitive. Ernst Widmer (1927–   ): Rondo Mobile. Klaus Huber
(1924–   ): Ein Hauch von Unzeit II. Han Ulrich Lehmann (1937–
    ): Piano Piece. Int. to M-D.

Cream of the Crop (SB   1974) 64pp. Outstanding piano pieces in a century of publishing.

Anne Cromwell's Virginal Book   1638 (Transcribed and edited by Howard
Ferguson—OUP   1975). Anne Cromwell was the first cousin of
Oliver Cromwell, and this edition of her Virginal Book provides a revealing glimpse of the kind of keyboard music that was played in the
home during the second quarter of the seventeenth century. The collection, which consists of fifty short arrangements of songs, dances,
and masque music, is a personal anthology of enjoyable keyboard
pieces. It is an important link between *Parthenia* (1612) and *Musicks
Hand-Maide* (1663). Some chording and octaves. Int. to M-D.

Czechoslovak Album for the Young (CFP 9418). Forty easy, progressive
pieces by nineteenth-century and contemporary composers from Smetana, Dvořák, Fibich, Janáček, and Martinů to present-day writers

such as Sarauer, Batñy, and Schäfer. Many folk-dance rhythms, much lyricism, and varied moods. Contains a short note about each composer. Easy to Int.

Early German Piano Music (Fodor Akos—EMB 1974) 52pp. Works by C. P. E. Bach, J. C. Bach, J. C. F. Bach, W. F. Bach, G. Böhm, J. J. Froberger, K. H. Graun, J. P. Kirnberger, J. L. Krebs, C. G. Neefe, J. Pachelbel, J. F. Reichardt, C. F. Schale, G. P. Telemann, G. C. Wagenseil, E. W. Wolf. A collection of some unusual Baroque keyboard works. Int.

Easy American Piano Classics (Stuart Isacoff—Consolidated Music Publishers 1978) 80pp. Vol.76 in series Music for Millions. Rags, blues, early jazz, marches, dances, and modern music from the Revolutionary War to the present. Int. to M-D.

Easy Graded Old English Masters (J. Ching—K. Prowse) 32pp. Works by Anonymous, John Blow, William Croft, Henry Purcell, William Byrd, Daniel Purcell, Thomas Arne, John Bull, and Jeremiah Clarke. Highly edited but effective on the piano. Int.

Easy Graded Old French and Flemish Masters (J. Ching—K. Prowse) 31pp. L. C. Daquin: La mélodieuse. F. Dandrieu: L'Empressée; Les Fifres; Les Tourbillons. F. Couperin: Le Moucheron; Les Moissonneurs. G. H. Fiocco: La Légère. J. P. Loeillet: Gigue g. J. P. Lully: Courente e. D. Raick: Gavotte f. J. P. Rameau: Gavotte a; La Villageoise; Les Tendres Plaintes. Highly edited but effective on the piano. Int. to M-D.

Easy Russian Piano Music (Maisie Aldridge—OUP) Book I: fourteen appealing, short pieces based on folk tunes and dances. Book II: slightly more difficult; contains pieces by Russian composers not too familiar in the U.S.A., e.g., L. Vlasova, A. Baltin, L. Revutsky. Easy.

Eleven Variations on a Theme by Glinka (AMP 7729 1976) 24pp. The theme is Vanya's song from the opera *Ivan Susanin.* "This set of eleven variations on a theme from the opera *Ivan Susanin* are meant to be a musical homage to Michael Glinka, the father of Russian music, on the occasion of the one hundredth anniversary of his death in 1957. The first composer to do so was Dmitri Shostakovitch, who wrote three variations for this cycle. The contributions of Shostakovitch and the seven other musicians are a lasting tribute to a composer who, like Verdi, is beloved by all his countrymen for his patriotic fervor as well as his musical genius" (from the score). Other composers represented are Kabalevsky, Eugen Kapp, Vissarion Shebalin, Andrei Eshpai, Rodion Shchedrin, Georgi Sviridov, and Yuri Levitin. M-D.

Encores of Great Pianists (Raymond Lewenthal—GS). 34 pieces by 27 well-known composers that have been used as encores by some of the greatest pianists from the past. An essay on the art of the encore and notes about each piece and who has performed it make this a most interesting collection. Beethoven: Polonaise Op.89; Ecossaises. Boro-

din: Scherzo. Busoni: Turandots Frauengemach ("Greensleeves").
Chaminade: Autrefois Op.87/4. Clementi: Finale from Sonata B♭
Op.47/2. Czerny: Etude A♭ Op.740/33. Delibes: Passepied from *Le
Roi l'a dit;* Pizzicato (Pizzicato Polka from *Sylvia*) (Joseffy). Godow-
sky: Alt Wien. Granados: Quejas ó la Maja y el Ruiseñor ("Laments,
or the Maiden and the Nightingale" from *Goyescas*). Grieg: An der
Wiege ("By the Cradle"). Guion: Turkey in the Straw. Leschetizky:
Arabesque en forme d'Etude Op.45/1. Levitski: Arabesque valsante
Op.6. Lewenthal: Toccata alla Scarlatti. Liszt: Valse Oubliée No.1.
Medtner: Fairy Tale Op.34/2. Mendelssohn: The Joyous Peasant
Op.102/5. Moszkowski: The Juggleress Op.52/4; Etude F Op.72/6.
Mozart: Serenade from *Don Giovanni* (Busoni). Philipp: Feux-Follets
("Jack o'Lanterns") Op.23/4. Prokofieff: March from *The Love of
Three Oranges*. Raff: La Fileuse ("The Spinner"). Schumann: Nacht-
stück Op.23/4; Romance Op.28/2; Contrabandista ("The Smug-
gler") (Tausig); Widmung ("Dedication") (Liszt). Shostakovitch:
Polka from the ballet *L'Age d'or*. Smetana: Polka Op.7. Weber:
Momento capriccioso Op.12. Most of the music is showy and difficult
but highly effective. Int. to D.

English Pastime Music, 1630–1660 (Martha Maas—A-R Editions 1974)
138pp. 109 small, unpretentious settings of songs and dances. The
harmonizations in this collection include melodies from the early editions of Playford's *The English Dancing Master* and from various song
books. Many of the pieces are known primarily from lute sources,
while others are found in a variety of arrangements including consort
versions and cittern pieces. This charming repertoire shows us some
of the music known to amateur keyboard players as well as to the
musicians who taught them and to the household musicians who provided music for social occasions. Int. to M-D.

English Piano Music for the Young Musician (György Balla—EMB) 49pp.
Contains one work from the Robertsbridge Codex, fourteen other short
anonymous pieces, and works by Hugh Ashton (Hornepype), J. Bar-
ret, Blow, Bull, Byrd, Clarke, Croft, Eccles, Giles Farnaby, Richard
Farnaby, Edmund Hooper, R. Johnson, Morley, Peerson, Daniel
Purcell, Henry Purcell, Tisdall. A few ornaments have been realized;
clean edition. Int. to M-D.

Etüden (Wolfgang Wendt—CFP 1971) Book I, 59pp. Book II, 55pp.
Pieces by various composers. Book I. Basic kinds of touch: portato,
legato, staccato. Book II. Portato, legato, and staccato in combinations. Introduction to other kinds of touch. M-D.

Favorite Sonatinas (W. Brendal, E. Fleishman—Thompson 1977). Special study edition with performance annotations and glossary. Clementi: Op.36/1, 2, 4. Kuhlau: Op.55/1, 2; Op.88/2. Int.

Five Eighteenth-Century Sonatas (Stoddard Lincoln—OUP 1975).
Johann Samuel Schroeter (ca.1752–1788), Sonata Op.1/1 C: three

movements; expressive slow movement; could almost have been written by J. C. Bach. Johann Jacob Paul Küffner (1727–1786), Sonata: two movements; displays refined taste and a gift for creating sensitive and subtle melodies. Leopold Anton Kozeluch (1747–1818), Sonata Op.2/3 c: slow, symphonic introduction returns at the end of the first movement; this is perhaps the finest work in the collection. Christian Ignatius Latrobe (1757–1836), Sonata Op.3/1 A: four movements; well constructed and charming. Jacob Kirkman (?–1812?), Sonata Op.3/3 E♭: two movements; fuses development and recapitulation in the main Allegro. (Kirkman's Op.3 is a collection of Six Lessons in an unusual arrangement of three neo-Handelian suites and three more modern sonatas in a true piano style.) These works, all dating from the 1780s, form a valuable addition to the repertoire of the early piano. They display characteristics of the English and Viennese styles. The increasing interest in the field is well served by illuminating comments on the music, its interpretation, and the types of instruments that were used. Sources are listed, and editorial marks are easily identified. An altogether fine collection of unknown and rarely heard music than can be most effectively realized on the fortepiano. M-D.

Four Piano Pieces (Price Milburn   1977) By New Zealand composers. Christopher Norton, Four-three: meter changes on almost every bar, lively. David Griffiths, Equation: chordal, carefully pedalled. Jack Speirs, Metamorphoses: strong contemporary writing, the most difficult of the four pieces. John M. Jennings, Abstract One: repeated notes, alternating quintal and quartal chords. M-D.

Four Pieces by Modern Polish Composers for Young Pianists (Compiled by Emma Altberg—PWM   1972) 31pp. Short compositions by Tadeusz Paciorkiewicz, Zofia Iszkowska, Feliks Radzkowski, and Hanna Skalska. Interesting pedagogic material. Easy to Int.

French Piano Music: An Anthology (I. Philipp—Dover   1977) 188pp. 44 short works from 1670 to 1906 representing 28 composers. Includes a wide range of compositions: courantes, passepieds, sarabandes, gigues, gavottes, preludes, minuets, waltzes, romances, scherzos, and caprices. Works of special interest include: Lully: Courante in e; F. Couperin: Les Papillons; Rameau: The Hen; Gossec: Gavotte; Saint-Saëns: Song without Words; Delibes: Passepied; Bizet: Le Retour; Massenet: Toccata; Fauré: Fourth Barcarolle; d'Indy: Scherzo from Sonata C. Other composers are J. C. de Chambonnières, André Campra, André-Cardinal Destouches, J. B. Loeillet, François Dagincourt, Louis-Claude Daquin, Johann Schobert, C.-H. Valentin Alkan, Georges Mathias, Théodore Dubois, Emmanuel Chabrier, Charles-Marie Widor, Benjamin Godard, Cécile Chaminade, Camille Erlanger, Gabriel Pierné, Isidor Philipp. Int. to M-D.

French Piano Music for the Young Musician (Péter Solymos—EMB 1973) 53pp. Attractive collection of music originally written for instruments other than the piano, ranging from three pieces in the 1530 collection by Attaignant to three harmonium pieces by Franck. Also contains a lute piece by Denis Gaultier and other works by Louis Couperin, François Couperin, Rameau, Dandrieu, Daquin, Lully, Marin Marais, and Chambonnières. Fingering given. Int.

French Piano Music of the Early 20th Century (Martin Canin—Sal 1976) 74pp. Déodat de Séverac: En Vacances ("Holiday Time") (suite of seven short Romantic pieces). Charles Koechlin: Petites Pièces faciles Op.41/1 (suite of ten pieces); 1ère Sonatine Op.59/1. Darius Milhaud: 4 Romances sans paroles. Florent Schmitt: Musiques Intimes Op.29/1, 3, 5 (suite of three pieces). Francis Poulenc: 5 Improvisations, Nos.3, 5, 6, 8, 12; Badinage. Excellent anthology of recital and teaching repertoire by five French composers who were all major figures during their lifetime. M-D.

From Russia for Youth—Contemporary Piano Music by Russian Composers (Boris Berlin—Harris 5044 1971) 24pp. Pieces by E. Aglinzev, K. Akimov, L. Barenboim, V. Gerstein, A. Goedicke, D. Kabalevsky, A. Khachaturian, S. Liakhovitskaya, N. Lubarsky, L. Lukomsky, Y. Medin, T. Salutrinskaya, P. Tchaikovsky, and other less-known composers. Easy.

Für Junge Pianisten (DVFM 1973) Book I, 37pp. Contemporary Pieces for Young Pianists. By Werner Richter, Peter Langhof, Helmut Reinbothe, Hans-Georg Marek, Jürgen Golle, Roland Buchwald, Andre Asriel, Kurt Schwaen, Wilfried Krätzschmar, Otto Reinhold, Rainer Lischka, Peter Hermann, and Gerhard Tittel. Easy. Book II, 53 pp. Works by 18 composers, many of those listed for Book I. Int. Book III. 34 pieces by 15 German composers and one Austrian. Titles in German. Int. to M-D. Book IV. 23 compositions by 10 different composers. M-D. These first four volumes would be very fine for students who have stretch problems. The pieces are not avant-garde but are in the manner of Bartók's *Mikrokosmos*. Brief biography on each composer. Book V. Works by seven contemporary German composers. Much more difficult than the preceding volumes. Contains new notational signs. Biographical notes in German. D.

Haru No Yarjoi (Anthology of Japanese Piano Music) (Ongaku No Tomo Sha) Vol.60 Sekai Dai Ongaku Zenshu, 225pp. Contains a broad sampling of twentieth-century Japanese piano music ranging from traditional to expressionistic (à la Schönberg). Shukichi Mitsukuri (1895–): 3 Piano Pieces after the Flower Op.16 (1. Night Rhapsody; 2. Sakura-Sakura; 3. Es ist März, der Frühling). Toroque Takagi (1904–): Five Homages (to Tchaikowsky, Waltar, Gershwin, Albeniz, Khachaturian). Toshitsugu Ogihara (1910–): 3 Piano Pieces (Moderato; Allegro; Andantino). Taminosuke Matsumoto (1914–): 7 Piano Pieces. Toshio Kashiwagi (1914–): 6 Piano Pieces (Moderato; Allegro moderato; Lento tranquillamente

con espressione; Tranquillamente; Delicatamente; Molto tranquillo).
Akira Ifukube (1915–   ): Bon-Odori (Nocturnal dance of the
Bon-Festival); Tanabata (Fête of Vega); Nebuta (Festal Ballad).
Roh Ogura (1916–   ): Sonatine (Allegro moderato; Canzonetta;
Rondo). Minao Shibata (1916–   ): Improvisation for Piano. Shin-
ichi Matsushita (1922–   ): 3 Piano Pieces. Takanobu Saitoh
(1924–   ): Prelude and Fugato; Promenade (3 movements).
Hajime Okumura (1925–   ): Capriccio pour Piano. Yasushi Aku-
tagawa (1925–   ): La Danse Op.1 (Suite pour piano—deux
danses avec un intermezzo). Michio Mamiya (1929–   ): 3 Inventions. Mutsuo Shishido (1929–   ): 2 Dances. Yutaka Makino
(1930–   ): Prelude and Fugue. Thoru Takemitsu (1930–   ):
3 Pieces. Makoto Moroi (1930–   ): Suite Classique (Allemande;
Courante; Sarabande-fantastique; Gavotte I & II; Menuet sentimental;
Gigue). Akira Miyoshi (1933–   ): Suite in Such Time (So Merry
is Dabbling!; A Witch Will Give You Some Sweets; Well Let's Play
in the Garden; Lions Live in Far and Away Lands; For His Mamma).
Contains biographical information in Japanese. Int. to D.

The Home Circle: A Collection of Piano-forte Music (Da Capo   1979)
216pp. Being a Repository of Music for Parlor and Drawing-Room
Recreations with a new foreword by Edward A. Berlin. Originally published in Boston in 1859, this anthology contains piano arrangements
of close to two hundred popular dances of the period—including
waltzes, marches, polkas, schottisches, mazurkas, cotillions, quadrilles,
and hornpipes. Int. to M-D.

Horizons—Music by Canadian Composers (Waterloo   1973) Book I.
Nine pieces aimed at acquainting the beginning piano student with the
sound of music that is not based on the traditional major or minor
scale. Materials drawn from various sources: modes, non-Western
scales, synthetic scales. Certain keyboard styles prevalent in twentieth-
century idioms are introduced. Explanatory notes and performance
suggestions are included for most pieces. Composers include: George
Fiala, Louis Applebaum, Violet Archer, Robert Fleming, Carleton
Elliott, Brian Cherney, Richard Johnston, Robert Turner, and Murray
Adaskin. Int. Book II. Slightly more difficult, follows same format.
Composers include: Anne Eggleston, John Beckwith, Samuel Dolin,
and Gerhard Wuensch. Int. to M-D.

Hungarian Piano Booklet (EMB, joint publication with Litolff   1974)
47pp. 37 pieces, with five color illustrations. Works by Balassa, Bartók, Bozay, Járdányi, Kadosa, Károlyi, Kodály, Kókai, Papp, Ránki,
Soproni, Sugár, Szervánszky, and Weiner. Int.

Intabulatura Nova   1551 (Dob) No.297 in the Diletto Musicale series.
Edited from the original tabulature by Friedrich Cerha, who has provided scholarly and interesting commentary. This was the first published collection of dances in Italy. It consists of 25 dances by "divers

most excellent composers," including galliards, pavans, passamezzi, and a saltarello. There is much charm in these little pieces. Interesting metrical relationships. Int.

Introduction to the Masterworks (Palmer, Lethco—Alfred 1976). A survey of the major periods: Baroque, classical, Romantic, and modern. Includes works from some of the major composers in each period. Also contains short discussions of musical practices. Includes pieces by J. Clarke, J. S. Bach, F. Couperin, D. Scarlatti, Händel, Haydn, W. A. Mozart, Clementi, Beethoven, Chopin, Schumann, Grieg, Bartók, Satie, Prokofieff, and Palmer. Int.

Italian Keyboard Music (Andras Pernye—EMB through TP) Vol.I. 29 pieces from the sixteenth and seventeenth centuries. Includes a few anonymous and little-known compositions. Carefully edited. Appendix lists other references. Int.

Italian Piano Music for the Young Musician (István Mariassy—EMB 1974) 54pp., colored illustrations. Anonymous: Gagliarda veneziana. Anerio: Gagliarda. D. Cimarosa: Sonata c. Clementi: Valse "il eco." Corelli: Gigue. Durante: Studio. Frescobaldi: Aria detta "La Frescobalda." Galuppi: Variazioni. Martini: Gavotte. Pergolesi: Allegretto. Rossini: Énchantillon du Chant de Noël a l'Italienne. D. Scarlatti: Sonatas f♯, g. Zipoli: Suite. The Clementi and the Rossini works are the only true piano music. The two Scarlatti Sonatas, the delightful Gigue by Corelli, and the Frescobaldi variations have the most interest. No fingering given. Int. to M-D.

Japanese Folk Airs on the Piano (Zen-On 1960) Vol.1: 13 pieces. Vol.2: 14 pieces. Varied moods, lengths, and figurations in these expressive, original, and effective folk tunes. Titles given in Japanese and English. Tempo markings included. The four arrangers are: R. Ito, K. Koyama, Y. Makino, and A. Tsukatani. Int. to M-D.

A Jefferson Music Book (J. S. Darling—University Press of Virginia 1976) 42pp. Facsimile reproductions of six pieces that are not readily available in modern editions: Samuel Arnold: Sonata a Op.12/11. J. C. Bach: Sonata A Op.10/4 with violin. C. F. Abel: Favorite Overture I B♭. Wenzel Wodiczka: Sonata B♭ Op.1/1. G. F. Handel: Suite d, Vol.2/4. J. Snow: Variations for the Gavot in Otho. These selections are typical of the music played and enjoyed by Thomas Jefferson and his family. All were included in Jefferson's collection of music at Monticello. Int. to M-D.

The Joy of Baroque (D. Agay—YMP 1974). 45 pieces of Baroque keyboard music, mostly written for the harpsichord, but much of it would sound well on the piano. An outstanding survey including many familiar names but some less familiar like: Daniel Speer, Johann H. Buttstedt, Valentin Rathgeber, John C. Pepusch, Johann Tischer, Johann Goldberg, Mattia Vento, and Leonardo Leo. A few editorial marks have been added. Int.

fugal playing. 27 short and easy fugues by German composers around 1700.

A Little Keyboard Book (J. S. Darling—University Press of Virginia 1972) 16pp. Eight tunes of Colonial Virginia for piano or harpsichord. Taken from the MS music books of the Bollings, once of Chellowe plantation, Buckingham County, Virginia. Int.

Magyar szerzök könnyü Zongoradarabjai (K. Váczi—Zenemukiado 1975) 35pp. Easy piano pieces by Hungarian composers. Compositions by András Borgulya, Tamás Daróczi Bárdos, Janos Decényi, György Geszler, Mihály Hajdu, Zoltán Horusitzky, Pál Járdányi, Pál Kadosa, Laszlo Kalmár, Rezsö Kokai, Istvan Loránd, Imre Mezo, Rezsö Sugár, Ferenc Szabo, Istvan Szelenyi, Endre Szervánsky, Sándor Szokolay, and Béla Tardos. Arranged in progressive order of difficulty. Easy to Int.

Magyar Szerzök Zongoramüvei (EMB 1975) 67pp. Piano Works by Hungarian Composers. Works by Anonymous, József Csermák, F. Liszt, B. Bartók, Z. Kodály, Pál Kadosa, Ferenc Farkas, József Soproni, Attila Bozay, Zoltán Jeny.

Manuscrits Autographes (Leduc). Twenty short pieces, all facsimiles of the autographs by "contemporary" French composers. L. A. Bourgault-Ducoudray: Berceuse Tendre. Henri Busser: Scène de Ballet. Louis Diemer: Pièce en forme de Menuet. Théodore Dubois: Chanson Lesbienne. Georges Falkenberg: Scherzetto. Benjamin Godard: Feuillet d'Album. Charles Gounod: Entrée de Fête. Joseph Guy-Ropartz: Feuillet d'Album. Reynaldo Hahn: Bacchante endormie. Georges Hüe: Coeur brisé. Vincent d'Indy: Tableaux de Voyage; Lac vert. Théodore Lack: Le Furet. Paul Lacombe: Menuet. Sylvio Lazzari: Petite Esquisse. Xavier Leroux: Les Perses. Emile Pessard: Le Papillon. Isidor Philipp: 1re Cantilène de Th. Dubois. Gabriel Pierné: Petite Gavotte. Camille Saint-Saëns: Fantasie sur l'Hymne National Russe. Paul Vidal: Lélio. Int. to M-D.

Meet Canadian Composers at the Piano (Thompson 1968) 24pp. Pieces by Boris Berlin, Claude Champagne, Eileen Ruthven Gilley, William Lea, Leonard Leacock, Godfrey Ridout, and Healey Willan. Easy to Int.

Meet Modern Music (Esther Abrams—Mer 1943). Almost all of the original titles have been changed. Vol.I: Bartók: Not Too Fast; Peasant's Song; Song of the Tramp. Goedicke: In a Quiet Mood. Gretchaninoff: Holidays; Mommy. Liapounov: Lullaby for a Doll. Prokofieff: Fairy Tale; Promenade. Rebikoff: Children Skating; Hurdy Gurdy; Playing Soldiers. Rhené-Baton: A Little Song; A Little Waltz. Satie: The Tulip Princess Says; Waltz of the Chocolate Bar; War Song of the Bean King. Sibelius: Valsette. Stravinsky: Just Walking. Easy to Int. Vol.II: Bartók: Dance Tune; Energy. Amado Carvajal: Miniature; Tristeza. René de Castera: The Cat Is Dead. E. Granados:

Theme and Two Variations; The Last Pavanne. Jacques-Dalcroze: The Battle. Samuel Maykapar: The Blacksmith. Prokofieff: Morning; Parade of the Grasshoppers. Abel Rufino: Campestre. Domingo Santa-Cruz: March of the Kittens. Stravinsky: Heavily. Int.

Meister der Romantik—Leichte Klavierstücke (W. Weismann—Litolff CL5033) 32pp. 24 short pieces by Brahms, Chopin, Grieg, Mendelssohn, Schubert, Schumann, Smetana, Tchaikowsky, and Weber. Contains some unusual literature, e.g., Brahms: Sarabande a; Sandmännchen. Smetana: L'Innocence. Schubert: Theme E. Int.

I miei primi Clavicembalisti (Montani—Ric ER2605) 12pp. J. S. Bach: Musetta; Minuetto; Marcia. F. Couperin: Le petit rien. B. Galuppi: Minuetto. G. F. Händel: Gavotte. J. P. Kirnberger: La birichina. H. Purcell: Preludio; Minuetto. J. P. Rameau: Le Lardon. A. Scarlatti: Minuetto. D. Scarlatti: Aria. Generally good editing. Easy to Int.

Miniature Preludes (Sonos) Vol.II of Music for Worship Services. Twenty pieces by five composers: Merrill Bradshaw, Newell Dayley, Jerry R. Jackman, Robert P. Manookin, and Reid Nibley. Written for the Mormon Church but could be used in any domination. Tasteful, on the quiet side. Int.

Modern Pieces for the Young Artist in Recital (Amsco) 95pp. Works by Albeniz, Bartók, Kabalevsky, Rachmaninoff, Ravel, Shostakovitch, and others. Not terribly modern but contains a broad spectrum of works. Fingered, no editor given. Int. to M-D.

Mosaics (Marguerite Miller—Sonos). Pieces by Paul Creston, Vincent Persichetti, Paul Cooper, Ross Lee Finney, Merrill Bradshaw, and others. Short pieces by some of the finest contemporary American composers that demonstrate new notation and "far out" sounds. Recording included. Editor encourages students to make up their own compositions using techniques employed in the various compositions. Int.

Music for Worship (Sonos 1971) Vol.I 12 pieces. Written to provide appropriate prelude music for the various organizations in the Mormon Church. MC, mainly lyric in character. Includes works by same composers as in Vol.II (*Miniature Preludes,* listed above). Easy-Int.

Music from the Days of George Washington (U.S. George Washington Bicentennial Commission 1931. Reprint AMS Press 1970) 61pp. Introduction by Carl Engle. In addition to other items this collection contains the following piano music: Philip Phile: The President's March; Washington's March; General Burgoyne's March; Brandywine Quick-Step; Successful Campaign. James Hewitt: The Battle of Trenton (abbreviated form). Alexander Reinagle: Sonata D (first movement); Minuet and Gavotte. Pierre Duport: Two Minuets. William Brown: Rondo. Int. to M-D.

Música vasca del siglo XVIII para tecla (UME 1972). Realización y adaptación de Antonio Ruiz-Pipó. 36pp. An anthology of eighteenth-century Spanish Basque keyboard music. Preface in Spanish, French, and English. Works by Oxinaga, Larrañaga, Gamarra, Echeverria, Lonbide, de Sostoa, Eguiguren, and others. Numerous additions of dynamics, ornamentation, and phrasing. Perhaps these pieces were originally conceived for the fortepiano. M-D.

Musical Christmas Cards (Hin 400a   1954) dedicated to and collected by Kathleen Cooper. Vol.I: Madeleine Dring: March—For the New Year. Isobel Dunlop: Le Petit Noël. Fernand Laloux: Prelude for Christmas. Serge Lancen: Jesus naît tendre et blême. Kathleen Richards: Allegretto pastorale. Lloyd Webber: Badinage de Noël. MC, modal. Int. to M-D.

Neue Klaviermusik Deutsche Demokratische Republik (New Piano Music of the German Democratic Republic) (Helge Jung—Gerig) Vol.I: Hanns Eisler (1898–1962): Allegretto. Ottmar Gerster (1897–1969): Improvisation. Friedrich Goldmann (1941–   ): Two Intermezzos. Siegfried Matthus (1934–   ): Invention and Fugue. Dieter Nowka (1924–   ): Sostenuto. Manfred Schubert (1937–   ): Serenata semplice. Johannes Paul Thilman (1906–1973): Capriccioso. Vol.II: Andre Asriel (1922–   ): Fugue C. Paul Dessau (1894–   ): Guernica. Hanns Eisler (1898–1962): Piano Piece Op. 8/2. Günter Kochan (1930–   ): Intermezzo and Fugue. Rudolf Wagner-Régney (1903–1969): Two Piano Pieces. This collection makes known and accessible a part of musical life in East Germany. It presents a representative cross section and an informative chronological survey. Arranged in progressive order of difficulty. M-D to D.

Neue Sonatinen für Klavier (CFP   1970) 44pp. Antonius Streichardt (1936–   ): Sonatine C. Friebert Streller (1931–   ): Sonatine. Peter Langhof (1933–   ): Sonatine 1961. Ruth Bodenstein-Hoyme (1924–   ): Sonatine 1967. Klaus Norberger (1938–   ): Sonatine. Roland Buchwald (1940–   ): Sonatine. Hermann Werner Finke (1911–   ): Sonatine a. Biographical notes in German. Int. to M-D.

Nine Little Lyric Pieces of the 19th and 20th Centuries (H. Kreutzer—BMC) 12pp. Z. Fibich: In the Morning. A. Gretchaninoff: An Ancient Poem Op.119/2. E. Grieg: Cradle Song for Gjendine Op.66/19. S. Heller: Prelude Op.81/4. D. Kabalevsky: Lullaby. T. Kirchner: Miniature Op.62/8. R. Schumann: Little Folk Song Op.68/9. D. Shostakovitch: Romanze. E. Sjögren, Elegy on the name "EBBA" Op. 41. Int.

Nineteenth-Century European Piano Music (John Gillespie—Dover 1977) 343pp. M. Clementi: Exercises 12–15 of *Gradus ad Parnassum*. C. Czerny: Song without Words Op.795/1; Etude mélodieuse Op. 795/3; Toccata C Op.92. J. L. Dussek: Sonata A♭ Op.70 ("The Return to Paris"). A. Dvořák: Nos.1–6 Silhouetten Op.8. G. Fauré: Thème et Variations Op.73. J. Field: Nocturnes Nos.2 c, 4 A. N.

Gade: Arabeske Op.27. E. Granados: selections from Spanish Dances. S. Heller: Drei deutsche Tänze; Toccatina. J. N. Hummel: Variations sur un thème d'Armide de Gluck Op.57. Short, distinctive and idiomatic works not often found in other anthologies. Includes bibliographic references and translations of tempi. M-D.

Organa Hispanica—Iberian Music of the 16th, 17th and 18th Centuries for Keyboard Instruments. Book II: *Portuguese Sonatas, Toccatas and Minuets of the 18th Century for Cimbalo* (Gerhard Doderer—Müller 1972). Preface in English, German, and Spanish. João de Sousa Carvalho: two sonatas (both require much hand crossing; the best works in the collection). Anonimus: Toccata C (superficial gaiety). Other minor works by Francisco Xavier Baptista, João Cordeiro da Silva, and Frei Manuel de Santo Elias. Int. to M-D. Book VI: *Spanish and Portuguese Sonatas of the 18th Century* (G. Doderer—Müller 1975) 36pp. For keyboard instruments. Preface in German, English, and Portuguese. Critical note in German. Contains eight sonatas by: Francisco Xavier Baptista, João Cordeiro da Silva, Alberto José Gomes da Silva, Vicente Rodriguez, Anselmo Viola, Félix Máximo López, Carlos Sexias, and Antonio Soler. The Sexias and Soler sonatas have appeared before, but the other six are appearing in a modern edition for the first time. All the sonatas are short, in one or two movements (except the Sexias, which has three). Thin textures, lively rhythms, mainly in two-part form. M-D.

Original Airs and Dances—A Collection of Short and Easy Eighteenth Century Pieces (H. Kreutzer—BMC) 23pp. J. S. Bach: Bourrée; Gigue; For Anna Magdalena; Aria. J. C. F. Bach: Menuet. Christoph Graupner: Air en Gavotte. G. F. Handel: Menuet; Passepied. J. W. Hässler: Allegro. Leopold Mozart: 6 pieces from *Notebook for Wolfgang.* W. A. Mozart: Menuet from Violin Sonata K.6; Air E♭; Menuet B♭; Menuet F; Andante; Contretanz G. Easy to Int.

Oxford Keyboard Classics (OUP). Howard Ferguson, general editor of the series. Based on the same didactic method of presentation as Ferguson's *Style and Interpretation* volumes. Each volume is devoted to a roughly chronological selection of works, edited from original MSS and first editions by a great keyboard composer. Each volume also provides an essay on the composer's stylistic background together with detailed notes on each work. See individual volumes listed under composers: J. S. Bach, Haydn, Liszt, Schubert.

Paraphrases on an Easy Theme (A. Tcherepnin—Belaieff 1959) 47pp. 24 variations and 17 small pieces based on the theme "Chopsticks." Composers who contributed to this unique collaborative collection include: Rimsky-Korsakow: 24 Variations and Finale. Liszt: Prélude. Borodin: Polka; March funèbre; Requiem; Mazurka. Cui: Valse. Liadow: Valse; Galop; Gigue; Cortège triomphal. Rimsky-Korsakow: Berceuse; Fughetta on BACH; Tarantelle; Menuet; Carillon; Fugue grotesque. N. Stcherbatcheff: Bigarrures. Also contains Petit supplément. Int. to M-D.

See: Guy Wuellner, "Franz Liszt's Prelude on Chopsticks," JALS, IV (December 1978):37–44.

The Performer's Analysis (Robert Dumm—Schroeder & Gunther 1972) 22pp. A series of analytic–interpretive lessons of piano masterworks. J. S. Bach: Scherzo S.844; Minuet S.843. G. F. Handel: Capriccio. M. Mussorgsky: Niania and I, Op. posth./1 from *Souvenirs d'enfance*. R. Glière: Album Leaf Op.31/11. E. MacDowell: An Elfin Round, Op. 7/6 from *Six Fancies*. Each piece is carefully analyzed, and directions for study are most helpful. A fine series. Int.

Le Petit Classique (M. Morhange-Motchane—Sal) 30pp. 22 short pieces from the Baroque and classical periods, each with technical exercises. Directions in French and English. Easy to Int.

Le Petit Romantique (M. Morchange-Motchane—Sal) 39pp. 20 short pieces from this period, each with technical exercises. Familiar and unfamiliar works. Int.

Piano Music for One Hand (Raymond Lewenthal—GS 1972). 34 studies, exercises, and pieces for the left hand. An extensive and outstanding preface deals with the character and place of these pages in the repertoire. 24 composers including: Alkan, J. S. Bach, C. P. E. Bach, Bartók, Hermann Berens, Ludwig Berger, Blumenfeld, F. Bonimici, Chopin Op.10/6 (transcribed by L. Godowsky), Czerny, R. Ganz, Godowsky, F. W. Greulich, Kalkbrenner, L. Köhler, Liszt, Eduard Marxsen, Moskowski, Reger, Reinecke, Saint-Saëns, Scriabin, Wilhelm Tappert, Géza Zichy. M-D to D.

Piano Music for the Young (Cleveland Composers Guild Publication Series —Galaxy) Vol.I: Eleven pieces by Starling Cumberworth, Frederick Koch, Klaus George Roy, Jane Young, Juli Nunlist, Bain Murray. Easy to Int. Vol.II: Eleven contemporary experimental pieces for the adventurous young pianist: Frank Boehnlein: A Moon Child's Piano Book (requires some sophisticated preparing of the piano, using bobby pins, pennies, pencils, etc.). Klaus George Roy: Three Turns of the Key (uses a twelve-tone row in its third piece). Raymond Wilding-White: Cartoon and Character Sketches (a four-piece suite). Easy to Int. with most of the pieces toward the Int. level.

Piano Music from Spain (AMP 1971). Fifteen pieces by Albeniz and Granados. Albeniz: Sevilla; Asturias; Córdoba; Rumores de la Caleta; Pavana-Capricho; Zortzico; Triana. Granados: Quejas ó la Maja y el Ruiseñor; Andaluza (Playera); Rondalla Aragonesa; El Invierno; Barcarola; Añoranza; Ecos de la Parranda; Zapateado. Excellent collection of some of the most popular pieces by these composers. Int. to M-D.

Piano Music in Nineteenth Century America (M. Hinson—Hinshaw 1975) Vol.I: Thomas Bethune (Blind Tom): Battle of Manassas.

Richard Hoffman: In Memoriam L. M. G. William Wallace: Nocturne
II. Anton Philip Heinrich: Song without Words (for Jenny Lind).
William Mason: Dance Antique Op.38. Vol.II: William H. Sherwood:
Prelude A Op.5/1. Louis M. Gottschalk: La Gallina (duet). Edward
MacDowell: Clair de Lune Op.37/1. John Knowles Paine: A Christ-
mas Gift Op.45. Arthur Foote: Zweite Suite Op.30 (Appassionato).
Full chords are prevalent in Vol.II. Programmatic and patriotic pieces
make up some of the most interesting music. "The Battle of Manassas"
is based on "The girl I left behind me," "Dixie," "Yankee Doodle,"
"Marseillaise," and the "Star Spangled Banner." Cluster chords, whistling, and train effects with the voice make this a most unusual fun
piece. M-D.

Piano Music Inspired by Folklore (P. Arma—Lemoine 1959). 24 pieces
by contemporary composers based on popular themes of 14 nationali-
ties. Includes works by Arma, Bartók, Sas, Tansman, Viski, and
others. Easy to Int.

Piano Music of Viceregal Mexico (Iinson, Martin—Hinshaw 1979).
Anonymous (c.1790): Sonata en Mi. Josc Aldana (1758–1810):
Minuet with Variations; Polaca. Much of the music heard in Mexico
during the late eighteenth and early nineteenth centuries conformed
with European standards. The music in this collection exudes charm
and elegance but does not exhibit traits that later came to be classed
as characteristically Mexican or Latin American. Aldana's Minuet and
Variations aptly represents this late viceregal music. The Polaca is a
most unusual example in that it is a simplified keyboard arrangement
of a movement from Beethoven's Serenade for String Trio Op.8. The
anonymous Sonata comes the closest to containing elements associated
with music by known Mexican-born composers of the period; influences of Scarlatti and Soler are evident. An altogether unusual collection. Int.

Piano Pieces by Children—A Collection of Piano Pieces by Gifted Children
(Ernst Lubin—Hyperion 1974) 55pp. By composers aged 4 to 16.
The pieces have a freshness and charm that could never have come
from adults. Int.

Piano Pieces by Soviet Composers for Children (Leonid Roisman—CFP)
3 vols. Edited with biographical notes in German, French, and English.
Most of the composers are unfamiliar in the USA; among them are the
following: Yossif Neumark, Moissej Weinberg, Grigori Frid, Dmitri
Blagoi, and Alexander Pirumow. Among the better-known composers
included are: Khatchaturian, Shostakovich, Maikapar, and Glière.
Vol.I: 40 pieces and biographies of the 30 represented composers.
Easy to Int. Vol.II: 27 pieces and biographies of 23 composers. Int.
Vol.III: 22 pieces with biographical notes on the composers. This is
the most difficult of the three volumes. A brilliant Toccata by Andrej
Eschpai and an Impromptu for left hand by Glière are two of the most

interesting works. Most of the pieces are short and effective. Int. to M-D.

Piano Recital (D. Agay—Amsco   1975). 54 varied pieces, most no longer than 4pp. each. Practical edition containing some unusual repertoire (e.g., Beethoven: Rondo Wo048; Heller: Etude Héroique: Moszkowski: Second Spanish Dance) in an attractive format. Int. to M-D.

Piano Spectrum (Herbert Connor—Reuter & Reuter   1966) 31pp. 26 original compositions for piano by 10 contemporary Scandinavian composers. Introduction and instructions for study included. Contains a cross section of styles from polyphonic to dance-like. Gottfrid Berg (1889–1970): Five Pieces. Laci Boldemann (1921–   ): Two Piano Pieces without Pedal. Hans Eklund (1927–   ): To an Obtuse Common Chord; Swatting Flies. Hallgrimur Helgason (1914–   ): A New Song; Icelandic Song; From a Fairytale Isle. Daniel Hellden (1917–   ): Rondo giocoso. Finn Höffding (1899–   ): Five Pieces. Edvin Kallstenius (1881–1967): Little Polka in Pentatone. Sparre Olsen (1903–   ): A 400-Year-Old Miners Hymn. Matti Rautio (1922–   ): Berceuse; Little Study in Boogie Woogie. Knudåge Riisager (1897–   ): Sarabande; Polytonal; Duet in Canon; Duet. MC. Int. to M-D.

Piano Works by French Composers (Margaret Gresh—GS   1977) 159pp. Bizet: L'Arlésienne: suites de concert Nos.1 and 2. Debussy: Suite bergamasque. Fauré: Romance sans paroles; First Barcarolle Op.26; Third Impromptu Op.34; Fourth Nocturne Op.36; Fourth Barcarolle Op.44; Sixth Barcarolle Op.70; Clair de lune Op.46/2; Improvisation Op.34/5; Berceuse Op.56/1. Ravel: Sonatine. Satie: Three Gnossiennes; Three Gymnopedies. Int. to M-D.

Piano Works by Russian Composers (Margaret Gresh—GS   1977) 176pp. Prokofiev: Prelude Op.12/7; Sonatina G Op.54/2. Scriabin: Preludes Opp.15, 22, 27, 35, 51/2, 56/1. Tschaikowsky: The Seasons Op.37a. Rachmaninoff: 10 preludes Op.23. Ippolitov-Ivanov: Caucasian sketches. M-D to D.

PKK Their Greatest Piano Solos (Prokofieff, Kabalevsky, Khachaturian) (A. Shealy—Ashley   1972) 192pp. Kabalevsky: Sonatina C Op. 13/1; 8 pieces from Op.27: Dance, Dance in the Garden; Etude A; Etude a; Scherzo; Sonatina a; Toccatina; Waltz; Rondo Op.59; A Warlike Dance; Preludes 1 and 2. Khachaturian: Dance g; Sabre Dance (*Gayne* Ballet); Sonate; Sonatinas a, C; Toccata; Valse Caprice. Prokofieff: A Story Op.3/1; Humoreske Op.3/2; Fantasy Op.3/4; Diabolical Suggestion Op.4/4; Toccata Op.11; Gavotte Op.25; March (from *The Love of Three Oranges*) Op.33; Paysage Op.59/2; Sonatina Pastorale Op.59/3; Moments Musicaux 1 and 2, Op.62/2, 3; Tarantella Op.65/4; Triumphant March (from *Peter and the Wolf*) Op. 67; Mephisto Waltz Op.96/3; Etude c; Morning; Waltz (from the ballet *Cinderella*). Int. to M-D.

Polonezy ze zbiorów Anny Marii Saskiej (Karol Hlawiczka—PWM 1971)
136pp. Polonaises from the collection of Anna Maria, Princess of
Saxony (second half of the eighteenth century). Vol.III: for harpsichord or piano. Edited with preface and editorial notes in Polish and
English. Vol.XXI in series Sources for the History of Polish Music.

Practical Music Book for Piano (Eckhart Sellheim—Hans Gerig). Anthology of pieces from the seventeenth to the twentieth century. Includes a recording (by Alfons Kontarsky) of all the examples in the
collection. Section one: pieces ranging from Schumann's Soldier's
March to his First Sonata for Children, Op.118, to less-known pieces
such as Marko Tajčević: First Suite; Bruno Bjelinsky: Alarm; Anatol
Vieru: The Mechanical Guitar. Easy to M-D. Section two: moves from
Mozart's Minuet D to Liszt's Valse Oubliée f♯ and less-known works
such as Günther Becker's Diverging and Converging Directions. Int.
to M-D.

Pro Musica Nova (Alfons Kontarsky—Hans Gerig 1972) 47pp. Studies
for playing avant-garde music for piano written since 1950. Contains
works by Pavle Merkù, Lucia Alcalay, Tilo Medek, Bojidar Dimov,
Norbert Linke, Yannis Ioannidis, Werner Heider, José Luis de Delás,
Günther Becker, Helmut Lachenmann, and Friedhelm Döhl. Two valuable appendixes with explanations in German and English. Some of
the pieces are highly suitable for public performance. M-D to D.

Purcell's Contemporaries (CFP Hin 9). Sixteen original short pieces by
masters of the seventeenth century: Daniel Purcell, Henry Purcell,
Blow, Clarke, Croft, Eccles, Loeillet, Barrett. Titles include: Airs,
Cibel, Gavotte, Hornpipe, Minuets, Rigaudon, Sarabandes, Theater
Tune, Trumpet Tunes. Int.

*Sergei Rachmaninoff, Anton Rubinstein, Nikolas Rimsky-Korsakoff—Their
Greatest Piano Solos* (Alexander Shealy—Copa 1972) 192pp. A
comprehensive collection of these composers' world-famous works in
their original form. Contains original works and arrangements.

Ragtime Classics (Paxton 1976) 36pp. Introduction by Charles Wilford.
Scott Joplin: The Easy Winners; Heliotrope Bouquet (with Louis
Chauvin). Tom Turpin: St. Louis Rag. Charles Hunter: Cotton Bolls.
Arthur Marshall: Kinklets. Joe Jordan: Nappy Lee. Joseph F. Lamb:
Sensation. James Scott: The Ragtime Betty. Lucian P. Gibson: Jinx
Rag. J. Hubert (Eubie) Blake: Fizz Water. M-D.

The Ragtime Current (EBM 1976) 56pp. Piano solos by a mainstream
of today's ragtime composers. Foreword by Rudi Blesh. William Albright: Sweet Sixteenths. Donald Ashwander: Astor Place Rag Waltz;
Friday Night. William Bolcom: Last Rag. Kathy Craig: Romantic
Rag. Milton Kaye: Amatory Hallucination Rag. Max Morath: One
for Norma; The New Black Eagle Buck. William Rowland: Tickled
Pink. Thomas A. Schmutzler: Shootin the Agate. Trebor Jay Tich-
enor: The Show-Me Rag. Terry Waldo: Yellow Rose Rag. M-D.

Renaissance to Rock: An Annotated Keyboard Collection of Renaissance, Baroque, Jazz and Popular Music (Nathan Bergenfeld—Hyperion 1975) 160pp. Everybody's Favorite Series No.157. In part with chord symbols. Works by Byrd, Couperin, Rameau, Scott Joplin, Cy Oliver, John Mehegan, Paul McCartney. Contains much commentary about each composer and his music. Styles are compared by pairing old with new. Bibliography and indexes. Int. to M-D.

Romanticos Espanoles (UME   1976) 48pp. Martin Sanchez Allu: La estrella perdida Op.23. Apolinar Brull: El laud (mazurka). Santiago de Masarnau: Desaliento (Ballada II) Op.25. Marcial del Adalid (1826–1881): La noce (balada) Op.29; Gratitud (nocturno) Op.47; Dos romanzas sin palabras; Variaciones a la antigua usanza. Int. to M-D.

Royal Collection (N. Fairbairn, Clive Unger-Hamilton—Nov   1977) 54pp. An historical album of music composed exclusively by Members of the Royal Family of Great Britain and Ireland. "In some of the pieces, the voice or instrument is unspecified; since this was often not a matter of particular importance, the performer should be prepared to be adaptable" (from the score). Pieces playable on the keyboard include: King James I of Scotland: The Duke of Perth's Reel; Lochleven Castle. King Henry VIII: Two instrumental pieces. Edward Augustus, 10th Duke of York; Two Minuets. Victoria, Duchess of Kent: Galoppade. Alfred, Duke of Edinburgh: The *Galatea* Valse No.1. Leopold, Duke of Albany: Fontainebleau Waltz No.1. King Edward VIII: Mallorca. Int. to M-D.

Russian Piano Music for the Young Musician (Lehel Both—EMB   1973) 50pp. Attractive collection featuring a number of miniatures by some of Russia's greatest Romantic composers, including Borodin, Mussorgsky, Tchiakowsky, Rachmaninoff, as well as less-known writers such as Dimitry Arakishvile (1873–1953), Sogomon Komitas (1869–1935), Miaskovsky, Maikapar, Goedicke, Liapounov (with an Allegretto that is fairly easy, for once), Drozdov, and Kopilov. Fingering added. Int. to M-D.

Scandinavian Aspect (Kjell Baekkelund, Bengt Johnsson—WH   1971) 46pp. Works by contemporary composers from Norway, Sweden, Denmark, and Finland. Egil Hovland: Raindrop Study. Tage Nielsen: Sun, Moon and Stars. Per Nørgärd: Journeys. Poul Rovsing Olsen: Three Etudes—I. Ride Through a Comet's Tail, II. The Asteroid's Song, III. Death Dance of a Variable Star. Erik Bergman: Spectrum, from the suite *Aspekter*. Einojuhani Rautavaara: Quinte. Sigurd Berge: Chorale. Finn Mortensen: Nocturne. Bengt Hambraeus: Musical Box. Arne Mellnäs: For You and Me. An interesting and valuable collection showing the great variety of stylistic and technical elements being used by contemporary Scandinavian composers. Most pieces contain detailed performance instructions. Varied keyboard techniques required. Most are avant-garde and are M-D to D.

Scriabin, Shostakovich, Stravinsky—Their Greatest Piano Solos (Alexander Shealy—Copa 1973) 192pp. A comprehensive collection of these composers' most famous works in their original form. This writer was not able to determine if all the pieces were definitely in their original form. Contains 16 works by Stravinsky (including pieces from *Petrushka, Firebird, L'Histoire du Soldat,* and *Le Sacre du Printemps*), 18 works by Scriabin, and 44 works by Shostakovich (including pieces from *L'Age d'or* and Fifth Symphony). Int. to M-D.

Select Piano Music for Advanced Grades (H. Kasschau—GS) 64pp. I. Albeniz: Cordova Op.232/4. Arthur L. Brown: Improvisation and Melody. Rudolf Friml: Valse Lucille. Leopold Godowsky: Alt-Wien. E. Granados: Intermezzo from the opera *Goyescas* (composed for the first performance at the Metropolitan Opera House, Jan. 28, 1916). Charles Griffes: The White Peacock. F. Grieg: Erotik Op.43/5. David Guion: Arkansas Traveler; The Harmonica-Player. Frank LaForge: Romance. M. Levitzki: Valse. Margaret Upcraft: Valse-Impromptu. M-D.

Selected Piano Compositions (A. Poláková, J. Novotný—Supraphon 1968) rev. by A. Wilde. Leoš Janáček: I.X.1905. Iša Krejčí: Tri Scherzina. Jaroslav Ježek: Toccata. M-D to D.

Seven Americans (Banowetz—General Words and Music). Works by Reid Nibley, Merrill Ellis, Felix Powell, Frank Stewart, John Kimmey, William Latham, and David Wheatley. Varied styles that include most recent trends. Includes pictures and short biographical sketches of each composer. M-D to D.

The Show-Booth for Bold Pianists (Schott & PWM 1972) 31pp. Music chosen by Wilfried Steinbrenner and Friedrich Wanek, illustrated by Zofia Darowska. 17 pieces of mainly twentieth-century works by Gretchaninov, Orff, Hindemith, Bartók, Stojanov, Lutoslawski, Prokofiev, and Luciuk. Beethoven, Mozart, and Weber are also represented by one piece each. 16 clever illustrations are an added attraction. Easy to Int.

Sonatas: Classics to Moderns (D. Agay—CMP 1974) 208pp. Vol.67 of *Music for Millions.* 17 sonatas by as many composers from D. Scarlatti to D. Kabalevsky. Each work is complete, in its original form, and is based on an authentic text. C. P. E. Bach: Sonata G W.62. J. C. Bach: Sonata B♭ Op.5/1. Beethoven: Sonata c Op.10/1. D. Bortniansky: Sonata F. D. Cimarosa: Sonata B♭. M. Clementi: Sonata D Op.26/3. J. L. Dussek: Sonata G Op.39/1, C.166. E. Grieg: Sonata e Op.7. G. F. Handel: Concerto G. J. Haydn, Sonata F Hob.XVI/23. D. Kabalevsky: Sonata III Op.46. W. A. Mozart: Sonata G K.283.

S. Prokofieff: Sonata III (from *Old Notebooks*) Op.28. D. Scarlatti: Sonata E L.23. F. Schubert: Sonata A Op.120. R. Schumann: Sonata for the Young G Op.118a. E. W. Wolf: Sonata E. An outstanding survey of the development of one of the most important of all instrumental forms. Int. to M-D.

Sonate e Sonatine (Carla Giudici—Carisch   1972). 14 sonatas and sonatinas. Beethoven: Sonatinas G, F. Clementi: Sonatinas Op.36/1, 6; Op.38/3. F. Kuhlau: Sonatina Op.55/1. J. L. Dussek: Sonatina Op. 20/1. Diabelli: Sonatina Op.151/2. J. Haydn: Sonatas Hob.XVI/9, 11, 4, 1. W. A. Mozart: Sonatas K.547, K.282. Int. to M-D.

Sonatinas (Ongaku No Tomo Sha   1966) Collection I, 109pp. Contains sonatinas by the Japanese composers Kazuko Hara (1935–   ), Tomojiro Ikenouchi (1906–   ), Akira Miyoshi (1933–   ), Hajime Okumura (1923–   ), Hisatada Otaka (1911–1951), Toroque Takagui (1904–   ), Akihiro Tsukatani (1919–   ), and Kazuo Yamada (1912–·   ). A few of the movements display an Oriental influence. Int. to M-D.

Sonatinas, the First Book for Young Pianists (M. Halford—Alfred   1977) 24pp. Sonatinas by Thomas Attwood, George Berg, Theodore Latour, and Matthew Camidge. Int.

Sonatinas, Sonatas, Pieces from the 18th through the 20th Centuries (Hans-Georg Schwerdtner—Schott 6695   1977) 115pp. Preface in English and German. Contains works by Handel, D. Scarlatti, Couperin, Galuppi, C. P. E. Bach, Benda, Cimarosa, J. C. Bach, Mozart, Haydn, Clementi, Beethoven, Kuhlau, Schubert, Mendelssohn, Chopin, Reger, Fibich, Kadosa, Bartók, Hindemith, Honegger, Françaix, Prokofiev, and Ligeti. Int. to M-D.

Sonatiny Ukrainskikh Sovetskikh Kompozitorov (Muzychna Ukraina 1972) 37pp. Sonatinas by Ukrainian Soviet composers. Works by: I. Berkovych, M. Stepanenko, Iu. Shchurovs'kyi, Tylyk, V. Klyn, Iu. Shamo, and L. Sokovnin.

Sonaty Sovetskikh Kompozitorov (Sovetskii Kompozitor   1972) 78pp. Sonatas by Soviet composers, Vol.I. Works by: V. Zolotukhin, E. Botiarov, D. Krivitskii, K. Volkov. Titles in Russian.

Spanish Piano Music for the Young Musician (György Balla—EMB 1974) 56pp. 14 works by Isaac Albeniz, Mateo Albeniz, Cabezón, Cantallos, Ferrer, Freixanet, Milán, Narváez, Felipe Rodriguez, Vicente Rodriguez, Serrano, Soler. The Sonata by Cantallos (born 1770?) is excellent though reminiscent of D. Scarlatti. The collection covers the sixteenth to the twentieth century, concluding with the Sevilla by I. Albeniz. Includes reproductions of paintings by Alonso Cano and Velazquez. M-D.

Swedish Profile (Trygve Nordwall—NMS   1974) 36pp. Ten pieces for piano by Blohmdahl, Bäck, Hambraeus, Johanson, Maros, Mellnäs, Nilsson, Rabe, Werlin, and Werle.

Themes and Variations (D. Agay—CMP 1974). Vol.77 of Music for Millions. 28 compositions by 24 composers representing a broad survey of theme and variation techniques. Agay: Variations on a Hebrew Folk Theme from *Mosaics*. J. S. Bach: Aria Variata alla Maniera Italiana. Bartók: Variations on a Slovakian Folk Tune from *For Children,* Book II. Beethoven: 7 Variations on "God Save the King" Wo0 78; 32 Variations c Wo0 80. Brahms: Variations on an Original Theme Op.21/1. Byrd: The Carman's Whistle. Jean F. Dandrieu: Wedding Feast of the Birds. Glinka: Variations on a Russian Folk Song. Goedicke: Theme and Variations Op.46. Granados: Theme, Variations and Finale from *Seis Estudios Espresivos*. Handel: Passacaglia from Suite VII g. Haydn: Variations "Un Piccolo Divertimento" Hob.XVII/6. Earl Hines: Jazz Improvisation on the song "Smoke Rings." Kabalevsky: Variations Op.40/2; Toccata Variations Op.40/1. Kuhlau: Variations on an Austrian Folk Song. Liszt: Praeludium ("Weinen, Klagen, Sorgen, Sagen") on an ostinato bass after J. S. Bach. Mendelssohn: Variations Sérieuses Op.54. Mozart: 6 Variations on an Air ("Mio Caro Adone") by Salieri, K.180; Variations on an Allegretto K.54. J. Pachelbel: Chorale and Variations ("Werde Munter Mein Gemute"). J. P. Rameau: Gavotte Variée—Gavotte with Variations. Sam Raphling: Improvisations on 2 American Folk Tunes. Schubert: Impromptu Op.142/3. Villa-Lobos: Preludio from Bachianas Brasileiras IV. Leo Weiner: Variations on a Hungarian Peasant Song Op.22. Tempo, dynamic, and expression marks added by the editor are discreet and tastefully handled. Int. to M-D.

Three Compositions (Mobart Music Publications) Vol.4, for piano solo. 20th Century Solo Instrumental Music Series. 31pp. David Winkler (1949–   ): Intermezzo. George Edwards (1943–   ): Two Bagatelles. Thomas S. James (1937–   ): Variations.

Le Trésor des Pianistes (complied by Jacques and Louise Farrenc—Leduc 1861–72; reprint Da Capo 1977). The most complete collection of keyboard music ever assembled. About 250 of the works are available separately (Leduc). See *Guide,* pp.715–17, for a complete listing of the works.

Index of Composers

Composer	Volume(s)	Composer	Volume(s)
Byrd (William)	II	Marcello (Benoît)	IX
Chambonnières (J. de)	II	Martini (le P. Jean-Baptiste)	IX
Chopin (Frédéric)	XXIII	Mattheson (Jean)	XI
Clementi (Muzio)	XVI	Mendelssohn-Bartholdy (Félix)	
Couperin (Louis)	III		XXIII
Couperin (François)	IV, V	Merulo (Claude)	II
Cramer (Jean-Baptiste)	XVIII	Mozart (W.-Amédée)	XVII
Crofurd	II	Muffat (Georges)	II
Dandrieu (François)	IX	Muffat (Théophile)	X
Daquin (Claude)	IX	Nichelmann (Christophe)	X
Duphly	XIV	Paradies (P.-Dominique)	XIV
Durante (François)	IX	Pasquini (Bernard)	III
Dussek (Louis)	XVIII	Pescetti (Jean-Baptiste)	IX
Eberlin (Ernest)	XI	Porpora (Nicolo)	VIII
Fasch (Chrétien)	XV	Purcell (Henri)	III
Frescobaldi (Jérôme)	II	Rameau (J. Philippe)	VIII
Froberger (Jacques)	III	Ries (Ferdinand)	XXIII
Gibbons (Orlando)	II	Scarlatti (Alexandre)	III
Goldberg (Théophile)	XI	Scarlatti (Dominique)	VI, VII
Haendel (G.-Frédéric)	V	Schaffrath (Christophe)	XI
Haessler (Wilhelm)	VI	Schwanenberg	XVIII
Haydn (Joseph)	XV	Smith (Christophe)	XI
Hummel (J.-Népomucène)	XXII	Steibelt (Daniel)	XVIII
Kerl (Gaspard de)	III	Telemann (Philippe)	IX
Kirnberger (J.-Philippe)	XIV	Weber (Ch.-Marie de)	XXIII
Krebs (J.-Louis)	IX	Wernicke (J.-G.)	XVIII
Kuhnau (Jean)	III	Zipoli (Dominique)	XI
Lindeman (O.-A.)	XVI		

See: Maurice Hinson, "Le Trésor des Pianistes," PQ, 72 (Summer 1970): 20–21, for a discussion of the background and development of the collection.

Tonstücke alter Meister (Hermann Wagner—Möseler 1972) 28pp. Works by: Telemann, Pachelbel, Händel, Kirnberger, J. C. Bach, and Fischer. Int. to M-D.

Twelve by Eleven (Hinson—Hinshaw 1978). Contains twelve original compositions written by eleven contemporary composers of the U.S. Stylistically, the pieces range from the Romantic heritage to post-serial techniques. Challenging and exciting new piano repertoire. Milton Babbitt: Playing for Time. Leslie Bassett: Mobile. Fred Coulter: Variations for Agnes. George Crumb: Dream Images. David Diamond: Prelude and Fugue II c. Richard Faith: Souvenir. Ross Lee Finney:

Medley. Lou Harrison: Homage to Milhaud, Reel; Homage to Henry Cowell. Nelson Keyes: Three Love Songs. Halsey Stevens: Notturno —Bellagio Adagio. Bruce Wise: Four Piano Pieces. For descriptions of each piece, see listing under composer's name. Int. to M-D.

20th Century Keyboard Masters (M. Nevin—Schroeder & Gunther 1972). Original piano works by modern composers for intermediate and early advanced levels. Compositions by Bartók, Debussy, Kabalevsky, Prokofieff, and others. Int. to M-D.

Twenty-Six Pieces from Three Centuries (Scarlatti to Prokofiev) (Karl Bradley—GS 1975) 106pp. Music by Albeniz, Blood, Bruckner, Chaminade, Dello Joio, German, Granados, Helm, Henselt, Herbert, Holst, Mozart, MacDowell, Moszkowski, Muczynski, Pachulski, Poldini, Prokofiev, Saint-Saëns, Schütt, Surinach, and Turina. Contains a wide variety of repertoire with some unusual items. Int. to M-D.

Twenty-Six Romantic and Contemporary Piano Pieces (Karl Bradley—GS 1975) 106pp. A fine collection of popular and some unusual works by Albeniz, Barber, Cowell, Debussy, Dvořák, Godard, Grainger, Griffes, Guion, V. Herbert, MacDowell, Muczynski, Nevin, Prokofiev, Rachmaninoff, Rossini, Sapellnikoff, Sarasate, Satie, R. Schumann, Scriabin, A. Tcherepnin, and Warlock. Int. to M-D.

Antonio Valente: Intavolatura de Cimbalo Naples 1576 (Charles Jacobs OUP 1973) 200pp. The earliest attributable Italian harpsichord source. The numerical musical notation employed is unique in Western music, and in this edition it has been transliterated into modern musical notation. The *Intavolatura* contains ricercars, sets of variations, dances, transcriptions of vocal music, a setting of plainsong, and the apparently earliest Italian keyboard fantasia. It is the earliest source of ground-bass technique and an early source for ornamentation in Italian keyboard literature. Also includes related music by Valenti's contemporaries: Rocco Rodia: Salve Regina. Diego Ortiz: 2 Salve Regina, in 4 parts and one in 5 parts. Thomas Crequillon: Pis ne me peut venir. Adrian Willaert: Qui la dira. Philippe de Monte: Sortez mes pleurs; and vocal models of his transcriptions. In the commentary, Jacobs discusses the contents of the collection and Valente's relationship to contemporary and Spanish musicians. Scholarly edition that contains some beautiful and unusual music.

Variations on a Theme of Diabelli (W. Newman—Music Treasure 1973). 50 variations by various composers. Int. to M-D.

The Virginalists, Selected Pieces for Piano (Jan Drath—PWM 1972) 45pp. A tasteful selection of fourteen short selections, mainly from the FVB: R. Johnson: Alman. Anonimus: Corranto; Daunce. S. Kennedy: Corrant. Byrd: The Trumpetts; The Bagpipe and the Drone; The Flute and the Droome; Ye Souldiers Dance; The Whislinge Carman. Anonimus; Callino Cusurame. Bull: The Irishe Ho-hoane. M. Peerson: The Primerose; The Fall of the Leafe. Anonimus: Muscadin. A two-page essay by Drath provides a questionable discussion of stylistic problems in playing ornaments in virginal music. Ornaments are realized on a staff above the score. Highly edited. Int. to M-D.

Waltzes (CFP 66735   1978). A collection of contemporary pieces for piano by Ashforth, Babbitt, Busby, Cage, Constanten, Felciano, Fennimore, Finney, Gena, Glass, Harrison, Helps, Imbrie, Kohn, Krauze, Mellnaes, Moran, Sessions, Shifrin, Stout, I. Tcherepnin, Thomson, Thorne, Tower, and Wuorinen. Int. to M-D.

The Young Pianist's Anthology of Modern Music (AMP   1972) 65pp. 42 works by contemporary composers including Bartók, Bernstein, Cowell, Creston, Grainger, Guarnieri, Harris, Haufrecht, Hovhaness, Kabalevsky, Krenek, George List, Muczynski, Pinto, Rodrigo, W. Schuman, S. Strohbach, Surinach, Takacs, Tansman. No commentary on composer's style or technical problems. Diverse styles. Easy-Int.

Yugoslav Youth Album (Marijan Lipovsek—CFP 9633a   1975). Book I. Preface in German and French. Contains 37 works by Pavel Sivic, Marijan Lipovsek, Matija Bravnicar, Mihovil Logar, Lucijan Marija Skerlanc, Marko Tajcevic, Stanojlo Rajicic, Karol Pahor, Marjan Kozina, Slavko Osterc, Igor Stuhec, Primoz Ramovs. Includes biographical notes and essential fingering. Wide variety of keys and moods. Int. to M-D.

Zeitgenössische Klaviermusik (Johen Beck—Möseler   1973) 72pp.

BIBLIOGRAPHY

This extension of the references that appear after individual composers or single compositions concentrates on English-language books, periodicals, and dissertations. These sources are most helpful when used in conjunction with the musical score. Careful attention has been directed toward dissertations, some of which are annotated. As a general rule, biographies have been excluded; however, selected ones focusing on the composer's music have been included. For a more complete list of books related to keyboard accompanying, aesthetics, analysis, biographies, church music, group piano, construction and design, history, lists of piano music, ornamentation, pedagogy and performance practices, see Maurice Hinson, *The Piano Teacher's Source Book* (Melville, NY: Belwin-Mills, 1979, 2d ed.).

Denes Agay. "The Search for Authenticity." *Clavier*, 14 (November 1965):29–31.

Putnam Aldrich. "Bach's Technique of Transcription and Improvised Ornamentation." MQ, 35 (January 1949):26–35.

———. "The 'Authentic' Performance of Baroque Music." In *Essays on Music in Honor of Archibald T. Davison*. Cambridge: Department of Music, Harvard University, 1957. Pp.161–71.

Ruth P. Andrews. "Preferred Editions." AMT, 21 (November–December 1971):30.

Paul Badura-Skoda. "Paul Badura-Skoda on the Schubert Sonatas," an interview with Dean Elder. *Clavier,* 12 (March 1973):7–16. Also includes score to Schubert Sonata E, D.157, edited by Elder.

Joseph Banowetz. "Master Lessons on a Liszt Hungarian Rhapsody." *Clavier,* 12 (March 1973):25–32. Discusses the Third Rhapsody and includes the score as edited by Banowetz.

Elsie B. Barnett. "An Annotated Translation of Moriz Rosenthal's *Franz Liszt, Memories and Reflections*." *Current Musicology,* 13 (1972): 29–37. "Rosenthal (1862–1946), one of Liszt's most famous pupils, describes Liszt as teacher, performer, and composer and gives his own opinions and impressions of Liszt and some of his contemporaries" (author).

Frances Bedford. "The Historical Significance of Harpsichord Compositions Written between 1913 and 1928." AMT, 22 (February–March 1973):25, 36.

David Blum. *Casals and the Art of Interpretation*. New York: Holmes & Meier, 1977. 223pp.

Alfred Brendel. *Musical Thoughts and Afterthoughts*. Princeton: Princeton University Press, 1976.

Arthur Briskier. *New Approach to Piano Transcriptions and Interpretation of J. S. Bach's Music*. New York: Carl Fischer, 1958.

Maurice J. E. Brown. "Schubert and Some Folk Songs." ML, 53 (April 1972):173–78. Discusses the use of folk songs in Schubert's piano and chamber music, citing two dances, D. 529 and D. 146, the *Divertissement à l'hongroise* D. 818m, the adagio D. 879, and the unfinished sonata in C major D. 845. Reports the new discoveries uncovered by the Neue Schubert Ausgabe.

John C. Byrt. "Form and Style in the Works of J. S. and C. P. E. Bach." Ph.D. diss., Oxford University, 1970. 2 vols., 380pp.

David Charlton. "Performance Practice around 1800." M&M, 23 (January 1975):22–24. A discussion that centers on the pros and cons of using contemporary instruments of the period.

Gilbert Chase. *The Music of Spain,* 2d rev. ed. New York: Dover Publications, 1959.

J. Bunker Clark. "The Renaissance of Early American Keyboard Music: A Bibliographic Review." *Current Musicology,* 18 (1974):127–32.

Michael Collins. "In Defense of the French Trill." JAMS, 26 (Fall 1973): 405–40.

C. F. Colt. "Early Pianos: Their History and Character." *Early Music,* 1 (January 1973):27–33.

Herbert Colvin. "Contemporary American Piano Music." AMT, 14 (January–February 1965).

Barry A. R. Cooper. "The Keyboard Suite in England before the Restoration." ML, 53 (July 1972):309–19.

———. "English Solo Keyboard Music of the Middle and Late Baroque." Ph.D. diss., Oxford University, 1974. 517pp.

Alfred Cortot. *French Piano Music*. London: Oxford University Press, 1932. Reprint, New York: Da Capo Press, 1977.

Thurston Dart. "Bach's Early Keyboard Music: A Neglected Source." AM, 42/3–4 (1970):236–38.

Fanny Davies. "About Schumann's Pianoforte Music." MT, 51 (1910): 493–94.

Maurice Dumesnil. *How to Play and Teach Debussy*. New York: Schroeder & Gunther, 1932.

———. "Debussy's Principles in Pianoforte Playing." *Etude,* 56 (March 1938):153.

Robert Ehle. "20th Century Music and the Piano." PQ, 96 (Winter 1976–77):28–31.

Dean Elder. "Bach Talk with Rosalyn Tureck." *Clavier,* 18 (January 1979):18–23.

Winsome Evans. "The Influence of the Pianoforte on 18th Century Keyboard Style." *Musicology,* 3 (1968–69):49–68.

Keith Fagan. "The Chopin Style." MO, 95 (February 1972):239, 241.

Albert Faurot. *Concert Piano Repertoire.* Metuchen, NJ: Scarecrow Press, 1974. 337pp.

James Friskin and Irwin Freundlich. *Music for the Piano: A Handbook of Concert and Teaching Material from 1580 to 1952.* New York: Rinehart, 1954. Reprint, New York: Dover, 1974.

Beatrice Ganz. "Problems of Articulation in Baroque Keyboard Music." *Bach,* 7 (April 1977):3–13.

Reginald R. Gerig. *Famous Pianists and Their Technique.* Washington, D.C.: Robert B. Luce, 1974.

James Goodfriend. "Going on Record—A Note on Performance." *Stereo Review,* 30 (May 1973):52–53.

Robert A. Hagopian. "The d'Indy and Dukas Piano Sonatas." DMA diss., Indiana University, 1975. 53pp.

———. "The Confluence of Artistic and Literary Sources in the Creation of Ravel's *Gaspard de la nuit.*" DMA diss., Indiana University, 1975. 37pp. "An interdisciplinary study of the interrelations of the three prose-poems of Aloysius Bertrand which Maurice Ravel chose to recreate in his own piano suite of the same name. Considers the entire set of Bertrand's poems in its overall influence on Ravel's creative style" (author, abridged).

Hal Haney. "Conversation with Harpsichordist Rosalyn Tureck." *Harpsichord* 8 (February–March–April 1975):8–11, 14–22.

Doris Hays. "Noise Poise." MJ, 35 (February 1977):14–17, 42. A discussion of avant-garde techniques used in playing the piano.

Sarah Carson Hegmann. "The Latin-American Piano Sonata in the Twentieth Century." Ph.D. diss., Indiana University, 1975. 142pp. "A study of sonatas or sonatinas representing most of the major countries and twentieth-century composers of Latin America; some are nationalistic in character, and others represent major twentieth-century compositional techniques. Categorizes the countries according to those of Indian, Negro, or cosmopolitan cultural influences; summarizes elements of tonality, harmony, melody, texture, rhythm, and form; and examines the position of the sonatas within the international musical sphere" (author, abridged).

Julius Herford. "Bach's Models of 'Good Inventiones'—How to Develop the Same Well." *Bach,* 4 (January 1973):16–20.

———. "J. S. Bach's Fugue in C Minor from *The Well-Tempered Clavier,* Book I." *Bach,* 4 (July 1973):36–40. An analysis.

Cecil Hopkinson. "A Postscript to the 18th-Century Editions of the Keyboard Compositions of Domenico Scarlatti." *Brio,* 7 (Spring 1970): 9–10.

Eric Frederick Jensen. "The Piano Capriccio, 1830–1860." MA thesis, Eastman School of Music, 1975. 66pp.

Keyboard Solos and Duos by Living British Composers: A Catalogue. London: Composers' Guild of Great Britain, 1974. 63pp.

George A. Kochevitsky. "The Performance of J. S. Bach's Keyboard Music." PQ, 54 (Winter 1965–66).

B'jarn Korsten. *Contemporary Norwegian Piano Music.* Oslo: Norsk Komponistforening, 1965. 3d enlarged and revised edition, 1976.

Olga Llano Kuehl. "The Piano Music of Spain, Its Flavor and Interpretation." *Clavier,* 15 (October 1976): 17–18, 20.

Patrick La Cerra. "The Keyboard Alman in Elizabethan England." *Clavier,* 16 (September 1977):24–34. Includes scores of seven almans.

Harry B. Lincoln. ed. *The Computer and Music.* Ithaca: Cornell University Press, 1970. 372pp. See essay that describes the experiments in analyzing and identifying the keyboard styles of Haydn, Mozart, and Beethoven.

Mark Lindley. "Authentic Instruments, Authentic Playing." MT, 118 (April 1977):285, 287–88.

Arthur Loesser. "Playing Bach on the Modern Piano." *Piano Teacher,* 1 (January–February 1959):5.

Ernest Lubin. "Another Lok at the Urtext." PQ, 98 (Summer 1977): 14, 16–17.

MENC. "Selective List of American Music for the Bicentennial Celebration—Piano." *Music Educators Journal,* 62 (April 1976):87–89, 98–104. A graded list by various contributors.

Timothy Miller. "Haydn Sonatas." Diss., Indiana University, 1957. A compilation with detailed analyses of the sonatas.

Hans-Christian Müller. "Sources and Their Line of Descent (Sources and Urtext)." PQ, 97 (Spring 1977):43–45.

Donald Arthur Myrvik. "Musical and Social Interaction for Composers and Performers: Differences between *Source* Music and the 1950 Avant-Garde." Diss., University of Minnesota, 1975. In 1970, in a significant number of new compositions—those published in *Source*—the relationship between the composer and the performer was substantially different from what it was for compositions written around 1950. While the nature of the interaction between performers and the composer in 1950 was authoritarian, in 1970 it was more often open and cooperative, and a new genre of cooperative music came into being. The composers' statements confirm this, and an analysis of the assignment of roles to performers illustrates an aspect of the shape of 1950 and 1970 music. Significant differences between the 1950 avant-garde and *Source* composers are found and discussed in this highly interesting dissertation.

Randolph Nicholas. "Tempo and Character." *Clavier,* 15 (March 1976): 46–47. Discusses Chopin's Prelude e and Beethoven's use of tempo and character terms.

Fritz Oberdoerffer. "On Urtext Editions." *Peters Notes 'The Newsletter of C. F. Peters,'* 1 (Fall/Winter 1976–77):5.

Michael J. Pizzuto. "A Comparison of the Finale of Chopin's Sonata in B-flat Minor and the Second Movement of A. Ginastera's Sonata for Piano." MMA diss., Chicago Conservatory College, 1975. 18pp.

Linton E. Powell. "Guitar Effects in Spanish Piano Music." PQ, 92 (Winter 1975–76): 40–44.

Johann J. Quantz. *On Playing the Flute.* Translated by Edward Reilly. New York: The Free Press, 1966. Reprint, New York: Schirmer Books, 1975.

Joseph Rezits and Gerald Deatsman. *The Pianist's Resource Guide: Piano Music in Print.* Park Ridge, Ill.: Pallma Music Corp., 1974, 1978. 1,491pp.

Charles Rosen. *The Classical Style: Beethoven, Haydn and Mozart.* New York: Viking, 1970. Reprint, New York: W. W. Norton, 1972.

Felix Salzer. ed. *The Music Forum,* Vol.IV. New York: Columbia University Press, 1976. 403pp. Articles of special interest to pianists: "Ornamentation," by Heinrich Schenker (originally published some 70 years ago; not previously available in English), which discusses the appoggiatura, trill, and turn, with many examples from the Baroque and classical literature; "Aspects of the Recapitulation in Beethoven's Piano Sonatas," by Roger Kamien; and "The Musical Significance of Beethoven's Fingerings in the Piano Sonatas," by Jeanne Bamberger. Also contains other highly interesting articles by Schenker, Carl Schacter, and Felix Salzer.

Walter Schenkman. "Clementi, Cramer, Czerny, Composers of Valuable Etude Material." CK, 3 (September 1977):14–16, 43.

Harold Schonberg. "The Far-Out Pianist." *Harper's Bazaar,* 130 (June 1960):49.

Adrienne Simpson. "Bohemian Piano Music of Beethoven's Time." MT, 1553 (July 1972):666–67. Deals with the four volumes of piano works published by Henle under this same title (Reicha, Steffan, Tomášek, and Voříšek).

Larry Sitsky. "Summary Notes for a Study on Alkan." *Studies in Music,* 8 (1974):53–91. Twenty sections, each of which could well be the subject of a separate essay. Musical examples including the following complete pieces: Gigue et Air de Ballet Op.24/1; Trois Airs à Cinq Temps et un à Sept Temps Op.32/2; Cinquième Recueil de Chants Op.70; Ancienne Mélodie de la Synagogue.

Ellsworth Snyder. "Avant-garde Piano: Non-traditional Uses in Recent Music." CK, 3 (April 1977):12–13.

Madeau Stewart. "Playing Early Pianos—A Lost Tradition?" *Early Music,* 1 (1973):93–95.

K. Marie Stolba. "Music in the Life of Thomas Jefferson." AMT, 25 (April–May 1976):6–8, 12.

Charles R. Suttoni. "Piano and Opera: A Study of the Piano Fantasies Written on Opera Themes in the Romantic Era." Ph.D. diss., New York University. 494pp. "A study of the piano fantasy on opera themes, particularly from 1830 to 1850. Relates the fantasy to the technical development of the piano and to the tradition of improvisation in the Classic and Romantic eras. Discusses Mozart, Clementi, Cramer, Beethoven, Hummel, Moscheles, Joseph Gelinek, Daniel Steibelt, Franz Hünten, Kalkbrenner, Henri Herz, Czerny, Thalberg, Liszt, and Busoni" (author, abridged).

Virgil Thomson. *American Music since 1910.* New York: Holt, Rinehart & Winston, 1970.

Rosalyn Tureck. "Toward a Unity of Performance and Musicology." *Current Musicology,* 14 (1972):164–72.

Alan Tyson. ed. *Beethoven Studies.* London: Oxford University Press, 1974. 260pp.

Hubert Unverricht. "Urtext for Practical Use." PQ, 88 (Winter 1974–75): 46–47.

Alphabetical List of Composers under
Nationality Designations

American

Adler
Agay
Ahnell
Ahrendt
Aitken
Albright
Alexander
Allanbrook
Anderson
Antheil
Applebaum, E.
Applebaum, S.
Ashton
Austin
Avinger
Avshalomov
Babbitt
Baker
Ballard
Barber
Barkin
Bartow
Bassett
Bastien
Bauer
Beach
Beeson
Berberian
Berger
Berkowitz
Bernstein
Berry
Bestor
Bevelander
Biggs
Binkerd
Blake
Blind Tom
Bolcom
Bonds
Boretz
Borishansky
Brings
Brown, E.
Brown, R.
Brunswick
Bull, C.
Bunger
Burge

Cage
Calabro
Carr
Carter
Castaldo
Cazden
Chabade
Chajes
Chasins
Childs
Cines
Constantinides
Cooper
Cope
Copland
Cortés
Cory
Coulter
Cowell
Creston
Crist
Croley
Crossman
Crumb
Cumming
Cunningham, A.
Cunningham, M.
Curran
Curtis-Smith
Dahl
Darzins
Davidovsky
Davis
Debusman
Dello Joio
Del Tredici
Dett
Diamond
Diemente
Diemer
Dowd
Downey
Drew
Eakin
Edwards, G.
Edwards, R.
Ehle
Elwell
Epstein
Erb

Evett
Faith
Farwell
de Filippi
Fine
Finney
Fisher
Fishman
Foldes
Foss
Franchetti
Franco
Fuleihan
Gamer
Ganz
Garland
de Gastyne
Gerschefski
Gershwin
Ghezzo
Giannini
Glanville-Hicks
Goldman
Gottschalk
Gould
Green, H.
Green, R.
Greene
Griffes
Gruenberg
Gutche
Haieff
Hakim
Hanson
Harrison
Hartley
Haubiel
Heinrich
Heiss
Helps
Hennagin
Hewitt
Hill
Hiller
Hoffman
Hoiby
Hopkins
Hovhaness
Howe
Hutcheson

Hutchison
Iatauro
Ives
Ivey
Jackson
James
Jannery
Jenni
Johnson, H.
Johnson, L.
Johnson, T.
Johnston
Joplin
Kam
Katins
Kay
Keats
Kennan
Keyes
Kim
Kirchner
Koch, F.
Koch, J.
Kohn
Kolb
Kosteck
Kraft
Kramer
Kupferman
Kurtz
Laderman
La Montaine
Lansky
Lazarof
Lee, Noël
Lee, Norman
Lees
Leichtling
Lessard
Levy, B.
Levy, E.
Lewis, M.
Lewis, P. T.
Lewis, R.
Lipschutz
Lombardo
Long
Luening
Lunetta
MacDowell

Black Composers

Women Composers

Archer
Aretz
Arrieu
Bacewicz
Bauld
Beach
Berberian
Bonds
Boyd
Bull, C.
de Campos
Capuis
de Carvalho
Catalanotto
Chaminade
Coulthard

Dziewulska
Fontyn
Garścia
Gartenlaub
Garztecka
Glanville-Hicks
Howe
Ivey
Johnson, H.
Jolas
Kolb
Last
LeFanu
Lipschutz
Lutyens
Maconchy

Mageau
Mana-Zucca
Mefano
Moore, D. R.
Moszumanska-
  Nazar
Musgrave
Newlin
Pentland
Pfeiffer
Philiba
Pierce
Prieto
Rainier
Ran
Schonthal

Schumann
Seeger
Setti
da Silva
Simonis
Simons
Smith, J.
Sohet-Boulnois
Sorel
Spagnolo
Szönyi
Szymanowska
Talma
Tate
Zechlin

Compositions for Piano and Tape

See under:
Babbitt
Bauld
Biggs
Brouwer
Childs
Davidovsky

Detoni
Dobrowolski
Escobar
Gehlhaar
Gerstel
Hutchison
Jackson

Johnson, B. E.
Kolb
Lanza
MacInnis
Nono
de Oliveira, W. C.
Reibel

Ross
Santoro
Schwartz
Smalley
Subotnick
Vieru
Wilding-White
Zupko

See: Barbara English Maris, "American Compositions for Piano and Tape-Recorded Sound," diss., Peabody Conservatory, 1976.

Compositions for Prepared Piano

See under:
Aperghis
Bedford
Bentzon
Bunger
Butterley
Cage
Capdenat
Cardew

Childs
Cope
Cowell
Crumb
Curtis-Smith
Ehle
Ghezzo
Greene, A.
Hovland (in

collection
*Scandinavian
Aspect*)
Hutchison
Kagel
Luciuk
Manoury
Nørgärd (in
collection

*Scandinavian
Aspect*)
Pierce
Polin
Quintanar
Stout
Szalonek
Wolff

See: Richard Bunger, "Prepared Piano—Part I, Its History, Development, and Practice," CK, 3 (July 1977):26–28. "Prepared Piano—Part II, Explorations in Sound," CK, 3 (August 1977):14–17, 36.
———. *The Well Prepared Piano*, revised and expanded edition (New York: Highgate Press, 1979).

New Dates

The following list supplies death dates of composers who have recently died as well as birth and death dates that were not available at the time of the first printing of *Guide to the Pianist's Repertoire.*

George Adams, 1904–1959
Karl Andersen, 1903–1970
Hans Eric Apostel, 1901–1972
Kurt Atterberg, 1887–1974
Esther Williamson Ballou, 1915–1973
David Barlow, 1927–1975
Jean Barraqué, 1928–1973
Philip Bezanson, 1916–1975
Boris Blacher, 1903–1975
Arthur Bliss, 1891–1975
Benjamin Britten, 1913–1976
Robert Casadesus, 1899–1972
Bainbridge Crist, 1883–1969
Luigi Dallapiccola, 1904–1975
Richard Donovan, 1891–1970
Sabin V. Dragoi, 1894–1968
S. C. Eckhardt-Gramatté, 1902–1974
Florin Eftimescu, 1919–
Bentsion Eliezer, 1920–
Oscar Esplá, 1886–1976
Alvin Etler, 1913–1973
Robert Evett, 1922–1975
Samuel Feinberg, 1890–1962
Richard Flury, 1896–1967
Janina Garścia, 1920–
Alois Hába, 1893–1973
Yoshio Hachimura, 1938–
Rhené Jacque, 1918–
Hanns Jelinek, 1901–1969
Karel Jirák, 1891–1972
Lockrem Johnson, 1924–1977
André Jolivet, 1905–1974
Mihail Jora, 1891–1971

Joseph Kaminski, 1903–1972
Lucrecia R. Kasilag, 1918–
Aram Khatchaturian, 1903–1978
Wiktor Labuński, 1895–1974
Benjamin Lees, 1924–
René Leibowitz, 1913–1972
Matthew Locke, ca.1622–1677
John McCabe, 1939–
George Frederick McKay, 1899–1970
Gian Francesco Malipiero, 1882–1973
Frank Martin, 1890–1974
Jean Martinon, 1910–1976
Georges Migot, 1891–1976
Darius Milhaud, 1892–1974
Lev Oborin, 1907–1973
Leo Ornstein, 1892–
Hall Overton, 1920–1972
Oedoen Partos, 1907–1977
Juan Carlos Paz, 1897–1972
Walter Piston, 1894–1976
Giovanni Benedetto Platti, 1697–1763
André Previn, 1930–
Knudaage Riisager, 1897–1974
Julius Schloss, 1902–1972
Tibor Serly, 1900–1978
Dmitri Shostakovitch, 1906–1975
Eric-Walter Sternberg, 1898–1974
Edward Steuermann, 1892–1964
Joseph Wagner, 1900–1974
Adolph Weiss, 1891–1971
Egon Wellesz, 1885–1974
Friedrich Wührer, 1900–1975